A BIBLICAL HEBREW REFERENCE GRAMMAR

A BIBLICAL HEBREW REFERENCE GRAMMAR

Second Edition

Christo H.J. van der Merwe
Jacobus A. Naudé
Jan H. Kroeze

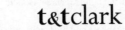
LONDON · NEW YORK · OXFORD · NEW DELHI · SYDNEY

T&T CLARK
Bloomsbury Publishing Plc
50 Bedford Square, London, WC1B 3DP, UK

BLOOMSBURY, T&T CLARK and the T&T Clark logo are trademarks
of Bloomsbury Publishing Plc

First published 2017
Reprinted 2018 (twice), 2019

Cover image © DEA / G. DAGLI ORTI/Getty

A catalogue record for this book is available from the British Library.

Library of Congress Cataloging-in-Publication Data
Van der Merwe, C. H. J., author. | Naudâe, J. A.,author. | Kroeze,
Jan, 1958-author.
A biblical Hebrew reference grammar / by ChristoH.J. van der Merwe,
Jacobus A.Naudâe & Jan Kroeze.
Second edition. | New York : BloomsburyT&T Clark, [2017] |
Includesbibliographical references and index.
LCCN 2017034085 (print) | LCCN 2017034785(ebook) | ISBN
9780567663344(epdf) | ISBN 9780567663320 (hc : alk. paper)
LCSH:Hebrew language--Grammar.
LCC PJ4556 (ebook) | LCC PJ4556 .V36 2017(print) | DDC
492.482/421--dc23
LC record available at https://lccn.loc.gov/2017034085

ISBN: HB: 978-0-5676-6332-0
PB: 978-0-5676-6333-7
ePDF: 978-0-5676-6334-4

Typeset by Forthcoming Publications (www.forthpub.com)
Printed and bound in Great Britain

To find out more about our authors and books visit www.bloomsbury.com
and sign up for our newsletters.

To
Walter T. Claassen
and
Cynthia L. Miller-Naudé

CONTENTS

Chapter 3
KEY TERMS AND CONCEPTS

Chapter 4
Verbs

Chapter 6
THE OTHER WORD CLASSES

Chapter 7
WORD ORDER

PREFACE TO THE FIRST EDITION

The contents of most modern introductory Biblical Hebrew (= BH) grammars are arranged according to didactic principles. For example, in these grammars the simple forms of the verb are often introduced at the very outset, followed by the simpler forms of the noun. The irregular stems of nouns and verbs are then dealt with bit by bit in the rest of the grammar. Although didactic principles should play a decisive role in structuring an introductory grammar, it often happens that such introductory grammars become the only source of information for second language readers of BH. Apart from the limited data available in these works, tracing in them information on a particular theme can be a very time-consuming process.

The aim of this grammar is to serve as a reference work at an intermediate level for exegetes and translators of the Hebrew Bible who have a basic knowledge of BH, but would like to use and broaden the knowledge they have acquired in an introductory course. It therefore strives, on the one hand, to systematize as briefly as possible the BH linguistic knowledge that is normally presented in introductory courses. On the other hand, it offers BH information beyond that of introductory courses in areas that are deemed relevant for exegetes and translators. For this reason, unlike an introductory grammar, it is not intended as a manual to be learned systematically. The intention is rather to present information concerning BH systematically for easy reference. It attempts neither to present information in terms of a single linguistic theory nor to be absolutely comprehensive. It also avoids discussing problems regarding the description of BH. It is a grammar trying to offer solutions to users who are not interested in the problems of describing BH. Although most of the examples come from the prose sections of the Bible, this volume represents, in the opinion of the authors, a major part of the BH linguistic information required by an exegete of the *Biblia Hebraica Stuttgartensia*. Footnotes and bibliographical references have been kept to a minimum.

This grammar is a team effort in the true sense of the word. Apart from the three authors, there have also been contributions by the Reverend Wouter van Wyk of the Rand Afrikaans University. Professor Cynthia Miller of the North Carolina State University (USA) and Ms Jackie du Toit of the University of the North provided valuable criticisms of the beta version. In editing the English edition (which was translated by Dr Edwin Hees of the Department of English at the University of Stellenbosch) Ms Helen Efthimiadis of the University of the North made numerous brilliant suggestions which we incorporated.

Although reference grammars are rarely compiled consistently in terms of a single linguistic framework or theory, the process of compiling such a grammar does not occur in a vacuum. In this grammar the following principles were consciously adopted:

1. This grammar is intended for a very specific audience, namely translators and exegetes of BH texts who wish to engage critically with existing translations and interpretations of the *Biblia Hebraica Stuttgartensia.*

2. The linguistic information has been structured and presented in such a way as to be accessible to an ordinary interpreter of a BH passage. For this reason (as far as possible) linguistic terms have been used that (1) may be familiar to users and/or (2) they will come across regularly in the type of literature they are going to consult. Thus, for example, the terms perfect, imperfect and waw consecutive imperfect are used (in place of linguistically more accurate terms) because they are used in Holladay's popular dictionary. In 'explaining' the phonological processes that occur in the conjugation of some weak verbal stems, didactic considerations carried more weight than the accurate representation of the diachronic development of a particular form. In this regard our use of the concept 'compensatory lengthening' may be called into question too.

3. More modern and possibly less familiar terms are used only in cases where they make a significant contribution towards a clearer understanding of the BH constructions in the authors' view, e.g. the terms postconstructus, fronting, focus particle, discourse marker, adjunct and complement.

4. In Chapter 3 the metalinguistic frame of reference that is relevant to this volume is explained. Although the linguistic structures of English and BH are by no means the same, English examples are used for didactic purposes.

5. The type of information presented must be useful to the above-mentioned audience in their exegesis of the BH text. For this reason a very wide definition of what constitutes the knowledge of a language has been adopted. On the one hand, knowledge of BH includes the ability to understand the organization (grammar) and meaning (semantics) of the language at the level of pronunciation, forms, phrases, clauses, sentences and texts. On the other hand, it also includes the ability to understand the use of the above-mentioned linguistic constructions (pragmatics and sociolinguistics). This volume is fairly traditional in its use (for didactic reasons) of The Verbs (Chapter 4), The Nouns (Chapter 5) and The Other Word Classes (Chapter 6) as three of its major categories at a macro level. At the lower levels, however, where relevant and where possible, the semantics and pragmatics of some constructions are dealt with. In a contemplated next volume most of the categories at the macro level, e.g. inter-sentence relationships, text types, speech acts and socio-linguistic conventions, will not be word-based.

6. Unnecessary detail has been avoided. If constructions with a low frequency have been mentioned for the sake of completeness, they are indicated as seldom or rare. A glossary of linguistic terms used here and/or which users of this grammar may encounter in other exegetical works may be found at the back of the grammar.

7. No attempt has been made to be linguistically innovative. Existing knowledge of BH has been incorporated. The grammars of Gesenius–Kautzsch–Cowley (1909), Richter (1978, 1979 and 1980), Waltke and O'Connor (1990) and Joüon–Muraoka (1991) have been used extensively. Nevertheless an attempt has been made throughout to utilize where relevant the findings of recent research in BH for the purposes of this grammar. The sections on construct relationships, pronouns, focus particles, some conjunctions and word order are examples in this regard. Furthermore, the linguistic interests of the authors (interests that range from the works of Noam Chomsky to Simon Dik and Deirdre Wilson) must certainly have played an unconscious role in the writing of this grammar. Even so, a deliberate attempt has been made to subordinate these interests to the primary purpose of this grammar.

8. English translations of the Hebrew text come mainly from the RSV. In cases where the RSV translation fails to illustrate a grammatical construction under discussion or was too archaic the RSV's translation was modified.

9. The authors want to acknowledge their indebtedness to the tradition of BH grammatical teaching in South Africa. Without it this grammar would not have been possible. Until the beginning of the 1970s B. Gemser's *Hebreeuse Spraakkuns* was used by most institutions where BH was taught. Since then scholars at the different institutions experimented with grammars that they had compiled themselves and distributed in the form of photocopied notes. Such grammars were compiled at the University of the Free State, Potchefstroom University of Christian Higher Education, University of Pretoria, University of South Africa and University of Stellenbosch. These grammars are important forerunners of this reference work and influenced the thoughts of the authors in more than one way.

10. The authors also want to express their appreciation to their mentors and/or other scholars who played a significant role in their careers as Hebrew linguists. Christo van der Merwe: Professors F.C. Fensham, W.T. Claassen, W. Richter, W. Gross, F.E. Deist, E. Talstra, Dr. A. Michel and Dr. A. Disse; Jackie Naudé: Professors F. du T. Laubscher, P. Nel, H. Borer and J. Oosthuizen; and Jan Kroeze: Professors E.J. Smit, H.F. van Rooy, J. Hoftijzer and Dr. P.J.J. van Huyssteen.

11. Steve Barganski of Sheffield Academic Press should be thanked for his contribution to (and patience in) the final editing of this book.

Preface to the Second Edition

The second edition of the Biblical Hebrew Reference Grammar is a thoroughly revised and enlarged version of the one published in 1999 which is still widely used by scholars, exegetes, Bible translators, teachers and students of the ancient language. While it retains its chapter divisions and overall structure which is intended to help users to easily access the information (viz. "Introduction," "Writing System," "Key Terms and Concepts," "Verbs," "Nouns," "The Other Word Classes" and "Word Order"), many of the sections are nearly completely revised and/or substantially enlarged. Insights gleaned from the wealth of recent publications in the field of the Biblical Hebrew verbal system, negation, the use of pronouns, quantifiers, prepositions, discourse particles, word order and left dislocation have been used to revise and rewrite many parts of the grammar. While it still strives to present a solution-oriented source of grammatical information to its users which is as theory neutral as possible, relevant recent developments in the field of general linguistics (e.g. formal grammar, historical linguistics, linguistic typology, cognitive linguistics, semantics, pragmatics and sociolinguistics) have also been taken into account in preparing this edition.

The foundations of Gesenius–Kautzsch–Cowley (1909), Richter (1978, 1979 and 1980), Waltke and O'Connor (1990), Joüon-Muraoka (1991) as well as its 2nd edition (2009) are still highly respected and maintained in many parts of this version. However, in the more than sixteen years since the first edition, the discipline of Biblical Hebrew has advanced in numerous ways. As a result, the second edition of this grammar presents some perspectives and insights not to be found in those earlier works; see, for example the following: the theoretical framework that underpins this grammar (Chapter 3), the sections on the semantics and pragmatics of the verbal system, quantifiers, negation, the prepositions, discourse markers (and many of the "other word classes"), word order and left dislocation. In the intervening years between the editions, our work and research into Biblical Hebrew grammar has both diverged and converged. Jan Kroeze has shifted his academic focus to computer science and information technology. Although he was not involved in the revision of the grammar for this second edition, his name is retained as one of the co-authors out of respect for his contribution to the first edition. As the other two co-authors revised every section of the grammar – one author doing the initial revisions and the other author providing substantive feedback – we found that in those places where we had differing viewpoints, further discussion and consultation produced a grammatical description that superceded particular theoretical viewpoints. We hope that the final product is a well-written and nuanced description of the state of the art of Biblical Hebrew.

The Hebrew texts that are used are still from the *Biblia Hebraica Stuttgartensia*. However, where relevant, readers are informed of some of the advances introduced by *Biblia Hebraica Quinta*.

Many of the translations of the first version were from the RSV. In this version, with its more than 1300 examples from the Hebrew Bible, the primary aim was to explain the Hebrew construction(s) under consideration as well as possible. In some cases (e.g. with the use of *wāw*), this was done at the expense of an idiomatic contextual rendering. Most of the translations in the new version are those of the authors, or sometimes adaptations from the NRSV. They are marked by asterisks. When any other English translation is used, the conventional abbreviation of that translation is provided.

In the first edition, rare examples of some categories were sometimes indicated. In this version, we attempted, where possible, to provide readers with the frequency of the occurrence of expressions or an indication of whether they can expect to find an expression and/or category of use frequent in the Hebrew Bible, or not.

The first version retained the traditional terms for grammatical items insofar as possible, e.g. the notions perfect, imperfect, *wāw* consecutive imperfect and *wāw* consecutive perfect. In this edition, new but already widely used terms are sometimes used next to the older terms (e.g. *qātal*/perfect and *yiqtōl*/ imperfect). In cases where it could be argued that retaining the older terms could give rise to confusion, unambiguous terms replace the older terms, e.g. *wayyiqtōl* for *wāw* consecutive imperfect and *wəqātal* for *wāw* consecutive perfect.

In the new version, a more consistent and precise system for the transcription of Hebrew words has been used.

The authors are indebted to many colleagues and students:

Christo van der Merwe: I would like to thank a number of colleagues who were always willing to share some of their ideas and/or unpublished articles with me. In this regard I want to thank in particular Reinier de Blois, Janet Dyk, Randall W. Garr, Gideon Kotze, Frank Polak, Pierre van Hecke, Eep Talstra, Gerrit van Steenbergen, Andy Warren, Ernst Wendland and Tamar Zewi. I also appreciate Barry Bandstra's willingness to read earlier drafts of some of the sections. I have to make special mention of Alexander Andrason. He opened my eyes to language as a dynamic and complex system and helped me to better understand how verbal systems across languages work. His brilliance, work ethic and willingness to share, debate and assist, has enriched my life as scholar since his arrival at Stellenbosch. I am also highly indebted to a number of my students in the Department of Ancient Studies: Ettienne Ellis and Eva Raal for reading and giving critical feedback on some of the earlier drafts, and Bill Bivin, Christian Locatell, Sebastian Floor, Kris Lyle, Yoseob Lee, Andrea Mena, Daniel Rodriguez, Steve Runge, Josh Westbury and C.-K. Yoo for conducting their postgraduate studies on topics that are directly relevant for this grammar. I appreciate that I could have learned so much from them and that we could use some of their insights in this grammar.

Jacobus Naudé: One stands on the shoulders of many persons who deserve thanks. It is impossible to list all the names of persons who impacted on and formed my thoughts and for whom I have huge appreciation; they are referred to in my publications. In particular, however, I want to acknowledge the following individuals for their contributions. I am grateful to Dean Forbes for his important work on statistical methods to study the diachrony of Biblical Hebrew and on a computerized approach to Biblical Hebrew corpus linguistics; to Robert Holmstedt for his unified approach on the edge constructions of Biblical Hebrew, to Gary Rendsburg for our joint work on negation in pre-modern Hebrew; and to the late Andrzej Zaborski for his insights on Afroasiatic linguistics. The interaction with the work of Ian Young, Robert Rezetko and Martin Ehrensvärd contributed to the nuancing of the theory of language change and diffusion. John Cook, Adina Moshavi and Tania Notarius enrich my Biblical Hebrew knowledge as members of the steering committee of Linguistics and Biblical Hebrew of the Society of Biblical Literature, which I chair. For this project I am influenced to a great extent by the academic contributions of four of my former students who are now colleagues. Discussions with Kobus Marais, my colleague at the University of the Free State in Translation Studies, on complexity and complex systems have provided an impetus for my work in applying complexity to Biblical Hebrew linguistics as early as 2007. I learned much from At Lamprecht, (Northwest University) who was the first student who embarked on cognitive linguistics and Biblical Hebrew in South Africa. The analysis of Cobus Snyman (University of Stellenbosch) on the negative in Biblical Hebrew inspired my work on quantification. Tshokolo J. Makutoane (University of the Free State) who works on the role of orality in biblical texts, opened my eyes to the description of language as a spoken system. Steve Modugno's recent study of LXX-Micah gave me insight in the role of ideology in language use. I also benefit from the contributions of the authors in the Linguistic Studies in Ancient West Semitic which I co-edited with Cynthia Miller-Naudé as well as from interaction with the Dinka Cam Bible translation team in Southern Sudan for which Cynthia and I are translation consultants. My deepest gratitude is reserved for my soulmate Cynthia Miller-Naudé. As a Joan of Arc, she has not only succeeded in creating in a very hostile academic environment a space for exercising Biblical Hebrew linguistics and Bible translation from which our work in general and this project in particular is advantaged, but she is also my inspiration in our 2275 days of married life (and counting). I am forever grateful for her steadfast love and support.

We are grateful to Bloomsbury for their willingness to publish this second edition and to our editor, Dominic Mattos, for his assistance and advice in editorial matters. We want to thank Duncan Burns for his commitment to prepare a manuscript of the highest standards – as well as his gracious patience with us. We thank the colleagues who generously provided robust reviews of our work as well as the three anonymous peer-reviewers engaged by the publisher; the final version is much better because of their feedback. Last, but certainly not least, we want to thank Cynthia Miller-Naudé for her enormous effort in closely scrutinizing not only the English that we used in this grammar, but also what we have to say about Biblical Hebrew. She also produced the subject index, the index of Hebrew words and performed the final proofreading of the entire book.

This work is based on research supported in part by the National Research Foundation of South Africa (Christo H. J. van der Merwe UID 85432 and Jacobus A. Naudé UID 85902). The grantholders acknowledge that opinions, findings and conclusions or recommendations expressed in any publication generated by the NRF supported research are those of the authors, and that the NRF accepts no liability whatsoever in this regard.

Chapter 1

INTRODUCTION

§1. Biblical Hebrew as a Semitic Language

The term "Biblical Hebrew" refers to the form of the language of the Hebrew Bible/Tanak/Old Testament as it appears in the printed editions that are in use today. It is based on a form of the biblical text found in medieval manuscripts that derives from a school of scholars in Tiberias known as the Masoretes (see §2.1). It is this form of the language that is represented in this grammar. However, Biblical Hebrew reflects to a large extent the varieties of Hebrew that were spoken in Israel from the beginning of the Iron Age (about 1200 BCE) to the Hellenistic era (about 165 BCE).

The languages that have a genetic relationship to Biblical Hebrew (that is, they descend from a common ancestor, namely Proto-Semitic) and that display similar common features (that is, they have similar structures and vocabulary) are known as the Semitic languages.[1] The geographical area of the Semitic languages includes the Arabian Peninsula and the fertile region which stretches in the form of a crescent from Iran in the northeast across Syria and Israel and Palestine in the northwest to Ethiopia in the southwest. The Semitic languages can be subdivided into East Semitic and West Semitic based primarily on verb forms.[2] East Semitic comprises Akkadian, the language of ancient Mesopotamia (roughly, modern Iraq), which was spoken from about 2600 BCE, and Eblaite of Tell Mardikh (Ebla) in Syria (2400 BCE). West Semitic includes the rest of the languages. Biblical Hebrew belongs to a subgroup of West Semitic languages called Northwest Semitic.

§1.1. Northwest Semitic

The earliest languages in the area traditionally known as Syro-Palestine are:

(1) Amorite (from about 2000 BCE), which is the language of members of nomadic groups which infiltrated the Levant, that is Syria, Lebanon, Israel, Palestine, and Jordan. Amorite is reflected in Amorite names mentioned in Akkadian texts.

---

1. The use of the term "Semitic" to refer to these languages is generally attributed to August Ludwig Schloezer (1735–1809) based upon Gen. 10:31; see Baasten (2003).

2. The traditional subdivisions into East and West Semitic languages is evident since the 1920s (see Bergsträsser [1923] 1983 and Brockelmann [1926] 1961).

(2) Ugaritic (from about 1450–1200 BCE), which is the language of Ugarit, a cosmopolitan city-state on the Syrian coast. Ugaritic is mostly written in a cuneiform alphabetic script.

(3) Canaanite, which included, among others, Hebrew (from about the tenth century BCE); Phoenician (from about the eleventh century BCE), spoken in the Phoenician city-states of the Levant and in Phoenician colonies throughout the Mediterranean; and, Moabite, Edomite and Ammonite (from about 850 BCE), spoken in Transjordan. Distinctive features of Canaanite, especially hybrid verbal forms and lexical glosses, can be traced back at least to the middle of the second millennium BCE in Akkadian cuneiform tablets dispatched from Syro-Palestinian vassals to their Egyptian overlord in Amarna.

(4) Aramaic, which consisted of distinct varieties in different regions of the Fertile Crescent. Aramaic was spoken since the tenth century BCE in Syria (Aram), with Damascus as an early cultural center. It was promoted by the Neo-Assyrian and Neo-Babylonian Empires and under the Persians it later became the official language of correspondence and common usage in the ancient Near East.

The family resemblances between Canaanite and Aramaic can be explained by gradual transitions within a dialect continuum with Phoenician at the one end and Aramaic at the other; between them are found Hebrew and the Transjordanian dialects.[3]

§1.2. West Semitic and Central Semitic

The group of languages called Northwest Semitic is subsumed together with Old South Arabian languages and Arabic under a group of languages called Central Semitic.[4] The Central Semitic languages together with the Modern South Arabian languages and the Ethiopian languages form West Semitic.

To summarize, Hebrew is a member of the Canaanite family of languages, which descends from the Northwest Semitic languages, which in turn are part of the larger Central Semitic language family and finally of the West Semitic division of the Semitic languages.[5]

---

3. See Garr (1985).
4. Central Semitic was first defined by Hetzron in 1972 (Faber 1997).
5. See Rubin (2010) and Kaltner and McKenzie (2002) for further introductory reading, and Hetzron (1997) and Lipiński (2001, 2014) for advanced reading.

§1.3. Semitic Languages and Afroasiatic

The Semitic languages also bear similarities to certain language groups, for example, ancient Egyptian, Cushitic of Ethiopia and neighboring countries, Berber of North Africa, and Chadic (of central and western sub-Saharan Africa including some 150 languages). This larger grouping of languages, which includes the Semitic languages, is currently classified as Afroasiatic.[6] (The term Hamito-Semitic, which inaccurately implies a binary split between Semitic and the other branches, was used in the past.) The relationship between and among the Afroasiatic languages can be demonstrated with features of the pronominal systems as well as with features of nominal and verbal morphology.

§2. Unity and Diversity in the Development of Hebrew

The first attestation of the term "Hebrew" being used to refer to the language occurs in the Mishnah (עברית) and in the Greek prologue to Ben Sira (Ecclesiasticus) (Εβραϊστί). In the Hebrew Bible itself the term יְהוּדִית "Judahite" is used (2 Kgs 18:26–28 = Isa. 36:11–13; 2 Chron. 32:18) to refer to the variety of Hebrew spoken in the kingdom of Judah. Although Hebrew demonstrates change and variation in the structure of the language, in many ways Hebrew has remained the same in its development. Hebrew is usually divided according to four different linguistic corpuses.[7]

§2.1. Biblical and Epigraphic Hebrew

Hebrew alphabetic writing was invented in Iron Age Israel (about 1200 BCE). Epigraphic Hebrew, which refers to the language preserved in inscriptions, exhibits essentially the same phonology and morphology as Biblical Hebrew. Although Biblical Hebrew is regarded by many as a language with its own characteristic features, it is not uniform. It was used over a period of about 1000 years. Any language changes over such a long period of time. Furthermore, archaizing techniques (i.e. the application of archaic forms) or modernization techniques (i.e. the replacement of older forms by contemporary forms) were sometimes adopted in the writing.

For the sake of convenience Biblical Hebrew has been subdivided into smaller categories:

---

6. The term "Afroasiatic" was coined by the linguist Greenberg (1952).

7. For further reading, see Rabin (1974), Kutscher (1982), Sáenz-Badillos (1993), Naudé (2003b), and Schniedewind (2013).

(1) Archaic Biblical Hebrew (1200–1000 BCE) is best reflected in the more ancient poetic works of the Hebrew Bible (e.g. The Blessing of Jacob [Gen. 49]).

(2) Israelian Hebrew is the language of the northern kingdom of Israel and is reflected in the Elijah–Elisha narratives (1 Kgs 17–2 Kgs 8) and the Samaria ostraca.

(3) Standard Biblical Hebrew (1000–587/586 BCE) is mainly the literary language of the Judean scribes as reflected in the prose sections of the pre-exilic period.

(4) Late Biblical Hebrew (539/538–165 BCE) is the language of the sections from the postexilic period. Late Biblical Hebrew shows similarities to the language of the Dead Sea Scrolls and Ben Sira and the latter is therefore also classified as Late Biblical Hebrew by some.

The term "Classical Hebrew" is used by some scholars to designate only Standard Biblical Hebrew. Some use it as a synonym for Biblical Hebrew. Others use it as a term for the Hebrew of the Hebrew inscriptions, the Hebrew Bible, the Dead Sea Scrolls and Ben Sira. Some include even Mishnaic or early Rabbinic Hebrew.

Originally Biblical Hebrew writing only consisted of consonants. In order to prevent the loss of the correct pronunciation, which was transmitted orally, around 600 CE a group of Jewish scholars began to devise a system of signs to record and standardize the received pronunciation. They were known as the "Masoretes" (from the Hebrew word מסר, which means "to hand down"). The work of the Masoretes was continued for many centuries by a large number of scholars. Several systems of vocalization were developed (see §5). The most important vocalization system is known as the Tiberian Masoretic system and is the product of the work of the Ben Asher family in Tiberias about 900 CE. The earliest complete text in which this system is preserved is the Leningrad Codex from the year 1008, which is now housed in the Russian National Library in St. Petersburg. The scientific editions of the Hebrew Bible in the series of *Biblia Hebraica* use the Leningrad Codex as their base text,[8]

---

8. Rudolf Kittel (1853–1929) initiated the plan for a critical edition of the Hebrew Bible in 1901 of which the first edition appeared in 1906. As its basis, Kittel chose the text of the Bomberg edition of Jacob ben Ḥayyim, the so-called Hebrew *Textus Receptus*. At the foot of the pages he included a concise critical apparatus with textual variants from other known Masoretic manuscripts and from the ancient translations, e.g. the Septuagint.

specifically the third edition of *the Biblia Hebraica Kittel* (1937),[9] *Biblia Hebraica Stuttgartensia* (1977)[10] and *Biblia Hebraica Quinta* (since 2004).[11] The Biblical Hebrew described in this grammar is thus, strictly speaking, the Masoretic Biblical Hebrew of the Ben Asher family. Therefore, some scholars prefer the term "Tiberian Hebrew" instead of "Biblical Hebrew."

§2.2. Rabbinic Hebrew

Despite the fact that Aramaic and Greek vernaculars were spoken by most Jews, the language of the liturgy which the rabbis used in synagogues was predominantly Hebrew. This form of post-biblical Hebrew, known as Rabbinic Hebrew, was in use from 165 BCE. It reflects its own characteristic features which distinguished it from Biblical Hebrew, but it also attests to the sustained usage of Hebrew. It was also the language of the Mishnah, known as Mishnaic Hebrew. Rabbinic Hebrew stopped being used as a living vernacular around the end of the second century CE, but survived for two or three centuries as a literary language.

§2.3. Medieval Hebrew

Medieval Hebrew was the language revitalized by Jewish scholars and writers in the Arab countries and Europe during the Middle Ages, starting with the Islamic expansion in the seventh century and lasting until the European

---

9. Paul Kahle (1875–1964) recognized the importance of the Leningrad Codex and persuaded Rudolf Kittel to use it as the textual base of the third edition of the *Biblia Hebraica*. The critical apparatus was divided into two sections, one with minor variants and less important items and one with real textual changes and more important items. Qumran variants from the Isaiah Scroll (1QIsa[a]) and the Habakkuk Commentary (1QpHab) were added in a different typeface as a third section of the critical apparatus, beginning with the seventh imprint of the third edition of *Biblia Hebraica Kittel* (from 1951 up until the mid-1970s).

10. *Biblia Hebraica Stuttgartensia* lists in a concise way the textual variants and suggested corrections together in a single critical apparatus at the foot of each page. The managing editors were Karl Elliger and Wilhelm Rudolph in cooperation with an international team of Old Testament experts.

11. The *Biblia Hebraica Quinta* continues in the tradition of Kittel's *Biblia Hebraica* and is designated as its fifth, completely revised edition after the first two editions of the *Biblia Hebraica Kittel*, followed by the third edition of *Biblia Hebraica Kittel* and *Biblia Hebraica Stuttgartensia*. It includes an accompanying commentary in which the editors elucidate their text-critical judgments. Adrian Schenker is the head of the Editorial Committee for the *Biblia Hebraica Quinta*.

Renaissance at the end of the fifteenth century. The fact that this form of the language borrowed heavily from Arabic distinguishes it from Rabbinic Hebrew. The language was used in a limited way in speech situations. However, by its extensive use in writing, Hebrew attained a level of richness and intensity in specific areas (e.g. an enlarged vocabulary) that was not known in earlier times. It never developed into a homogeneous system because Medieval Hebrew is a revival of linguistic usages and traditions, developed according to each writer's judgment.

§2.4. Modern Hebrew

Modern Hebrew is the language that was revived as a vernacular of the emigrant Jewish community in Palestine towards the end of the nineteenth century, although it is claimed that this new phase of the language had already begun in the sixteenth century. It is a further development of the earlier forms of Hebrew. In 1948 it became one of the official languages of the new State of Israel.

§3. Overview of the Grammatical Treatment of Biblical Hebrew

§3.1. Early Jewish Grammarians (1000–1500 CE)

The earliest signs of the grammatical description of Hebrew may be found in the marginal notes of rabbis in midrashic studies dating from the eighth century CE. Furthermore, the Masoretes, whose work culminated in the tenth century CE, conducted their vocalization of Biblical Hebrew texts in terms of a particular oral grammatical tradition.

The first written Biblical Hebrew grammars appeared in Spain – a center of Jewish intellectual activity – between 1000 and 1200 CE. They were written in the scientific language of the day, namely Arabic. The Jewish grammarians based their description of Jewish grammar on the model used for the description of Arabic. The fruit of their labors culminated in the works of grammarians such as Abraham ibn Ezra and David Qimḥi. At a later stage these works became influential in other European centers as well. For example, Martin Luther probably learned Biblical Hebrew from David Qimḥi's grammar.

§3.2. Christian Biblical Hebrew Grammarians (1500–1750 CE)

During the Reformation, Christians dominated the study of Biblical Hebrew grammar. The linguistic model used for the description of Biblical Hebrew was no longer Arabic but Latin. The study of grammar and the study of rhetoric, formerly seen as one, became two separate disciplines. As the emphasis fell on Biblical Hebrew grammar, knowledge concerning the wealth of Biblical Hebrew rhetorical conventions was lost.

The study of Biblical Hebrew grammar flourished in the sixteenth century, especially in humanist circles. Reuchlin's *Rudimenta linguae hebraicae* (1506) is regarded as one of the influential works of this period. In the seventeenth century, however, humanist interest in Biblical Hebrew waned, so that Biblical Hebrew was confined to an auxiliary role in support of theology.

§3.3. Historical and Comparative Biblical Hebrew Grammars (1750–1960)

The most significant Biblical Hebrew grammar after Reuchlin's is that of Schultens, entitled *Institutiones* (1737). This work laid the basis for the study of Biblical Hebrew as a Semitic language. The main purpose of this grammar was to ascertain what light the other Semitic languages could cast on the understanding of Biblical Hebrew.

One of the most highly esteemed and most authoritative Biblical Hebrew grammars – that of Gesenius – appeared for the first time in 1807. There have been 28 subsequent editions. The last seven were produced by Kautzsch and in 1910 Cowley produced an English version. *Gesenius' Hebrew Grammar* by Gesenius–Kautzsch–Cowley remains a standard Biblical Hebrew reference work to this day.

In the nineteenth century linguists not only devoted much attention to the comparison of languages, but also tried to explain the various degrees of similarity between languages. By paying particular attention to the sequence of sound changes within languages that belong to the same family, sound rules were identified which could then be used to draw up a family tree of a language group. This approach to the study of language is known as historical-comparative linguistics. Brockelmann's *Grundriss der vergleichenden Grammatik der semitischen Sprachen* (1908–1913) is regarded as a benchmark of Semitic historical-comparative grammar (Brockelmann [1926] 1961).

The historical-comparative approach led to the following Biblical Hebrew grammars. König's comprehensive grammar, *Historisch-kritisches Lehr-gebäude der hebräischen Sprache*, which appeared in three volumes between 1881 and 1897 (König [1881–1897] 1979), drew on the work of the older Jewish grammars. This work is still highly regarded today. Bauer–Leander's *Historische Grammatik der hebräischen Sprache* (Bauer and Leander [1922] 1991) and Bergsträsser's 29th edition of Gesenius (Bergsträsser 1929) were the crowning glory of the attempts to utilize the principles of the historical-comparative method to describe Biblical Hebrew.

Historical-comparative linguistics was particularly useful in providing a framework for studying the phonology and morphology of language. This is one of the reasons the works of Bauer–Leander and Bergsträsser have hardly any description of Biblical Hebrew syntax. Syntactic constructions were mostly explained in terms of psychological considerations, as in Brockel-mann's *Hebräische Syntax* (1956).

§3.4. Modern Biblical Hebrew Grammarians (1960–2000)[12]

Since the 1920s the historical-comparative method has been superseded by a structuralist approach initiated by the linguist Ferdinand de Saussure. According to this approach, language is a structural system. It is the relationship between its various components at a particular period in history – the so-called synchronic level – that must be studied separately from the historical development of the language – the so-called diachronic level. Although the structuralist approach to the description of language revolutionized linguistics and led to a host of new theories on language, it did not have an immediate influence on Biblical Hebrew grammar. Works such as those by Andersen, *The Sentence in Biblical Hebrew* (1974), and Richter, *Grundlagen einer althebräischen Grammatik* (1978, 1979, 1980), paved the way in this regard.

The grammar by Waltke and O'Connor, *An Introduction to Biblical Hebrew Syntax* (1990), describes a large variety of Biblical Hebrew syntactic construc-tions. They use not only broad structural principles for this purpose, but also draw on the more traditional descriptions of Biblical Hebrew. In the process of doing so, this work also provides a useful taxonomy of Biblical Hebrew constructions, as well as a sound review of current Biblical Hebrew grammatical research.

---

12. See also Van der Merwe (1989, 1994 and 2003).

A Grammar of Biblical Hebrew (1991) by Muraoka is a revision of a French grammar published in 1923 by Joüon. It is cast in the form of a traditional grammar and explains some Biblical Hebrew syntactic constructions psychologically. However, Muraoka specifically attempts to incorporate the insights of modern grammarians, including those who published their research in Modern Hebrew. Some of the categories that he uses, as well as some of the arguments he presents in his grammar, indicate that aspects of the structuralist approach have been adopted.

The works of Waltke and O'Connor and of Joüon–Muraoka are still regarded as standard reference works. For this reason this reference grammar refers to both these studies for further reference in many instances. It must be borne in mind, however, that both grammars deal with the sentence as the largest unit of linguistic description. Furthermore, neither of these grammars utilizes the insights of generative grammar, which dominated linguistics in the second half of the twentieth century.

Noam Chomsky began generative grammar as a rule system but changed it to a principles and parameters approach in the late 1970s. The Principles and Parameters Model (or, Government and Binding Theory) is a syntactic model of human language centered around universal principles argued to be common to all languages, and specific, distinct sets of parameters whose values are fixed in one of a limited number of ways to derive the particular grammar of a specific language, for example Biblical Hebrew. Thus, it provides a program for language typology. In the early 1990s the fact that language may be designed economically is suggested by various kinds of minimalist considerations and this constituted the next development in generative grammar, the Minimalist Program (see Naudé 2006). Although the community of scholars studying Modern Hebrew from the generative perspective is fairly large (see Borer 2013), only a few scholars pursue the study of Biblical Hebrew within the framework of generative grammar (see Naudé 2013c); this asymmetry between Modern and Biblical Hebrew was also apparent with respect to structuralist linguistic approaches of the early twentieth century. The generative studies of Coetzee (1999), DeCaen (1995), Holmstedt (2002, 2016), Malone (1993), Naudé (1993), and Snyman (2004) contributed to the study of, *inter alia*, the following phenomena in Biblical Hebrew: the nature and distribution of subjects, pronouns and pronominal clitics, resumption, constituent order, syntax of relative clauses, scope of negation and the syntax and semantics of verbless predicates.

Functional Grammar as a linguistic theory was devised in the 1970s by proponents such as Simon Dik and Michael Halliday as an alternative to the abstract, formalized view of language presented by generative grammar. Functional Grammar is geared to the study of language as communication. It sees meaning in the writer's linguistic choices and systematically relates these choices to a wider sociocultural framework. The functional grammar framework is utilized by Biblical Hebrew scholars like Buth (1995), Heimerdinger (1999), Rosenbaum (1997) and Winther-Nielsen (1995).

Since the 1980s the following have also been regarded as part of the knowledge of a language: the way in which sentences are used to create texts (text linguistics), the ways people use utterances to execute actions and the relationship between language and its context of use (pragmatics) and the factors that determine *which* linguistic constructions are adopted by *which* role-playing members of a particular society, *when* they are adopted and the *reasons* for their adoption (sociolinguistics). The analysis of, and description of systematic patterns in texts, i.e. discourse analysis, has been particularly influential in the study of Biblical Hebrew (Bergen 1994; Bodine 1992; Longacre 2003).

§3.5. Biblical Hebrew Grammar in the Twenty-first Century

Apart from a second edition of Joüon–Muraoka in 2006 and a "Second Reprint of the Second Edition, with Corrections" in 2009, no major Biblical Hebrew reference grammar has been published in the twenty-first century thus far.

Although one runs the risk of oversimplification, some broad trends can be distinguished either in the study of Biblical Hebrew, or in linguistics, which are of relevance for the study of the ancient language. First, the empirical rigor provided by structuralist, generative and/or functional approaches continues to encourage many Biblical Hebrew scholars to use syntagmatic and paradig-matic distributional patterns as the foundation of their research. Advances in computer technology and the availability of sophisticated linguistic databases, which speed up the tagging and compilation of datasets, without doubt are playing a crucial role in this regard and will continue to do so in the future.

Second, cognitive linguistics has emerged with a greater focus on language as a "means of organizing, processing and conveying" informational struc-tures in the minds of humans (Geeraerts and Cuykens 2007: 5). Language is regarded as an integrated part of human cognition and communication. If one wants to understand how language works, one has to use, among other things, insights into the working of the brain and models of human cognition as a point of departure, and study how language is used in communication processes and modeled by its users in particular speech communities. The dynamic nature of language necessitates sophisticated models of how the meaning of linguistic constructions work – on the one hand, how they develop and may change, and, on the other hand, how they should be interpreted in specific instances of use. In fact, the issue of the "meaning" of constructions constitutes the heart of the linguistic enterprise for cognitive linguists. Furthermore, the reality of the fuzziness of language often makes it difficult to operate only with neat categories that state necessary and sufficient conditions for their members. Family relationships between items may also be sufficient to postulate a category. Some members of a category may be prototypical members whereas other members may be non-prototypical members.

Cognitive linguistics has provided one way to integrate the developments in the linguistics and Biblical Hebrew mentioned in the last paragraph of §3.4 (Van der Merwe 2003). Although cognitive linguistics represents no unified model that can be used uncritically to understand Biblical Hebrew better, some sections of this grammar have benefitted from its alternative approach to categorization and how the meaning of linguistic constructions may develop (e.g. §19–21, §39–40, §46–48).

Third, many Biblical Hebrew scholars embrace insights of modern linguistic approaches, and/or experiment with the use of those insights to better describe the ancient language. The *Encyclopedia of Hebrew Language and Linguistics* (Khan 2013b) illustrates the value that various modern linguistic models have had for the better understanding of a wide range of constructions and notions in Hebrew in all its diachronic stages.

Fourth, some traditional models for identifying and describing the diachronic phases of Biblical Hebrew have been challenged (Young, Rezetko, and Ehrensvärd 2008). This prompted a heavy debate, in which many of the new hypotheses were refuted and linguistic models for language change and variation were highlighted (Miller-Naudé and Zevit 2012). The debate continues (e.g. Rezetko and Young 2014), but it has illustrated, on the one hand, the complexities of describing an ancient language, and, on the other hand, the indispensability of construing the diachronic phases in the Hebrew Bible in the light of cross-linguistic models of linguistic change. One particularly useful linguistic concept for describing diachronic change in Biblical Hebrew is grammaticalization, the process by which a lexical item becomes fossilized as a grammatical item (Miller 1996: 179–212; Rubin 2005).

Fifth, recently a case has been made for conceiving of language as a complex, adaptive, dynamic system (Ellis and Larsen-Freeman 2009). These developments have significant implications for the study of the grammar of Biblical Hebrew (Naudé 2012a and 2012b). Language is construed as a system that consists of multiple agents (the speakers in the speech community) interacting with one another. The system is adaptive, that is, speakers' behavior is based on their past interactions, while current and past interactions together feed into future behavior. Cognition, consciousness, experience, embodiment, brain, self, human interaction, society, culture, and history are all intertwined in rich, complex, and dynamic ways in language. The structures of language emerge from interrelated patterns of experience, social interactions, and cognitive mechanisms as synchronic patterns of use at numerous levels (phonology, lexis, syntax, semantics, pragmatics, discourse, genre, etc.). They also emerge as dynamic, diachronic patterns of language change (linguistic cycles of grammaticalization, pidginization, creolization, etc.), as ontogenic developmental patterns in child language acquisition and as global geo-political patterns of language growth and decline, dominance and loss, etc.

Sixth, typological studies of language have demonstrated that there are a limited number of possible constructions among the world's languages. Determining how Biblical Hebrew relates to cross-linguistic variation provides an important means for understanding grammatical features of Biblical Hebrew, as well as a means for teaching students, especially non-Western students, Biblical Hebrew (Naudé and Miller-Naudé 2011).

Seventh, the nature of formal, written language in the ancient Near East as a function of scribal activity alongside the vernacular oral tradition within which it is embedded (Polak 1998, 2003; Rollston 2010; Sanders 2009; Schniedewind 2004) has implications for the study of the grammar of Biblical Hebrew.

Chapter 2

Writing System

§4. Consonants

§4.1. Forms of the Hebrew Consonants

The Hebrew alphabet consists of twenty-three characters (some with alternative graphic signs), which represent consonants only. The table below gives the name, form, transliteration and approximate pronunciation of each consonant.

Note the following:

(1) Hebrew is written from right to left with lines running from the top to the bottom of the page.

(2) Transliteration means that the distinctive characters of the Hebrew writing system are represented using characters of the Latin (Roman) alphabet that express approximately equivalent sounds. In cases where no equivalents exist, special transliteration symbols have been devised with the help of certain diacritical signs, for example, a dot under an h, /ḥ/ (letter 8), a wedge over the s, /š/ (letter 22).[1]

---

1. Transcriptions of Hebrew proper names that are found in the Septuagint exhibit phonological differences from the Tiberian Masoretic tradition. For example, the transcription for the name Gaza in Gen. 10:19 is written as Γάζα in the Septuagint and as עַזָּה in the Tiberian Masoretic tradition. The Septuagint transcription of gamma (Γ) for ʿayin (ע) preserves some of the original Semitic sound (voiced pharyngeal fricative) which is not reflected by the Tiberian Masoretic tradition. However, the voiceless pharyngeal fricative at the beginning of the name *Hannah* in 1 Sam. 1:2 is preserved in the Tiberian Masoretic tradition as חַנָּה but not in the transcription as reflected in the Septuagint Ἄννα (see also Khan 2013a: 55–57).

Table 1. *Consonants*

No.	Name	Form		Transliteration	Sound value
		Usual	*Final*		
1	*ʾālep̄*	א		/ʾ/	A very light glottal stop corresponding to the Greek *spiritus lenis*. Even before a vowel it is lost to the ear, like the *h* in *hour*.
2	*bêṯ*	בּ		/b/	[b] as in **b**ank
		ב		/ḇ/	[v] as in ne**v**er
3	*gimel*	גּ		/g/	[g] as in **g**o
		ג		/ḡ/	
4	*dāleṯ*	דּ		/d/	[d] as in **d**oor
		ד		/ḏ/	
5	*hē ʾ*	ה		/h/	[h] as in **h**and
6	*wāw*	ו		/w/	[v] as in **v**ote
7	*zayin*	ז		/z/	[z] as in **z**one
8	*ḥêṯ*	ח		/ḥ/	lo**ch** (velar as in Scots)
9	*ṭêṯ*	ט		/ṭ/	[t] as in **t**ime
10	*yôḏ*	י		/y/	[y] as in **y**ear
11	*kap̄*	כּ	ך	/k/	[k] as in **k**eep
		כ		/ḵ/	[x] as in Ba**ch** (palatal as in German)
12	*lāmeḏ*	ל		/l/	[l] as in **l**ine
13	*mêm*	מ	ם	/m/	[m] as in **m**ain
14	*nûn*	נ	ן	/n/	[n] as in **n**oon
15	*sāmeḵ*	ס		/s/	[s] as in **s**ilver
16	*ʿayin*	ע		/ʿ/	A hard glottal stop formed at the back of the throat. It may be heard in certain pronunciations of words like *bottle* and *battle* in which the glottal stop replaces the normal *t*.

No.	Name	Form		Transliteration	Sound value
		Usual	Final		
17	*pē᷎*	פ		/p/	[p] as in **pay**
		פ	ף	/p̄/	[f] as in **f**ace
18	*ṣāḏê*	צ	ץ	/ṣ/	[ts] as in ca**ts**
19	*qôp̄*	ק		/q/	[k] as in **k**eep
20	*rêš*	ר		/r/	[r] as in **r**ope
21	*śîn*	שׂ		/ś/	[s] as in **s**ilver
22	*šîn*	שׁ		/š/	[š] as in **sh**oe
23	*tāw*	ת		/t/	[t] as in **t**ime
		ת		/t̄/	

§4.2. Special Features of the Hebrew Consonants

4.2.1. *Letters with two forms*

Five Hebrew consonants have alternative forms when they appear at the end of a word. These are called final letters or end consonants.

Table 2. *Final Forms of Consonants*

Beginning or middle of word	כ/כּ	מ	נ	פ/פּ	צ
End of word	ך	ם	ן	ף	ץ
Number of letter on chart	11	13	14	17	18

4.2.2. *Letters with two alternative pronunciations*

Six of the Hebrew consonants, namely בּ (2), ג (3), ד (4), כ (11), פ (17) and ת (23), represent allophones. In other words, the same letter is used to indicate either a plosive or a fricative pronunciation. The plosive pronunciation involves a complete stopping of the air as it passes through the mouth. The fricative pronunciation allows the air to pass through a narrow passage of the mouth.

There is, however, no possibility of confusion as the plosives are marked by a diacritical point, the *dāḡēš* (§8.2).

בּ	גּ	דּ	כּ	פּ	תּ
/b/	/g/	/d/	/k/	/p/	/t/

The fricatives are written without the *dāḡēš*:

ב	ג	ד	כ/ך	פ/ף	ת
/ḇ/ [v]	/ḡ/ [g]	/ḏ/[d]	/ḵ/	/p̄/ [f]	/ṯ/ [t]

The fricative pronunciation of ג, ד and ת has fallen out of use, and they are currently pronounced like their plosive counterparts.

The distinction between the plosives and the fricatives is clear:

plosives always written with a *dāḡēš*,
always after a consonant,
regularly at the beginning of a word;
fricatives always written without the *dāḡēš*
always after a vowel.

Because it is sometimes necessary to refer as a group to the six consonants that may take the *dāḡēš lene* (weak *dāḡēš*), they are arranged alphabetically and furnished with vowels to form a catchword, namely: *beḡaḏkep̄aṯ*.

4.2.3. *Letters with homogeneous pronunciation*

In the following examples various groups of letters are pronounced more or less similarly:

גּ	(3)	and	ג	like	g	in	go
דּ	(4)	and	ד	like	d	in	door
תּ	(23)	and	ת	like	t	in	time
א	(1)	and	ע (16)	like	a glottal stop		
ב	(2)	and	ו (6)	like	v	in	never/vote
ח	(8)	and	כ/ך (11)	like	ch	in	Loch/Bach
ט	(9)	and	ת/ת (23)	like	t	in	time
כ	(11)	and	ק (19)	like	k	in	keep
ס	(15)	and	שׂ (21)	like	s	in	silver

Although these groups of signs have more or less the same pronunciation now, their sound values originally differed (that is, distinctive pronunciations originally existed for all the signs of the alphabet). These differences are reflected in the orthography.

4.2.4. *Letters with the same place of articulation*

It is useful to group sounds that share the same or similar articulation (i.e. they are produced in the same location or in the same manner in the mouth).

4.2.4.1. *Gutturals*

Gutturals are a group of consonants articulated at the back of the throat, namely: א (1), ה (5), ח (8) and ע (16).

- א must not be confused with the English "a" or Greek alpha (α). The latter two are vowels, while א is a consonant.
- א and ע are not pronounced at the beginning of a word; א is not pronounced at the end of a word.
- In the middle of a word א and ע are pronounced as a glottal stop, made by the complete stoppage of breath in the throat, almost like the "stop" between the two instances of the letter "e" in re-enact.

The consonant ר (20) bears certain similarities to the four gutturals and is usually grouped with them.

Should certain vowel changes become necessary in a word as, for example, when a plural is formed, the deviation from the normal is predictable within this group of consonants, namely:

- When a sound rule requires a vowel to be reduced, the vowel attached to a guttural will be reduced to a half vowel (also referred to as a composite *šǝwāʾ*) (§5.2.1.4).
- When a sound rule requires the doubling of a consonant, this doubling will occur neither with the gutturals nor with ר (§8.2.2).

4.2.4.2. *Dentals/Alveolars*

Dentals/alveolars are a group of consonants articulated when the tongue obstructs the air flow against the upper teeth or alveolar ridge (the ridge just behind the teeth on the roof of the mouth):

ד / ד (4), ט (9) and ת / ת (23)
ל (12), נ (14) and ר (20)

- When a word begins with a dental consonant, the deviation from any customary change in this group is predictable.
- When a conjugation results in two dental consonants occurring in immediate succession, the first dental becomes assimilated to the second dental.[2]

4.2.5. *Letters articulated in a similar fashion*

4.2.5.1. *Sibilants*

Sibilants are a group of consonants formed when the speech canal is narrowed and the air stream is forced through with a hissing sound, namely

שׁ (22), ז (7), ס (15) and שׂ (21)

When a word begins with a hissing sound, the deviation from the customary change in this group is predictable, e.g.:

- When a conjugation results in a sibilant occurring immediately after a dental, *metathesis*[3] of the sibilant and the dental occurs.

4.2.5.2. *Glides*

Glides are a group of consonants formed by limited obstruction to the air flow, namely

ה (5), ו (6) and י (10)

The obstruction is so limited that these consonants have more in common with vowels than with consonants. The result is that a vowel and the glide immediately following it sometimes become fused, so that the glide becomes associated with specific vowel sounds (see §5.1):

---

2. *Assimilation* is a phonological process which usually takes place when one consonant which closes a syllable passes over into another consonant beginning the next syllable, so forming with it a strengthened letter. In this process the sounds of the two consonants are equalized. Note, for example, the case of nasal assimilation in which *ten mice* is pronounced as *tem mice*. Assimilation is not restricted to dentals.

3. *Metathesis* is a phonological process in which two sounds are reversed (e.g. the pronunciation of the word *ask* as /aks/ in some dialects of English).

ה	e	as in	there
	ey	as in	café
	o	as in	more
	a	as in	father
ו	o	as in	more
	oo	as in	book
י	i	as in	machine
	ey	as in	café
	e	as in	there

In certain cases the א (1) has lost its consonantal character. In such cases א is also associated with specific vocalic sound values:

א	o	as in	more
	a	as in	father
	ey	as in	café

Biblical Hebrew was originally written only with consonants. This could easily lead to ambiguities; for example,

ים could be interpreted as /yām/ ("sea") or /yōm/ ("day").

In order to ensure that the reader would distinguish between the forms, one of the above-mentioned glides – namely ו – was used with the latter form to indicate the presence of an [ō] vowel between the two consonants: יום. This ensured the reading of the latter form as /yôm/. The form without the glide was read as /yām/.

When the glides (ה, ו and י) represent vowels and not consonants, they are called vowel indicators (*matres lectionis*, "mothers of reading") (§5.2.2.1).

§5. Vowels

A group of Jewish scholars, the Masoretes, did important work between 600 and 1000 CE in preserving and transmitting the text of the Hebrew Bible. Three groups of Masoretes were active, namely, in Babylon, Palestine and Tiberias. Their most important task was transmitting the consonantal text with the utmost accuracy.[4] To ensure that the oral tradition did not weaken further

---

4. The consonantal text that was incorporated into the Tiberian Masoretic tradition is a textual tradition that was transmitted with precision since at least the third century BCE. In contrast, Qumran scribal practice does not reflect a tradition of precise and conservative copying, but rather exhibits interventions by the scribe (see Tov 2004: 250–54). In

and to combat uncertainty and ambiguity, they devised vowel signs (or points) and added them to the consonantal text to precisely fix or establish the pronunciation and thus the meaning of the text of the Hebrew Bible. The highly meticulous work of the Masoretes gave rise to the term for the careful biblical text that they produced, the Masoretic text.[5] As indicated in §2.1, the tradition from Tiberias, the so-called Tiberian vocalization, is used in the scientific editions of the Hebrew Bible, namely the third edition of *Biblia Hebraica Kittel* (1937), *Biblia Hebraica Stuttgartensia* (1977), and *Biblia Hebraica Quinta* (since 2004).[6]

When the Masoretes introduced the system of vowel signs, the Hebrew Bible had already been committed to writing in consonants with vowel indicators (mothers of reading or *matres lectionis*) added to the consonants (§4.2.5.2). The Masoretes left the consonantal text unchanged and simply added the vowel signs to the existing letters. In most cases a vowel sign was placed under a consonant, in one case above the consonant and in others next to the consonant. In Biblical Hebrew the consonant is normally read first followed by the vowel accompanying it (§6.2).

§5.1. Forms of the Hebrew Vowels

The signs that represent vowels are given in the table below (shown with the letter ט or ה). The combination of vowel signs and vowel indicators is also given.

---

addition to these texts a number of texts were brought to Qumran from elsewhere which are closer to the Septuagint and the Samaritan tradition (Tov 2001: 107). Therefore the Qumran scrolls attest to a multiplicity of texts that co-existed with the one which is found in the Tiberian Masoretic tradition.

5. The scroll was the ancient form of manuscript used for public liturgical reading in synagogues. As a result it was regarded as unacceptable by the Masoretes to add the various written components of the Masoretic tradition such as vocalization, accents and marginal notes to scrolls. By contrast, codices were used for study purposes and non-liturgical reading and so the Masoretes felt free to introduce into these types of manuscript the newly developed written Masoretic components (Khan 2013a: 6–11).

6. The Tiberian Masoretic tradition concerns the consonantal text, layout of the text, indications of divisions of paragraphs, vocalization, accent signs, marginal notes, treatises and orally transmitted reading tradition. The accent and vocalization signs, but not the reading tradition that the signs represented, and the majority of textual notes and treatises were developed by the Masoretes. The other components are inherited from earlier traditions (Khan 2013a: 3–4). See Schäfer and Voss (2008: 4–15) for an introduction to the scholarly editions.

Table 3. *Vowels*

No.	Name	Form	Transliteration	Sound value (Modern Hebrew)
1	qāmeṣ	טָ טָה	/ā/ /â/	father
2	pataḥ	טַ	/a/	father
3	ḥaṭēp̄ pataḥ	חֲ	/ᵃ/	father
4	ḥôlem	טֹ טֹ, טֹה	/ō/ /ô/	more
5	qāmeṣ ḥāṭûp̄	טָ	/o/	hot
6	ḥaṭēp̄ qāmeṣ	חֳ	/ᵒ/	hot
7	ṣērê	טֵ טֵה, טֵי	/ē/ /ê/	café[7]
8	saḡôl	טֶ טֶי טֶה	/e/ /é/ /ê/	pen
9	ḥaṭēp̄ saḡôl	חֱ	/ᵉ/	pen
10	šûreq	טוּ	/û/	put
11	qibbûṣ	טֻ	/u/	put
12	ḥîreq	טִ טִי	/i/ or /ī/ /î/	hit
13	audible šəwāᶜ	טְ	/ə/	above

§5.2. Classification of Vowels and their Characteristics

5.2.1. *Classification of vowels*

It is generally held that the Tiberian vowel system indicated only the sound value or quality of a particular vowel and that it did not give a reliable representation of its length or quantity.[8] The Tiberian vowels are classified phonologically by some grammarians as listed below.

---

7. In American circles the *ṣērê* is pronounced like the diphthong in *they*. According to Joüon–Muraoka §6h, the *ṣērê* may also be pronounced like the vowel in *pen*.

8. See Khan (2013a: 43–65) concerning the prevalent reading traditions and vocalization.

5.2.1.1. *Short vowels*

טַ (2), טֹ (5 = o), טֶ (8), טִ (11) and טֻ (12)

5.2.1.2. *Changeable (ordinary) long vowels*

טָ (1 = ā), טֹ (4), טֵ (7)

5.2.1.3. *Unchangeable long vowels*

טָה (1), טוֹ, טֹה (4), טֵי, טֵה (7), טִי, טֶה (8), טוּ (10), טִי (12)

5.2.1.4. *Extra short vowels (half vowels)*

חַ (3), חֱ (6), חֳ (9), טְ (13)

5.2.2. *Characteristics of vowels*

5.2.2.1. *Vowel indicators (matres lectionis)*

It was stated in §4.2.5.2 that the glides ה, ו and י (and marginally א) could represent consonants as well as specific vowels, i.e. they could be used as vowel indicators; for example:

ה   for /ô/, /â/ and /ê/
ו   for /ô/ and /û/
י   for /î/, /ê/ and /é/

Therefore, in the consonantal text that predated the Masoretes, the ה, ו and י could sometimes represent a consonant and sometimes a vowel. The Masoretes resolved this ambiguity through their system of vowel points as follows:

(1) In Biblical Hebrew every consonant within a word must be accompanied by a vowel sign except for the final consonant of a word, which does not necessarily have to be accompanied by a vowel sign. When one of these glides represented a consonant, the Masoretes simply placed a vowel sign beneath it.

(2) Where a glide represented a vowel indicator the Masoretes combined their own vowel sign with the vowel indicator. In other words, when one of these four letters follows another consonant and only one vowel sign accompanies the two characters, the second character is functioning as a vowel indicator.

(3) ה, ו and י are used as vowel indicators solely in combination with specific vowel signs as indicated in §5.1.

Examples:

- The ה is used as a vowel indicator only at the end of the word, for example, סוּסָה (§9.2).
- In the word אָהֵב a vowel follows the ה within a word and thus ה cannot be regarded as a vowel indicator.
- There can be no confusion with the ו because a new sign is always created when the vowel and the vowel indicator are joined, namely וֹ and וּ.

The unchangeable long vowels are formed in combination with the vowel indicators (§5.2.2.1).

5.2.2.2. *Full and defective modes of writing*

In some instances a vowel may be represented by two different forms simultaneously. This is due to the fact that vowel signs were added to the text only after it had been fixed in consonants and vowel indicators.

(1) Vowel indicators were used in some words to refer to a particular vowel before the Masoretic vocalization. During the vocalization process another vowel sign referring to the same vowel was added to the vowel indicator. When a vowel sign is combined with a vowel indicator in this way, one speaks of the "full mode of writing" or *scriptio plena*.

(2) If the vowel is written without a vowel indicator, one speaks of the "defective mode of writing" or *scriptio defectiva*. There is no difference in the pronunciation of the two modes of writing.

The same word can sometimes be written in the full mode and sometimes in the defective mode of writing, e.g.:

קָדוֹשׁ	or	קָדֹשׁ
טוֹב	or	טֹב

In general, *scriptio defectiva* tends to be used in earlier Biblical Hebrew texts whereas *scriptio plena* tends to be used in later Biblical Hebrew. For example, the name "David" is always written דָּוִד in the earlier book of Kings, but as דָּוִיד in the later book of Chronicles.

5.2.2.3. *Distribution of the half vowels*

The first vowel of some words is a half vowel, namely an audible *šəwāʾ*, e.g.:

לְבוּשׁ

It was stated in §4.2.4.1 that a deviation from the customary change is predictable with the gutturals (א, ה, ח and ע). One of the characteristics of the gutturals is that they may not be vocalized with the audible *šəwāʾ*. Instead of the audible *šəwāʾ* the gutturals are vocalized with *ḥaṭēp̄* vowels.

The *ḥaṭēp̄* vowels are also half vowels. The Masoretic signs for the *ḥaṭēp̄* vowels are a combination of the *šəwāʾ* sign with the *pataḥ*, the *qāmeṣ* or the *səḡôl*. This produces the *ḥaṭēp̄* vowels, namely:

ḥaṭēp̄ pataḥ (3)	*חֲמוֹר	>	חֲמוֹר
ḥaṭēp̄ qāmeṣ (6)	*הֲלִי	>	הֲלִי
ḥaṭēp̄ səḡôl (9)	*אֱמֶת	>	אֱמֶת

The question may arise as to which one of the *ḥaṭēp̄* vowels takes the place of the *šəwāʾ*:

(1) In the case of the examples above the *ḥaṭēp̄* vowel is part of the actual composition of each word and must be learned as such.

(2) In other cases a sound rule may require the pronunciation of an audible *šəwāʾ* immediately after a guttural. A *ḥaṭēp̄ pataḥ* usually replaces the *šəwāʾ* in such a case.

§6. Diphthongs

Diphthongs are sounds formed when two different vowels are combined into one syllable. In Biblical Hebrew diphthongs may be formed in the two ways listed below.

§6.1. With ׳ after a Vowel

When ׳ follows certain vowels, they are pronounced as diphthongs. In the following table the diphthong is written after the consonant ט as an example:

Consonant	Combination	Pronunciation
׳	טִי	**Tie**
	טֶי	**Sky**
	טֹיו	**Boy**
	טוּי	**Gluey**

Note the following:

- When טִי is followed by a *wāw*, as in טִיו, the combination is pronounced as /tâv/.

§6.2. The Transitional *Paṭaḥ* or *Paṭaḥ Furtivum*

6.2.1. *Characteristics*

The consonants ה, ח and ע are articulated by moving the base of the tongue in the direction of the wall of the throat. This unusual articulation at the end of a closed syllable (§7.1.1) is strenuous. The vowel that produces the least stress on the speech organs in pronouncing ח or ע at the end of a closed syllable is the "a" (/ā/ or /a/), e.g.:

יָדַע   and   אָח

When one of the *other* long vowels appears before ה, ח and ע in the last syllable, a transitional vowel becomes necessary to facilitate pronunciation. In these cases the *paṭaḥ* is utilized as the transitional vowel.

Not /rûḥ / but   /rûaḥ /
Not /kōḥ/ but   /kōaḥ/

It is important to note that this *paṭaḥ* does not begin a new syllable, but only denotes a transition in the current syllable. The combination of the preceding vowel with the *paṭaḥ* creates a diphthong before the final consonant.

The *paṭaḥ furtivum* is written as follows:

רוּחַ   and   כֹּחַ

Although the *paṭaḥ* is written after the final consonant, it is pronounced between this consonant and vowel preceding it. This *paṭaḥ* is called the *transitional paṭaḥ* or *paṭaḥ furtivum* (the *paṭaḥ* that slides in).

6.2.2. *Distribution*

The *paṭaḥ furtivum* is a *paṭaḥ* that occurs at the end of a word when:

(1) The final consonant of a word is ה, ח and ע and

(2) The preceding vowel is not a *paṭaḥ* or a *qāmeṣ*, e.g.:

רֵעַ   and   רוּחַ

but   שָׁלַח

Because ע and ח in רֵעַ and רוּחַ were not originally furnished with a *paṭaḥ*, the insertion of the *paṭaḥ furtivum* became necessary. In שָׁלַח, however, the ח is preceded by a *paṭaḥ* and the insertion of the *paṭaḥ furtivum* is thus unnecessary.

§7. Syllables and Accents

§7.1. Types of Syllables

7.1.1. *Terminology: Open and closed syllables*

The word *syllable* denotes a combination of consonants and vowels that produces a word or a segment of a word in a single effort of articulation, i.e. the smallest grouping of sounds in a word that can be pronounced as a unit. The following distinctions are usually made with regard to syllables:

(1) *Open syllables*   An open syllable ends in a vowel.

(2) *Closed syllables*   A closed syllable ends in a consonant.

Table 4. *Examples of English Open and Closed Syllables*

Open syllable	Closed syllable
go	got
CV	CVC
spa	spank
CCV	CCVCC
mi-ni	mind-ful
CV–CV	CVCC–CVC

Every language has its own rules according to which vowels and consonants are combined into syllables. In English, for example, a cluster of two consonants commonly occurs at the beginning or end of a syllable, as in **blank** or **art**.

7.1.2. *Hebrew syllables*

The following rules apply to syllables in Hebrew:

(1) A syllable always begins with a consonant (see §31.1.1.(1)(b) and (c) for an exception).

(2) A syllable may be open or closed.

(3) There are usually no consonant clusters within a syllable, i.e. a syllable begins with only one consonant and a closed syllable ends with only one consonant.

Examples of syllables:

- One open syllable   לוֹ
- One closed syllable   בַּת
- Two open syllables   סוּ-סָה   <   סוּסָה
- Two syllables, one open and one closed   כָּ-תַב   <   כָּתַב

§7.2. Accentuation

7.2.1. *Rules*

The following rules may serve as broad guidelines for accentuation in Biblical Hebrew:

(1) In a *word* the accent usually falls on the *final* (ultimate) syllable.

(2) In words with the vowel pattern סֶסֶ, סֶסֶ, סֶס or סָס the accent falls on the second-last (penultimate) syllable (see §27.3)

(3) In a *clause* the accent usually falls on the stressed syllable of the last word.

The stressed syllable is referred to as the tone syllable and the two preceding it are referred to as the pretonic and the propretonic syllables, respectively.

7.2.2. *Examples*

The Masoretes designed a system for noting the accentuation of all the words in Biblical Hebrew. This complex system is dealt with in §9.5. Where it becomes essential in this grammar to indicate the accentuation of a particular word, the sign [ʻ] will be used to mark the accented syllable, e.g.:

(1) שְׁמוֹ

(2) מֶלֶךְ

(3) רֹ-מֶ-שֶׂת

(4) אָ-מַר

(5) הוֹ-צִי-אָם

7.2.3. *Additional or secondary accentuation*

In Biblical Hebrew certain words have a secondary accent. Words consisting of three syllables, with the primary accent on the final syllable, often receive a secondary accent on the third and last syllable. The Masoretic sign that indicates secondary accent is a vertical line to the left of the first vowel. This sign is called the *meteḡ* (§9.1) and denotes that the syllable is held open, e.g.:

$$ כָּתְבָה \qquad = \qquad כָּ-תְ-בָה $$

§7.3. Distribution of Vowels in Syllables

There is a clear correlation between the classification of the Masoretic vowel signs and their use in syllables:

(1) Extra short vowels always occur in open, unaccented syllables, e.g.:

שְׁמוֹ   his name

(2) Short vowels usually occur in closed, unaccented syllables, e.g.:

מִדְבָּר   desert

(3) Short vowels can also occur in open, accented syllables, e.g.:

קַיִן   Cain

(4) Long vowels usually occur in open syllables regardless of whether the syllable is accented or not, e.g.:

בָּנָה   he built

(5) Long vowels can also occur in closed, accented syllables, e.g.:

מִדְבָּר   desert

§8. Masoretic Signs with a Double Function

§8.1. *Šəwāʾ*

8.1.1. *Audible šəwāʾ*

The *šəwāʾ* has already been encountered as the sign of the extra short vowel (§5.2.1.4) as in

לְבוֹשׁ   garment

This *šəwāʾ* is called the audible *šəwāʾ* or *šəwāʾ mobile*. It acts as the "vowel" of an open syllable.

CV   =   סְ

The distribution of the audible *šəwāʾ* is as follows:

(1) The *šəwāʾ* is audible in the first syllable of a word, as in:

בְּרִית   =   בְּ-רִית

(2) The *šəwāʾ* is audible after a syllable with a long vowel, as in:

סוּסְכֶם   =   סוּ-סְ-כֶם

(3) The *šəwāʾ* is audible after a syllable that held open, as in:

כֵּתְבָה   =   כֵּ-תְ-בָה

Note the following:

(a) Should two audible *šəwāʾ*'s be found in two consecutive open syllables, they fuse into one closed syllable with the vowel /◌ִ/, e.g.:

*כְּשְׁמוּאֵל   becomes   כִּשְׁמוּאֵל

(b) If the second open syllable begins with the consonant י, the י loses its consonantal value and becomes a vowel indicator, e.g.:

*בְּיְהוּדָה   becomes   בִּיהוּדָה

(c) If a guttural with a *ḥaṭēp* vowel is preceded by an open syllable with an audible *šəwāʾ* as the vowel, this open syllable takes the full vowel corresponding to the *ḥaṭēp* vowel, e.g.:

*בְּחֲלוֹם   becomes   בַּחֲלוֹם

8.1.2. *Silent šəwā³*

The *šəwā³* is also used for another purpose, namely to note the end of a closed syllable in the middle of a word, such as

מִשְׁפָּט	=	מִשׁ-פָּט
מִדְבָּר	=	מִד-בָּר

This *šəwā³* is called the silent *šəwā³* or *šəwā³ quiescens.* It is an orthographical aid used to indicate a closed syllable within a word and the absence of a vowel in that position.

$$\text{CVC} \quad = \quad \text{סַס}$$

The distribution of the silent *šəwā³* is as follows:

(1) The *šəwā³* is usually silent after a short vowel, e.g.:

מִדְבָּר	=	מִד-בָּר
כָּתַבְתָּ	=	כָּ-תַב-תָּ

When a word ends with a closed syllable, the final consonant is usually not accompanied by a Masoretic sign, e.g. כָּתַב. In the following cases, however, a deviation from the norm occurs:

(2) A silent *šəwā³* is also placed in a final *kap̄* in order to distinguish the latter from a final *nûn*, e.g. הָלַךְ.

(3) A silent *šəwā³* is also placed under a double final *tāw* e.g. אַתְּ. (The doubling of the final *tāw* is simply orthographic. It is not articulated. Words ending with a double consonant are usually written with a single consonant, e.g. עַם *ʿam* < *ʿamm.*)

(4) What appears to be a consonant cluster may sometimes be found at the end of a word. The cluster originated from the combination of a closed and an open syllable, with the vowel of the latter syllable having lost its sound. In this case a silent *šəwā³* occurs underneath each of the consonants, e.g. כָּתַבְתְּ.

(5) A sound rule may lead to a silent *šəwā³* appearing after a guttural. In such cases a *ḥaṭēp̄* vowel may appear in the place of the silent *šəwā³*, e.g. יֶחֱזַק (§5.2.1.4).

8.1.3. *Medial šəwāʾ*

The medial *šəwāʾ* is used in syllables in which the vowel is no longer pronounced but in which its effect remains so that the subsequent *beḡaḏkepat* letters do not have a plosive *dāḡēš*, e.g.:

מַלְכֵי   /malkê/   instead of   /maləkê/

Historically the word מַלְכֵי derives from מַלֲכֵי in which the *kap* is preceded by a vowel. In the historical development of this word the vowel became silent and the *kap* was pronounced directly after the *lāmed*. To indicate the original presence of a vowel before the *kap*, the Masoretes did not place a plosive *dāḡēš* in the *beḡaḏkepat* letter.

The *šəwāʾ* sign that replaces the original vowel is known as the medial *šəwāʾ* or the *šəwāʾ medium*. For pronunciation purposes the medial *šəwāʾ* is a silent *šəwāʾ* and the *beḡaḏkepat* letter following it is a fricative.

§8.2. *Dāḡēš*

8.2.1. *Plosive dāḡēš (dāḡēš lene)*

The *dāḡēš* has already been encountered as the diacritical point that occurs only in the *beḡaḏkepat* letters and which distinguishes the plosives from the fricatives (§4.2.2). This form of the *dāḡēš* is called the plosive *dāḡēš* or *dāḡēš lene* (weak *dāḡēš*).

The distribution of the plosive *dāḡēš* may be determined as follows:

(1) It usually occurs at the beginning of a word, as in:

בְּרִית   =   בְּ-רִית

(2) It occurs after a closed syllable, as in:

מִדְבָּר   =   מִדְ-בָּר

כָּתַבְתָּ   =   כָּ-תַבְ-תָּ

8.2.2. *Doubling dāḡēš (dāḡēš forte)*

The *dāḡēš* is also used for another purpose, namely to indicate the doubling of a consonant:

הַסּוּס	= הַס-סוּס	Two closed syllables
עַמּוּד	= עַמ-מוּד	Two closed syllables
צַדִּיק	= צַד-דִּיק	Two closed syllables

This *dāḡēš* is called the doubling *dāḡēš* or the *dāḡēš forte* (strong *dāḡēš*). The consonant which is doubled is written once only and then punctuated with the doubling *dāḡēš*. The doubled consonant thus simultaneously ends one syllable and begins the next one.

The distribution of the strong *dāḡēš* may be determined as follows:

- The *dāḡēš* found in consonants that follow a vowel is a doubling *dāḡēš*. This vowel is usually short.

$$צַדִּיק \quad = \quad צַד-דִיק$$
$$עַמּוּד \quad = \quad עַמ-מוּד$$

The gutturals and ר normally do not double (§4.2.4.1). Under certain conditions which would normally require doubling, the gutturals and ר are therefore not doubled. One of two conditions results: either no changes are made (e.g. נִחַת without doubling is written instead of *niḥḥat*), or, the preceding vowel is changed, for example, בֵּרֵךְ is written instead of בִּרֵךְ*. The former process is called "virtual doubling"; the latter process is called "compensatory lengthening," because a short vowel is replaced with a long vowel in most cases.

8.2.3. *Conjunctive dāḡēš*

When a word ends on an unaccented /ā/, /â/ or /ê/ and the first syllable of the next word is accented, the first consonant of the second word is written with a conjunctive *dāḡēš*, as in:

$$שָׁבִיתָ שֶּׁבִי$$
$$שִׂימָה לָּנוּ$$

This *dāḡēš* is called the conjunctive *dāḡēš* or the *dāḡēš conjunctivum*. It is generally understood that this *dāḡēš* does not indicate the doubling of the consonant, but it has not been possible to ascertain its precise function as yet.

8.2.4. *Disjunctive dāḡēš*

This *dāḡēš* does not indicate the doubling of the consonant, but serves to distinguish the audible *šəwāʾ* from the silent *šəwāʾ*, as in:

$$עֲקְבֵי \qquad /ʿiqəbê/ \quad \text{instead of} \quad /ʿiqbê/$$

The distribution of the disjunctive *dāḡēš* can be determined as follows: short vowels usually occur in closed, unaccented syllables (§7.3). In some cases a short vowel may appear in an open syllable as in the word עֲקְבֵי. In such cases, when the short vowel is followed by an audible *šəwā²*, confusion could arise concerning the pronunciation of that particular word. A disjunctive *dāḡēš* is placed in the consonant between the short vowel and the *šəwā²* sign.

8.2.5. *Qenemlui letters*

It sometimes happens that the doubling of the consonant is dropped, as in the י of

$$\text{וַיְהִי}\quad \text{/wayəhî/}\quad <\quad \text{וַיְּהִי}\quad \text{/wayyəhî/}$$

This is due to the fact that the doubling of certain consonants is dropped when they are followed by an audible *šəwā²*. This occurs with י, ו, ל, מ, נ and ק, the so-called *qenemlui* letters, and the sibilants (§4.2.5.1).

§8.3. *Qāmeṣ*

8.3.1. *Phonetic values*

The *qāmeṣ* sign indicates two possible sound values (different pronunciations):

> **a** as in the English word father
> **o** as in the English word hot

The latter is called the *qāmeṣ ḥāṭûp̄* or the *short qāmeṣ*.

8.3.2. *Distribution*

The distribution of the *qāmeṣ* and the *qāmeṣ ḥāṭûp̄* can be determined as follows:

(1) The /◌ָ/ occurring in closed, unaccented syllables is the *qāmeṣ ḥāṭûp̄* and represents /o/.

(2) The /◌ָ/ occurring in all other syllables (i.e. open syllables or closed accented syllables) is the *qāmeṣ* and represents /ā/.

(3) Wherever uncertainty may arise concerning the correct interpretation of the /◌ָ/, the *meṯeḡ* (§9.1) is used whenever a syllable must be left open and vocalized with a *qāmeṣ*.

(4) A /◌ָ/ followed by a /◌ָ/ is read as a *qāmeṣ ḥāṭûp̄*, in spite of the fact that it occurs in an open syllable, e.g. פָּעֳלִי /po⁽ᵒ⁾lî/.

8.3.3. *Examples of distribution*

(1) The first syllable is open and unaccented; the vowel is a *qāmeṣ*, e.g.:

כָּתַב   כָּ-תַב

(2) The last syllable is closed but accented; the vowel is a *qāmeṣ*, e.g.:

מִדְבָּר   מִדְ-בָּר

(3) The syllable is closed but accented; the vowel is a *qāmeṣ*, e.g.:

אָב   אָב

(4) The first syllable is open and accented; the vowel is a *qāmeṣ*, e.g.:

כָּתְבָה   כָּ-תְ-בָה

(5) The first syllable is closed and unaccented; the vowel is a *qāmeṣ ḥāṭûp̄*, e.g.:

חָכְמָה   חָכְ-מָה

(6) The penultimate syllable is open and accented; the vowel is a *qāmeṣ*. The last syllable is closed and unaccented; the vowel is a *qāmeṣ ḥāṭûp̄*, e.g.:

וַיָּקָם   וַיָ-יָ-קָם

§8.4. ו Sign

The ו sign can function either as the vowel *šûreq* or as a double consonant *wāw*. If it appears after a consonant, it is a *šûreq* (e.g. בָּרוּךְ); if it appears after a short vowel, it is a double *wāw* (e.g. צִוָּה) (§5.2.2.1).

§9. Additional Masoretic Signs

§9.1. *Meṯeḡ*

The *meṯeḡ* (◌ֽ) is a small vertical line that is written underneath the consonant and to the left of the vowel (in *Biblia Hebraica Stuttgartensia* it is sometimes written to the right of the vowel). Its purpose is to indicate a secondary or additional accent in a word (§7.2.3).

The *meṯeḡ* should not be confused with the *sillûq* which only appears under the last word of the verse (§9.5.2).

One of the orthographic functions of the *meṯeḡ* is to distinguish between the *qāmeṣ* and *qāmeṣ ḥāṭûp̄* (§8.3). The *qāmeṣ ḥāṭûp̄* is a short vowel in a closed, unaccented syllable (§7.3.(3)). The *qāmeṣ*, by contrast, usually appears as a long vowel in an accented syllable. The *meṯeḡ* is used with the *qāmeṣ* in any position where doubt may arise in order to ensure that it will not be interpreted as a *qāmeṣ ḥāṭûp̄*.

For example, אָכְלָה can be interpreted as /ʾāḵəlâ/ (she ate) or as /ʾoḵlâ/ (food). In order to eliminate confusion the *meṯeḡ* is used in the first instance, namely אָֽכְלָה, to indicate that /◌ָ/ is stressed and cannot be interpreted as a *qāmeṣ ḥāṭûp̄*. In the latter case, namely אָכְלָה, /◌ָ/ occurs in a closed, unaccented syllable. The *meṯeḡ* is absent and therefore the *qāmeṣ* must be interpreted as a *qāmeṣ ḥāṭûp̄*.

In this grammar the *meṯeḡ* is used only when a distinction has to be made between *qāmeṣ* and *qāmeṣ ḥāṭûp̄*.

In *Biblia Hebraica Stuttgartensia* the *meṯeḡ* is not used consistently:

(1) The *qāmeṣ* and *ṣērê* are regularly replaced by half vowels in open pretonic or propretonic syllables. Because the occurrence of the *qāmeṣ* and *ṣērê* in these positions would be anomalous, they are usually marked with a *meṯeḡ*, e.g.:

אָֽנֹכִי

בֵּֽרַכְתַּ֫נִי

(2) Although the principle is not applied consistently, any pretonic or propretonic vowel may be marked with the *meṯeḡ*, e.g.:

הֹֽושִׁיעֵ֫נִי

(3) Short vowels usually occur in closed syllables before the primary accent. Should this not be the case, the vowel is marked with a *meṯeḡ*, e.g.:

תַּֽעֲמֹד

(4) A short vowel with a *meṯeḡ* in what appears to be a closed syllable is an indication that the normal doubling of the following consonant has been dropped:

הַֽמְרַגְּלִים   instead of   הַמְרַגְּלִים

§9.2. *Mappîq*

In §5.2.2.1 it was stated that the letter ה could act as a vowel indicator. To ensure that a consonant ה at the end of a word is not accidentally interpreted as a ה used as a vowel indicator, the Masoretes placed a point inside the ה to distinguish it from the ה vowel indicator.

ה as consonant:	גָּבַהּ	He is high
	סוּסָהּ	her [male] horse
ה as vowel indicator:	סוּסָה	mare

This diacritical point is called the *mappîq* and it only occurs in the ה. It must not be confused with the *dāḡēš*.

§9.3. *Maqqēp̄*

The *maqqēp̄* is a hyphen that joins a short word to the word that follows it. The *maqqēp̄* is written as follows:

לֹא־דָרְשָׁה   She did not seek

The two words joined in this way form a single accentual unit. The accent then falls on the last part of the unit – usually on the last syllable of that part.

§9.4. *Sôp̄ Pāsûq*

The *sôp̄ pāsûq*, which looks like a boldly printed colon [:], is the sign that indicates the end of a verse.

§9.5. Accent Signs

9.5.1. *Introduction*

In addition to their vowel system, the Masoretes also developed a system of accents.

9.5.1.1. *Functions*

The accent system indicates:

(1) the stressed syllable of a word, which can be crucial to determine the correct interpretation, e.g.: שָׁבוּ "they captured" (Gen. 34:29) but שָׁבוּ "they returned" (Josh. 2:22);

(2) the place where long or short pauses occur in a clause;

(3) which words belong together; and

(4) cantillation for liturgical purposes.

9.5.1.2. *Accents for prose and for poetry*

There are two accent systems:

(1) one for the prose sections and

(2) one for three poetic books, namely Psalms, Job and Proverbs.

The most important accent signs are, however, more or less the same for both.

9.5.1.3. *Conjunctive and disjunctive accents*

Two groups of accent signs may be distinguished, namely *conjunctive* (joining) and *disjunctive* (separating) accents. They are used as follows:

(1) The accent sign indicates the position of the stressed syllable in a word. In Biblical Hebrew the final syllable (and in certain cases also the penultimate) is usually accented. The accent sign is normally placed above or below the first consonant of the accented syllable. In some cases accent signs are placed at the beginning or end of the word – these are the so-called prepositive and postpositive accents.

(2) The conjunctive and disjunctive accents often follow each other in a fixed order. The resultant sequence of accents was used to group together the words of the Biblical Hebrew text. This grouping of words facilitated the recitation of the Hebrew Bible in the synagogues and was thus similar to punctuation in modern publications.

9.5.2. *Most important conjunctive and disjunctive accents*

A list of the most important conjunctive and disjunctive accents is given below.

9.5.2.1. *Prose system*

Table 5. *Main Disjunctive Accents in Prose*

Name	Form	Remarks
sillûq (סִלּוּק)	סססּ	Identifies the final accented syllable of a verse. With the *sôp̄ pāsûq* (סוֹף פָּסוּק) (§9.4), it indicates the end of the verse. It is written below the accented syllable.
ʾaṯnāḥ (אַתְנָח)	סססֿ	Indicates the main pause in a verse. It is placed to the left of the vowel in the accented syllable of the word preceding the pause. It divides the verse into two.

Name	Form	Remarks
ṭipḥā' (טִפְחָא)	סֹסֽ	Indicates either the main pause in short verses or the final pause before a *sillûq* or *'aṭnāḥ*.
zāqēp̄ qāṭôn (זָקֵף קָטוֹן)	סֹסֽ	A long unit with *'aṭnāḥ* as main subdivision is further subdivided by a *zāqēp̄ qāṭôn*.
səḡôltâ' (סְגוֹלְתָּא)	סֹּסֽ	Postpositional. Indicates the first of two main pauses in a verse. It is written to the left and above the last letter of the word preceding the pause.
rəḇîaʿ (רְבִיעַ)	סֹסֽ	Subdivides sections indicated by *zāqēp̄ qāṭôn*, *səḡôltâ'* or *ṭipḥā'*. It may also be used to mark the focal point of a clause.

Table 6. *Weaker Disjunctive Accents*

Name	Form	Remarks
paštā' (פַּשְׁטָא)	סֹסֽ	Postpositional. If the accent does not fall on the final syllable of the word, it is repeated on the accented syllable.
zarqā' (זַרְקָא)	סֹּסֽ	Postpositional
gereš (גֵּ֜רֶשׁ)	סֹסֽ	

Table 7. *Main Conjunctive Accents*

Name	Form	Remarks
mûnaḥ (מוּנַח)	סְסֽ	
məhuppāḵ (מְהֻפָּךְ)	סְסֽ	
mêrəḵā' (מֵירְכָא)	סְסֽ	

Table 8. *Less Strong Conjunctive Accents*

Name	Form	Remarks
təlîšā' qəṭannâ (תְּלִישָׁא קְטַנָּה)	סֹּסֽ	Postpositional
'azlā' (אַזְלָא)	סֹּסֽ	

9.5.2.2. *Poetry system*

Table 9. *Main Disjunctive Accent in Poetry*

Name	Form	Remarks
ʿôlê wəyôrēḏ (עוֹלֶה וְיוֹרֵד)	סֹסֶס	Placed on the accented syllable and on the preceding syllable of the word preceding the pause.

9.5.2.3. *Common combinations of accents*

(1) *ʾaṯnāḥ* and *sillûq*

וַיֹּאמֶר אֱלֹהִים יְהִי אוֹר וַיְהִי־אוֹר: And God said, "Let there be light." And there was light (Gen. 1:3).*

(2) *mêrəḵāʾ, ṭiᵖḥāʾ, mûnaḥ* and *ʾaṯnāḥ*

וַיֹּאמֶר אֱלֹהִים יְהִי אוֹר   And God said, "Let there be light" (Gen. 1:3).*

(3) *məhuppāḵ, pašṭāʾ* and *zāqēᵖ qāṭôn*

וַיֹּאמֶר יְהוָֹה אֶל־קַיִן...   And the LORD said to Cain... (Gen. 4:9).*

(4) *mûnaḥ, zarqāʾ, mûnaḥ* and *səḡôltāʾ*

וַיָּרַח יְהוָֹה אֶת־רֵיחַ הַנִּיחֹחַ   And the LORD smelled the soothing aroma (Gen. 8:21).*

(5) *mûnaḥ* and *rəḇîaʿ*

וַיֹּאמֶר אֱלֹהִים...   And God said... (Gen. 1:24).

(6) *təlišāʾ qəṭannâ, ʾazlāʾ* and *gereš*

וַיִּצֶר יְהוָֹה אֱלֹהִים...   And the LORD God formed...(Gen. 2:19).*

§9.6. Pausal Forms

A word that occurs at the end of a verse or section of a verse is pronounced with particular emphasis on the accented syllable. Consequently, short vowels in this syllable may lengthen and long vowels that have been reduced may return to their original form (§7.3). These forms are known as pausal forms and occur particularly with the *sillûq*, *ʾatnāḥ* and *zāqēp qāṭôn*.

In the following example, the *pataḥ* in מַיִם has changed to a *qāmeṣ* (מָיִם), at the end of each verse section due to the influence of the accents *ʾatnāḥ* and *sillûq*.

וַיֹּאמֶר אֱלֹהִים יְהִי רָקִיעַ בְּתוֹךְ הַמָּיִם	And then God said: "Let there be
וִיהִי מַבְדִּיל בֵּין מַיִם לָמָיִם׃	a dome in the midst of the waters and let it divide the waters from the waters" (Gen. 1:6).*

§9.7. *Kəṯîḇ* and *Qərê* Readings

The Masoretes sometimes believed that a word should be pronounced in a way that differed from the traditional consonantal text. Because they did not wish to alter the consonantal text itself, they recorded variant readings in the margin. These variant readings as indicated by the Masoretes are also printed in the margins of the third edition of *Biblia Hebraica Kittel*, *Biblia Hebraica Stuttgartensia* and *Biblia Hebraica Quinta*.

The variant form in the margin is called the *qərê* reading (from the Aramaic word קְרֵי "to be read") and the corresponding written form in the text is referred to as the *kəṯîḇ* reading (from the Aramaic word כְּתִיב "written"). The *qərê* reading was normally preferred to the *kəṯîḇ* reading. The vocalization of the *kəṯîḇ* reading in the margin was placed below the *kəṯîḇ* form in the text. A small circle above the relevant word in the text informs the reader to refer to the *qərê* reading in the margin. In the margin a small *qōp* (an abbreviation of קְרֵי) is placed under the word to be read to indicate that it is the *qərê* reading.

For example:

(1) In the text of Ps. 54:7 the form יָשׁוּב is found. The pre-Masoretic consonantal text had ישוב which indicates יָשׁוּב (or possibly יָשׁוֹב), the Qal form. The Masoretes understood instead that the word should rather be read יָשִׁיב (*Hipʿîl*) at this point. Rather than change the *wāw* of the consonantal text to a *yôḏ*, they vocalized the consonants ישוב in the text as יָשׁוּב (which is neither a real word nor pronounceable) and placed the consonants ישיב in the margin as the *qərê* ("read") variant to be vocalized as יָשִׁיב.

(2) Some words are so frequently pronounced differently from the written text that they are not explained in the margin. The most important of these is the name of God. In Biblical Hebrew God's name is written as יהוה and was probably pronounced "Yahweh" in ancient times. At a certain stage,

it was considered wrong to pronounce God's name and the word אֲדֹנָי "my Lord" was always read in the place of the name יהוה. The Masoretes retained the consonants of the name יהוה out of respect for the text, but always appended to them the vowels of the word אֲדֹנָי as an indication of how the word should be read. This produced the form יְהֹוָה, which the Leningrad Codex (and thus the third edition of *Biblical Hebraica, Biblia Hebraica Stuttgartensia* and *Biblia Hebraica Quinta*) represents as יְהוָה. Jews pronounce this form as /ˣdōnāy/ (see also §24.3.3.(7)(c)).

§9.8. Other Masoretic Markers

9.8.1. *Paragraph markers*

To facilitate reading, the text in codices is written in columns. In the Tiberian manuscripts the convention was to write three columns of equal width on each page. The poetic books (e.g. Psalms, Proverbs and Job) have a distinctive layout in two columns with interspersed spaces within the columns. Except for the interspersed spaces within the columns of poetic texts, this convention is not followed in the *Biblia Hebraica* series. However, the layout of the columns of some poetical sections are followed in *Biblia Hebraica Quinta*.[9] For example, the "space over space and text over text" format is found in Deuteronomy 32:

--------------------   ---------------------

--------------------   ---------------------

The "space over text and text over space" format is found in Judges 5:

--------------------   ---------------------

-----------   --------------------   ------------

--------------------   ---------------------

A further component of the Tiberian Masoretic tradition is the division of text into paragraphs (known as *pisqāʾôt* or *pārāššīyyôt*) according to content. Paragraphs were originally indicated by spaces in the text.

Two types of paragraphs are found. The "open" paragraph or *pǝṯûḥâ* begins on a new line. The "closed" paragraph or *sǝṯûmâ* begins later on the same line in which the previous paragraph ended.

---

9. Some lists in *Biblia Hebraica Quinta* retain the formatting of the *Leningrad Codex* (e.g. Ezra 2:43–57; Neh. 7:8–59).

Table 10. *Paragraph Markers*

Pəṯûḥâ	Səṯûmâ	
.... פ	.... ס	.... ס
....	....	....

As has been the practice from the beginning of the *Biblia Hebraica* series, open and closed paragraphs are not indicated in the various printed editions by the spacing of lines, but by the insertion of the letter פ in the space to mark a *pəṯûḥâ*, which is a major division in content, and the insertion of the letter ס to mark a *səṯûmâ*, which is a sub-division of the *pəṯûḥâ*. In the *Biblia Hebraica Quinta* a complete table of the occurrences of the paragraph markers is included in the introduction to each book.

9.8.2. *Liturgical chapter markers*

The Pentateuch was divided in two different ways for liturgical readings.

9.8.2.1. *Sēḏer*

According to *Palestinian tradition* the Pentateuch is recited in a cycle of three years. For this purpose it was divided into 154 or 167 segments. Each segment is called a *sēḏer* and is marked by a ס in the margin. Different manuscripts, however, vary in the number of *səḏārîm*. There are a total of 452 *səḏārîm* in the Leningrad Codex.

9.8.2.2. *Pārāšâ*

According to *Babylonian tradition* the Pentateuch is recited in an annual cycle and is thus divided into 54 parts. Each part is called a *pārāšâ* and is indicated by the letters פרש in the margin.

In *Biblia Hebraica Stuttgartensia* the symbols for *sēḏer* and *pārāšâ* always appear in the inner margin (i.e. in the middle of the bound book). In *Biblia Hebraica Quinta*, however, these symbols appear in the outer margins.

9.8.3. *Critical signs in the text*

The Masoretes made use of certain critical signs in the text

- to focus attention on the text itself,
- to indicate instances of uncertainty in the correctness of the text,
- to indicate where the text had been improved.

These critical signs could take the following forms.

9.8.3.1. *Large letters (literae majusculae)*

Some letters were deliberately enlarged when a passage deserved special attention.

שְׁמַע יִשְׂרָאֵל   Hear, O Israel, the LORD is our God,
יְהוָה אֱלֹהֵינוּ יְהוָה| אֶחָד   the LORD is one (Deut. 6:4).*

9.8.3.2. *Small letters (literae minusculae)*

Some letters were deliberately decreased in size when the form of the word was not standard. This feature is not represented in *Biblia Hebraica Stuttgartensia*.

9.8.3.3. *Suspended letters (literae suspensae)*

Some letters were deliberately written above the line either when there was uncertainty about that particular section or when that section had been improved.

וִיהוֹנָתָן בֶּן־גֵּרְשֹׁם בֶּן־מְנַשֶּׁה   and Jonathan, the son of Gershom, *the son of Moses* **or** *the son of Menassah* (Judg. 18:30)*

9.8.3.4. *Inverted nûn (nûn inversum)*

An inverted *nûn* was added to a section that did not fit into the context and had to be placed in brackets, as it were.

...בְּנָסְעָם מִן־הַמַּחֲנֶה ׃נ ס   [34] [34]...whenever they set forth from the camp.

וַיְהִי בִּנְסֹעַ הָאָרֹן[35] [35]And whenever the ark set out, וַיֹּאמֶר מֹשֶׁה...   Moses said...

...רִבְבוֹת אַלְפֵי יִשְׂרָאֵל ׃נ פ[36] [36]...the ten thousand thousands of Israel (Num. 10:34–36).*

9.8.3.5. *Extraordinary points (puncta extraordinaria)*

Points were placed above doubtful letters.

...וַיֹּאמְרוּ אֵלָיו   And they asked [lit. said *to*] *him*... (Gen. 18:9).*

The various other Masoretic markers (e.g. the signals for reading sections, enlarged letters, suspended letters, the inverted *nûn*) are printed in *Biblia Hebraica Stuttgartensia* and *Biblia Hebraica Quinta* as they appear in the Leningrad Codex, as has been the practice since the third edition of *Biblia Hebraica Kittel*.

9.8.4. *Critical comments that supplement the text*

9.8.4.1. *Masoretic endnotes (Masora finalis)*

Lists were added at the end of every book in the Hebrew Bible (with the exception of 1 Samuel, 1 Kings, Ezra, and 1 Chronicles, which originally were paired with 2 Samuel, 2 Kings, Nehemiah and 2 Chronicles, respectively). These lists contained information about the number of verses in a book, but could also contain additional information. The note at the end of Deuteronomy, for example, mentions the following:

- The book has 955 verses.
- The middle-point of the book is עַל־פִּי in 17:10.
- There are 31 *sǝḏārîm* in the book.
- It also states that the Pentateuch consists of 5,845 verses, 158 *sǝḏārîm*, 79,856 words and 400,945 letters.

These Masoretic comments were a form of quality control against which a new manuscript could be checked.

9.8.4.2. *Masoretic marginal notes (Masora marginalis)*

(1) *Masora parva*
In addition to establishing a fixed pronunciation and meaning, the Masoretes also endeavored to secure the biblical text against mistakes in copying and to correct existing errors. These marginal notes are called the *Masora parva* (or small Masora). In addition to *qǝrê* readings (§9.7), *Masora parva* refers to the notes containing commentary on the text, non-textual traditions, rare words and the center of whole books or larger sections. They also contain statistical information such as the following:

- (a) Words that appear only once in the Hebrew Bible are marked by the letter ל, which is the abbreviation for the Aramaic לָא לִית/לֵית ("There is no other").
- (b) Words/phrases used twice are marked by ב (the Hebrew notation for the numeral two) and those used three times by ג, etc.

The *Masora parva* was printed for the first time as part of the text in the third edition of *Biblia Hebraica Kittel* (1937), although without further treatment or explanation. For *Biblia Hebraica Stuttgartensia* the commentary of the *Masora parva* is placed in the outer margin (i.e. on the right-hand side of even-numbered pages and on the left-hand side of odd-numbered pages). It is written mostly in Aramaic.[10]

Small circles written above words in the text identify those portions of the text on which commentary is provided in the *Masora parva* on the adjacent line. Should more than one word in the same line be marked by such a circle, points are used to distinguish the marginal notes belonging to the various words. The small numbers in the *Masora parva* refer to the *Masora magna*.

The basic principle of representation of the *Masora parva* in the *Biblia Hebraica Quinta* is diplomatic with respect to what is actually written in the Leningrad Codex. This means that where the Masora of the Leningrad Codex is not consistent with the text in the manuscript, it will not be corrected, as was the practice especially in *Biblia Hebraica Stuttgartensia*. A glossary of common abbreviations used in the *Masora parva* is included in the *Biblia Hebraica Quinta* to aid readers in understanding those notes. Notes from the *Masora parva* that cannot be translated reliably using the glossary are trans-lated in the commentary section.

(2) *Masora magna*

Along with the lesser collection of notes, the *Masora parva*, the Masoretes also compiled lists of entire passages which are included at the top and the foot of the pages of the Masoretic manuscripts, and which are referred to as the *Masora magna* (or large Masora). The *Masora magna* was not dealt with in the publication of the third edition of *Biblia Hebraica Kittel*. Concerning the *Biblia Hebraica Stuttgartensia*, the *Masora magna* is not found in the same volume as the text, but is found in a separate volume, the *Massorah Gedolah*, critically edited by Gerard E. Weil (Weil 1971). This volume represents a fully corrected version of the *Masora magna* of the Leningrad Codex, rather than a diplomatic representation of what was actually written in the manuscript. The *Masora magna* of a particular text may be accessed by means of the *Masora parva*. A circle above a word refers to the *Masora parva*. A small number in the *Masora parva* refers to the note at the bottom of the page (just above the critical apparatus). This note refers to a particular entry in the *Massorah Gedolah*.

---

10.   A glossary of masoretic terms is provided in Kelley et al. (1998: 69–193).

In the *Biblia Hebraica Quinta* the *Masora magna* are reproduced in a diplomatic representation of what was actually written in the manuscript and are laid out in a separate register below the base text. The number of the chapter and verse to which the note refers is inserted ahead of the note. There is no particular signal in the text to indicate that a word has a note in the *Masora magna*, although these notes typically occur for words already noted in the *Masora parva*. In order to aid the reader in connecting notes in the *Masora magna* with the relevant words or phrases in the text, the notes are given in the order of the words in the biblical text even when this requires departing from the order of the notes on a given page of the Leningrad Codex. Translations of notes in the *Masora magna* are available in the commentary section, as are comments on difficult notes or notes that do not correspond to the text of Leningrad Codex.

Chapter 3

KEY TERMS AND CONCEPTS

§10. Aspects of Language Structure

In order to study Biblical Hebrew grammar it is necessary to know the meta-language (i.e. the technical terminology used to describe the observed features of the language) because it provides the means for explaining language structure (e.g. the terminology of linguistic categories). Additionally, some insight is necessary into the nature and various relationships between the aspects of language structure. The metalanguage used has not been deduced from the atomistic study of an individual language, but from broad cross-linguistic comparisons. This chapter provides a basic grammatical orientation to these matters.[1] Please note that using English examples does not imply that the structures of English and Biblical Hebrew are the same.

Language structure can be described in terms of the phonetic and phono-logical, morphological, syntactic, semantic and pragmatic, and textual aspects. These core aspects of language are influenced by matters like style (the way a specific author make a unique selection from the range of grammatical possibilities to the purpose of the communication), the relation of language to society (the way language is constructed by and in turn helps to construct society) and the mental or cognitive processes underlying the production, perception and comprehension of speech.

§10.1. Phonetic and Phonological Aspects

The phonetic aspect refers to the various speech sounds which are found in the world's languages. Each language, however, selects a small sub-set of sounds and uses them within the language in order to convey meaning. This system of sound-combination is studied as the phonological aspect of a language. Certain features of the sound aspect of Biblical Hebrew language structure (i.e. its phonology) are addressed in §4–9. Reference is also made to certain phonological processes such as *assimilation* (§4.2.4.2) and *metathesis* (§4.2.5.1).

---

1. For further reading Crystal (2008) and Finch (2005) are recommended.

§10.2. Morphological Aspect

A morpheme is the smallest linguistic unit that bears grammatical meaning. Morphemes may be prefixes, suffixes or words. The structure or form of words is studied as the morphological aspect of a language. Words belong to different classes, called word categories (or word classes or parts of speech). A basic morphological orientation with regard to the different categories of words is provided in §11. Some of these word categories may be inflected to provide additional grammatical information. Words are inflected through the addition of prefixes and/or suffixes. For example, in Biblical Hebrew there are suffixes that indicate that certain nouns are masculine while others are feminine. Furthermore, the possessive pronoun (e.g. "my," "your") is not independent of the noun to which it relates but is added to the noun in the form of a suffix.

§10.3. Syntactic Aspect

The syntax of a language describes how words are combined to form phrases and sentences. For this general grammatical orientation, §12 presents a review of the sentence and its structure.

§10.4. Semantic and Pragmatic Aspects

The semantic contribution of a word or construction refers to the minimum contribution that it makes towards an understanding of the context. The following construction indicates *possession*:

The palace *of* the king.

The move towards a linguistic typology of language description has the implication that cross-linguistic comparison largely proceeds on semantic or functional grounds rather than formal categories.

Pragmatics refers to the relationship between language and its context of use as well as language as intentional, purposive social behavior. For example, pragmatics includes the conventions according to which speakers belonging to a particular culture *do* various things in particular ways with language. Thus speakers can perform an action with the words that they utter, e.g.:

Look, I *appoint* you to rule over the whole of Egypt.

By attention to pragmatics, the role of non-linguistic information such as background information and personal perspectives in the interpretation of sentences can be included in the grammatical description of language.

In this grammar semantic and/or pragmatic aspects are distinguished only where they are relevant for distinguishing grammatical forms or functions.

§10.5. Textual Aspect

In a written document sentences are usually organized to form larger units or texts. Texts written in Biblical Hebrew can be broadly divided into prose or poetry. The communicative purpose of a text determines its form and content. A prose text such as a narrative, for example, looks very different from a piece of legislation. For this reason a distinction is made between different *types of texts* (or *discourse types*). The way in which sentences are organized to form coherent texts is also determined by the conventions of a particular society.

§11. Word Categories in Biblical Hebrew

Traditionally, words have been divided into word categories (or classes) such as noun, verb, adjective, adverb, etc. In current linguistic thought, there are different approaches to word categories.[2] Generative linguistics views word categories as involving clusters of features (e.g. a noun has the features [+N, -V] whereas an adjective has the features [+N, +V]). Lexical categories are those whose members have descriptive content (e.g. nouns, verbs, adjective); the members of functional categories lack descriptive content and are used instead to indicate grammatical properties (e.g. determiners, pronouns). Grammatical categories may also be described as open or closed. Open categories are those whose membership is, in principle, unlimited; closed categories are those with a limited and fixed number of members (e.g. functional members). In functional grammar, languages are classified as having either rigid categories (in which a part of speech is used for one function) or flexible categories (in which a part of speech may be used for more than one function). In cognitive linguistics, categories are seen as prototypical entities based upon human cognition. Category membership is gradient: some members of the category are more prototypical, while others are peripheral. In typological linguistics,

---

2. As representative of the various approaches, see Radford (2004: 33–63) for generative syntax, Hengeveld and Van Lier (2010) for functional grammar, Taylor (2003) for cognitive linguistics, and Haspelmath (2012) for typological linguistics; see the overview of the various approaches in Miller-Naudé and Naudé (2017).

grammatical categories are not cross-linguistically valid. Instead, categories are purely semantic and must be determined for each language. In this grammar, aspects of each of the approaches to grammatical categorization will be employed at various points. However, in general, words are divided into the following categories:

- Verbs (V)
- Nouns (N)
- Adjectives (A)
- Prepositions (P)
- Conjunctions
- Adverbs (Adv)
- Predicators of existence (existential words)
- Interrogatives
- Discourse markers
- Interjections

The focus on the traditional, morphologically based grammatical categories relates to the pedagogical goals of the grammar in assisting students to understand how the various forms of Biblical Hebrew are used in the Hebrew Bible.

§11.1. Verbs

Verbs express the action, condition or existence of a person or thing. Verbs have the following characteristics.

11.1.1. *Valency*

Valency describes the number of arguments (or expressions) that are required by a verb to form a complete predication. Verbs may be divided into two syntactic groups on the basis of valency, namely, transitive verbs (i.e. verbs that take a direct object, e.g. the English verb *kill* requires an indication of who or what was killed) and intransitive verbs (i.e. verbs that do not take a direct object, e.g. the English verb *sleep*) (see §12.3).

11.1.2. *Tense and aspect*

Tense indicates the temporal orientation of an action, which may include the present, future or past, e.g.:

David *plays* the harp.
David *will play* the harp.
David *played* the harp.

Aspect indicates whether the action is complete or incomplete. The terms perfective or imperfective (respectively) are sometimes used to denote the aspect of a verb, e.g.:

God *made* the earth (it is a complete action).
God (continually) *sustains* creation.

In Biblical Hebrew, the temporal and aspectual aspects of verbs are conveyed both by verbal forms and by syntactic structures.

11.1.3. *Modality*

Modality refers to (the orientation of a speaker concerning) the actuality and/or actualization of a process. Various types of modality are distinguished.

11.1.3.1. *Indicative*

The indicative refers to a fact in the form of a statement or question. This is regarded as the unmarked (or neutral) form, e.g.:

David plays the harp.
Does David play the harp?

11.1.3.2. *Epistemic modality*

Epistemic modality refers to the speaker's certainty or uncertainty about the actuality of a matter, e.g.:

You *must* be a man of God. You healed my son.
You *may* be right.

Languages sometimes either make use of auxiliary verbs (e.g. *must, may*) or of specific conjugations to express epistemic modality. Biblical Hebrew does not have either auxiliary verbs or specific conjugations to express epistemic modality, but uses the same conjugation forms as the indicative (see §19.3).

11.1.3.3. *Deontic modality*

Deontic modality refers to the speaker's command, directive, instruction, order, commission, prompting or request, e.g.:

> *Play* the harp.

11.1.4. *Voice*

Voice indicates the way in which the action of the verb is related to the subject. In the *active* voice the subject is the agent which performs the action, e.g.:

> David *plays* the harp.

In the *passive* voice the action is oriented towards the patient of the action, e.g.:

> The harp *is played* by David.

11.1.5. *Conjugations*

Among the most important conjugations in Biblical Hebrew are the following:

• *Qātal/Perfect*	כָּתַב	he wrote
• *Yiqtōl/Imperfect*	יִכְתֹּב	he will write
• *Imperative*	כְּתֹב	write!
• *Infinitive construct*	כְּתֹב	to write
• *Infinitive absolute*	כָּתוֹב	[translation is contextually determined]
• *Participle*	כֹּתֵב	(he is) writing

11.1.6. *Congruency features (or agreement markers)*

Congruency features are markers indicating grammatical agreement. Finite verbs in Biblical Hebrew have congruency features with their subject, indicating gender (masculine or feminine), number (singular and plural), person (the speaker [first person], the addressee [second person] and neither speaker nor addressee [third person]). All the verbal conjugations in Biblical Hebrew except the infinitives (which have no congruency features) and participles (with no indication of person) display all these congruency features of the subject. Adjectives display congruency features with the noun they modify with respect to determination (definite and indefinite), gender (masculine and feminine) and number (singular and plural; nouns marginally display the dual), but not person.

11.1.7. *Finite/Non-Finite*

A finite verb is marked for person and may stand on its own in an independent sentence. It indicates formal contrasts in time and mood. Non-finite verbs, in contrast with finite verbs, occur only in dependent clauses and lack indications of person, time and mood. All Biblical Hebrew verb conjugations except the infinitives and participles are finite.

§11.2. Nouns

Nouns may be divided into the following main classes:

11.2.1. *Substantives*

Substantives refer to people, places, things, ideas, conditions, qualities or feelings. The following subcategories are distinguished in Biblical Hebrew:

- *Proper nouns* denote the names of a specific person, place or thing, e.g. David, Jerusalem, Passover, etc.
- *Common nouns* are the words that denote objects, e.g. table, tree, altar, etc.
- *Collective nouns* are common noun that denote classes or groups made up of many individual members, e.g. herd, cattle, forest, etc.
- *Abstract nouns* are common nouns that refer to qualities, traits or ideas, e.g. love, illness, work, etc.

In Biblical Hebrew common nouns are qualified in terms of gender (masculine and feminine) and number (singular, plural or dual). A common noun may be morphologically marked as definite or indefinite. In addition to common nouns that are marked as definite with the definite article, proper names, pronouns, and possessed nouns are considered to be inherently definite because they refer to specific individuals within the speech context.

11.2.2. *Pronouns*

A pronoun is used as a substitute for a noun or noun phrase. A pronoun is not a specific name for an object. The identification of a pronoun with a particular noun is determined partly by congruency features and partly by its position in a sentence or paragraph. Consider, for example, the following sentence:

God chose David and blessed *him.*

The personal object pronoun "him" refers to David and cannot be interpreted as referring to God.

Pronouns may be classified as follows:

- *Personal* pronouns (subject):   I, you, etc.
- *Personal* pronouns (object):   me, you, etc.
- *Possessive* pronouns: my, your, his, her, etc.
- *Demonstrative* pronouns: this, that, these, those
- *Interrogative* pronouns: who, what, etc.
- *Relative* pronouns: which, whose, etc.
- *Indefinite* pronouns: everyone, all, etc.
- *Reflexive* pronouns: myself, yourself, etc.[3]
- *Reciprocal* pronouns: each other, one another, etc.

A personal pronoun usually refers to a person or thing that has already been mentioned. Such a person or thing is called the *antecedent* of the pronoun. Biblical Hebrew has a set of independent personal pronouns used as the subject of a sentence. Personal pronouns as objects and possessive pronouns do not occur as separate words but are found in the form of pronominal suffixes affixed to verbs, nouns and other types of words. Reflexive and reciprocal pronouns are *anaphora*, which implies that they must have a fixed antecedent in the same sentence (as opposed to the case of personal pronouns), e.g.:

David saves *himself* from the hand of Saul.

For that reason, the following sentence is not grammatical:

*David saves *herself* from the hand of Saul.[4]

11.2.3. *Numerals*

There are two kinds of numerals:

- *Cardinal* numerals indicate a specific amount or quantity, e.g.:
  three women

---

3. Biblical Hebrew does not have direct equivalents for the English reciprocal (e.g. one another) and reflexive (e.g. myself) pronouns. Biblical Hebrew uses other means to express them, namely, the Niṗʿal and Hitpaʿēl stem formations (§16.2.3.(2) and §16.6.2) as well as lexical means such as נֶפֶשׁ "soul" and עֶצֶם "bone" and the לְ with pronominal suffixes (see §36.1.6.2.(3)(e)).

4. The asterisk indicates that this is an ungrammatical sentence. In English *herself* requires a female antecedent within the sentence.

- *Ordinal* numerals indicate sequence or order, e.g.:

    in the *tenth* year on the *seventieth* day

§11.3. Adjectives

An adjective is a word that qualifies a noun, pronoun or substantive (a substantive is any word or group of words that is used grammatically as a noun). In Biblical Hebrew the adjective usually agrees with the word it qualifies according to most of its congruency features.

The qualification can be attributive, e.g.:

> The *good* king

or predicative, e.g.:

> The king is *good.*

In Biblical Hebrew the adjective has no morphologically distinguished degrees of comparison (e.g. *faster* and *fastest* are, respectively, the comparative and superlative degrees of the adjective *fast*). The semantic effect normally obtained by means of degrees of comparison is expressed through other constructions (§30.4).

Although adjectives in Biblical Hebrew have sometimes been classified as a sub-category of nouns, in this grammar they are dealt with as an independent word class (§30.1).

§11.4. Prepositions

A preposition is used to relate a succeeding noun or a pronoun to another word or group of words. It does so in such a way that the preposition and the subsequent noun or pronoun become directly associated with the remaining words of the sentence, e.g.:

> He places the firewood *on* Isaac's shoulders.
> They wandered *around* the city.

Prepositions express position in time or space or any similar abstract relationship (§39.1.4).

§11.5. Conjunctions

A conjunction joins words, phrases or sentences in such a way that they form a unit. There are two types of conjunctions (§40.1.2).

11.5.1. *Coordinating conjunctions*

A coordinating conjunction joins grammatically equivalent items such as nouns or independent phrases, e.g.:

> John *and* Mary walk.
> John walks *and* Mary rides.

11.5.2. *Subordinating conjunctions*

A subordinating conjunction joins a subordinate sentence (i.e. a sentence that does not stand independently) to the main sentence.

> You are cursed, *because* you abandoned the LORD.

§11.6. Adverbs

An adverb is used to modify an adjective, a verb or another adverb with respect to time, manner, place, e.g.:

> You are *still* speaking to the king.
> You speak *little*.
> You speak *outside*.

These adverbs are called *ordinary adverbs* in this grammar (§40.1.3.1). Adverbs can also qualify sentences, e.g.:

> *Truly*, Sarah will bear a son.

Such adverbs will be called *modal words* in this grammar (§40.1.3.2). Some adverbs place the focus on the item or phrase that follows them. The referent for these adverbs is a qualification or limitation of another referent, e.g.:

> Let me speak *just* this once.

This class is called *focus particles* (§40.1.3.4). Negatives, that is, words which negate sentences (apart from existential sentences), are also regarded as adverbs in this grammar (§40.1.3.5 and §41).

§11.7. Predicators of Existence

Biblical Hebrew has predicators of existence (or, existentials) that express the existence or non-existence of (mostly) impersonal items (§43); they can be translated as *there is/there is not*, e.g.:

> *There is* wheat in Egypt.
> *There are no* people to cultivate the land.

§11.8. Discourse Markers

Speakers use discourse markers to comment on the content of a sentence (or sentences) from the perspective of a meta-level (§40.1.4). In this way the sentence or sentences are anchored in the discourse. In Biblical Hebrew, discourse markers always precede the sentence(s) to which they refer. They often draw attention to the contents of the succeeding sentence(s), affording this/these sentence(s) greater prominence within its/their larger context, e.g.:

> *Look*, I am going to do something.

§11.9. Interrogatives

Apart from the interrogative pronouns that mark content questions (§42.3), Biblical Hebrew has an interrogative that marks sentences requiring a yes–no answer (§42.2). This interrogative has no lexical equivalent in English.

§11.10. Interjections and Oaths

An interjection is an expression inserted between the other words of a sentence but which has no grammatical link to them. Often it indicates some sudden emotional reaction, e.g. *Ah, Oh, Alas* (§44).

Oaths (§38 and §45) may or may not be preceded by an oath formula, e.g.:

> *As the LORD lives.*

§12. Sentences in Biblical Hebrew

§12.1. Definition

A sentence is a meaningful series of words that has at least a subject and a predicate. Since a sentence is made of words and a formal relationship/ coherence holds between the words, a sentence is a unit that can be analyzed structurally. In linguistics the term *clause* is used in ways that partially overlap with the usage of *sentence*.

§12.2. Syntactical Units of the Sentence

Words may be grouped together into larger units known as *phrases*. The following kinds of phrases are important here:

- *Noun phrase* (NP)   the boys
- *Verb phrase* (VP)   ate the bread
- *Adverbial phrase* (AP)   when they walked
- *Prepositional phrase* (PP)   to the fields

§12.3. Relationships between Syntactical Units of the Sentence

All clauses are built up of phrases that have a particular relationship with one another. Clauses may maximally be simple sentences. A simple sentence (S)[5] can be divided into a noun phrase (NP) and a verb phrase (VP).

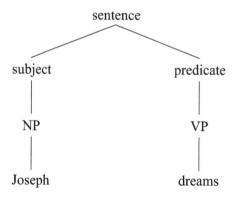

---

5. The convention to refer to the highest node or maximal projection in a tree diagram as "sentence" is retained here.

The preceding diagram represents the most basic relationships in a sentence, corresponding to the traditional division of the sentence into subject and predicate. The predicate may be used with a direct object, for example,

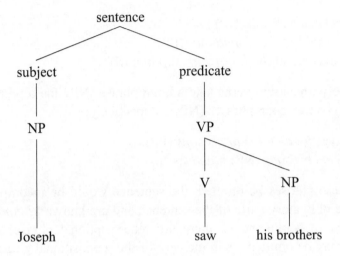

or an indirect object, for example,

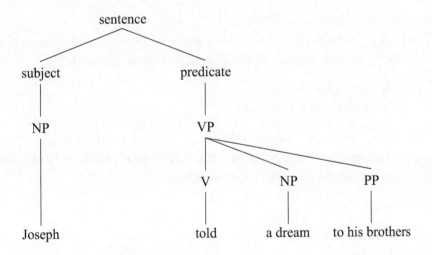

The type and number of phrases selected by a verb (V) are determined by the nature of the verb (see also §22). Intransitive verbs do not select any phrases.

[Jacob] sleeps Ø (Ø = nothing, i.e. no object follows the verb).

Transitive verbs may take a noun phrase (NP), a prepositional phrase (PP) or a complement clause (S),[6] respectively. Clauses may thus be syntactically less than a simple sentence because of embedding, e.g. a complement clause, a relative clause or a subordinate clause:

> [Joseph] relates *a dream* (NP).
> [Jacob] is afraid *of the Canaanites* (PP).
> [Joseph] knows that *the LORD will help him* (S).

Ditransitive (doubly transitive) verbs take a noun phrase (NP) and a prepositional phrase (PP) or two noun phrases (NPs), respectively:

> [Jacob] gives *bread* (NP) *to his sons* (PP).
> [Jacob] gives *his sons* (NP) *bread* (NP).

Should any of these phrases be omitted, the sentence would be incomplete. These phrases are obligatory parts of the sentence and are known as *complements*. In contrast to complements, there are other, optional phrases in a sentence, which may be omitted, as in the case of the prepositional phrase in the following sentence:

> Jacob sleeps *in Bethel* (PP).

These phrases are known as *adjuncts*.

The subject in the first sentence above may also be expanded. A noun phrase (NP) may be extended by an article or a prepositional phrase (PP):

> *The* man dreams.
> The man *in the tent* dreams.

In principle, the noun phrase (NP) may be extended infinitely through recursive processes, that is, processes that can be applied infinitely in number. The following are examples of such processes:

- Coordination

  > Joseph *and* Rebecca dream.

- Adjectival qualification

  > The *handsome* man dreams.

---

6. No formal distinction is made between the symbolizing of clauses and sentences; both are symbolized by S.

- Apposition

    Jacob, *the traitor*, dreams.

- Qualification by means of a relative clause

    Jacob, *who lived in Canaan*, dreams.

- Qualification by means of a construct relationship

    The son *of Jacob* dreams.

Similarly, prepositional phrases (PP) and adjective phrases (AP) can be extended:

> Jacob gives bread to his hungry sons *who are watching over his sheep*.
> The charming, *handsome* man dreams.

§12.4. Typical Characteristics of Biblical Hebrew Syntax

Clauses may also syntactically be less than a simple sentence when they have implicit constituents, for instance, an absent overt subject or an elliptical verb. Sometimes they are also called sentences if they refer to the highest node or maximal projection in a tree diagram. Typical features of Biblical Hebrew syntax in this regard are described below:

12.4.1. *Absent subject*

The pronominal subject may be absent in certain cases. In such cases a trace of the subject has remained and must be assumed; the assumed subject is sometimes referred to as a "null subject." The following form is thus a complete clause or sentence even though no visible subject exists:

> כָּתַב
> wrote–[he]
> he wrote

12.4.2. *Free inversion of the subject, or any other constituent*

Biblical Hebrew is often regarded as a so-called VSO (= **V**erb, **S**ubject, **O**bject) language, i.e. the verb normally precedes the subject and object. However, free inversion means that the subject (or any other constituent) can be placed either before or after the verb phrase, e.g.:

(1)   כָּתַב אָב
        wrote–[he] father
        a father wrote

(2)   אָב כָּתַב
        father wrote–[he]
        a father wrote

Although the sequence in (2) is not predicate (verb) followed by subject, it still forms a clause or sentence. This process can, however, have semantic implications (see §46–47).

12.4.3. *Nominal clause (verbless clause)*

These are clauses in Biblical Hebrew that do not contain a finite form of the verb. The English copulative verb *is* must be added to them to produce an accurate translation:

> Jacob [is] old.
> Jacob [is] a farmer.
> Jacob [is] in the tent.

In such clauses the non-verbal complement forms the predicate. In the clauses above the non-verbal complements consist of an adjective (*old*), a noun phrase (*a farmer*) and a prepositional phrase (*in the tent*). A nominal clause therefore consists of: Subject + Predicate. They are also called nominal or verbless sentences if they refer to the highest node or maximal projection in a tree diagram.

§12.5. Types of Sentences

When they are the highest node or maximal projection in a tree diagram, the following types of sentences may be identified in Biblical Hebrew:

12.5.1. *Simple sentence*

(1) Nominal sentence (§12.4)

(2) Verbal sentence, e.g.:

   Statements

> He gave bread to the boy.

Interrogatives[7]

Content questions (also referred to as WH-questions)

Who buys wheat?

Questions expecting a yes–no answer (also referred to as polar questions)

Did you buy wheat?

Commands

Pick it up!/You may not pick it up.

You must pick it up/You must not pick it up.
Let us pick it up/Let us not pick it up.

12.5.2. *Extended sentence*

The extension forms part of the main clause (or matrix clause) and expands a part of the sentence, for example, the subject or the object of the sentence. In the next sentence the subordinate clause is an extension of the subject, the NP, Jacob.

Jacob, *who lives in Canaan*, loved Joseph.

12.5.3. *Complex sentence*

Complex sentences consist of one or more clauses related to the so-called main clause (or matrix clause).

Coordinate clause

At first Joseph was strict with his brothers, *then he treated them well.*

Subordinate clause

When Joseph saw his brothers, he immediately recognized them.

---

7. Interrogatives do not always pose questions, e.g. in the case of rhetorical questions. In such cases a question like "Were you not the one who bought the wheat?" can be used to say, "You were, indeed, the one who bought the wheat."

A basic difference between subordinate and coordinate clauses is that speakers normally do not carry out speech acts in subordinate clauses. In other words, a speaker does not make a statement, pose a question or make an appeal in a subordinate clause. Examples of subordinate clauses in Biblical Hebrew are found in the following sentences:

> Conditional sentences (syntactical composition: Protasis [conditional clause] + Apodosis [main or matrix clause])
>
> *If you believe*, you will receive mercy.
>
> Circumstantial sentence (syntactical composition: circumstantial clause + main or matrix clause)
>
> *When he was old*, he returned.

The subordinate clauses above, also called *supplement* clauses, are distinguished from subordinate clauses that can act as complements in a sentence, for example, as its subject or object. These so-called *complement* clauses are more integrally linked to their main or matrix clauses than the supplement clauses, e.g.:

> God sees *that you love him* (object).
> *To give* (subject) is your duty.

To summarize, clauses are called sentences if they refer to the highest node or maximal projection in a tree diagram. However, they are often syntactically less than a simple sentence. This happens, for example, when they are embedded as clause constituents as complement clauses, used as supplement clauses or when they extend a constituent as a relative clause.

§13. Beyond the Sentence

Sentences are used to create texts, usually by means of utilizing conventions regarding cohesion and rhetorical organization.

§13.1. Textual Cohesion

Every language community has its own conventions that determine the form that their texts should take in order to be understood as coherent texts. This includes conventions regarding the manner in which semantic links are made between the relevant people and things in a text, e.g.:

(1) *Reference to people and things.* In English a text initially refers to persons by mentioning their names and positions, e.g. *Elijah, man of God*. Subsequently only their names will often be used, i.e. *Elijah*. In Biblical Hebrew, however, the person's name and position will often be repeated.

(2) *The use of pronouns.* In Biblical Hebrew texts the name of a person will be used explicitly much more often than it would in English. The direct translation of Gen. 41:15–16 reads "And Pharaoh said to Joseph…and Joseph answered *Pharaoh*." In English, the second explicit reference to Pharaoh would be replaced with a pronoun: "…and Joseph answered *him*."

§13.2. Rhetorical Organization

Sentences are organized to form texts. The rhetorical organization of texts is not always the same, however. That is why different types of texts may be distinguished:

- Narrative texts
- Descriptive texts
- Argumentative/discursive texts
- Prescriptive or instructional texts.

Naturally, a mixture of the different kinds of texts may also occur.

Language communities have various conventions that govern the way different types of texts are begun, the way they proceed, and the way they are concluded. This is why these conventions are regarded as part of the "organizational" structure of a language. For example, narrative texts in Biblical Hebrew often conclude with a summary of the narrative, namely "And so this (or that) happened."

Poetic texts in Biblical Hebrew differ from prose texts in the use of parallelism (semantically and/or grammatically corresponding lines), in the use of verbal ellipsis, and in the reduced use of the so-called prose particles (the definite article, the relative clause marker, the definite object marker).

§13.3. Information Structure

The information structure of a text relates both to the sentence level and to the level of the text. Information on both levels may be identified as thematic information (that which is "given" or assumed in the discourse) and rhematic information (that which is "new" and is not assumed in the prior discourse). See also §47.1.

Chapter 4

VERBS

§14. Overview

Biblical Hebrew verbs are derived from a stem or root consisting of three consonants.[1] These roots never occur on their own in Biblical Hebrew texts but are always provided with affixes (that is, prefixes, infixes and/or suffixes) which indicate that they belong to:

(1) A specific stem formation (also referred to as a verbal stem). For example, in the Qal the root כתב is vocalized with the vowel pattern /ֹ‍ֹ/, also known as an infix. The verb is then read as כָּתַב. If the same root begins with a ה- prefix and has the infix /‍ִי/, i.e. הִכְתִּיב, one knows that it is a Hip̄ʿîl stem formation. There are seven main stem formations in Biblical Hebrew:

> Qal, Nip̄ʿal, Piʿēl, Puʿal, Hitpaʿēl, Hip̄ʿîl and Hop̄ʿal.

(2) A particular conjugation of a stem formation. For example, the תִי- suffix of the word כָּתַבְתִּי indicates the *qātal*/perfect form of a verb; while the -יִ prefix of the word יִכְתֹּב indicates the *yiqtōl*/imperfect form. The following conjugations are found in Biblical Hebrew:

> *Qātal/Perfect, Yiqtōl/Imperfect, Imperative, Jussive, Cohortative, Infinitive Construct, Infinitive Absolute and Participle.*

(3) A specific feature or mark of congruency (person, gender, number, where applicable) in the conjugation. For example, in the *qātal*/perfect and the *yiqtōl*/imperfect the suffixes and prefixes are used to indicate a difference in person (subject of the verb). The congruency features distinguished in Biblical Hebrew are the following:

---

1. See Naudé (2003a) for an overview of the viewpoints concerning the nature of the stem and root in Semitic.

	Singular	*Plural*
3rd person	he, she	they (m. and f.)
2nd person	you (m. and f.)	you (m. and f.)
1st person	I	we

These sets of affixes are usually clearly discernible in the regular stems. In other words, it is usually easy to recognize the stem (or root), stem formation and conjugation of a particular verb form. In the so-called irregular stems, however, a whole range of phonological processes must be considered, which makes it more difficult to recognize the stem and/or stem formation. These processes are related to the phonetic features of the irregular stems.

In English a graphic unit never comprises more than one lexical item or word. This is not the case in Biblical Hebrew. Not only is the subject part of the verb, but a verb can also contain a pronominal suffix that refers to the object of the verb. This suffix is a separate lexical item and has nothing to do with the verbal system as such. Yet the suffix influences the vocalization of the verb – a factor that has to be taken into account in order to understand the vocalization of a verb.

In Biblical Hebrew there are also certain verb chains and sequences associated with the *qātal*/perfect, *yiqtōl*/imperfect and imperative forms. In describing the meaning of these sequences the context or discourse must be taken into account more systematically than with the other conjugations.

Each of the above features of the Biblical Hebrew verb will be discussed in the following sections.

§15. Morphology of the Basic Paradigm

Seeing that, morphologically speaking, the Qal paradigm has the simplest form and is normally the first to be learned, it will be used to describe the basic morphology of the Biblical Hebrew verb.

§15.1. *Qātal*/Perfect (Suffix Conjugation)[2]

Qātal/perfect forms[3] refer, broadly speaking, to complete events or facts that often can be translated with the past tense (§19.2). The *qātal*/perfect has the following forms:

---

2. The reason for referring to the same form by three different terms is explained in §19.1.

3. Unless stated otherwise, "perfect" refers only to the perfect forms of a Biblical Hebrew verb in this grammar.

כָּתַב	3 m. sing.	he wrote
כָּתְבָה	3 f. sing.	she wrote
כָּתַבְתָּ	2 m. sing.	you (m.) wrote
כָּתַבְתְּ	2 f. sing.	you (f.) wrote
כָּתַבְתִּי	1 sing.	I wrote
כָּתְבוּ	3 pl.	they wrote
כְּתַבְתֶּם	2 m. pl.	you (m. pl.) wrote
כְּתַבְתֶּן	2 f. pl.	you (f. pl.) wrote
כָּתַבְנוּ	1 pl.	we wrote

Note the following characteristics:

(1) Person is indicated by means of suffixes. Although there is no suffix in the third masculine singular, the infix sufficiently identifies it as a Qal *qātal/* perfect.

(2) In the case of the first singular, first plural and third plural no distinction is made between the masculine and feminine forms.

(3) The suffix of the *qātal*/perfect is either consonantal, e.g. כָּתַבְתִּי, or vocalic, e.g. כָּתְבוּ.

(4) The vowel pattern of the Qal *qātal*/perfect is /ǪǪ/. However, the following exceptions are to be found:

(a) Before vocalic suffixes the /Ǫ/ becomes an audible *šəwāʾ* (/Ǫ/) due to the fact that vocalic suffixes are always accented. The /Ǫ/ changes in the syllable nearest to a changeable vowel due to the accent shift produced by the addition of the suffix, for example, כָּתַב plus הǪ becomes כָּתְבָה and not כָּתַבָה (§7.3.(1)).

(b) The consonantal suffixes תֶּם- (second masculine plural) and תֶּן- (second feminine plural) carry the accent and consequently the /Ǫ/ in the first syllable is reduced to *šəwāʾ* (§7.3.(1)).

(5) In the third feminine singular and third plural forms the /Ǫ/ acquires a *meteḡ* which indicates that the syllable carries an additional accent and that /Ǫ/ must be read as /ā/ (§9.1).

§15.2. *Yiqtōl*/Imperfect (Prefix Conjugation)

Yiqtōl/imperfect[4] forms refer, broadly speaking, to incomplete events that often could be translated with the present or future tense (§19.3).

The *yiqtōl*/imperfect has the following forms:

יִכְתֹּב	3 m. sing.	he will write
תִּכְתֹּב	3 f. sing.	she will write
תִּכְתֹּב	2 m. sing.	you (m.) will write
תִּכְתְּבִי	2 f. sing.	you (f.) will write
אֶכְתֹּב	1 sing.	I will write
יִכְתְּבוּ	3 m. pl.	they (m.) will write
תִּכְתֹּבְנָה	3 f. pl.	they (f.) will write
תִּכְתְּבוּ	2 m. pl.	you (m. pl.) will write
תִּכְתֹּבְנָה	2 f. pl.	you (f. pl.) will write
נִכְתֹּב	1 pl.	we will write

Note the following characteristics:

(1) Person is indicated by means of prefixes as well as by suffixes in certain cases.

(2) The prefix forms a closed syllable with the first stem consonant, and the vowel pattern of the Qal *yiqtōl*/imperfect is usually /◌ ◌/.

   (a) Before consonantal suffixes the /◌/ remains unchanged, e.g. תִּכְתֹּבְנָה.

   (b) Before vocalic suffixes the /◌/ becomes an audible *šəwā*', e.g. תִּכְתְּבוּ.

(3) On a morphological level, no distinction is made between masculine and feminine forms in the case of the first singular and the first plural.

(4) The second masculine singular and the third feminine singular have the same morphological form. The context in which the words are used always provides clues towards making the necessary distinction. The same applies to the second feminine plural and third feminine plural forms.

(5) A distinction is made between a masculine and a feminine form in the third person.

---

4. Unless stated otherwise, in this study "*yiqtōl*" refers to the "long *yiqtōl*" (§19.3).

§15.3. Imperative

The meaning of the imperative can broadly be described as a direct command to the second person (§19.5.1.1). For indirect commands in the first person and the third person the cohortative and jussive forms, respectively, are used (see §19.5.1.2–3). The following imperative forms can be distinguished:

כְּתֹב	2 m. sing.	(You) write!
כִּתְבִי	2 f. sing.	(You) write!
כִּתְבוּ	2 m. pl.	(You) write!
כְּתֹבְנָה	2 f. pl.	(You) write!

Note the following characteristics:

(1) The forms of the imperative are the same as the *yiqtōl*/imperfect second person without the prefix, e.g.: תִּכְתְּבִי "you will write" minus the prefix is כְּתְבִי "write!"

(2) There is an /ǐ/ vowel in the imperative feminine singular and masculine plural. It results from the fusion of two audible *šəwāʾ*s, e.g.: כִּתְבִי > כְּתְבִי > תִּכְתְּבִי

§15.4. Cohortative

The meaning of the cohortative can broadly be described as an indirect command to the first person (§19.5.1.2). In the cohortative the suffix הָ is added to the *yiqtōl*/imperfect of the first person. The final stem vowel which occurs before this vocalic suffix is reduced. This phenomenon is found in every stem formation with the exception of the Hip̄ʿîl where the /ǐ/ occurring before the vowel suffix is retained (§16.7).

אֶכְתְּבָה	1 sing.	Let me write
נִכְתְּבָה	1 pl.	Let us write

§15.5. Jussive

The meaning of the jussive can broadly be described as an indirect command to the third person. The jussive form is also used with אַל in negative commands to the second person (§19.5.2.1). The jussive often appears as a shorter form of the *yiqtōl*/imperfect. However, this shorter form can only be found in certain cases as, for example, in the Hiṗʿîl where the /ʾ◌/ of the conjugation forms without suffixes is "shortened" to /◌/ (§16.7.1.2.(6)). The shorter form also occurs with II-*wāw* / II-*yôḏ* (§18.8.3.5.(5)) and III-*hēʾ* verbs. (See §18.5.4 for these shorter or so-called apocopated forms.)

יִכְתֹּב	3 m. sing.	Let him write/may he write
תִּכְתֹּב	3 f. sing.	Let her write/may she write
יִכְתְּבוּ	3 m. pl.	Let them write/may they (m.) write
תִּכְתֹּבְנָה	3 f. pl.	Let them write/may they (f.) write

§15.6. Infinitive Construct

In Biblical Hebrew a distinction is made between two infinitive forms, namely the infinitive construct (or, declinable infinitive) and the infinitive absolute (or, undeclinable infinitive). The infinitive construct is a verbal noun that expresses action without referring to the time of the action or the person doing the action (§20.1).

כְּתֹב   (no person indicated)   to write

Note the following characteristics:

(1) The infinitive construct usually has the same form as the masculine singular imperative.
(2) The infinitive construct is often used with a pronominal suffix or a preposition (§17.5).

§15.7. Infinitive Absolute

The infinitive absolute (undeclinable infinitive) has the following form:

כָּתוֹב   (no person indicated)   to write

Note the following characteristics:

(1) The infinitive absolute is usually characterized by a /î/ in the final syllable (§20.2).
(2) The infinitive absolute does not decline.

§15.8. Participle ·

In Biblical Hebrew the participle is a verbal adjective that functions as a verb, noun or adjective (§20.3). The participle has the following forms:

כֹּתֵב	m. sing.	writing
כֹּתֶבֶת	f. sing.	writing
כֹּתְבִים	m. pl.	writing
כֹּתְבוֹת	f. pl.	writing

Note the following characteristics:

(1) The nominal grammatical morphemes added to the participle correspond with those used for the adjective (§30.1).

(2) כֹּתְבָה is also used for the feminine singular participle, but it does not occur frequently.

§16. Stem Formations

§16.1. Names of the Stem Formations

Biblical Hebrew has seven stem formations in which verbs may appear. In Modern Hebrew the term *binyanim* (literally "buildings") is used to describe these forms.

The Qal stem formation is the simplest, requiring only the verb stem for its various forms/conjugations. The other stem formations are morphological extensions of this stem. These extended forms may express various semantic associations with the Qal, such as passive, causative, etc. This semantic relationship with the Qal must not, however, be taken for granted. Each stem formation should rather be regarded as an independent form, the meaning of which must be learned separately. The third masculine singular *qātal*/perfect of the stem פָּעַל has been used as a pattern to illustrate the so-called derived or extended stem formations. Hence the paradigm:

פָּעַל Qal	פִּעֵל Piʿēl	הִפְעִיל Hiṗʿîl
נִפְעַל Niṗʿal	פֻּעַל Puʿal	הָפְעַל Hoṗʿal
	הִתְפַּעֵל Hitpaʿēl	

This paradigm is used to name each of the derived stem formations. The Qal stem formation is also alternatively called the Pāʿal based on its morphological shape. (The name Qal derives from a root meaning "to be light or insignificant.")

The idea that the more complex stem formations are derivations of the Qal led grammarians to assume that the Qal forms also reflect the most basic meaning of a verb and that the meanings of the other stem formations could thus be derived from it. Although this is often the case, recent research has clearly indicated that this assumption is untenable. This is one of the reasons why the above system is no longer used in some more recent Biblical Hebrew grammars. See also Richter (1978: 73).

The following system may also be used for denoting the stem formations:

Qal	=	G (for German *Grundstamm* "basic stem")
Niṗʿal	=	N (for the stem with *n*- prefix)
Piʿēl	=	D (for the doubled stem)
Puʿal	=	Dp (for the passive of the doubled stem)
Hitpaʿēl	=	Dt (for the doubled stem with *t*- infix)
Hiṗʿîl	=	H (for the stem with *h*- prefix)
Hoṗʿal	=	Hp (for the passive of the stem with *h*- prefix)

In this grammar the traditional categories will be used.

§16.2. Morphology and Semantics of the Qal

16.2.1. *Morphology*

The morphology of the Qal stem formation has already been dealt with in §15.

16.2.1.1. *Paradigm*

Table 11 provides a summary of the complete paradigm.

Table 11. *The Paradigm of the Qal Stem Formation*

QAL		ā-a	ā-ē	ā-ō
Qātal/Perfect sing.	3 m.	כָּתַב	כָּבֵד	קָטֹן
	3 f.	כָּתְבָה	כָּבְדָה	קָטְנָה
	2 m.	כָּתַֽבְתָּ	כָּבֵֽדְתָּ	קָטֹֽנְתָּ
	2 f.	כָּתַבְתְּ	כָּבֵדְתְּ	קָטֹנְתְּ
	1 c.	כָּתַֽבְתִּי	כָּבֵֽדְתִּי	קָטֹֽנְתִּי
Pl.	3 c.	כָּתְבוּ	כָּבְדוּ	קָטְנוּ
	2 m.	כְּתַבְתֶּם	כְּבַדְתֶּם	קְטָנְתֶּם
	2 f.	כְּתַבְתֶּן	כְּבַדְתֶּן	קְטָנְתֶּן
	1 c.	כָּתַֽבְנוּ	כָּבֵֽדְנוּ	קָטֹֽנוּ
Yiqtōl/Imperfect sing.	3 m.	יִכְתֹּב	יִכְבַּד	יִקְטַן
	3 f.	תִּכְתֹּב	תִּכְבַּד	תִּקְטַן
	2 m.	תִּכְתֹּב	תִּכְבַּד	תִּקְטַן
	2 f.	תִּכְתְּבִי	תִּכְבְּדִי	תִּקְטְנִי
	1 c.	אֶכְתֹּב	אֶכְבַּד	אֶקְטַן
Pl.	3 m.	יִכְתְּבוּ	יִכְבְּדוּ	יִקְטְנוּ
	3 f.	תִּכְתֹּֽבְנָה	תִּכְבַּֽדְנָה	תִּקְטֹֽנָה
	2 m.	תִּכְתְּבוּ	תִּכְבְּדוּ	תִּקְטְנוּ
	2 f.	תִּכְתֹּֽבְנָה	תִּכְבַּֽדְנָה	תִּקְטֹֽנָה
	1 c.	נִכְתֹּב	נִכְבַּד	נִקְטַן
Imp. sing.	2 m.	כְּתֹב	כְּבַד	קְטַן
	2 f.	כִּתְבִי	כִּבְדִי	קְטְנִי
Imp. pl.	2 m.	כִּתְבוּ	כִּבְדוּ	קְטְנוּ
	2 f.	כְּתֹֽבְנָה	כְּבַֽדְנָה	קְטֹֽנָה
Coh. sing.	1 c.	אֶכְתְּבָה	אֶכְבְּדָה	אֶקְטְנָה
Juss. sing.	3 m.	יִכְתֹּב	יִכְבַּד	יִקְטַן

QAL			
	ā-a	*ā-ē*	*ā-ō*
Inf. cs.		כְּתֹב	כְּבֹד	קְטֹן
Inf. abs.		כָּתוֹב	כָּבוֹד	קָטוֹן
Part. act.		כֹּתֵב	כָּבֵד	קָטֹן
Part. pass.		כָּתוּב		

16.2.1.2. *Important morphological features*

(1) In the *qātal*/perfect the vowel pattern is /◌ֲ◌ַ/ (כָּתַב)[5]
or /◌ֲ◌ֵ/ (כָּבֵד)
or /◌ֲ◌ֹ/ (קָטֹן).

- Before the vocalic suffixes, the /◌ַ/, /◌ֵ/, /◌ֹ/ in the second stem syllable are reduced to an audible *šəwāʾ* (§8.1.1) (קָטְנָה, כָּבְדָה, כָּתְבָה).
- The consonantal suffixes תֶּם- (second masculine plural) and תֶּן- (second feminine plural) draw the accent to themselves. The first syllable consequently loses its accent. The /◌ָ/ in the first syllable is reduced to an audible *šəwāʾ* (כְּתַבְתֶּם).

(2) In the *yiqtōl*/imperfect the vowel pattern is /◌ ◌ֹ/ (יִכְתֹּב) or /◌ ◌ַ/ (יִלְמַד).[6] The /◌ֹ/ becomes an audible *šəwāʾ* before vocalic suffixes (תִּכְתְּבוּ).

(3) In the imperative and infinitive construct the vowel pattern is /◌ֲ◌ֹ/ (כְּתֹב).

(4) In the participle the vowel in the first syllable is /◌ֹ/ (כֹּתֵב).

(5) The cohortative form occurs in the singular and plural of the first person. It is formed by adding the ◌ָה suffix to the *yiqtōl* first singular (אֶכְתְּבָה) and plural (נִכְתְּבָה).

(6) The jussive form looks like a shorter version of the *yiqtōl*/imperfect form. However, this "shorter" form, referred to as a short *yiqtōl*, is often not distinguished from the *yiqtōl*/imperfect form, e.g. the jussive and *yiqtōl*/imperfect form of כתב is the same, viz. יִכְתֹּב. In contrast, these forms are distinguished in some weak verbs; see §18.5.4.

---

5. The vowels /◌ֲ◌/ used for the third masculine singular are known as the stem vowels of the *qātal*/perfect. In the *yiqtōl*/imperfect only the vowel in the second syllable, e.g. the /◌ֹ/ of the Qal *yiqtōl*/imperfect, is regarded as a stem vowel.

6. The prefix, i.e. the consonant and the vowel added to the stem, is also called a preformative.

(7) In a *wāw* consecutive + *yiqtōl*/imperfect construction, also referred to as the *wayyiqtōl* (§21.2), the "*yiqtōl*/imperfect" is in reality not a *yiqtōl*/imperfect form, but a short *yiqtōl*. In some cases, however, this short *yiqtōl*/jussive form may change as well. This is due to a shift of accent caused by the addition of the וֹ (see §18.5.4.(6) and §18.8.3.5.(7)).

Note the following:

(a) The difference discernable in the vocalic form of the above verb stems is analogous to the division of verbs into two syntactic groups, namely transitive – the *qātal* and *yiqtōl* patterns, and intransitive – the *qātēl* (e.g. כָּבֵד "he was heavy") and *qātōl* (e.g. קָטֹן "he was small") patterns with their corresponding *yiqtal* forms (e.g. יִכְבַּד and יִקְטַן). In the Qal certain verbs have both a *qātēl* and a *qātal* form and are accordingly both intransitive or transitive, respectively.

לָבֵשׁ יְהוָה The Lord *is robed* (Ps. 93:1).

אֲשֶׁר לָבַשׁ בְּבֹאוֹ אֶל־הַקֹּדֶשׁ that *he put on* when he went into the holy place (Lev. 16:23).

(b) Certain transitive *yiqtal* forms also exist, e.g. רכב (ride), למד (learn) and שכב (sit).

There is considerable evidence that a Qal passive form also existed in a pre-Masoretic Biblical Hebrew phase. However, the Masoretes only acknowledged the active Qal. The only Qal passive form that still occurs fairly regularly in Biblical Hebrew is the Qal passive participle.[7]

16.2.2. *Semantics*

The Qal stem formation has no specific meaning per se. Verbs occurring in this stem formation can, at most, be divided into the following semantic categories:

(1) Action verbs in which the subject performs some or other action. These verbs are also referred to as fientive verbs.

(2) Stative verbs express the condition or state of the subject, e.g. "he was heavy"; "he was small."

---

7. See Waltke and O'Connor §22.6 and Siebesma (1991) for a more complete discussion of the Qal passive.

§16.3. Morphology and Semantics of the Nipͨal

16.3.1. *Morphology*

16.3.1.1. *Paradigm*

Table 12. *The Paradigm of the Nipͨal*

NIPͨAL		Singular	Plural
Qātal/Perfect	3 m.	נִכְתַּב	נִכְתְּבוּ
	3 f.	נִכְתְּבָה	
	2 m.	נִכְתַּ֫בְתָּ	נִכְתַּבְתֶּם
	2 f.	נִכְתַּבְתְּ	נִכְתַּבְתֶּן
	1 c.	נִכְתַּ֫בְתִּי	נִכְתַּ֫בְנוּ
Yiqtōl/Imperfect	3 m.	יִכָּתֵב	יִכָּתְבוּ
	3 f.	תִּכָּתֵב	תִּכָּתַ֫בְנָה
	2 m.	תִּכָּתֵב	תִּכָּתְבוּ
	2 f.	תִּכָּתְבִי	תִּכָּתַ֫בְנָה
	1 c.	אֶכָּתֵב	נִכָּתֵב
Imp.	m.	הִכָּתֵב	הִכָּתְבוּ
	f.	הִכָּתְבִי	הִכָּתַ֫בְנָה
Coh.		אֶכָּתְבָה	
Juss.		יִכָּתֵב	
Inf. cs.		הִכָּתֵב	
Inf. abs.		הִכָּתֹב/נִכְתֹּב	
Part.		נִכְתָּב	

16.3.1.2. *Important morphological features*

(1) In the *qātal*/perfect -נְ is prefixed to the stem. This prefix forms a closed syllable with the first stem consonant. The vowel pattern is /ֹ ֹ/ (נִכְתַּב).

　(a) With the vocalic suffixes the second stem vowel is reduced (נִכְתְּבוּ).

　(b) With the consonantal suffixes both stem vowels are retained (נִכְתַּבְתִּי).

(3) In the *yiqtōl*/imperfect the vowel pattern is /ֹ ֹ ֹ/ (יִכָּתֵב).

　(a) The first consonant of the stem doubles. The doubling occurs as a result of the assimilation of the *nûn* of the Niᵖᶜal with the first stem consonant (יִכָּתֵב).

　(b) With vocalic suffixes the /ֹ/ is reduced to /ֹ/ (תִּכָּתְבִי).

　(c) With consonantal suffixes the /ֹ/ changes to /ֹ/ (תִּכָּתַבְנָה).

(4) The prefix in the imperative and infinitive construct is הִ- (הִכָּתֵב).

(5) The participle is similar in appearance to the *qātal*/perfect third masculine singular. However, the stem vowel of the participle is /ֹ/ (נִכְתָּב) and not /ֹ/ (נִכְתַּב).

16.3.2. *Semantics*

About 60% of the verb stems that have a Niᵖᶜal form are semantically related to the Qal form of the verb stem. However, 10% are semantically related to stems in the Piᶜēl, and 10% to stems in the Hiᵖᶜîl; while 10% have no semantic relationship to any other active stem formation.[8]

The semantic relationships most often realized are the following:

(1) The passive (mostly of the Qal)

כָּל־מְלָאכָה לֹא־יֵעָשֶׂה בָהֶם　No work *shall be done* on them (Exod. 12:16).*

(2) The reflexive (mostly of the Qal)
　This category is also called the "double status" Niᵖᶜal because the subject of the verb is both the agent and the patient of the verbal action. Within this category, it is possible to distinguish between:

8.　For more statistics, see Siebesma (1991: 92–96).

(a) Ordinary reflexive

> וְאִנָּקְמָה מֵאוֹיְבַי And I *will avenge myself* on my foes (Isa. 1:24).*

(b) Reciprocal

> וְכִי־יִנָּצוּ אֲנָשִׁים... And when men *strive with one another*... (Exod. 21:22).*

For the distinction between the Nip̄ʿal and the Hitpaʿēl, see §16.6.2.

(3) Some verbs occur in the Nip̄ʿal, but not in the Qal, and then express an active meaning of the verb, e.g. נִלְחַם (he fought), נִסְתַּר (he crept away), נִמְלַט (he slipped away).

§16.4. Morphology and Semantics of the Piʿēl

16.4.1. *Morphology*

16.4.1.1. *Paradigm*

Table 13. *Paradigm of the Piʿēl*

PIʿĒL		Singular	Plural
Qātal/Perfect	3 m.	כִּתֵּב	כִּתְּבוּ
	3 f.	כִּתְּבָה	
	2 m.	כִּתַּבְתָּ	כִּתַּבְתֶּם
	2 f.	כִּתַּבְתְּ	כִּתַּבְתֶּן
	1 c.	כִּתַּבְתִּי	כִּתַּבְנוּ
Yiqtōl/Imperfect	3 m.	יְכַתֵּב	יְכַתְּבוּ
	3 f.	תְּכַתֵּב	תְּכַתֵּבְנָה
	2 m.	תְּכַתֵּב	תְּכַתְּבוּ
	2 f.	תְּכַתְּבִי	תְּכַתֵּבְנָה
	1 c.	אֲכַתֵּב	נְכַתֵּב
Imp.	m.	כַּתֵּב	כַּתְּבוּ
	f.	כַּתְּבִי	כַּתֵּבְנָה

	PI‘ĒL		
		Singular	*Plural*
Coh.		אֶכְתְּבָה	
Juss.		יְכַתֵּב	
Inf. cs.		כַּתֵּב	
Inf. Abs.		כַּתֵּב/כַּתּוֹב	
Part.		מְכַתֵּב	

16.4.1.2. *Important morphological features*

(1) The doubling of the second stem consonant (יְכַתֵּב ,כִּתֵּב).

(2) In the *qātal*/perfect the stem vowel of the first syllable is /ִ◌/ (כִּתֵּב).

(3) In the *qātal*/perfect third masculine singular the second stem vowel is usually /ֵ◌/ (כִּתֵּב), but it may sometimes also be /ַ◌/ (לְמַד). In the rest of the *qātal*/perfect paradigm it is /ַ◌/ (כִּתַּבְנוּ).

   (a) Before vocalic suffixes the second stem vowel reduces to /ְ◌/ (כִּתְּבוּ).

   (b) Before consonantal suffixes the vowel pattern is /ַ◌ְ◌/ (כִּתַּבְנוּ).

(4) In the *yiqtōl*/imperfect the prefix vowel is /ְ◌/ (תְּכַתֵּב) and the vowel pattern is /ְ◌ַ◌ֵ/ (יְכַתֵּב).

   (a) Before vocalic suffixes the second stem vowel reduces to /ְ◌/ (תְּכַתְּבוּ).

   (b) Before consonantal suffixes the vowel pattern remains /ְ◌ַ◌ֵ/ (תְּכַתֵּבְנָה).

(5) In the *yiqtōl*/imperfect first common singular the prefix vowel is /ֶ◌/ (אֲכַתֵּב) and not /ְ◌/.

(6) In the imperative and the infinitive construct the vowel pattern is /ַ◌ֵ/ (כַּתֵּב).

(7) In the participle the prefix is מְ- (מְכַתֵּב).

(8) Other patterns of the Pi‘ēl also occur without another stem formation being constituted, e.g. Pô‘ēl, Pil‘ēl, Pə‘alal and Pilp‘ēl, mostly relating to types of weak verbs.[9]

---

9. See Waltke and O'Connor §21.2.3.

16.4.2. *Semantics*

All the verbs that occur in the Qal stem formation do not necessarily have conjugations in the Piᶜēl. Similarly all the verbs occurring in the Piᶜēl stem formation do not necessarily have conjugations in the Qal, e.g. דִּבֶּר (he spoke) and בִּקֵּשׁ (he sought). Should a verb occur both in the Qal and the Piᶜēl, there may be a correspondence of meaning. However, the nature of this correspondence differs with each lexical root.

16.4.2.1. *Factitive*

In some cases the Piᶜēl is used to express the factitive/causative sense of verbs that occur in the Qal. The Piᶜēl indicates the cause that places an object in the condition to which the Qal form (with a stative meaning) of the same stem refers, e.g.:

וְאִם־בְּנֵי עַמּוֹן יֶחֶזְקוּ מִמְּךָ Qal: And if the Ammonites *are* too *strong* for you (2 Sam. 10:11).*

אֲשֶׁר־חִזְּקוּ אֶת־יָדָיו לַהֲרֹג אֶת־אֶחָיו Piᶜēl: who *strengthened* his hands to slay his brothers (Judg. 9:24).*

Note that the Hip̄ᶜîl also has a causative function. However, it differs from that of the Piᶜēl (§16.7.2).

16.4.2.2. *Resultative*

The Qal may describe the action of the verb as a process that occurs, while the Piᶜēl describes the result of that process.

וּפָרַשְׂתָּ אֵלָיו כַּפֶּךָ Qal: And *you stretch out* your hands toward him (Job 11:13).*

פֵּרַשְׂתִּי יָדַי כָּל־הַיּוֹם Piᶜēl: *I spread out* my palms all day (Isa. 65:2).*

The nature of this semantic difference between the Qal and Piᶜēl forms of a verb is difficult to determine and is sometimes difficult to reflect in English.

16.4.2.3. *Denominative*

The Piʿēl refers to the action of the official referred to in the noun with the same stem consonants; for example, the verb כָּהֵן (he served as a priest) refers to the action of the official to which the noun כֹּהֵן (priest) refers. (See also Waltke and O'Connor §24.4.)

> וְכִהֵן לִי   so that he *may serve as priest* for
> me (Exod. 40:13).*

The Piʿēl must be regarded as an independent stem formation, the meaning of which must be determined independently. There may be a similarity with the Qal, but this cannot be taken for granted.

§16.5. Morphology and Semantics of the Puʿal

16.5.1. *Morphology*

16.5.1.1. *Paradigm*

Table 14. *Paradigm of the Puʿal*

PUʿAL			
		Singular	*Plural*
Qātal/Perfect	*3 m.*	כֻּתַּב	כֻּתְּבוּ
	3 f.	כֻּתְּבָה	
	2 m.	כֻּתַּבְתָּ	כֻּתַּבְתֶּם
	2 f.	כֻּתַּבְתְּ	כֻּתַּבְתֶּן
	1 c.	כֻּתַּבְתִּי	כֻּתַּבְנוּ
Yiqtōl/Imperfect	*3 m.*	יְכֻתַּב	יְכֻתְּבוּ
	3 f.	תְּכֻתַּב	תְּכֻתַּבְנָה
	2 m.	תְּכֻתַּב	תְּכֻתְּבוּ
	2 f.	תְּכֻתְּבִי	תְּכֻתַּבְנָה
	1 c.	אֲכֻתַּב	נְכֻתַּב
Juss.		יְכֻתַּב	
Inf. cs.			
Inf. abs.		כֻּתֹּב	
Part.		מְכֻתָּב	

16.5.1.2. *Important morphological features*

(1) The doubling of the second stem consonant and the vowel /ֻ/ below the first consonant of the stem (כֻּתַּב ,יְכֻתַּב).

(2) In the *qātal*/perfect the vowel pattern is /ַֻ/ (כֻּתַּב).

(3) In the *yiqtōl*/imperfect the vowel pattern is /ְַֻ/ (יְכֻתַּב).

- With consonantal suffixes the /ְַֻ/ pattern is retained (תְּכֻתַּבְנָה).
- With vocalic suffixes the /ַ/ changes to /ְ/ (תְּכֻתְּבוּ).

(4) No imperative forms occur in the Puʿal.

(5) In the participle the prefix is מְ- and the vowel pattern /ְַֻ/ (מְכֻתַּב). Note that 40% of all Puʿal forms in the Hebrew Bible are participles.

(6) Other patterns of the Puʿal also occur without another stem formation being constituted, e.g. Poʿal, Puʿlal, and Pôlpal, mostly relating to types of weak verbs. (See Waltke and O'Connor §21.2.3.)

16.5.2. *Semantics*

The Puʿal is in all respects the passive of the Piʿēl.

וַיְבַקְשׁוּ שְׁלֹשָׁה־יָמִים וְלֹא מְצָאֻהוּ	Piʿēl: And for three days *they sought* (him), but did not find him (2 Kgs 2:17).*
וַיְבֻקַּשׁ הַדָּבָר...	Puʿal: And when the affair was *investigated*… (Est. 2:23).*

However, in certain cases the passive voice of the Piʿēl may be expressed by the Niᵽʿal, rather than by the Puʿal.

כָּבְדָה מְאֹד יַד הָאֱלֹהִים שָׁם	Qal: The hand of God *was* very *heavy* there (1 Sam. 5:11).
כִּי־מְכַבְּדַי אֲכַבֵּד	Piʿēl: For those who honor me, *I will honor* (1 Sam. 2:30).
וְעַל־פְּנֵי כָל־הָעָם אֶכָּבֵד	Niᵽʿal: And before all the people *I will be honored* (Lev. 10:3).*

§16.6. Morphology and Semantics of the Hitpaʿēl

16.6.1. *Morphology*

16.6.1.1. *Paradigm*

Table 15. *Paradigm of the Hitpaʿēl*

HIṬPĀʿĒL				
			Singular	Plural
Qātal/Perfect	3 m.		הִתְכַּתֵּב	הִתְכַּתְּבוּ
	3 f.		הִתְכַּתְּבָה	
	2 m.		הִתְכַּתַּ֫בְתָּ	הִתְכַּתַּבְתֶּם
	2 f.		הִתְכַּתַּבְתְּ	הִתְכַּתַּבְתֶּן
	1 c.		הִתְכַּתַּ֫בְתִּי	הִתְכַּתַּ֫בְנוּ
Yiqtōl/Imperfect	3 m.		יִתְכַּתֵּב	יִתְכַּתְּבוּ
	3 f.		תִּתְכַּתֵּב	תִּתְכַּתֵּ֫בְנָה
	2 m.		תִּתְכַּתֵּב	תִּתְכַּתְּבוּ
	2 f.		תִּתְכַּתְּבִי	תִּתְכַּתֵּ֫בְנָה
	1 c.		אֶתְכַּתֵּב	נִתְכַּתֵּב
Imp.	m.		הִתְכַּתֵּב	הִתְכַּתְּבוּ
	f.		הִתְכַּתְּבִי	הִתְכַּתֵּ֫בְנָה
Coh.			אֶתְכַּתְּבָה	
Juss.			יִתְכַּתֵּב	
Inf. cs.			הִתְכַּתֵּב	
Inf. Abs.			הִתְכַּתֵּב	
Part.			מִתְכַּתֵּב	

16.6.1.2. *Important morphological features*

(1) The middle stem consonant doubles and -תְ is the prefix throughout all its conjugations (הִתְכַּתֵּב).

(2) In the *qātal*/perfect the prefix is -הִת (הִתְכַּתֵּב).

(3) In the *qātal*/perfect the vowel pattern is /◌ְ◌ַ/ (הִתְכַּתֵּב).

    (a) Before consonantal suffixes the /◌ֵ/ changes to /◌ַ/ (הִתְכַּתֵּבְנָה).

    (b) Before vocalic suffixes the /◌ֵ/ is reduced to /◌ְ/ (הִתְכַּתְּבוּ).

(4) In the *yiqtōl*/imperfect the prefix is יִת- (יִתְכַּתֵּב), תִּת- (תִּתְכַּתֵּב) etc.

(5) In the imperative the prefix is הִת- (הִתְכַּתֵּב).

(6) In the participle the prefix is מִת- (מִתְכַּתֵּב).

Note the following:

    (a) When a verb beginning with a sibilant (§4.2.5.1) is conjugated in the Hitpaʿēl, metathesis occurs between the sibilant and the ת of the ית/הת prefix, for example, *הִשְׁתַּמֵּר becomes הִשְׁתַּמֵּר (guard yourself against or refrain from).

    (b) When the first stem consonant is צ, metathesis as well as assimilation takes place. For example, התצדק becomes *הצתדק as a result of metathesis and *הצתדק becomes הצטדק (justify yourself) as a result of assimilation (§4.2.4.2).

    (c) When a verb beginning with a ת, ד or ט is conjugated in the Hitpaʿēl, the ת of the הת prefix assimilates to the verbal root, i.e. *תתדבר becomes תדבר.

    (d) Other patterns of the Hitpaʿēl also occur without another stem formation being constituted, e.g. Hitpôʿēl, Hitpaʿlēl, Hitpôʿlal, Hitpalpēl. (See Waltke and O'Connor §26.1.1.)

16.6.2. Semantics

The Hitpaʿēl usually indicates a reflexive or reciprocal action.

> וְהִתְקַדִּשְׁתֶּם וִהְיִיתֶם קְדֹשִׁים   And *consecrate yourselves* and be holy (Lev. 11:44).*

As discussed above (§16.3.2), the Nip̄ʿal also may indicate reflexive or reciprocal action. The distinction between the Nip̄ʿal and Hitpaʿēl has been described as follows.[10] The Nip̄ʿal focuses on the resulting state of the action, whereas the Hitpaʿēl focuses on the process:

> לֹא תְטַמְּאוּ בָּהֶם וְנִטְמֵתֶם בָּם: *Do* not *become defiled* (Hitpaʿēl) by them and thus *be defiled* by them (Nip̄ʿal) (Lev. 11:43).*

---

10. See Benton (2008).

The Hitpaᶜēl also sometimes simply indicates an active meaning of a verb that does not appear in the Qal.

הִתְפַּלֵּל בְּעַד־עֲבָדֶיךָ   *Pray* for your servants (1 Sam. 12:19).*

The Hitpaᶜēl must be regarded as an independent stem formation, the meaning of which must be learned separately.[11]

§16.7. Morphology and Semantics of the Hip̄ᶜîl

16.7.1. *Morphology*

16.7.1.1. *Paradigm*

Table 16. *Paradigm of the Hip̄ᶜîl*

		Singular	Plural
HIP̄ᶜÎL			
		Singular	*Plural*
Qātal/Perfect	3 m.	הִכְתִּיב	הִכְתִּיבוּ
	3 f.	הִכְתִּיבָה	
	2 m.	הִכְתַּבְתָּ	הִכְתַּבְתֶּם
	2 f.	הִכְתַּבְתְּ	הִכְתַּבְתֶּן
	1 c.	הִכְתַּבְתִּי	הִכְתַּבְנוּ
Yiqtōl/Imperfect	3 m.	יַכְתִּיב	יַכְתִּיבוּ
	3 f.	תַּכְתִּיב	תַּכְתֵּבְנָה
	2 m.	תַּכְתִּיב	תַּכְתִּיבוּ
	2 f.	תַּכְתִּיבִי	תַּכְתֵּבְנָה
	1 c.	אַכְתִּיב	נַכְתִּיב
Imp.	m.	הַכְתֵּב	הַכְתִּיבוּ
	f.	הַכְתִּיבִי	הַכְתֵּבְנָה
Coh.		אַכְתִּיבָה	
Juss.		יַכְתֵּב	

---

11. See Waltke and O'Connor §26.2–4 and Joüon–Muraoka §53i.

HIP̄ʿÎL		
	Singular	*Plural*
Inf. cs.	הַכְתֵּיב	
Inf. abs.	הַכְתֵּב	
Part.	מַכְתֵּיב	

16.7.1.2. *Important morphological features*

(1) In the *qātal*/perfect the prefix is הִ- (הִכְתֵּיב). This prefix forms a closed syllable with the first stem consonant.

(2) In the *qātal*/perfect the vowel pattern is /ִ ֵ◌/ (הִכְתֵּיב).

    (a) With the vocalic suffixes the unchangeable long second vowel of the stem vowel, /ִי◌/ (הִכְתֵּיבָה), is retained.

    (b) With the consonantal suffixes, however, the second stem vowel is /ַ◌/ (הִכְתַּבְתָּ).

(3) In the *yiqtōl*/imperfect the vowel of the prefix is /ַ◌/. The ה prefix, however, falls away completely (תַּכְתֵּיב).

    (a) In the *yiqtōl*/imperfect the vowel pattern is /ַ ֵ◌/ (תַּכְתֵּיב).

    (b) With consonantal suffixes the stem vowel /ֵ◌/ changes to /ְ◌/ (תַּכְתֵּבְנָה).

    (c) With vowel suffixes the vowel pattern remains unaltered (תַּכְתֵּיבוּ).

(4) In the imperative feminine singular, masculine plural and feminine plural, and the infinitive construct the prefix is הַ- and the stem vowel /ֵ◌/ (הַכְתֵּיב, הַכְתֵּיבוּ).

(5) In the infinitive absolute and imperative masculine singular the stem vowel is /ֵ◌/ (הַכְתֵּב).

(6) In the jussive form the stem vowel /ֵ◌/ changes to /ֵ◌/ (תַּכְתֵּב). As opposed to the other stem formations, the shorter form of the jussive is thus always readily recognizable.

(7) In the participle the prefix is מַ- and the stem vowel /ִי◌/ (מַכְתֵּיב).

Note: the Hip̄ʿîl is the only stem formation in which the forms of the imperative masculine singular and the infinitive construct differ.

16.7.2. *Semantics*

(1) The Hip̄ʿîl stem formation mostly indicates the causative sense of verbs occurring in the Qal.

In other words, the subject of the stem in the Hip̄ʿîl causes the object of that verb to act as subject in the idea expressed by the stem.[12]

וְאֵלֶּה אֲשֶׁר־נָחֲלוּ בְנֵי־יִשְׂרָאֵל	Qal: And these are what the Israelites *inherited* (Josh. 14:1).*
תַּנְחִיל אֶת־הָעָם הַזֶּה אֶת־הָאָרֶץ	Hip̄ʿîl: You *will cause* this people *to inherit* the land (Josh. 1:6).*

In Josh. 1:6 "people" is grammatically the object of the Hip̄ʿîl form of נחל. However, it is also semantically the agent (subject) of the verbal idea, i.e. it is the "people" who inherit.

(2) The Hip̄ʿîl may also be used to express the causative of verbs that occur in the Nip̄ʿal.

וַאֲשֶׁר נִשְׁבַּע־לִי	Nip̄ʿal: And who *swore* to me (Gen. 24:7).*
כַּאֲשֶׁר הִשְׁבִּיעֶךָ	Hip̄ʿîl: As he *made* you *swear* (Gen. 50:6).

(3) A causative link between the Qal and the Hip̄ʿîl cannot always be deduced from the translation of a verb, e.g., Qal פָּקַד (he visited) versus Hip̄ʿîl הִפְקִיד (he appointed).

(4) Some verbs occur in the Hip̄ʿîl, but not in the Qal, e.g. הִשְׁלִיךְ (he threw), הִשְׁכִּים (he rose early) and הִשְׁמִיד (he eradicated). These verbs do not have a causative meaning.

Note the following:

(a) The factitive expressed by the Piʿēl also has a causative nuance.

וְאֶת־אֶלְעָזָר בְּנוֹ קִדְּשׁוּ	And, Eleazar, his son, *they consecrated* [lit. *they caused* Eleazar, his son, *to be holy*] (1 Sam. 7:1).*

---

12. See Waltke and O'Connor §27 and Joüon–Muraoka §54.

(b) When a verb is used in the Piˤēl, it indicates an action that leads to an object ending up in a certain condition. That object does not do the action referred to by the verbal idea.

The Hip̄ˤîl must be regarded as an independent stem formation, the meaning of which must be learned separately.

§16.8. Morphology and Semantics of the Hop̄ˤal

16.8.1. *Morphology*

16.8.1.1. *Paradigm*

Table 17. *Paradigm of the Hop̄ˤal*

HOP̄ˤAL		Singular	Plural
Qātal/Perfect	*3 m.*	הָכְתַּב	הָכְתְּבוּ
	3 f.	הָכְתְּבָה	
	2 m.	הָכְתַּ֫בְתָּ	הָכְתַּבְתֶּם
	2 f.	הָכְתַּבְתְּ	הָכְתַּבְתֶּן
	1 c.	הָכְתַּ֫בְתִּי	הָכְתַּ֫בְנוּ
Yiqtōl/Imperfect	*3 m.*	יָכְתַּב	יָכְתְּבוּ
	3 f.	תָּכְתַּב	תָּכְתַּ֫בְנָה
	2 m.	תָּכְתַּב	תָּכְתְּבוּ
	2 f.	תָּכְתְּבִי	תָּכְתַּ֫בְנָה
	1 c.	אָכְתַּב	נָכְתַּב
Imp.	*m.*		
	f.		
Coh.			
Juss.		יָכְתַּב	
Inf. cs.			
Inf. abs.		הָכְתַּב	
Part.		מָכְתָּב	

16.8.1.2. *Important morphological features*

(1) In the *qātal*/perfect the prefix is -הָ. This prefix forms a closed syllable with the first stem consonant (הָכְתַּב); the vowel is therefore *qāmeṣ ḥāṭûp̄* /o/ and not *qāmeṣ* /ā/ (§8.3.2).

(2) In the *qātal*/perfect the vowel pattern is /◌ ◌/ (הָכְתַּב).

- With vocalic suffixes the /◌/ changes to /◌/ (הָכְתְּבוּ).

(3) In the *yiqtōl*/imperfect the vowel of the prefix is /◌/ (a *qāmeṣ ḥāṭûp̄*), but the prefix -הָ falls away (תָּכְתַּב, יָכְתַּב).

(4) In the *yiqtōl*/imperfect the vowel pattern is /◌ ◌/ (יָכְתַּב).

- With vocalic suffixes the /◌/ changes to /◌/ (יָכְתְּבוּ).

(5) In the participle the prefix is -מָ and the stem vowel /◌/ (מָכְתָּב).

16.8.2. *Semantics*

(1) The primary function of the Hop̄ʿal stem formation is to express *the passive sense of the Hip̄ʿîl.*

וַתַּשְׁכִּבֵהוּ בְּחֵיקָהּ	Hip̄ʿîl: And *laid* him in her bosom (1 Kgs 3:20).*
וְהֻשְׁכַּב בְּתוֹךְ עֲרֵלִים	Hop̄ʿal: And *he shall be laid* among the uncircumcised (Ezek. 32:32).*

(2) In certain cases the passive sense of the Hip̄ʿîl may be expressed *by the Nip̄ʿal.*

אִם־לֹא תַשְׁמִידוּ הַחֵרֶם מִקִּרְבְּכֶם	Hip̄ʿîl: Unless *you destroy* the devoted things from among you (Josh. 7:12).
וְנִשְׁמַדְתִּי אֲנִי וּבֵיתִי	Nip̄ʿal: And *I shall be destroyed,* both I and my household (Gen. 34:30).*

§16.9. Stem Formations: Complete Paradigm

Table 18. *Paradigm of All the Stem Formations*

	QAL	NI.	PI.	PU.	HTP.	HI.	HO.
Sing.				Qātal/Perfect			
3 m.	כָּתַב	נִכְתַּב	כִּתֵּב	כֻּתַּב	הִתְכַּתֵּב	הִכְתִּיב	הָכְתַּב
3 f.	כָּתְבָה	נִכְתְּבָה	כִּתְּבָה	כֻּתְּבָה	הִתְכַּתְּבָה	הִכְתִּיבָה	הָכְתְּבָה
2 m.	כָּתַבְתָּ	נִכְתַּבְתָּ	כִּתַּבְתָּ	כֻּתַּבְתָּ	הִתְכַּתַּבְתָּ	הִכְתַּבְתָּ	הָכְתַּבְתָּ
2 f.	כָּתַבְתְּ	נִכְתַּבְתְּ	כִּתַּבְתְּ	כֻּתַּבְתְּ	הִתְכַּתַּבְתְּ	הִכְתַּבְתְּ	הָכְתַּבְתְּ
1 c.	כָּתַבְתִּי	נִכְתַּבְתִּי	כִּתַּבְתִּי	כֻּתַּבְתִּי	הִתְכַּתַּבְתִּי	הִכְתַּבְתִּי	הָכְתַּבְתִּי
Pl.							
3 c.	כָּתְבוּ	נִכְתְּבוּ	כִּתְּבוּ	כֻּתְּבוּ	הִתְכַּתְּבוּ	הִכְתִּיבוּ	הָכְתְּבוּ
2 m.	כְּתַבְתֶּם	נִכְתַּבְתֶּם	כִּתַּבְתֶּם	כֻּתַּבְתֶּם	הִתְכַּתַּבְתֶּם	הִכְתַּבְתֶּם	הָכְתַּבְתֶּם
2 f.	כְּתַבְתֶּן	נִכְתַּבְתֶּן	כִּתַּבְתֶּן	כֻּתַּבְתֶּן	הִתְכַּתַּבְתֶּן	הִכְתַּבְתֶּן	הָכְתַּבְתֶּן
1 c.	כָּתַבְנוּ	נִכְתַּבְנוּ	כִּתַּבְנוּ	כֻּתַּבְנוּ	הִתְכַּתַּבְנוּ	הִכְתַּבְנוּ	הָכְתַּבְנוּ
Sing.				Yiqtōl/Imperfect			
3 m.	יִכְתֹּב	יִכָּתֵב	יְכַתֵּב	יְכֻתַּב	יִתְכַּתֵּב	יַכְתִּיב	יָכְתַּב
3 f.	תִּכְתֹּב	תִּכָּתֵב	תְּכַתֵּב	תְּכֻתַּב	תִּתְכַּתֵּב	תַּכְתִּיב	תָּכְתַּב
2 m.	תִּכְתֹּב	תִּכָּתֵב	תְּכַתֵּב	תְּכֻתַּב	תִּתְכַּתֵּב	תַּכְתִּיב	תָּכְתַּב
2 f.	תִּכְתְּבִי	תִּכָּתְבִי	תְּכַתְּבִי	תְּכֻתְּבִי	תִּתְכַּתְּבִי	תַּכְתִּיבִי	תָּכְתְּבִי
1 c.	אֶכְתֹּב	אֶכָּתֵב	אֲכַתֵּב	אֲכֻתַּב	אֶתְכַּתֵּב	אַכְתִּיב	אָכְתַּב
Pl.							
3 m.	יִכְתְּבוּ	יִכָּתְבוּ	יְכַתְּבוּ	יְכֻתְּבוּ	יִתְכַּתְּבוּ	יַכְתִּיבוּ	יָכְתְּבוּ
3 f.	תִּכְתֹּבְנָה	תִּכָּתַבְנָה	תְּכַתֵּבְנָה	תְּכֻתַּבְנָה	תִּתְכַּתַּבְנָה	תַּכְתֵּבְנָה	תָּכְתַּבְנָה
2 m.	תִּכְתְּבוּ	תִּכָּתְבוּ	תְּכַתְּבוּ	תְּכֻתְּבוּ	תִּתְכַּתְּבוּ	תַּכְתִּיבוּ	תָּכְתְּבוּ
2 f.	תִּכְתֹּבְנָה	תִּכָּתַבְנָה	תְּכַתֵּבְנָה	תְּכֻתַּבְנָה	תִּתְכַּתַּבְנָה	תַּכְתֵּבְנָה	תָּכְתַּבְנָה
1 c.	נִכְתֹּב	נִכָּתֵב	נְכַתֵּב	נְכֻתַּב	נִתְכַּתֵּב	נַכְתִּיב	נָכְתַּב

	QAL	NI.	PI.	PU.	HTP.	HI.	HO.
Sing.	Imperative						
2 m.	כְּתֹב	הִכָּתֵב	כַּתֵּב		הִתְכַּתֵּב	הַכְתֵּב	
2 f.	כִּתְבִי	הִכָּתְבִי	כַּתְּבִי		הִתְכַּתְּבִי	הַכְתִּיבִי	
Pl.							
2 m.	כִּתְבוּ	הִכָּתְבוּ	כַּתְּבוּ		הִתְכַּתְּבוּ	הַכְתִּיבוּ	
2 f.	כְּתֹבְנָה	הִכָּתַבְנָה	כַּתֵּבְנָה		הִתְכַּתֵּבְנָה	הַכְתֵּבְנָה	
Sing.	Cohortative						
1 c.	אֶכְתְּבָה	אִכָּתְבָה	אֲכַתְּבָה		אֶתְכַּתְּבָה	אַכְתִּיבָה	
Sing.	Jussive						
3 m.	יִכְתֹּב	יִכָּתֵב	יְכַתֵּב	יְכֻתַּב	יִתְכַּתֵּב	יַכְתֵּב	יָכְתַּב
	Infinitive						
cs.	כְּתֹב	הִכָּתֵב	כַּתֵּב		הִתְכַּתֵּב	הַכְתִּיב	
abs.	כָּתוֹב	נִכְתֹב	כַּתֵּב	כֻּתֹב	הִתְכַּתֵּב	הַכְתֵּב	הָכְתֵּב
	Participle						
act.	כֹּתֵב		מְכַתֵּב		מִתְכַּתֵּב	מַכְתִּיב	
pass.	כָּתוּב	נִכְתָּב		מְכֻתָּב			מָכְתָּב

§17. Pronominal Suffixes Added to Verbs

§17.1. Introduction

In Biblical Hebrew the definite object of a clause is usually preceded by the so-called accusative/object marker אֶת/אֶת־. Should this object be pronominalized, i.e. should the noun be replaced with a pronoun, the pronoun may be added either to the אֶת or to the verb of the clause. These two forms are variants and there is no readily apparent difference in meaning between them.

וְהִכְרַתִּי אֹתוֹ מִקֶּרֶב עַמּוֹ   And I will cut *him* off from among his people (Lev. 20:3).*

וְהִכְרַתִּיו מִתּוֹךְ עַמִּי   And I will cut *him* off from the midst of my people (Ezek. 14:8).*

There is basically one set of suffixes that is added to the *qātal*/perfect, *yiqtōl*/imperfect and imperative. This set of suffixes, which is used in all stem formations, appears in the table below:

Table 19. *Object Suffixes for Qātal/Perfect, Yiqtōl/Imperfect and Imperative*

1 sing.	נִי-	me	1 pl.	נוּ-	us
2 m. sing.	ךָ-	you	2 m. pl.	כֶם-	you
2 f. sing.	ךְ-	you	2 f. pl.	כֶן-	you
3 m. sing.	הוּ-\וֹ	him	3 m. pl.	ם- הֶם-	them
3 f. sing.	הָ\הָ	her הָ-	3 f. pl.	ן- הֶן-	them

The addition of the pronominal suffixes to verbs results in accent shifts and vowel changes within the verbs.

The following variables must be taken into account:

(1) Whether the verbs end in a consonant or a vowel.

(2) Verbs that end in consonants take a connecting vowel.

(3) *Qātal*/Perfect forms take /◌/ or /◌/ and *yiqtōl*/imperfect as well as imperative forms take /◌/ or /◌/ as the connecting vowel. The suffixes כֶם-, כֶן- and ךָ-, however, do not take a connecting vowel.

(4) Suffixes are light or heavy. The heavy consonantal suffixes כֶם-, כֶן-, הֶם- and הֶן- always attract the accent to themselves resulting in the reduction of the changeable long vowels in preceding syllables.

(5) The so-called "energic" *nûn* suffix sometimes occurs with *yiqtōl*/imperfect forms and imperatives. It has no semantic value.

§17.2. Suffixes Added to *Qātal*/Perfect Forms

17.2.1. *Qātal/Perfect forms ending in vowels*

17.2.1.1. *List of forms*

(1) The following *qātal*/perfect forms usually end in a vowel:

שָׁמַרְתִּי, שָׁמְרוּ, שָׁמַרְנוּ

(2) The following *qātal*/perfect forms are adapted to end in a vowel:

    (a) The תְּ ending of the second feminine singular becomes תִי, i.e. שָׁמַרְתִּי instead of שָׁמַרְתְּ. This form thus has the same appearance as the first singular.

    (b) The final *nûn* and *mēm* of the second feminine and masculine plural fall away and the /ọ/ is replaced with ֹי, e.g.: שְׁמַרְתּוּ instead of שְׁמַרְתֶּם and שְׁמַרְתֶּן.

(3) The following *qātal*/perfect forms usually end in a vowel but are adapted to end in a consonant:

    (a) The הָ֯ ending of the third feminine singular is replaced by ת֯. Normal vowel changes that accompany the addition of an element such as a suffix occur, e.g.: שְׁמָרַת instead of שְׁמָרָה.

    (b) The תָ- ending of the second masculine singular contracts to תְּ-, e.g.: שְׁמַרְתְּ- instead of שָׁמַרְתָּ.

17.2.1.2. *Basic vowel changes*

(1) When one of the pronominal suffixes is added to a *qātal*/perfect that ends in a vowel, the /ọ/ in the first open syllable is reduced to /ọ/, e.g.:

$$\text{שָׁמַרְנוּ} \quad \text{plus suffix is:} \quad \text{-שְׁמַרְנוּ}$$

(2) If the second syllable is open, the original stem vowel /ọ/ is revived and changes to /ọ/, e.g.:

$$\text{שָׁמְרוּ} \quad \text{plus suffix is:} \quad \text{-שְׁמָרוּ}$$

(3) If the first syllable is closed, its vowel does not changed, e.g.:

$$\text{בְּקַשׁוּנִי}$$

(4) If there is an unchangeable long vowel in the second open syllable, no vowel change occurs, e.g.:

$$\text{הִכְרִיתוּנִי}$$

17.2.1.3. *Set of suffixes*

The so-called basic set (§17.1).

17.2.2. *Qātal/Perfect forms ending in consonants*

17.2.2.1. *List of forms*

(1) The following *qātal*/perfect forms usually end in a consonant:

שָׁמַר

(2) The following *qātal*/perfect forms are constructed to end in a consonant:

    (a) The הָ◌ ending of the third feminine singular is replaced by תָ◌.
    Normal vowel changes which accompany the addition of an element
    such as a suffix occur, e.g.: שְׁמָרַת- instead of שָׁמְרָה.

    (b) The תָ- ending of the second masculine singular contracts to תְ-, e.g.:
    שְׁמַרְתְ- instead of שָׁמַרְתָ.

17.2.2.2. *Basic vowel changes*

The vowel changes are similar to those of the forms ending in vowels, e.g.:

שָׁמַר   plus suffix is: שְׁמָר-

17.2.2.3. *Set of suffixes*

Table 20. Suffixes to Qātal/Perfect Ending in Consonants

1 sing.	נִי◌	me	1 pl.	נוּ◌	us
2 m. sing.	ךָ◌	you	2 m. pl.	כֶם◌	you
2 f. sing.	ךְ◌ ךָ◌	you	2 f. pl.	כֶן◌	you
3 m. sing.	הוּ◌/-וֹ	him	3 m. pl.	ם◌	them
3 f. sing.	הָ◌	her	3 f. pl.	ן◌	them

17.2.3. *Summary of qātal/perfect forms with pronominal suffixes*

Table 21. *Qātal/Perfect Base Forms for Suffixes*

1 sing.	שָׁמַרְתִּי-	1 pl.	שְׁמַרְנוּ-
2 m. sing.	שְׁמַרְתְּ-	2 m. pl.	שְׁמַרְתּוּ-
2 f. sing.	שְׁמַרְתִּי-	2 f. pl.	שְׁמַרְתּוּ-
3 m. sing.	שְׁמָר-	3 m. pl.	שְׁמָרוּ-
3 f. sing.	שְׁמָרַת-	3 f. pl.	שְׁמָרוּ-

§17.3. Suffixes Added to *Yiqtōl*/Imperfect Forms

17.3.1. *Yiqtōl/Imperfect forms ending in vowels*

17.3.1.1. *List of forms*

Forms that normally end in a vowel:

תִּכְתֹּבְנָה ,תִּכְתְּבוּ ,יִכְתְּבוּ ,תִּכְתְּבִי

17.3.1.2. *Basic vowel changes*

Since the forms to which the suffixes are added contain virtually no changeable vowels, relatively few changes occur when the pronominal suffixes are added. Sometimes ו is written as /◌ֹ/, e.g.:

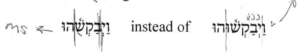

ms ← וַיְבַקְשֹׁהוּ　　　instead of　　　וַיְבַקְשׁוּהוּ

17.3.1.3. *Set of suffixes*

This set is the same as the basic set in §17.1.

17.3.2. *Yiqtōl/Imperfect forms ending in consonants*

17.3.2.1. *List of forms*

Forms that usually end in a consonant:

נִכְתֹּב ,אֶכְתֹּב ,תִּכְתֹּב ,יִכְתֹּב

17.3.2.2. *Basic vowel changes*

(1) The changeable stem vowel, /◌/, changes to a *šəwāʾ* in open syllables, e.g.:

יִשְׁמְרֵנִי   instead of   יִשְׁמֹרֵנִי

(2) Before the suffixes ־ךָ, ־כֶם and ־כֶן the /◌/ changes to /◌/ (*qāmeṣ ḥāṭûp̄*), e.g.:

יִשְׁמָרְכֶם   instead of   יִשְׁמֹרְכֶם

17.3.2.3. *Set of suffixes*

This set looks similar to the set given in §17.2.2.3. The connecting vowels here, however, are /◌/ and /◌/. A partial set of *variant suffixes* also exists in which a *nûn* is inserted between the basic set and the verb. The *nûn* always assimilates with the suffix. The following two sets of suffixes may thus be added to *yiqtōl*/imperfect forms ending in consonants:

Table 22. *Suffixes to Yiqtōl/Imperfect Ending in Consonants*

1 sing.	◌ֵנִי	◌ֵנִּי	1 pl.	◌ֵנוּ	◌ֵנּוּ
2 m. sing.	◌ְךָ	◌ֶּךָ	2 m. pl.	◌ְכֶם	
2 f. sing.	◌ְךְ		2 f. pl.	◌ְכֶן	
3 m. sing.	◌ֵהוּ	◌ֶנּוּ	3 m. pl.	◌ֵם	
3 f. sing.	◌ֶהָ ◌ֵהָ	◌ֶנָּה	3 f. pl.	◌ֵן	

Note the following:

(1) The unusual *dāḡēš* in the *kap̄* of the second masculine singular, ◌ֶּךָ, reflects the *nûn* that has assimilated with the second masculine singular suffix.

(2) The third masculine singular and the first plural of the alternative suffixes with the assimilated *nûn* look alike.

(3) These suffixes are not added to *wayyiqtōl* forms.

(4) In poetry the pronominal suffixes ־מוֹ and ־מוּ are sometimes used for the third masculine plural.

(5) A connecting syllable with a *nûn* (the energic *nûn*) is sometimes placed before the singular suffixes, e.g. יַעַבְרֶנְהוּ (Jer. 5:22).

§17.4. Suffixes Added to Imperative Forms

Since the form of the imperative is derived from the *yiqtōl*/imperfect, the imperative takes the same connecting vowels and undergoes the same vowel changes as the *yiqtōl*/imperfect forms (see §15.3).

Note however that the masculine singular form to which the suffix is added is קָטְל and not קְטֹל.

§17.5. Suffixes Added to Infinitives

The infinitive construct takes the set of pronominal suffixes normally added to nouns (see §15.6 and §26.1), namely:

Table 23. *Suffixes Added to Infinitives*

1 sing.	ִי◌	me	1 pl.	◌ֵנוּ	us
2 m. sing.	◌ְךָ	you	2 m. pl.	◌ְכֶם	you
2 f. sing.	◌ֵךְ	you	2 f. pl.	◌ְכֶן	you
3 m. sing.	וֹ	him	3 m. pl.	◌ָם	them
3 f. sing.	◌ָהּ	her	3 f. pl.	◌ָן	them

Note the following:

(1) Distinctive verbal suffixes for referring to the object and the subject of the infinitive are used only in the first person, e.g. קָטְלֵנִי (to kill me) and קָטְלִי (my killing).

(2) The form of the infinitive to which suffixes are added is קָטְל- and not קְטֹל.

(3) Sometimes the form of the infinitive to which suffixes are added is קְטֹל-, e.g. נׇפְלוֹ (2 Sam. 1:10). At other times the form is קָטְל- and not קְטֹל-, e.g. אֲכׇלְךָ (Gen. 2:17).

§18. Morphology of the Irregular (Weak) Verbs

§18.1. Notation of Irregular Verbs

Irregular (or, "weak") verbs are verbs that deviate in systematic ways in their conjugations from the pattern of the regular (or, "strong") verb which has been dealt with so far (§16). The deviations occur only in certain groups of verbs. Even so, weak verbs do not conjugate erratically, but according to rules determined by the phonetic features of one or more of their stem consonants. The following systems of notation have been introduced when referring to specific types of weak verbs.

The three consonants that comprise most of the weak verbs in Biblical Hebrew are identified from right to left either with the consonants of the פעל verb stem or with Roman numerals. The position of a weak consonant as the first, second of third consonant of a particular verb stem is indicated either by means of the consonants פעל or by means of a Roman numeral, e.g.:

Traditional Description				*Modern Alternative*			
ל	ע	פ		III	II	I	
ר	מ	ע	*pēʾ* guttural	ר	מ	ע	I-guttural
ל	א	שׁ	*ʿayin* guttural	ל	א	שׁ	II-guttural
ח	ל	שׁ	*lāmed* guttural	ח	ל	שׁ	III-guttural
ל	כ	א	*pēʾ ʾālep*	ל	כ	א	I-ʾālep
א	צ	מ	*lāmed ʾālep*	א	צ	מ	III-ʾālep
ה	נ	ב	*lāmed hēʾ*	ה	נ	ב	III-hēʾ
ל	פ	נ	*pēʾ nûn*	ל	פ	נ	I-nûn
ב	שׁ	י	*pēʾ wāw / pēʾ yôd*	ב	שׁ	י	I-wāw / I-yôd
ם	ו	ק	*ʿayin wāw*	ם	ו	ק	II-wāw
ם	י	שׁ	*ʿayin yôd*	ם	י	שׁ	II-yôd
ב	ב	ס	*ʿayin ʿayin*	ב	ב	ס	Double II or geminate

Hēʾ's and *ʾālep*s, which are not pronounced, behave differently from the other gutturals (§4.2.5.2 and §5.2.2.1). *Hēʾ* in position III is not usually pronounced while *ʾālep* is not pronounced in positions I and III. For this reason a distinction is made between *ʾālep* and *hēʾ* as gutturals in general and the following types of weak verbs:

- I-*ʾālep*
- III-*ʾālep*
- III-*hēʾ*

Rêš, which is not a guttural, acts like a guttural, whether in positions I, II or III (§4.2.4.1).

It often happens that a verb stem has two irregular consonants, e.g.:

נָכָה (he hit)

The verb is both I-*nûn* and III-*hē*.

There are also a few verbs that occur frequently and which are irregular in additional respects. The way in which they conjugate cannot be determined solely by the phonetic features of their particular consonants. These verbs will be considered individually:

היה (is), חיה (live), חוה (bend), נתן (give),
לקח (take) and הלך (go).

§18.2. Guttural Verbs

18.2.1. *General rules*[13]

(1) After a guttural, audible *šəwā* is replaced by a *ḥaṭēp̄ šəwā* (§5.2.2.3).

עֲמֹד	instead of	עְמֹד
שֶׁחֲטוּ	instead of	שֶׁחְטוּ

(2) A guttural may be followed by a silent *šəwā* which is often replaced by a *ḥaṭēp̄* vowel corresponding to the preceding full vowel (§8.1.2).

הֶעֱמִיד	instead of	הֶעְמִיד
יַעֲמֹד	instead of	יַעְמֹד

(3) Gutturals and *rêš* (normally) cannot be doubled. If a guttural is supposed to be doubled, "compensatory lengthening" often occurs in the preceding syllable (§8.2.2).

בֵּרֵךְ	instead of	בֵּרֵּךְ
יְבָרֵךְ	instead of	יְבָרֵּךְ
בֹּחַר	instead of	בֹּחַּר

---

13. For a more complete description of the morphology of the gutturals, see Joüon–Muraoka §67–70.

18.2.2. *I-guttural*

18.2.2.1. *Paradigm*

Table 24. *I-guttural Verbs*

	QAL	QAL	NI.	HI.	HO.
Root Gloss	עמד stand	חזק become strong		עמד stand	
Sing.			Qātal/Perfect		
3 m.	עָמַד	חָזַק	נֶעֱמַד	הֶעֱמִיד	הָעֳמַד
3 f.	עָמְדָה	חָזְקָה	נֶעֶמְדָה	הֶעֱמִׁידָה	הָעֳמְדָה
2 m.	עָמַֹדְתָּ	חָזַֹקְתָּ	נֶעֱמַֹדְתָּ	הֶעֱמַֹדְתָּ	הָעֳמַֹדְתָּ
2 f.	עָמַדְתְּ	חָזַקְתְּ	נֶעֱמַדְתְּ	הֶעֱמַדְתְּ	הָעֳמַדְתְּ
1 c.	עָמַֹדְתִּי	חָזַֹקְתִּי	נֶעֱמַֹדְתְּ ׳	הֶעֱמַֹדְתִּי	הָעֳמַֹדְתִּי
Pl.					
3 c.	עָמְדוּ	חָזְקוּ	נֶעֶמְדוּ	הֶעֱמִׁידוּ	הָעֳמְדוּ
2 m.	עֲמַדְתֶּם	חֲזַקְתֶּם	נֶעֱמַדְתֶּם	הֶעֱמַדְתֶּם	הָעֳמַדְתֶּם
2 f.	עֲמַדְתֶּן	חֲזַקְתֶּן	נֶעֱמַדְתֶּן	הֶעֱמַדְתֶּן	הָעֳמַדְתֶּן
1 c.	עָמַֹדְנוּ	חָזַֹקְנוּ	נֶעֱמַֹדְנוּ	הֶעֱמַֹדְנוּ	הָעֳמַֹדְנוּ
Sing.			Yiqtōl/Imperfect		
3 m.	יַעֲמֹד	יֶחֱזַק	יֵעָמֵד	יַעֲמִיד	יָעֳמַד
3 f.	תַּעֲמֹד	תֶּחֱזַק	תֵּעָמֵד	תַּעֲמִיד	תָּעֳמַד
2 m.	תַּעֲמֹד	תֶּחֱזַק	תֵּעָמֵד	תַּעֲמִיד	תָּעֳמַד
2 f.	תַּעַמְדִי	תֶּחֶזְקִי	תֵּעָמְדִי	תַּעֲמִֹידִי	תָּעֳמְדִי
1 c.	אֶעֱמֹד	אֶחֱזַק	אֵעָמֵד	אַעֲמִיד	אָעֳמַד
Pl.					
3 m.	יַעַמְדוּ	יֶחֶזְקוּ	יֵעָמְדוּ	יַעֲמִֹידוּ	יָעֳמְדוּ
3 f.	תַּעֲמֹֹדְנָה	תֶּחֱזַֹקְנָה	תֵּעָמַֹדְנָה	תַּעֲמֵֹדְנָה	תָּעֳמַֹדְנָה
2 m.	תַּעַמְדוּ	תֶּחֶזְקוּ	תֵּעָמְדוּ	תַּעֲמִֹידוּ	תָּעֳמְדוּ
2 f.	תַּעֲמֹֹדְנָה	תֶּחֱזַֹקְנָה	תֵּעָמַֹדְנָה	תַּעֲמֵֹדְנָה	תָּעֳמַֹדְנָה
1 c.	נַעֲמֹד	נֶחֱזַק	נֵעָמֵד	נַעֲמִיד	נָעֳמַד

	QAL	QAL	NI.	HI.	HO.
Sing.			*Imperative*		
2 m.	עֲמֹד	חֲזַק	הֵעָמֵד	הַעֲמֵד	
2 f.	עִמְדִי	חִזְקִי	הֵעָמְדִי	הַעֲמִידִי	
Pl.					
2 m.	עִמְדוּ	חִזְקוּ	הֵעָמְדוּ	הַעֲמִידוּ	
2 f.	עֲמֹדְנָה	חֲזֹקְנָה	הֵעָמַדְנָה	הַעֲמֵדְנָה	
Sing.			*Cohortative*		
	אֶעֶמְדָה			אַעֲמִידָה	
Sing.			*Jussive*		
	יַעֲמֹד	יֶחֱזַק		יַעֲמֵד	
			Infinitive		
cs.	עֲמֹד	חֲזֹק	הֵעָמֵד	הַעֲמִיד	הָעֳמֵד
abs.	עָמוֹד	חָזוֹק	נַעֲמוֹד	הַעֲמֵד	הָעֳמֵד
			Participle		
act.	עֹמֵד	חָזֵק		מַעֲמִיד	
pass.	עָמוּד		נֶעֱמָד		מָעֳמָד

18.2.2.2. Qal

(1) In the *qātal*/perfect

- Most conjugations are like those of the strong verbs. The only difference is that the audible *šəwāʾ* under the guttural becomes a *ḥaṭēp šəwāʾ* in the second masculine and feminine plural (§5.2.2.3).

עֲמַדְתֶּן   instead of   עֲמַדְתֶּן

(2) In the *yiqtōl*/imperfect

- The prefix vowel of the *yiqtōl*/imperfect, /ⵔ/, is replaced with /ⵔ/.

יַעֲמֹד   instead of   יְעֲמֹד

- The silent *šəwā'* after the I-guttural is always replaced by a *ḥaṭēp̄ šəwā'*.

יַעֲמֹד   instead of   יַעְמֹד

- When a vocalic suffix is added, the final stem vowel is reduced. As a result, a hypothetical form arises in which the *ḥaṭēp̄* vowel is followed by an audible *šəwā'*. The *ḥaṭēp̄* vowel and the audible *šəwā'* then fuse into one syllable with the full vowel corresponding to the *ḥaṭēp̄*.

יַעַמְדוּ   instead of   יַעֲמְדוּ

- In the first person the /◌/ is retained. It is not replaced with /◌/.

אֶעֱמֹד   instead of   אַעֲמֹד

(3) In verbs beginning with ח

- The vowel of the prefix is /◌/ and not /◌/. The *ḥaṭēp̄*, which replaces the silent *šəwā'* after the guttural in some cases, is then a *ḥaṭēp̄ səḡôl*.

יֶחֱזַק   instead of   יִחְזַק

(4) I-*'ālep̄* verbs

- In some I-*'ālep̄* verbs, for example אהב and אסף, the vowel of the prefix is /◌/ instead of /◌/.

יֶאֱסֹף   instead of   יִאְסֹף

- If a vocalic suffix is added to these forms in the *yiqtōl*/imperfect, the /◌/ becomes a /◌/. In the process the /◌/ vowel of the prefix also assimilates into a /◌/. In other words, the following process occurs: יַאַסְפוּ > יַאֲסְפוּ > יֶאֱסְפוּ.

יַאַסְפוּ   instead of   יֶאֶסְפוּ

18.2.2.3. *Nip̄ʿal*

(1) In the *qāṭal*/perfect

- The prefix is -נֶ and not -נִ. A *ḥaṭēp̄ səḡôl* sometimes occurs in the place of the silent *šəwā'* after the guttural.

נֶעֱמַד   instead of   נֶעְמַד

- When a vocalic suffix is added, the last stem vowel is reduced. A hypothetical form is then created in which the *ḥaṭēp̄* vowel is followed by an audible *šəwā᾽*. The *ḥaṭēp̄* vowel and the audible *šəwā᾽* then fuse (into a single syllable with the full vowel of the *ḥaṭēp̄*). Here it is a *səḡôl*.

נֶעֶמְדוּ   instead of   נֶעֶמְדוּ

(2) In the *yiqṭōl*/imperfect and imperative

- The vowel of the prefix /◌ֶ/ changes to /◌ֵ/ as a result of "compensatory lengthening" (§8.2.2). The vowel pattern is then /◌ֵ◌ֲ◌/.

יֵעֶמֵד   instead of   יַעֲמֵד

הֵעֶמֵד   instead of   הַעֲמֵד

18.2.2.4. *Piʿēl, Puʿal and Hiṯpaʿēl*

In I-guttural verb stems these stem formations are conjugated like regular verb stems.

18.2.2.5. *Hip̄ʿîl*

(1) In the *qāṭal*/perfect

- The vowel of the prefix is /◌ֶ/ and not /◌ַ/.

הֶעֱמִיד   instead of   הַעְמִיד

- A *ḥaṭēp̄ səḡôl* occurs in the place of the silent *šəwā᾽* after the guttural.

הֶעֱמִיד   instead of   הֶעְמִיד

(2) In the *yiqṭōl*/imperfect

- The vowel of the prefix (/◌ַ/) is the same as that of the strong verbs (תַּעֲמִיד).
- A *ḥaṭēp̄ paṭaḥ* sometimes occurs instead of the silent *šəwā᾽* after the guttural.

תַּעֲמִיד   instead of   תַּעְמִיד

18.2.2.6. *Hop̄ʿal*

In the *qātal*/perfect and the *yiqtōl*/imperfect the vowel of the prefix /◌/ is the same as that of the strong verb verbs, but a *ḥaṭēp̄ qāmeṣ* occurs instead of the silent *šəwāʾ* after the guttural.

הָעֳמַד   instead of   הָעְמַד

יָעֳמַד   instead of   יָעְמַד

18.2.3. *II-guttural*

18.2.3.1. *Paradigm*

Table 25. *II-guttural Verbs*

	QAL	NI.	PI.	PU.	HTP.
Root Gloss	שחט slaughter		ברך bless		
Sing.			Qātal/Perfect		
3 m.	שָׁחַט	נִשְׁחַט	בֵּרֵךְ	בֹּרַךְ	הִתְבָּרֵךְ
3 f.	שָׁחֲטָה	נִשְׁחֲטָה	בֵּרְכָה	בֹּרְכָה	הִתְבָּרְכָה
2 m.	שָׁחַטְתָּ	נִשְׁחַטְתָּ	בֵּרַכְתָּ	בֹּרַכְתָּ	הִתְבָּרַכְתָּ
2 f.	שָׁחַטְתְּ	נִשְׁחַטְתְּ	בֵּרַכְתְּ	בֹּרַכְתְּ	הִתְבָּרַכְתְּ
1 c.	שָׁחַטְתִּי	נִשְׁחַטְתִּי	בֵּרַכְתִּי	בֹּרַכְתִּי	הִתְבָּרַכְתִּי
Pl.					
3 c.	שָׁחֲטוּ	נִשְׁחֲטוּ	בֵּרְכוּ	בֹּרְכוּ	הִתְבָּרְכוּ
2 m.	שְׁחַטְתֶּם	נִשְׁחַטְתֶּם	בֵּרַכְתֶּם	בֹּרַכְתֶּם	הִתְבָּרַכְתֶּם
2 f.	שְׁחַטְתֶּן	נִשְׁחַטְתֶּן	בֵּרַכְתֶּן	בֹּרַכְתֶּן	הִתְבָּרַכְתֶּן
1 c.	שָׁחַטְנוּ	נִשְׁחַטְנוּ	בֵּרַכְנוּ	בֹּרַכְנוּ	הִתְבָּרַכְנוּ
Sing.			Yiqtōl/Imperfect		
3 m.	יִשְׁחַט	יִשָּׁחֵט	יְבָרֵךְ	יְבֹרַךְ	יִתְבָּרֵךְ
3 f.	תִּשְׁחַט	תִּשָּׁחֵט	תְּבָרֵךְ	תְּבֹרַךְ	תִּתְבָּרֵךְ
2 m.	תִּשְׁחַט	תִּשָּׁחֵט	תְּבָרֵךְ	תְּבֹרַךְ	תִּתְבָּרֵךְ
2 f.	תִּשְׁחֲטִי	תִּשָּׁחֲטִי	תְּבָרְכִי	תְּבֹרְכִי	תִּתְבָּרְכִי
1 c.	אֶשְׁחַט	אֶשָּׁחֵט	אֲבָרֵךְ	אֲבֹרַךְ	אֶתְבָּרֵךְ

	QAL	NI.	PI.	PU.	HTP.
Pl.	*Yiqtōl/Imperfect*				
3 m.	יִשְׁחֲטוּ	יִשָּׁחֲטוּ	יְבָרְכוּ	יְבֹרְכוּ	יִתְבָּרְכוּ
3 f.	תִּשְׁחַטְנָה	תִּשָּׁחַטְנָה	תְּבָרֵכְנָה	תְּבֹרַכְנָה	תִּתְבָּרֵכְנָה
2 m.	תִּשְׁחֲטוּ	תִּשָּׁחֲטוּ	תְּבָרְכוּ	תְּבֹרְכוּ	תִּתְבָּרְכוּ
2 f.	תִּשְׁחַטְנָה	תִּשָּׁחַטְנָה	תְּבָרֵכְנָה	תְּבֹרַכְנָה	תִּתְבָּרֵכְנָה
1 c.	נִשְׁחַט	נִשָּׁחֵט	נְבָרֵךְ	נְבֹרַךְ	נִתְבָּרֵךְ
Sing.	*Imperative*				
2 m.	שְׁחַט	הִשָּׁחֵט	בָּרֵךְ		הִתְבָּרֵךְ
2 f.	שַׁחֲטִי	הִשָּׁחֲטִי	בָּרְכִי		הִתְבָּרְכִי
Pl.					
2 m.	שַׁחֲטוּ	הִשָּׁחֲטוּ	בָּרְכוּ		הִתְבָּרְכוּ
2 f.	שְׁחַטְנָה	הִשָּׁחַטְנָה	בָּרֵכְנָה		הִתְבָּרֵכְנָה
Sing.	*Cohortative*				
	אֶשְׁחֲטָה	אֶשָּׁחֲטָה	אֲבָרְכָה		אֶתְבָּרְכָה
Sing.	*Jussive*				
	יִשְׁחַט	יִשָּׁחֵט	יְבָרֵךְ		
	Infinitive				
cs.	שְׁחֹט	הִשָּׁחֵט	בָּרֵךְ		הִתְבָּרֵךְ
abs.	שָׁחוֹט	נִשְׁחוֹט	בָּרֵךְ בָּרֹךְ		הִתְבָּרֵךְ
	Participle				
act.	שֹׁחֵט		מְבָרֵךְ		מִתְבָּרֵךְ
pass.	שָׁחוּט	נִשְׁחָט		מְבֹרָךְ	

18.2.3.2. *Qal*

(1) In the *qātal*/perfect

- Most of the conjugations are like those of the strong verbs. The only difference is that the audible /◌/ under the guttural becomes a *ḥaṭēp̄* vowel with the vocalic suffixes.

  שָׁחֲטוּ   instead of   שָׁחְטוּ

(2) In the *yiqtōl*/imperfect

- The expected vowel after the guttural is replaced with a /◌/ in an accented closed syllable. The vowel pattern is then /◌ ◌/.

  יִשְׁחַט   instead of   יִשְׁחֹט

(3) In the infinitive

- The /◌/ after the infinitive is, however, retained.

  שְׁחֹט   instead of   שְׁחַט

(4) In the Qal imperative

- The first consonant has /◌/ rather than /◌/.

  שַׁחֲטוּ   instead of   שְׁחֲטוּ

18.2.3.3. *Piˤēl, Puˤal and Hiṯpaˤēl*

In the II-guttural and II-*rêš* verbs the middle consonant (normally) cannot double and "compensatory lengthening" occurs.

(1) In the Piˤēl *qātal*/perfect

- The /◌/ changes to a /◌/ and the vowel pattern is /◌◌/.

  בֵּרֵךְ   instead of   בִּרֵךְ

(2) In the Piˤēl *yiqtōl*/imperfect

- The /◌/ changes to a /◌/ and the vowel pattern is /◌◌◌/.

  יְבָרֵךְ   instead of   יְבָרֵךְ

(3) In the Puʿal *qātal*/perfect

- The /ǫ̣/ changes to a /ǒ/ and the vowel pattern is /ǫǒ/.

בֹּרַךְ   instead of   בֵּרַךְ

18.2.3.4. *Hip̄ʿil and Hop̄ʿal*

The II-guttural verbs conjugate like the strong verbs.

18.2.4. *III-guttural*

18.2.4.1. *Paradigm*

Table 26. *III-guttural Verbs*

	QAL	NI.	PI.	PU.	HTP.	HI.	HO.
Root Gloss	שלח send				פתח open	שלח send	
Sing.				Qātal/Perfect			
3 m.	שָׁלַח	נִשְׁלַח	שִׁלַּח	שֻׁלַּח	הִתְפַּתַּח	הִשְׁלִיחַ	הָשְׁלַח
3 f.	שָׁלְחָה	נִשְׁלְחָה	שִׁלְּחָה	שֻׁלְּחָה	הִתְפַּתְּחָה	הִשְׁלִיחָה	הָשְׁלְחָה
2 m.	שָׁלַחְתָּ	נִשְׁלַחְתָּ	שִׁלַּחְתָּ	שֻׁלַּחְתָּ	הִתְפַּתַּחְתָּ	הִשְׁלַחְתָּ	הָשְׁלַחְתָּ
2 f.	שָׁלַחַתְּ	נִשְׁלַחַתְּ	שִׁלַּחַתְּ	שֻׁלַּחַתְּ	הִתְפַּתַּחַתְּ	הִשְׁלַחַתְּ	הָשְׁלַחַתְּ
1 c.	שָׁלַחְתִּי	נִשְׁלַחְתִּי	שִׁלַּחְתִּי	שֻׁלַּחְתִּי	הִתְפַּתַּחְתִּי	הִשְׁלַחְתִּי	הָשְׁלַחְתִּי
Pl.							
3 c.	שָׁלְחוּ	נִשְׁלְחוּ	שִׁלְּחוּ	שֻׁלְּחוּ	הִתְפַּתְּחוּ	הִשְׁלִיחוּ	הָשְׁלְחוּ
2 m.	שְׁלַחְתֶּם	נִשְׁלַחְתֶּם	שִׁלַּחְתֶּם	שֻׁלַּחְתֶּם	הִתְפַּתַּחְתֶּם	הִשְׁלַחְתֶּם	הָשְׁלַחְתֶּם
2 f.	שְׁלַחְתֶּן	נִשְׁלַחְתֶּן	שִׁלַּחְתֶּן	שֻׁלַּחְתֶּן	הִתְפַּתַּחְתֶּן	הִשְׁלַחְתֶּן	הָשְׁלַחְתֶּן
1 c.	שָׁלַחְנוּ	נִשְׁלַחְנוּ	שִׁלַּחְנוּ	שֻׁלַּחְנוּ	הִתְפַּתַּחְנוּ	הִשְׁלַחְנוּ	הָשְׁלַחְנוּ
Sing.				Yiqtōl/Imperfect			
3 m.	יִשְׁלַח	יִשָּׁלַח	יְשַׁלַּח	יְשֻׁלַּח	יִתְפַּתַּח	יַשְׁלִיחַ	יָשְׁלַח
3 f.	תִּשְׁלַח	תִּשָּׁלַח	תְּשַׁלַּח	תְּשֻׁלַּח	תִּתְפַּתַּח	תַּשְׁלִיחַ	תָּשְׁלַח
2 m.	תִּשְׁלַח	תִּשָּׁלַח	תְּשַׁלַּח	תְּשֻׁלַּח	תִּתְפַּתַּח	תַּשְׁלִיחַ	תָּשְׁלַח
2 f.	תִּשְׁלְחִי	תִּשָּׁלְחִי	תְּשַׁלְּחִי	תְּשֻׁלְּחִי	תִּתְפַּתְּחִי	תַּשְׁלִיחִי	תָּשְׁלְחִי
1 c.	אֶשְׁלַח	אֶשָּׁלַח	אֲשַׁלַּח	אֲשֻׁלַּח	אֶתְפַּתַּח	אַשְׁלִיחַ	אָשְׁלַח

	QAL	NI.	PI.	PU.	HTP.	HI.	HO.
Pl.	Yiqtōl/Imperfect						
3 m.	יִשְׁלְחוּ	יִשָּׁלְחוּ	יְשַׁלְּחוּ	יְשֻׁלְּחוּ	יִתְפַּתְּחוּ	יַשְׁלִיחוּ	יֻשְׁלְחוּ
3 f.	תִּשְׁלַחְנָה	תִּשָּׁלַחְנָה	תְּשַׁלַּחְנָה	תְּשֻׁלַּחְנָה	תִּתְפַּתַּחְנָה	תַּשְׁלַחְנָה	תֻּשְׁלַחְנָה
2 m.	תִּשְׁלְחוּ	תִּשָּׁלְחוּ	תְּשַׁלְּחוּ	תְּשֻׁלְּחוּ	תִּתְפַּתְּחוּ	תַּשְׁלִיחוּ	תֻּשְׁלְחוּ
2 f.	תִּשְׁלַחְנָה	תִּשָּׁלַחְנָה	תְּשַׁלַּחְנָה	תְּשֻׁלַּחְנָה	תִּתְפַּתַּחְנָה	תַּשְׁלַחְנָה	תֻּשְׁלַחְנָה
1 c.	נִשְׁלַח	נִשָּׁלַח	נְשַׁלַּח	נְשֻׁלַּח	נִתְפַּתַּח	נַשְׁלִיחַ	נֻשְׁלַח
Sing.	Imperative						
2 m.	שְׁלַח	הִשָּׁלַח	שַׁלַּח		הִתְפַּתַּח	הַשְׁלַח	
2 f.	שִׁלְחִי	הִשָּׁלְחִי	שַׁלְּחִי		הִתְפַּתְּחִי	הַשְׁלִיחִי	
Pl.							
2 m.	שִׁלְחוּ	הִשָּׁלְחוּ	שַׁלְּחוּ		הִתְפַּתְּחוּ	הַשְׁלִיחוּ	
2 f.	שְׁלַחְנָה	הִשָּׁלַחְנָה	שַׁלַּחְנָה		הִתְפַּתַּחְנָה	הַשְׁלַחְנָה	
Sing.	Cohortative						
	אֶשְׁלְחָה	אֶשָּׁלְחָה	אֲשַׁלְּחָה		אֶתְפַּתְּחָה	אַשְׁלִיחָה	
Sing.	Jussive						
	יִשְׁלַח	יִשָּׁלַח	יְשַׁלַּח		יִתְפַּתַּח	יַשְׁלַח	
	Infinitive						
cs.	שְׁלֹחַ	הִשָּׁלַח	שַׁלַּח		הִתְפַּתַּח	הַשְׁלִיחַ	הָשְׁלַח
abs.	שָׁלוֹחַ	נִשְׁלוֹחַ	שַׁלֵּחַ		הִתְפַּתֵּחַ	הַשְׁלֵחַ	הָשְׁלֵחַ
	Participle						
act.	שֹׁלֵחַ		מְשַׁלֵּחַ		מִתְפַּתֵּחַ	מַשְׁלִיחַ	
pass.	שָׁלוּחַ	נִשְׁלָח		מְשֻׁלָּח			מָשְׁלָח

18.2.4.2. *General characteristics*

(1) In a syllable that ends in a guttural

- The vowel is usually /◌ַ/. It replaces the expected vowel.

  שְׁלַח instead of שְׁלֵח

- The same process occurs if a consonantal suffix is added (שְׁלַחְנָה).

(2) With zero or vocalic suffixes

- If the expected vowel in a syllable that ends in a guttural is /◌ִי/, /◌ִ/ or /◌ֵ/ (i.e. unchangeably long), or if it is /◌ֹ/ or /◌ֻ/, it is not replaced with /◌ַ/. A transitional *pataḥ* is placed between the normal stem vowel and the guttural (§6.2).

Piel inf abs

| שַׁלֵּחַ | instead of | שַׁלֵּח |
| יַשְׁלִיחַ | instead of | יַשְׁלִיח |

(3) In the *qātal*/perfect

- In the second feminine singular the silent *šǝwāʾ* under the guttural is replaced with a /◌ַ/.

| שָׁלַחַתְּ | instead of | שָׁלַחְתְּ |

(4) In the *yiqtōl*/imperfect

- The stem vowel before the consonantal suffixes is /◌ַ/.

| תִּשְׁמַ֫עְנָה | instead of | תִּשְׁמֹ֫עְנָה |
| תִּשְׁמַ֫עְנָה | instead of | תִּשְׁמֵ֫עְנָה |

(5) In the participle

- The feminine singular does not have the expected /◌ֶ◌ֶ/ pattern. Its vowel pattern is /◌ַ◌ַ/.

| שֹׁמַ֫עַת | instead of | שֹׁמֶ֫עַת |

§18.3. I-ʾālep̄ Verbs

In Biblical Hebrew the א has a very weak consonantal character. At the end of a closed syllable the א has become silent (§4.2.5.2). The preceding short vowel changes to compensate for the loss of the א.

This phenomenon is limited to the Qal *yiqtōl*/imperfect form of only five verbs, namely אָכַל (he ate), אָמַר (he said), אָבַד (he perished), אָבָה (he was willing), אָפָה (he baked).[14] The verbs אָחַז (he held fast), אָהַב (he loved) and אָסַף (he collected) also have I-ʾālep̄ variants in addition to the usual forms for I-guttural verbs (§18.1 and §18.2). For example, אָהַב has the I-guttural form יֶאֱהַב (Prov. 3:12) and the I-ʾālep̄ form וָאֹהַב (Mal. 1:2).

---

14. For a more complete discussion, see Joüon–Muraoka §73.

(1) The usual vowel of the prefix /ְ◌/ becomes /◌ֹ/.

יֹאמַר   instead of   יְאֹמֹר

(2) In the *yiqtōl*/imperfect prefix of the first singular the א of the verb stem has fallen away in writing.

אֹמַר   instead of   אֶאֱמַר

(3) In the second syllable the usual stem vowel /◌ֹ/ is replaced with /◌ַ/ or /◌ָ/. The latter is usually the pausal form.

יֹאמַר   instead of   יְאֹמֹר
יֹאכֵל   instead of   יְאֹכֹל

(4) All the other forms of the I-*ʾālep* verbs are regular. The infinitive construct of the verb stem אמר with the preposition לְ is, however, an exception (see §20.1.5).

לֵאמֹר   instead of   לֶאֱמֹר

(5) The *wayyiqtōl* of אמר is also an exception. The /◌ַ/ in the second syllable changes to /◌ֶ/, due to the accent shift. With the pausal forms (§9.6), the /◌ַ/ vowel returns.

וַיֹּאמֶר   instead of   וַיֹּאמַר

§18.4. III-*ʾālep* Verbs

18.4.1. *Introduction*

In Biblical Hebrew the א has a very weak consonantal character. At the end of a closed syllable the א often becomes silent (§4.2.5.2 and §5.2.2.1). To compensate for the loss of the א the preceding short vowels are changed. Although the א looks like a vowel indicator in this case, it is actually a silent consonant that appears with a changed vowel. At the beginning of a syllable, however, the א retains its consonantal character.

The general statement above implies that the *ʾālep̄* is not pronounced when a verb ends with the *ʾālep̄* or when a III-*ʾālep̄* appears before a consonantal suffix (namely the תִי-, תָ-, תְ-, נוּ- of a *qātal*/perfect, the נָה- and ן- of a *yiqtōl*/imperfect), for example, הִמְצִיא (but הִמְצִיאוּ).

18.4.2. *Paradigm*

Table 27. *III-ʾālep̄ Verbs*

	QAL	NI.	PI.	PU.	HTP.	HI.	HO.
Root Gloss				מצא find			
Sing.				*Qātal/Perfect*			
3 m.	מָצָא	נִמְצָא	מִצֵּא	מֻצָּא	הִתְמַצֵּא	הִמְצִיא	הֻמְצָא
3 f.	מָצְאָה	נִמְצְאָה	מִצְּאָה	מֻצְּאָה	הִתְמַצְּאָה	הִמְצִיאָה	הֻמְצְאָה
2 m.	מָצָאתָ	נִמְצֵאתָ	מִצֵּאתָ	מֻצֵּאתָ	הִתְמַצֵּאתָ	הִמְצֵאתָ	הֻמְצֵאתָ
2 f.	מָצָאת	נִמְצֵאת	מִצֵּאת	מֻצֵּאת	הִתְמַצֵּאת	הִמְצֵאת	הֻמְצֵאת
1 c.	מָצָאתִי	נִמְצֵאתִי	מִצֵּאתִי	מֻצֵּאתִי	הִתְמַצֵּאתִי	הִמְצֵאתִי	הֻמְצֵאתִי
Pl.							
3 c.	מָצְאוּ	נִמְצְאוּ	מִצְּאוּ	מֻצְּאוּ	הִתְמַצְּאוּ	הִמְצִיאוּ	הֻמְצְאוּ
2 m.	מְצָאתֶם	נִמְצֵאתֶם	מִצֵּאתֶם	מֻצֵּאתֶם	הִתְמַצֵּאתֶם	הִמְצֵאתֶם	הֻמְצֵאתֶם
2 f.	מְצָאתֶן	נִמְצֵאתֶן	מִצֵּאתֶן	מֻצֵּאתֶן	הִתְמַצֵּאתֶן	הִמְצֵאתֶן	הֻמְצֵאתֶן
1 c.	מָצָאנוּ	נִמְצֵאנוּ	מִצֵּאנוּ	מֻצֵּאנוּ	הִתְמַצֵּאנוּ	הִמְצֵאנוּ	הֻמְצֵאנוּ
Sing.				*Yiqtōl/Imperfect*			
3 m.	יִמְצָא	יִמָּצֵא	יְמַצֵּא	יְמֻצָּא	יִתְמַצֵּא	יַמְצִיא	יֻמְצָא
3 f.	תִּמְצָא	תִּמָּצֵא	תְּמַצֵּא	תְּמֻצָּא	תִּתְמַצֵּא	תַּמְצִיא	תֻּמְצָא
2 m.	תִּמְצָא	תִּמָּצֵא	תְּמַצֵּא	תְּמֻצָּא	תִּתְמַצֵּא	תַּמְצִיא	תֻּמְצָא
2 f.	תִּמְצְאִי	תִּמָּצְאִי	תְּמַצְּאִי	תְּמֻצְּאִי	תִּתְמַצְּאִי	תַּמְצִיאִי	תֻּמְצְאִי
1 c.	אֶמְצָא	אֶמָּצֵא	אֲמַצֵּא	אֲמֻצָּא	אֶתְמַצֵּא	אַמְצִיא	אֻמְצָא

	QAL	NI.	PI.	PU.	HTP.	HI.	HO.
Pl.	Yiqtōl/Imperfect						
3 m.	יִמְצְאוּ	יִמָּצְאוּ	יְמַצְּאוּ	יְמֻצְּאוּ	יִתְמַצְּאוּ	יַמְצִיאוּ	יֻמְצְאוּ
3 f.	תִּמְצֶּאנָה	תִּמָּצֶאנָה	תְּמַצֶּאנָה	תְּמֻצֶּאנָה	תִּתְמַצֶּאנָה	תַּמְצֶאנָה	תֻּמְצֶאנָה
2 m.	תִּמְצְאוּ	תִּמָּצְאוּ	תְּמַצְּאוּ	תְּמֻצְּאוּ	תִּתְמַצְּאוּ	תַּמְצִיאוּ	תֻּמְצְאוּ
2 f.	תִּמְצֶּאנָה	תִּמָּצֶאנָה	תְּמַצֶּאנָה	תְּמֻצֶּאנָה	תִּתְמַצֶּאנָה	תַּמְצֶאנָה	תֻּמְצֶאנָה
1 c.	נִמְצָא	נִמָּצֵא	נְמַצֵּא	נְמֻצָּא	נִתְמַצֵּא	נַמְצִיא	נֻמְצָא
Sing.	Imperative						
2 m.	מְצָא	הִמָּצֵא	מַצֵּא		הִתְמַצֵּא	הַמְצֵא	
2 f.	מִצְאִי	הִמָּצְאִי	מַצְּאִי		הִתְמַצְּאִי	הַמְצִיאִי	
Pl.							
2 m.	מִצְאוּ	הִמָּצְאוּ	מַצְּאוּ		הִתְמַצְּאוּ	הַמְצִיאוּ	
2 f.	מְצֶּאנָה	הִמָּצֶאנָה	מַצֶּאנָה		הִתְמַצֶּאנָה	הַמְצֶאנָה	
Sing.	Cohortative						
1.	אֶמְצְאָה	אֶמָּצְאָה				אַמְצִיאָה	
Sing.	Jussive						
3 m.	יִמְצָא	יִמָּצֵא				יַמְצֵא	
	Infinitive						
cs.	מְצֹא	הִמָּצֵא	מַצֵּא		הִתְמַצֵּא	הַמְצִיא	הֻמְצָא
abs.	מָצוֹא	נִמְצֹא	מַצֵּא		הִתְמַצֵּא	הַמְצֵא	הֻמְצֵא
	Participle						
act.	מֹצֵא		מְמַצֵּא		מִתְמַצֵּא	מַמְצִיא	
pass.	מָצוּא	נִמְצָא		מְמֻצָּא			מֻמְצָא

18.4.3. *General characteristics*

(1) Where there are no suffixes the א becomes silent. An /◌/ before the א
changes to /◌/.

מָצָא instead of מְצָא

(2) Where there are vocalic suffixes, the א functions as a consonant and the verb stem conjugates regularly (הַמְצִיאוּ).

(3) Where there are consonantal suffixes the א becomes silent and the Qal *qātal*/perfect and *yiqtōl*/imperfect take an /אֹ/ (מָצָאתָ, מְצָאתֶם):

- The *qātal*/perfect of all the other stem formations takes an /אֵ/ (הִמְצֵאתָ, נִמְצֵאתָ).
- The *yiqtōl*/imperfect of all the other stem formations takes an /אֶ/ (תְּמַצֶּאנָה, תִּמְצֶאנָה) vowel.

In other words:

- In the Niṗʿal /ֵ/ is used where one would expect /ָ/.

  נִמְצֵאתָ   instead of   נִמְצָאתָ

- In the Hiṗʿîl /ֵ/ is used where one would expect /ִי/.

  הִמְצֵאתָ   instead of   הִמְצִיאתָ

- The Hiṗʿîl third singular masculine form is regular, however (e.g. הִמְצִיא).

(4) The vowels of the Qal infinitive construct look just like those of a regular verb stem.

  מְצֹא   instead of   מְצָא

(5) In stative verbs with /ָֹ/ (§16.2) the /ָ/ in the Qal *qātal*/perfect is retained (מָלֵאתִי, מָלֵא).

(6) The א sometimes falls away.

  מָלֵתִי   instead of   מָלֵאתִי

(7) As many of the conjugations of the III-*hē²* and III-*²ālep* verbs sound identical, some III-*hē²* verbs are vocalized as III-*²ālep* and vice versa, e.g.:

- The III-*hē²* verb אתה (to come) sometimes looks like the verb stem אתא in the Qal *qātal*/perfect third masculine singular.

  אָתָא   instead of   אָתָה

- The III-*²ālep* verb כלא (to restrain) looks like the verb כלה (be finished) in the Qal *qātal*/perfect first singular.

  כָּלֵאתִי   as   כָּלִיתִי

  instead of   כָּלֵאתִי

§18.5. III-*hē*ʾ Verbs

18.5.1. *Introduction*

The term III-*hē*ʾ refers specifically to verbs in the Qal *qātal*/perfect third masculine singular that end in a ה vowel indicator, for example, שָׁתָה (to drink), etc. At an early stage of the language these verbs ended in a *yôḏ* or *wāw*. In other words they were originally III-*yôḏ* and III-*wāw* verbs. These consonants fell away either through elision or were retained as vowel indicators before consonantal suffixes. Verbs that originally ended in *hē*ʾ and reflect the consonantal character of the *hē*ʾ with a *mappîq* (e.g. גבה "be high") are not recognized as III-*hē*ʾ verbs.

18.5.2. *Paradigm*

Table 28. *III-hē*ʾ *Verbs*

	QAL	NI.	PI.	PU.	HTP.	HI.	HO.
Root Gloss	גלה reveal						
Sing.	Qātal/Perfect						
3 m.	גָּלָה	נִגְלָה	גִּלָּה	גֻּלָּה	הִתְגַּלָּה	הִגְלָה	הָגְלָה
3 f.	גָּלְתָה	נִגְלְתָה	גִּלְּתָה	גֻּלְּתָה	הִתְגַּלְּתָה	הִגְלְתָה	הָגְלְתָה
2 m.	גָּלִיתָ	נִגְלֵיתָ	גִּלִּיתָ	גֻּלֵּיתָ	הִתְגַּלֵּיתָ	הִגְלֵיתָ	הָגְלֵיתָ
2 f.	גָּלִית	נִגְלֵית	גִּלִּית	גֻּלֵּית	הִתְגַּלֵּית	הִגְלֵית	הָגְלֵית
1 c.	גָּלִיתִי	נִגְלֵיתִי	גִּלִּיתִי	גֻּלֵּיתִי	הִתְגַּלֵּיתִי	הִגְלֵיתִי	הָגְלֵיתִי
Pl.							
3 c.	גָּלוּ	נִגְלוּ	גִּלּוּ	גֻּלּוּ	הִתְגַּלּוּ	הִגְלוּ	הָגְלוּ
2 m.	גְּלִיתֶם	נִגְלֵיתֶם	גִּלִּיתֶם	גֻּלֵּיתֶם	הִתְגַּלֵּיתֶם	הִגְלֵיתֶם	הָגְלֵיתֶם
2 f.	גְּלִיתֶן	נִגְלֵיתֶן	גִּלִּיתֶן	גֻּלֵּיתֶן	הִתְגַּלֵּיתֶן	הִגְלֵיתֶן	הָגְלֵיתֶן
1 c.	גָּלִינוּ	נִגְלֵינוּ	גִּלִּינוּ	גֻּלֵּינוּ	הִתְגַּלֵּינוּ	הִגְלֵינוּ	הָגְלֵינוּ

	QAL	NI.	PI.	PU.	HTP.	HI.	HO.
Sing.	*Yiqtōl/Imperfect*						
3 m.	יִגְלֶה	יִגָּלֶה	יְגַלֶּה	יְגֻלֶּה	יִתְגַּלֶּה	יַגְלֶה	יָגְלֶה
3 f.	תִּגְלֶה	תִּגָּלֶה	תְּגַלֶּה	תְּגֻלֶּה	תִּתְגַּלֶּה	תַּגְלֶה	תָּגְלֶה
2 m.	תִּגְלֶה	תִּגָּלֶה	תְּגַלֶּה	תְּגֻלֶּה	תִּתְגַּלֶּה	תַּגְלֶה	תָּגְלֶה
2 f.	תִּגְלִי	תִּגָּלִי	תְּגַלִּי	תְּגֻלִּי	תִּתְגַּלִּי	תַּגְלִי	תָּגְלִי
1 c.	אֶגְלֶה	אֶגָּלֶה	אֲגַלֶּה	אֲגֻלֶּה	אֶתְגַּלֶּה	אַגְלֶה	אָגְלֶה
Pl.							
3 m.	יִגְלוּ	יִגָּלוּ	יְגַלּוּ	יְגֻלּוּ	יִתְגַּלּוּ	יַגְלוּ	יָגְלוּ
3 f.	תִּגְלֶינָה	תִּגָּלֶינָה	תְּגַלֶּינָה	תְּגֻלֶּינָה	תִּתְגַּלֶּינָה	תַּגְלֶינָה	תָּגְלֶינָה
2 m.	תִּגְלוּ	תִּגָּלוּ	תְּגַלּוּ	תְּגֻלּוּ	תִּתְגַּלּוּ	תַּגְלוּ	תָּגְלוּ
2 f.	תִּגְלֶינָה	תִּגָּלֶינָה	תְּגַלֶּינָה	תְּגֻלֶּינָה	תִּתְגַּלֶּינָה	תַּגְלֶינָה	תָּגְלֶינָה
1 c.	נִגְלֶה	נִגָּלֶה	נְגַלֶּה	נְגֻלֶּה	נִתְגַּלֶּה	נַגְלֶה	נָגְלֶה
Sing.	*Imperative*						
2 m.	גְּלֵה	הִגָּלֵה	גַּלֵּה		הִתְגַּלֵּה	הַגְלֵה	
2 f.	גְּלִי	הִגָּלִי	גַּלִּי		הִתְגַּלִּי	הַגְלִי	
Pl.							
2 m.	גְּלוּ	הִגָּלוּ	גַּלּוּ		הִתְגַּלּוּ	הַגְלוּ	
2 f.	גְּלֶינָה	הִגָּלֶינָה	גַּלֶּינָה		הִתְגַּלֶּינָה	הַגְלֶינָה	
Sing.	*Jussive*						
	יִגֶל	יִגָּל	יְגַל		יִתְגַּל	יַגֶל	
	Infinitive						
cs.	גְּלוֹת	הִגָּלוֹת	גַּלּוֹת	גֻּלּוֹת	הִתְגַּלּוֹת	הַגְלוֹת	הָגְלוֹת
abs.	גָּלֹה	נִגְלֹה	גַּלֵּה	גֻּלֹּה	הִתְגַּלֵּה	הַגְלֵה	הָגְלֵה
	Participle						
act.	גֹּלֶה		מְגַלֶּה		מִתְגַּלֶּה	מַגְלֶה	
pass.	גָּלוּי	נִגְלֶה		מְגֻלֶּה			מָגְלֶה

18.5.3. *General characteristics*

A particular systemization is evident in all the conjugations of the III-*hē'*
verbs. This systematization can best be appreciated if all the conjugations are
arranged according to their suffixes.

(1) In forms where no suffix is added, the endings are as follows:

- The *qātal*/perfect ends in הָ◌.

Qal	גָּלָה
Ni.	נִגְלָה
Pi.	גִּלָּה
Hi.	הִגְלָה

- The *yiqtōl*/imperfect ends in הֶ◌.

Qal	יִגְלֶה
Ni.	יִגָּלֶה
Hi.	יַגְלֶה

- The imperative ends in הֵ◌.

Qal	גְּלֵה
Ni.	הִגָּלֵה
Hi.	הַגְלֵה

- The infinitive ends in תוֹ-.

Qal	גְּלוֹת
Ni.	הִגָּלוֹת
Pi.	גַּלּוֹת
Hi.	הַגְלוֹת

- The masculine singular participle ends in הֶ◌. The construct form of
  the participle ends in הֵ◌.

Qal	בֹּנֶה
Ni.	נִגְלֶה
Hi.	מַבְנֶה

(2) Forms in which a suffix beginning with a vowel is added:

- With all the stem formations the third feminine singular form of the *qātal*/perfect is formed by replacing the final ה with an older feminine ת ending and then adding the suffix הָׁ.

בָּנְתָה   instead of   בָּנְהָה

- In all the other cases the III-*hē*ʾ and the preceding vowel or audible *šəwāʾ* fall away and the suffix is added immediately after the second stem consonant.

גָּלוּ   instead of   גָּלְהוּ

- The object suffixes (§17) are also added directly after the second stem consonant.

גָּלַנִי   and   גָּלָה

(3) In forms where a *suffix beginning with a consonant* is added, the original י replaces the ה. The י fuses with the preceding vowel resulting in the following connecting vowels:

- The Qal, Piʿēl, Hip̄ʿîl and Hitpaʿēl have /יׁ/ as connecting vowel.

Qal   גָּלִיתָ

Hi.   הִגְלִיתָ

- The *qātal*/perfect of the Nip̄ʿal, Puʿal and Hop̄ʿal have /יׁ/ as connecting vowel.

Ni.   נִבְנֵיתָ

Pu.   בֻּנֵּיתָ

Ho.   הֻבְנֵיתָ

- In the *yiqtōl*/imperfect and imperative of all the stem formations the connecting vowel is /יׁ/ (בְּנֶינָה, תִּבְנֶינָה).

18.5.4. *Short forms of III-hēʾ verbs*

An accent shift normally takes place in the jussive and *wayyiqtōl*. In the III-*hē*ʾ verbs this shift results in the *hē*ʾ falling away, for example, יִגְלֶה is "shortened" to יִגֶל. A list of the most common "short" forms, i.e. jussive or *wayyiqtōl* is given below. Note that the third person short form of a particular verb can differ from that of its second person.

(1) In the Qal there are four apocopated forms.

	Long	and	Short
3 m. sing.	יִשְׁבֶּה		וַיֵּשֶׁב
3 m. sing.	יִבְכֶּה		וַיֵּבְךְּ
3 m. sing.	יִרְבֶּה		וַיִּרֶב
2 m. sing.	תִּפְנֶה		וַתֵּפֶן

(2) III-*hē* verbs that have a guttural as the first or second stem consonant in the Qal, have their own apocopated forms.

	Long	and	Short
3 m. sing.	יַעֲלֶה		וַיַּעַל
3 m. sing.	יֶחֱרֶה		וַיִּחַר
3 m. sing.	יִרְאֶה		וַיַּרְא
2 m. sing.	תִּרְאֶה		וַתֵּרֶא

(3) The Niṗ‘al stem formation has one apocopated form.

2 m. sing.	תִּגָּלֶה	תִּגָּל

(4) The Pi‘ēl stem formation has one apocopated form.

3 m. sing.	יְכַלֶּה	וַיְכַל

(5) The Hiṗ‘îl stem formation has two apocopated forms.

3 m. sing.	יַשְׁקֶה	וַיַּשְׁקְ
3 m. sing.	יַרְבֶּה	וַיֶּרֶב

(6) III-*hē* verbs that have a guttural as first stem consonant in the Hiṗ‘îl also have another apocopated form.

יַעֲלֶה	וַיַּעַל

§18.6. I-*nûn* Verbs

18.6.1. *Introduction*

When a *nûn* appears at the end of a closed syllable, it often assimilates with the next consonant (§4.2.4.2).

18.6.2. *Paradigm*

Table 29. *I-nûn Verbs*

	QAL	QAL	NI.	PI.	HTP.	HI.	HO.
Root Gloss	נפל fall	נגש approach					
Sing.	Qātal/Perfect						
3 m.	נָפַל	נָגַשׁ	נִגַּשׁ			הִגִּישׁ	הֻגַּשׁ
3 f.	נָפְלָה	נָגְשָׁה	נִגְּשָׁה			הִגִּישָׁה	הֻגְּשָׁה
2 m.	נָפַלְתָּ	נָגַשְׁתָּ	נִגַּשְׁתָּ			הִגַּשְׁתָּ	הֻגַּשְׁתָּ
2 f.	נָפַלְתְּ	נָגַשְׁתְּ	נִגַּשְׁתְּ			הִגַּשְׁתְּ	הֻגַּשְׁתְּ
1 c.	נָפַלְתִּי	נָגַשְׁתִּי	נִגַּשְׁתִּי			הִגַּשְׁתִּי	הֻגַּשְׁתִּי
Pl.							
3 c.	נָפְלוּ	נָגְשׁוּ	נִגְּשׁוּ			הִגִּישׁוּ	הֻגְּשׁוּ
2 m.	נְפַלְתֶּם	נְגַשְׁתֶּם	נִגַּשְׁתֶּם			הִגַּשְׁתֶּם	הֻגַּשְׁתֶּם
2 f.	נְפַלְתֶּן	נְגַשְׁתֶּן	נִגַּשְׁתֶּן			הִגַּשְׁתֶּן	הֻגַּשְׁתֶּן
1 c.	נָפַלְנוּ	נָגַשְׁנוּ	נִגַּשְׁנוּ			הִגַּשְׁנוּ	הֻגַּשְׁנוּ
Sing.	Yiqtōl/Imperfect						
3 m.	יִפֹּל	יִגַּשׁ	יִנָּגֵשׁ			יַגִּישׁ	יֻגַּשׁ
3 f.	תִּפֹּל	תִּגַּשׁ	תִּנָּגֵשׁ			תַּגִּישׁ	תֻּגַּשׁ
2 m.	תִּפֹּל	תִּגַּשׁ	תִּנָּגֵשׁ			תַּגִּישׁ	תֻּגַּשׁ
2 f.	תִּפְּלִי	תִּגְּשִׁי	תִּנָּגְשִׁי			תַּגִּישִׁי	תֻּגְּשִׁי
1 c.	אֶפֹּל	אֶגַּשׁ	אֶנָּגֵשׁ			אַגִּישׁ	אֻגַּשׁ

	QAL	QAL	NI.	PI.	HTP.	HI.	HO.
Pl.				*Yiqtōl/Imperfect*			
3 m.	יִפְּלוּ	יִגְּשׁוּ	יִנָּגְשׁוּ			יַגִּישׁוּ	יֻגְּשׁוּ
3 f.	תִּפֹּלְנָה	תִּגַּשְׁנָה	תִּנָּגַשְׁנָה			תַּגֵּשְׁנָה	תֻּגַּשְׁנָה
2 m.	תִּפְּלוּ	תִּגְּשׁוּ	תִּנָּגְשׁוּ			תַּגִּישׁוּ	תֻּגְּשׁוּ
2 f.	תִּפֹּלְנָה	תִּגַּשְׁנָה	תִּנָּגַשְׁנָה			תַּגֵּשְׁנָה	תֻּגַּשְׁנָה
1 c.	נִפֹּל	נִגַּשׁ	נִנָּגֵשׁ			נַגִּישׁ	נֻגַּשׁ
Sing.				*Imperative*			
2 m.	נְפֹל	גַּשׁ	הִנָּגֵשׁ			הַגֵּשׁ	
2 f.	נִפְלִי	גְּשִׁי	הִנָּגְשִׁי			הַגִּישִׁי	
Pl.							
2 m.	נִפְלוּ	גְּשׁוּ	הִנָּגְשׁוּ			הַגִּישׁוּ	
2 f.	נְפֹלְנָה	גַּשְׁנָה	הִנָּגַשְׁנָה			הַגֵּשְׁנָה	
				Cohortative			
Sing.	אֶפְּלָה	אֶגְּשָׁה				אַגִּישָׁה	
				Jussive			
Sing.	יִפֹּל	יִגַּשׁ				יַגֵּשׁ	
				Infinitive			
cs.	נְפֹל	גֶּשֶׁת	הִנָּגֵשׁ			הַגִּישׁ	הֻגַּשׁ
abs.	נָפוֹל	נָגוֹשׁ	הִנָּגֵשׁ			הַגֵּשׁ	הֻגֵּשׁ
				Participle			
act.	נֹפֵל	נֹגֵשׁ				מַגִּישׁ	
pass.		נָגוּשׁ	נִגָּשׁ				מֻגָּשׁ

18.6.3. *General characteristics*

(1) In stem formations and conjugations that have a prefix, the first *nûn* often assimilates with the next consonant which then doubles as a result.

יִצֹּר   instead of   יִנְצֹר

(2) If the second consonant of the verb stem is a guttural, no assimilation occurs.

יְנַחֵם   instead of   יְחֵם

(3) The distinction between the /◌/ and the /◌/ in the Qal *yiqtōl*/imperfect has an important effect on the imperative and the infinitive construct.

- Verbs with /◌/ in the *yiqtōl*/imperfect have a regular imperative and infinitive construct.

נְפֹל   from   יִנְפֹּל

- Verbs with /◌/ in the *yiqtōl*/imperfect have an imperative without the *nûn*.

גַּשׁ   from   יִגַּשׁ

- Their infinitive construct forms also have no *nûn* but they do take a ת suffix. The infinitive construct formed has a /◌/ vowel pattern which is typical of segholates.

גֶּשֶׁת   instead of   נְגֹשׁ

When a pronominal suffix is added to these infinitives, they usually manifest a /◌/ like segholates with an i-stem, e.g. גִּשְׁתִּי (§27.3.3.(4)).

(4) In the Niṗ‘al

Assimilation of the first *nûn* occurs in the *qātal*/perfect, participle and infinitive construct in addition to the usual forms of assimilation, e.g. נִגַּשׁ (§4.2.4.2).

(5) In Pi‘ēl, Pu‘al and Hiṭpa‘ēl

No assimilation occurs in any of the Pi‘ēl, Pu‘al and Hiṭpa‘ēl conjugations. Here the I-*nûn* verb stem conjugates like a regular strong verb, e.g. נִבֵּל.

(6) In Hiṗ‘îl

Assimilation occurs in all the forms of the Hiṗ‘îl, e.g. יַגִּישׁ, הִגִּישׁ.

(7) In Hoṗ‘al

Assimilation occurs in all the forms of the Hoṗ‘al. Furthermore, the vowel of the prefix is /◌/ and not /◌/.

הֻגַּשׁ   instead of   הָנְגַּשׁ

§18.7. I-*yôḏ* and I-*wāw* Verbs

18.7.1. *Introduction*

These two classes must be considered together because of their historical development.

Old Hebrew	יטב*	ושב*
Biblical Hebrew (Qal *qātal*/perfect)	יטב	ישב
Biblical Hebrew (Hip̄ʿîl *qātal*/perfect)	היטיב	הושיב

The Old Hebrew verb ושב* became ישב in the Qal *qātal*/perfect of Biblical Hebrew, but the historical distinction between יטב and ושב can still be seen in the Hip̄ʿîl. In the following discussion a distinction will be made between verbs that were originally I-*yôḏ* verbs, such as יטב, and verbs which were originally I-*wāw* verbs, such as ישב.

18.7.2. *Paradigm*

Table 30. *I-wāw and I-yôḏ Verbs*

	QAL	QAL	NI.	HI.	HO.	QAL	HI.
			I-*wāw*			I-*yôḏ*	
Root Gloss	ישב sit	ירש take posses-sion		ישב sit		יטב be good	
Sing.				Qātal/Perfect			
3 m.	יָשַׁב	יָרַשׁ	נוֹשַׁב	הוֹשִׁיב	הוּשַׁב	יָטַב	הֵיטִיב
3 f.	יָשְׁבָה	יָרְשָׁה	נוֹשְׁבָה	הוֹשִׁיבָה	הוּשְׁבָה	יָטְבָה	הֵיטִיבָה
2 m.	יָשַׁבְתָּ	יָרַשְׁתָּ	נוֹשַׁבְתָּ	הוֹשַׁבְתָּ	הוּשַׁבְתָּ	יָטַבְתָּ	הֵיטַבְתָּ
2 f.	regular	regular	נוֹשַׁבְתְּ	הוֹשַׁבְתְּ	הוּשַׁבְתְּ	regular	הֵיטַבְתְּ
1 c.			נוֹשַׁבְתִּי	הוֹשַׁבְתִּי	הוּשַׁבְתִּי		הֵיטַבְתִּי
Pl.							
3 c.	regular	regular	נוֹשְׁבוּ	הוֹשִׁיבוּ	הוּשְׁבוּ	regular	הֵיטִיבוּ
2 m.			נוֹשַׁבְתֶּם	הוֹשַׁבְתֶּם	הוּשַׁבְתֶּם		הֵיטַבְתֶּם
2 f.			נוֹשַׁבְתֶּן	הוֹשַׁבְתֶּן	הוּשַׁבְתֶּן		הֵיטַבְתֶּן
1 c.			נוֹשַׁבְנוּ	הוֹשַׁבְנוּ	הוּשַׁבְנוּ		הֵיטַבְנוּ

	QAL	QAL	NI.	HI.	HO.	QAL	HI.
Sing.	— Yiqtōl/Imperfect						
3 m.	יֵשֵׁב	יִירַשׁ	יִוָּשֵׁב	יוֹשִׁיב	יוּשַׁב	יִיטַב	יֵיטִיב
3 f.	תֵּשֵׁב	תִּירַשׁ	תִּוָּשֵׁב	תּוֹשִׁיב	תּוּשַׁב	תִּיטַב	תֵּיטִיב
2 m.	תֵּשֵׁב	תִּירַשׁ	תִּוָּשֵׁב	תּוֹשִׁיב	תּוּשַׁב	תִּיטַב	תֵּיטִיב
2 f.	תֵּשְׁבִי	תִּירְשִׁי	תִּוָּשְׁבִי	תּוֹשִׁיבִי	תּוּשְׁבִי	תִּיטְבִי	תֵּיטִיבִי
1 c.	אֵשֵׁב	אִירַשׁ	אֶוָּשֵׁב	אוֹשִׁיב	אוּשַׁב	אִיטַב	אֵיטִיב
Pl.							
3 m.	יֵשְׁבוּ	יִירְשׁוּ	יִוָּשְׁבוּ	יוֹשִׁיבוּ	יוּשְׁבוּ	יִיטְבוּ	יֵיטִיבוּ
3 f.	תֵּשַׁבְנָה	תִּירַשְׁנָה	תִּוָּשַׁבְנָה	תּוֹשֵׁבְנָה	תּוּשַׁבְנָה	תִּיטַבְנָה	תֵּיטַבְנָה
2 m.	תֵּשְׁבוּ	תִּירְשׁוּ	תִּוָּשְׁבוּ	תּוֹשִׁיבוּ	תּוּשְׁבוּ	תִּיטְבוּ	תֵּיטִיבוּ
2 f.	תֵּשַׁבְנָה	תִּירַשְׁנָה	תִּוָּשַׁבְנָה	תּוֹשֵׁבְנָה	תּוּשַׁבְנָה	תִּיטַבְנָה	תֵּיטַבְנָה
1 c.	נֵשֵׁב	נִירַשׁ	נִוָּשֵׁב	נוֹשִׁיב	נוּשַׁב	נִיטַב	נֵיטִיב
Sing.	— Imperative						
2 m.	שֵׁב	רַשׁ	הִוָּשֵׁב	הוֹשֵׁב			הֵיטֵב
2 f.	שְׁבִי	רְשִׁי	הִוָּשְׁבִי	הוֹשִׁיבִי			הֵיטִיבִי
Pl.							
2 m.	שְׁבוּ	רְשׁוּ	הִוָּשְׁבוּ	הוֹשִׁיבוּ			הֵיטִיבוּ
2 f.	שֵּׁבְנָה	רֵשְׁנָה	הִוָּשַׁבְנָה	הוֹשֵׁבְנָה			הֵיטַבְנָה
Sing.	— Cohortative						
1 s.	אֵשְׁבָה	אִירְשָׁה					
Sing.	— Jussive						
3 m.	יֵשֵׁב			יוֹשֵׁב		יִיטַב	יֵיטֵב
	— Infinitive						
cs.	שֶׁבֶת	רֶשֶׁת	הִוָּשֵׁב	הוֹשֵׁב	הוּשַׁב	יְטֹב	הֵיטִיב
abs.	יָשׁוֹב	יָרוֹשׁ	הִוָּשֵׁב	הוֹשֵׁב		יָטוֹב	הֵיטֵב
	— Participle						
act.	יֹשֵׁב	יֹרֵשׁ		מוֹשִׁיב		יֹטֵב	מֵיטִיב
pass.	יָשׁוּב	יָרוּשׁ	נוֹשָׁב		מוּשָׁב	יָטוּב	

18.7.3. *Original I-yôḏ verbs*

Only seven verbs belonging to this category occur in the Bible, namely יבשׁ (dry up), ינק (suckle), ישׁר (be honest), יטב (be good), יקץ (be awake), ילל (scream), and ימן (go to the right).[15] If the *yôḏ* were to appear at the end of a closed syllable under normal circumstances, i.e. by analogy with the regular verb, it would function as a vowel indicator (§5.2.2.1).

(1) In the Qal

A characteristic of this verb stem is that the I-*yôḏ* is retained in all the conjugations; see the Qal *yiqṭōl*/imperfect third masculine singular.

יֵיטַב   instead of   יֵטַב

(2) In the Hip̄ʿîl

The *qāṭal*/perfect the vowel of the prefix /ֶ/ is replaced with /ֵ/.

הֵיטִיב   instead of   הֵיטִיב

(3) In the Hip̄ʿîl

The *yiqṭōl*/imperfect and participle the usual vowel of the prefix /ַ/ becomes /ֵ/.

יֵיטִיב   instead of   יַיְטִיב

מֵיטִיב   instead of   מַיְטִיב

18.7.4. *Original I-wāw verbs*

Original I-*wāw* verbs include ישׁב (sit), ילד (give birth), ירד (go down), ידע (know) and יצא (go out). In conjugating these verbs the original *wāw* is sometimes retained, but each stem formation will be considered separately.

18.7.4.1. *Qal with an active meaning*

(1) In the *qāṭal*/perfect

• The I-*wāw* is replaced by a *yôḏ*. In other respects this verb stem conjugates regularly.

יָשַׁב   instead of   וְשַׁב

---

15. Joüon–Muraoka §76.

(2) In the *yiqtōl*/imperfect

- Fusion of the *yiqtōl*/imperfect prefix and the *wāw* of the verb stem leads to the vowel of the prefix /○/ changing to /○/.

       יֵשֵׁב   instead of   יִוְשֵׁב

- The stem vowel of the *yiqtōl*/imperfect is /○/ and not /○/.

       יֵשֵׁב   instead of   יֵשֹׁב

(3) In the *wayyiqtōl*, the /○/ vowel in the last syllable changes to /○/ due to the accent shift that accompanies the addition of the conjunction.

       וַיֵּ֫שֶׁב   instead of   וַיֵּשֵׁב

(4) In the imperative

- The ו falls away.

       שֵׁב   instead of   וְשֵׁב

(5) In the infinitive construct

- The ו falls away, but a ת suffix is added to the remaining consonants. These consonants are vocalized as follows:

       שֶׁ֫בֶת   instead of   וְשֵׁב

- The infinitive construct with a pronominal suffix behaves like a typical segholate with an i-stem, e.g. שִׁבְתִּי (§27.3.3.(4)).

18.7.4.2. *Qal with a stative meaning*

In the *yiqtōl*/imperfect of these forms the י of the verb stem, which has replaced the ו, does not fuse with the prefix.

       יִירָא   instead of   יְרָא

Note the following:

(1) The *yiqtōl*/imperfect and infinitive construct of the stative verb יָכֹל (he is able), which occurs only in the Qal, are completely irregular. They conjugate as if they are Hōpʿal *yiqtōl*/imperfect forms, e.g.:

Qātal/Perfect	יָכֹל
Yiqtōl/Imperfect	יוּכַל
Infinitive construct	יְכֹלֶת

(2) With the exception of the Qal *qātal*/perfect, the verb הלך conjugates in the Qal and the Hip̄ʿîl stem formations like a typical original I-*wāw* verb (Table 30).

(3) In some of the I-*yôḏ* verbs where the middle consonant is a צ, the *yôḏ* assimilates when it appears at the end of a closed syllable, just like the I-*nûn* verbs. There are only six such verbs in the Hebrew Bible, namely יצב (take a position), יצק (cast), יצע (spread out), יצת (set alight), יצג (place), יצר (form, make) (Joüon–Muraoka §77). Note that יצא (go out) is not regarded as part of this group (Joüon–Muraoka §75g).

(4) The verb ידע (know) which has both an original I-*wāw* and a guttural as third stem consonant, has a /◌/ vowel pattern in the Qal *yiqtōl*/imperfect. The /◌/ before the guttural is also observable in the imperative and infinitive construct, e.g.:

Qal *yiqtōl*/imperfect	יֵדַע
Qal imperative	דַּע
Qal infinitive construct	דַּעַת

18.7.4.3. *Nip̄ʿal*

The original *wāw* is retained in all the conjugations of the Nip̄ʿal stem formation.

(1) The *wāw* of the verb stem is retained as a vowel indicator in the *qātal*/ perfect and participle.

נוֹלַד   instead of   נְוְלַד

(2) The *wāw* of the verb stem is retained as a consonant in the *yiqtōl*/imperfect, imperative, infinitive construct and infinitive absolute, e.g. יִוָּשֵׁב.

(3) The *yiqtōl*/imperfect first singular, however, takes a /◌/ instead of a /◌/ vowel in the prefix.

אִוָּשֵׁב   instead of   אֶוָּשֵׁב

18.7.4.4. *Piˤēl, Puˤal and Hitpaˤēl*

In these stem formations the I-*wāw* verbs conjugate like the regular verbs.

(1) In the Piˤēl and Puˤal a consonantal *yôḏ* appears as the first stem consonant, e.g. יִשֵּׁב, יִלְּדָה.

(2) In the Hitpaˤēl the original *wāw* is usually retained as a consonant, e.g. יִתְוַכַּח.

18.7.4.5. *Hiป̄ˤîl and Hoป̄ˤal*

The "original" I-*wāw* is retained here. In the Hiป̄ˤîl the *wāw* is retained as a ִי vowel indicator and in the Hoป̄ˤal as a ֹו vowel indicator, e.g. הוּשַׁב, הוֹשִׁיב.

18.7.5. *Mixed forms*

A number of I-*yôḏ* verbs do not conjugate consistently either as original I-*yôḏ* or original I-*wāw* verbs. They have forms that correspond with both these groups. In the Qal stem formation these verbs usually follow the pattern of the original I-*yôḏ* verbs. In the remaining stem formations they usually follow the pattern of the original I-*wāw*, e.g.:

Qal *yiqtōl*/imperfect	יִירַשׁ
Qal imperative	רֵשׁ
Qal infinitive construct	רֶשֶׁת
Hiป̄ˤîl *qātal*/perfect	הוֹרִישׁ

§18.8. II-*wāw* and II-*yôḏ* Verbs

18.8.1. *Introduction*

The weak consonantal character of the *wāw* and the *yôḏ* (§4.2.5.2 and §5.2.2.1) may also be observed in verbs with *wāw* and *yôḏ* as middle consonants. The *wāw* and *yôḏ* have fallen out of the written form in certain cases, while in other cases they function as vowel indicators.

18.8.2. *Paradigm*

Table 31. *II-wāw and I-yôḏ Verbs*

	QAL	QAL	QAL	NI.	HI.	HO.	QAL
Root Gloss	קום get up	מות die	בוש be ashamed	קום get up			שׂים put down
Sing.	*Qātal/Perfect*						
3 m.	קָם	מֵת	בּוֹשׁ	נָקוֹם	הֵקִים	הוּקַם	שָׂם
3 f.	קָ֫מָה	מֵ֫תָה	בּוֹשָׁה	נָק֫וֹמָה	הֵקִ֫ימָה	הוּקְמָה	שָׂ֫מָה
2 m.	קַ֫מְתָּ	מַ֫תָּה	בֹּשְׁתָּ	נְקוּמֹ֫תָ	הֲקִימֹ֫תָ	הוּקַ֫מְתָּ	שַׂ֫מְתָּ
2 f.	קַמְתְּ	מַתְּ	בֹּשְׁתְּ	נְקוּמֹת	הֲקִימוֹת	הוּקַמְתְּ	שַׂמְתְּ
1 c.	קַ֫מְתִּי	מַ֫תִּי	בֹּשְׁתִּי	נְקוּמֹ֫תִי	הֲקִימֹ֫תִי	הוּקַ֫מְתִּי	שַׂ֫מְתִּי
Pl.							
3 c.	קָ֫מוּ	מֵ֫תוּ	בּוֹשׁוּ	נָק֫וֹמוּ	הֵקִ֫ימוּ	הוּקְמוּ	שָׂ֫מוּ
2 m.	קַמְתֶּם	מַתֶּם	בָּשְׁתֶּם	נְקוֹמֹתֶם	הֲקִימֹתֶם	הוּקַמְתֶּם	שַׂמְתֶּם
2 f.	קַמְתֶּן	מַתֶּן	בָּשְׁתֶּן	נְקוֹמֹתֶן	הֲקִימֹתֶן	הוּקַמְתֶּן	שַׂמְתֶּן
1 c.	קַ֫מְנוּ	מַ֫תְנוּ	בֹּשְׁנוּ	נְקוּמֹ֫נוּ	הֲקִ֫ימֹנוּ	הוּקַ֫מְנוּ	שַׂ֫מְנוּ
Sing.	*Yiqtōl/Imperfect*						
3 m.	יָקוּם	יָמוּת	יֵבוֹשׁ	יִקּוֹם	יָקִים	יוּקַם	יָשִׂים
3 f.	תָּקוּם	תָּמוּת	תֵּבוֹשׁ	תִּקּוֹם	תָּקִים	תּוּקַם	תָּשִׂים
2 m.	תָּקוּם	תָּמוּת	תֵּבוֹשׁ	תִּקּוֹם	תָּקִים	תּוּקַם	תָּשִׂים
2 f.	תָּק֫וּמִי	תָּמ֫וּתִי	תֵּב֫וֹשִׁי	תִּקּ֫וֹמִי	תָּקִ֫ימִי	תּוּקְמִי	תָּשִׂ֫ימִי
1 c.	אָקוּם	אָמוּת	אֵבוֹשׁ	אֶקּוֹם	אָקִים	אוּקַם	אָשִׂים
Pl.							
3 m.	יָק֫וּמוּ	יָמ֫וּתוּ	יֵב֫וֹשׁוּ	יִקּ֫וֹמוּ	יָקִ֫ימוּ	יוּקְמוּ	יָשִׂ֫ימוּ
3 f.	תָּקוּמֶ֫ינָה	תָּמוּתֶ֫ינָה	תֵּב֫וֹשְׁנָה	/	תָּקִימֶ֫ינָה תָּקֵ֫מְנָה	תּוּקַ֫מְנָה	תָּשִׂימֶ֫ינָה
2 m.	תָּק֫וּמוּ	תָּמ֫וּתוּ	תֵּב֫וֹשׁוּ	תִּקּ֫וֹמוּ	תָּקִ֫ימוּ	תּוּקְמוּ	תָּשִׂ֫ימוּ
2 f.	תָּקוּמֶ֫ינָה	תָּמוּתֶ֫ינָה	תֵּב֫וֹשְׁנָה	/	תָּקִימֶ֫ינָה תָּקֵ֫מְנָה	תּוּקַ֫מְנָה	תָּשִׂימֶ֫ינָה
1 c.	נָקוּם	נָמוּת	נֵבוֹשׁ	נִקּוֹם	נָקִים	נוּקַם	נָשִׂים

	QAL	QAL	QAL	NI.	HI.	HO.	QAL
Sing.	Imperative						
2 m.	קוּם	מוּת	בּוֹשׁ	הִקּוֹם	הָקֵם		שִׂים
2 f.	קוּמִי	מוּתִי	בּוֹשִׁי	הִקּוֹמִי	הָקִימִי		שִׂימִי
Pl.							
2 m.	קוּמוּ	מוּתוּ	בּוֹשׁוּ	הִקּוֹמוּ	הָקִימוּ		שִׂימוּ
2 f.	קֹמְנָה	מֹתְנָה	בֹּשְׁנָה	הִקֹּמְנָה	הָקֵמְנָה		
Sing.	Cohortative						
1 s.	אָקוּמָה	אָמוּתָה	אֵבוֹשָׁה		אָקִימָה		אָשִׂימָה
	Jussive						
3 s.	יָקֹם	יָמֹת	יֵבוֹשׁ		יָקֵם		יָשֵׂם
	Infinitive						
cs.	קוּם	מוּת	בּוֹשׁ	הִקּוֹם	הָקִים	הוּקַם	שִׂים
abs	קוֹם	מוֹת	בּוֹשׁ	הִקּוֹם	הָקֵם	הוּקַם	שׂוֹם
	Participle						
act.	קָם	מֵת	בּוֹשׁ		מֵקִים		שָׂם
pass.	קוּם			נָקוֹם		מוּקָם	

18.8.3. *Characteristics*

18.8.3.1. *General features*

(1) In the stem syllable (i.e. the syllable that begins with the first stem consonant) the *wāw* or *yôḏ* falls way or functions as a vowel indicator, e.g. תָּקוּם and קָם, תָּמוּת and מֵת.

(2) A connecting vowel occurs before the consonantal suffixes.

- In the *qātal*/perfect it is /i/

         הֲקִימֹותִי   instead of   הֲקִימְתִּי

- and in the *yiqṭōl*/imperfect it is /ֶי/.

         תְּקוּמֶינָה   instead of   תָּקֹומְנָה

(3) The vowel of the prefix is long and is found in an open syllable. This long vowel reduces should a connecting vowel occur in the verb.

הֲקִימֹׄתִי   instead of   הֲקִימֹׄתִי

תְּקוּמֶֽינָה   instead of   תְּקוּמֶֽינָה

(4) The II-*yôḏ* verbs are, with the exception of the Qal *yiqṭōl*/imperfect, imperative and infinitive construct, identical to the II-*wāw* verbs in all respects, e.g. קָם and שָׂם.

- In these exceptions the *yôḏ*, instead of the *wāw*, functions as a vowel indicator (as the only distinguishing feature of II-*yôḏ* verbs), e.g. קָם and תָּקוּם, but שִׂים and תָּשִׂים.

Note the following:

(a) The II-*yôḏ* verbs are considerably fewer in number than the II-*wāw* verbs. The II-*yôḏ* verbs that occur most frequently are דִּין (judge), בִּין (understand), גִּיל (shudder), רִיב (strive), שִׁיר (sing), and שִׁית (put down).

(b) Certain II-*wāw* verbs retain the characteristics of verbs having three stem consonants, namely גּוַע (dwindle away), צָוה (command), קוה (hope), היה (be), and חיה (live).

18.8.3.2. *Qal*

(1) In the *qāṭal*/perfect

(a) In the *qāṭal*/perfect third masculine singular and the third feminine singular forms the *wāw* and *yôḏ* have fallen away in the stem syllable, e.g. קָם and קָמָה.

- A long vowel occurs before vocalic suffixes and forms without suffixes, e.g. קָם and קָֽמָה.
- This long vowel changes before consonantal suffixes, e.g. קַֽמְתָּ and שַֽׂמְתָּ.

(b) The vowels of the stative *qāṭal*/perfect form correspond to the vowels in the second syllable of verbs with three stem consonants, e.g. מֵת as קָ-טוֹן, בּוֹשׁ as כָּ-בֵד.

(c) When the normal suffixes of the *qāṭal*/perfect are added to verbs such as מֵת, the /◌ֵ/ is replaced by /◌ַ/, e.g. מֵתָה as קַֽמְתָּ. (The ת doubles because the verb stem ends on a ת and the suffix begins with a ת.) In stative verbs such as בּוֹשׁ, however, the /◌/ is retained (בֹּשְׁתָּ).

(4) In the *yiqtōl*/imperfect
- The vowel of the prefix is /ǎ/ instead of /ĭ/.

תָּקוּם	instead of	תִּקוּם
תָּשִׂים	instead of	תִּשִׂים

(5) In the imperative and infinitive construct
- The II-*wāw* verbs take /ū/ as stem vowel, e.g. קוּם and קוּמִי and
- The II-*yôḏ* verbs take / î/ as stem vowel, e.g. שִׂים and שִׂימִי.

(6) In the infinitive absolute
- The stem vowel of the infinitive absolute is /ô/ like that of the regular verbs, e.g. קוֹם as כָּתוֹב.

(7) In the jussive
- The long /û/ of the II-*wāw* changes to /ō/.

תָּקֹם	instead of	תָּקוּם

- The /î/ of the II-*yôḏ* changes to /ē/.

תָּשֵׂם	instead of	תָּשִׂים

(8) In the *wayyiqtōl*
- The /ō/ of the II-*wāw* changes to /ǎ/ (*qāmeṣ ḥāṭuр̄*).

וַתָּ֫קָם	instead of	וַתָּקוּם

- The /ē/ of the II-*yôḏ* changes to /ē/.

וַתָּ֫שֶׂם	instead of	וַתָּשֶׂם

(9) In the participle
- The masculine singular participle and the *qāṭal*/perfect third masculine singular are identical in form, viz. קָם.
- Although the corresponding feminine forms also seem to be identical, the accent in the *qāṭal*/perfect falls on the first syllable (קָ֫מָה) while it falls on the final syllable in the participle (קָמָ֫ה).

18.8.3.3. *Nip̄ʿal*

(1) In the *qātal*/perfect

- Since the prefix in the *qātal*/perfect does not form a closed syllable with the first stem consonant, the prefix is -נָ and not -נִ.

נָקוֹם   instead of   נִקוֹם

- The stem vowel of the *qātal*/perfect is /î/ (נָקוֹם) or /î/ (נְקוּמֹתִי) and not /ǒ/ (נָקֹם).
- With the consonantal suffixes the connecting vowel /ô/ is inserted between the suffix and the final stem consonant. As a result of the accompanying accent shift, the prefix /ā/ is reduced to /ǎ/.

נְקוּמֹתִי   instead of   נָקוּמְתִי

נְקוּמֹתִי   instead of   נָקוּמְתִי

(2) In the *yiqtōl*/imperfect

The *yiqtōl*/imperfect is highly irregular. The vowel of the prefix is /ǐ/. The next consonant doubles and the *wāw* functions as the vowel indicator /î/, e.g. יִקּוֹם as יִכָּתֵב.

18.8.3.4. *Piʿēl, Puʿal and Hitpaʿēl and Pôʿlēl, Pôʿlal, and Hitpôʿlēl*

Instead of the Piʿēl, Puʿal, and Hitpaʿēl stem formations, the II-*wāw* and II-*yôd̠* verbs have a Pôʿlēl, Pôʿlal, and Hitpôʿlēl stem formation, respectively. It is clear from the names of these stem formations that the final stem consonant is repeated.

Table 32. *Pôʿlēl, Pôʿlal and Hitpôʿlēl*

	PÔʿLĒL	*PÔʿLAL*	*HITPÔʿLĒL*
Sing.	*Qātal/Perfect*		
3 m.	קוֹמֵם	קוֹמַם	הִתְקוֹמֵם
3 f.	קוֹמְמָה	(קוֹמְמָה[16])	(הִתְקוֹמְמָה)
2 m.	קוֹמַ֫מְתָּ	קוֹמַ֫מְתָּ	הִתְקוֹמַ֫מְתָּ
2 f.	(קוֹמַמְתְּ)	(קוֹמַמְתְּ)	(הִתְקוֹמַמְתְּ)
1 c.	קוֹמַ֫מְתִּי	קוֹמַמְתִּי	הִתְקוֹמַ֫מְתִּי

---

16. Forms in brackets are theoretical constructs. They are not attested in the Hebrew Bible.

	PÔʿLĒL	*PÔʿLAL*	*HITPÔʿLĒL*
Pl.	*Qātal/Perfect*		
3 c.	קוֹמֲמוּ	קוֹמֲמוּ	הִתְקוֹמֲמוּ
2 m.	(קוֹמַמְתֶּם)	(קוֹמַמְתֶּם)	(הִתְקוֹמַמְתֶּם)
2 f.	קוֹמַמְתֶּן	קוֹמַמְתֶּן	הִתְקוֹמַמְתֶּן
1 c.	(קוֹמַ֫מְנוּ)	(קוֹמַ֫מְנוּ)	(הִתְקוֹמַ֫מְנוּ)
Sing.	*Yiqtōl/Imperfect*		
3 m.	יְקוֹמֵם	יְקוֹמַם	יִתְקוֹמֵם
3 f.	תְּקוֹמֵם	(תְּקוֹמַם)	תִּתְקוֹמֵם
2 m.	תְּקוֹמֵם	תְּקוֹמַם	תִּתְקוֹמֵם
2 f.	(תְּקוֹמֲמִי)	תְּקוֹמֲמִי	תִּתְקוֹמֲמִי
1 c.	אֲקוֹמֵם	אֲקוֹמַם	אֶתְקוֹמֵם
Pl.			
3 m.	יְקוֹמֲמוּ	יְקוֹמֲמוּ	יִתְקוֹמֲמוּ
3 f.	תְּקוֹמֵ֫מְנָה	תְּקוֹמַ֫מְנָה	תִּתְקוֹמֵ֫מְנָה
2 m.	תְּקוֹמֲמוּ	(תְּקוֹמֲמוּ)	תִּתְקוֹמֲמוּ
2 f.	תְּקוֹמֵ֫מְנָה	תְּקוֹמַ֫מְנָה	תִּתְקוֹמֵ֫מְנָה
1 c.	נְקוֹמֵם	(נְקוֹמַם)	(נִתְקוֹמֵם)
Sing.	*Imperative*		
2 m.	קוֹמֵם		
2 f.	(קוֹמֲמִי)		
Pl.			
2 m.	קוֹמֲמוּ		
2 f.	(קוֹמֵ֫מְנָה)		
	Infinitive		
cs.	קוֹמֵם		
abs.			
	Participle		
	מְקוֹמֵם	מְקוֹמָם	

General features of the Pôʿlēl, Pôʿlal and Hitpôʿlēl and the similarities between
them.

(1) In the *qātal*/perfect
- Only a -הִת is added before the forms of the Pôʿlēl to form the Hitpôʿlēl.
- The Pôʿlal can be distinguished from the Pôʿlēl only in the third
  masculine singular.
- Before vocalic suffixes the two matching consonants are separated
  with a *ḥaṭēp̄* vowel rather than with an audible *šəwā*ʾ.

(2) In the *yiqṭōl*/imperfect
- In the *yiqṭōl*/imperfect the Pôlēl conjugates regularly.
- In the *yiqṭōl*/imperfect of the Hitpôʿlēl a יִת- prefix replaces the יְ- prefix
  of the Pôʿlēl.
- In the *yiqṭōl*/imperfect of the Pôʿlal a /◌ֳ/ occurs in the place of the
  Pôʿlēl's /◌ֹ/.

(3) In the imperative
- The forms of the imperative, infinitive and participle are derived in the
  usual way.

18.8.3.5. *Hip̄ʿîl*

(1) In the Hip̄ʿîl *qātal*/perfect and *yiqṭōl*/imperfect the *wāw* falls away and a
vowel indicator /י/ occurs in the stem syllable.

הֵקִים   instead of   הֵקוֹם

(2) In the *qātal*/perfect
- The vowel of the prefix is /◌ֵ/ instead of /◌ֱ/.

הֵקִים   instead of   הֱקִים

- The prefix vowel is reduced when a connecting vowel is inserted later
  in the verb, e.g. הֲקִימֹ֫ותָ.

(3) In the *yiqṭōl*/imperfect
- The vowel of the prefix is /◌ָ/ instead of /◌ֵ/.

תָּקִים   instead of   תַּקִים

- The vowel of the prefix is reduced when a connecting vowel is used
  later in the verb, e.g. תְּקִימֶ֫ינָה.

(4) In the participle
- The prefix vowel of the participle is /ְ◌/ and not /ַ◌/.

  מֵקִים   instead of   מַקִים

(5) In the jussive
- The stem vowel in the second syllable /ִי◌/ changes to /ֵ◌/.

  תָּקֶם   instead of   תָּקִים

(6) In the imperative
- The prefix vowel of the imperative is also /ָ◌/. The imperative and infinitive construct may also be derived in the usual way, e.g. הָקֵם.

(7) In the *wayyiqtōl*
- In the *wayyiqtōl* /ֵ◌/ of the jussive form referred to in (5) above, changes to /ֶ◌/ due to the accent shift that accompanies the *wayyiqtōl*.

  וַתָּקֶם   instead of   וַתָּקֵם

- Should the II-*wāw* verb end with a guttural or *rêš*, the stem vowel /ֵ◌/ changes to /ַ◌/.

  וַיֹּסַר   instead of   וַיָּסֵר

18.8.3.6. *Hop̄ʿal*

In the *qātal*/perfect and *yiqtōl*/imperfect /וּ/ functions as the vowel for the prefix instead of /ָ◌/.

  הוּקַם   instead of   הָקַם
  יוּקַם   instead of   יְקַם

§18.9. Geminate Verbs

18.9.1. *Introduction*

The term "geminate verbs" refers to verbs that have identical second and third stem consonants, e.g. סבב (surround), בזז (capture). They bear certain similarities to the II-*wāw* verbs. The features of the geminate verbs in the Qal,

Niᵽ'al, Hiᵽ'îl, and Hoᵽ'al stem formations may be systematically described as follows:

(1) A connecting vowel occurs before the consonantal suffix. In the *qātal*/ perfect it is /ǐ/ and in the *yiqtōl*/imperfect it is /ᵊ◌/.

(2) The prefix vowel in an open syllable is long.

(3) The long vowel is reduced if a connecting vowel occurs in the verb.

(4) In the conjugations that have no suffixes, the third root consonant usually falls away, while the middle consonant usually doubles in forms which have either vocalic or consonantal suffixes. (The first two stem consonants constitute the stem syllable.)

(5) The accent usually falls on the stem syllable. When a connecting vowel is added, the vowel is usually accented. In a closed unaccented syllable a vowel change occurs, e.g.: /◌/ becomes /◌/ and /ǐ/ becomes /ᵊ◌/.

18.9.2. *Paradigm*

Table 33. *Geminate Verbs*

	QAL	QAL	QAL	NI.	HI.	HI.	HO.
Root Gloss	סבב surround		קלל be swift	סבב surround			
Sing.	Qātal/Perfect						
3 m.	סַב	סָבַב	קַל	נָסַב	הֵסַב	הֵסֵב	הוּסַב
3 f.	סַבָּה	סָבְבָה סָבְבָה	קַלָּה	נָסַבָּה	הֵסֵבָּה	הֵסֵבָּה	הוּסַבָּה
2 m.		סַבּוֹתָ	קַלּוֹתָ	נְסַבּוֹתָ		הֲסִבּוֹתָ	הוּסַבּוֹתָ
2 f.		סַבּוֹת	קַלּוֹת	נְסַבּוֹת		הֲסִבּוֹת	הוּסַבּוֹת
1 c.		סַבּוֹתִי	קַלּוֹתִי	נְסַבּוֹתִי		הֲסִבּוֹתִי	הוּסַבּוֹתִי
Pl.							
3 c.	סַבּוּ	סָבְבוּ	קַלּוּ	נָסַבּוּ	הֵסַבּוּ		
2 m.		סַבּוֹתֶם	קַלּוֹתֶם	נְסַבּוֹתֶם		הֲסִבּוֹתֶם	הוּסַבּוֹתֶם
2 f.		סַבּוֹתֶן	קַלּוֹתֶן	נְסַבּוֹתֶן		הֲסִבּוֹתֶן	הוּסַבּוֹתֶן
1 c.		סַבּוֹנוּ	קַלּוֹנוּ	נְסַבּוֹנוּ		הֲסִבּוֹנוּ	הוּסַבּוֹנוּ

Aramaism (handwritten annotation with arrow pointing to third QAL column)

	QAL	QAL	QAL	NI.	HI.	HI.	HO.
Sing.				*Yiqtōl/Imperfect*			
3 m.	יָסֹב	יִסֹב	יֵקַל	יִסַּב	יָסֵב	יָסֵב	יוּסַב יֻסַּב
3 f.	תָּסֹב	תִּסֹב	תֵּקַל	תִּסַּב		תָּסֵב	תּוּסַב
2 m.	תָּסֹב	תִּסֹב	תֵּקַל	תִּסַּב		תָּסֵב	תּוּסַב
2 f.	תָּסֹבִּי	תִּסְבִּי	תֵּקַלִּי	תִּסַּבִּי		תָּסֵבִּי	תּוּסְבִּי
1 c.	אָסֹב	אֶסֹב	אֵקַל	אֶסַּב		אָסֵב	אוּסַב
Pl.							
3 m.	יָסֹבּוּ	יִסְבוּ	יֵקַלּוּ	יִסַּבּוּ	יָסֹבּוּ	יָסֵבּוּ	יוּסַבּוּ
3 f.	תְּסֻבֶּינָה	תָּסֹבְנָה	תְּקַלֶּינָה	תִּסַּבֶּינָה		תְּסִבֶּינָה	תּוּסַבֶּינָה
2 m.	תָּסֹבּוּ	תִּסְבוּ	תֵּקַלּוּ	תִּסַּבּוּ		תָּסֵבּוּ	תּוּסַבּוּ
2 f.	תְּסֻבֶּינָה	תָּסֹבְנָה	תְּקַלֶּינָה	תִּסַּבֶּינָה		תְּסִבֶּינָה	תּוּסַבֶּינָה
1 c.	נָסֹב	נִסֹב	נֵקַל	נִסַּב		נָסֵב	נוּסַב
Sing.				*Imperative*			
2 m.		סֹב		הִסַּב		הָסֵב	
2 f.		סֹבִּי		הִסַּבִּי		הָסֵבִּי	
Pl.							
2 m.		סֹבּוּ		הִסַּבּוּ		הָסֵבּוּ	
2 f.		סֻבֶּינָה		הִסַּבֶּינָה		הֲסִבֶּינָה	
Sing.				*Cohortative*			
	אָסֹבָּה	אֶסֹבָה	אֵקְלָה				
Sing.				*Jussive*			
	יָסֹב	יִסֹב	יֵקַל	יִסַּב		יָסֵב	
				Infinitive			
cs.		סֹב	קַל	הִסֵּב		הָסֵב	
abs.		סָבוֹב	קָלוֹל	הִסּוֹב		הָסֵב	
				Participle			
act.	סֹבֵב	סוֹבֵב	קַל			מֵסֵב	
pass.		סָבוּב		נָסָב			מוּסָב

18.9.3. *General characteristics*

18.9.3.1. *Qal*

A clear distinction must be made between the forms of geminate verbs that have an active meaning and those that have a stative meaning. Here are some of the verbs that occur frequently.

Statives		Actives	
חָתַת	to be destroyed	אָרַר	to curse
מָרַר	to be bitter	בָּלַל	to mix
קָלַל	to be quick	גָּלַל	to roll away
רָעַע	to be bad	מָדַד	to measure
שָׁמֵם	to be desolate	סָבַב	to surround
		שָׁדַד	to destroy

(1) *Qal with active meaning*

   (a) In the Qal *qātal*/perfect

     • In the Qal *qātal*/perfect third masculine singular, third feminine singular and third plural, variants occur according to rule, viz. the identical second and third consonants may be visibly repeated (סָבְבָה or סָבֲבָה).

     • However, the repetition may also be indicated by means of a *dāḡēš* in the second consonant (סַבָּה).

     • Sometimes the third consonant falls away and sometimes it is retained, e.g. סָבַב and סַב.

   (b) In the *yiqtōl*/imperfect

     • The vowel of the prefix is /◌̣/ and /◌/ occurs in the stem syllable, e.g. תָּסֹב.

     • Variants that conjugate like I-*nûn* verbs also occur, e.g. תָּסֹב as תִּפֹּל.

   (c) In the *wayyiqtōl*

     • The accent shift that accompanies the *wayyiqtōl* results in the /◌/ in the second syllable changing to /◌̣/.

וַתָּ֫סָב   instead of   וַתָּסֹב

(d) The imperative, infinitive construct and participle may be derived regularly, e.g. סֹב.

(2) *Qal with a stative meaning*

    (a) The third consonant falls away in:

- The *qātal*/perfect third masculine singular, the masculine singular participle

           תַּם   instead of   תָּמֵם

- the imperative

           תַּם   instead of   תְּמַם

- and the infinitive

           תֹּם   instead of   תְּמַם

    (b) The prefix vowel of the *yiqtōl*/imperfect is /◌/ and not /◌/. A /◌/ also occurs in the stem syllable.

           יֵתַם   instead of   יִתַם

18.9.3.2. *Niṗʿal*

(1) In the Niṗʿal the geminate root always occurs in its shortened form, e.g. נָסַבָּה not נָסַבְבָה.

(2) The prefix vowel of the *qātal*/perfect and participle changes to /◌/.

           נָסַב   instead of   נִסַב

           נָסָב   instead of   נִסָב

(3) The stem vowel of the *yiqtōl*/imperfect, imperative and infinitive is /◌/.

           תִּסַּב   instead of   תִּסֵּב

18.9.3.3. *Piʿēl, Puʿal and Hitpaʿēl / Pôʿēl, Pôʿal, and Hitpôʿēl*

Geminate verbs have Pôʿēl, Pôʿal and Hitpôʿēl stem formations instead of the Piʿēl, Puʿal, Hitpaʿēl, respectively. The former stem formations are characterized by the vowel indicator /î/ between the first and second stem consonants.

(1) The conjugation of verbs in these formations is identical in all respects to the Pôʿlēl, Pôʿlal, and Hitpôʿlēl stem formations of the II-*wāw* verbs (§18.8.3.4).

- Pôʿēl *qātal*/perfect third masculine singular, e.g. סוֹבֵב.
- Pôʿēl *yiqtōl*/imperfect third masculine singular, e.g. יְסוֹבֵב.

(2) The following forms may also be derived regularly:

- Pôʿēl imperative masculine singular, e.g. סוֹבֵב.
- Pôʿēl infinitive construct, e.g. סוֹבֵב.
- Pôʿēl participle, e.g. מְסוֹבֵב.

(3) Some geminate verbs have either regular Piʿēl forms or conjugations that duplicate the first two stem consonants instead of a Pôʿēl stem formation. The duplicated stem formations are called the Pilpēl and Hitpalpēl.

- Piʿēl *qātal*/perfect third masculine singular, e.g. גִּלֵּל.
- Pilpēl *qātal*/perfect first singular, e.g. גִּלְגַּלְתִּי.
- Hitpalpēl *qātal*/perfect third masculine plural, e.g. הִתְגַּלְגְּלוּ.

18.9.3.4. *Hip̄ʿîl*

(1) The stem vowel of all Hip̄ʿîl conjugations is / $\circ$ /.

יָסֵב	instead of	יָסִיב
מֵסֵב	instead of	מֵסִיב

(2) The prefix vowel of the *qātal*/perfect changes to / $\circ$ /.

הֵסֵב	instead of	הֵסֵב

(3) The prefix vowel of the *yiqtōl*/imperfect, infinitive construct and imperative, / $\circ$ /, changes to / $\circ$ /.

יָסֵב	instead of	יַסֵב
הָסֵב	instead of	הַסֵב

(4) When a suffix that begins with a consonant is added, the stem vowel of the *yiqtōl*/imperfect changes to / $\circ$ /.

הֲסֻבּוֹנוּ	instead of	הֲסֻבּוֹנוּ

(5) The forms of the imperative and infinitive may be derived regularly, e.g. הָסֵב.

(6) The prefix vowel of the participle is /◌/ and not /◌/.

מֵסֵב   instead of   מַסֵב

(7) The accent shift that accompanies the *wayyiqtōl* leads to the /◌/ in the final syllable changing to /◌/ in the Hip̄ʿîl.

וַיָּסֶךְ   instead of   וַיְסֵךְ

(8) In verbs with a guttural as second and third stem consonants:

- the /◌/ before the final guttural in the third masculine singular is replaced by a /◌/.

הֵרַע   instead of   הֵרֵע

- "Compensatory lengthening" occurs in conjugations where the guttural is meant to double. The /◌/ changes to /◌/.

הֲרֵעוֹתָ   instead of   הַרֵעוֹתָ

18.9.3.5. *Hop̄ʿal*

The Hop̄ʿal is formed by analogy with the II-*wāw* verbs

(1) *Qātal*/Perfect, e.g. הוּסַב as הוּקַם.

(2) *Yiqtōl*/Imperfect, e.g. יוּסַב as יוּקַם.

(3) Infinitive construct, e.g. הוּסַב as הוּקַם.

(4) Participle, e.g. מוּסָב as מוּקָם.

§18.10. Verbs with More than One Irregular Consonant

The following types occur fairly frequently:

- I-ʾālep̄ and III-*hē*ʾ, e.g.   אבה   (willing) (Table 33a)
- I-*nûn* and III-ʾālep̄, e.g.   נשׂא   (raise up/carry) (Table 33b)
- I-*wāw* and III-*hē*ʾ, e.g.   ירה   (shoot) (Table 33c)
- I-*wāw* and III-ʾālep̄, e.g.   יצא   (go out) (Table 33d)
- I-*yôd* and III-ʾālep̄, e.g.   ירא   (fear) (Table 33e)
- II-guttural and III-*hē*ʾ, e.g.   ראה   (see) (Table 33f)
- II-*wāw* and III-ʾālep̄, e.g.   בוא   (come) (Table 33g)
- I-*nûn* and III-*hē*ʾ, e.g.   נטה   (stretch out) (Table 33h)

Table 33a. *I-ʾālep̄ and VerbsIII-hē² Verbs*

	QAL	NI.	PI.	PU.	HI.	HO.
Qāṭal	אָבָה					
Yiqṭōl	יֹאבֶה					
Juss.	יֹאבֶה					
Wayyiqṭōl	וַיֹּאבֶה					
Imp.						
Inf. cs.						
Inf. abs.						
Part.	אֹבִים					

Table 33b. *I-nûn and III-ʾālep̄ Verbs*

	QAL	NI.	PI.	PU.	HI.	HO.
Qāṭal	נָשָׂא	נִשָּׂא			הִשִּׂיא	
Yiqṭōl	יִשָּׂא	As III-ʾālep̄ verb stem			יַשִּׂיא	
Juss.	יִשָּׂא				יַשֵּׂא	
Wayyiqṭōl	וַיִּשָּׂא				וַיַּשֵּׂא	
Imp.	שָׂא				הַשֵּׂא	
Inf. cs.	שְׂאֵת				הַשִּׂיא	
Inf. abs.	נָשׂוֹא				הַשֵּׂא	
Part.	נֹשֵׂא				מַשִּׂיא	

Table 33c. *I-wāw and III-hē Verbs*

	QAL	NI.	PI.	PU.	HI.	HO.
Qātal	יָרָה				הוֹרָה	
Yiqtōl		יִיָּרֶה			יוֹרֶה	
Juss.					יוֹר	
Wayyiqtōl					וַיּוֹר	
Imp.	יְרֵה					
Inf. cs.						
Inf. abs.	יָרֹה					
Part.	יֹרֶה				מוֹרֶה	

Table 33d. *I-wāw and III-ʾāleḡ Verbs*

	QAL	NI.	PI.	PU.	HI.	HO.
Qātal	יָצָא				הוֹצִיא	הוּצָא
Yiqtōl	יֵצֵא				יוֹצִיא	יוּצָא
Juss.	יֵצֵא				יוֹצֵא	
Wayyiqtōl	וַיֵּצֵא				וַיּוֹצֵא	וַיּוּצָא
Imp.	צֵא				הוֹצֵא	
Inf. cs.	צֵאת				הוֹצִיא	הוּצָא
Inf. abs.	יָצוֹא				הוֹצֵא	
Part.	יֹצֵא				מוֹצִיא	מוּצָא

Table 33e. *I-yôḏ and III-ʾāleḡ Verbs*

	QAL	NI.	PI.	PU.	HI.	HO.
Qātal	יָרֵא					
Yiqtōl	יִירָא	תִּוָּרֵא				
Juss.	יִירָא					
Wayyiqtōl	וַיִּירָא					

stative

	QAL	NI.	PI.	PU.	HI.	HO.
Imp.	יְרָא					
Part.	יְרָא					

Table 33f. *II-guttural and III-hē° Verbs (*ירא vs. ראה*)*

	QAL	NI.	PI.	PU.	HI.	HO.
Qātal	רָאָה				הֶרְאָה	
Yiqtōl	יִרְאֶה				יַרְאֶה	
Juss.	יֵרֶא				יַרְא	
Wayyiqtōl	וַיִּרְאֶה וַתֵּרֶא וַיֵּרְא				וַיַּרְאֶה וַיַּרְא	
Imp.	רְאֵה					
Inf. cs.	רְאוֹת				הַרְאוֹת	
Inf. abs.	רָאֹה					
Part.	רֹאֶה				מַרְאֶה	

Table 33g. *II-wāw and III-°ālep Verbs*

	QAL	NI.	PI.	PU.	HI.	HO.
Qātal	בָּא				הֵבִיא	הוּבָא
Yiqtōl	יָבֹא				יָבִיא	יוּבָא
Juss.	יָבֹא				יָבֵא	
Wayyiqtōl	וַיָּבֹא				וַיָּבֵא	וַיּוּבָא
Imp.	בֹּא				הָבֵא	
Inf. cs.	בֹּא				הָבִיא	הוּבָא
Inf. abs.	בּוֹא				הָבֵא	
Part.	בָּא				מֵבִיא	מוּבָא

Table 33h. *I-nûn and III-hē° Verbs*

	QAL	NI.	PI.	PU.	HI.	HO.
Qātal	נָטָה				הִטָּה	הֻטָּה
Yiqtōl	יִטֶּה				יַטֶּה	יֻטֶּה
Juss	יֵט				יֵט	
Wayyiqtōl	וַיֵּט				וַיֵּט	וַיֻּט
Imp.	נְטֵה				הַטֵּה	
Inf. abs.	נָטֹה				הַטֵּה	הֻטֵּה
Inf. cs.	נְטוֹת				הַטּוֹת	הֻטּוֹת
Part.	נֹטֶה				מַטֶּה	מֻטֶּה

§18.11. Others: הלך and לקח, נתן, חוה, חיה, היה

Table 34. הלך *and* לקח, נתן, חוה, חיה, היה

	QAL		QAL	NI.	QAL pass.	QAL	NI.	QAL
Sing.				*Qātal/Perfect*				
3 m.	הָיָה	חָיָה	נָתַן	נִתַּן	נֻתַּן	לָקַח	נִלְקַח	הָלַךְ
3 f.	הָיְתָה		נָתְנָה	נִתְּנָה		לָקְחָה	נִלְקְחָה	
2 m.	הָיִיתָ	חיה as	נָתַתָּ	נִתַּתָּ		לָקַחְתָּ	נִלְקַחְתָּ	regular
2 f.	הָיִית		נָתַתְּ	נִתַּתְּ		regular	נִלְקַחְתְּ	
1 c.	הָיִיתִי		נָתַתִּי	נִתַּתִּי			נִלְקַחְתִּי	
Pl.								
3 c.	הָיוּ		נָתְנוּ	נִתְּנוּ			נִלְקְחוּ	
2 m.	הֱיִיתֶם		נְתַתֶּם	נִתַּתֶּם			נִלְקַחְתֶּם	
2 f.	הֱיִיתֶן		נְתַתֶּן	נִתַּתֶּן			-	
1 c.	הָיִינוּ		נָתַנּוּ	נִתַּנּוּ			נִלְקַחְנוּ	

	QAL		QAL	NI.	QAL pass.	QAL	NI.	QAL
Sing.				*Yiqtōl/Imperfect*				
3 m.	יִהְיֶה		יִתֵּן	יִנָּתֵן	יֻתַּן	יִקַּח	יִלָּקַח	יֵלֵד
3 f.	תִּהְיֶה		תִּתֵּן	תִּנָּתֵן	תֻּתַּן	תִּקַּח	תִּלָּקַח	תֵּלֵד
2 m.	תִּהְיֶה		תִּתֵּן	תִּנָּתֵן	תֻּתַּן	תִּקַּח	תִּלָּקַח	תֵּלֵד
2 f.	תִּהְיִי		תִּתְּנִי	תִּנָּתְנִי	תֻּתְּנִי	תִּקְחִי	תִּלָּקְחִי	תֵּלְכִי
1 c.	אֶהְיֶה		אֶתֵּן	אֶנָּתֵן	אֻתַּן	אֶקַּח	אֶלָּקַח	אֵלֵד
Pl.								
3 m.	יִהְיוּ		יִתְּנוּ	יִנָּתְנוּ	יֻתְּנוּ	יִקְחוּ	יִלָּקְחוּ	יֵלְכוּ
3 f.	תִּהְיֶינָה		תִּתֵּנָּה			תִּלַּקַחְנָה		תֵּלַכְנָה
2 m.	תִּהְיוּ		תִּתְּנוּ	תִּנָּתְנוּ	תֻּתְּנוּ	תִּקְחוּ	תִּלָּקְחוּ	תֵּלְכוּ
2 f.	תִּהְיֶינָה		תִּתֵּנָּה			תִּלַּקַחְנָה		תֵּלַכְנָה
1 c.	נִהְיֶה		נִתֵּן	נִנָּתֵן	נֻתַּן	נִקַּח	נִלָּקַח	נֵלֵד
Sing.				*Imperative*				
2 m.	הֱיֵה		תֵּן	הִנָּתֵן		קַח	הִלָּקַח	לֵד
2 f.	הֲיִי		תְּנִי	הִנָּתְנִי		קְחִי	הִלָּקְחִי	לְכִי
Pl.								
2 m.	הֱיוּ		תְּנוּ	הִנָּתְנוּ		קְחוּ	הִלָּקְחוּ	לְכוּ
2 f.			תֵּנָּה			קַחְנָה	הִלָּחְנָה	לֵכְנָה
Sing.				*Cohortative*				
			אֶתְּנָה			אֶקְחָה		אֵלְכָה
Sing.				*Jussive*				
	יְהִי		יִתֵּן			יִקַּח		
				Infinitive				
cs.	הֱיוֹת		תֵּת	הִנָּתֵן		קַחַת	הִלָּקַח	לֶכֶת
abs.			נָתוֹן	הִנָּתֹן		לָקוֹחַ	הִלָּקַח	הָלוֹךְ
				Participle				
act.			נֹתֵן			לֹקֵחַ		הֹלֵךְ
pass.			נָתוּן	נִתָּן		לָקוּחַ	נִלְקָח	

18.11.1. היה *and* חיה *(Table 34)*

Apart from the conjugation patterns normally associated with I and III-gutturals, this verb stem also has several unique features.

(1) /ֱ/ is found with the I-guttural where one would expect /ֲ/.

הֱיִיתֶם	instead of	הֲיִיתֶם
הֱיֹות	instead of	הֲיֹות

(2) In the *yiqtōl*/imperfect the vowel of the prefix is not influenced by the I-guttural.

יִהְיֶה	instead of	יֶהְיֶה

(3) The II-*yôḏ* never becomes a vowel indicator except in the case of (short) jussive forms.

יְהִי	instead of	יִהְיֶה

18.11.2. חוה

For a very long time הִשְׁתַּחֲוָה was regarded as a Hitpaʿēl form of שחה in which *metathesis* had occurred (§4.2.5.1). However, research into Ugaritic, a Semitic language closely related to Biblical Hebrew, has clearly indicated that it is a relic from an earlier stage of the language. One is here dealing with a verb stem חוה that is used in a stem formation to which a /*hišt-*/ or /*yišt-*/ syllable is added. Only one verb stem in Biblical Hebrew occurs in this stem formation, namely חוה. The most common meaning of this verb stem is "to bow down." This stem formation is called the *Hištap̄ʿēl*.

Table 35. *Most Frequent Hištap̄ʿēl Forms of* הוה

	Qātal	*Yiqtōl*	*Imp.*	*Part.*	*Inf. cs.*
3 m. sing.	הִשְׁתַּחֲוָה	יִשְׁתַּחֲוֶה			
2 m. sing.	הִשְׁתַּחֲוִיתָ	תִּשְׁתַּחֲוֶה			
1 sing.	הִשְׁתַּחֲוֵיתִי	אֶשְׁתַּחֲוֶה			
3 m. pl.	הִשְׁתַּחֲווּ	יִשְׁתַּחֲווּ			

	Qātal	Yiqtōl	Imp.	Part.	Inf. cs.
2 m. pl.	הִשְׁתַּחֲוִיתֶם	תִּשְׁתַּחֲווּ	הִשְׁתַּחֲווּ		
1 pl.	הִשְׁתַּחֲוִינוּ	נִשְׁתַּחֲוֶה			
					הִשְׁתַּחֲוֹת
m. sing.				מִשְׁתַּחֲוֶה	
m. pl.				מִשְׁתַּחֲוִים	

The *wayyiqtōl* is formed by adding the conjunction -וַ to the *yiqtōl*, in which case the first consonant doubles. The following are the forms for the third masculine singular and second masculine singular:

| *וַיִּשְׁתַּחֲוֶה | וַיִּשְׁתַּחוּ | "and he bowed" |
| *וַתִּשְׁתַּחֲוֶה | וַתִּשְׁתַּחוּ | "and you bowed" |

18.11.3. נתן *(Table 33)*

(1) The *qātal*/perfect conjugates regularly. Note that the final *nûn* assimilates with the ת of the suffixes.

נָתַתָּ instead of נָתַנְתָּ

(2) The stem vowel of the *yiqtōl*/imperfect is /$\circ$/ as though this were a I-*wāw* verb stem.

יִתֵּן instead of יִתֹּן

In addition to the assimilation of the first *nûn*, the final *nûn* also assimilates with the subsequent consonantal suffix, נְתַתֶּם and תְּתָּנִי.

(3) In the infinitive construct and imperative the I-*nûn* of the verb stem falls away (or it may be derived regularly from the *yiqtōl*/imperfect).

תֵּת instead of נְתֹן

(4) נתן also has conjugations in the Hŏp̄ʿal *yiqtōl*/imperfect. However, these forms are traditionally interpreted as passive *yiqtōl*/imperfect forms of the Qal stem formation, e.g. יֻתַּ. (Joüon–Muraoka §58a and §72i). Table 33 reflects the traditional interpretation.

(5) The infinitive construct is formed with a ת suffix.

- The infinitive construct looks like a typical monosyllabic noun, e.g. תֵּת (§27.4). When the pronominal suffix is added to the infinitive it has an i-stem, e.g. תִּתִּי.

18.11.4. לקח *(Table 34)*

לקח behaves as if it were a I-*nûn* verb:

(1) The *qātal*/perfect paradigm conjugates normally, e.g. לָקַח and לְקָחְתִּי.

(2) In the *yiqtōl*/imperfect conjugation the ל assimilates, like the I-*nûn*, with the subsequent consonant, e.g. יִקַּח and אֶקַּח.

(3) The imperative is derived regularly from the *yiqtōl*/imperfect.

קַח   instead of   לְקֹח

(4) In the infinitive construct the ל of the verb stem falls away, and a suffix ת is added. לקח then looks like a typical segholate noun with a guttural as middle consonant (§27.3).

קַחַת   instead of   לְקֹח

(5) לקח also has conjugations in the Puʿal *yiqtōl*/imperfect. However, these forms have been interpreted traditionally as Qal passive *yiqtōl*/imperfect forms, e.g. יֻקַּח.

18.11.5. הלך *(Table 34)*

(1) The *qātal*/perfect paradigm conjugates as expected, e.g. הָלַךְ and הָלַכְתָּ.

(2) With the exception of the Qal *qātal*/perfect הלך conjugates in the Qal and Hiᵖʿîl like a typical I-*wāw* verb.

- The *yiqtōl*/imperfect forms look like I-*wāw* verbs, e.g. יֵלֵךְ as יֵשֵׁב.
- In the imperative the ה of the verb stem falls away, e.g. לֵךְ and לְכִי.
- In the infinitive the ה of the verb stem falls away, and a suffix ת is added, e.g. לֶכֶת. לֶכֶת then has the appearance of a typical segholate noun (§27.3).

§19. Syntax and Semantics of Finite Verbs[17]

§19.1. Introduction

19.1.1. *Statistics*

Explaining the nature of the Biblical Hebrew verbal system has been a challenge to grammarians throughout the ages. The crux of the problem is the relatively wide range of possible interpretations of the *qātal*/perfect (13,874 times), *wəqātal* (6,378 times), *yiqtōl*/imperfect (14,299 times), as well as the *wayyiqtōl* (14,972 times) and *wəyiqtōl* (1,335 times).[18] McFall (1982: 186–87) illustrates this issue by listing how the *qātal*/perfect and *yiqtōl*/imperfect forms are interpreted in the Revised Standard Version.

Qātal	*13,874*	*Yiqtōl*	*14,299*
Past	10,830	Past	774
Present	2,454	Present	3,376
Future	255	Future	5,451
Non-past modal	56	Non-past modal	200
Past modal	115	Past modal	423
Imperative	17	Imperative	2,133
Juss./coh.	38	Juss./coh.	789
Non-verbal form	109	Non-verbal form	153

19.1.2. *Tense or time system*

When a language possesses the *grammatical* means of referring to the time at which the action denoted by the verb took place, that language has a *tense system*. For example, in English there are present, past and future tense verbal forms.

> She *drinks* the coffee.
> She *drank* the coffee.
> She *will drink* the coffee.

The word "drink" conjugates in the *past tense* ("drank") and *present tense* ("drinks"), while the *future tense* makes use of an auxiliary ("will").

---

17. See also §21.
18. These statistics are based on McFall (1982: 186–87). See also Waltke and O'Connor §29.1c.

Such a "tense" system can be very sophisticated;[19] it may have a variety of different forms that refer to different anterior events, as is the case of English, for example:

Simple past	She *drank* the coffee.
Present perfect	She *has drunk* the coffee.
Past perfect	She *had drunk* the coffee (when he arrived).
Future perfect	She *will have drunk* the coffee (when he arrives).

The verb in each of the above sentences indicates an event that is anterior (or, prior) to the moment of speaking. In the case of *She has drunk*, reference is made to an anterior event which still has relevance at the moment of speaking In the case of *She had drunk* the coffee, reference is made to an anterior event that is relevant at a particular point in the past, i.e. when he arrived; this is called the past perfect. In the case of *She will have drunk*, an event anterior to a point of time in the future is referred to; this is called the future perfect.

In contrast to English, other languages may have much simpler systems or more complicated systems. For example, Afrikaans is a simple system – it has no grammatical means of differentiating between the *simple past*, the *present perfect* or the *past perfect*. In other words, the English sentences above will have no direct Afrikaans equivalent in translation. The particular moment in the past to which the Afrikaans sentence refers (literally "she has drunk the coffee") must therefore be determined from the greater context or specified with additional words.

19.1.3. *Aspect system*

Instead of indicating time through a grammatically realized tense, some languages use verbal forms primarily to indicate whether an event is viewed as a whole or not. Languages which have the *grammatical* means of indicating that how an event is viewed are described as having an *aspect system*. Consider the following example. In answer to the question:

What did you do last night?

---

19. Strictly speaking, a system of grammatically indicating time that is relative both to the moment of an utterance (i.e. past, present or future) and to a system of anteriority (i.e. anterior events that are relevant at a particular point) is a blended system. In a blended system, events may be anterior to and relevant in the present (present perfect), past (past perfect) or future (future perfect).

one could answer:

> I finished reading my book; or
> I was reading my book.

The first answer views the action of reading as complete and as a whole; the second answer views the same action as on-going. In Russian one would use the perfective form of the verb "read" instead of the lexeme "finished" to indicate that the action has been completed and viewed as a whole. The imperfective form of the verb would be used to indicate that the action was ongoing (i.e. not viewed as a whole).

19.1.4. *Time and aspect in Biblical Hebrew*

Various opinions exist as to whether Biblical Hebrew has a tense or an aspect system. Medieval Jewish grammarians, like some recent grammarians who adopt their point of view, were of the opinion that the Biblical Hebrew verb system is primarily a tense based system. The *qātal*/perfect form (§15.1) thus refers to *past time* and the *yiqtōl*/imperfect form (§15.2) to the *future* and *present*.[20]

A different interpretation of the *qātal*/perfect and the *yiqtōl*/imperfect forms views these two verbal forms as indicating primarily aspect, rather than moments in time. In the aspectual model, the *qātal*/perfect and *yiqtōl*/imperfect indicate the perfective and imperfective semantic categories respectively. By using the *qātal*/perfect, speakers, on the one hand, describe an action as complete and viewed as a whole from their perspective. By using the *yiqtōl*/imperfect, on the other hand, speakers represent an event that is not viewed as a whole. This explains why Biblical Hebrew speakers can use a *yiqtōl*/imperfect form to refer to a habitual action in the past, e.g.:

> וְכֵן יַעֲשֶׂה שָׁנָה בְשָׁנָה   And this is what *he used to do* year by year (1 Sam. 1:7).*

Notice that a tense based explanation of the *yiqtōl*/imperfect (as future or present tense) has difficulty explaining this verse. The terms perfect(ive) and imperfect(ive), which were intended to refer to the aspectual functions of Biblical Hebrew verbs, became so entrenched that they are still used today

---

20. Joüon–Muraoka §111a uses "for want of better terms, the common and disparate terms *perfect* and *future*, which at least have the advantage of being short and of reflecting the reality in the majority of cases."

by some grammarians to refer to the forms themselves.[21] Terms such as suffix conjugation and prefix conjugation, as well as *qātal* and *yiqtōl*, were therefore introduced with the specific purpose of providing neutral terms for referring to verbal forms.

19.1.5. *Theoretical model*

The following distinctions with regard to the *qātal*/perfect and *yiqtōl*/imperfect will serve as the points of departure in this grammar:

(1) Any semantic functions mentioned here have a bearing only on free-standing *qātal*/perfect and *yiqtōl*/imperfect forms. (For the functions of verb sequences such as *wayyiqtōl* and *wəqātal*, see §21.2 and §21.3.)

(2) The aspectual distinctions with regard to complete and incomplete actions correlate more or less with the above distinction (with some exceptions), namely:

qātal/perfect	= past time	= complete event
yiqtōl/imperfect	= non-past time	= incomplete action

(3) The following distinction is typically made with respect to time (with some clear exceptions):

qātal/perfect	= past time
yiqtōl/imperfect	= non-past time

The conjugations in Biblical Hebrew do not distinguish between different moments in past time (e.g. the ordinary past, the distant past and the perfect) or between the present time, the future and modality. These distinctions, which naturally appear in the translations of a Biblical Hebrew text in tense languages such as English, are exclusively determined by the context and the lexical signification of the verb.

---

21. This was the case with Van der Merwe, Naudé and Kroeze (1999) as well as Köhler and Baumgartner (1988) and many electronic databases. As a semantic category the term "perfect" is ambiguous. It is used as an anterior category, i.e., to refer to an anterior event with current relevance in a present, past or future time frame. However, it is also used as an aspectual category, i.e., to refer to a complete event – a perfective. For a discussion of the semantic value of the notion "perfect" and the necessity to clearly distinguish between the semantic categories "perfect" and "perfective," see Crystal (2008: 356), as well as De Haan (2011: 456–58).

(4) Biblical Hebrew speakers and narrators had a choice with respect to the perspective from which they described an action. This could be done from the perspective of the narrator or the narrator could present the action from the perspective of his characters. In the latter case it is sometimes difficult to translate the *qātal*/perfect with the past tense and the *yiqtōl*/imperfect with the present or future tense (§19.2.1.2.(3) and §19.3.2, respectively).

(5) It is assumed that each verbal conjugation has a semantic potential. The nature of each conjugation's semantic potential can sometimes be explained as a result of the historical development of that conjugation. In recent years, scholars have posited a variety of models as to how these developments could have taken place and why the different "meanings" of each of the conjugations may be regarded as senses which are in a polysemous relationship.[22]

In a reference grammar at an intermediate level, ease of reference has a higher priority than a logical, coherent explanation of the polysemous relationship between the various senses. For this reason, the senses will, whenever possible, be presented in terms of the more prototypical uses. This includes an indication of the typical contexts in which these senses could be expected. The possible polysemous relationship between senses will, whenever possible, be referred to in footnotes.

19.1.6. *Some parameters*

Since the meaning of the Biblical Hebrew verbal forms is different (and often broader) than that of other languages, some guidelines for translation can be proposed. The following heuristic parameters for the identification of specific senses may be useful:

(1) What is the lexical value of the root lexeme? For example, is a telic or atelic event referred to, or is reference made to a state?

(2) Can it be argued that an event is construed by a narrator or speaker as a complete whole or not?

(3) Is the verbal form used in direct discourse or in the narration of a narrator? Or, is it used in a proverb or a psalm?

---

22. This grammar benefitted much from the so-called path theory; see Bybee et al. (1994), as well as Bybee (2010 and 2011). Andersen (2000) and Cook (2002) were the first scholars who viewed the Biblical Hebrew verbal system from the perspective of the path theory. Cook (2012) represents a substantial revision of Cook (2002). We are also indebted to a range of studies conducted by Andrason (2010, 2011a, 2011b, 2011c, 2011d, 2012a, 2012b, 2012c, 2013) and Andrason and Van der Merwe (2015).

(4) Does the utterance have a modal tone, e.g. does it express a wish or condition (often with a particle), is it a directive, or is it a statement made (see §11.1.3)?

(5) Is it possible to establish the relationship in time between the event referred to by the conjugation and an event referred to in a previous clause and/or a subsequent clause?

(6) In the light of (5), what is the time frame of the broader speech event in which the verbal form is used? Is it past, present or future? Or is the point in time irrelevant, e.g. in a timeless saying.

(7) Are there any temporal adjuncts or quantifiers in the clause that have implications for the interpretation of the semantic value of the conjugation, e.g. "We ate the manna *within an hour*" (complete action) and "We ate all the manna" (telic) vs. "We ate manna *for forty years*" (atelic, habitual).

§19.2. *Qātal*/Perfect (Suffix Conjugation)

19.2.1. *Anterior events*

The *qātal*/perfect typically refers to an event x that happened prior to (i.e. before) another event or situation y.

19.2.1.1. *Past perfective*

Referring to a *situation in the past as a whole* is one of the prototypical uses of *qātal*/perfect.

This use of *qātal*/perfect is frequently attested in clauses with a fronted constituent (#*a*) or a negative particle (#*b*). In narration, it often acts as a counterpart to a *wayyiqtōl* (#*a-b*).

a	וַיִּקְרָא אֱלֹהִים ׀ לָאוֹר יוֹם וְלַחֹשֶׁךְ קָרָא לָיְלָה	And God called the light "Day," and the darkness *he called* "Night" (Gen. 1:5).*
b	וַיֶּחֱזַק לֵב פַּרְעֹה וְלֹא שָׁמַע אֲלֵהֶם	And Pharaoh's heart was hard, and *he did* not *listen* to them (Exod. 7:13).*

19.2.1.2. *Perfect*

The *qātal*/perfect often refers to events that happened *prior to a point y*, and the effects of what happened are *still relevant at point y*.

(1) In direct discourse, the point y is often *the moment of speaking* (#a-b). In English, this use of the *qātal*/perfect is translated as a present perfect, i.e. "has/have …" (#a-b).

a	וַיִּשְׁלַ֣ח פַּרְעֹ֗ה וַיִּקְרָא֙ לְמֹשֶׁ֣ה וּֽלְאַהֲרֹ֔ן וַיֹּ֥אמֶר אֲלֵהֶ֖ם חָטָ֣אתִי הַפָּ֑עַם יְהוָה֙ הַצַּדִּ֔יק וַאֲנִ֥י וְעַמִּ֖י הָרְשָׁעִֽים	Then Pharaoh summoned Moses and Aaron, and said to them, "This time *I have sinned*; the LORD is in the right [lit. the righteous one], and I and my people are in the wrong [lit. the wrong ones]" (Exod. 9:27).*
b	וַיֹּ֤אמֶר אֲלֵהֶם֙ יִצְחָ֔ק מַדּ֖וּעַ בָּאתֶ֣ם אֵלָ֑י וְאַתֶּם֙ שְׂנֵאתֶ֣ם אֹתִ֔י וַתְּשַׁלְּח֖וּנִי מֵאִתְּכֶֽם׃	And Isaac said to them, "Why *have you come* to me, seeing that you hate me and have sent me away from you?" (Gen. 26:27).*

(2) In narrative, the point y is often *events in the past* (past perfect). This use of *qātal*/perfect is very frequent with clauses introduced by כִּי (#a) or אֲשֶׁר (#b) In English this use of *qātal*/perfect is translated as a past perfect. i.e. "had …" In some languages it is grammaticalized as a pluperfect.

a	וְלֹא־יָדַ֣ע יַעֲקֹ֔ב כִּ֥י רָחֵ֖ל גְּנָבָֽתַם	Now Jacob did not know that Rachel *had stolen* them (the gods) (Gen. 31:32).*
b	וַיִּבֶן֩ יְהוָ֨ה אֱלֹהִ֧ים ׀ אֶת־הַצֵּלָ֛ע אֲשֶׁר־לָקַ֥ח מִן־הָֽאָדָ֖ם לְאִשָּׁ֑ה	And the LORD God fashioned the rib which *he had taken* from the man into a woman (Gen. 2:22).*

(3) In a few rare instances, the point y may be in a *future time frame* (future perfect). The *qātal*/perfect that is governed by עַד (#a), עַד אִם (#b) and עַד אֲשֶׁר אִם (#c) refers to situations that are prior to other events.

a	לֹ֣א אֹכַ֔ל עַ֖ד אִם־דִּבַּ֣רְתִּי דְּבָרָ֑י	I will not eat until *I have told* my errand (Gen. 24:33).

b	וַתֹּאמֶר גַּם לִגְמַלֶּיךָ אֶשְׁאָב עַד אִם־כִּלּוּ לִשְׁתֹּת	She said, "I will draw for your camels also, until *they have finished* drinking" (Gen. 24:19).
c	לֹא אֶעֱזָבְךָ עַד אֲשֶׁר אִם־עָשִׂיתִי אֵת אֲשֶׁר־דִּבַּרְתִּי לָךְ:	I will not leave you until *I have done* what I have promised you (Gen. 28:15).

19.2.1.3. *Anterior events in conditional sentences*

In these cases no reference is made to actual past events. From the perspective of the characters or the hypothetical world, anterior events are involved.

Qātal may be used in the protases of conditions with the particles אִם and in some cases כִּי. In these cases, the *qātal*/perfect form refers to real and possible conditions that logically and/or temporally precede the event described in the apodosis (#*a*). In a few rare cases, *qātal*/perfect is used in both the protasis and apodoses of unreal (hypothetical) conditions with לוּ (#*b*). In a few rare instances, the apodosis is elided. This leads to the expression of an unrealizable wish (#*c*).

a	אִם־נָא מָצָאתִי חֵן בְּעֵינֶיךָ אַל־נָא תַעֲבֹר מֵעַל עַבְדֶּךָ	If *I have found* favor in your eyes do not pass by your servant (Gen. 18:3).*
b	לוּ חָפֵץ יְהוָה לַהֲמִיתֵנוּ לֹא־לָקַח מִיָּדֵנוּ עֹלָה וּמִנְחָה	If the LORD *had meant* to kill us, *he would not have accepted* a burnt offering and a grain offering from our hands (Judg. 13:23).*
c	לוּ־מַתְנוּ בְּאֶרֶץ מִצְרַיִם אוֹ בַּמִּדְבָּר הַזֶּה לוּ־מָתְנוּ	If only we *had died* in the land of Egypt or if only *we had died* in this wilderness (Num. 14:2).*

19.2.2. *States of affairs*

A state of affairs or a condition is often expressed through a morphologically stative verb. A stative verb cannot express a "once-off," complete action. It always carries a certain element of duration, which may be either a condition or the result of an activity The time frame is determined by the context. In direct speech a stative verb in the *qātal*/perfect often indicates a condition at the moment of speaking (#a-b). In narration, a condition in the past may be referred to (#c). In a few rare cases, *qātal*/perfect can be used to describe a future condition (#d). A stative verb in *qātal*/perfect may also indicate an event that is the result of an activity (#e).

a	וַיֹּאמֶר הִנֵּה־נָא זָקַנְתִּי לֹא יָדַעְתִּי יוֹם מוֹתִי	And he said, "Look, *I am old*; *I do* not *know* the day of my death" (Gen. 27:2).*
b	וְאֶעֱשֶׂה אֹתָם מַטְעַמִּים לְאָבִיךָ כַּאֲשֶׁר אָהֵב	so that I may prepare from them savory food for your father, such as *he likes* (Gen. 27:9).
c	וַתַּעַשׂ אִמּוֹ מַטְעַמִּים כַּאֲשֶׁר אָהֵב אָבִיו	And his mother prepared savory food, such as his father *loved* (Gen. 27:14).
d	כִּי־מָלְאָה הָאָרֶץ דֵּעָה אֶת־יְהוָה	For the earth *will be full* of the knowledge of the LORD (Isa. 11:9).
e	כָּבְדָה מְאֹד יַד הָאֱלֹהִים שָׁם	The hand of God *was* (i.e. *it became*) very *heavy* there (1 Sam. 5:11).

19.2.3. *Performative actions*

A performative action refers to an action that is "performed" by virtue of uttering a speech. In Biblical Hebrew performative events are represented with a *qātal*/perfect verb (#a). Lexemes that are not verbs of speech may also be used as performatives (#b-c).

a	הִגַּדְתִּי הַיּוֹם לַיהוָה אֱלֹהֶיךָ כִּי־בָאתִי אֶל־הָאָרֶץ	*I hereby declare* today to the LORD your God that I have come into the land (Deut. 26:3).*
b	לֹא־אֲדֹנִי שְׁמָעֵנִי הַשָּׂדֶה נָתַתִּי לָךְ וְהַמְּעָרָה אֲשֶׁר־בּוֹ לְךָ נְתַתִּיהָ	No, my lord, hear me; the field *I hereby give* you, and the cave that is in it, to you *I give* it (Gen. 23:11).*
c	הִנֵּה שָׁלַחְתִּי לְךָ שֹׁחַד כֶּסֶף וְזָהָב	Look, *I am hereby sending* you a present of silver and gold (1 Kgs 15:19).*

19.2.4. *Events that are not time-bound*

Habitual actions are typically referred to by means of the *yiqtōl*/imperfect or participle. However, *qātal*/perfect is sometimes used to refer to an event that is not time-bound – these are also called gnomic events (#*a-b*).[23]

a	גְּמָלַתְהוּ טוֹב וְלֹא־רָע כֹּל יְמֵי חַיֶּיהָ	*She does* him good, and not harm, all the days of her life (Prov. 31:12).
b	בִּקֶּשׁ־לֵץ חָכְמָה וָאָיִן וְדַעַת לְנָבוֹן נָקָל	A scoffer *seeks* wisdom in vain, but knowledge is easy for the one who understands (Prov. 14:6).

19.2.5. *Rare and controversial uses*

19.2.5.1. *Prophetic qātal/perfect*

Future events are represented as if they have already happened or are immanent.

לָכֵן גָּלָה עַמִּי מִבְּלִי־דָעַת	Therefore my people *go* (or, *will go*) into exile without knowledge (Isa. 5:13).*

19.2.5.2. *Precative*

Even though there are only a few rare instances, many scholars argue that the *qātal*/perfect may express a realizable wish – the so-called precative mood. However, in most of these instances it is also possible to postulate that one of the more typical senses of the *qātal*/perfect (e.g. present perfect) is involved. Compare the renderings of Ps. 31:6 by the NIV and NRSV.

בְּיָדְךָ אַפְקִיד רוּחִי פָּדִיתָה אוֹתִי יְהוָֹה אֵל אֱמֶת	(NIV) Into your hands I commit my spirit; *deliver* me, LORD, my faithful God. (NRSV) Into your hand I commit my spirit; *you have redeemed* me, O LORD, faithful God.

---

23. The gnomic use of the *qātal*/perfect most probably developed, among other things, from its present perfect sense. In other words, an uninterrupted activity that began in the past and continued to the present became a fact about somebody (Andrason 2013).

§19.3. *Long Yiqtōl (Prefix Conjugation Long Forms)*

The long *yiqtōl*/imperfect form is used predominantly in direct discourse.

19.3.1. *Future events or expectations*

The most typical use of the *yiqtōl*/imperfect in direct discourse is to refer to events or expectations in the *future*.

וַיֹּאמֶר יְהוָה אֶל־מֹשֶׁה עַתָּה תִרְאֶה אֲשֶׁר אֶעֱשֶׂה לְפַרְעֹה כִּי בְיָד חֲזָקָה יְשַׁלְּחֵם וּבְיָד חֲזָקָה יְגָרְשֵׁם מֵאַרְצוֹ:	And the LORD said to Moses, "Now *you will see* what I will do to Pharaoh, because with a strong hand *he will release* them, and with a strong hand *he will drive* them out from his land" (Exod. 6:1).*

19.3.2. *Past events*

The *yiqtōl*/imperfect refers in specific contexts to past events (seldom).

(1) In dependent clauses (e.g. with אֲשֶׁר or כִּי), the *yiqtōl*/imperfect refers to a future event from a past perspective.

וֶאֱלִישָׁע חָלָה אֶת־חָלְיוֹ אֲשֶׁר יָמוּת בּוֹ...	And when Elisha had fallen sick with the illness of which *he was to die*... (2 Kgs 13:14).*

(2) When following (בְּ)טֶרֶם (#*a*) or עַד (#*b*), the *yiqtōl*/imperfect refers to events posterior to a main action in a past temporal context.

a	וּלְיוֹסֵף יֻלַּד שְׁנֵי בָנִים בְּטֶרֶם תָּבוֹא שְׁנַת הָרָעָב	To Joseph two sons were born before the year of the famine *came* (Gen. 41:50).*
b	יֹּדֹם הַשֶּׁמֶשׁ וְיָרֵחַ עָמָד עַד־יִקֹּם גּוֹי אֹיְבָיו	The sun stood still, and the moon stopped, till the nation *avenged* itself on its enemies (Josh. 10:13).*

(3) In a few rare cases, following אָז,[24] a *yiqtōl*/imperfect refers to simple past events.

אָז יַעֲלֶה חֲזָאֵל מֶלֶךְ אֲרָם At that time Hazael, king of Aram, *went up* (2 Kgs 12:18).*

19.3.3. *Habitual actions*

A frequentative habitual action is often referred to by means of a *yiqtōl*/imperfect. This happens typically in narrative in a past tense time frame (#*a*). A habit that prevailed at the time of the narrator's statement (i.e. present time frame) may also be involved (#*b*).

a   <div dir="rtl">כָּכָה יַעֲשֶׂה אִיּוֹב כָּל־הַיָּמִים:</div> This is what Job *always did* (Job 1:5).

b   <div dir="rtl">עַל־כֵּן לֹא־יֹאכְלוּ בְנֵי־יִשְׂרָאֵל
אֶת־גִּיד הַנָּשֶׁה אֲשֶׁר עַל־כַּף
הַיָּרֵךְ עַד הַיּוֹם הַזֶּה</div> Therefore the Israelites *do not eat* the thigh muscle that is on the hip socket until today [lit. unto this day] (Gen. 32:33).*

19.3.4. *Progressive continuous events*

The *yiqtōl*/imperfect refers in discourse sometimes to a progressive continuous action, in both present (#*a*) and past tense time frames (#*b*).

a   <div dir="rtl">וַיִּמְצָאֵהוּ אִישׁ וְהִנֵּה תֹעֶה
בַשָּׂדֶה וַיִּשְׁאָלֵהוּ הָאִישׁ
לֵאמֹר מַה־תְּבַקֵּשׁ</div> And a man found him and look! He *was wandering* in the fields! The man asked him, "What *are you seeking*?" (Gen. 37:15).*

b   <div dir="rtl">וַיֹּאמֶר לָהֶם בָּרוּךְ מִפִּיו
יִקְרָא אֵלַי אֵת כָּל־הַדְּבָרִים
הָאֵלֶּה וַאֲנִי כֹּתֵב עַל־הַסֵּפֶר
בַּדְּיוֹ:</div> And Baruch answered them, "He *was dictating* all these words to me [lit. from his mouth he read to me all these words], and I was writing them with ink on the scroll" (Jer. 36:18).*

---

24. Although אָז is typically followed by a *yiqtōl*/imperfect, there are some instances where אָז is followed by a *qātal*/perfect, e.g. Judg. 8.3 (§40.6.(1)).

19.3.5. *Modal uses*

Biblical Hebrew does not have modal auxiliary verbs such as *can/could*, *shall*, *would*, *will*, *may*, etc. The root of the concept "modality" lies in the distinction made between the form of the indicative, subjunctive and optative "moods" of Greek and Latin verbs. Each one of these modalities refers to a certain subjective judgment regarding the actuality of an event. The indicative refers to a certain reality (factual event) and is regarded as the unmarked form, for example, "Peter sings well." The subjunctive and optative, by contrast, refer to non-real events. An event is non-real if a speaker is not certain about the actuality of the events referred to, for example, "Peter should (be able to) sing well." A speaker is sometimes uncertain about the relationship between a subject and its predicate, for example, the sentence "Peter may sing now" indicates that the speaker does not know whether Peter is actually going to sing. For this reason all directive actions, i.e. commands, instructions, orders, etc., are also classified as expressions of modality (§11.1.3).

The *yiqtōl/imperfect* can be used to indicate one of the modalities listed below.

19.3.5.1. *Directives*

A directive is a speech act by which speakers want to make their listeners do something. Typically, a speaker wants his/her hearer to conform to his/her wish.[25] This may be in the form of a request (#*a*), a prohibition (#*b-c*), an indirect command in the third person (jussive) (#*d*) or first person (cohortative) (#*e*).

In Biblical Hebrew the *yiqtōl/imperfect* is used with לֹא (#*b-c*) to express an (absolute) prohibition ("you *must* not…"). By contrast, אַל is typically used with the jussive to express the nuance of a temporally binding prohibition ("you *should* not…") (§19.5.1.3).

a	תְּחַטְּאֵנִי בְאֵזוֹב וְאֶטְהָר תְּכַבְּסֵנִי וּמִשֶּׁלֶג אַלְבִּין:	*Purify* me with hyssop, and I shall be clean. *Wash* me, and I shall be whiter than snow (Ps. 51:9).*
b	וַיֹּאמֶר לֹא תִשְׁלָחוּ:	And he said, "*Do not send* (them)" (2 Kgs 2:16).*

---

25. Waltke and O'Connor §31 classify instances "where the action of the subject is contingent on the will of the speaker" as "volitional uses."

c   לֹא תִּרְצָח   *You shall not murder* (Exod. 20:13).

d   וַיֹּאמֶר אֱלֹהִים יִקָּווּ הַמַּיִם   And God said, "*Let* the waters מִתַּחַת הַשָּׁמַיִם אֶל־מָקוֹם under the sky *be gathered* together אֶחָד וְתֵרָאֶה הַיַּבָּשָׁה into one place, and *let* the dry land *appear*" (Gen. 1:9).

e   לְכָה דוֹדִי נֵצֵא הַשָּׂדֶה   Come, my beloved, let us go out to נָלִינָה בַּכְּפָרִים: the fields; *let us spend the night* in the villages (Song 7:12).*

19.3.5.2. *Desirability of events*

The event referred to may have the character of an obligation (*#a*) or permission (*#b*).

a   וְהוֹרֵיתִי אֶתְכֶם אֵת אֲשֶׁר   And I will teach you what *you* תַּעֲשׂוּן: *should do* (Exod. 4:15).*

b   וַיְצַו יְהוָה אֱלֹהִים עַל־הָאָדָם   And the LORD God commanded the לֵאמֹר מִכֹּל עֵץ־הַגָּן אָכֹל man, "*You may* freely *eat* of every תֹּאכֵל: tree of the garden" (Gen. 2:16).

19.3.5.3. *Possibility of events*

This use of the *yiqtōl*/imperfect is typically associated with particles that prompt the sense of possibility. The particle אוּלַי (*#a*) is typical. In real conditions with the particles אִם (*#b*) and כִּי (*#c*) in the protasis, *yiqtōl*/imperfect connotes the idea of probability and contingency. In a few rare cases, the *yiqtōl*/imperfect may be found with the hypothetical unreal conjunction לוּ (*#d*) When the apodosis is missing, a wish is expressed (*#e*).

a   אוּלַי יִתְעַשֵּׁת הָאֱלֹהִים לָנוּ   Perhaps your god [lit. the god] *will* וְלֹא נֹאבֵד *spare* us a thought so that we do not perish (Jonah 1:6).*

b   לֹא אַשְׁחִית אִם־אֶמְצָא שָׁם   I will not destroy it if *I find* forty-five אַרְבָּעִים וַחֲמִשָּׁה there (Gen. 18:28).

c   כִּי¹ יְבִיאֲךָ יְהוָה אֱלֹהֶיךָ   ¹*When* the LORD your God *brings* אֶל־הָאָרֶץ...²וְהִכִּיתָם הַחֲרֵם you into the land...²and you defeat תַּחֲרִים אֹתָם them, then you must utterly destroy them (Deut. 7:1–2).

d   וַיִּרְאוּ אֲחֵי־יוֹסֵף כִּי־מֵת   When the brothers of Joseph
אֲבִיהֶם וַיֹּאמְרוּ לוּ יִשְׂטְמֵנוּ realized that their father was
יוֹסֵף וְהָשֵׁב יָשִׁיב לָנוּ אֵת dead, they said, "*If* Joseph *would*
כָּל־הָרָעָה אֲשֶׁר גָּמַלְנוּ *(still) bear a grudge* against us,
אֹתוֹ: he will certainly repay us all the
harm which we did to him" (Gen.
50:15).*

e   וַיֹּאמֶר אַבְרָהָם אֶל־הָאֱלֹהִים And Abraham said to God, "If only
לוּ יִשְׁמָעֵאל יִחְיֶה לְפָנֶיךָ Ishmael *might live* in your sight!"
(Gen. 17:18).*

Also conveying the notion of contingency are instances where the particles
לְמַעַן (#*f*), בַּעֲבוּר (#*g*) and פֶּן (#*h*) are used to mark the possible purpose of what
is said in a matrix clause.

f   כַּבֵּד אֶת־אָבִיךָ וְאֶת־אִמֶּךָ Honor your father and your mother
לְמַעַן יַאֲרִכוּן יָמֶיךָ עַל הָאֲדָמָה so that your days *may be long* on
אֲשֶׁר־יְהוָה אֱלֹהֶיךָ נֹתֵן לָךְ: the land which the LORD your God
is giving you (Exod. 20:12).*

g   וַיֹּאמֶר יְהוָה אֶל־מֹשֶׁה הִנֵּה Then the LORD said to Moses,
אָנֹכִי בָּא אֵלֶיךָ בְּעַב הֶעָנָן "Look, I am going to come to you
בַּעֲבוּר יִשְׁמַע הָעָם בְּדַבְּרִי in a dense cloud, so that the people
עִמָּךְ *may hear* when I speak with you"
(Exod. 19:9).*

h   וְאָנֹכִי לֹא אוּכַל לְהִמָּלֵט הָהָרָה But I cannot flee to the mountains,
פֶּן־תִּדְבָּקַנִי הָרָעָה וָמַתִּי lest the disaster *overtakes* me and
I die (Gen. 19:19).*

19.3.5.4. *Capability of subjects to perform actions*

אֵיכָה אֶשָּׂא לְבַדִּי טָרְחֲכֶם How *can I bear* all by myself your
וּמַשַּׂאֲכֶם וְרִיבְכֶם: troubles, burdens and disputes?
(Deut. 1:12).*

19.3.6. *Problem cases*

There are a number of instances, especially in the poetic sections, where a *yiqtōl* is used where one would have expected a *qātal*/perfect. These instances are probably remnants of the non-jussive short *yiqtōl*, a form that is also to be found in *wayyiqtōl*.

וַיַּרְעֵם בַּשָּׁמַיִם ׀ יְהוָה וְעֶלְיוֹן יִתֵּן קֹלוֹ	And the Lᴏʀᴅ thundered in the heavens, and the Most High *uttered* his *voice* (Ps. 18:14).*
צָרָה וְיָגוֹן אֶמְצָא:	*I encountered* distress and anguish (Ps. 116:3).*

§19.4. Short *Yiqtōl* (Prefix Conjugation Short Form)

The short *yiqtōl* has traditionally been described as the "jussive" form (§15.5 and §19.5.1.3).

The epithet "short," qualifying the *yiqtōl*, differentiates it from a morphologically similar construction, known as "*yiqtōl*" or "long *yiqtōl*" (§19.3). It is not always possible to distinguish morphologically between long and short *yiqtōl* forms. This can be done only with the Hip̄ʿil and some weak verbs, e.g. the III-*hē*ʾ (see §18.5.4).

The short *yiqtōl* occurs predominantly in the third person in positive or negative clauses and in the second person in negative clauses. The negative used with the short *yiqtōl* is predominantly אַל; this construction is the usual way to express a negative command (the imperative form cannot be negated; see §19.5.2.1).

Short *yiqtōl* forms typically have a directive function (§19.5.1.3). In poetic sections, short *yiqtōl*s are sometimes used in non-jussive contexts (§19.3.6).[26]

---

26. Short *yiqtōl* forms have non-jussive meanings in a few rare cases, both in the third person and the second person, e.g. Pss. 25:9; 47:4; 90:3; 104:20; 107:29; Isa. 12:1 and Joel 2:2. Waltke and O'Connor §34.2.1c wisely remark in this regard: "These unexpected jussive forms may be due to the confusion between the form groups or to textual corruptions; or they may represent vestiges of an earlier verbal system. Some grammarians explain them on rhythmical grounds. Because of this minor formal confounding, it is best in problem passages of this nature to be governed by sense rather than by forms."

§19.5. Directive Forms and Functions

A directive is an utterance whose purpose is to get somebody to do something (Crystal 2008: 147; see also §11.1.3.3). In Biblical Hebrew, the following kinds of directives are morphologically distinguished: imperatives, cohortatives, and jussives (short *yiqtōl*). The imperatives are directives to the second person, cohortatives are directives to the first person and jussives are directives to the second or third person.

19.5.1. *Directive forms*

19.5.1.1. *Imperative*

Imperative forms are attested 4,261 times in the Hebrew Bible. The following types of directives may be expressed by an imperative. Only context can help one decide on the type of directive involved in each case.

(1) Commands
    More than 50% of all imperatives in the Hebrew Bible are commands or instructions by God (#*a*) or people (#*b*) who have some kind of authority over the addressees (Jenni 2005b: 252).

a	כַּבֵּד אֶת־אָבִיךָ וְאֶת־אִמֶּךָ	*Honor* your father and your mother (Exod. 20:12).
b	וַיֹּאמֶר אֲלֵהֶם לְכוּ דִרְשׁוּ בְּבַעַל זְבוּב אֱלֹהֵי עֶקְרוֹן	And he (the king) said to them, "*Go consult* Baal-Zebub, the god of Ekron" (2 Kgs 1:2).*

(2) Appeals and requests

a	וַיֹּאמֶר אֲבִימֶלֶךְ אֶל־יִצְחָק לֵךְ מֵעִמָּנוּ כִּי־עָצַמְתָּ־מִמֶּנּוּ מְאֹד:	And Abimelech said to Isaac, "*Move away* from us, for you have become too powerful for us" (Gen. 26:16).*
b	חָנֵּנִי וּשְׁמַע תְּפִלָּתִי	*Be merciful* to me and *hear* my prayer (Ps. 4:2).*

(3) Imperatives of preparation
    Some frequently occurring lexemes lose their typical semantic values when they are used within the context of other main imperatives which they introduce.

(a) רֵאֵה[27]

The imperative of רֵאֵה may be used in appeals to addressees to intellectually apprehend a situation or event. In most cases, the speaker intends this command as an encouragement to the addressee and/or as the ground of a directive to the addressee.

רְאֵה נָתַתִּי לִפְנֵיכֶם	*See,* I have set the land before you;
אֶת־הָאָרֶץ בֹּאוּ וּרְשׁוּ	go in and take possession of the
אֶת־הָאָרֶץ אֲשֶׁר נִשְׁבַּע	land that I swore to your ancestors
יְהוָה לַאֲבֹתֵיכֶם	(Deut. 1:8).

(b) Verbs of movement

When they precede another directive, the imperatives of the following verbs of movement, קוּם (#a), הלך (#b), בוא (#c) and יהב (#d), have become desemantisized and have acquired a preparatory sense.

a	קוּם קַח אֶת־אִשְׁתְּךָ וְאֶת־שְׁתֵּי בְנֹתֶיךָ	*Get going* [lit. *arise*]! Take your wife and your two daughters (Gen. 19:15).*
b	לְכוּ וְנֵלְכָה עַד־הָרֹאֶה	*Come* [lit. *go*], and let us go to the seer (1 Sam. 9:9).
c	בֹּאוּ וְנָבוֹא יְרוּשָׁלַםִ	*Come,* and let us go to Jerusalem (Jer. 35:11).
d	הָבָה | נִבְנֶה־לָּנוּ עִיר	*Come,* let us build for ourselves a city (Gen. 11:4).

19.5.1.2. *Cohortative*

The Biblical Hebrew cohortative form is associated with an affix ־ָה that is suffixed to a first person singular or plural short *yiqtōl* (§19.4). The cohortative form is attested 527 times in the Hebrew Bible. Of these, 352 are first person singular, while 175 are first person plural.

---

27. The Qal imperative form of the root רֵאֵה appears 143 times in the Hebrew Bible. Of these 143 instances, in only 36 instances is רֵאֵה used as a type of pointing device. When used like this, רֵאֵה is almost synonymous to הֵן and הִנֵּה (see §40.21 and §40.22). The interpretations proposed for רֵאֵה are argued for in more detail in Van der Merwe (2011a).

In addition, 88 pseudo-cohortatives are attested. They are *wayyiqtōl* forms with the הָ suffix and occur primarily in Daniel, Ezra and Nehemiah. No special semantic value of this construction, beyond that of a *wayyiqtōl*, has yet been identified (Jenni 2005a: 176–77).

The cohortative form typically expresses a directive in the first person.

(1) Directive (frequent)

   (a) Proposals

   וְעַתָּה לְכָה נִכְרְתָה בְרִית | So now, come *let us make* [lit.
   אֲנִי וָאַתָּה | *let us cut*] a covenant, you and I (Gen. 31:44).*

   (b) Requests

   וְעַתָּה נֵלֲכָה־נָּא דֶּרֶךְ שְׁלֹשֶׁת | So now, please *let us make* [lit. *let
   יָמִים בַּמִּדְבָּר | us go*] a three-days' journey into the wilderness (Exod. 3:18).*

(2) Declarations of intent

   In poetry (predominantly the Psalms), a specialized use of the cohortative can be distinguished. In a typical cultic setting, removed from normal dialogue, the cohortative is used as a self-encouragement to praise God.

   אוֹדֶה יְהוָה בְּכָל־לִבִּי אֲסַפְּרָה | *I will give* thanks to the LORD with
   כָּל־נִפְלְאוֹתֶיךָ: | my whole heart; *I will tell* of all your wonderful deeds (Ps. 9:2).

(3) Expression of wishes (rare)

   וְאָמַרְתָּ אֹכְלָה בָשָׂר | And you will say: "*I want to eat* meat" (Deut. 12:20).*

19.5.1.3. *Jussive*

The jussive (short *yiqtōl*, see §19.4) is typically an indirect command in the third (and sometimes the second) person. The jussive form in the second person is often used to express a negative directive. The negative used with the jussive is אַל.

The following types of directives can be expressed by the jussive form. Only context can give an indication as to which type of directive is involved in each case.

(1) Directives

    (a) Commands

        a   וַיֹּאמֶר אֱלֹהִים תּוֹצֵא   And God said, "*Let* the earth *bring*
              הָאָרֶץ נֶפֶשׁ חַיָּה לְמִינָהּ   *forth* living creatures of every
                                 kind" (Gen. 1:24).

        b   אַל־תֹּאכַל לֶחֶם   *Do not eat* bread and *do not drink*
                  וְאַל־תֵּשְׁתְּ מָיִם   water (1 Kgs 13:22).*

    (b) Requests

        a   יָשָׁב־נָא עַבְדְּךָ וְאָמֻת   Please *let* your servant *return* so
                          בְּעִירִי   that I can die in my own town
                                   (2 Sam. 19:37).*

        b   וָאֶתְפַּלֵּל אֶל־יְהוָה וָאֹמַר   And I prayed to the L<small>ORD</small> and
            אֲדֹנָי יְהוִֹה אַל־תַּשְׁחֵת עַמְּךָ   said, "Lord God, *do not destroy*
                          וְנַחֲלָתְךָ   the people who are your very own
                                   possession" (Deut. 9:26).*

    (c) Proposals

        a   וַיָּשֻׁבוּ אֶל־יְהוֹשֻׁעַ וַיֹּאמְרוּ   And they returned to Joshua and
             אֵלָיו אַל־יַעַל כָּל־הָעָם   said to him, "*Do not let* the whole
                                   army *go up*" (Josh. 7:3).*

        b   יֵלֶךְ־נָא הַמֶּלֶךְ וַעֲבָדָיו   *Let* the king and his servants
                       עִם־עַבְדֶּךָ:   please *go* with your servant
                                   (2 Sam. 13:24).*

(2) Expression of wishes

                       יְחִי הַמֶּלֶךְ:   *Long live* the king! (1 Sam. 10:24).

19.5.2. *Modifying directives*

19.5.2.1. *Negation of directives*

In many languages the grammatical forms of positive and negative directives are not the same. In Biblical Hebrew, second person positive commands are expressed by means of imperative forms. Negative commands are expressed by אַל + second person short *yiqtōl* (jussive form) or לֹא + long *yiqtōl* (imperfect form) (§19.3.5.1). The former construction typically involves urgent, here-and-now commands (#*a*) and the latter, timeless prohibitions (#*b*). When a third person jussive (#c)[28] or a first person cohortative is negated (#d), אַל is typically used.[29]

a	אַל־תֹּאכַל לֶחֶם וְאַל־תֵּשְׁתְּ מָיִם	*Do not eat* bread and *do not drink* water (1 Kgs 13:22).*
b	לֹא תִּגְנֹב:	*You shall not steal* (Exod. 20:15).
c	אִישׁ אַל־יֵרָא בְּכָל־הָהָר	Nobody *should be seen* on the whole mountain (Exod. 34:3).*
d	וְאַל־נַקְשִׁיבָה אֶל־כָּל־דְּבָרָיו:	and *let us not heed* any of his words (Jer. 18:18).

19.5.2.2. *Directive forms and the particle* נָא

The particle נָא occurs about 400 times in the Hebrew Bible. It can be added to any of the directive forms, i.e., the imperative (#a), jussive (#b) and cohortative (#c). In negative requests, נָא typically follows אַל (#d). In courteous requests that are connected to a condition, נָא may be placed directly after the particle אִם in the protasis of the condition. The נָא may also be placed after a הִנֵּה which points an addressee to a state of affairs which is the grounds for an ensuing polite request (#f and #a).

It appears that the particle נָא is used, *inter alia*, to express a polite request (#a-b, d). In some cases, such a nuance is hard to postulate (#c, #f).

a	אִמְרִי־נָא אֲחֹתִי אָתְּ	*Please say* you are my sister (Gen. 12:13).*
b	יֵלֶךְ־נָא אֲדֹנָי בְּקִרְבֵּנוּ	*Let* the Lord *please go* in our midst (Exod. 34:9).*
c	אַגִּידָה־נָּא לָכֶם אֵת אֲשֶׁר־עָשׂוּ לָנוּ אֲרָם	*Let me tell* you what the Arameans have prepared against us (2 Kgs 7:12).*
d	אַל־נָא תִקְבְּרֵנִי בְּמִצְרָיִם:	*Please do not bury* me in Egypt (Gen. 47:29).*
e	אִם־נָא מָצָאתִי חֵן בְּעֵינֶיךָ וְעָשִׂיתָ לִּי אוֹת	If now I have found favor in your eyes, then *please show* me a sign (Judg. 6:17).*
f	הִנֵּה־נָא יָדַעְתִּי כִּי אִשָּׁה יְפַת־מַרְאֶה אָתְּ	Look, I do know that you are a good-looking woman (Gen. 12:11).*

---

28. For a few rare exceptions, see Waltke and O'Connor §34.2.1d.
29. Contrast Gen. 37:21 with לֹא negating the cohortative.

19.5.2.3. *Imperatives with* הָ◌

In all stem formations an הָ◌ suffix may be added to the first person singular and plural *yiqtōl*/imperfect (#*a*) as well as the imperative masculine singular (#*b*). The resultant directive forms are known as cohortatives (#*a*, see also §19.5.1.2) and "emphatic" (or "long") imperatives (#*b*), respectively.[30] The exact function of the latter form is not clear.[31]

a	וְנִשְׁלְחָה וְנִרְאֶה:	And *let us send* and see (2 Kgs 7:13).*
b	מִכְרָה כַיּוֹם אֶת־בְּכֹרָתְךָ לִי:	First [lit. as today] *sell* me your birthright (Gen. 25:31).

§20. Syntax and Semantics of Non-finite Verb Forms

Finite verbal forms (§11.1.7) are marked for person, gender, and number. Non-finite verbal forms lack one or more of these markers: participles are not marked for person; infinitives are not marked for gender or number.

§20.1. Infinitive Construct

20.1.1. *Introduction*

The infinitive construct expresses an action without referring to person, gender, number, or tense/aspect. For this reason, the infinitive is not usually used independently as the main verb of a clause. An infinitive almost always occurs in relation to another verb.

A characteristic of infinitive construct forms is that in some respects they act syntactically like nouns:

(1) They are similar to nouns in that they may be governed by prepositions, e.g.:

וַיְהִי כְמָלְכוֹ הִכָּה אֶת־כָּל־בֵּית יָרָבְעָם	And *as soon as he (Baasha) was king*, he killed all the house of Jeroboam (1 Kgs 15:29).*

They also take pronominal suffixes (§17.5).

---

30. The combination of a directive ending in הָ◌- followed by נָא is also attested. Of the 301 imperatives with הָ◌-, 26 are followed by נָא.
31. See Fassberg (1999) for a possible explanation.

(2) The infinitive construct forms differ from nouns in that they are not morphologically marked for *gender or number*. They may express actions and states (as finite verbs do).

(3) In Biblical Hebrew the infinitive construct, unlike a finite verb, is not *negated* by לֹא or אַל but by בְּלִי, בִּלְתִּי, or לְבִלְתִּי.

הֲמִן־הָעֵץ אֲשֶׁר צִוִּיתִיךָ לְבִלְתִּי אֲכָל־מִמֶּנּוּ אָכָלְתָּ׃	Have you eaten of the tree of which I commanded you *not to eat*? (Gen. 3:11).

The functions of an infinitive refer either to the syntactic function that it fulfills in a clause, or to the semantic and syntactic relationship between the infinitive and the finite verb; this relationship is often indicated by means of a preposition.[32]

20.1.2. *As part of the subject of a nominal clause*

The infinitive may be used with (#*a*) or without (#*b*) the preposition לְ.

a	וְאִם רַע בְּעֵינֵיכֶם לַעֲבֹד אֶת־יְהוָה...	And if it is wrong in your eyes *to serve the* LORD... (Josh. 24:15).*
b	טוֹב תִּתִּי אֹתָהּ לָךְ מִתִּתִּי אֹתָהּ לְאִישׁ אַחֵר	It is better that I give her to you [lit. good is *my giving* her to you] than that I should give her to any other man (Gen. 29:19).

20.1.3. *As part of a predicate*

See also §39.11.(3).

(1) Part of the predicate of a nominal clause.

a	שֹׁמֵר תְּבוּנָה לִמְצֹא־טוֹב	The one who preserves under-standing *is likely to find prosperity* (Prov. 19:8).*
b	וַיְהִי הַשֶּׁמֶשׁ לָבוֹא	and as the sun was *about to go down* (Gen. 15:12).*

---

32. For uses of the preposition לְ plus infinitive construct, see §39.11.(3).

(2) Part of the predicate (i.e. embedded as the complement) of a verbal clause. The infinitive is embedded as the complement of some verbs that require a complement (object) to form a complete predicate (#a-e). Sometimes, the preposition לְ is absent (#d-e).

a	אֲדֹנָי יְהוִה אַתָּה הַחִלּוֹתָ לְהַרְאוֹת אֶת־עַבְדְּךָ אֶת־גָּדְלְךָ	O LORD God you yourself have begun *to show* your servant your greatness (Deut. 3:24).*
b	וַיְמַהֵר פַּרְעֹה לִקְרֹא לְמֹשֶׁה וּלְאַהֲרֹן	And Pharaoh hurriedly *summoned* [lit. he hurried *to summon*] Moses and Aaron (Exod. 10:16).*
c	וַיֹּסִפוּ בְּנֵי יִשְׂרָאֵל לַעֲשׂוֹת הָרַע בְּעֵינֵי יְהוָה	And the Israelites again *did* [lit. added *to do*] what was evil in the eyes of the LORD (Judg. 3:12).*
d	מַדּוּעַ מִהַרְתֶּן בֹּא הַיּוֹם	Why *have* you *come* so soon today? [lit. Why have you hurried *to come* today?] (Exod. 2:18).*
e	לֹא אֵדַע צֵאת וָבֹא	I do not know *what to do* [lit. I do not know *going out and coming in*] (1 Kgs 3:7).*

20.1.4. *As part of an adjunct*

20.1.4.1. *Adjunct of purpose, explication or result*

For more detail about the type of main verbs that are typically involved, see §39.11.(3)(b).

(1) Purpose (very frequent)

וַיָּבֹא הַבַּיְתָה לַעֲשׂוֹת מְלַאכְתּוֹ	And he went into the house *to do* his work (Gen. 39:11).*

(2) Explicative (frequent)

וַיֶּאֱהַב שְׁלֹמֹה אֶת־יְהוָה לָלֶכֶת בְּחֻקּוֹת דָּוִד אָבִיו	And Solomon loved the LORD *by walking* in the statutes of David his father (1 Kgs 3:3).*

(3) Consequence (seldom)

> חָלָה חִזְקִיָּהוּ לָמוּת   Hezekiah became *terminally* ill
> [lit. Hezekiah became ill *to die*]
> (2 Kgs 20:1).*

20.1.4.2. *Adjunct of time*

The construction reflects the moment in time at which the events indicated by the finite verb occur. The specific moment in time proposed here is indicated, *inter alia*, by the preposition used.

(1) When used with the preposition בְּ, the action depicted by the infinitive construct is *simultaneous* with that of the main clause.

It is simultaneous in the sense that the action referred to by the בְּ + infinitive construction constitutes a stretch of time within which the action in the main clause takes place. This construction can be translated "as," "when," or "while" (§39.6.(2)).

> בְּלֶכְתְּךָ הַיּוֹם מֵעִמָּדִי וּמָצָאתָ   *When you depart* from me today
> שְׁנֵי אֲנָשִׁים   you will meet two men (1 Sam. 10:2).

(2) When used with the preposition כְּ, the action of the infinitive construct occurs *just before* the events described in the main clause.

This construction can be translated "the moment when" or "as soon as" (§39.10.(4) and §40.25.(2)(b)).

> וַיְהִי כְמָלְכוֹ הִכָּה אֶת־כָּל־בֵּית יָרָבְעָם   And *as soon as he (Baasha) was king*, he killed all the house of Jeroboam (1 Kgs 15:29).*

(3) When the preposition עַד is used, then the action of the main clause sentence occurs *in the period extending to* the events described by the infinitive construct.

The construction may be translated "until" (§39.19.(2)).

> עַד־בֹּאֲכֶם עַד־הַמָּקוֹם הַזֶּה: *until you came* to this place (Deut. 1:31).*

(4) When the preposition אַחֲרֵי is used, then the action in the main clause occurs *after* the events in the infinitive construct.

    The construction may be translated "after" (§39.2.(2)).

...אַחֲרֵי הַכֹּתוֹ אֵת סִיחֹן *After he had defeated* Sihon… (Deut. 1:4).

(5) The preposition מִן is used when the action of the main clause occurs *from the inception of* the events implied by the infinitive construct.

    The construction may be translated with "from (the time) when" (§39.14.(1)(f)).

מֵהָחֵל חֶרְמֵשׁ בַּקָּמָה תָּחֵל
לִסְפֹּר שִׁבְעָה שָׁבֻעוֹת Begin to count the seven weeks *from the time you first put the sickle to the standing grain* (Deut. 16:9).*

20.1.5. לֵאמֹר

The infinitive construct form לֵאמֹר usually acts as a complementizer, marking reported speech.[33]

    It is significant that the form of לֵאמֹר is not what one would expect the infinitive construct of a I-ʾālep̄ root to be, namely לֶאֱמֹר, on analogy to לֶאֱכֹל (§18.3). Rather, it is an infinitive construct that has become grammaticalized as a complementizer.

(1) לֵאמֹר is predominantly used to *mark reported speech* in the following contexts:

- where no dialogue is involved,

וַיַּגֵּד שָׁפָן הַסֹּפֵר לַמֶּלֶךְ לֵאמֹר
סֵפֶר נָתַן לִי חִלְקִיָּה הַכֹּהֵן And Shaphan the secretary informed the king *as follows*, "Hilkiah, the priest, has given me a book" (2 Kgs 22:10).*

וַיִּשְׁמַע הָעָם הַחֹנִים לֵאמֹר קָשַׁר
זִמְרִי וְגַם הִכָּה אֶת־הַמֶּלֶךְ And the troops who were encamped heard *the following information* [lit. heard *saying*], "Zimri has conspired, and also has killed the king" (1 Kgs 16:16).*

---

33. The insights of this section are from Miller (1996); see also Miller-Naudé and Naudé 2016b.

- or where the main verb is not a verb of saying.

וַיָּבֹ֙אוּ֙ כָל־מִצְרַ֔יִם אֶל־יוֹסֵ֖ף לֵאמֹ֑ר הָֽבָה־לָּ֣נוּ לֶ֔חֶם And all the Egyptians came to Joseph, *saying*, "Give us food!" (Gen. 47:15).*

The use of לֵאמֹר to introduce direct speech can be contrasted with quotative frames (or dialogue introducers) like the finite forms of אמר that usually mark reported speech in dialogues, for example:

וַיֹּ֙אמֶר֙ אֲבִימֶ֣לֶךְ אֶל־אַבְרָהָ֔ם מֶ֣ה רָאִ֔יתָ כִּ֥י עָשִׂ֖יתָ אֶת־הַדָּבָ֣ר הַזֶּ֑ה ¹⁰ וַיֹּ֙אמֶר֙ אַבְרָהָ֔ם כִּ֣י אָמַ֔רְתִּי... ¹¹

¹⁰ And Abimelech *said* to Abraham, "What were you thinking [lit. seeing] of, that you did this thing?" ¹¹ Abraham *said*, "Because I said..." (Gen. 20:10–11).*

(2) לֵאמֹר as a normal infinitive construct.
Although in the above-mentioned cases לֵאמֹר has lost its normal function as an infinitive, it does not mean that לֵאמֹר cannot be used as an infinitive at all. In other words, it may also have one of the uses listed in §20.1.3. However, this use of לֵאמֹר is, in comparison to its use as a complementizer, relatively infrequent.

וַיֹּ֙סֶף֙ ע֤וֹד אַבְנֵר֙ לֵאמֹ֣ר אֶל־עֲשָׂהאֵ֔ל ס֥וּר לָֽךְ And Abner *said* again [lit. added *to say*] to Asahel, "Turn away from following me" (2 Sam. 2:22).*

§20.2. Infinitive Absolute

20.2.1. *Overview*

The infinitive absolute differs from the infinitive construct in terms of both form and function. In contrast to the infinitive construct, the infinitive absolute, as a rule, does not combine with any other grammatical or lexical morpheme. In other words, it cannot take a pronominal suffix. The infinitive absolute is only rarely governed by a preposition. This happens in a few cases where it functions like an infinitive construct or a noun (§20.2.5–6).

The infinitive absolute occurs about 865 times in the Hebrew Bible.[34] In more than 50% of the cases, the infinitive absolute is followed by a finite verb with the same root. In only 31 instances is the infinitive absolute preceded by a finite verb.[35]

In comparison with Samuel and Kings, the infinitive absolute construction is used much less frequently in Chronicles. Instances where the construction functions as a directive, which abound in Classical Biblical Hebrew, are, however, completely absent in Chronicles (Kim 2009: 105).

From the perspective of all its uses, it is clear that the infinitive absolute is an *adverbial specifier* par excellence. The senses of the infinitive absolute can be linked to the types of syntactical constructions in which it is used, namely:

- The infinitive absolute with a finite verb of the same lexical stem
- The infinitive absolute substituting for a finite verb
- The infinitive absolute used as an adverb
- The infinitive absolute used as an infinitive construct
- The infinitive absolute used as a noun

20.2.2. *Infinitives absolute with a finite verb*

20.2.2.1. *Introduction*

This syntactic construction represents over 55% of the examples. It is occasioned by the collocation of an infinitive absolute and a finite verb. Often the infinitive absolute and the finite verb share the same stem formation; however, they sometimes differ, especially in instances where the finite verb is in the Niṗʿal and the infinitive absolute is in the Qal (#*a*).

a	וְאִם־גָּנֹב יִגָּנֵב מֵעִמּוֹ יְשַׁלֵּם לִבְעָלָיו	And if it *was indeed stolen* from him, he must compensate its owner (Exod. 22:11).*[36]

As has been indicated above, cases in which the infinitive absolute *precedes* the finite verb are much more common than those in which the infinitive absolute *follows* the finite verb. However, when the infinitive absolute is

---

34. The statistics are from Callaham (2010: 1).

35. This construction is referred to as the "tautological infinite" (Kim 2009) or the "paronomastic infinitive" (Callaham 2010). In this grammar we will simply use the term "infinitive absolute construction."

36. For more examples and other patterns, see Waltke and O'Connor §35.2.1d.

used with a *wayyiqtōl*, imperative, or participle, the infinitive absolute always *follows* the verbal form.

When the infinitive absolute precedes the finite verb, the negative particle has to precede the finite verb (#b), thus intervening between the infinitive absolute and the finite verb. However, focus particles tend to immediately precede the infinitive absolute, regardless of whether the infinitive absolute precedes (#c) or follows (#d) the finite verb.

b	וּמֵאָ֞ז בָּ֣אתִי אֶל־פַּרְעֹה֮ לְדַבֵּר֒ בִּשְׁמֶ֔ךָ הֵרַ֖ע לָעָ֣ם הַזֶּ֑ה וְהַצֵּ֥ל לֹא־הִצַּ֖לְתָּ אֶת־עַמֶּֽךָ	And since I came to Pharaoh to speak in your name, he mistreated this people, but *you have not delivered* your people *at all* (Exod. 5:23).*
c	וַתֹּאמַ֕רְןָ אִ֣ישׁ מִצְרִ֔י הִצִּילָ֖נוּ מִיַּ֣ד הָרֹעִ֑ים וְגַם־דָּלֹ֤ה דָלָה֙ לָ֔נוּ	And they said, "An Egyptian man saved us from the hand of the shepherds, and *he* even *diligently draws* water for us" (Exod. 2:19).*
d	הֲל֧וֹא נָכְרִיּ֛וֹת נֶחְשַׁ֥בְנוּ ל֖וֹ כִּ֣י מְכָרָ֑נוּ וַיֹּ֥אכַל גַּם־אָכ֖וֹל אֶת־כַּסְפֵּֽנוּ׃	Are we not regarded by him as foreigners? After all, he sold us, and then *completely wasted* our money (Gen. 31:15).*

20.2.2.2. *Semantic-pragmatic functions*[37]

(1) Confirms the factuality of an event

This typically happens in contexts where a speaker is of the opinion that the factuality of an event or state of affairs is not certain or not beyond any doubt.

The construction is used to confirm (#a), or express the conviction (#b) of speakers, that something will or must happen (#c) – or not happen – in the future. In rhetorical questions, the potential realization of an event is sometimes strongly denied (#d). In a context where typically a number of possible scenarios are postulated or implied (i.e. if x…, then y), the factuality of a possible but relatively less likely or expected condition is to be considered (#e).

a	וְאַ֨בְרָהָ֔ם הָי֧וֹ יִֽהְיֶ֛ה לְג֥וֹי גָּד֖וֹל וְעָצ֑וּם	And Abraham *will certainly become* a great and powerful nation (Gen. 18:18).*

---

37. See also Van der Merwe (2013a).

b	כִּי יָדַעְתִּי אַחֲרֵי מוֹתִי כִּי־הַשְׁחֵת תַּשְׁחִתוּן	For I know that after my death *you will surely act corruptly* (Deut. 31:29).
c	סָקוֹל יִסָּקֵל הַשּׁוֹר	The ox *must be stoned* (Exod. 21:28).*
d	הַהַצֵּל הִצִּילוּ אֱלֹהֵי הַגּוֹיִם אִישׁ אֶת־אַרְצוֹ מִיַּד מֶלֶךְ אַשּׁוּר:	Have any of the gods of the nations *ever delivered* his land out of the hand of the king of Assyria? (2 Kgs 18:33).*
e	¹⁵וּבְשַׂר זֶבַח תּוֹדַת שְׁלָמָיו בְּיוֹם קָרְבָּנוֹ יֵאָכֵל לֹא־יַנִּיחַ מִמֶּנּוּ עַד־בֹּקֶר: ¹⁶וְאִם־נֶדֶר ׀ אוֹ נְדָבָה זֶבַח קָרְבָּנוֹ בְּיוֹם הַקְרִיבוֹ אֶת־זִבְחוֹ יֵאָכֵל וּמִמָּחֳרָת וְהַנּוֹתָר מִמֶּנּוּ יֵאָכֵל: ¹⁷וְהַנּוֹתָר מִבְּשַׂר הַזָּבַח בַּיּוֹם הַשְּׁלִישִׁי בָּאֵשׁ יִשָּׂרֵף: ¹⁸וְאִם הֵאָכֹל יֵאָכֵל מִבְּשַׂר־זֶבַח שְׁלָמָיו בַּיּוֹם הַשְּׁלִישִׁי לֹא יֵרָצֶה	¹⁵ The meat of his thanksgiving peace offering must be eaten on the day of his offering; he must not set any of it aside until morning. ¹⁶ If his offering is a votive or freewill sacrifice, it may be eaten on the day he presents his sacrifice, and also the leftovers from it may be eaten on the next day, ¹⁷ but the leftovers from the meat of the sacrifice must be burned up in the fire on the third day. ¹⁸ If some of the meat of his peace offering sacrifice *is ever eaten* on the third day it will not be accepted (NET Lev. 7:15–18).

(2) Specify the extreme mode of an event[38]
   In contexts where the factuality of an event is either discourse active, assumed, or not contested, the intensity or extreme nature of an event is specified (#a-b).

a	כִּי אָמְרוּ אַךְ נִגּוֹף נִגָּף הוּא לְפָנֵינוּ כַּמִּלְחָמָה הָרִאשֹׁנָה	So that they thought, "Surely *they are completely defeated* before us, as in the first battle" (Judg. 20:39).*
b	וַתִּתְפַּלֵּל עַל־יְהוָה וּבָכֹה תִבְכֶּה:	And she prayed to the LORD while *she was weeping bitterly* (1 Sam. 1:10).*

---

38. This category of use is significantly less frequent in the Hebrew Bible than those referred to in modal contexts. See also Callaham (2010: 224).

20.2.3. *Infinitives absolute substituting for finite verbs*[39]

It sometimes appears as if an infinitive absolute is the substitute of a finite verb. However, this use is restricted to contexts where the person, number, tense, aspect and/or mode of the infinitive absolute can "easily" be inferred from its immediate context.

About 66% of the 193 so-called independent infinitives absolute occur in prose and 34% in poetry.[40]

20.2.3.1. *Following an assertion or directive*

The infinitive absolute typically specifies asyndetically the manner of an event or state of affairs (#a) or the directive (#b) that has been referred to in the immediately preceding context by means of a finite verb. In these cases, the construction with the infinitive absolute functions adverbially – similar to those instances described in §20.2.4.

a	לֵךְ וּפִתַּחְתָּ הַשַּׂק מֵעַל מָתְנֶיךָ וְנַעַלְךָ תַחֲלֹץ מֵעַל רַגְלֶיךָ וַיַּעַשׂ כֵּן הָלֹךְ עָרוֹם וְיָחֵף:	"Go, and loose the sackcloth from your loins and take your sandals off your feet," and he did so, *walking* naked and barefoot (Isa. 20:2).*
b	שְׁאַל־לְךָ אוֹת מֵעִם יְהוָה אֱלֹהֶיךָ הַעְמֵק שְׁאָלָה אוֹ הַגְבֵּהַּ לְמָעְלָה:	Ask a sign of the LORD your God; *let it be deep* as Sheol or *high* as heaven (Isa. 7:11).

20.2.3.2. *Heading directives*

The infinitive absolute is used at the head of commands or instructions. This happens predominantly after a verb of saying (#a). The infinitive absolute of הָלֹךְ also often introduces a sequence of specific instructions (#b).[41]

---

39. This section benefitted much from Garr (2009).

40. The notion "independent" could be misleading since the infinitives absolute typically draw their person, number and tense, aspect or mood from a finite verb in its immediate context. See also Van der Merwe and Andrason (2014).

41. This use of הָלֹךְ resembles a similar use of the Qal imperative form לֵךְ (§19.5.1.1.(3)(b)) which points the addressees' attention to the immediately following directives.

a   וָאֲצַוֶּה אֶת־שֹׁפְטֵיכֶם בָּעֵת   And I charged your judges at that
הַהִוא לֵאמֹר שָׁמֹעַ   time, "*Hear* the cases between your
בֵּין־אֲחֵיכֶם וּשְׁפַטְתֶּם   fellow tribe members, and judge
צֶדֶק   righteously" (Deut. 1:16).*

b   הָלוֹךְ וְדִבַּרְתָּ אֶל־דָּוִד   *Go* and say to David (2 Sam. 24:12).

20.2.4. *Infinitives absolute used like adverbs*

20.2.4.1. *Verb + infinitive absolute + infinitive absolute*

(1) Main verb x + infinitive absolute x + infinitive absolute y
The infinitive absolute x + infinitive absolute y adverbially describes the
mode of the finite verb. The mode is that aspect that describes the simultaneity of two actions and, in particular, what happened while a subject was
moving in a direction (#a-b).

a   וַיֵּלֶךְ הָלוֹךְ וְאָכֹל   And he went on, *eating as he went*
[lit. he went, *going* and *eating*]
(Judg. 14:9).

b   וַיֵּצֵא יָצוֹא וָשׁוֹב   And it went *to and fro* [lit. and it
went out, *going out* and *returning*]
(Gen. 8:7).

The lexical stem הלך often expresses a figurative movement, so that the
expression indicates a progression in time, rather than physical movement
(#c).

c   וַיֵּלֶךְ דָּוִד הָלוֹךְ וְגָדוֹל   And David became *greater and
greater* (2 Sam. 5:10).

In certain cases (#d) the lexical stem of the infinitive absolute is not a verb
of motion, but the construction reflects the same kind of simultaneity as
described in the cases above.

d   וַיַּכֵּהוּ הָאִישׁ הַכֵּה וּפָצֹעַ:   And the man struck him, *continuously striking and wounding* him
(1 Kgs 20:37).*

(2) Main verb y + infinitive absolute of הלך + infinitive absolute y
The infinitive absolute of הלך vividly expresses the gradual progression
of the main verb. The stem of the main verb is repeated in the infinitive

absolute after the infinitive absolute הָלוֹךְ (#*a*). In a few cases the stem of the main verb differs from that of the second infinitive absolute (#*b*).

a	וַיָּשֻׁבוּ הַמַּיִם מֵעַל הָאָרֶץ הָלוֹךְ וָשׁוֹב	And the waters *gradually* receded from the earth (Gen. 8:3).
b	וְהַמַּיִם הָיוּ הָלוֹךְ וְחָסוֹר עַד הַחֹדֶשׁ הָעֲשִׂירִי	And the waters *continued* to abate until the tenth month (Gen. 8:5).*

Sometimes הַשְׁכֵּם is used instead of the infinitive absolute form of הלך. The construction adverbially describes the action of the finite verb as being persistent (#*c*).[42]

c	וָאֲדַבֵּר אֲלֵיכֶם הַשְׁכֵּם וְדַבֵּר	And I *kept on speaking* to you (Jer. 7:13).*

(3) Main verb z + infinitive absolute of root x + infinitive absolute of root y

	בַּיּוֹם הַהוּא אָקִים אֶל־עֵלִי אֵת כָּל־אֲשֶׁר דִּבַּרְתִּי אֶל־בֵּיתוֹ הָחֵל וְכַלֵּה:	On that day I will fulfil against Eli all that I have spoken concerning his house, *from the beginning to the end* [lit. *beginning and finishing*] (1 Sam. 3:12).*

20.2.4.2. *Infinitives absolute used like "full-blown" adverbs*

The nature of the adverbial modification of this category is determined exclusively by the lexical value of the stem that is in the infinitive absolute. This infinitive absolute is usually in the Hip̄ʿîl, e.g. הֵיטֵב (well, thoroughly), הַרְבֵּה (many), הַשְׁכֵּם (early) and הַרְחֵק (far).

The lexeme with the infinitive absolute morphology modifies the predicate (#*a*). Often the lexeme in the infinitive absolute form is itself modified by מְאֹד (#*b*).

a	וְדָרַשְׁתָּ...הֵיטֵב	And you shall inquire...*thoroughly* (Deut. 13:15).*
b	וָאֶשְׁגֶּה הַרְבֵּה מְאֹד:	And I have made a very *great* mistake (1 Sam. 26:21).*

---

42. With one exception, all instances of this category occur in the book of Jeremiah, viz. Jer. 7:25; 23:14; 25:3, 4; 26:5; 29:19; 35:14, 15; 44:4; 2 Chron. 36:15 (a report about Jeremiah, see v. 12).

20.2.5. *Infinitives absolute used like an infinitive construct (rare)*

וַיֵּשֶׁב הָעָם לֶאֱכֹל וְשָׁתוֹ   And the people sat down to eat and *drink* (Exod. 32:6).

20.2.6. *Infinitives absolute used like nouns*

וְגַם־הַרְבֵּה נָפַל מִן־הָעָם   and also *many* of the army fell (2 Sam. 1:4).*

§20.3. Participle

20.3.1. *Introduction*

The participle is a verbal form with nominal features which occurs more than 9,600 times in the Hebrew Bible.

It may take a definite article, and it may occur in the *status constructus*. When participles decline for gender and number, the declensions accord with those of nouns and adjectives. Both nominal and verbal pronominal affixes are suffixed to participles. Participles are typically negated by אֵין, but may be negated by לֹא.[43]

Biblical Hebrew has active and passive participles. The latter are typically indicated by the "passive" stem formation, e.g. Nip̄ʿal, Puʿal, and Hop̄ʿal. Only the Qal stem formation has morphologically distinguished active and passive participles (see §16 for morphology).

20.3.2. *Syntax*

Syntactically, the participle in Biblical Hebrew may function as (1) the predication of a clause, (2) the modification of a noun phrase or clause, or (3) like a noun.

20.3.2.1. *As main predication of a clause*[44]

(1) Unmarked configuration: Subject + predicate (§46.2.2.1)
   The most typical configurations are those where the subject of the verb is a lexicalized noun or noun phrase (*#a*) or an independent personal pronoun

---

43. See Miller-Naudé and Naudé (2015b).
44. If one considers the formal structure of these participle clauses, they could be regarded as nominal clauses. See also §46.2.2 and §47.3.1.

(#*b*). The pronominal subject suffix may also be suffixed to a particle, e.g. הִנֵּה (#*c*).

a	וִיהוֹנָתָן וַאֲחִימַעַץ עֹמְדִים בְּעֵין־רֹגֵל וְהָלְכָה הַשִּׁפְחָה וְהִגִּידָה לָהֶם	And Jonathan and Ahimaaz *were waiting* at Enrogel; a maidservant went and informed them (2 Sam. 17:17).*
b	הוּא יֹשֵׁב בִּסְדֹם	He *was living* in Sodom (Gen. 14:12).*
c	הִנְנִי עֹמֵד עַל־שְׂפַת הַיְאֹר:	Look, I *was standing* on the bank of the Nile (Gen. 41:17).*

(2) Marked configurations (see also §46.2.2.2)

The participial predicate may precede the subject. This happens predominantly in clauses introduced by כִּי or אִם (#*a-b*), but may also occur when these particles are not present (#*c-d*), as well when a complement precedes the participial predicate (#*e*). These kinds of fronting are not restricted to participial clauses; for the semantic-pragmatic function of these fronted constructions, see §47.2.

a	כִּי יֹדֵעַ אֱלֹהִים כִּי בְּיוֹם אֲכָלְכֶם מִמֶּנּוּ וְנִפְקְחוּ עֵינֵיכֶם	For God *knows* that on the day when you eat from it, your eyes will be opened (Gen. 3:5).*
b	וְאִם־מָאֵן אַתָּה לְשַׁלֵּחַ הִנֵּה אָנֹכִי נֹגֵף אֶת־כָּל־גְּבוּלְךָ בַּצְפַרְדְּעִים:	And if you *refuse* to let them go, look, I am going to plague your whole territory with frogs (Exod. 7:27).*
c	עֲזֻבוֹת עָרֵי עֲרֹעֵר	The towns of Aroer *are deserted* (Isa. 17:2).*
d	וַיֹּאמֶר לָהֶן רֹאֶה אָנֹכִי אֶת־פְּנֵי אֲבִיכֶן כִּי־אֵינֶנּוּ אֵלַי כִּתְמֹל שִׁלְשֹׁם	And he said to them, "I *see* the face of your father: he is not treating me as before" (Gen. 31:5).*
e	אֶת־אַחַי אָנֹכִי מְבַקֵּשׁ	I *am looking* for my brothers (Gen. 37:16).*

20.3.2.2. *As modification of a noun phrase or a clause*

(1) Modifying noun phrases

Participles are often used like adjectives that are in an attributive relationship with nouns. Typically the participle headed by a definite article agrees with the definite noun phrase it modifies attributively (#*a*). The noun phrase and its modifying participle may also be indefinite (#*b*). Also frequent are cases where the participle in the construct form governs the constituents that are required by the valency of the participle's verbal root (#*c*). In these instances, it would seem that the construction in Hebrew is a zero relative clause (a relative clause without the relative marker).[45]

a	וְשָׁכַחְתָּ אֶת־יְהוָה אֱלֹהֶיךָ הַמּוֹצִיאֲךָ מֵאֶרֶץ מִצְרָיִם	And you forget the Lord your God *who brought you* from Egypt (Deut. 8:14).*
b	אֲרִי־נֹהֵם וְדֹב שׁוֹקֵק מֹשֵׁל רָשָׁע עַל עַם־דָּל	A *roaring* lion or a *charging* bear is a wicked person, ruling over helpless people (Prov. 28:15).*
c	וְאֶת־הַלְוִיִּם מְשָׁרְתֵי אֹתִי	And the Levites *who serve* me (Jer. 33:22).*

(2) Modifying clauses

A participle clause may be used to describe the manner of an action.

וַיִּתֵּן אֶל־הָגָר שָׂם עַל־שִׁכְמָהּ	And he gave it to Hagar, *putting* it on her shoulder (Gen. 21:14).*

20.3.2.3. *Functioning like a noun*

(1) The participle specifies entities by means of the action(s) they perform or the state(s) they are in.

Often the participle is headed by a definite article, and the entity that is referred to acts as the subject of the clause (#*a*). The participle may also be used in a reference to the object of a clause (#*b*).

a	וְהַנִּשְׁאָרִים הֶרָה נָּסוּ	*And the rest* [lit. *those who remained over*] fled to the mountain (Gen. 14:10).
b	וָאֶשְׁמַע אֵת מִדַּבֵּר אֵלָי	And I heard *someone speaking* to me (Ezek. 2:2).*

(2) The use of the participle to specify certain entities may become conventionalized so that the participle functions as a substantive.

This use of a participle form often refers to professions (#*a-b*).

---

45. See Miller-Naudé and Naudé (2015b).

a   שֹׁפְטִים וְשֹׁטְרִים תִּתֶּן־לְךָ   You must appoint *judges and officers* (Deut. 16:18).*

b   וַיִּשְׁמַע יִתְרוֹ כֹהֵן מִדְיָן חֹתֵן   And Jethro, the *priest* of Midian
           מֹשֶׁה אֵת כָּל־אֲשֶׁר עָשָׂה   and father-in-law of Moses, heard
           אֱלֹהִים לְמֹשֶׁה   of everything God had done for
           Moses (Exod. 18:1).*

20.3.3. *Semantics*

(1) Continuous actions (events)

The prototypical semantic value of the participle in Classical Biblical Hebrew is that of continuous action that takes place simultaneously with the reference time of an event. The reference time may be the same as the speech time of the event, i.e. the present (#*a*), a point in the past (#*b*) or in the future (#*c*).

a   וַיֹּאמֶר אֶת־אַחַי אָנֹכִי מְבַקֵּשׁ   And he said, "I *am looking* for my
           brothers" (Gen. 37:16).*

b   וִיהוֹנָתָן וַאֲחִימַעַץ עֹמְדִים   And Jonathan and Ahimaaz *were*
           בְּעֵין־רֹגֵל וְהָלְכָה הַשִּׁפְחָה   *waiting* at Enrogel; a maidservant
           וְהִגִּידָה לָהֶם   went and informed them (2 Sam.
           17:17).*

c   עוֹדָךְ מְדַבֶּרֶת שָׁם עִם־הַמֶּלֶךְ   While you are still *speaking* there
           וַאֲנִי אָבוֹא אַחֲרָיִךְ   with the king, I will come in after
           you (1 Kgs 1:14).*

(2) Habitual events

The participle may refer to habitual events, with (#*a*) or without היה (#*b*).

a   מִיכָה הַמּוֹרַשְׁתִּי הָיָה נִבָּא   Micah of Moresheth *used to*
           בִּימֵי חִזְקִיָּהוּ מֶלֶךְ־יְהוּדָה   *prophesy* in the days of Hezekiah
           king of Judah (Jer. 26:18).*

b   וְהָעֹרְבִים מְבִיאִים לוֹ לֶחֶם   And the ravens *brought* him bread
           וּבָשָׂר בַּבֹּקֶר וְלֶחֶם וּבָשָׂר   and meat in the morning, and bread
           בָּעֶרֶב וּמִן־הַנַּחַל יִשְׁתֶּה   and meat in the evening; and he
           would drink from the wadi (1 Kgs
           17:6).*

(3) Future events

The participle's most typical use in future contexts is that of the immediate future of something that is certainly going to happen (#*a-b*).

a   כִּי־מַשְׁחִתִים אֲנַחְנוּ   For we *are about to destroy* this אֶת־הַמָּקוֹם הַזֶּה   place (Gen. 19:13).

b   וַיֹּאמֶר לוֹ הִנְּךָ מֵת עַל־הָאִשָּׁה   And he said to him, "Look, you אֲשֶׁר־לָקַחְתָּ   *are about to die* on account of the woman you have taken" (Gen. 20:3).*

§21. Verb Chains and Sequences

§21.1. Introduction

Verb chains are constituted by finite verbs that are immediately preceded by a *wāw*.[46] This, however, applies only to cases of the verb in the *qātal*/perfect, *yiqtōl*/imperfect, imperative, jussive or cohortative.

Some verb chains constitute what is called a *verb sequence*. Introductory grammars often distinguish between the following "sequences":

qātal/perfect	+	*wayyiqtōl*	Consecutive events in the past
yiqtōl/imperfect	+	*wəqātal*	Consecutive events in the future
directive	+	*wəqātal*	Consecutive commands
yiqtōl/imperfect	+	*wəyiqtōl*	Purpose
directive	+	*wəyiqtōl*	Purpose

Grammarians agree, however, that the above scheme can be refined. A variety of other factors and problems are involved in identifying verb sequences and their respective functions. This requires a far more nuanced scheme than the one given above.

§21.2. *Wayyiqtōl*

A significant feature of the semantic potential of the *wayyiqtōl* construction is that it displays semantic values similar to that of *qātal*/perfect. In narration, a *wayyiqtōl* predominantly refers to complete events in the past (past perfective)

---

46. For a typology of the diachronic developments concerning *wayyiqtōl* and *wəqātal*, see Naudé (1994a, 2001, 2003b, 2012a, 2012b).

and events in the simple past tense.[47] In discourse, a *wayyiqtōl* may also have a past or present perfect value, in poetry a present tense, and in proverbs a gnomic value.[48]

21.2.1. *In narration*[49]

We make a distinction between instances where a *wayyiqtōl* refers to sequential events and those where no sequentiality is involved. This distinction implies that a *wayyiqtōl* form does not necessarily mark sequential events.

21.2.1.1. *Sequential events*

(1) *Wayyiqtōl* as the *foreground* of a narration or narrated discourse (very frequent)

Wayyiqtōl appears predominantly in narration (#*a*) (or narrated discourse, see §21.2.2) where it introduces principal events of the narrative story (foreground of the narration). It typically refers to logically and/or temporarily consecutive actions (#*b*) which are anterior to the present time sphere, predominantly as complete past events (perfective past) (#*a-b*) and sometimes as simple past events (#*c*). The logical sequence may be one of contrast (#*d*).

a	וַיֵּלֶךְ אִישׁ מִבֵּית לֵוִי וַיִּקַּח אֶת־בַּת־לֵוִי	¹ Now a man from the house of Levi *went* and *married* a Levite woman.
	וַתַּהַר הָאִשָּׁה וַתֵּלֶד בֵּן וַתֵּרֶא אֹתוֹ כִּי־טוֹב הוּא וַתִּצְפְּנֵהוּ שְׁלֹשָׁה יְרָחִים	² The woman *conceived* and *bore* a son; *and when she saw* that he was a fine baby, *she hid* him three months.
	³ וְלֹא־יָכְלָה עוֹד הַצְּפִינוֹ וַתִּקַּח־לוֹ תֵּבַת גֹּמֶא וַתַּחְמְרָה בַחֵמָר וּבַזָּפֶת וַתָּשֶׂם בָּהּ אֶת־הַיֶּלֶד וַתָּשֶׂם בַּסּוּף עַל־שְׂפַת הַיְאֹר	³ When she could hide him no longer *she got* a papyrus basket for him, *and* *plastered* it with bitumen and pitch; *she put* the child in it *and placed* it among the reeds on the bank of the river (Exod. 2:1–3).

---

47. The section benefitted from Andrason (2011c), Cook (2012), and Joosten (2012: 164–92). Some of the examples that are used are taken from these works.

48. A few rare instances have been identified where *wayyiqtōl* forms are used "to represent future actions as already accomplished" (Joosten 2012: 188). See Num. 35:16, Jer. 38:9, and Joel 2:23.

49. According to Joosten (2012: 164), in classical prose, 99% of *wayyiqtōl* forms occur in narrative or narrated discourse.

b	וְהָאָדָ֗ם יָדַ֖ע אֶת־חַוָּ֣ה אִשְׁתּ֑וֹ	Now the man knew his wife Eve,
	וַתַּ֙הַר֙ וַתֵּ֣לֶד אֶת־קַ֔יִן וַתֹּ֕אמֶר	*and she conceived and bore* Cain.
	קָנִ֥יתִי אִ֖ישׁ אֶת־יְהוָֽה	*She then said,* "I have produced a man with the help of the LORD" (Gen. 4:1).*
c	וַיֵּרְד֤וּ אֲבֹתֵ֙ינוּ֙ מִצְרַ֔יְמָה	And our ancestors *went down* to
	וַנֵּ֥שֶׁב בְּמִצְרַ֖יִם יָמִ֣ים רַבִּ֑ים	Egypt, *and we lived* in Egypt a long
	וַיָּרֵ֧עוּ לָ֛נוּ מִצְרַ֖יִם וְלַאֲבֹתֵֽינוּ	time; and the Egyptians *oppressed* us and our ancestors (Num. 20:15).*
d	וַיָּקֻ֙מוּ֙ כָל־בָּנָ֤יו וְכָל־בְּנֹתָיו֙	*And* all his sons and all his daughters
	לְנַחֲמ֔וֹ וַיְמָאֵ֖ן לְהִתְנַחֵ֑ם	*rose* up to comfort him; *but he refused* to be comforted (Gen. 37:35).*

(2) *Wayyiqtōl* at the *beginning* of a narrative (or section)[50]

(a) *Without* an explicit temporal indication

A *wayyiqtōl* verb can introduce a new narrative or section of a narrative. In these instances it is usually accompanied by an introduction of the characters of the new story and a change of location. Verbs of motion and communication occur regularly.

וַיֹּ֤אמֶר יְהוָה֙ אֶל־אַבְרָ֔ם	*Now* the LORD *said* to Abram, "Get
לֶךְ־לְךָ֛ מֵאַרְצְךָ֖	yourself out, away from your land" (Gen. 12:1).*

(b) *With* explicit temporal indication

When a *temporal indication* is involved, the clause with *wayyiqtōl* is usually preceded by וַיְהִֽי. However, this new section follows as a rule on preceding events. In other words, an entirely new narrative is seldom introduced like this. The subsequent foreground events of the narrative are then introduced *by a subsequent wayyiqtōl form* (#*a*). A *nominal clause*, a *yiqtōl/imperfect* or an x *qātal/perfect may be inserted* between the temporal indication and the *wayyiqtōl* to give more *background information* (#*b*). Rarely a *wayyiqtōl* introduces the foreground of the narrative after a temporal indication that is not introduced by וַיְהִי (#*c*).

---

50. Joosten (2012: 164) correctly observes: "The corpus of classical Hebrew prose presents itself as one long story stretching from the creation of the world to the exile of Judah. Apart from Gen. 1:1, there are hardly any absolute beginnings."

a   וַיְהִי בָּעֵת הַהִוא וַיֹּאמֶר   And at that time Abimelech *said*...
אֲבִימֶלֶךְ...   (Gen. 21:22).*

b   וַיְהִי אַחַר הַדְּבָרִים הָאֵלֶּה   And after these events, God him-
וְהָאֱלֹהִים נִסָּה אֶת־אַבְרָהָם   self tested Abraham and said to
וַיֹּאמֶר אֵלָיו אַבְרָהָם   him, "Abraham!" (Gen. 22:1).

c   בַּיֹּום הַשְּׁלִישִׁי וַיִּשָּׂא אַבְרָהָם   On the third day Abraham *lifted up*
אֶת־עֵינָיו וַיַּרְא אֶת־הַמָּקֹום   *his eyes* and *saw* the place afar off
מֵרָחֹק: (Gen. 22:4).*

(3) *Wayyiqtōl* as part of the background or descriptive information *within* a
narrative (seldom)
In these cases, the *wayyiqtōl* typically has the same value as the verbal
form it continues, e.g. habitual activities (#a) or in few rare instances
events anterior to the main narrative (#b).

a   וְלֹא־הָלְכוּ בָנָיו בִּדְרָכָו וַיִּטּוּ   Yet his sons did not follow in his
אַחֲרֵי הַבָּצַע וַיִּקְחוּ־שֹׁחַד וַיַּטּוּ   ways, *but turned aside* after gain;
מִשְׁפָּט   *they took* bribes *and perverted*
justice (1 Sam. 8:3).

b   וּפְלִשְׁתִּים בָּאוּ וַיִּנָּטְשׁוּ בְּעֵמֶק   Now the Philistines had come *and*
רְפָאִים: *spread out* in the valley of Rephaim
(2 Sam. 5:18).

(4) *Wayyiqtōl* at the *end* of a narrative
A *wayyiqtōl* form may be used to present an event that is viewed as
complete (i.e. a past perfective) to summarize a preceding section.

וַיְכֻלּוּ הַשָּׁמַיִם וְהָאָרֶץ   *Thus* the heavens and the earth
were finished (Gen. 2:1).

21.2.1.2. *Non-Sequential events and states of affairs*

(1) Simultaneous events and states of affairs (seldom).
Sometimes *wayyiqtōl* forms are used to describe a situation in the past that
sets the scene of a subsequent narrative (#a-b).

a   וְהִיא יוֹשֶׁבֶת תַּחַת־תֹּמֶר דְּבוֹרָה בֵּין הָרָמָה וּבֵין בֵּית־אֵל בְּהַר אֶפְרָיִם וַיַּעֲלוּ אֵלֶיהָ בְּנֵי יִשְׂרָאֵל לַמִּשְׁפָּט: She used to sit under the palm of Deborah between Ramah and Bethel in the hill country of Ephraim; *and* the Israelites *came up* to her for judgment (Judg. 4:5).

b   וַתִּשָּׁחֵת הָאָרֶץ לִפְנֵי הָאֱלֹהִים וַתִּמָּלֵא הָאָרֶץ חָמָס: *Now* the earth *was corrupt* in God's sight, *and* the earth *was filled* with violence (Gen. 6:11).

(2) Explicative commentary (rare).

וְאֵלֶּה הָיוּ בְּנֵי אָהֳלִיבָמָה בַת־עֲנָה בַת־צִבְעוֹן אֵשֶׁת עֵשָׂו וַתֵּלֶד לַעֲשָׂו אֶת־יְעִישׁ וְאֶת־יַעְלָם וְאֶת־קֹרַח   And these were the sons of Esau's wife Oholibamah, daughter of Anah daughter of Zibeon: *she bore* to Esau Jeush, Jalam, and Korah (Gen. 36:14).*

(3) Referring to retrospective material, in other words, events that had happened at an earlier stage (past perfect / pluperfect) (rare).

וַיְדַבֵּר אֲלֵהֶם אֲבִיהֶם אֵי־זֶה הַדֶּרֶךְ הָלָךְ וַיִּרְאוּ בָנָיו אֶת־הַדֶּרֶךְ   And their father said to them, "Which way did he go?" His sons *had seen* the way (1 Kgs 13:12).*

(4) Successive *wayyiqtōl*s referring to one event (seldom).
This use of the *wayyiqtōl* occurs typically with verbs of saying (#a)[51] and roots like מהר, יסף and שוב (#b). In most cases it can be argued that a type of fixed expression is involved.

a   וַיַּעַן כָּל־הָעָם וַיֹּאמְרוּ טוֹב הַדָּבָר   Then all the people *answered and said*, "The word is good!" (1 Kgs 18:24).*

b   וַתֹּאמֶר שְׁתֵה אֲדֹנִי וַתְּמַהֵר וַתֹּרֶד כַּדָּהּ עַל־יָדָהּ וַתַּשְׁקֵהוּ:   And she said, "Drink, my lord." Then she *quickly lowered* [lit. *made quick and lowered*] her jar upon her hand and gave him a drink (Gen. 24:18).*

---

51. Miller (1996) argues that instances like #a represent a standard convention.

21.2.2. *In discourse*

Direct speech never opens with a *wayyiqtōl*. In narrative discourse, of course, sequential past perfective events (#*a*) or simple past events (#*b*) are referred to.

a וַיְהִי כְשָׁמְעוֹ כִּי־הֲרִימֹתִי קוֹלִי
וָאֶקְרָא וַיַּעֲזֹב בִּגְדוֹ אֶצְלִי וַיָּנָס
וַיֵּצֵא הַחוּצָה

And when he heard me raise my voice and cry out, *he left* his garment beside me, *and fled* outside (Gen. 39:15).

b וָאָבֹא הַיּוֹם אֶל־הָעָיִן וָאֹמַר...

So *I came* today to the spring, and *said*... (Gen. 24:42).*

In discourse, relatively often no sequentiality can be postulated, e.g. the expressions with *wayyiqtōl* explicate an aspect of the content of a preceding utterance (#*c-d*).

c וַיֹּאמֶר לָבָן לְיַעֲקֹב מֶה עָשִׂיתָ
וַתִּגְנֹב אֶת־לְבָבִי וַתְּנַהֵג אֶת־
בְּנֹתַי כִּשְׁבֻיוֹת חָרֶב

And Laban said to Jacob, "What have you done? *You have deceived* me [lit. you stole my heart] and carried away my daughters like captives of the sword" (Gen. 31:26).*

d וַתֹּאמֶר אֲבָל אִשָּׁה־אַלְמָנָה אָנִי
וַיָּמָת אִישִׁי

And she answered, "Alas, I am a widow; my husband *has died*" (2 Sam. 14:5).*

21.2.3. *In poetry and proverbs*[52]

In poetry, a *wayyiqtōl* sometimes refers to an actual present (#*a*). It often has the meaning of a general-persistent present, i.e. a gnomic value (#*b*), in proverbial sayings. In the latter cases, the *wayyiqtōl* is typically the second of a parallel poetic line with a *qātal*/perfect form in the first line. Cook aptly observes about this: "the temporally successive meaning that comes to be associated with narrative *wayyiqtōl* through pragmatic implicature because of its dominant use in prose narrative is capitalized on in poetic discourse to mark departures from the normal parallelistic, nontemporally successive structure of Hebrew poetry" (Cook 2012: 304).

---

52. Cook (2012: 298) correctly observes about the use of *wayyiqtōl* in poetry, "That the form is indeed native to prose narrative is underscored by its rarity in poetry or (more narrowly) verse." For more detail, see Cook (2012: 298–304).

a   לָכֵן שָׂמַח לִבִּי וַיָּגֶל כְּבוֹדִי   Therefore my heart is glad, *and* my soul [lit. honor] *rejoices* (Ps. 16:9).

b   אָהַבְתָּ צֶּדֶק וַתִּשְׂנָא רֶשַׁע   You love righteousness *and hate* wickedness (Ps. 45:8).

c   בַּצָּרָה קָרָאתָ וָאֲחַלְּצֶךָ   In this [lit. the] trouble you called, *and I rescued* you (Ps. 81:8).*

§21.3. *Wəqātal*

This construction reflects a combination of the formation **qātal* and an original coordinating **wa*. Although the **qātal* is the same one underlying the Bible Hebrew *qātal*/perfect conjugation,[53] the *wəqātal* construction did not develop in the same way.[54]

Since the semantic development of the *wəqātal* needs to be understood primarily in terms of the contexts where it is "contaminated," its semantic description is structured accordingly.

21.3.1. *In discourse*

The *wəqātal* is often used in dialogue and typically refers to events in the foreground.

21.3.1.1. *Contingent uses*[55]

(1) Consecutive (either logical or temporal) future

Most basic are instances where the clause introduced by a *wəqātal* is the apodosis of a condition (#a). Often, the future consecutive connotation is present in contexts where no conditional is involved (#b-c). Sometimes *wəqātal* introduces (#d) or is part (#e) of the protasis of a conditional; in these cases the *wəqātal* refers to future actions of which the completion determines other prospective events.

---

53. It is theoretically possible that at an early stage of Biblical Hebrew, i.e. before the *wayyiqtōl* began to fulfil this function, the *wəqātal* was the usual form of referring to narratives in the past. What we do know is that in the later books *wayyiqtōl* loses this role and *wəqātal* occurs in places where one would have expected *wayyiqtōl* (Joüon–Muraoka §119z).

54. It is hypothesized that the formation acquired a modal sense due to a process called context-induced reinterpretation (also referred to as "modal contamination"). See Heine et al. (1991) and Andrason (2011b, 2012b).

55. "Contingent use" means that in order to understand the meaning of a *wəqātal* construction it has to be linked to a clause in the preceding context.

a   וְאִם־אֵין מוֹשִׁיעַ אֹתָנוּ **וְיָצָאנוּ** אֵלֶיךָ

And, if there is no one to save us, *we will give ourselves* up [lit. *we will go up*] to you (1 Sam. 11:3).*

b   עַבְדְּךָ יֵלֵךְ **וְנִלְחַם** עִם־הַפְּלִשְׁתִּי הַזֶּה

Your servant will go *and fight* with this Philistine (1 Sam. 17:32).

c   לָכֵן אֱמֹר לִבְנֵי־יִשְׂרָאֵל אֲנִי יְהוָה **וְהוֹצֵאתִי** אֶתְכֶם מִתַּחַת סִבְלֹת מִצְרַיִם

Therefore say to the Israelites, "I am the LORD, *and I will send* you out from the burdens of the Egyptians" (Exod. 6:6).*

d   וַנֹּאמֶר אֶל־אֲדֹנִי לֹא־יוּכַל הַנַּעַר לַעֲזֹב אֶת־אָבִיו **וְעָזַב** אֶת־אָבִיו **וָמֵת**:

And we said to my lord, "The boy cannot leave his father, [lit. and] *if he leaves* his father, [lit. and] his father [lit. he] *will die*" (Gen. 44.22).*

e   וְעַתָּה אִם־שָׁמוֹעַ תִּשְׁמְעוּ בְּקֹלִי **וּשְׁמַרְתֶּם** אֶת־בְּרִיתִי **וִהְיִיתֶם** לִי סְגֻלָּה מִכָּל־הָעַמִּים

Now, therefore, if you will obey faithfully my voice *and will keep* my covenant, *you will be* my treasured possession out of all the peoples (Exod. 19:5).*

(2) Consecutive directives (frequent)

When following an explicit directive (#*a-c*), the value of *wəqātal* depends on the value of the preceding verbal category. In (#*a*) the *wəqātal* follows an imperative; in (#*b*) it follows a *yiqtōl*/imperfect; and in (#*c*) it follows a cohortative.

a   וַיֹּאמֶר אֲלֵהֶם עֲלוּ זֶה בַּנֶּגֶב **וַעֲלִיתֶם** אֶת־הָהָר

And he said to them, "Go up there into the Negeb, *and go up* into the hill country" (Num. 13:17).*

b   שֵׁשֶׁת יָמִים תַּעֲבֹד **וְעָשִׂיתָ** כָּל־מְלַאכְתֶּךָ:

For six days you shall labor *and do* all your work (Exod. 20:9).

c   וַתֹּאמֶר אֲלַקֳטָה־נָּא **וְאָסַפְתִּי** בָעֳמָרִים אַחֲרֵי הַקּוֹצְרִים

And she said, "Please let me glean *and gather* among the sheaves behind the harvesters" (Ruth 2:7).*

(3) Consecutive modal future (occasional)

Often *wəqātal* functions as a modal future, i.e. it has both a temporal and modal connotation (#*a*). Both of these values are also present in instances where the *wəqātal* clause refers to the purpose of preceding utterances (#*b*).

a וְשָׁאֲלוּ לְךָ לְשָׁלוֹם וְנָתְנוּ   And they will greet you and give
לְךָ שְׁתֵּי־לֶחֶם וְלָקַחְתָּ מִיָּדָם: you two loaves of bread, which
you shall accept from their hand
(1 Sam. 10:4).*

b הִנֵּה שָׁלַחְתִּי אֵלֶיךָ אֶת־נַעֲמָן   Look, I have sent to you Naaman,
עַבְדִּי וַאֲסַפְתּוֹ מִצָּרַעְתּוֹ   my servant, *that you may cure* him
of his leprosy (2 Kgs 5:6).*

21.3.1.2. *Non-contingent uses*

In a few cases, *wəqātal* has lost its typical contingency character and functions as a semantically independent construction referring to a future event, especially in poetry.

וְיָצָא חֹטֶר מִגֵּזַע יִשַׁי וְנֵצֶר   And a shoot *shall come* out from
מִשָּׁרָשָׁיו יִפְרֶה   the stump of Jesse, and a branch
shall grow out of his roots (Isa. 11:1).*

21.3.2. *In narration*

In contrast with its use in discourse, in narration, *wəqātal* refers to *comments* and *background information* (i.e. information that is not part of the foreground). The most typical semantic value of *wəqātal* in narration is iterative-habitual actions in the past.

¹⁵וַיִּשְׁפֹּט שְׁמוּאֵל אֶת־יִשְׂרָאֵל   ¹⁵ And Samuel judged Israel all
כֹּל יְמֵי חַיָּיו: ¹⁶וְהָלַךְ מִדֵּי שָׁנָה   the days of his life. ¹⁶ *He went* on
בְּשָׁנָה וְסָבַב בֵּית־אֵל וְהַגִּלְגָּל   a circuit year by year to Bethel,
וְהַמִּצְפָּה וְשָׁפַט אֶת־יִשְׂרָאֵל   Gilgal, and Mizpah; *and he judged*
אֵת כָּל־הַמְּקוֹמוֹת הָאֵלֶּה: Israel in all these places (1 Sam. 7:15–16).*

§21.4. *Wəyiqtōl*

Besides linking clauses, this construction has no semantic function in itself.

תַּעְתִּיר אֵלָיו וְיִשְׁמָעֶךָ   You will make your prayer to him,
and he will hear you (Job 22:27).*

§21.5. Sequences of Directives

21.5.1. *Introduction*

Wāw + a jussive, imperative or cohortative can follow any other directive or question. The following combinations are thus possible:

imperative	+	*wāw*	+	cohortative/imperative/jussive
cohortative	+	*wāw*	+	cohortative/imperative/jussive
jussive	+	*wāw*	+	cohortative/imperative/jussive
question	+	*wāw*	+	cohortative/imperative/jussive

Note that directives without a *wāw* also occur. For the semantic functions of directives, see §19.5.

21.5.2. *Imperative + (wāw) + directive form*

21.5.2.1. *Imperative + (wāw) imperative*

Imperative sequences – asyndetic and syndetic, alike – could be used by speakers to command (#*a-b*), request (#*c*), invite (#*d*), propose (#*e*), bless (#*f*), or encourage (#*g*). The addresses could be of any status, i.e. higher (#*c-f*) or lower (#*a-b*, *g-h*) than the speakers. Each directive typically conveys what a speaker wants, and each has the same volitive force (Oakes 2011: 52–53). Some frequently occurring lexemes (e.g. קוּם) may lose their full lexical meaning (#*a*). See also §19.5.1.1.(3)(b) for the so-called imperatives of preparation.

Two imperatives in sequence may be in a resultative relationship (#*h*). This is often the case where the addressee is not in a position to heed the directive. See also Jenni (2005b: 238–40).

a	וַיֹּאמֶר קִישׁ אֶל־שָׁאוּל בְּנוֹ קַח־נָא אִתְּךָ אֶת־אַחַד מֵהַנְּעָרִים וְקוּם לֵךְ בַּקֵּשׁ אֶת־הָאֲתֹנֹת׃	And Kish said to Saul his son, "*Take* with you one of the servants, *get ready* (and) *go* and *look* for the donkeys" (1 Sam. 9:3).*
b	עֲלֵה אֱכֹל וּשְׁתֵה	*Go up, eat* and *drink* (1 Kgs 18:41).
c	הַטֵּה יְהוָה׀ אָזְנְךָ וּשֲׁמָע פְּקַח יְהוָה עֵינֶיךָ וּרְאֵה וּשְׁמַע אֵת דִּבְרֵי סַנְחֵרִיב	*Incline*, O LORD, your ear and *listen*; *open*, O LORD, your eyes and *see*. And, *hear* the words of Sennacherib (2 Kgs 19:16).*

d	וַיְדַבֵּר הַמֶּלֶךְ אֶל־אִישׁ הָאֱלֹהִים בֹּאָה־אִתִּי הַבַּיְתָה וּסְעָדָה	And the king spoke to the man of God, "*Come* with me to my house and *have something to eat*" (1 Kgs 13:7).*
e	וַתֹּאמֶר אֵלָיו סוּרָה אֲדֹנִי סוּרָה אֵלַי אַל־תִּירָא	And she said to him, "*Turn aside*, my lord, *turn aside* to me. Do not be afraid" (Judg. 4:18).*
f	וְאַתֶּם פְּרוּ וּרְבוּ שִׁרְצוּ בָאָרֶץ וּרְבוּ־בָהּ	And you, *be fruitful* and *multiply*; *abound* on the earth and *multiply* on it (Gen. 9:7).*
g	חִזְקוּ וְאִמְצוּ	*Be bold* and *strong* (Deut. 31:6).*
h	זֹאת עֲשׂוּ וִחְיוּ	*Do* this *so that you may* [lit. *and*] *live* (Gen. 42:18).*

21.5.2.2. *Imperative + (wāw) jussive form*

The purpose of a request may be expressed by means of the *wāw* + jussive construction.

הַעְתִּירוּ אֶל־יְהוָה וְיָסֵר הַצְפַרְדְּעִים מִמֶּנִּי	Entreat the LORD *so that he takes* the frogs away from me (Exod. 8:4).*

21.5.2.3. *Imperative + wəqātal*

The *wəqātal* forms are typically used in instructions to specify the details of an instruction referred to by means of the initial imperative. This construction is nearly always uttered by speakers towards addressees with a lower status (Oakes 2011: 57).

וַיֹּאמֶר אֲלֵהֶם עֲלוּ זֶה בַּנֶּגֶב וַעֲלִיתֶם אֶת־הָהָר	And he said to them, "Go up there into the Negeb, *and go up* into the hill country" (Num. 13:17).*

21.5.2.4. *Imperative + (wāw) imperative + wəqātal*

When a series of imperative forms are used and they are followed by a *wəqātal* as final member, the *wəqātal* typically refers to the purpose of the directives.

וּרְאוּ וּדְעוּ מִכֹּל הַמַּחֲבֹאִים אֲשֶׁר יִתְחַבֵּא שָׁם וְשַׁבְתֶּם אֵלַי אֶל־נָכוֹן And establish precisely the places where he used to hide [lit. And look and know among all the hiding places where he used to hide himself] *so that you can come back* to me with reliable information (1 Sam. 23:23).*

21.5.3. *Cohortative* + *(wāw)* + *directive form*

The purpose of a contemplated action is typically expressed.

אָסֻרָה־נָּא וְאֶרְאֶה... I must go across *to see* [lit. *and see*]... (Exod. 3:3).*

21.5.4. *Jussive* + *(wāw)* + *directive form*

The purpose of a request is typically expressed.

יִתְּנוּ־לִי מָקוֹם...וְאֵשְׁבָה שָּׁם Let a place be given to me...*that I may dwell* there (1 Sam. 27:5).*

§22. Valency of Verbs

The valency of a verb refers to the number of complements a verb may select (§12.3 and §33.2). A verb may select one or more complements, e.g.:

(1) One complement: Verb + subject

וַיָּמָת שָׁאוּל And Saul died (Gen. 36:38).*

(2) Two complements: Verb + subject + object

כִּי הָרַג שָׁאוּל אֵת כֹּהֲנֵי יְהוָה: that Saul had killed the priests of the Lord (1 Sam. 22:21).

(3) Three complements: Verb + subject + object + indirect object

וַיִּתֵּן יְהוֹנָתָן אֶת־כֵּלָיו אֶל־הַנַּעַר And Jonathan gave his weapons to the boy (1 Sam. 20:40).*

Chapter 5

NOUNS

§23. Introduction

The noun class (*nomen – nomina*) includes the following main categories (see also §11.2):

- Nouns (substantives)
- Pronouns (*pronomina*)
- Numerals

Although adjectives largely correspond morphologically to nouns, in this grammar they are classified in a separate category from nouns on the basis of syntactic criteria.[1] However, because of the similarity of adjectives to nouns, they will be dealt with in this chapter (see §11.3).

Nouns are words that indicate the names of people, places, things or feelings. The following sub-categories of nouns may be distinguished in Biblical Hebrew:

- Proper names
  These are the names of

God/gods	יהוה	LORD
people	דָּוִד	David
places	יְרוּשָׁלַֽיִם	Jerusalem
nations/groups	יִשְׂרָאֵל	Israel
happenings	פֶּֽסַח	Passover

- Common nouns/generic names
  These are common nouns for types of

things	שֻׁלְחָן	table
plants	עֵץ	tree

---

1. See Baker (2003) on lexical categories in general and Miller-Naudé and Naudé (2016a, 2017) on the issues involved in the adjective as a syntactic category in Biblical Hebrew.

animals	עֵז	goat
people	יֶלֶד	child

- Collective nouns
  These are words in the singular that name a group consisting of multiple members.

animals	צֹאן	sheep and goats

- Abstract nouns
  These are the names given to non-concrete things such as

qualities	אַהֲבָה	love
conditions	חֳלִי	illness
actions	עֲבוֹדָה	work

§24. Congruency Features of Nouns

§24.1. Morphology of Congruency Features

Nouns (including proper nouns) are characteristically third person entities and govern a verb in the third person form as subject. They are also marked in terms of gender, i.e. masculine or feminine, and number, i.e. singular, plural or dual (§11.1.6). The gender and number of nouns may be recognized by the following endings:

	Masculine	*Feminine*
Singular	-	◌ָה
Plural	◌ִים	וֹת
Dual	◌ַיִם	◌ָתַיִם

- The masculine singular has no ending – it is a zero or unmarked form.
- Other typical feminine singular endings are וּת, וֹת, ◌ַאת, ◌ָאת, ◌ֶת, ◌ַת.
- The masculine plural ending is sometimes replaced by ◌ִין, e.g.: יָמִין (days; Dan. 12:13), מְלָכִין (kings; Prov. 31:3). (This ending is borrowed from Aramaic.)

§24.2. Gender

24.2.1. *Gender at morphological, syntactic and semantic levels*

Gender is a feature allocated to nouns *on the basis of their form* **or** *on the basis of the way they combine with other elements in a clause.* Some languages (such as English and Afrikaans) have masculine and feminine words (e.g. actor and actress), but they do not affect the constructions of phrases or clauses. Compare for example:

> The fine *actor* plays the role.
> The fine *actress* plays the role.

The forms of the adjective (*fine*) and verb (*plays*) have not changed, even though the gender of the subject has changed from masculine to feminine. Most words do not even have specific masculine or feminine endings, e.g., *man/wife/boy/girl*. In these languages one is inclined to look at real life to determine a word's gender – *son* is masculine, *daughter* is feminine and *tree* is neuter. This background creates a problem for the Biblical Hebrew student because Biblical Hebrew allocates a "grammatical gender" to each noun and grammatical gender does not necessarily correspond to the sex of the item in real life. When the gender of a noun is described in Biblical Hebrew, the level of description must be indicated, namely morphological, syntactic or semantic:

(1) On the *morphological* level gender is indicated by means of an ending (§24.1).

(2) On the syntactic level gender is indicated by means of the congruency features of words (such as adjectives and verbs), e.g.

> הָעִיר הַגְּדֹלָה   the big city (Gen. 10:12).*

Note that עִיר "city" is grammatically feminine even though it is does not have the feminine morphological ending. As a result, it is modified by a grammatically feminine adjective.

Indicating gender at the morphological and syntactic levels is also known as "grammatical gender."

(3) On the *semantic* level gender refers to the actual sex (in real life).
In Biblical Hebrew two genders are identified on the morphological and syntactic level, namely masculine and feminine. The result is that things that are neuter in real life must be described in terms of these two categories. Thus עִיר (city) is grammatically feminine, but מָקוֹם (place)

is normally grammatically masculine. There is no logical reason for allocating gender to inanimate objects. Hebrew does not have a morphologically distinguished neuter form as Latin and Greek do.

(4) *Different combinations* of morphological, syntactic and semantic gender are possible in Biblical Hebrew.

  (a) *Gender agrees at all levels.* That is, if the form is masculine, it refers to a male animal. If the word is the subject of a verb, then the verb will also be masculine. Similarly, the feminine form refers to a female animal, etc.

סוּס   stallion

סוּסָה   mare

  (b) On the semantic level the gender is neuter (i.e. it does not refer to a male or female living person or animal); nevertheless it is masculine or feminine on the morphological and syntactic level, e.g.

הֵיכָל   a palace (masculine)

תּוֹרָה   a law (feminine)

Thus הֵיכָל has a masculine form and תּוֹרָה a feminine form (morphological gender). If these words are qualified by an adjective, הֵיכָל governs the masculine form of an adjective and תּוֹרָה the feminine form, e.g.

הֵיכָל טוֹב   a good palace

תּוֹרָה טוֹבָה   a good law

  (c) Some words are *feminine on the semantic and syntactic level, but masculine on the morphological level*, for example, נָשִׁים (women) is a masculine form but refers to female persons. It also takes the feminine form of the adjective, e.g.

נָשִׁים טוֹבוֹת   good women

  (d) Some nouns are morphologically masculine, syntactically feminine and semantically neuter, e.g.

עִיר   a city

עִיר טוֹבָה   a good city

(e) The gender of a word remains unchanged on the syntactic level, even though the *morphological form sometimes varies*, for example, מָקוֹם which is masculine in the singular on the morphological and syntactic level, becomes feminine in the plural on the morphological level (מְקוֹמוֹת), but remains masculine on the syntactic level.

(f) Some words may be syntactically masculine or feminine in the singular and exhibit only one syntactic gender in the plural.

דֶּרֶךְ is, for example, syntactically masculine or feminine in the singular but always masculine in the plural. However, syntactic gender is the most important and is the kind of gender that is indicated in Hebrew lexicons.

The most important combinations are summarized in the following table:

Hebrew forms	Morphological gender	Syntactic gender	Semantic gender
אִישׁ/אֲנָשִׁים	m.	m.	Male
מַלְכָּה/מְלָכוֹת	f.	f.	Female
עִיר/עָרִים	m.	f.	Neuter
אֶרֶץ/אֲרָצוֹת	sing. m. / pl. f.	f.	Neuter
חֲלוֹם/חֲלוֹמוֹת	sing. m. / pl. f.	m.	Neuter
אָב/אָבוֹת	sing. m. / pl. f.	m.	Male
אִשָּׁה/נָשִׁים	sing. f. / pl. m.	f.	Female
דֶּרֶךְ/דְּרָכִים	m.	sing. m. or f. / pl. m.	Neuter
יָד/יָדַיִם/יָדוֹת	sing. m. / du. m./ pl. f.	f.	Neuter
יוֹם/יָמִים/יוֹמַיִם	m.	m.	Neuter
רֶגֶל/רַגְלַיִם/רְגָלִים	m.	f.	Neuter
קֹהֶלֶת	f.	m.	Male

24.2.2. *Gender features of inanimate objects*

(1) Nouns with a *masculine form* (i.e. morphologically masculine nouns). Most nouns that are morphologically masculine are also masculine on the syntactic level. There are, however, exceptions.

(a) Nouns with a *spatial reference* are usually syntactically feminine, even though they lack feminine endings.

אֶרֶץ earth

תֵּבֵל world

עִיר city

(b) Nouns that refer to *natural elements and forces* are usually syntactically feminine, even though they lack feminine endings.

אֶבֶן stone

רוּחַ wind

אֵשׁ fire

(c) Nouns that refer to *implements* are usually syntactically feminine, even though they lack feminine endings.

חֶרֶב sword

כּוֹס cup

נַעַל sandal

(d) Nouns that refer to *paired parts of the body* are usually syntactically feminine, even though they lack feminine endings.

אֹזֶן ear

עַיִן eye

יָד hand

An exception is שַׁד (breast) which is masculine on the syntactic level.

(e) With *place names*, gender on the syntactic level is often not determined by the proper noun itself, but by the presumed generic term associated with it.

- בֵּית־לֶחֶם and בֵּית־אֵל are morphologically and syntactically masculine because בַּיִת is morphologically and syntactically masculine.

- בָּבֶל, יְהוּדָה and יְרוּשָׁלַיִם are syntactically feminine because מַמְלָכָה (kingdom), אֶרֶץ (country) and עִיר (city), respectively, are syntactically feminine.

- פְּרָת (the Euphrates river) is syntactically masculine even though פְּרָת is morphologically feminine. The reason for this is that the generic term נָהָר (river) is syntactically masculine.

(f) When words are used *figuratively* their gender may sometimes vary from that of their literal use on the syntactic level.

- עַיִן (literally "*eye*," feminine, but figuratively "*engraving surface*," masculine).

(2) Nouns that have a *feminine form* (i.e. morphologically feminine nouns)

(a) *Abstract* nouns are morphologically feminine.

גְּבוּרָה power

יְשָׁרָה sincerity

נְדִיבוֹת noble things (plural)

An exception is חַיִל (power), which is morphologically masculine.

(b) *Collective* nouns are often also morphologically feminine.

אֹרְחָה caravan

דַּלָּה (the) poor

אֹיֶבֶת enemy

(c) A single member of a *collective* is often also morphologically feminine.

אֳנִיָּה ship

as opposed to

אֳנִי fleet

Compare, however, the following exception:

דָּגָה fish (collective)

as opposed to

דָּג a fish

(d) When an *infinitive* is used as a noun, it is often regarded as morphologically feminine.

דֵּעַת knowledge, to know

(e) A noun used *figuratively* is often morphologically feminine.

יוֹנֶקֶת a young shoot, sapling

as opposed to

יוֹנֵק suckling/child

Most nouns with feminine forms are also feminine on the level of syntax and semantics.

(3) Gender doublets

Some nouns that refer to inanimate objects have masculine and feminine forms with the same meaning – this applies to abstract concepts as well as concrete things.

אָשָׁם/אַשְׁמָה debt

מַתָּן/מַתָּנָה gift

24.2.3. *Characteristics of gender in animate objects*

(1) Natural pairs

(a) Sometimes there is no morphological indication of the gender of the elements in semantically marked opposite gender pairs.

אָב father

אֵם mother

(b) The gender of some semantically related pairs is marked morphologically by a masculine and a feminine form.

פַּר bull, ox

פָּרָה cow

(2) Epicene nouns

Some nouns are called *epicene nouns*, meaning that they have only one form for both masculine and feminine referents.

(a) Some words bear semantic reference to a mixed gendered group, but are either morphologically masculine or feminine.

כֶּלֶב dog (masculine form refers to both male and female)

יוֹנָה dove (feminine form refers to both male and female)

(b) Some epicene nouns that have a masculine form are syntactically feminine.

גְּמַלִּים מֵנִיקוֹת nursing camels

(c) The word for god(s)/goddess(es) אֱלֹהִים is also regarded as an epicene noun.

(3) Precedence of the masculine gender on syntactic level

When masculine and feminine word forms are combined, the masculine gender is accorded precedence on the syntactic level (see §35.(8)).

זָכָר וּנְקֵבָה בָּרָא אֹתָם׃　Male and female he created *them* (m.)

(Gen. 1:27).

This syntactic precedence is possibly due to the function of the masculine form as an unmarked gender, especially in the plural for mixed groups.

§24.3. Number[2]

24.3.1. *Number as a grammatical and extra-linguistic concept*

Number is a *grammatical (morphological and syntactic) characteristic* of nouns, but also refers to the extra-linguistic reality (the semantic aspect of number). Morphologically, nouns in Biblical Hebrew have singular, plural and dual forms. The dual forms in Biblical Hebrew are mainly reserved for objects that occur in pairs (such as parts of the body) and for certain indications of time.

(1) Morphological characteristics of number in general

    (a) Some words have *all three forms of number*.

יָד　hand

יָדַיִם　two hands

יָדוֹת　hands

    (b) Others have *only a singular and dual form* – the dual form is then used for the plural.

אֹזֶן　ear

אָזְנַיִם　ears

    (c) Some words have *only a dual form*.

מָתְנַיִם　hips

---

2. See Waltke and O'Connor §7.

(2) Syntactic characteristics of number in general

    (a) Syntactically a singular noun in subject position takes a singular form of the verb (§35).

        וַיַּשְׁכֵּם אֲבִימֶלֶךְ בַּבֹּקֶר And *Abimelech rose early* in the morning (Gen. 20:8).*

    (b) A plural subject takes a plural verb.

        וַיִּירְאוּ הָאֲנָשִׁים מְאֹד: And *the men were* very much *afraid* (Gen. 20:8).

    (c) There are *exceptions*, for example, when a noun with a plural form has a singular meaning.

        וַיֹּאמֶר אֱלֹהִים... And *God said*... (Gen. 1:3).*

    (d) Dual subjects take plural verbs because Biblical Hebrew verbs have no dual forms.

        אַל־יִרְפּוּ יָדֶיךָ: Let not *your hands* (dual form) *grow weak* (plural form) (Zeph. 3:16).*

(3) The semantics of number in general

Number is a grammatical feature of nouns that does not always correspond to extra-linguistic reality. For example, collective nouns are singular nouns that refer to more than one object, e.g.: עוֹף (birds) and הָעָם (the people). On the other hand, Hebrew also makes use of the plural noun פָּנִים to refer to the singular "face." In the case of the latter type, the morphological number *sometimes* corresponds to the syntactic number *and sometimes does not*.

        פָּנַי יֵלֵכוּ וַהֲנִחֹתִי לָךְ: *My presence* [lit. *my face* (plural)] *will go* (plural) with you, and I will give you rest (Exod. 33:14).

        וְיָדְעוּ הָעָם כֻּלּוֹ And all *the people* (singular) *will know* (plural) (Isa. 9:8).*

Furthermore, the allocation of grammatical number to concepts differs from language to language.

24.3.2. *Syntactic and semantic aspects of the singular form*

(1) With nouns referring to countable objects, the singular refers to *one example of many* (the so-called numerical singular).

אִישׁ   a man

בַּיִת   a house

(2) With collective nouns the singular is used to refer to *a group* (the so-called collective singular).

צֹאן   sheep

אָדָם   people, humanity

עוֹף   birds

דָּגָה   fish

Collective nouns in subject positions may govern the singular or plural form of the verb. See §35 for possible reasons.

יֹאכְלוּ עוֹף הַשָּׁמַיִם   *The birds of heaven will eat* (plural) (1 Kgs 14:11).*

עוֹף הַשָּׁמַיִם יוֹלִיךְ אֶת־הַקּוֹל   *The birds of heaven will carry* (singular) your voice [lit. the voice] (Eccl. 10:20).*

(a) Some nouns are used *almost exclusively in the singular* as collective nouns.

פְּרִי   fruit

דֶּשֶׁא   grass

רֶמֶשׂ   creeping things

בְּהֵמָה   animals

טַף   children

רֶכֶב   war-chariots

(b) Nouns that often occur in the plural form can, however, also sometimes be used *in the singular collective*.

אִישׁ   men

אִשָּׁה   women

עֵץ   trees

(3) The singular noun occurring after cardinal numbers, after כֹּל and other words indicating quantity, *refers to a class or a group*. Gentilic nouns (names of people or groups) are also often used in the singular.

וּשְׁלֹשִׁים וּשְׁנַיִם מֶלֶךְ	and thirty-two kings [lit. king] (1 Kgs 20:1)*
וְלָרֽאוּבֵנִי...אָמַר יְהוֹשֻׁעַ...	And to the *Reubenites* [lit. the Reubenite]...Joshua said... (Josh. 1:12).*
כָּל־זְכוּרְךָ	all your males [lit. male] (Exod. 34:23)

Note, however, that when כֹּל precedes a singular indefinite noun, the nuance is "every" or "each."[3]

וְכָל־פֶּה דֹּבֵר נְבָלָה	And every mouth speaks folly (Isa. 9:16).*

See also §24.3.3.(8).

(4) When the same noun is repeated in the singular – with or without the conjunction וְ or with a preposition – it has a *distributive sense* (§29.3(7)).

שָׁנָה שָׁנָה	*year by year* [lit. year year] (Deut. 14:22)*
דּוֹר־וָדוֹר	*generation after generation* (i.e. *every* generation) (Deut. 32:7)*
שָׁנָה בְשָׁנָה	*year* on year (Deut. 15:20)*
בַּבֹּקֶר בַּבֹּקֶר	*morning by* morning (Exod. 16:21)

(5) When the same noun is repeated syndetically in the singular (i.e. with a conjunction), it expresses *diversity.*

בְּלֵב וָלֵב יְדַבֵּרוּ׃	They speak with a *double* heart (i.e. deceitfully) (Ps. 12:3).*

---

3. See Naudé (2011a and 2011b).

(6) Repetition of the same noun can also indicate *exclusivity* or *intensity* (§29.3(8)).

זָהָב זָהָב   *pure* gold (2 Kgs 25:15)*

בַּדֶּרֶךְ בַּדֶּרֶךְ אֵלֵךְ   I will go *only* by the road (Deut. 2:27).*

24.3.3. *Syntactic and semantic aspects of the plural form*

(1) With nouns referring to countable objects the plural indicates more than one or two specimens (the so-called *numerical plural*).

אֲנָשִׁים   men

מְלָכִים   kings

(2) The repetition of the same noun in the plural indicates *intensification*.

עָשֹׂה הַנַּחַל הַזֶּה גֵּבִים | גֵּבִים: I will make this wadi [dry river bed] *full of pools* (2 Kgs 3:16).

(3) The plural form of a singular collective noun indicates *a disruption or processing of the collective*. With nouns referring to crops it often indicates the processed state.

דָּם   blood

דָּמִים   blood*shed*

שְׂעֹרָה   barley (in the fields)

שְׂעֹרִים   *cooked* barley

(4) The plural forms of some nouns indicate that the referent of the noun is *large, complex or manifold* (the so-called plurals of extension).

מַיִם   water

אֹהָלִים   camp, dwelling

as opposed to

אֹהֶל   tent (often a religious use)

Some nouns that refer to *body parts* are used only in the plural as plurals of extension.

פָּנִים   face

(5) The plural form of some nouns indicates *a repeated series of actions or a habit*. It can have an abstract meaning.

זְנוּנִים prostitution

כּוֹס תַּנְחוּמִים cup of consolation (Jer. 16:7)

(6) With abstract nouns the plural often refers to a *characteristic or condition*.

בִּינוֹת understanding

בְּחֻרִים youth

זְקֻנִים old age

(7) The plural form of some nouns refers to a *special or exalted person*, or superior deity or person, the so-called *honorific plural* (*pluralis majestatis*).

הָאֱלֹהִים gods/God

(a) The plural forms of *participles* are also sometimes used as honorific plurals in reference to God or people.

עֹשָׂי my Maker (Job 35:10)

(b) The plural form of some nouns that refer to animals is sometimes used as an honorific plural to designate *a whole species*.

וְעַל־עַיִר בֶּן־אֲתֹנוֹת׃ and on a colt, the foal of donkeys (Zech. 9:9)

(c) The honorific plural is also used in reference to *people*.

בְּעָלִים boss, master

אֲדֹנִים lord

The word אֲדֹנָי (Lord, as the name of the God of Israel) must be distinguished from both אֲדֹנִי (my master) and אֲדֹנַי (my lord), which are used to refer to people.

(8) When כֹּל precedes a definite plural noun, it has the nuance of the totality of the specific group.

When it precedes an indefinite plural noun, it has the nuance of each and every member of the group (see also §24.3.2(3)).

כָּל־הַנְּתִינִים וּבְנֵי עַבְדֵי שְׁלֹמֹה שְׁלֹשׁ מֵאוֹת תִּשְׁעִים וּשְׁנָיִם	*All* (i.e. *the total*) of the temple servants and the sons of Solomon's servants – three hundred and ninety-two (Ezra 2:58)*
כָּל־שֻׁלְחָנוֹת מָלְאוּ קִיא צֹאָה	*All* tables (i.e. *each and every one*) are covered with filthy vomit (Isa. 28:8).*

24.3.4. *Syntactic and semantic aspects of the dual form*

(1) The dual occurs especially in nouns referring to *body parts* that occur in pairs.

אָזְנַיִם	two ears
עֵינַיִם	two eyes

    (a) The dual is also used for *nouns* that refer to objects that usually occur in pairs.

נַעֲלַיִם	a pair of sandals [lit. two sandals]

    (b) The plural form of nouns that have dual forms referring to body parts is often used *metaphorically*.

יָדַיִם	two hands

        but

יָדוֹת	handles [lit. hands (of a pot)]

(2) The dual form of nouns is also used for *measurable time and measuring units*.

אַמָּה	cubit
אַמָּתַיִם	two cubits
אַמּוֹת	cubits
יוֹם	day
יוֹמַיִם	two days
יָמִים	days

(3) Although מַיִם and שָׁמַיִם *look like dual forms*, they should be regarded as plural forms.

(4) Some nouns have dual forms without there being any obvious reason for this.

צָהֳרַיִם midday (noon)

מִצְרַיִם Egypt

יְרוּשָׁלַיִם Jerusalem

§24.4. Definiteness

Definiteness may be regarded as a congruency feature of nouns. In English a distinction is made between the definite article *the* and the indefinite article *a*. Biblical Hebrew has a grammatical equivalent only for the definite article.

24.4.1. *Expression of indefiniteness/definiteness*

The indefiniteness or definiteness of Biblical Hebrew nominal forms is morphologically determined as follows:

(1) A noun is *indefinite* if:

    (a) An article or pronominal suffix is not affixed to it and it is not followed by a definite noun in a construct relation (§25.3).

    (b) אֶחָד or אַחַת is used, however, to mark a certain or specific someone or something.

אִישׁ אֶחָד a *certain* man (Judg. 13:2)

(2) A noun is *definite* if:

    (a) It is definite in itself

      •   a proper name

וַיְבַקֵּשׁ לַהֲרֹג אֶת־מֹשֶׁה And he sought to kill *Moses* (Exod. 2:15).*

      •   a pronoun

וַיֵּשֶׁב בַּמְּעָרָה הוּא וּשְׁתֵּי בְנֹתָיו And *he* dwelt in a cave with his two daughters [lit. *he* dwelt in a cave, *he* and *his* two daughters] (Gen. 19:30).*

- a title

וַיַּמְלִכוּ כָל־יִשְׂרָאֵל אֶת־עָמְרִי   And all Israel made Omri, *the com-*
שַׂר־צָבָא עַל־יִשְׂרָאֵל   *mander of the army*, king over
Israel (1 Kgs 16:16).*

- a common noun that has acquired the value of a proper noun

וַיָּשֶׁת עֲלֵיהֶם תֵּבֵל׃   And he set on them *the world*
(1 Sam. 2:8).*

(b) It has the definite article הַ

(c) A pronominal suffix is affixed to it

(d) It is in *status constructus* and followed by a definite noun

הָשֵׁב אֵשֶׁת־הָאִישׁ   Restore the man's wife [lit. *the wife*
of the man] (Gen. 20:7).*

Note the following:

(i) Biblical Hebrew differs from English in its use of the definite article.
The function of the article must thus be determined carefully, especially
in translation.

(ii) The use of the article is a relatively recent phenomenon in Semitic
languages and is therefore often omitted in poetic sections.

24.4.2. *Form of the article*

The basic form of the article is הַ. The article is directly attached to the front
of the relevant noun resulting in the doubling of the first consonant of that
word.

מֶלֶךְ + הַ   the + king

הַמֶּלֶךְ   the king

The following exceptions occur:[4]

(1) The gutturals (א, ה, ח, ע) and ר (as a rule) cannot be doubled (§4.2.4.1).
When a definite noun begins with one of these consonants, the /◌/ of the
article changes or lengthens to compensate for the doubling that can no
longer occur.

---

4. See also Waltke and O'Connor §13.3 and Bekins (2013).

These changes may be presented systematically as follows:

The first vowel is not a qāmeṣ			The first vowel is a qāmeṣ		
אִישׁ	א		אָדָם	א	
רֹאשׁ	ר	הָ	רָשָׁע	ר	הָ
עִיר	ע		עָפָר	ע	
הֵיכָל	ה		הָרִים	ה	
חֶרֶב	ח	הַ	חָכָם	ח	הֶ

(2) The first consonant of the noun also does not double in the following instances:

(a) In words beginning with יְ or מְ the doubling usually falls away (§8.2.5).

הַיְלָדִים the children

(b) In words beginning with יְ and followed by a ה or ע, the doubling does occur.

הַיְּהוּדִים the Jews

(c) In words beginning with מְ and followed by a ה, ע or ר the doubling does occur.

הַמְּרֵעִים the mischief-makers

(3) The vocalization of some nouns changes when the article is added to them.

אֶרֶץ land
הָאָרֶץ the land
אֲרוֹן ark
הָאָרוֹן the ark

(4) When the bound prepositions (בְּ, כְּ and לְ) appear before the article, the prepositions and the article combine to form a single syllable, e.g.: בַּ instead of בְּהַ, לַ instead of לְהַ, כַּ instead of כְּהַ.

בַּמֶּלֶךְ by the king
לַמֶּלֶךְ for the king
כַּמֶּלֶךְ like the king

24.4.3. *Syntactic functions of the article*[5]

(1) The article is sometimes used to designate *a specific addressee* (§34.4).

חֵי־נַפְשְׁךָ הַמֶּלֶךְ By the life of your inner being, *O king* (1 Sam. 17:55).*

However, the article is not necessary for specifying an addressee. (See also Miller 2010a and 2010b.)

(2) The article is used in the place of a relative marker to construct a *relative clause*.

(a) With *a finite verb* (rare and usually in Late Biblical Hebrew)

עַמְּךָ הַנִּמְצְאוּ־פֹּה your people *who are present* here (1 Chron. 29:17).

(b) Apparently with a *participle* (§20.3.2.2.(2)).

לַיהוָה הַנִּרְאֶה אֵלָיו: to the LORD, *who had appeared* to him (Gen. 12:7).

(3) The article is used to construct *the superlative*.

כִּי־אַתֶּם הַמְעַט מִכָּל־הָעַמִּים: For you were *the fewest* of all peoples (Deut. 7:7).

(4) It *marks* an adjective or demonstrative pronoun as *grammatically congruent* with a noun.

וַנֵּלֶךְ אֵת כָּל־הַמִּדְבָּר הַגָּדוֹל And we went through all that *great* desert (Deut. 1:19).*

24.4.4. *Semantic functions of the article*[6]

(1) The article makes a *demonstrative* semantic contribution when used with nouns referring to time.

הַיּוֹם today [lit. the day] (Gen. 4:14)

---

5. See Waltke and O'Connor §13.5.2.
6. See Waltke and O'Connor §13.5.1.

(2) The definite noun focuses attention on the referent's *identity.* The following constructions are important here:

(a) A common noun with an article can refer to a *unique referent* (i.e. there is only one of its kind).

הַשֶּׁמֶשׁ the sun

(b) A common noun with an article can refer to a *specific referent* that has, for example, been mentioned before. This contributes towards creating a coherent text. To put it another way, if there were no indication that a particular referent had already been mentioned, the text would seem awkward (or incoherent).

וַיִּקַּח בֶּן־בָּקָר...[7] [7]And he took a calf...

[8]וַיִּקַּח חֶמְאָה וְחָלָב וּבֶן־הַבָּקָר [8]then he took curds, and milk, and *the calf* (Gen. 18:7–8).*

(3) Things that are *implied by the context* take the article, even if they have not been mentioned before.

וַתְּעַר כַּדָּהּ אֶל־הַשֹּׁקֶת And she emptied her jar into *the trough* (Gen. 24:20).*

(4) The article is used *generically to designate* a class of persons or things that are definite in themselves.

אַךְ אֶת־זֶה לֹא תֹאכְלוּ... But you shall not eat these...*the* אֶת־הַגָּמָל...וְאֶת־הַשָּׁפָן camel...and *the rock badger* (Lev. 11:4–5).*

הַכּוֹכָבִים *the stars* (Gen. 15:5)

הַכְּנַעֲנִי *the Canaanite(s)*

בָּאֵשׁ with [lit. *the*] *fire* (Josh. 11:9)

בַּסַּנְוֵרִים with [lit. *the*] *blindness* (Gen. 19:11)

This construction is used particularly in comparisons, e.g.

כְּלֵב הָאַרְיֵה like the heart of *a* [lit. *the*] *lion* (2 Sam. 17:10)

(5) The article is used to mark a common noun as a *proper noun.*

הַיְאֹר *The River* = the Nile River

§25. Declension of the Noun

§25.1. Construct State

25.1.1. *General*

Unlike most of the other Semitic languages, Biblical Hebrew no longer has noun cases. A Biblical Hebrew noun thus does not "decline" as a Greek or Latin noun; i.e. it does not have different endings for the nominative, vocative, accusative, genitive, dative and ablative cases. In other words, the morphology of the noun in Biblical Hebrew does not indicate its grammatical role in the sentence.

Only the forms of the personal pronoun indicate the grammatical role of the pronoun within the sentence:

	Subject	Direct Object	Possessive	Indirect Object
Equivalent case in languages with case	"Nominative"	"Accusative"	"Genitive"	"Dative"
1 sing.	אֲנִי	אוֹתִי	◌ִי	לִי
	I	me	my	to me
3 m. sing.	הוּא	אוֹתוֹ	◌ֹ-	לוֹ
	he	him	his	to him

25.1.2. *Terminology: Status absolutus and status constructus*

Biblical Hebrew has adopted other strategies to compensate for the loss of noun cases. There is, for example, the *construct relation*. It is a linguistic phenomenon in Biblical Hebrew that involves two nouns that could be expressed in English as follows:

> The horse of the king.

In its simplest form it consists of a *status constructus* form of the noun and a *status absolutus* form.

St. cs.	St. abs.
the horse	of the king
the God	of the heavens

The *status absolutus* is the normal form of the word.

The *status constructus* is a special form of the word that is used to indicate that it forms a construction (in the broadest sense of the word) with the word(s) that follow it. This is called the *construct relationship* or סְמִיכוּת (support). The *status constructus* is also called the נִסְמָךְ (supported) and the word that follows it the סֹמֵךְ (supporter). The סֹמֵךְ is the equivalent of the genitive in Greek and Latin and other Semitic languages.

The construct word(s) and the absolute word form a phrasal unit and are called a *construct chain.* The construct chain as a whole may have any syntactic role in the sentence, e.g. subject (#*a-c*), direct object, indirect object (with a preposition), etc.

a	יְהוָה אִישׁ מִלְחָמָה	The LORD is *a man of war* (i.e. a warrior) (Exod. 15:3).
b	וַיֹּאמְרוּ אֱלֹהֵי הָעִבְרִים נִקְרָא עָלֵינוּ	And they said, "The God of the Hebrews himself revealed himself to us" (Exod. 5:3).*
c	וַתֵּרֶב חָכְמַת שְׁלֹמֹה מֵחָכְמַת כָּל־בְּנֵי־קֶדֶם	And the *wisdom of Solomon* was greater than *the wisdom of all of the Kedemites* (1 Kgs 5:10).*

Note the following:

(1) The *status constructus* has different endings from the *status absolutus* in all the numbers and genders, except the masculine singular (which has no endings) and the feminine plural (where it is the same as the absolute). The masculine dual *status constructus* ending and masculine plural *status constructus* endings look the same. (See the second table in §25.2.)

(2) The construct phrase as a whole is either definite or indefinite. The definiteness is determined by whether or not the absolute form is definite. An absolute form is definite if it has the definite article, if it has a pronominal suffix or if it is a proper name (see §24.4.1).

(3) A *status constructus* form loses its main accent and this is why vowel reduction often occurs, e.g.: דָּבָר becomes דְּבַר (see §7.3 and the tables of noun forms in §27).

(4) Sometimes the *status constructus* is joined to the *status absolutus* with the *maqqēp̄*, e.g.: בֶּן־ (son of) (see §9.3).

(5) The Masoretic accents (§9.5) can also indicate the distinction between the *status absolutus* and the *status constructus.* A conjunctive accent can indicate a construct relationship, but a disjunctive accent indicates that the word is in the *status absolutus.*

§25.2. Morphology of the *Status Absolutus* and *Status Constructus*

Biblical Hebrew nouns can have the following endings:

	Masculine		Feminine	
	st. abs.	*st. cs.*	*st. abs.*	*st. cs.*
singular	-	-	◌ָה	◌ַת
plural	◌ִים	◌ֵי	וֹת	וֹת
dual	◌ַֽיִם	◌ֵי	◌ָתַֽיִם	◌ָתֵי

If endings are "added" to unchangeable nouns, the results are:

	Masculine		Feminine	
	st. abs.	*st. cs.*	*st. abs.*	*st. cs.*
singular	סוּס stallion	סוּס stallion of	סוּסָה mare	סוּסַת mare of
plural	סוּסִים stallions	סוּסֵי stallions of	סוּסוֹת mares	סוּסוֹת mares of
dual	סוּסַֽיִם two stallions	סוּסֵי two stallions of	סוּסָתַֽיִם two mares	סוּסָתֵי two mares of

Vowel reduction or other changes also occur in most nouns – the relevant rules and paradigms will be dealt with in §26 and §27. Not all the forms described in §26 and §27 occur in the Hebrew Bible, but they have been theoretically reconstructed in order to form a complete paradigm.

§25.3. Nouns in Construct Relationships

25.3.1. *Syntactic features*

(1) A noun in the *status constructus* never takes the definite article הַ.

(2) In order to express a possessive relationship between nouns which differ in definiteness, a construction with the preposition לְ is used instead of the construct phrase, e.g.

מִזְמוֹר לְדָוִד   a psalm of David [lit. a psalm to David]

(3) A construct relationship is *usually inseparable.*
On rare occasions, a constituent may intervene between the elements of the construct phrase. In such a case one speaks of a *broken* construct relationship. Such elements include, *inter alia*, the following:

(a) The *hē² locale* (see §28.1)

וַיָּבֵא הָאִישׁ אֶת־הָאֲנָשִׁים בֵּיתָה   And the man brought the men to

יוֹסֵף: the house *of Joseph* (Gen. 43:17).*

(b) Prepositions

אֶת־אַחַד מֵהַנְּעָרִים   one *of the servants* (1 Sam. 9:3)*

(c) אֵת

לְיֵשַׁע אֶת־מְשִׁיחֶךָ   for the salvation *of your anointed* (Hab. 3:13)*

(d) Certain verb forms (rare)

דֶּרֶךְ יְרַצְּחוּ־שֶׁכְמָה   They murder on the *way to/of Shechem* (Hos. 6:9).*

(e) The so-called enclitic *mêm* (see §28.2).[7]

יְהוָה־אֱלֹהִי־ם צְבָאוֹת   Lord, God *of hosts* (Ps. 59:6)
(MT reads אֱלֹהִים)

(4) Additional syntactic features of the construct relationship

    (a) *Usually two coordinated constructs cannot occur with one status constructus.* Instead, two construct phrases are used.

אֶל־תְּפִלַּת עַבְדְּךָ וְאֶל־תְּחִנָּתוֹ   to the prayer and supplication *of your servant* [lit. to the prayer *of your servant* and to his supplication] (1 Kgs 8:28)*

    There are, however, some *exceptions.*

מִבְחַר וְטוֹב־לְבָנוֹן   the choice and the best of *Lebanon* [lit. the choice of and best *of Lebanon*] (Ezek. 31:16)

---

7. See Waltke and O'Connor §9.8 and §28a.

(b) One *status constructus* cannot usually govern two coordinated *status absolutus* forms either.

Where this does occur, the *status constructus* is usually repeated.

אֱלֹהֵי הַשָּׁמַיִם וֵאלֹהֵי הָאָרֶץ *the God* of the heaven and the earth [lit. *the God* of the heaven and *the God* of the earth] (Gen. 24:3)*

In some cases the *status constructus* is not repeated, especially if the two *absolute forms* are closely related.

בְּעֵינֵי אֱלֹהִים וְאָדָם: in the eyes *of God and humans* (Prov. 3:4)*

(c) A prepositional phrase or verb phrase sometimes follows a noun in the *status constructus*.

יֹשְׁבֵי בְּאֶרֶץ צַלְמָוֶת those who dwelt *in the land* of deep darkness (Isa. 9:1).*

כָּל־יְמֵי הִתְהַלַּכְנוּ אִתָּם all the days *that we went with them* [lit. all the days *of our going with them*] (1 Sam. 25:15).*

(d) A pronominal suffix that semantically belongs to the word that is in *status constructus* occurs at the end of the construct phrase, i.e. on the *status absolutus* form. It must, however, be translated as a part of the *status constructus*. In order to determine the element to which the pronominal suffix belongs, the textual context needs to be taken into account.

הַר קָדְשִׁי *my* holy mountain [lit. the mountain of *my* holiness] (Isa. 11:9)

25.3.2. *Possible combinations in construct relationship*

(1) Instances where definiteness agrees

סוּסַת מַלְכָּה *a* mare of *a* queen

סוּסַת הַמַּלְכָּה *the* mare of *the* queen

(a) In a construct chain all the members of the chain are in the *status constructus* except the last.

The last member, however, always stands in the ordinary form or the *status absolutus*. The definiteness or indefiniteness of the *status absolutus* applies to all the other parts of the construct phrase.

יִרְאַת סוּסַת מַלְכָּה   *a* fear of *a* mare of *a* queen

יִרְאַת סוּסַת הַמַּלְכָּה   *the* fear of *the* mare of *the* queen

(b) Both the *status constructus* and *status absolutus* may be singular or plural.

דְּבַר הַנָּבִיא   the word of the prophet

דְּבַר הַנְּבִיאִים   the word of the prophets

דִּבְרֵי הַנָּבִיא   the words of the prophet

דִּבְרֵי הַנְּבִיאִים   the words of the prophets

(c) The *status constructus* can be a participle.

שֹׁמֵר הַתּוֹרָה   *the guardian* (participle) of the law

(d) The *status constructus* can be an adjective.

טוֹבַת הַנָּשִׁים   *the good* (adjective) of the women

(2) Should the *status constructus* and the *status absolutus* *differ in definiteness*, the construct relationship cannot be used, but the preposition לְ is used to express the "possessive construction."

סוּסָה לַמַּלְכָּה   a mare of the queen

הַסּוּסָה לְמַלְכָּה   the mare of a queen

הַסּוּסָה לְמַלְכָּה הַגְּדוֹלָה   the large mare of a queen

סוּסָה לַמַּלְכָּה גְּדוֹלָה   a large mare of the queen

(3) The *preposition* לְ can also be used in cases where there is *no difference in definiteness*.

In such cases it can assist in determining which element is being qualified. The following constructions are thus possible:

• סוּסַת הַמַּלְכָּה הַגְּדוֹלָה

                    or   *the large mare* of the queen

הַסּוּסָה הַגְּדוֹלָה לַמַּלְכָּה

- סוּסַת הַמַּלְכָּה הַגְּדוֹלָה

  or   the mare of *the large queen*

  הַסּוּסָה לַמַּלְכָּה הַגְּדוֹלָה

- סוּסַת מַלְכָּה גְדוֹלָה

  or   *a large mare* of a queen

  סוּסָה גְדוֹלָה לְמַלְכָּה

- סוּסַת מַלְכָּה גְּדוֹלָה

  or   a mare of *a large queen*

  סוּסָה לְמַלְכָּה גְּדוֹלָה

§25.4. Syntactic-Semantic Relationships in Construct Relationships

The *status constructus* is used to express many other relationships beside that of possession–possessor.

The *status constructus* and *status absolutus* can occur in the following relationships:

25.4.1. *Relationships of Possession*

(1) Possession (concrete object)–possessor

> בֵּית הַמֶּלֶךְ   the house of the king

(2) Possession (body part)–possessor

> שִׂפְתֵי הַמֶּלֶךְ   the lips of the king

(3) Possession (characteristic)–possessor

> הֲדָרַת־הַמֶּלֶךְ   the majesty of the king

(4) Kinship/relationship–possessor

> בְּנֵי הַמֶּלֶךְ   the sons of the king

(5) Possessor–possession

> בַּעַל הַבַּיִת   the owner of the house

25.4.2. *Subject and object relations*

(1) Verbal notion–subject

בִּרְכַּת יהוה the blessing of (or, by) the LORD

(2) Verbal notion (passive)–agent

הֲרוּגֵי הָאִשָּׁה the murdered (ones) of the woman

(3) Verbal notion–object

יִרְאַת יהוה the fear of (for) the LORD

25.4.3. *Partitive relationships*

(1) Part–divided whole

בְּנֵי הַנְּבִיאִים the members of (among) the prophet guild

(2) Superlative part–divided whole

טוֹב הַבָּנִים the best (good) of (among) the sons

(3) Specification of undivided whole

כָּל־הַבָּנִים all of the sons (all the sons)

25.4.4. *Equalizing relationships*

(1) Entity–synonym

שִׂמְחַת גִּיל joy of (viz.) rejoicing

(2) Entity–class (genus)

כְּסִיל אָדָם a fool of (viz.) a person

(3) Entity–type (species)

זִבְחֵי שְׁלָמִים sacrifices of (viz.) peace offerings

(4) Entity–name

נְהַר פְּרָת the river of (viz.) the Euphrates

(5) Entity–characteristic (description, attribute, quality)

אִמְרֵי בִינָה   words of (with) insight

25.4.5. *Adverbial relationships*

(1) Entity–aim, goal or result

אַבְנֵי־קֶלַע   stones of (meant for) a sling

(2) Entity–manner

אוֹצְרוֹת רֶשַׁע   riches of (acquired through) injustice

(3) Entity–cause or reason

מְזֵי רָעָב   exhausted (ones) of (due to) hunger

(4) Entity–means (instrument)

חַלְלֵי־הַחֶרֶב   the wounded (ones) of (by means of) the sword

(5) Entity–duration of time

בֶּן־שָׁנָה   a son of a year (a one year old)

(6) Entity–direction

יוֹרְדֵי בוֹר   the (ones) going down (into the) pit

(7) Entity–origin

שְׁלַל הֶעָרִים   the loot of (from) the cities

25.4.6. *Other relationships*

(1) Product–material

כְּלֵי כֶסֶף   vessels of silver

(2) Product–author, creator, source, origin

סֵפֶר הָאִישׁ   the book of (by) the man

(3) Characteristic–with regard/respect to (specification)

אֱוִיל שְׂפָתַיִם   foolish of (with respect to) lips

(4) Entity–interested (favored/injured) party

מוֹקֵשׁ הָאָדָם the trap of (for, to the detriment of) a person

(5) Container–content

חֵמַת מַיִם a bag of (full of) water

§26. Nouns with Pronominal Suffixes

§26.1. Morphology of Nouns with Pronominal Suffixes

Suffixes are elements added to the end of a word. Biblical Hebrew has different types of suffixes:

(1) Finite *verbs* have suffixes that designate the person, gender and number of the subject (§15). In addition, *object suffixes* may also be affixed to them (§17).

(2) With *nouns* the distinction between the singular, plural and dual, masculine and feminine, *status absolutus* and *status constructus* is also expressed by means of suffixes (§24 and §25). These suffixes are called *endings*. In contrast to the classical languages, however, *person suffixes* also occur with nouns. These *pronominal suffixes/enclitic personal pronouns* may be regarded as the possessive equivalent of the separate personal pronoun. One could even speak of *genitive* suffixes here as morphologically distinguishable endings do indeed occur. *Whenever further reference is made to "suffixes" here, the possessive pronominal suffixes are understood.*

The following distinctions must be maintained in the declension of nouns:

- Words with masculine forms and words with feminine forms
- Words in the singular, plural or dual

There are six unique sets of pronominal suffixes (Table 36):

Set 1 is used with *masculine singular* nouns.
Set 2 is used with *feminine singular* nouns.
Set 3 is used with *masculine plural* nouns.
Set 4 is used with *feminine plural* nouns.
Set 5 is used with *masculine dual* nouns.
Set 6 is used with *feminine dual* nouns.

The consonant and vowel pattern of a noun influences the declension.

Note the following:

The characteristics of nouns with suffixes may be systematized as follows (always compare the full declension of a noun in Table 36):

(a) The endings of the *status absolutus* and *status constructus* in the singular, dual and plural of nouns with masculine and feminine forms are unique (§25.2).

(b) The pronominal suffixes occurring with masculine singular nouns constitute the so-called *basic paradigm* in Biblical Hebrew.

(c) The *heavy suffixes* are כֶם-, כֶן-, הֶם- and הֶן-. All other pronominal suffixes are *light suffixes*.

(d) If a closed syllable has developed from an open syllable, for example, after applying the rule of *šəwāʾ*, the syllable is considered half-closed and the *beḡaḏkeḏaṯ* letter following it does not get a *dāḡēš*, for example, when the heavy suffixes are added to singular nouns (see Table 36, e.g. תּוֹרַתְכֶם).

(e) Masculine dual nouns use the same set of suffixes that is used with plural, masculine nouns.

(f) The suffixes used with feminine nouns can be deduced from the suffixes used with masculine nouns as follows:

Singular: *status absolutus* הָ becomes תָ before light suffixes
                  status constructus תַ appears before heavy suffixes

Dual: *status absolutus* (תַיִם) // the form תָ before the light suffixes (which look just like the suffixes in masculine plural nouns)

               status constructus (תֵי) // the form תַ before the heavy suffixes (which look just like those used with masculine plural nouns)

Plural: *status absolutus* = *status constructus* (תוֹ) = the form occurring before all suffixes (which look just like those used with masculine plural nouns)

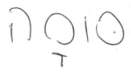

Table 36. *Complete Declension of the Noun*

Masculine Singular			Feminine Singular		
st. abs.			st. abs.		◌ָה
st. cs.			st. cs.		◌ַת
with sing. suffix	1 c.	◌ִי	with sing. suffix	1 c.	◌ָתִי
	2 m.	◌ְךָ		2 m.	◌ָתְךָ
	2 f.	◌ֵךְ		2 f.	◌ָתֵךְ
	3 m.	◌ֵהוּ ,◌וֹ		3 m.	◌ָתוֹ
	3 f.	◌ָ ,◌ָהּ		3 f.	◌ָתָהּ
with pl. suffix	1 c.	◌ֵ֫נוּ	with pl. suffix	1 c.	◌ָתֵ֫נוּ
	2 m.	◌ְכֶם		2 m.	◌ָתְכֶם
	2 f.	◌ְכֶן		2 f.	◌ָתְכֶן
	3 m.	◌ֵהֶם ,◌ָם		3 m.	◌ָתָם
	3 f.	◌ֵהֶן ,◌ָן		3 f.	◌ָתָן
Masculine Dual			Feminine Dual		
st. abs.		◌ַ֫יִם	st. abs.		◌ָתַ֫יִם
st. cs.		◌ֵי	st. cs.		◌ָתֵי
with sing. suffix	1 c.	◌ַי	with sing. suffix	1 c.	◌ָתַי
	2 m.	◌ֶ֫יךָ		2 m.	◌ָתֶ֫יךָ
	2 f.	◌ַ֫יִךְ		2 f.	◌ָתַ֫יִךְ
	3 m.	◌ָיו ,◌ָו ,◌ֵיהוּ		3 m.	◌ָתָיו
	3 f.	◌ֶ֫יהָ		3 f.	◌ָתֶ֫יהָ
with pl. suffix	1 c.	◌ֵ֫ינוּ	with pl. suffix	1 c.	◌ָתֵ֫ינוּ
	2 m.	◌ֵיכֶם		2 m.	◌ָתֵיכֶם
	2 f.	◌ֵיכֶן		2 f.	◌ָתֵיכֶן
	3 m.	◌ֵיהֶם ,◌ֵימוֹ		3 m.	◌ָתֵיהֶם
	3 f.	◌ֵיהֶן		3 f.	◌ָתֵיהֶן

Masculine Plural			Feminine Plural		
st. abs.		ִים	st. abs.		וֹת
st. cs.		ֵי	st. cs.		וֹת
with sing. suffix	1 c.	ַי	with sing. suffix	1 c.	וֹתַי
	2 m.	ֶיךָ		2 m.	וֹתֶיךָ
	2 f.	ַיִךְ		2 f.	וֹתַיִךְ
	3 m.	ֵיהוּ, ־וֹ, ־ָיו		3 m.	וֹתָיו
	3 f.	ֶיהָ		3 f.	וֹתֶיהָ
Plural	1 c.	ֵינוּ	*Plural*	1 c.	וֹתֵינוּ
	2 m.	ֵיכֶם		2 m.	וֹתֵיכֶם
	2 f.	ֵיכֶן		2 f.	וֹתֵיכֶן
	3 m.	ֵיהֶם		3 m.	וֹתֵיהֶם
	3 f.	ֵיהֶן		3 f.	וֹתֵיהֶן

§26.2. Syntactic and Semantic Functions of Pronominal Suffixes

The pronominal suffixes fulfil the syntactic function of an adjectival qualification occurring with a noun – *in the same way as does the second element* (the *status absolutus*) *of a construct relationship*. Like the *status absolutus*, pronominal suffixes are used to express many underlying syntactic and semantic relations. Because a pronominal suffix can replace any noun, almost all the distinctions made with the *status constructus* are possible here (§25.4).

§27. Noun Patterns and Suffixes

Nouns can be divided into various groups on the basis of the vowel changes that occur with declensions. The endings and suffixes given above lead to systematized vowel changes in each group. The general sound rules remain valid, namely the rule of *šəwā'* (§8.1), the rules of gutturals (§4.2.4.1) and the *beḡaḏkep̄aṭ* rules (§8.2).

§27.1. Declension of Nouns with Unchangeable Vowels

The endings and suffixes are added to the simplest form of the word with no further changes. תּוֹרָה serves as the example for the feminine forms of this group.

Table 37. *Nouns with Unchangeable Vowels*

Masculine Singular			Feminine Singular		
Gloss		horse	Gloss		law
st. abs.		סוּס	st. abs.		תּוֹרָה
st. cs.		סוּס	st. cs.		תּוֹרַת
with sing. suffix	1 c.	סוּסִי	with sing. suffix	1 c.	תּוֹרָתִי
	2 m.	סוּסְךָ		2 m.	תּוֹרָתְךָ
	2 f.	סוּסֵךְ		2 f.	תּוֹרָתֵךְ
	3 m.	סוּסוֹ		3 m.	תּוֹרָתוֹ
	3 f.	סוּסָהּ		3 f.	תּוֹרָתָהּ
with pl. suffix	1 c.	סוּסֵנוּ	with pl. suffix	1 c.	תּוֹרָתֵנוּ
	2 m.	סוּסְכֶם		2 m.	תּוֹרַתְכֶם
	2 f.	סוּסְכֶן		2 f.	תּוֹרַתְכֶן
	3 m.	סוּסָם		3 m.	תּוֹרָתָם
	3 f.	סוּסָן		3 f.	תּוֹרָתָן
Masculine Dual			Feminine Dual		
st. abs.		סוּסַיִם	st. abs.		תּוֹרָתַיִם
st. cs.		סוּסֵי	st. cs.		תּוֹרָתֵי
with sing. suffix	1 c.	סוּסַי	with sing. suffix	1 c.	תּוֹרָתַי
	2 m.	סוּסֶיךָ		2 m.	תּוֹרָתֶיךָ
	2 f.	סוּסַיִךְ		2 f.	תּוֹרָתַיִךְ
	3 m.	סוּסָיו		3 m.	תּוֹרָתָיו
	3 f.	סוּסֶיהָ		3 f.	תּוֹרָתֶיהָ

Masculine Dual			Feminine Dual		
with pl. suffix	1 c.	סוּסֵ֫ינוּ	with pl. suffix	1 c.	תּוֹרָתֵ֫ינוּ
	2 m.	סוּסֵיכֶם		2 m.	תּוֹרֺתֵיכֶם
	2 f.	סוּסֵיכֶן		2 f.	תּוֹרֺתֵיכֶן
	3 m.	סוּסֵיהֶם		3 m.	תּוֹרֺתֵיהֶם
	3 f.	סוּסֵיהֶן		3 f.	תּוֹרֺתֵיהֶן
Masculine Plural			Feminine Plural		
st. abs.		סוּסִים	st. abs.		תּוֹרֺת
st. cs.		סוּסֵי	st. cs.		תּוֹרֺת
with sing. suffix	1 c.	סוּסִי	with sing. suffix	1 c.	תּוֹרֺתִי
	2 m.	סוּסֶ֫יךָ		2 m.	תּוֹרֺתֶ֫יךָ
	2 f.	סוּסַ֫יִךְ		2 f.	תּוֹרֺתַ֫יִךְ
	3 m.	סוּסָיו		3 m.	תּוֹרֺתָיו
	3 f.	סוּסֶ֫יהָ		3 f.	תּוֹרֺתֶ֫יהָ
with pl. suffix	1 c.	סוּסֵ֫ינוּ	with pl. suffix	1 c.	תּוֹרֺתֵ֫ינוּ
	2 m.	סוּסֵיכֶם		2 m.	תּוֹרֺתֵיכֶם
	2 f.	סוּסֵיכֶן		2 f.	תּוֹרֺתֵיכֶן
	3 m.	סוּסֵיהֶם		3 m.	תּוֹרֺתָם\ ֵיהֶם
	3 pl.	סוּסֵיהֶן		3 f.	תּוֹרֺתָן\ֵיהֶן

§27.2. Declension of Nouns with Changeable Long Vowels

27.2.1. *Forms of declensions*

The rules regarding vowel changes in this group may be summarized by means of the following scheme. The first column indicates the position of the changeable long vowel in a word and the others indicate the changes that this vowel undergoes:

Example	Noun Sing. st. abs.	Noun Sing. st. cs. or heavy suffix	Noun Pl. st. cs. or heavy suffix	All other sing. or pl.
פָּקִיד	a. _◌	_◌	_◌	_◌
מְדַבֵּר	b. ◌_	◌_	◌_	◌_
שֹׁמֵר	c. ◌_	◌ / ◌	◌_	◌_

Example	Noun Sing. st. abs.		Noun Sing. st. cs. or heavy suffix	Noun Pl. st. cs. or heavy suffix	All other sing. or pl.
	d. (ii)	(i)			
דָּבָר	◌	◌			
זָקֵן	◌	◌			
לֵבָב	◌	◌			

(i) Treated like the /◌/ of a.

(ii) Treated like the /◌/ of b (where the /◌/ of b is retained, the /◌/ in d is also retained).

27.2.2. *Forms of nouns with changeable long vowels*

(1) Nouns with /◌/ in the penultimate (second-last) syllable

See Table 38a פָּקִיד

(2) Nouns with /◌/ in the final syllable

See Table 38b מְדַבֵּר

(3) Nouns with /◌/ in the final syllable

See Table 38c שֹׁמֵר

(4) Nouns with /◌/ in the last two syllables

See Table 39a דָּבָר

(5) Nouns with /◌/ in the final and /◌/ in the penultimate syllable

See Table 39b זָקֵן

(6) Nouns with /◌/ in the final and /◌/ in the penultimate syllable

See Table 39c לֵבָב

(7) Feminine nouns with /◌/ in the last two syllables

See Table 40 שָׁנָה

(8) Trisyllabic feminine nouns with a *šəwāʾ* in the first syllable, /◌̣/ in the second syllable and with the feminine ending ה◌ in the final syllable

See Table 41   צְדָקָה

(9) Nouns with gutturals in this group

See Table 42

(10) Monosyllabic nouns with a changeable vowel

See Table 43

Table 38. *Nouns with Changeable Long Vowels*

		Table 38a	Table 38b	Table 38c
		Nouns with /◌̣/ in the penultimate syllable	Nouns with /◌̣/ in the final syllable	Nouns with /◌̣/ in the final syllable
		פָּקִיד	מִדְבָּד	שֹׁמֵר
Gloss		commissioner/ officer	desert	guardian/guard
		Singular		
st. abs.		פָּקִיד	מִדְבָּד	שֹׁמֵר
st. cs.		פְּקִיד	מִדְבַּד	שֹׁמֵר
with sing. suffix	*1 c.*	פְּקִידִי	מִדְבָּרִי	שֹׁמְרִי
	2 m.	פְּקִידְךָ	מִדְבָּרְךָ	שֹׁמֶרְךָ
	2 f.	פְּקִידֵךְ	מִדְבָּרֵךְ	שֹׁמְרֵךְ
	3 m.	פְּקִידוֹ	מִדְבָּרוֹ	שֹׁמְרוֹ
	3 f.	פְּקִידָהּ	מִדְבָּרָהּ	שֹׁמְרָהּ
with pl. suffix	*1 c.*	פְּקִידֵנוּ	מִדְבָּרֵנוּ	שֹׁמְרֵנוּ
	2 m.	פְּקִידְכֶם	מִדְבַּרְכֶם	שֹׁמֶרְכֶם
	2 f.	פְּקִידְכֶן	מִדְבַּרְכֶן	שֹׁמֶרְכֶן
	3 m.	פְּקִידָם	מִדְבָּרָם	שֹׁמְרָם
	3 f.	פְּקִידָן	מִדְבָּרָן	שֹׁמְרָן

		Table 38a	Table 38b	Table 38c
		Nouns with /Ǫ/ in the penultimate syllable	Nouns with /Ǫ/ in the final syllable	Nouns with /Ǫ/ in the final syllable
		Plural		
st. abs.		פְּקִידִים	מְדַבְּרִים	שֹׁמְרִים
st. cs.		פְּקִידֵי	מְדַבְּרֵי	שֹׁמְרֵי
with sing. suffix	1 c.	פְּקִידַי	מְדַבְּרַי	שֹׁמְרַי
	2 m.	פְּקִידֶיךָ	מְדַבְּרֶיךָ	שֹׁמְרֶיךָ
	2 f.	פְּקִידַיִךְ	מְדַבְּרַיִךְ	שֹׁמְרַיִךְ
	3 m.	פְּקִידָיו	מְדַבְּרָיו	שֹׁמְרָיו
	3 f.	פְּקִידֶיהָ	מְדַבְּרֶיהָ	שֹׁמְרֶיהָ
with pl. suffix	1 c.	פְּקִידֵינוּ	מְדַבְּרֵינוּ	שֹׁמְרֵינוּ
	2 m.	פְּקִידֵיכֶם	מְדַבְּרֵיכֶם	שֹׁמְרֵיכֶם
	2 f.	פְּקִידֵיכֶן	מְדַבְּרֵיכֶן	שֹׁמְרֵיכֶן
	3 m.	פְּקִידֵיהֶם	מְדַבְּרֵיהֶם	שֹׁמְרֵיהֶם
	3 f.	פְּקִידֵיהֶן	מְדַבְּרֵיהֶן	שֹׁמְרֵיהֶן

Table 39. *Nouns with Changeable Long Vowels (Continued 1)*

		Table 39a	Table 39b	Table 39c
		Nouns with /Ǫ/ in the final and penultimate syllables	Nouns with /Ǫ/ in the final and /Ǫ/ in the penultimate syllables	Nouns with /Ǫ/ in the final and /Ǫ/ in the penultimate syllables
		דָּבָר	זָקֵן	לֵבָב
Gloss		thing, word	old man/elder	heart
		Singular		
st. abs.		דָּבָר	זָקֵן	לֵבָב
st. cs.		דְּבַר	זְקַן	לְבַב

		Table 39a	Table 39b	Table 39c
		Nouns with /Ǫ/ in the final and penultimate syllables	*Nouns with /Ǫ/ in the final and /Ǫ/ in the penultimate syllables*	*Nouns with /Ǫ/ in the final and /Ǫ/ in the penultimate syllables*
Singular				
with sing. suffix	1 c.	דְּבָרִי	זְקֵנִי	לְבָבִי
	2 m.	דְּבָרְךָ	זְקֵנְךָ	לְבָבְךָ
	2 f.	דְּבָרֵךְ	זְקֵנֵךְ	לְבָבֵךְ
	3 m.	דְּבָרוֹ	זְקֵנוֹ	לְבָבוֹ
	3 f.	דְּבָרָהּ	זְקֵנָהּ	לְבָבָהּ
with pl. suffix	1 c.	דְּבָרֵנוּ	זְקֵנֵנוּ	לְבָבֵנוּ
	2 m.	דְּבַרְכֶם	זְקַנְכֶם	לְבַבְכֶם
	2 f.	דְּבַרְכֶן	זְקַנְכֶן	לְבַבְכֶן
	3 m.	דְּבָרָם	זְקֵנָם	לְבָבָם
	3 f.	דְּבָרָן	זְקֵנָן	לְבָבָן
Plural				
st. abs.		דְּבָרִים	זְקֵנִים	לְבָבוֹת
st. cs.		דְּבְרֵי	זְקְנֵי	
with sing. suffix	1 c.	דְּבָרַי	זְקֵנַי	
	2 m.	דְּבָרֶיךָ	זְקֵנֶיךָ	
	2 f.	דְּבָרַיִךְ	זְקֵנַיִךְ	
	3 m.	דְּבָרָיו	זְקֵנָיו	
	3 f.	דְּבָרֶיהָ	זְקֵנֶיהָ	
with pl. suffix	1 c.	דְּבָרֵינוּ	זְקֵנֵינוּ	
	2 m.	דִּבְרֵיכֶם	זִקְנֵיכֶם	
	2 f.	דִּבְרֵיכֶן	זִקְנֵיכֶן	
	3 m.	דִּבְרֵיהֶם	זִקְנֵיהֶם	
	3 f.	דִּבְרֵיהֶן	זִקְנֵיהֶן	לְבָבֶהֶן

Table 40. *Nouns with Changeable Long Vowels (Continued 2)*

	St. abs.	St. cs.	Light suffix 1 sing.	Heavy suffix 2 m. pl.
	Feminine nouns with /◌ָ/ in the final two syllables			
Gloss	year			
Sing.	שָׁנָה	שְׁנַת	שְׁנָתִי	שְׁנַתְכֶם
Pl.	שָׁנִים/שָׁנוֹת	שְׁנֵי/שְׁנוֹת	שְׁנוֹתַי	שְׁנוֹתֵיכֶם

Table 41. *Nouns with Changeable Long Vowels (Continued 3)*

		Trisyllabic feminine nouns with a šəwāʾ in the first, a /◌ָ/ in the second and with the feminine ending הָ◌ in the final syllable
		צְדָקָה
Gloss		righteousness/justice
	Singular	
st. abs.		צְדָקָה
st. cs.		צִדְקַת
with sing. suffix	1 c.	צִדְקָתִי
	2 m.	צִדְקָתְךָ
	2 f.	צִדְקָתֵךְ
	3 m.	צִדְקָתוֹ
	3 f.	צִדְקָתָהּ
with pl. suffix	1 c.	צִדְקָתֵנוּ
	2 m.	צִדְקַתְכֶם
	2 f.	צִדְקַתְכֶן
	3 m.	צִדְקָתָם
	3 f.	צִדְקָתָן

		Trisyllabic feminine nouns with a šəwāʾ in the first, a /Ọ/ in the second and with the feminine ending הָ֯ *in the final syllable*
		Plural
st. abs.		צְדָקוֹת
st. cs.		צְדָקוֹת
with sing. suffix	1 c.	צִדְקוֹתִי
	2 m.	צִדְקוֹתֶ֫יךָ
	2 f.	צִדְקוֹתַ֫יִךְ
	3 m.	צִדְקוֹתָיו
	3 f.	צִדְקוֹתֶ֫יהָ
with pl. suffix	1 c.	צִדְקוֹתֵ֫ינוּ
	2 m.	צִדְקוֹתֵיכֶם
	2 f.	צִדְקוֹתֵיכֶן
	3 m.	צִדְקוֹתֵיהֶם
	3 m.	צִדְקוֹתָם
	3 f.	צִדְקוֹתֵיהֶן
	3 f.	צִדְקוֹתָן

Table 42. *Nouns with Changeable Long Vowels (Continued 4)*

	St. abs.	St. cs.	Light suffix 1 sing.	Heavy suffix 2 m. pl.
	Nouns with gutturals			
Gloss	land, country			
Sing.	אֲדָמָה	אַדְמַת	אַדְמָתִי	
Pl.	אֲדָמוֹת			
Gloss	wise (adjective)			
Sing.	חָכָם	חֲכַם	חֲכָמִי	חֲכַמְכֶם
Pl.	חֲכָמִים/חֲכָמוֹת	חַכְמוֹת/חַכְמֵי	חֲכָמַי	חַכְמֵיכֶם

	St. abs.	St. cs.	Light suffix 1 sing.	Heavy suffix 2 m. pl.
		Nouns with gutturals		
Gloss	village			
Sing.	חָצֵר	חֲצַר	חֲצֵרִי	
Pl.	חֲצֵרוֹת/חֲצֵרִים	חַצְרוֹת/חַצְרֵי	חֲצֵרַי	חַצְרֵיכֶם
Gloss	meeting, meeting place			
Sing.	מוֹעֵד	מוֹעֵד	מוֹעֲדִי	
Pl.	מוֹעֲדִים	מוֹעֲדֵי	מוֹעֲדַי	מוֹעֲדֵיכֶם
Gloss	messenger			
Sing.	מַלְאָךְ	מַלְאַךְ	מַלְאָכִי	
Pl.	מַלְאָכִים	מַלְאֲכֵי	מַלְאָכַי	
Gloss	river, stream			
Sing.	נָהָר	נְהַר	נַהֲרִי	נַהַרְכֶם
Pl.	נְהָרוֹת/נְהָרִים	נַהֲרוֹת/נַהֲרֵי	נְהָרַי	נַהֲרֵיכֶם
Gloss	meeting, gathering			
Sing.	עֵדָה	עֲדַת	עֲדָתִי	
Gloss	grapes			
Sing.	עֵנָב			
Pl.	עֲנָבִים	עִנְּבֵי		
Gloss	riches			
Sing.	עָשִׁיר			
Pl.	עֲשִׁירִים	עֲשִׁירֵי	עֲשִׁירַי	
Gloss	side			
Sing.	צֵלָע	צֶלַע/צֵלַע	צַלְעִי	
Pl.	צְלָעִים/צְלָעוֹת	צַלְעוֹת		
Gloss	hair			
Sing.	שֵׂעָר	שַׂעַר/שְׂעַר	שְׂעָרִי	
Pl.	none	none	none	

Table 43. *Nouns with Changeable Long Vowels (Continued 5)*

	Monosyllabic nouns with changeable vowels			
	St. abs.	St. cs.	Light suffix 1 sing.	Heavy suffix 2 m. pl.
Gloss	son			
Sing.	בֵּן	בֶּן־/בֶּן־	בְּנִי	בִּנְכֶם
Pl.	בָּנִים	בְּנֵי	בָּנַי	בְּנֵיכֶם
Gloss	blood			
Sing.	דָּם	דַּם	דָּמִי	דִּמְכֶם
Pl.	דָּמִים	דְּמֵי	דָּמַי	דְּמֵיכֶם
Gloss	hand			
Sing.	יָד	יַד	יָדִי	יֶדְכֶם
Pl.	יָדוֹת	יְדוֹת	יְדוֹתַי	
Gloss	tree			
Sing.	עֵץ	עֵץ	עֲצִי	
Pl.	עֵצִים	עֲצֵי	עֲצִי	

§27.3. Declension of Segholate Nouns

27.3.1. *Introduction*

The segholates are nouns that have a characteristic *səḡôl* in their final syllable. Most segholates have two syllables in the singular *status absolutus*. The first syllable may have a /ọ/, /ọ/ or /ọ/ as vowel. Segholates originally had only one syllable, which is called the stem form. The stem vowels are /ọ/ (a-stem), /ọ/ (i-stem) and /ọ/ or /ọ/ (u-stem). The stem form recurs in large sections of the declension.

27.3.2. *Forms of declensions*

(1) Singular *status constructus*, masculine and feminine

    (a) Masculine *status absolutus* = masculine *status constructus* (Tables 44a-c).

מֶלֶךְ   and   מֶלֶךְ

(b) Feminine *status absolutus* = feminine *status constructus*, but the feminine ending הָ becomes תָ (Table 47).

מַלְכָּה   to   מַלְכַּת

With trisyllabic segholates the following changes occur: הֶָ becomes תֶֶ (Table 48).

מַמְלָכָה   to   מַמְלֶכֶת

(2) Plural *status absolutus*, masculine and feminine

    (a) All three types (בֹּקֶר, סֵפֶר, מֶלֶךְ) take on a stem form that has the same appearance, e.g.: מְלָכִים (Tables 44a-c). The latter form corresponds with the plural of דָּבָר (see Table 39a).

מֶלֶךְ   and   מְלָכִים

סֵפֶר   and   סְפָרִים

בֹּקֶר   and   בְּקָרִים

    (b) The same stem form also occurs with the feminine words where *only* the ending differs.

מְלָכוֹת   or   מַלְכָּה

The feminine plural words such as מְלָכוֹת were probably formed by analogy with the masculine plural forms (see also Joüon–Muraoka §97Ab).

מְלָכוֹת   such as   מְלָכִים

(3) Plural *status constructus*, masculine and feminine

    (a) Here the original stem form recurs before the ending and the first syllable is half closed (§8.1.3).

מַלְכ   in   מַלְכֵי

סִפְר   in   סִפְרֵי

בְּקְר   in   בִּקְרֵי

(b) The feminine plural *status constructus* forms were probably formed by analogy with the masculine plural

מַלְכוֹת   as   מַלְכֵי

(4) Dual *status absolutus* and *status constructus*, masculine and feminine
Here the original stem form returns before the ending, but the first syllable is fully closed, e.g.: בִּרְכַּיִם

(5) Segholate forms with pronominal suffixes

Masculine	Feminine
Singular	Singular
stem (closed) + all suffixes	stem (closed) + all suffixes
Dual	Dual
stem (closed) + all suffixes	stem (closed) + all suffixes
Plural	Plural
st. abs. (lengthened form like דְּבָרִים) + light suffixes	*st. abs.* (lengthened form)
st. cs. (stem, half closed) + heavy suffixes	*st. cs.* (stem, half-closed) + all suffixes

(6) Plus the following rules:
   (a) The application of sound rules (§4.2.4, §5.2 and Table 46).
   (b) Contraction of the glides ו and י as *middle* consonant: with the singular *status constructus* and before all suffixes as well as with the plural *status constructus* and before heavy suffixes or all suffixes (§4.2.4, §5.2.2.1 and Table 49).

(7) Some exceptions:
   (a) With words that have י as final consonant, the lengthened form occurs throughout in the plural (Table 49).

גְּדִי   and   גְּדָיִים

   (b) With words that have ו as final consonant, where the stem form occurs throughout in the plural (Table 49).

שָׁלוּ   and   שַׁלְוִים

27.3.3. *Forms of segholate nouns*

(1) Words with an original short /ǫ/ (a-stem) that acquired a /ǫ/ in both syllables

See Table 44a   מֶלֶךְ

(2) Words with an original short /ǫ/ (i-stem) that became /ǫ/ and have a /ǫ/ in the second syllable

See Table 44b   סֵפֶר

(3) Segholates with an original short /ǫ/ or /ǫ/ (u-stem), and with a /ǫ/ in the second syllable

See Table 44c   בֹּקֶר

(4) Segholates that look just like the a-stems in the singular *status absolutus* and *status constructus*, but nevertheless conjugate further like the i-stems

See Table 45   קֶבֶר

(5) Segholate nouns with gutturals

See Table 46   עֶבֶד

(6) Feminine segholate nouns

See Table 47   מַלְכָּה

(7) Trisyllabic segholate nouns

See Table 48   מִשְׁמֶרֶת

(8) Nouns with a glide י or ו as middle or final consonant

See Table 49   חַיִל

Table 44. *Segholate Nouns*

		Table 44a	Table 44b	Table 44c
		Segholates with an original short /ǫ/	*Segholates with an original short* /ǫ/	*Segholates with an original short* /ǫ/ *or* /ǫ/ *(o)*
		מֶלֶךְ	סֵפֶר	בֹּקֶר
Gloss		king	scroll	morning
Singular				
st. abs.		מֶלֶךְ	סֵפֶר	בֹּקֶר
st. cs.		מֶלֶךְ	סֵפֶר	בֹּקֶר

		Table 44a	Table 44b	Table 44c
		Segholates with an original short /ǫ/	Segholates with an original short /ǫ/	Segholates with an original short /ǫ/ or /ǫ/ (o)
with sing. suffix	1 c.	מַלְכִּי	סִפְרִי	בְּקָרִי
	2 m.	מַלְכְּךָ	סִפְרְךָ	בְּקָרְךָ
	2 f.	מַלְכֵּךְ	סִפְרֵךְ	בְּקָרֵךְ
	3 m.	מַלְכּוֹ	סִפְרוֹ	בְּקָרוֹ
	3 f.	מַלְכָּהּ	סִפְרָהּ	בְּקָרָהּ
with pl. suffix	1 c.	מַלְכֵּנוּ	סִפְרֵנוּ	בְּקָרֵנוּ
	2 m.	מַלְכְּכֶם	סִפְרְכֶם	בְּקָרְכֶם
	2 f.	מַלְכְּכֶן	סִפְרְכֶן	בְּקָרְכֶן
	3 m.	מַלְכָּם	סִפְרָם	בְּקָרָם
	3 f.	מַלְכָּן	סִפְרָן	בְּקָרָן
Plural				
st. abs.		מְלָכִים	סְפָרִים	בְּקָרִים
st. cs.		מַלְכֵי	סִפְרֵי	בְּקָרֵי
with sing. suffix	1 c.	מְלָכַי	סְפָרַי	בְּקָרַי
	2 m.	מְלָכֶיךָ	סְפָרֶיךָ	בְּקָרֶיךָ
	2 f.	מְלָכַיִךְ	סְפָרַיִךְ	בְּקָרַיִךְ
	3 m.	מְלָכָיו	סְפָרָיו	בְּקָרָיו
	3 f.	מְלָכֶיהָ	סְפָרֶיהָ	בְּקָרֶיהָ
with pl. suffix	1 c.	מְלָכֵינוּ	סְפָרֵינוּ	בְּקָרֵינוּ
	2 m.	מַלְכֵיכֶם	סִפְרֵיכֶם	בְּקָרֵיכֶם
	2 f.	מַלְכֵיכֶן	סִפְרֵיכֶן	בְּקָרֵיכֶן
	3 m.	מַלְכֵיהֶם	סִפְרֵיהֶם	בְּקָרֵיהֶם
	3 f.	מַלְכֵיהֶן	סִפְרֵיהֶן	בְּקָרֵיהֶן

Table 45. *Segholate Nouns (I-Class)*

	St. abs.	St. cs.	Light suffix 1 sing.	Heavy suffix 2 m. pl.
	Segholates that look like the a-stems in the singular status absolutus and status constructus, but decline like the i-stems			
Gloss	grave			
Sing.	קֶבֶר	קֶבֶר	קִבְרִי	קִבְרְכֶם
Pl.	קְבָרִים	קִבְרֵי	קְבָרַי	קִבְרֵיכֶם

Table 46. *Segholate Nouns (with Gutturals)*

	St. abs.	St. cs.	Light suffix 1 sing.	Heavy suffix 2 m. pl.
	Segholates with gutturals			
Gloss	seed, posterity			
Sing.	זֶרַע	זֶרַע	זַרְעִי	זַרְעֲכֶם
Pl.	זְרָעִים	זַרְעֵי	זְרָעַי	זַרְעֵיכֶם
Gloss	month, new moon			
Sing.	חֹדֶשׁ	חֹדֶשׁ	חָדְשִׁי	חָדְשְׁכֶם
Pl.	חֳדָשִׁים	חָדְשֵׁי	חֳדָשַׁי	חָדְשֵׁיכֶם
Gloss	young boy, servant			
Sing.	נַעַר	נַעַר	נַעֲרִי	נַעַרְכֶם
Pl.	נְעָרִים	נַעֲרֵי	נְעָרַי	נַעֲרֵיכֶם
Gloss	eternity			
Sing.	נֵצַח	נֵצַח	נִצְחִי	נִצְחֲכֶם
Pl.	נְצָחִים	נִצְחֵי	נְצָחַי	נִצְחֵיכֶם
Gloss	slave, servant			
Sing.	עֶבֶד	עֶבֶד	עַבְדִּי	עַבְדְּכֶם
Pl.	עֲבָדִים	עַבְדֵי	עֲבָדַי	עַבְדֵיכֶם

Segholates with gutturals				
	St. abs.	*St. cs.*	*Light suffix 1 sing.*	*Heavy suffix 2 m. pl.*
Gloss	valley, lowlands			
Sing.	עֵמֶק	עֵמֶק	עֶמְקִי	עֶמְקְכֶם
Pl.	עֲמָקִים	עִמְקֵי	עֲמָקַי	עֲמְקֵיכֶם
Gloss	deed, (handi)work			
Sing.	פֹּעַל	פֹּעַל	פָּעֳלִי	פָּעָלְכֶם
Pl.	פְּעָלִים	פָּעֳלֵי	פְּעָלַי	פָּעֳלֵיכֶם
Gloss	spear			
Sing.	רֹמַח	רֹמַח	רָמְחִי	רָמְחֲכֶם
Pl.	רְמָחִים	רָמְחֵי	רְמָחַי	רָמְחֵיכֶם

Table 47. *Feminine Segholate Nouns*

Feminine segholates				
	St. abs.	*St. cs.*	*Light suffix 1 sing.*	*Heavy suffix 2 m. pl.*
Gloss	queen			
Sing.	מַלְכָּה	מַלְכַּת	מַלְכָּתִי	מַלְכַּתְכֶם
Pl.	מְלָכוֹת	מַלְכוֹת	מַלְכוֹתַי	מַלְכוֹתֵיכֶם
Gloss	baldness			
Sing.	קָרְחָה	קָרַחַת	קָרְחָתִי	קָרַחְתְּכֶם
Pl.	קָרָחוֹת	קָרְחוֹת	קָרְחוֹתַי	קָרְחוֹתֵיכֶם
Gloss	joy, gladness			
Sing.	שִׂמְחָה	שִׂמְחַת	שִׂמְחָתִי	שִׂמְחַתְכֶם
Pl.	שְׂמָחוֹת	שִׂמְחוֹת	שִׂמְחוֹתַי	שִׂמְחוֹתֵיכֶם

Table 48. *Segholate Nouns with Three Syllables*

With trisyllabic segholate nouns the first syllable is unchangeable and the last two syllables decline like the other segholates.

	Trisyllabic segholate nouns			
	St. abs.	*St. cs.*	*Light suffix 1 sing.*	*Heavy suffix 2 m. pl.*
Gloss	skull			
Sing.	גֻּלְגֹּלֶת	גֻּלְגֹּלֶת	גֻּלְגָּלְתִּי	גֻּלְגָּלְתְּכֶם
Pl.	גֻּלְגְּלוֹת	גֻּלְגְּלוֹת	גֻּלְגְּלוֹתַי	גֻּלְגְּלוֹתֵיכֶם
Gloss	(wet-)nurse			
Sing.	מֵינֶקֶת	מֵינֶקֶת	מֵינִקְתִּי	מֵינִקְתְּכֶם
Pl.	מֵינִקוֹת		מֵינִקוֹתַי	
Gloss	kingdom			
Sing.	מַמְלָכָה	מַמְלֶכֶת	מַמְלַכְתִּי	מַמְלַכְתְּכֶם
Pl.	מַמְלָכוֹת	מַמְלְכוֹת	מַמְלְכוֹתַי	מַמְלְכוֹתֵיכֶם
Gloss	guard			
Sing.	מִשְׁמֶרֶת	מִשְׁמֶרֶת	מִשְׁמַרְתִּי	מִשְׁמַרְתְּכֶם
Pl.	מִשְׁמָרוֹת	מִשְׁמְרוֹת	מִשְׁמְרוֹתַי	מִשְׁמְרוֹתֵיכֶם

Table 49. *Segholate Nouns with Glides*

Some nouns with a glide, that is, י or ו, as middle or final consonant do not look like segholates in the singular *status absolutus* and *status constructus*, but in the rest of the declension it is clear that they decline in the same way.

	Nouns with a י or ו glide as middle or final consonant			
	St. abs.	*St. cs.*	*Light suffix 1 sing.*	*Heavy suffix 2 m. pl.*
Gloss	lion			
Sing.	אֲרִי	אֲרִי	אֲרִיִי	אַרְיְכֶם
Pl.	אֲרָיִים	אַרְיֵי	אֲרָיַי	אַרְיֵיכֶם

	St. abs.	St. cs.	Light suffix 1 sing.	Heavy suffix 2 m. pl.
	Nouns with a ' or ו glide as middle or final consonant			
Gloss	kid/goat			
Sing.	גְּדִי	גְּדִי	גְּדְיִי	גְּדְיִכֶם
Pl.	גְּדָיִים	גְּדָיֵי	גְּדָיֵַ	גְּדָיֵיכֶם
Gloss	olive			
Sing.	זַיִת	זֵית	זֵיתִי	זֵיתְכֶם
Pl.	זֵיתִים	זֵיתֵי	זֵיתֵי	זֵיתֵיכֶם
Gloss	power, strength			
Sing.	חַיִל	חֵיל	חֵילִי	חֵילְכֶם
Pl.	חֲיָלִים	חֵילֵי	חֵילַַי	חֵילֵיכֶם
Gloss	death			
Sing.	מָוֶת	מוֹת	מוֹתִי	מוֹתְכֶם
Pl.	מוֹתִים	מוֹתֵי	מוֹתֵי	מוֹתֵיכֶם
Gloss	sickness			
Sing.	חֳלִי	חֳלִי	חֳלְיִי	חֳלְיְכֶם
Pl.	חֳלָיִים	חֳלָיֵי	חֳלָיַַי	חֳלָיֵיכֶם
Gloss	prosperity			
Sing.	שָׁלוּ	שָׁלוּ	שָׁלְוִי	שָׁלְוְכֶם
Pl.	שָׁלְוִים	שָׁלְוֵי	שָׁלְוַַי	שָׁלְוֵיכֶם

§27.4. Declension of Monosyllabic Nouns with Double Final Consonants

27.4.1. *Formation of declensions*

Some monosyllabic nouns originally had two identical final consonants. The double final consonants recur when a suffix is added to the noun.

(1) Forming the singular *status constructus* (masculine)

    Status absolutus singular = *status constructus* singular

(2) Forming the plural *status absolutus* and *status constructus* and the form of the word (singular and plural) with all pronominal suffixes

    (a) The stem vowel has shortened where possible (/ $\circ$ / becomes / $\circ$ /, / $\circ$ / becomes / $\circ$ / and / $\circ$ / becomes / $\circ$ /)

חֵץ	becomes	חִצִּי
עֹז	becomes	עָזִּי

    (b) The final consonant doubles when endings or pronominal suffixes are added.

חֵץ	and	חִצִּי

With stems ending in a guttural or *rêš* no doubling occurs. Accordingly compensation occurs in the preceding syllable.

שֹׁר	but	שֹׁרִי

    (c) With bisyllabic words that have the characteristics of monosyllabic nouns, the changeable vowel reduces in the first syllable if a suffix is added.

גָּמָל	but	גְּמַלִּי

27.4.2. *Forms of monosyllabic nouns with double final consonants*

(1) Monosyllabic words with a / $\circ$ / (a-stems) and where the final consonant was originally double

    See Table 50a   עַם

(2) Monosyllabic words with a / $\circ$ / (i-stems) and where the final consonant was originally double

    See Table 50b   חֵץ

(3) Monosyllabic words with a / $\circ$ / (u-stems) and where the final consonant was originally double

    See Table 50c   עֹז

(4) Monosyllabic words that originally had their final consonants doubled and involve gutturals

    See Table 51   חֹר

(5) Bisyllabic words with the characteristics of monosyllabic words (rare)

     See Table 52   גָּמָל

(6) Monosyllabic words with feminine endings in the plural

     See Table 53   אֵם

Table 50. *Monosyllabic Nouns*

		Table 50a	Table 50b	Table 50c
		Monosyllabic words with a /Ọ/ *(a-stems)*	*Monosyllabic words with a* /Ọ/ *(i-stems)*	*Monosyllabic words with a* /Ọ/ *(u-stems)*
		עַם	חֵץ	עֹז
Gloss		people/nation	arrow	strength, power
Singular				
st. abs.		עַם	חֵץ	עֹז
st. cs.		עַם	חֵץ	עֹז/עָז
with sing. suffix	1 c.	עַמִּי	חִצִּי	עֻזִּי
	2 m.	עַמְּךָ	חִצְּךָ	עֻזְּךָ
	2 f.	עַמֵּךְ	חִצֵּךְ	עֻזֵּךְ
	3 m.	עַמּוֹ	חִצּוֹ	עֻזּוֹ
	3 f.	עַמָּהּ	חִצָּהּ	עֻזָּהּ
with pl. suffix	1 c.	עַמֵּנוּ	חִצֵּנוּ	עָזֵּנוּ/עֻזֵּנוּ
	2 m.	עַמְּכֶם	חִצְּכֶם	עֻזְּכֶם
	2 f.	עַמְּכֶן	חִצְּכֶן	עֻזְּכֶן
	3 m.	עַמָּם	חִצָּם	עֻזָּם
	3 f.	עַמָּן	חִצָּן	עֻזָּן

		Table 50a	Table 50b	Table 50c
		Monosyllabic words with a /Ǫ/ *(a-stems)*	*Monosyllabic words with a* /Ǫ/ *(i-stems)*	*Monosyllabic words with a* /Ǫ/ *(u-stems)*
		Plural		
st. abs.		עַמִּים	חִצִּים	עֻזִּים
st. cs.		עַמֵּי	חִצֵּי	עֻזֵּי
with sing. suffix	1 c.	עַמַּי	חִצַּי	עֻזַּי
	2 m.	עַמֶּיךָ	חִצֶּיךָ	עֻזֶּיךָ
	2 f.	עַמַּיִךְ	חִצַּיִךְ	עֻזַּיִךְ
	3 m.	עַמָּיו	חִצָּיו	עֻזָּיו
	3 f.	עַמֶּיהָ	חִצֶּיהָ	עֻזֶּיהָ
with pl. suffix	1 c.	עַמֵּינוּ	חִצֵּינוּ	עֻזֵּינוּ
	2 m.	עַמֵּיכֶם	חִצֵּיכֶם	עֻזֵּיכֶם
	2 f.	עַמֵּיכֶן	חִצֵּיכֶן	עֻזֵּיכֶן
	3 m.	עַמֵּיהֶם	חִצֵּיהֶם	עֻזֵּיהֶם
	3 f.	עַמֵּיהֶן	חִצֵּיהֶן	עֻזֵּיהֶן

Table 51. *Monosyllabic Nouns with Final Doubled Guttural Consonant*

	St. abs.	St. cs.	Light suffix 1 sing.	Heavy suffix 2 m. pl.
	Monosyllabic words that originally had their final consonants doubled and involve gutturals			
Gloss	cave, hole			
Sing.	חֹר	חֹר	חֹרִי	חֹרְכֶם
Pl.	חֹרִים	חֹרֵי	חֹרַי	חֹרֵיכֶם
Gloss	chief/leader			
Sing.	שַׂר	שַׂר	שָׂרִי	שַׂרְכֶם
Pl.	שָׂרִים	שָׂרֵי	שָׂרַי	שָׂרֵיכֶם

Table 52. *Bisyllabic Nouns with Features of Monosyllabic Nouns*

	St. abs.	St. cs.	Light suffix 1 sing.	Heavy suffix 2 m. pl.
Gloss	camel			
Sing.	גָּמָל	גְּמַל	גְּמַלִּי	גְּמַלְּכֶם
Pl.	גְּמַלִּים	גְּמַלֵּי	גְּמַלַּי	גְּמַלֵּיכֶם
Gloss	people, nation			
Sing.	לְאֹם	לְאֹם	לְאֻמִּי	לְאֻמְּכֶם
Pl.	לְאֻמִּים	לְאֻמֵּי	לְאֻמַּי	לְאֻמֵּיכֶם
Gloss	fortress			
Sing.	מָעוֹז	מָעוֹז	מָעֻזִּי	מָעֻזְּכֶם
Pl.	מָעֻזִּים	מָעֻזֵּי	מָעֻזַּי	מָעֻזֵּיכֶם

Table 53. *Monosyllabic Nouns with Feminine Plural Endings*

	St. abs.	St. cs.	Light suffix 1 sing.	Heavy suffix 2 m. pl.
Monosyllabic words with original double final consonant that have feminine endings in the plural				
Gloss	mother			
Sing.	אֵם	אֵם	אִמִּי	אִמְּכֶם
Pl.	אִמּוֹת	אִמּוֹת	אִמֹּתַי	אִמֹּתֵיכֶם

§27.5. Declension of Nouns that End in הָ

27.5.1. *Introduction*

The characteristic feature of nouns in this group is that they end in הָ in the singular *status absolutus*. They are usually bisyllabic and the first syllable can have a changeable or unchangeable vowel.

27.5.2. *Forms of declensions*

(1) Forming the singular *status constructus* (masculine)

הֶ (מִקְנֶה) becomes הֶ (מִקְנֶה) (Table 54).

(2) Forming the plural *status absolutus* and *status constructus* and the form of the word (singular and plural) with all pronominal suffixes

   (a) The ending הֶ is dropped and the endings and pronominal suffixes are added to the stem, e.g.: מִקְנִי.

   (b) The third masculine singular and third feminine singular suffixes in the singular noun differ from those of the other main groups.

מִקְנֵהוּ	instead of	מִקְנוֹ
מִקְנֶהָ	instead of	מִקְנָה

(3) With words in which the vowel of the first syllable is changeable (e.g. קָצֶה), vowel reduction occurs in the singular *status constructus* (קְצֵה) and plural *status constructus* and also before heavy suffixes with the plural noun (קְצֵיכֶם).

27.5.3. *Forms of nouns that end in* הֶ

(1) Bisyllabic nouns that end in הֶ and have a closed first syllable

   See Table 54a   מִקְנֶה

(2) Bisyllabic nouns that end in הֶ and have a /ֶ/ in an open first syllable

   See Table 54b   קָצֶה

Table 54. *Nouns that End in* הֶ

		Table 54a	Table 54b
		Bisyllabic nouns that end in הֶ *which have a closed first syllable*	*Bisyllabic nouns that end in* הֶ *which have a /ֶ/ in first syllable that is open*
		מִקְנֶה	קָצֶה
Gloss		stock	end, border
Singular			
st. abs.		מִקְנֶה	קָצֶה
st. cs.		מִקְנֶה	קְצֵה

		Table 54a	Table 54b
		Bisyllabic nouns that end in הָ *which have a closed first syllable*	*Bisyllabic nouns that end in* הָ *which have a /◌ָ/ in first syllable that is open*
Singular			
with sing. suffix	*1 c.*	מִקְצִי	קָצִי
	2 m.	מִקְצְךָ	קָצְךָ
	2 f.	מִקְצֵךְ	קָצֵךְ
	3 m.	מִקְצֵׄהוּ	קָצֵׄהוּ
	3 f.	מִקְצֶׄהָ	קָצֶׄהָ
with pl. suffix	*1 c.*	מִקְצֵׄנוּ	קָצֵׄנוּ
	2 m.	מִקְצְכֶם	קָצְכֶם
	2 f.	מִקְצְכֶן	קָצְכֶן
	3 m.	מִקְצָם	קָצָם
	3 f.	מִקְצָן	קָצָן
Plural			
st. abs.		מִקְצִים	קָצִים
st. cs.		מִקְצֵי	קָצֵי
with sing. suffix	*1 c.*	מִקְצַי	קָצַי
	2 m.	מִקְצֶׄיךָ	קָצֶׄיךָ
	2 f.	מִקְצַׄיִךְ	קָצַׄיִךְ
	3 m.	מִקְצָיו	קָצָיו
	3 f.	מִקְצֶׄיהָ	קָצֶׄיהָ
with pl. suffix	*1 c.*	מִקְצֵׄינוּ	קָצֵׄינוּ
	2 m.	מִקְצֵיכֶם	קָצֵיכֶם
	2 f.	מִקְצֵיכֶן	קָצֵיכֶן
	3 m.	מִקְצֵיהֶם	קָצֵיהֶם
	3 f.	מִקְצֵיהֶן	קָצֵיהֶן

§27.6. Declensions of Irregular Nouns

Even though these nouns are classified as irregular, several repeated patterns occur. The greatest irregularity lies in the fact that these words cannot be classified in one specific group – precisely because they often have the characteristics of more than one group.

Table 55. *Irregular Nouns*

	St. abs.	St. cs.	Light suffix 1 sing.	Heavy suffix 2 m. pl.
Gloss	father			
Sing.	אָב	אֲבִי	אָבִי	אֲבִיכֶם
Pl.	אָבוֹת	אֲבוֹת	אֲבוֹתַי	אֲבוֹתֵיכֶם
Gloss	brother			
Sing.	אָח	אֲחִי	אָחִי	אֲחִיכֶם
Pl.	אַחִים	אֲחֵי	אַחַי	אֲחֵיכֶם
Gloss	sister			
Sing.	אָחוֹת	אֲחוֹת	אֲחוֹתִי	אֲחוֹתְכֶם
Pl.	אֲחָיוֹת	אַחְיוֹת	אַחְיוֹתַי	אַחְיוֹתֵיכֶם
Gloss	man			
Sing.	אִישׁ	אִישׁ	אִישִׁי	אִישְׁכֶם
Pl.	אֲנָשִׁים	אַנְשֵׁי	אֲנָשַׁי	אַנְשֵׁיכֶם
Gloss	woman			
Sing.	אִשָּׁה	אֵשֶׁת	אִשְׁתִּי	אִשְׁתְּכֶם
Pl.	נָשִׁים	נְשֵׁי	נָשַׁי	נְשֵׁיכֶם
Gloss	beast			
Sing.	בְּהֵמָה	בֶּהֱמַת	בְּהֶמְתִּי	בְּהֶמְתְּכֶם
Pl.	בְּהֵמוֹת	בַּהֲמוֹת		
Gloss	house			
Sing.	בַּיִת	בֵּית	בֵּיתִי	בֵּיתְכֶם
Pl.	בָּתִּים	בָּתֵּי	בָּתַּי	בָּתֵּיכֶם

	St. abs.	*St. cs.*	*Light suffix* *1 sing.*	*Heavy suffix* *2 m. pl.*
			Irregular nouns	
Gloss	son			
Sing.	בֵּן	בֶּן־ / בֵּן	בְּנִי	בִּנְכֶם
Pl.	בָּנִים	בְּנֵי	בָּנַי	בְּנֵיכֶם
Gloss	daughter			
Sing.	בַּת	בַּת	בִּתִּי	בִּתְּכֶם
Pl.	בָּנוֹת	בְּנוֹת	בְּנוֹתַי	בְּנוֹתֵיכֶם
Gloss	sin			
Sing.	חַטָּאת	חַטַּאת	חַטָּאתִי	חַטַּאתְכֶם
Pl.	חַטָּאוֹת	חַטֹּאת	חַטֹּאתַי	חַטֹּאתֵיכֶם
Gloss	day			
Sing.	יוֹם	יוֹם	יוֹמִי	יוֹמְכֶם
Pl.	יָמִים	יְמֵי	יָמַי	יְמֵיכֶם
Gloss	container, vessel, implement			
Sing.	כְּלִי	כְּלִי	כֶּלְיִי	כֶּלְיְכֶם
Pl.	כֵּלִים	כְּלֵי	כֵּלַי	כְּלֵיכֶם
Gloss	tunic			
Sing.	כֻּתֹּנֶת	כְּתֹנֶת	כֻּתָּנְתִּי	כֻּתָּנְתְּכֶם
Pl.	כֻּתֳּנֹת	כָּתְנֹת	כֻּתֳּנֹתַי	
Gloss	water			
Pl.	מַיִם	מֵימֵי / מֵי	מֵימַי	מֵימֵיכֶם
Gloss	city			
Sing.	עִיר	עִיר	עִירִי	עִירְכֶם
Pl.	עָרִים	עָרֵי	עָרַי	עָרֵיכֶם
Gloss	tree			
Sing.	עֵץ	עֵץ	עֵצִי	עֵצְכֶם
Pl.	עֵצִים	עֲצֵי	עֵצַי	עֲצֵיכֶם

Irregular nouns				
	St. abs.	*St. cs.*	*Light suffix* 1 sing.	*Heavy suffix* 2 m. pl.
Gloss	mouth			
Sing.	פֶּה	פִּי	פִּי	פִּיכֶם
Pl.	פֵּיוֹת / פִּיּוֹת	פִּיפִיּוֹת		
Gloss	head, chief			
Sing.	רֹאשׁ	רֹאשׁ	רֹאשִׁי	רֹאשְׁכֶם
Pl.	רָאשִׁים	רָאשֵׁי	רָאשַׁי	רָאשֵׁיכֶם
Gloss	ear of grain			
Sing.	שִׁבֹּלֶת			
Pl.	שִׁבֳּלִים	שִׁבֳּלֵי		
Gloss	name			
Sing.	שֵׁם	שֵׁם־ / שֶׁם	שְׁמִי	שִׁמְכֶם
Pl.	שֵׁמוֹת	שְׁמוֹת	שְׁמוֹתַי	שְׁמוֹתֵיכֶם
Gloss	heaven			
Pl.	שָׁמַיִם	שְׁמֵי	שָׁמַי	שְׁמֵיכֶם

§28. Other Modifications of Nouns

§28.1. *Hē'* Locale

The *hē' locale* (or locative *hē'*) is formed by adding the suffix הָ֫ to a place name and some common nouns to indicate the goal of a movement. It can occur with or without the article when it occurs with common nouns. It also occurs with directional adverbs.

יְרוּשָׁלַיִם	Jerusalem	יְרוּשָׁלַיְמָה	to Jerusalem
הַר	mountain	הָהָרָה	to the mountain
אֶ֫רֶץ	earth	אַ֫רְצָה	to (the) earth
שָׁם	there	שָׁ֫מָּה	(to) there

When added to a feminine noun ending in *-h*, the *-h* becomes *-t* in a manner analogous to the addition of pronominal suffixes to feminine nouns:

תִּרְצָה   Tirzah   תִּרְצָתָה   to Tirzah

The *hēʾ locale* ending is never accented and is thereby distinguished from the feminine ending הָ◌ as well as from a noun with a feminine singular suffix:

אֶרֶץ	earth	אַרְצָה	to (the) earth
		אֲדָמָה	land
אֶרֶץ	earth	אַרְצָה	her earth

The *hēʾ locale* may intervene between the *status constructus* and the *status absolutus* in a construct chain (§25.3.1.(3)(a)):

אַרְצָה כְּנַעַן   to the land of Canaan

§28.2. Enclitic *Mêm*

The enclitic *mêm* is an archaic suffix occasionally affixed to the end of a word. It is known in cognate Semitic languages, especially Ugaritic. In the vocalization of the Hebrew Bible by the Masoretes, the enclitic *mêm* was sometimes confused with the masculine plural ending ◌ִים, the third masculine plural suffix ◌ָם or the preposition מִן. It occurs with virtually all word types. The meaning and function of this *mêm* are, however, unknown.

    Some scholars believe that in the following case the enclitic *mêm* has been confused with the plural ending (§25.3.1.(3)(e)). By reading an enclitic *mêm*, the problem of a broken construct chain is avoided.

יְהוָה־אֱלֹהִים | (אֱלֹהֵי־ם read)   The Lord *God of* hosts (Ps. 59:6)
צְבָאוֹת

§28.3. Gentilic Suffixes

Nouns may be modified by a so-called "gentilic" suffix to indicate ethnic identity (#*a*), patronymics (#*b*) and occasionally social affiliations (#*c*).[8]

---

   8. Gesenius–Kautzsch–Cowley §86h link this suffix also to the ordinal numerals (see §37.3), although this is dubious.

a וָאֹמַר אַעֲלֶה אֶתְכֶם מֵעֳנִי
מִצְרַיִם אֶל־אֶרֶץ הַכְּנַעֲנִי וְהַחִתִּי
וְהָאֱמֹרִי וְהַפְּרִזִּי וְהַחִוִּי וְהַיְבוּסִי
אֶל־אֶרֶץ זָבַת חָלָב וּדְבָשׁ:

And I have said I will take you up from the affliction of Egypt to the land of *the Canaanite and the Hittite and the Amorite and the Perizzite and the Hivite and the Jebusite* to a land flowing with milk and honey (Exod. 3:17).*

b וַיַּעַן שָׁאוּל וַיֹּאמֶר הֲלוֹא בֶן־
יְמִינִי אָנֹכִי מִקַּטַנֵּי שִׁבְטֵי יִשְׂרָאֵל
וּמִשְׁפַּחְתִּי הַצְּעִרָה מִכָּל־
מִשְׁפְּחוֹת שִׁבְטֵי בִנְיָמֵן

And Saul answered, "Am I not a *Benjaminite* from the smallest tribe of Israel and my family is the most insignificant of all of the families of the tribe of Benjamin?" (1 Sam. 9:21).*

c לְעַם נָכְרִי לֹא־יִמְשֹׁל לְמָכְרָהּ
בְּבִגְדוֹ־בָהּ:

To a *foreign* people he must not sell her because he has treated her unfairly (Exod. 21:8).*

When a patronymic is composed of more than one lexical word, the lexical compound is decomposed into its two original parts when the gentilic suffix is added (compare בֶּן־יְמִינִי "Benjaminite" and בִּנְיָמֵן "Benjamin" in #b). If the definite article is added to the gentilic adjective, it is added to the second part of the compound (#d).

d אֵהוּד בֶּן־גֵּרָא בֶּן־הַיְמִינִי

Ehud, the son of Gera, *the Benjaminite* (Judg. 3:15)*

Grammatically, the gentilic suffix modifies a noun so that it becomes an adjective. Like other adjectives, the gentilic suffix may exhibit congruency features for gender and number – masculine singular (#e), feminine singular (#f), masculine plural (#g) and feminine plural (#h).

e עִבְרִי Hebrew (man) (m.s.)

f עִבְרִיָּה Hebrew (woman) (f.s.)

g עִבְרִים Hebrews (i.e. Hebrew men/people) (m.pl.)

h עִבְרִית Hebrews (i.e. Hebrew women) (f.pl.)

On the use of the singular gentilic to refer to a group, see §24.3.2.(3).

§29. Nouns in Appositional Relationships

An appositional relationship means that two elements in a particular clause have the same referent. The second element modifies the first in some way. Together the two elements form a construction that can function as a clause constituent (i.e. subject, object, etc.). They usually agree in number and gender, but not necessarily in person or definiteness. The first element is the head of the construction. Apposition has a wider use in Biblical Hebrew than in English. A word in apposition may often be better translated with an adjective or prepositional phrase.

§29.1. Types of Appositional Constructions

(1) A proper name can stand in apposition to another noun.

הַמֶּלֶךְ דָּוִד the king, *David* (2 Sam. 7:18)*

(2) A noun with pronominal suffix can stand in apposition to a proper name.

שָׂרָה אִשְׁתּוֹ Sarah, *his wife* (Gen. 20:2)*

(3) One noun can stand in apposition to another noun.

אִשָּׁה אַלְמָנָה a woman, *a widow* (1 Kgs 7:14)*

(4) A lexicalized noun can also stand in apposition to a pronominal suffix.

וַתִּרְאֵהוּ אֶת־הַיֶּלֶד And she saw him, *the child* (Exod. 2:6).*

(5) The same element can be repeated in apposition (see 24.3.1(4)).

    (a) *Two identical nouns* may occur directly after each other.

זַרְעֶךָ הַיֹּצֵא הַשָּׂדֶה שָׁנָה שָׁנָה: your seed which comes forth from the field *year by year* (Deut. 14:22).*

In a similar construction a *preposition* can occur with the second noun.

לִפְנֵי יְהוָה אֱלֹהֶיךָ תֹאכֲלֶנּוּ שָׁנָה בְשָׁנָה You shall eat it before the Lord your God year *on year* (Deut. 15:20).*

    (b) An identical *adverb* can also be repeated in apposition.

אַל־תַּרְבּוּ תְדַבְּרוּ גְּבֹהָה גְבֹהָה Talk no more so *very proudly* [lit. *proudly proudly*] (1 Sam. 2:3).

§29.2. Syntactic Functions of Nouns in Apposition

Syntactically speaking an appositional element is always an adjectival modification. It thus functions on the same level as attributive adjectives (§30), *status absolutus* forms (§25) and relative clauses (§36.3).

Within vocative expressions, appositional noun phrases do not necessarily agree in definiteness (see Miller-Naudé 2014):

וַיֹּאמֶר אֵלַי דָּנִיֵּאל אִישׁ־חֲמֻדוֹת... And he said to me, *"O Daniel, precious man..."* (Dan. 10:11).*

§29.3. Semantic Functions of Nouns in Apposition

The second member of the phrase *elucidates* the first in one of the following ways:

(1) The second member designates the role/capacity of the first member.

שָׂרָה אִשְׁתּוֹ Sarah, *his wife* (Gen. 20:2)*

(2) The second member specifies the status of the first member.

אִשָּׁה אַלְמָנָה a woman, *a widow* (1 Kgs 7:14)*

(3) The second member reveals a characteristic/quality of the first member.

אֲמָרִים אֱמֶת words, *truth* (i.e. *true* words) (Prov. 22:21)*

(4) The second member specifies the material from which the first member is made.

הַבָּקָר הַנְּחֹשֶׁת the cattle, *the bronze* (i.e. the cattle made of bronze) (2 Kgs 16:17)*

(5) The second member specifies the substance, a measuring unit or number of the first member.

וְסָאתַיִם שְׂעֹרִים...סְאָה־סֹלֶת and a measure of *fine meal*...and two measures of *barley* (2 Kgs 7:1)*

(6) The second member specifies the pronominal reference of the first member.

וַתִּרְאֵהוּ אֶת־הַיֶּלֶד And she saw him, *the child* (Exod. 2:6).*

(7) When the same word is repeated, the construction indicates distribution (see also §24.3.2.(4)).

זַרְעֶךָ הַיֹּצֵא הַשָּׂדֶה שָׁנָה שָׁנָה: your seed which comes forth from the field *year by year* (Deut. 14:22).*

(8) When the same word is repeated, the construction implies the high degree – positive or negative – of intensity of a referent or a quality referred to (see also §24.3.2.(6)).

זָהָב זָהָב   *pure* gold [lit. *gold gold*] (2 Kgs 25:15)*

(9) When the same word is repeated (with the *wāw* copulative), the construction indicates diversity (see §24.3.2.(5) and §40.23.4.1.(4)).

אֶבֶן וָאֶבֶן   two *kinds of* weights [lit. *stone and stone*] (Deut. 25:13)

§30. Modification of the Noun by the Adjective

§30.1. Morphology of the Adjective

Like the construct and appositional constructions, the use of the adjective is but one of the ways in which nouns may be modified. Adjectives describe or qualify nouns (see §11.3).

30.1.1. *Declension of the adjective*

The basic paradigm for the declension of adjectives is as follows:

	Masculine	Feminine
	st. abs.	st. abs.
Singular	טוֹב	טוֹבָה
Plural	טוֹבִים	טוֹבוֹת

Additional vowel reductions and consonantal changes can also occur in the stem.[9]

Gloss	Singular		Plural	
	Masculine	*Feminine*	*Masculine*	*Feminine*
good	טוֹב	טוֹבָה	טוֹבִים	טוֹבוֹת
great	גָּדוֹל	גְּדוֹלָה	גְּדוֹלִים	גְּדוֹלוֹת
wise	חָכָם	חֲכָמָה	חֲכָמִים	חֲכָמוֹת
many	רַב	רַבָּה	רַבִּים	רַבּוֹת
bitter	מַר	מָרָה	מָרִים	מָרוֹת
bad	רַע	רָעָה	רָעִים	רָעוֹת
beautiful	יָפֶה	יָפָה	יָפִים	יָפוֹת
small	קָטֹן	קְטַנָּה	קְטַנִּים	קְטַנּוֹת

Note the following:

(1) Modification by an adjective can be *attributive* (e.g. the *good* king, §30.2) or *predicative* (e.g. the king is *good*, §30.3).

(2) Adjectives do not indicate person in their morphology. The same form is used in apposition or predicatively with subjects of the first, second or third person.

(3) Adjectives are either masculine or feminine.

(4) Adjectives can only be singular or plural. The plural is used to modify a dual noun.

(5) An adjective agrees with its noun at least in number and gender.

30.1.2. *Patterns of adjectives with pronominal suffixes*

The morphological patterns of adjectives are similar to those of nouns (see §26–27).

---

9. See also Lambdin (1971: 13).

§30.2. Attributive Modification[10]

An attributive adjective modifies a noun and has the following *syntactic* characteristics:

30.2.1. *Subordination*

The adjectival modification is *subordinate* to its noun and can never be one of the main elements (i.e. the subject or object) of a clause:

כָּתַב אִישׁ טוֹב   A *good* man wrote.

אִישׁ טוֹב is the subject (constituent) of the verb כָּתַב. אִישׁ is the head of the subject phrase and טוֹב is an adjectival modification of it.

30.2.2. *Congruency*

(1) An attributive adjective agrees with its noun in number, gender and definiteness.

(2) The article of the adjective is sometimes omitted, possibly because adjectives are regarded as inherently definite, e.g. the numerals one and two, אַחֵר and רַבִּים.

הַגּוֹיִם רַבִּים   *many* nations (Ezek. 39:27)

(3) The attributive adjective does take the article with a noun that has no article, but which can nevertheless be regarded as inherently definite. This also occurs with numerals.

וְיוֹם הַשְּׁבִיעִי   and the *seventh* day (Exod. 20:10).*
שֶׁבַע פָּרֹת הַטֹּבֹת   the seven *good* cows (Gen. 41:26)

(4) An adjective often agrees *ad sensum* with its noun – in this way a collective singular noun may take a plural adjective and an honorific plural may take a singular adjective (see §24.3.1.(3)).

צֹאן רַבּוֹת   *large* flocks (Gen. 30:43)
אֱלֹהִים צַדִּיק   *righteous* God (Ps. 7:10)

---

10. See also Waltke and O'Connor §14.1–14.3.

(5) The adjective agrees with the syntactic gender of the noun regardless of its morphological form (see §24.2).

הַשָּׁנִים הַטֹּבֹת הַבָּאֹת הָאֵלֶּה these *good* years that are coming (Gen. 41:35).

(6) The masculine is preferred syntactically. In a series of nouns with different genders, the adjective modifying them is masculine. When two adjectives follow a feminine noun, the second one may be masculine.

חֻקִּים וּמִצְוֹת טוֹבִים *Good* (m.) statutes (m.) and commandments (f.) (Neh. 9:13)

בְּאֶרֶץ־צִיָּה וְעָיֵף in a *dry* (f.) *and weary* (m.) land (f.) (Ps. 63:2)

(7) An adjective cannot modify a proper noun directly, but must be preceded by an appropriate common noun. The noun with its adjective are in apposition to the proper noun (see §29).

נִינְוֵה הָעִיר הַגְּדוֹלָה Nineveh, the *great* city (Jon. 1:2)*

(8) The adjective does not have a dual form. Dual nouns usually take a plural attributive adjective.

עֵינַיִם עִוְרוֹת *blind* (pl.) eyes (du.) (Isa. 42:7)*

30.2.3. *Position in relation to the noun*

(1) In Biblical Hebrew an adjective usually follows the noun

מַלְכָּה טוֹבָה a *good* queen
הַמַּלְכָּה הַטּוֹבָה The *good* queen
מְלָכוֹת טוֹבוֹת *good* queens
הַמְּלָכוֹת הַטּוֹבוֹת The *good* queens

(2) The adjective רַב sometimes precedes the noun.

רַבּוֹת בָּנוֹת *many* daughters (Prov. 31:29)*

(3) An attributive adjective that modifies a word in the *status constructus* follows the entire construct phrase (§25.3.1.(3)).

סוּס הַמַּלְכָּה הַגָּדוֹל the *big* horse of the queen

סוּסַת הַמַּלְכָּה הַגְּדוֹלָה the *big* mare of the queen / the mare of the *big* queen

This sometimes means that the reader does not know whether the adjective modifies the *status constructus* or the *status absolutus* (if the gender and number of both are the same). In such cases the broader context usually makes the meaning clear.

30.2.4. *Attributive modification of an implied noun*

Adjectives can modify an implied noun:

וּלְלָבָן שְׁתֵּי בָנוֹת שֵׁם הַגְּדֹלָה לֵאָה וְשֵׁם הַקְּטַנָּה רָחֵל: Now Laban had two daughters; the name of the *elder* (daughter) was Leah and the name of *the younger* (daughter) was Rachel (Gen. 29:16).

In poetry, the adjective may occur on a separate poetic line from the noun it modifies:

וַתֹּאמְרוּ לֹא־כִי עַל־סוּס נָנוּס But you said, "No! On *horse(s)* we will flee."

עַל־כֵּן תְּנוּסוּן Therefore you shall flee!

וְעַל־קַל נִרְכָּב "And on *swift* (horses) we will ride."

עַל־כֵּן יִקַּלּוּ רֹדְפֵיכֶם: Therefore your pursuers will be swift! (Isa. 30:16).*

Adjectives in this type of construction have sometimes been called "substantives" because they seem to function like nouns,[11] but it is best to see this construction as an extension of the attributive use of adjectives.[12]

Adjectives modifying implied nouns exhibit the same characteristics of attributive adjectives modifying nouns:

---

11. See Waltke and O'Connor §14.3.3.
12. See Miller-Naudé and Naudé (2016a, 2017).

(1) They can function as the *status constructus* or the *status absolutus* in a construct phrase and they can take pronominal suffixes.

קְטֹן בָּנָיו the *young* (one) of his sons (i.e. the *youngest* of his sons) (2 Chron. 21:17)*

יֵין הַטּוֹב the wine of the *good* (wine) (i.e. the best wine) (Song 7:10)*

יְראוּ אֶת־יהוָה קְדֹשָׁיו כִּי־אֵין
מַחְסוֹר לִירֵאָיו: Fear the LORD, *O his holy* (ones), for there is no lack for those who fear him! (Ps. 34:10).*

(2) An adjective modifying an implied noun can stand in apposition to another noun (§29).

צַדִּיק עַבְדִּי *a righteous* (one), my servant (Isa. 53:11)*

(3) An adjective modifying an implied noun can sometimes function adverbially (the so-called accusative of specification).

יֹאכְלוּ בְנֵי־יִשְׂרָאֵל אֶת־לַחְמָם
טָמֵא The people of Israel shall eat their bread (as) *unclean* (bread) (Ezek. 4:13).*

§30.3. Predicative Modification

A predicative adjective functions as the predicate of a sentence and has the following syntactic characteristics:

30.3.1. *Subordination*

(1) As opposed to an attributive adjective, a predicative adjective is syntactically the main element of a nominal (or verbless) clause.

אֲדֹנִי חָכָם My lord *is wise* (2 Sam. 14:20).*

(2) It is also the head of a nominal complement in a clause with a copulative verb.

וּדְבַר־יהוָה הָיָה יָקָר And the word of the LORD *was rare* (1 Sam. 3:1).*

30.3.2. *Congruence*

A predicative adjective agrees with its subject noun in number and gender, but is *always indefinite*.

30.3.3. *Position in relation to the noun*

In Biblical Hebrew it *usually follows* the subject, but it *can also precede it*. In the first case – if the noun is indefinite – it is ambiguous and could be interpreted as an attributive construction. Here are some examples:

מַלְכָּה טוֹבָה	A queen *is good* / a *good* queen
טוֹבָה מַלְכָּה	*Good* is a queen.
הַמַּלְכָּה טוֹבָה	The queen *is good*.
טוֹבָה הַמַּלְכָּה	*Good* is the queen
מְלָכוֹת טוֹבוֹת	Queens *are good* / *good* queens.
טוֹבוֹת מְלָכוֹת	*Good are* queens.
הַמְּלָכוֹת טוֹבוֹת	The queens *are good*.
טוֹבוֹת הַמְּלָכוֹת	*Good are* the queens.

§30.4. Degrees of Comparison

In addition to the positive degree (e.g. "I am big"), languages usually also make provision for a comparative degree (e.g. "I am bigger than you"), and a superlative degree (e.g. "I am the biggest"). In Biblical Hebrew the positive degree is expressed with a predicative adjective (§30.3) or stative verb (§16.2.2.(2)).

The adjective in Biblical Hebrew has no forms to indicate the degrees of comparison. The semantic effect normally created by the degrees of comparison is effected by means of other constructions,[13] namely:

30.4.1. *Comparative degree*

The preposition מִן is used to indicate *the standard* against which an object is being compared (§39.14.(3)(a)).

חָכָם אַתָּה מִדָּנִיֵּאל	You are wiser *than Daniel* (Ezek. 28:3).*

---

13. See Waltke and O'Connor §14.5.

30.4.2. *Superlative degree*

(1) The *absolute superlative*, which manifests the outstanding feature, condition or state of something or someone can be expressed by:

(a) A singular noun in the *status constructus* preceding the indefinite plural form of the same word.

הֲבֵל הֲבָלִים   *utmost* vanities [lit. vanity *of vanities*] (Eccl. 1:2)*

(b) The same construction as above, for example, expressed *through synonyms*.

שִׂמְחַת גִּילִי   my *exceeding* joy [lit. joy *of my rejoicing*] (Ps. 43:4)

(c) The *adverbial modifications* מְאֹד or עַד־מְאֹד following the adjective.

וְהַנַּעֲרָה יָפָה עַד־מְאֹד   And the girl was *very beautiful* (1 Kgs 1:4).*

(d) The use of *divine or royal terms* in a construct relationship.

נְשִׂיא אֱלֹהִים   a *mighty* prince [lit. a prince *of gods*] (Gen. 23:6)

בֵּית זְבֻל   an *exalted* house [lit. a house *of a prince*] (1 Kgs 8:13)

(e) The use of מוּת (die), מָוֶת (death) and שְׁאֹל (underworld) (for absolute superlatives in a negative sense).

כִּי־עַזָּה כַמָּוֶת אַהֲבָה   For love is strong *as death* (i.e. *enormously strong*) (Song 8:6).

(2) The *comparative superlative* refers to an individual or object that surpasses all the others in the group in some way. The group can sometimes be omitted or assumed. This is expressed by:

(a) A *definite article* with the adjective

הִנֵּה בִתִּי הַגְּדוֹלָה   Here is my *eldest* daughter [lit. here is my daughter, *the large* (one)] (1 Sam. 18:17).*

(b) An adjective made definite by a pronominal suffix or construct relationship

מִקְטַנָּם וְעַד־גְּדוֹלָם from the *least* to the *greatest* [lit. from *their small* (one) to *their large* (one)] (Jer. 6:13)*

(c) A definite adjective preceding *a prepositional phrase with* בְּ (rare)

הַיָּפָה בַּנָּשִׁים *the fairest* among women [lit. *the fair* (one) among the women] (Song 1:8)*

(d) A singular noun in the *status constructus* followed by a definite plural form of the same word

שִׁיר הַשִּׁירִים *the most beautiful* song [lit. the song *of the songs*] (Song 1:1)*

(e) A predicative adjective following by מִכֹּל and a noun phrase

וְהַנָּחָשׁ הָיָה עָרוּם מִכֹּל חַיַּת הַשָּׂדֶה Now the serpent was *the shrewdest of all* the wild creatures [lit. *shrewd from* all of the wild creatures] (Gen. 3:1).*

(f) *Definite abstract terms* for features/qualities like רֵאשִׁית, מִבְחָר, טוֹב

וּמִבְחַר שָׁלִשָׁיו and his *choice* officers [lit. *the chosen* (one) of his officers] (Exod. 15:4)*

§31. Coordination of Nouns

Coordination can be defined as the addition of a second element at the same level as the first element. Coordinated elements must be of the same grammatical category.

§31.1. Forms of Coordination

31.1.1. *Conjunction* וְ

(1) The *morphology* of וְ (see §40.23.2)
The conjunction וְ is the most common coordinating conjunction. וְ takes the following forms before nouns:[14]

---

14. See Gemser (1968: 23).

(a) It is affixed to the next word.

אִישׁ וְסוּס   a man and a horse

(b) Before ב, ו, מ, פ it becomes וּ.

סוּס וּפָרָשׁ   a horse and a rider

(c) Before a syllable with an audible *šəwā'* it also becomes וּ.

וּסְדֹם   and Sodom

(d) It combines with the syllable יְ to form וִי.

וִירִיחוֹ   and Jericho (יְרִיחוֹ)

(e) With concepts that *are closely related* (provided the first syllable of the second word is stressed), it becomes וָ.

יוֹם וָלַיְלָה   day and night

(f) Before a syllable with a *ḥaṭēp* vowel וַ acquires the corresponding full vowel.

וַאֲרִי   and a lion

(2) The *syntax* of וְ (see also §40.23.3)
וְ has the following distribution:

(a) In a series of conjunctions וְ *can be repeated before each element.*

וַיְהִי־לוֹ צֹאן־וּבָקָר וַחֲמֹרִים   And he had sheep *and* oxen *and*
וַעֲבָדִים וּשְׁפָחֹת וַאֲתֹנֹת וּגְמַלִּים: male donkeys *and* menservants *and* maidservants *and* female donkeys *and* camels (Gen. 12:16).*

(b) In some cases וְ may occur before the last element of a list only.

מִן־הָאֱמֹרִי הַחִתִּי הַפְּרִזִּי הַחִוִּי   of the Amorites, the Hittites, the
וְהַיְבוּסִי   Perizzites, the Hivites, *and* the Jebusites (1 Kgs 9:20)

(c) In a series of semantically paired words וֹ can also occur *to join the pairs*.

נֹתְנֵי לַחְמִי וּמֵימַי צַמְרִי וּפִשְׁתִּי
שַׁמְנִי וְשִׁקּוּיָֽי:

who give me my bread *and* my water, my wool *and* my flax, my oil *and* my drink (Hos. 2:7).*

(d) In a series of entities וֹ can also *be omitted entirely* (asyndetic).

בִּימֵי עֻזִּיָּה יוֹתָם אָחָז יְחִזְקִיָּה

in the days of Uzziah, Jotham, Ahaz, Hezekiah (Hos. 1:1)*

(e) In a word chain וֹ can sometimes be *affixed to the first and second element* (rare). See also §31.1.3.(1).

וּבְיִשְׂרָאֵל וּבָאָדָם

both in Israel *and* among all humankind (Jer. 32:20)*

31.1.2. *Conjunction* אוֹ *(or)*

אוֹ usually occurs between elements of a word chain (see §40.3). (See also אִם, §40.11.(1)(c).)

וְכִי־יִגַּח שׁוֹר אֶת־אִישׁ אוֹ
אֶת־אִשָּׁה וָמֵת...

And when an ox gores a man *or* a woman to death... (Exod. 21:28).*

31.1.3. *Double conjunctions*

(1) וֹ...וֹ (§40.23.3.1.(2))

אֲשֶׁר־שַׂמְתָּ אֹתוֹת וּמֹפְתִים
בְּאֶרֶץ־מִצְרַיִם עַד־הַיּוֹם הַזֶּה
וּבְיִשְׂרָאֵל וּבָאָדָם

Who did signs and wonders in the land of Egypt until this day *both* in Israel *and* among all humankind (Jer. 32:20).*

(2) אוֹ(וֹ)...אוֹ (§40.3)

כִּי־פָשָׂה הַנֶּגַע בַּבֶּגֶד אוֹ־בַשְּׁתִי
אוֹ־בָעֵרֶב אוֹ בְעוֹר

If the disease has spread in the garment *or* in the warp, *or* in the woof, *or* in the skin (Lev. 13:51).*

(3) אִם(וֹ)...אִם (§40.11.(1)(c))

זֹבְחֵי הַזֶּבַח אִם־שׁוֹר אִם־שֶׂה

those offering a sacrifice, *whether* it be ox *or* sheep (Deut. 18:3).*

(4) גַּם...גַּם (§40.20.(3))

גַּם־תֶּבֶן גַּם־מִסְפּוֹא רַב עִמָּנוּ   We have *both* plenty of straw *and* fodder [lit. with us] (Gen. 24:25).*

§31.2. Syntactic Functions of Coordinated Nouns

Syntactically coordinated nouns form a unit, namely, a coordinate noun phrase. Like appositional and attributive constructions, a coordinate noun phrase can fulfil any syntactic function within a clause, e.g., subject, direct object, indirect object, adjunct, copulative predicate, etc. Within the coordinate phrase itself the coordinating elements are on the same syntactic level. As opposed to construct, attributive and appositional constructions, it is impossible to single out one unit as the head of the coordinate phrase and identify the others as the modifications.

For the *semantic functions* of coordinating conjunctions, see §40.

§32. Nouns as Complements of Prepositions

§32.1. Syntactic Characteristics of Prepositions

Prepositions are words that designate the relationships between verbs and nouns or between nouns themselves. *They precede the nouns they govern.* (For the morphological processes that can occur when prepositions are affixed to nouns, see §39.1.2.) The noun accompanying the preposition is the preposition's *complement.* The preposition and its complement together form a *prepositional phrase* (the abbreviation PP is commonly used to refer to this phrase).

Prepositions may *also take pronominal suffixes* in the place of nouns as complements (§39.1.1).

Should a preposition govern more than one complement, it is *normally repeated before each complement* (#a). There are, however, cases where the preposition is written before the first complement only (#b).

a   לֶךְ־לְךָ מֵאַרְצְךָ וּמִמּוֹלַדְתְּךָ   Get yourself out *away from* your
     וּמִבֵּית אָבִיךָ   land, and *away from* your relatives and *away from* the house of your father (Gen. 12:1).*

b   הַחֵפֶץ לַיהוָה בְּעֹלוֹת וּזְבָחִים   Has the LORD as great delight *in burnt offerings and sacrifices?* (1 Sam. 15:22).

For the *semantic functions* of prepositions, see §39.1.4 and §39.2–22.

§32.2. Syntactic Functions of Prepositional Phrases

Prepositional phrases are used in a variety of syntactic positions (§39.1.3).

(1) A prepositional phrase can function as predicate (as adverbial modification that may not be omitted) of a nominal clause.

> אֲרִי בֵּין הָרְחֹבוֹת׃   A lion is *in* [lit. *between*] *the streets* [lit. *the plains*] (Prov. 26:13).*

(2) A prepositional phrase can function as complement of a verb (§32.1).

(a) As direct object (prepositional object)
The prepositions לְ, אֶל־ and בְּ can mark the direct object.

> וַיִּבְחַר בָּכֶם   And he chose *you* (Deut. 7:7).*

(b) As indirect object
The prepositions לְ, אֶל־, אֵת, עַל can mark the indirect object.

> לְזַרְעֲךָ אֶתֵּן אֶת־הָאָרֶץ הַזֹּאת   *To your descendants* I will give this land (Gen. 12:7).*

(c) As complement of a prepositional verb

> וְהוּא נִלְחַם בְּמֶלֶךְ מוֹאָב הָרִאשׁוֹן   And he had fought *against the former king of Moab* (Num. 21:26).*

(3) A prepositional phrase can function as an adjunct (§32.1)

(a) As optional adverbial modifier

> וַיִּזְבַּח יַעֲקֹב זֶבַח בָּהָר   And Jacob offered a sacrifice *on the mountain* (Gen. 31:54).*

(b) As the agent of a passive verb. It can be marked by בְּ, לְ, מִן.

> שֹׁפֵךְ דַּם הָאָדָם בָּאָדָם דָּמוֹ   Whoever sheds the blood of a human – *by a human* shall his blood be shed (Gen. 9:6).*
> יִשָּׁפֵךְ

(4) A prepositional phrase can function as an adjectival modification.

> אִישׁ מִבֵּית לֶחֶם יְהוּדָה   a man of [lit. *from*] Bethlehem Judah (Ruth 1:1)*

§33. Nouns as Complements and Adjuncts of Verbs

§33.1. Introduction: Terminological Orientation

Verbs may govern nouns directly, i.e. without the help of prepositions. In other words, nouns are nominal elements of the verb phrase that can be complements or adjuncts (§12.3). *Complements* cannot be omitted without changing the meaning of the clause or without making the clause ungrammatical.[15] Direct objects are examples of complements. *Adjuncts*, however, add information to the core of the clause and may be omitted without changing the basic meaning of the clause. Direct objects and adjuncts especially may also be expressed by prepositional phrases.

In some of the other Semitic languages which indicate case on nouns, complements and adjuncts are marked by the *accusative*.[16] The accusative expresses the direct object and the so-called adverbial accusative. By analogy some Biblical Hebrew grammars speak of the accusative to refer both to complements and to adjuncts.

In contrast to the languages referred to above, Biblical Hebrew does not have cases (§25.1). The reader is thus dependent on clause analysis to determine what the syntactic function of the ordinary form of the word is. Even though word order is not absolutely rigid in Biblical Hebrew, it can sometimes help in determining these functions. The direct object and adjunct will usually follow the verb and subject. If the direct object is definite, it is usually preceded by the object marker אֵת/אֶת־. Nominal adjuncts can also be marked by it, but this occurs more rarely.

Nouns that are governed directly by verbs thus have two possible *syntactic functions*: complement (direct object and other complements) and adjunct.

§33.2. Complements

The number and type of complements in a clause is determined, or more technically speaking "selected," by the verb of the clause (§22). The following types and combinations of nominal complements occur in Biblical Hebrew.

33.2.1. *One object*

The direct object is the complement of a transitive verb. It is the receiver of the action of the transitive verb. It could have one of the following *semantic functions* (*inter alia*):

---

15. The complement of a verb may be omitted, but then only when it can be inferred from the context of the sentence. This phenomenon is referred to as *ellipsis*.

16. See also Waltke and O'Connor §10.1–2.

(1) The direct object is the patient of an action.

    (a) An *affected* patient exists before and apart from the action.

        וַיִּקַּח יְהוָה אֱלֹהִים אֶת־הָאָדָם   And the LORD God took *the human* (Gen. 2:15).*

    (b) The *effected* patient is the product or result of the action. It thus comes into being through the action concerned and did not exist before that action occurred. Upon completion of the action it exists as a concrete object apart from the action.

        נִלְבְּנָה לְבֵנִים   Let us make *bricks* (Gen. 11:3).

    (c) Sometimes the noun, which apparently functions as object, has the same root as the verb (the so-called internal object). However, the related entity in most cases is an adjunct (§33.3.(5)).

        זִקְנֵיכֶם חֲלֹמוֹת יַחֲלֹמוּן   Your old men shall dream *dreams* (Joel 3:1).

        שָׁם | פָּחֲדוּ פָחַד   There they were gripped by terror [lit. There they feared (*with*) *a fear*] (Ps. 14:5).*

(2) The direct object is the interested party with respect to the action.

        וְאָיַבְתִּי אֶת־אֹיְבֶיךָ וְצַרְתִּי אֶת־צֹרְרֶיךָ:   And I will be an enemy *to your enemies* (interested party – put at disadvantage) and an adversary *to your adversaries* (Exod. 23:22).*

(3) The direct object is the person addressed by the action.

        וַיִּקְרָא אֶת־עֵשָׂו | And he called *Esau* (Gen. 27:1).*

(4) The direct object is the agent of the action (rare).

        לֹא תִנָּשֵׁנִי: You will not be forgotten *by me* (Isa. 44:21).

Note the following:

(a) Verbs that are transitive in Biblical Hebrew are not necessarily so in English, and *vice versa*.

(b) Some verbs may govern their direct objects either directly or by a preposition. The latter are called prepositional objects. Both constructions sometimes occur with the same verb, sometimes with different nuances.

וַיִּבְחַ֤ר בְּזַרְעָם֙ אַחֲרֵיהֶ֔ם	And he chose *their descendants after them* (Deut. 10:15).*
וַיִּבְחַר־ל֣וֹ ל֗וֹט אֵ֚ת כָּל־כִּכַּ֣ר הַיַּרְדֵּ֔ן	So Lot chose for himself *the entire Jordan Valley* [lit. *all of the Jordan Valley*] (Gen. 13:11).*

33.2.2. *Two objects*

Where verbs govern two complements as objects, they may have the following semantic functions (*inter alia*):

(1) With verbs of address one direct object is the person addressed and the other the patient.

וַיְצַוֵּ֕ם אֵ֚ת כָּל־אֲשֶׁ֛ר דִּבֶּ֥ר יְהוָ֖ה אִתּֽוֹ	And he commanded *them* <u>all that the LORD had spoken to him</u> (Exod. 34:32).*

(2) With verbs of giving or taking one of the direct objects is the receiver and the other is the patient.

וְנָתַתִּ֛י אֶת־חֵ֥ן הָֽעָם־הַזֶּ֖ה	And I will give *this people* <u>favor</u> (Exod. 3:21).*

(3) With verbs where the status, role or name of someone is changed, one object is the old and the other is the new status, role or name.

וַיָּ֧שֶׂם אֶת־בָּנָ֛יו שֹׁפְטִ֖ים	And he made *his sons* <u>judges</u> (1 Sam. 8:1).
וַיִּקְרְא֥וּ שְׁמ֖וֹ עֵשָֽׂו׃	So they called *his name* <u>Esau</u> (Gen. 25:25).*

(4) Causative and factitive verbs also take two objects. The one is the object of the causative idea, and the other is the object of the action.

וְהַרְאֵיתִי גוֹיִם מַעְרֵךְ   And I will show *nations* <u>your nakedness</u> (Nah. 3:5).*

33.2.3. *Other nominal complements*

Nouns that are non-objects may also act as complements with the following verbs:

(1) With verbs of remaining

וְהוּא יֹשֵׁב פֶּתַח־הָאֹהֶל   And he sat *at the entrance of his tent* (Gen. 18:1).*

(2) With verbs of movement

וַיָּבֹאוּ אֶרֶץ כְּנַעַן   And they came *to the land of Canaan* (Gen. 45:25).*

(3) With stative verbs that refer to a condition of being full or covered

יְדֵיכֶם דָּמִים מָלֵאוּ:   Your hands are full of *blood* (Isa. 1:15).

§33.3. Adjuncts

Adjuncts are optional, non-verbal parts of the verb phrase. Nouns can act as adjuncts. Nominal adjuncts in Biblical Hebrew take the ordinary form of the noun. They are sometimes (very rarely) marked with the object marker אֶת/ת־. They can perform several semantic functions, such as indicating time, place, manner and specification. (In other Semitic languages with case endings these are referred to as the *adverbial accusative*.)

Nominal adjuncts can fulfil the following semantic functions (*inter alia*):

(1) Indicate time

    (a) Specific point(s) in time

הַשָּׁנָה אַתָּה מֵת   *This very year* you shall die (Jer. 28:16).*

(b) Duration

שֵׁשֶׁת יָמִים תַּעֲבֹד֙   *For six days* you shall labor (Exod. 20:9).*

(2) Indicate means/method

וְהִכֵּיתִי אֶת־הָאָרֶץ חֵרֶם: And I shall smite the land *with a curse* (Mal. 3:24).*

(3) Indicate specification

רַק לְעֵת זִקְנָתוֹ חָלָה אֶת־רַגְלָיו: Except that in his old age he was diseased *in his feet* (1 Kgs 15:23).*

(4) Indicate material

עַמּוּדָיו עָשָׂה כֶסֶף   Its posts he made *of silver* (Song 3:10).*

(5) Repeating the verbal idea
This occurs with a noun that is directly governed by a verb and which has either the same root or approximately the same meaning as the verb. The so-called internal adjunct (often referred to as the internal object, *schema etymologicum* or *figura etymologica*) normally has *no semantic meaning*.

וַיַּחֲלֹם יוֹסֵף חֲלוֹם   And Joseph had a dream (Gen. 37:5).*

The internal adjunct is sometimes used to describe the *intensity* of the verbal idea by means of an adjective.

וַיִּצְעַק צְעָקָה גְּדֹלָה וּמָרָה עַד־מְאֹד   And he cried out with *an exceedingly great and bitter cry* (Gen. 27:34).*

וְקָרְאוּ בְאָזְנַי קוֹל גָּדוֹל   And they cry in my ears *with a loud voice* (Ezek. 8:18).*

§33.4. "Object Marker" אֵת/אֶת־

33.4.1. *Morphology*

The marker has the form אֵת when it is written apart from the subsequent word and אֶת־ if it is affixed to the noun with a *maqqēp*.[17] Pronominal suffixes may be added to the marker (§36.1). The paradigm is as follows:

---

17. For a fuller discussion of אֵת/אֶת־, see Waltke and O'Connor §10.3.

Person	Singular		Plural	
1 c.	אֹתִי	me	אֹתָ֫נוּ	us
2 m.	אֹתְךָ	you	אֶתְכֶם	you
2 f.	אֹתָךְ	you	אֶתְכֶן	you
3 m.	אֹתוֹ	him	אֹתָם	them
3 f.	אֹתָהּ	her	אֹתָן	them

33.4.2. *Syntax*

(1) In general, it marks the definite direct object of transitive verbs. This is also why it is called the object marker.

וַיַּעַשׂ אֱלֹהִים אֶת־חַיַּת הָאָרֶץ   And God made *the beasts of the earth* (Gen. 1:25).*

(2) More specifically, it is used when the information status of the object is high within the discourse structure, specifically, when the object is identifiable, animate and persistent within the context (Bekins 2014).

וַיַּרְא[11] אִישׁ מִצְרִי מַכֶּה   [11]He saw *an Egyptian* beating a
אִישׁ־עִבְרִי מֵאֶחָיו:[12]וַיִּפֶן כֹּה וָכֹה   Hebrew man, one of his kinsman.
וַיַּרְא כִּי אֵין אִישׁ וַיַּךְ אֶת־הַמִּצְרִי   [12]He turned this way and that and
וַיִּטְמְנֵהוּ בַּחוֹל: seeing no one, he struck down *the Egyptian* and hid him in the sand (Exod. 2:11b–12).*

(3) Indefinite objects are usually unmarked.

וְנוֹדִיעָה אֶתְכֶם דָּבָר   And we will show you *a thing* (1 Sam. 14:12).*

(4) There are exceptions, however. Sometimes definite direct objects are not marked (#a), while indefinite direct objects are marked (#b).

a   וְהַדֶּלֶת סָגַר אַחֲרָיו: And he shut *the door* after him (Gen. 19:6).*

b   אִם־נָשַׁךְ הַנָּחָשׁ אֶת־אִישׁ...   If the serpent bit *any man*... (Num. 21:9).*

(5) In a list of definite direct objects אֶת/אֶת־ is usually repeated before each
one (#*a*), but it can also sometimes be affixed to the first one only (when
they are regarded as a group) (#*b*).

a	וַיַּכּוּ אֶת־הַכְּנַעֲנִי וְאֶת־הַפְּרִזִּי׃	And they defeated *the Canaanites and the Perizzites* (Judg. 1:5).*
b	וַיִּתֵּן יְהֹוָה אֶת־הַכְּנַעֲנִי וְהַפְּרִזִּי בְּיָדָם	And the Lord gave *the Canaanites and the Perizzites* into their hand (Judg. 1:4).

(6) אֶת/אֶת־ can also be used to distinguish a group within a list.
In such cases אֶת/אֶת־ can stand, for example, before the first two units of
a word chain, but not before the third because the second and third units
form a group. Compare (#*a*) and (#*b*).

a	וְאֶת־שְׂדוֹתֵיכֶם וְאֶת־כַּרְמֵיכֶם וְזֵיתֵיכֶם הַטּוֹבִים יִקָּח	And he will take your fields and *your best* vineyards *and* olive orchards (1 Sam. 8:14).*
b	וְאֶת־עַבְדֵיכֶם וְאֶת־שִׁפְחוֹתֵיכֶם וְאֶת־בַּחוּרֵיכֶם הַטּוֹבִים וְאֶת־חֲמוֹרֵיכֶם יִקַּח וְעָשָׂה לִמְלַאכְתּוֹ׃	And he will take your menservants and maidservants, and *your best young men* and your donkeys, and put them to his work (1 Sam. 8:16).*

(7) With other complements and adjuncts אֶת/אֶת־ occurs less frequently, but
it is used, for example, after verbs of movement and of fullness as well as
with an adjunct referring to a duration in time.

הֵם יָצְאוּ אֶת־הָעִיר	They left *the city* (Gen. 44:4).*
וַיִּמָּלֵא אֶת־הַחָכְמָה	And he was very *skillful* [lit. *full of wisdom*] (1 Kgs 7:14).*
מַצּוֹת יֵאָכֵל אֵת שִׁבְעַת הַיָּמִים	Unleavened bread shall be eaten *for seven days* (Exod. 13:7).

(8) אֶת/אֶת־ is even used to mark subjects (rare).

(a) In clauses with a verb

וְאֶת־הַבַּרְזֶל נָפַל אֶל־הַמָּיִם	And *his ax head* [lit. *the iron*] fell into the water (2 Kgs 6:5).*

(b) In nominal clauses (rare)

> הַמְעַט־לָ֫נוּ אֶת־עֲוֺן פְּעוֹר   Have we not had enough *of the sin of Peor*? (Josh. 22:17).*

(9) Some verbs exhibit variation between the use of אֶת/אֶת־ and the use of a preposition to mark their objects.

The use of the object marker occurs when the object is completely affected, whereas the preposition is used to indicate that the object is partially affected or that the action is in progress (imperfective aspect) (Bekins 2014: 147–54).

> וְאַחֲרֵי־כֵן קָרָא אֶת־כָּל־דִּבְרֵי הַתּוֹרָה   And after that, he read *all the words of the law* (Josh. 8:34).*

> וְהָיְתָה עִמּוֹ וְקָרָא בוֹ כָּל־יְמֵי חַיָּיו   And it must be with him and he must read *from it* all the days of his life (Deut. 17:19).*

§34. Nouns as Subjects, Predicates and Vocatives

§34.1. Nouns as Subjects of Verbal Clauses

A noun can function as the subject of a clause.[18] If the clause has a verb, its person, number and gender are determined by the subject. Since finite verbs have affixes which indicate the person, number and gender of the subject, one could also say that an explicit subject is a repetition of, or more precisely, a specification of the "built-in" subject.

> וַתֹּאמֶר רָחֵל...   And *she* said, (namely), *Rachel...* (Gen. 30:8).*

The position of the subject in a verbal clause is as follows (see also §46.1):

(1) With asyndetic verbal clauses and with consecutive clauses the subject usually follows the verb directly.

> דָּבְקָה נַפְשִׁי אַחֲרֶיךָ   *My soul* clings to you (Ps. 63:9).

---

18. See Waltke and O'Connor §8.3 for a more traditional discussion of the so-called nominative function.

(2) If the complement of the verb is a preposition plus a pronominal suffix, it usually stands between the verb and the subject (see §46.1.3.1.(1)).

וַיִּבְחַר־לוֹ לוֹט אֵת כָּל־כִּכַּר הַיַּרְדֵּן   So Lot chose *for himself* the entire Jordan Valley [lit. all of the Jordan Valley] (Gen. 13:11).*

(3) With so-called split subjects the coordinate noun phrase that specifies the subject may stand at the end of a clause (see also §36.1.1.2.(3) and Naudé 1999).

וַיֵּלֶךְ אִישׁ מִבֵּית לֶחֶם יְהוּדָה...   And a man of [lit. from] Bethlehem
הוּא וְאִשְׁתּוֹ וּשְׁנֵי בָנָיו: in Judah went..., *he and his wife and his two sons* (Ruth 1:1).*

(4) If the subject precedes the verb, this construction may express specific semantic and pragmatic functions (§47.2).

§34.2. Nouns as Subject of Verbless (Nominal) Clauses

(1) The subject usually stands first in the clause.
Verbless (nominal) clauses may have the following structure:

(a) *Noun* + predicative adjective (see §30.3)

וִידֵי מֹשֶׁה כְּבֵדִים   *And Moses' hands* grew weary (Exod. 17:12).*

(b) *Noun* + prepositional phrase

וַאֲדָמָה עַל־רֹאשׁוֹ   *And earth* is upon his head (2 Sam. 15:32).*

(c) *Noun* + predicator of existence

וְאָדָם אַיִן לַעֲבֹד אֶת־הָאֲדָמָה: And there was no *human* to till the ground (Gen. 2:5).*

(2) If the subject does not precede the predicate, specific semantic-pragmatic functions may be involved
For the functions of word order in verbless (nominal) clauses, see §47.3.

§34.3. Nouns as Predicates of Verbless (Nominal) Clauses

In verbless clauses which consist of two noun phrases, the semantic function of *identification* or of *classification* can be realized.

(1) In an *identifying* clause both the subject and the predicate are definite.

אָנֹכִי עֵשָׂו   I am *Esau* (Gen. 27:19).

(2) In a *classifying* clause the subject is definite and the predicate indefinite.

גּוּר אַרְיֵה יְהוּדָה   Judah is *a lion's whelp* (Gen. 49:9).

§34.4. Nouns as Vocatives (Form of Address)

In languages with case (see §25.1), a noun that is used to designate the addressee within direct speech is in the vocative case. In Biblical Hebrew, there is no vocative case, but a noun, noun phrase or proper name may function like a vocative by designating the addressee.[19] Although the addressee is often designated by the ordinary form of the noun with the article (see §24.4.3.(1)), the article is not always present. The vocative constituent often stands in apposition to a pronoun in the second person or to the built-in subject of an imperative. In other respects it is syntactically separate from the rest of the clause. Syntactically it can be regarded as an adjunct.

בֶּן־מִי אַתָּה הַנָּעַר   Whose son are you, *young man?* (1 Sam. 17:58).

הַחֵרְשִׁים שְׁמָעוּ   Hear, *you deaf* (Isa. 42:18).*

§34.5. Nouns as Dislocated, Fronted or Extraposed Constituents

A noun or noun phrase may occur at the beginning or end of the clause, outside of its normal position within the clause (see Naudé 1990, 1994a, 1994b; Van der Merwe 2013b; Holmstedt 2014). There are four main constructions.[20]

---

19. See Miller (2010a and 2010b).

20. Another construction which is like fronting in that it does not have resumption within the clause, but like left dislocation in that it is separated from the matrix clause by *wāw* is discussed in §48.1.1.(3).

(1) A *fronted* constituent occurs at the initial edge of the clause and does not have resumption within the clause.[21]

אֶת־הָאֱלֹהִים הִתְהַלֶּךְ־נֹחַ:   *With God*, Noah walked (Gen. 6:9).*

(2) A *left dislocated* constituent occurs beyond the initial edge of the clause and has resumption within the clause.

הָאִשָּׁה אֲשֶׁר נָתַתָּה עִמָּדִי הִוא   *The woman whom you gave to be with*
נָתְנָה־לִּי מִן־הָעֵץ וָאֹכֵל: *me*, <u>she</u> gave to me from the tree, and I ate (Gen. 3:12).*

(3) A *right dislocated* constituent occurs beyond the final edge of the clause and has resumption within the clause.

וַיַּךְ אֹתָם בַּעֳפֹלִים   And he afflicted <u>them</u> with tumors –
אֶת־אַשְׁדּוֹד וְאֶת־גְּבוּלֶיהָ:   *Ashdod and its vicinity* (1 Sam. 5:6).*

(4) An *extraposed* constituent occurs at the final edge of the clause and does not have resumption within the clause.

וְהִנֵּה רִבְקָה יֹצֵאת אֲשֶׁר יֻלְּדָה   And look, <u>Rebekah</u> was coming out,
לִבְתוּאֵל בֶּן־מִלְכָּה אֵשֶׁת נָחוֹר   *who was born to Bethuel the son of*
אֲחִי אַבְרָהָם   *Milcah, the wife of Nahor, Abraham's brother* (Gen. 24:15).*

Fronted and dislocated constituents may be used to indicate the topic or focus of the sentence that follows. For more details about these constructions, see §47.1 and §48.2.

§35. Congruence between Subject and Predicate

Congruence between the subject and predicate of clauses in Biblical Hebrew has the following characteristics:

(1) Normally the subject determines the person, gender and number of the predicate. (In the example below the subject is italicized.)

וַיִּבְחַר־לוֹ לוֹט אֵת כָּל־כִּכַּר הַיַּרְדֵּן   So *Lot* chose for himself the entire Jordan Valley [lit. all the Jordan Valley] (Gen. 13:11).*

---

21. The construction is also referred to as a "topicalized constituent," see Holmstedt (2014).

(2) If the subject is dual, the predicate is in the plural.

אַל־יִרְפּוּ יָדֶיךָ   Let not *your hands* (dual form) *grow weak* (plural form) (Zeph. 3:16).*

(3) If the subject is a collective singular noun, the predicate can be either singular or plural.

וְיָדְעוּ הָעָם כֻּלּוֹ   And *all the people* will know (Isa. 9:8).*

יֹאכְלוּ עוֹף הַשָּׁמַיִם   *The birds* of heaven will eat (1 Kgs 14:11).*

עוֹף הַשָּׁמַיִם יוֹלִיךְ אֶת־הַקּוֹל   *The birds* of heaven will carry your [lit. the] voice (Eccl. 10:20).*

(4) Plural subjects that refer to people can take a singular predicate if the statement bears upon the individual members of the group. This is called the distributive or individualizing singular.

מְבָרֲכֶיךָ בָרוּךְ   Blessed be *the ones who bless you* (Num. 24:9).*

(5) Plural nouns with a singular meaning, such as royal plurals, often govern the predicate in the singular.

וַיֹּאמֶר אֱלֹהִים...   And *God* (pl.) said (s.)... (Gen. 1:3).*

(6) If the predicate precedes the subject (usually in an asyndetic clause), the simplest form of the predicate is often used.

חָזַק מִמֶּנּוּ הַמִּלְחָמָה   *The battle* became too heavy for him (i.e. was going against him) (2 Kgs 3:26).*

(7) If the subject of the verb consists of a *status constructus* phrase, the verb is sometimes congruent with the absolute noun if it is the actual topic of the clause (*constructio ad sensum*).

נֶגַע צָרַעַת כִּי תִהְיֶה...   When a man is afflicted with a plague of... (Lev. 13:9).*

(8) If a subject consisting of more than one word precedes the predicate, the predicate is in the plural. If one part of the subject is masculine and the other part feminine, the predicate will be masculine.

> וְאַבְרָהָם וְשָׂרָה זְקֵנִים   And *Abraham and Sarah* were old (Gen. 18:11).*

(9) If a compound subject consisting of coordinated noun phrases or personal names follows the predicate, the predicate can be congruent with the first word/phrase of the compound subject. If such a predicate is followed by additional predicates, they will be in the plural.

> וַתַּעַן רָחֵל וְלֵאָה וַתֹּאמַרְנָה...   Then *Rachel* answered, as well as Leah, and *they* said... (Gen. 31:14).*

(10) If a preposition with pronominal suffix occurs between the predicate and the compound subject, the predicate often agrees with the compound subject, i.e. the predicate is in the plural.

> וַיֵּרְדוּ אֵלָיו מֶלֶךְ יִשְׂרָאֵל וִיהוֹשָׁפָט   And *the king of Israel, Jehoshaphat,*
> וּמֶלֶךְ אֱדוֹם: and *the king of Edom* went down to him (2 Kgs 3:12).*

(11) If a compound subject consists of a coordinate independent subject pronoun and a noun, the subject appears after the finite verb.
The congruence of subject and predicate may take the following forms (Naudé 1993, 1994a, 1994b, 1999, 2001; see also §36.1.1.2.(3)):

(a) The independent personal pronoun shows complete agreement in person, gender and number with the predicate:

> וַיַּכְבֵּד לִבּוֹ הוּא וַעֲבָדָיו: And *he* hardened his heart, *he and his servants* (Exod. 9:34).*

(b) The independent personal pronoun shows agreement in person and gender with the predicate:

> וַיֹּאכְלוּ וַיִּשְׁתּוּ הוּא וְהָאֲנָשִׁים   And *they* ate and they drank, *he*
> אֲשֶׁר־עִמּוֹ   *and the men who were with him* (Gen. 24:54).*

(c) The independent personal pronoun shows agreement in number and gender with a subject noun phrase that appears immediately after the predicate:

וַיֵּצֵא עוֹג מֶלֶךְ־הַבָּשָׁן לִקְרָאתֵנוּ And *Og, the king of Bashan*, went
הוּא וְכָל־עַמּוֹ לַמִּלְחָמָה אֶדְרֶעִי: out against us, *he and all his people*, for battle at Edrei (Deut. 3:1).*

(d) The coordinate subject with an independent personal pronoun may be preceded or followed by a prepositional phrase (or object phrase/clause, adverbial phrase/clause, or relative clause) but cannot be interrupted by it:

וַיַּעַל הוּא וְזִקְנֵי יִשְׂרָאֵל לִפְנֵי And *he* went up, *he and the elders*
הָעָם הָעָי: *of Israel*, before the people at Ai (Josh. 8:10).*

(e) The coordinate subject with an independent personal pronoun may be interrupted or followed by a prepositional phrase containing a pronominal suffix referring to the independent personal pronoun:

וּבָאתָ אֶל־הַתֵּבָה אַתָּה וּבָנֶיךָ And you shall come into the ark,
וְאִשְׁתְּךָ וּנְשֵׁי־בָנֶיךָ אִתָּךְ: *you and your sons and your wife and the wives of your sons with you* (Gen. 6:18).*

(f) If the predicate is a participle the independent personal pronoun of the coordinate subject must be preceded by an initial component (a noun or a pronoun) which agrees in number and gender with the repeated pronoun:

וְהוּא שֹׁתֶה הוּא וְהַמְּלָכִים And *he* was drinking, *he and the*
בַּסֻּכּוֹת *kings*, in the booths (1 Kgs 20:12).*

(g) The independent personal pronoun as part of the coordinate subject may not be overtly expressed:

וַתֵּצֵא מִן־הַמָּקוֹם אֲשֶׁר And she went out from the place
הָיְתָה־שָׁמָּה וּשְׁתֵּי כַלֹּתֶיהָ where she was (she) *and her two*
עִמָּהּ *daughters-in-law with her* (Ruth 1:7).*

§36. Pronouns

Pronouns are a closed class of words (lexemes) that can be used in the place of a noun or noun phrase in certain contexts (§11.2). Pronouns are deictics in that the meaning of their referent is determined in part by the speech context. Because pronouns stand for a noun or noun phrase, their referent must also be determined by the syntactic and/or discourse-pragmatic context in which they occur. The sentence in which a pronoun appears is thus always part of a larger whole.

In Biblical Hebrew, there are three groups of pronouns, properly speaking – personal pronouns (which deictically refer to persons or things), demonstrative pronouns (which deictically identify items as near or far from the deictic center) and interrogative pronouns (which function to introduce questions). Complementizers or relative markers introduce relative clauses (which modify nouns) are not strictly speaking pronouns but are included here because of the traditional nomenclature "relative pronoun." Indefinite pronouns occur in other languages (including English); the variety of lexical items and constructions used to convey similar concepts in Biblical Hebrew are included here.

§36.1. Personal Pronouns

A noun (or noun phrase) may be replaced by a pronoun (i.e. pronominalization) or it may be omitted (i.e. pronominalization by deletion) if it is not specified as conveying "new" information but rather conveys "old information." The replacement is optional in some cases and grammatically required in other cases. The rationale behind this replacement is obvious – by using pronouns, languages avoid the unnecessary repetition of nouns or noun phrases, for example, not "Jacob loved Joseph. *Jacob* made *Joseph* a cloak with long sleeves," but "Jacob loved Joseph. *He* made *him* a cloak with long sleeves." Pronominalization thus provides a way to refer to nouns or noun phrases which have already been mentioned in the discourse. The identity-of-reference of the pronoun with the noun or noun phrase is established by grammatical agreement. A personal pronoun usually refers to a person or thing that has already been mentioned. This person or thing is called the *antecedent* of the pronoun. Personal pronouns are inherently *deictic*, in that their semantic referent must be determined from the speech context.

In Biblical Hebrew pronouns are morphologically either independent words (i.e. the independent personal pronouns) or suffixes. The latter are not separate words, but pronominal suffixes affixed to verbs, nouns and other word types, the so-called enclitic pronouns (see §17, §26 and §27).

36.1.1. *Independent Personal Pronouns*

36.1.1.1. *Morphology*

The following independent personal pronouns occur in Biblical Hebrew:

Person	Singular		Plural	
1 c.	אֲנִי/אָנֹכִי	I	אֲנַ֫חְנוּ	we
2 m.	אַתָּה	you	אַתֶּם	you
2 f.	אַתְּ	you	אַתֵּן	you
3 m.	הוּא	he	הֵ֫מָּה/הֵם	they
3 f.	[22]הִיא	she	הֵ֫נָּה	they

36.1.1.2. *Syntax*[23]

(1) Independent personal pronouns function as the grammatically required subject of a clause that does not have a subject specified as part of the finite verb, e.g. a verbless (nominal) clause or a clause in which the predicate is a participle.

וַיֹּ֫אמֶר אַבְרָהָם אֶל־שָׂרָה אִשְׁתּוֹ   And Abraham said concerning
אֲחֹ֫תִי הִוא   Sarah his wife, "*She* is my sister" (Gen. 20:2).*

הֵ֫מָּה עֹלִים֙ בְּמַעֲלֵה הָעִ֔יר   *They* were going up the hill to the city (1 Sam. 9:11).*

(2) Finite verbal forms have a subject specified as part of the verbal form.
An independent personal pronoun may optionally be used with such finite verbs for semantic and pragmatic effects as described in §36.1.1.3. The independent subject pronoun precedes a *finite verb* that is not in the so-called consecutive form.

אָנֹכִ֗י נָתַ֤תִּי שִׁפְחָתִי֙ בְּחֵיקֶ֔ךָ   I *myself* gave my maid to your embrace (Gen. 16:5).*

---

22. A rare form of the feminine independent pronoun is הוא, which is found only in the Pentateuch. It is spelled in the consonantal text like the masculine pronoun but pointed by the Masoretes as a feminine pronoun (Joüon–Muraoka §39c).

23. This section benefitted much from Naudé (1996b, 1999, 2001, 2002a and 2013b).

The independent personal pronoun follows a finite verb that is in the *wayyiqtōl* or *wəqātal* form because no constituent can precede these forms.

וְזָכַרְתִּי אֲנִי אֶת־בְּרִיתִי אוֹתָךְ   And *I* myself will remember my covenant with you (Ezek. 16:60).*

(3) An independent personal pronoun may be coordinated with other subject phrases and occur after the finite verb (see §35.(11)).

וַיַּעַל אַבְרָם מִמִּצְרַיִם הוּא וְאִשְׁתּוֹ   And *Abram* went up from Egypt, *he* and his wife (Gen. 13:1).*

The pronominal affixes on the finite verb comprise the grammatical subject of the sentence. The independent pronoun coordinated with the noun phrase are adjuncts of the verb. The status of the coordinated pronoun and noun phrase can be clearly seen in instances where an independent pronoun also serves as the topic of the sentence.

וַיֹּאמֶר אֱלֹהִים אֶל־אַבְרָהָם וְאַתָּה   And God said to Abraham, "*As for*
אֶת־בְּרִיתִי תִשְׁמֹר אַתָּה וְזַרְעֲךָ   *you*, you shall keep my covenant,
אַחֲרֶיךָ לְדֹרֹתָם: *you and your descendants after you throughout their generations*" (Gen. 17:9).*

(4) The third person masculine singular independent personal pronoun may occur as the third member of a verbless (nominal) clause, in addition to the subject and predicate.

This construction is sometimes called a "tripartite nominal clause."

הֲלֹא אַתָּה־הוּא יְהוָה אֱלֹהֵינוּ   Are you not the LORD our God? (Jer. 14:22).*

The pronoun is always third person in this construction even when the subject of the verbless (nominal) clause is not, as illustrated in the above example. Various interpretations of this third person pronoun have been given. Naudé (1994a, 1994b, 2002a, 2002b, 2013b) argues that the pronoun is a pronominal clitic which is prosodically dependent upon the preceding subject, because it does not have stress or it is joined to the subject with a conjunctive accent. It is used to disambiguate subject and predicate in verbless (nominal) clauses as a "last resort" strategy.[24]

---

24. For other approaches, see Brockelmann (1956), who views the pronoun as a copula, Zewi (2000), who views the pronoun only as resumption of a left dislocated element, and

In the following example, the third-person pronoun disambiguates the sentence so that it must be understood as a verbless (nominal) clause ("you are my king, O God") and not as an extensive vocative expression ("you, my king, O God"):

אַתָּה־הוּא מַלְכִּי אֱלֹהִים   You are my king, O God (Ps. 44:5).*

In cases where there is stress on the third-person pronoun with a disjunctive accent, it is a left dislocation construction.

יְהוָה הוּא הָאֱלֹהִים   The LORD, *he* is God (Deut. 4:35).*

(5) An independent personal pronoun may indicate the scope of a focused constituent, with or without focus particles (see §40.20).

a	בִּי־אֲנִי אֲדֹנִי הֶעָוֺן	Upon *me alone*, my lord, be the guilt (1 Sam. 25:24).
b	פֶּן־יָמוּת גַּם־הוּא כְּאֶחָיו	otherwise *he too* might die, like his brothers! (Gen. 38:11).*
c	וַתְּהִי עָלָיו גַּם־הוּא רוּחַ אֱלֹהִים	And the spirit of God came upon *him also* (1 Sam. 19:23).*

36.1.1.3. *Semantic-pragmatic functions*

The use of the independent personal pronoun is often syntactically motivated (see §36.1.1.2.(1) and (4) above). However, apart from cases where they are grammatically required, independent personal pronouns are predominately used to express semantic-pragmatic functions. This happens in particular in those cases where the pronouns appear to be used superfluously (see §36.1.1.2.(2) above). The independent subject pronoun can be used as follows:

(1) It indicates the *focus* of an utterance confirming the personal or exclusive role of the referent of the pronoun in an event (see also §47.2.1.(2)(b)).

אָנֹכִי נָתַתִּי שִׁפְחָתִי בְּחֵיקֶךָ   *I myself* gave my maid to your embrace (Gen. 16:5).*

Holmstedt and Jones (2014), who view the pronoun as either a copula or as a resumptive element depending upon the context.

This use of the pronoun often occurs in *contexts where speakers boast* about what *they* have done.

> אֲנִי הֶעֱשַׁרְתִּי אֶת־אַבְרָם   *I* (or *it is I who*) made Abram rich (Gen. 14:23).*

The construction is also used in cases where *pledges or promises* are made, or where someone is being *confronted* with what he or she has done.

> וַיֹּאמֶר אָנֹכִי אֲשַׁלַּח גְּדִי־עִזִּים   And he said: *I* will (*personally*) send you a kid (Gen. 38:17).*

When the third person masculine singular form of the pronoun occurs as a pronominal clitic after the subject of a nominal clause (see §36.1.1.2.(4)), the pronoun apparently also indicates the focus of the utterance. It confirms the identification of a referent as a particular somebody or something.

> הֲלֹא אַתָּה־הוּא יְהוָה אֱלֹהֵינוּ   Are *you (and nobody else)* not the LORD our God? (Jer. 14:22).*

(2) It reactivates entities (e.g. characters) that are compared or contrasted (see also §47.2.1.(1)(a)).

> הוּא יְשׁוּפְךָ רֹאשׁ וְאַתָּה   *He (on the one hand)* shall bruise
> תְּשׁוּפֶנּוּ עָקֵב   your head, and *you (on the other hand)* shall bite his heel (Gen. 3:15).*

Both entities need not be explicitly mentioned.

> וְאַתָּה תָּבוֹא אֶל־אֲבֹתֶיךָ בְּשָׁלוֹם   But *you* shall go to your fathers in peace (in contrast to the nations referred to in Gen. 15:14) (Gen. 15.15).

(3) In terms of indicating time, it may signal that an anterior construction is involved. In terms of discourse structure, it introduces the presentation of background information (see also §47.2.1.(3)(c)).

This construction has *a discourse active referent* as fronted subject and a proposition that has a pluperfect or preperfect relationship with the main line of the narration.

וַיְהִ֞י כִּרְא֤וֹת מֶֽלֶךְ־הָעַי֙...וַיְשְׁכִּ֜ימו And as soon as the king of Ai saw
וַיֵּצְא֞וּ אַנְשֵֽׁי־הָעִ֤יר לִקְרַאת־יִשְׂרָאֵל֙ this... the men of the city went out
לַמִּלְחָמָ֔ה...וְה֣וּא לֹ֣א יָדַ֔ע כִּי־אֹרֵ֥ב early to meet Israel in battle...; but
ל֖וֹ מֵאַחֲרֵ֥י הָעִֽיר *he* did not know that there was an
ambush against him behind the city
(Josh. 8:14).*

(4) It signals a specific type of temporal construction. This construction is used to refer to two simultaneous (or nearly simultaneous) actions (§47.2.1.(5)).

a הִנֵּ֥ה עוֹדָ֛ךְ מְדַבֶּ֥רֶת שָׁ֖ם Look, while you are still *speaking*
עִם־הַמֶּ֑לֶךְ וַאֲנִ֛י אָב֥וֹא אַחֲרַ֖יִךְ there with the king, *I* will come in
after you (1 Kgs 1:14).*

b הֵ֜מָּה בָּ֣אוּ בְּאֶ֣רֶץ צ֗וּף וְשָׁא֛וּל When *they* came to the land of
אָמַ֥ר לְנַעֲר֖וֹ... Zuph, Saul said to his servant...
(1 Sam. 9:5).*

36.1.2. *Pronominal Suffixes Added to Verbs*[25]

36.1.2.1. *Morphology (§17)*

36.1.2.2. *Syntactic-semantic functions*

Pronominal suffixes affixed to finite verbs function as:

(1) The *object* of the clause (most common use)

וַיִּשְׁלָחֵ֙הוּ֙ מֵעֵ֣מֶק חֶבְר֔וֹן So he sent *him* from the valley of Hebron (Gen. 37:14).

(2) The *indirect object* of the clause (less common use)

וַהֲשִׁבֵ֥נִי דָּבָ֑ר And bring *me* word again (Gen. 37:14).*

---

25. Also called the "object suffix."

Biblical Hebrew allows deleted (or, zero) pronouns only in the cases of objects (Naudé 2013b).

וַיַּשְׁכֵּם אַבְרָהָם | בַּבֹּקֶר וַיִּקַּח־לֶחֶם
וְחֵמַת מַיִם וַיִּתֵּן אֶל־הָגָר   So Abraham rose early in the morning and took bread and a skin of water and gave (*them*) to Hagar (Gen. 21:14).*

See also the use of pronominal suffixes on the definite object marker to refer to the object (§33.4 and §36.1.4).

36.1.3. *Pronominal Suffixes Added to Infinitival Verb Forms*

36.1.3.1. *Morphology (§17.5)*

36.1.3.2. *Syntactic-semantic functions*

(1) The *subject* of an infinitive clause.

וְהָיָה בִכְזִיב בְּלִדְתָּהּ אֹתוֹ:   And she was in Chezib when *she* bore him (Gen. 38:5).*

(2) The *object* in an infinitive clause.

לַהֲמִיתוֹ   to kill *him* (Gen. 37:18).

(3) The *indirect object* in an infinitive clause.

וְלֹא יָכְלוּ דַּבְּרוֹ לְשָׁלֹם: And they could not speak peaceably *to him* (Gen. 37:4).*

36.1.4. *Pronominal Suffixes Added to* אֵת

36.1.4.1. *Morphology (§33.4.1)*

36.1.4.2. *Syntactic-semantic functions (§33.4.2)*

36.1.5. *Pronominal Suffixes Added to Nouns*

36.1.5.1. *Morphology (§26–§27)*

36.1.5.2. *Syntactic-semantic functions*

(1) Pronominal suffixes indicate possession. See also §25.4.

> וְהִנֵּה קָמָה אֲלֻמָּתִי And suddenly *my* sheaf arose (Gen. 37:7).*

(2) Pronominal suffixes expressing resumption of a nominal constituent (Naudé 1991, 1996a, 1996b, 2013b).

> (a) A pronominal suffix may be used to express resumption of a nominal constituent in a relative clause after a preposition.

> > הַמָּקוֹם אֲשֶׁר אַתָּה עוֹמֵד עָלָיו The place on which you are standing אַדְמַת־קֹדֶשׁ הוּא: is holy ground [lit. *the place* which you are standing upon *it*, it is holy ground] (Exod. 3:5).

> (b) A pronominal suffix may be used to express resumption of a nominal constituent in a relative clause after a noun.

> > וְאַתָּה חָלָל רָשָׁע נְשִׂיא יִשְׂרָאֵל But you vile, wicked prince of אֲשֶׁר־בָּא יוֹמוֹ בְּעֵת עֲוֹן קֵץ: Israel whose day has come [lit. which *his* day has come], the time of final punishment (Ezek. 21:25).*

> (c) A pronominal suffix may be used to express resumption of a dislocated element.

> > צָפוֹן וְיָמִין אַתָּה בְרָאתָם *North and South*, you created *them* (Ps. 89:13).*

> (d) A pronominal suffix may be used to express resumption in a floated quantifier construction (see Naudé 2011a, 2011b).

> > יֹצְרֵי־פֶסֶל כֻּלָּם תֹּהוּ *The makers of idols*, all *of them*, are nothing (Isa. 44:9).*

36.1.6. *Pronominal Suffixes Added to Prepositions*

36.1.6.1. *Morphology (§39.1.1)*

36.1.6.2. *Syntactic-semantic functions*

(1) The position of the syntactic antecedent of a pronominal suffix determines the nature of the pronominal suffix. If the syntactic antecedent occurs in the same clause as the pronominal suffix, the pronominal suffix has a reflexive (anaphoric) nature and is usually translated with *self* (*himself, herself,* etc.).

| אֶת־בְּנֵיכֶם יִקָּח וְשָׂם לוֹ | He will take your sons and *he* will appoint them for *himself* (1 Sam. 8:11).* |

(2) If the syntactic antecedent does not function in the same clause as the pronominal suffix, the pronominal suffix has a pronominal nature and is usually translated with *him/her/them*.

| וְהִמְלַכְתָּ לָהֶם מֶלֶךְ | and appoint a king *over them* (1 Sam. 8:22).* |

(3) With the preposition לְ, the pronominal suffixes play especially important syntactic roles (see Naudé 1997, 2013a):

   (a) To indicate the indirect object of the clause.

| וְאֶתְּנָה לְךָ אַלְפַּיִם סוּסִים | And I will give *to you* two thousand horses (2 Kgs 18:23).* |

   (b) To indicate a possessive dative.

| קָרָאתִי מִצָּרָה לִי אֶל־יְהוָה | I cried out from my distress [lit. distress (*belongs*) *to me*] to the LORD (Jon. 2:3).* |

   (c) To indicate the experiencer dative.

| וְטוֹב לָךְ | so that it may be good *for you* (Deut. 19:13).* |

   (d) To indicate the dative of interest by marking the person indicated by the pronoun as benefitting or being disadvantaged.

| וְאֵיךְ נֶהְפַּכְתְּ לִי סוּרֵי הַגֶּפֶן נָכְרִיָּה׃ | And how have you changed *to my disadvantage* and become a wild vine? (Jer. 2:21).* |

(e) To indicate reflexive pronouns.[26]

עַתָּה קֻמוּ וְעִבְרוּ לָכֶם אֶת־נַחַל Now rise up and move *yourselves*
זָרֶד through the Zered Gorge (Deut.
2:13).*

For additional syntactic functions, see §39.1.3.
For the semantic functions, see §39.1.4 and 39.2–22.

36.1.7. *Pronominal Suffixes Added to* הִנֵּה

36.1.7.1. *Morphology* (see §40.22.2)

36.1.7.2. *Syntactic-semantic functions* (see §40.22.4)

36.1.8. *Pronominal Suffixes Added to* עוֹד

36.1.8.1. *Morphology* (see §40.37)

36.1.8.2. *Syntactic-semantic functions* (see §40.37.(1)-(7))

36.1.9. *Pronominal Suffixes Added to* אַיִן *and* יֵשׁ

36.1.9.1. *Morphology* (see §41.2)

36.1.9.2. *Syntactic-semantic functions* (see §41.2 and §43.2–3)

§36.2. Demonstrative Pronouns

36.2.1. *Morphology*

Demonstrative pronouns are deictic (or "showing") words that can take the place of a noun or a noun phrase (NP), for example, "Here is the document; *this* is what you must read." Like adjectives they can also modify an NP, for example, "You must help *this* child." A distinction is usually drawn between *near* and *distant* demonstrative pronouns. Distinctions are also drawn between masculine and feminine, and the singular and the plural of the demonstrative pronouns. In Biblical Hebrew the following sets of pronouns are distinguished:

---

26. See also §11.2.2 n. 3.

	Near	*Distant*
	this/these	that/those
m. sing.	זֶה, זוּ, זֹה	הוּא
f. sing.	זֹאת	הִיא
m. pl.	אֵלֶּה	הֵמָּה/הֵם
f. pl.		הֵנָּה

The Biblical Hebrew "distant" demonstrative pronouns above are, however, called quasi-demonstrative pronouns because they cannot stand in every syntactic position, for example, הוּא cannot be used as the object of a clause. Yet זֶ can be used as the object, for example, קְרָא נָא־זֶה "Read *this*" (Isa. 29:11).[27]

36.2.2. *Syntax and semantics functions of "near" demonstrative pronouns*

(1) The demonstrative pronoun can stand in the place of an NP.

שִׁלְחוּ־נָא אֶת־זֹאת מֵעָלֵי Send *this* (woman) out of my presence (2 Sam. 13:17).*

(2) A demonstrative pronoun can modify a noun. It can be used attributively or predicatively.

(a) The demonstrative pronoun is used just like the adjective.
In other words, it usually *follows* the noun and *agrees* with it in definiteness, gender and number. In such cases the demonstrative pronoun is used *attributively*.

a כִּי־אֹתְךָ רָאִיתִי צַדִּיק לְפָנַי בַּדּוֹר For I have seen that you alone are הַזֶּה׃ righteous before me in *this* generation (Gen. 7:1).

When an independent pronoun is defined by both an adjective and a demonstrative pronoun, the adjective *precedes* the demonstrative pronoun.

b הַגּוֹי הַגָּדוֹל הַזֶּה *this* great nation (Deut. 4:6).

---

27. For a more exhaustive discussion, see Waltke and O'Connor §17.3 and Joüon–Muraoka §143j.

(b) Sometimes the demonstrative pronoun *precedes* the noun and does not agree with it in *definiteness*.

> כִּי־זֶה| מֹשֶׁה הָאִישׁ אֲשֶׁר הֶעֱלָנוּ   as for *this* Moses, the man who brought us up (Exod. 32:1).

(c) The predicative use of the demonstrative pronoun corresponds with the predicative use of the adjective; in other words, it can be placed before the noun and it agrees with it in gender and number.

> וְאֵלֶּה תּוֹלְדֹת אַהֲרֹן   And *these* are the generations of Aaron (Num. 3:1).*

(d) Sometimes people are modified in such a way that the nuance of *belonging to a group* is expressed.

> כִּי־קָרָא יְהוָה לִשְׁלֹשֶׁת הַמְּלָכִים הָאֵלֶּה   For the LORD has called *these* three kings (2 Kgs 3:10).*

(3) The demonstrative pronoun can function like a relative pronoun. (See §36.3.3)

> הַר־צִיּוֹן זֶה| שָׁכַנְתָּ בּוֹ:   Mount Zion, *where* you came to dwell [lit. *this* (*which*) you dwell on it] (Ps. 74:2).

(4) Demonstrative pronouns (usually in pairs) function as reciprocal pronouns.

> וְקָרָא זֶה אֶל־זֶה   And *one* called to *another* [lit. *this* (one) called to *this* (one)] (Isa. 6:3).

(5) The demonstrative pronoun is sometimes used tautologically after הִנֵּה.

> וְהִנֵּה־זֶה מַלְאָךְ נֹגֵעַ בּוֹ   And look, an angel touched him (1 Kgs 19:5).*

(6) Demonstrative pronouns combined with interrogative pronouns sometimes express the discontent of the speaker about a state of affairs in the form of a rhetorical question (see also §42.3.1.(1)).

> מַה־זֹּאת עֲשִׂיתֶם   *What* is *this* you have done?! (Judg. 2:2).*

(7) Sometimes זֶה is used to emphasize the frequency of an event or action.

| וַיְנַסּוּ אֹתִי זֶה עֶשֶׂר פְּעָמִים | And yet they have put me to the proof *these* ten times (Num. 14:22).* |

36.2.3. *Syntax and semantics of "distant" demonstrative pronouns*

(1) The demonstrative pronoun can modify a noun.

| *a* | וְהֵבֵאתִי עַל־הָאָרֶץ הַהִיא | And I will bring upon *that* land (Jer. 25:13).* |

It is used especially to refer to *a specific point in time* in the future or the past.

| *b* | בַּיּוֹם הַהוּא יָסִיר אֲדֹנָי... | In *that* day the Lord will take away... (Isa. 3:18). |
| *c* | בַּיּוֹם הַהוּא כָּרַת יְהוָה אֶת־אַבְרָם בְּרִית | On *that* day the LORD made a covenant with Abram (Gen. 15:18). |

(2) In contrast to the "near" demonstrative pronouns, the "distant" demonstrative pronoun is only used attributively.

§36.3. Relative Complementizer

In Biblical Hebrew a noun may be modified by a *relative clause*, which is usually introduced by a *relative complementizer*.[28] The following relative complementizers occur in Biblical Hebrew: אֲשֶׁר and -שֶׁ. The latter is found especially in the later books of the Bible (e.g. Ezra and Ecclesiastes). It also occurs in early texts, e.g. Judg. 5:7. In the intermediate period, however, -שֶׁ is not used. Other syntactic units which are not primarily relative

---

28. In the first edition of this grammar (as in many Biblical Hebrew grammars), the relative complementizer was described as a relative *pronoun*. Because the relative complementizer does not exhibit any agreement with the noun that it modifies, the term relative complementizer (or the more general term, relative marker) is preferable. The lexical arrangement of this grammar, however, dictated leaving the discussion of the relatives in this chapter. The discussion in this section is based upon Naudé (1996a) and Holmstedt (2013a and 2016).

complementizers, but function as such in introducing relative clauses are: זֶה, זוֹ and זוּ and the article הַ. A feature of all the relative complementizers in Biblical Hebrew is that they do not exhibit any congruency features with the nouns they modify.

36.3.1. אֲשֶׁר

36.3.1.1. *Syntax*

(1) The antecedent of אֲשֶׁר may be the implied subject, object or adjunct of the subordinate clause

a	הָעֵץ אֲשֶׁר בְּתוֹךְ־הַגָּן	the tree *which* (it) is in the midst of the garden (Gen. 3:3).*
b	אֱלֹהִים אֲחֵרִים אֲשֶׁר לֹא יָדַעְתָּ	other gods *which* you have not known (them) (Deut. 13:7).*
c	בַּיּוֹם הַהוּא אֲשֶׁר תָּבֹא	on that day *when* you go (*in it*) (1 Kgs 22:25).

(2) The antecedent may be implied but not expressed – the relative clause is headless (or, free or independent).

וַיֹּאמֶר לַאֲשֶׁר עַל־בֵּיתוֹ...	And he said to (the one) who was over his house… (Gen. 43:16).*

(3) The relative complementizer may be implied but not expressed – the relative clause is a zero relative (or, the relative is unmarked).

מָה־הַדָּבָר הַזֶּה עָשִׂיתָ לָּנוּ	What is this thing (which) you did to us? (Judg. 8:1).*

(4) The antecedent of אֲשֶׁר may be *resumed* within the relative clause by means of a pronominal element.

a	זֹאת הָאָרֶץ אֲשֶׁר תִּתְנַחֲלוּ אֹתָהּ בְּגוֹרָל	This is the land which you shall inherit *it* by lot (Num. 34:13).*
b	הָאָרֶץ אֲשֶׁר אַתָּה שֹׁכֵב עָלֶיהָ	the land *on which* you lie [lit. the land which you are lying upon *it*] (Gen. 28:13).
c	אֶת־הָאֲדָמָה אֲשֶׁר לֻקַּח מִשָּׁם	the ground *from which* he was taken [lit. the ground which he was taken *from there*] (Gen. 3:23).

(5) אֲשֶׁר occurs in a number of syntactic constructions in which it is not a relative complementizer, but rather a subordinating conjunction to introduce:

(a) A *complement* clause after verbs of observation, mental processes or speech

a   וַיַּרְא שָׁאוּל אֲשֶׁר־הוּא מַשְׂכִּיל מְאֹד...   And when Saul saw *that* he had great success... (1 Sam. 18:15).*

b   וַיֹּאמֶר שָׁאוּל אֶל־שְׁמוּאֵל אֲשֶׁר שָׁמַעְתִּי בְּקוֹל יְהוָה   And Saul said to Samuel (*that*): I have obeyed the voice of the LORD (1 Sam. 15:20).*

(b) Result (rare)

הִנֵּה | נָתַתִּי לְךָ לֵב חָכָם וְנָבוֹן אֲשֶׁר כָּמוֹךָ לֹא־הָיָה לְפָנֶיךָ   Look, I give you a wise and discerning mind [lit. heart], *so that* there has been none like you before you (1 Kgs 3:12).*

(c) Purpose (rare)

וְשָׁמַרְתָּ אֶת־חֻקָּיו וְאֶת־מִצְוֹתָיו אֲשֶׁר אָנֹכִי מְצַוְּךָ הַיּוֹם אֲשֶׁר יִיטַב לְךָ וּלְבָנֶיךָ אַחֲרֶיךָ   And you shall keep his statutes and his commandments, which I command you today, *that* it may go well with you, and with your children after you (Deut. 4:40).*

(d) Cause (rare)

נָתַן אֱלֹהִים שְׂכָרִי אֲשֶׁר־נָתַתִּי שִׁפְחָתִי לְאִישִׁי   God has rewarded me *because* I gave my maid to my husband (Gen. 30:18).*

(e) Motivation (rare)

מֵעֲמָלֵקִי הֱבִיאוּם אֲשֶׁר חָמַל הָעָם עַל־מֵיטַב הַצֹּאן וְהַבָּקָר   They have brought them from the Amalekites; *for* the people spared the best of the sheep and the cattle (1 Sam. 15:15).

(f) A real condition (rare)

אֲשֶׁר תִּשְׁמְעוּ אֶל־מִצְוֹת יְהוָה   if you obey the commandments
אֱלֹהֵיכֶם אֲשֶׁר אָנֹכִי מְצַוֶּה   of the LORD your God, which I
אֶתְכֶם הַיּוֹם: command you today (Deut. 11:27).*

36.3.1.2. *Semantics*

(1) Relative clauses may restrictively or non-restrictively modify their antecedent. Non-restrictive relative clauses are also known as appositive relative clauses.

   (a) In a *restrictive* relative clause, the relative clause provides information that allows the hearer to identify the antecedent from among all other possible referents.

וּמִפְּרִי הָעֵץ אֲשֶׁר בְּתוֹךְ־הַגָּן   and from the fruit of the tree *which* is in the midst of the garden (Gen. 3:3).*

   (b) Relative clauses may *non-restrictively* modify their antecedent. The relative clause provides additional information concerning the antecedent, but does not serve to identify the antecedent from among other possible referents.

הִשָּׁמֶר לְךָ פֶּן־תִּשְׁכַּח   Take care lest you forget the LORD,
אֶת־יְהוָה אֲשֶׁר הוֹצִיאֲךָ   *who* brought you out of the land of
מֵאֶרֶץ מִצְרַיִם מִבֵּית עֲבָדִים: Egypt, out of the house of slavery (Deut. 6:12).*

(2) Restrictive relative clauses require an antecedent that is a definite noun phrase; non-restrictive relative clauses may have any kind of antecedent.

(3) Indefinite antecedents must be semantically definite in order to be modified by a non-restrictive relative clause.

וְלֹא־תָקִים לְךָ מַצֵּבָה אֲשֶׁר   And you shall not erect for yourself
שָׂנֵא יְהוָה אֱלֹהֶיךָ:   a memorial stone, *which* the LORD your God hates (Deut. 16:22).*

(4) Unmarked relative clauses imply that the relative clause is restrictive.

וַיִּזְבְּחוּ לַיהוָה בַּיּוֹם הַהוּא מִן־הַשָּׁלָל הֵבִיאוּ בָּקָר שְׁבַע מֵאוֹת וְצֹאן שִׁבְעַת אֲלָפִים: And they sacrificed to the LORD on that day from the spoil (*that*) they had brought: seven hundred oxen and seven thousand sheep (2 Chron. 15:11).*

36.3.2. -שֶׁ

Relative clauses with -שֶׁ share the same syntactic and semantic features of relative clauses with אֲשֶׁר:

(1) The relative clause with -שֶׁ may optionally exhibit resumption with its antecedent.

a כַּחוֹל שֶׁעַל־שְׂפַת הַיָּם as the sand *which* is upon the sea-shore (without resumption) (Judg. 7:12).*

b אַשְׁרֵי הָעָם שֶׁיְהוָה אֱלֹהָיו: Happy are the people whose God is the LORD [lit. which the LORD is *its* God] (with resumption) (Ps. 144:15).

(2) -שֶׁ may be used with an implied antecedent.

אַשְׁרֵי שֶׁאֵל יַעֲקֹב בְּעֶזְרוֹ Happy is *he whose* help is the God of Jacob [lit. Happy is (the one) which the God of Jacob is his help] (with resumption) (Ps. 146:5).*

(3) -שֶׁ may introduce relative clauses which have a restrictive (#a) or non-restrictive (#b) relationship to their antecedents.

a וְשָׂנֵאתִי אֶת־הַחַיִּים כִּי רַע עָלַי הַמַּעֲשֶׂה שֶׁנַּעֲשָׂה תַּחַת הַשָּׁמֶשׁ So I hated life, because the work *which* is done under the sun was grievous to me (Eccl. 2:17).*

b בָּרוּךְ יְהוָה שֶׁלֹּא נְתָנָנוּ טֶרֶף לְשִׁנֵּיהֶם: Blessed be the LORD, *who* has not given us as prey to their teeth (Ps. 124:6).

36.3.3. זֶה/זֹה/זוֹ/זוּ

Relative clauses may be marked with one of the old demonstrative pronouns זֶה/זֹה/זוֹ/זוּ. This is an archaic use, which was replaced by אֲשֶׁר and -שֶׁ. These relative clauses share the same syntactic and semantic features of relative clauses that have been identified with אֲשֶׁר.

(1) The relative clause with זֶה/זֹה/זוֹ/זוּ may exhibit resumption with its antecedent (#*a*) or not (#*b*).

a   הַר־צִיּוֹן זֶה | שָׁכַנְתָּ בּוֹ:   Mount Zion, *where* you dwelt [lit. *which* you dwell on *it*] (Ps. 74:2).

b   יַעֲלוּ הָרִים יֵרְדוּ בְקָעוֹת   The mountains rose, the valleys אֶל־מְקוֹם זֶה | יָסַדְתָּ לָהֶם: sank down to the place *that* you appointed for them (Ps. 104:8).*

(2) זֶה/זֹה/זוֹ/זוּ may be used with an implied antecedent.

      וְזֶה־אָהַבְתִּי נֶהְפְּכוּ־בִי: and (those) *which* I loved have turned against me (Job 19:19).*

(3) זֶה/זֹה/זוֹ/זוּ may introduce relative clauses which have a restrictive (#*a*) or a non-restrictive (#*b*) relationship to their antecedents.

a   וְעֵדֹתִי זוֹ אֲלַמְּדֵם   and my testimonies *which* I shall teach them (Ps. 132:12).*

b   הֲלוֹא יְהוָה זוּ חָטָאנוּ לוֹ   Was it not the LORD against *whom* we sinned? [lit. the LORD, *who* we sinned against *him*] (Isa. 42:24 *kǝtib*).*

36.3.4. -ה

The definite article -ה (or more likely a particle homonymous with the definite article) also serves as a relative complementizer. It commonly occurs in relative clauses consisting of a verbless (or, nominal) clause with a participial (#*a*) or predicative adjective. It also occurs before finite verbs and particularly *qātal*/perfect forms in the later books (#*b*).

a   לַיהוָה הַנִּרְאֶה אֵלָיו   to the LORD, *who* appeared to him (Gen. 12:7).*

b   וְכֹל | אֲשֶׁר בְּעָרֵינוּ הַהֹשִׁיב   and all those in our cities *who* have נָשִׁים נָכְרִיּוֹת   taken foreign wives (Ezra 10:14).*

This type of relative clause shows important restrictions: (1) the antecedent is always the implicit subject within the relative clause; (2) negation, fronted constituents and interrogative elements do not occur; (3) there is no resumptive element within the relative clause.

However, this type of relative clause may exhibit either restrictive (#c) or non-restrictive (#d) semantics.

| c | וַיַּעַן נָבָל אֶת־עַבְדֵי דָוִד וַיֹּאמֶר מִי דָוִד וּמִי בֶן־יִשָׁי הַיּוֹם רַבּוּ עֲבָדִים הַמִּתְפָּרְצִים אִישׁ מִפְּנֵי אֲדֹנָיו: | And Nabal answered David's servants, "Who is David? Who is the son of Jesse? There are many servants these days *who* are breaking away from their masters" (1 Sam. 25:10).* |
| d | וְחִכִּיתִי לַיהוָה הַמַּסְתִּיר פָּנָיו מִבֵּית יַעֲקֹב וְקִוֵּיתִי־לוֹ: | And I will wait for the LORD, *who* is hiding his face from the house of Jacob, and I will hope in him (Isa. 8:17).* |

§36.4. Interrogative Pronouns (see §42.3)

§36.5. Indefinite Pronouns

Biblical Hebrew uses a variety of words and constructions to express meanings similar to English indefinite pronouns (e.g. *anyone, everyone, everything, someone, whatever*). In linguistic terms, these structures relate to quantification.

36.5.1. כֹּל

The quantifier כֹּל may express four meanings, depending upon the definiteness and number of the noun which follows it.[29]

(1) כֹּל with a singular indefinite noun expresses "every" in the sense of "each and every individual."

Its semantic nuance is non-specific and implicitly inclusive.

| אֱלֹהִים שׁוֹפֵט צַדִּיק וְאֵל זֹעֵם בְּכָל־יוֹם: | God is a righteous judge, and a God who has indignation *each and every day* (Ps. 7:12).* |

---

29. This section is based on Naudé (2011a, 2011b) and Naudé and Miller-Naudé (2015).

(2) כֹּל with a plural indefinite noun expresses "each and every one." Like the previous category, its semantic nuance is non-specific and implicitly inclusive.

> כָּל־שֻׁלְחָנוֹת מָלְאוּ קִיא צֹאָה   *All* tables (*each and every one*) are covered with filthy vomit (Isa. 28:8).*

(3) כֹּל with a singular definite noun expresses "the totality of the individual members of the specific group or set."

> *a*   וְגַם כָּל־הָאָדָם שֶׁיֹּאכַל   And also *all* humankind should eat
> וְשָׁתָה וְרָאָה טוֹב בְּכָל־עֲמָלוֹ   and drink and take pleasure in all
> מַתַּת אֱלֹהִים הִיא   his toil – it is a gift of God (Eccl. 3:13).

> *b*   כָּל־הַיּוֹם הִתְאַוָּה תַאֲוָה   *All day long* (i.e. the total day)
> וְצַדִּיק יִתֵּן וְלֹא יַחְשֹׂךְ:   the wicked covet, but the righteous give and do not hold back (Prov. 21:26).

(4) כֹּל with a plural definite noun expresses "the totality of the specific group" and conveys the nuance of "all."

> *a*   כָּל־הַנְּתִינִים וּבְנֵי עַבְדֵי שְׁלֹמֹה   *All* (the total) of the temple ser-
> שְׁלֹשׁ מֵאוֹת תִּשְׁעִים וּשְׁנָיִם: vants and the sons of Solomon's servants – three hundred and ninety-two (Ezra 2:58).*

כֹּל may also occur after the constituent to which it refers. A resumptive pronominal suffix occurs on כֹּל to refer to the preceding constituent:

> *b*   הֶן־אַתֶּם כֻּלְּכֶם חֲזִיתֶם   Look, you, *all of you*, have seen it yourselves (Job 27:12).*

36.5.2. מַה *and* מִי

The interrogative pronouns מַה (#*a*) and מִי (#*b*) may be used as complementizers in indefinite expressions. Sometimes מִי is followed by אֲשֶׁר (#*c*) or even אֲשֶׁר הָאִישׁ (#*d*).

a   מַה־תֹּאמַר נַפְשְׁךָ וְאֶעֱשֶׂה־לָּךְ:   *Whatever* you want [lit. *whatever* your soul says] I will do for you (1 Sam. 20:4).*

b   מִי־יָרֵא וְחָרֵד יָשֹׁב   *Whoever* is fearful and trembling, let him return (Judg. 7:3).

c   מִי אֲשֶׁר חָטָא־לִי אֶמְחֶנּוּ   *Whoever* has sinned against me, מִסִּפְרִי: I will blot him out of my book (Exod. 32:33).*

d   מִי־הָאִישׁ אֲשֶׁר בָּנָה   *Whoever* that has built a new בַיִת־חָדָשׁ...   house... (Deut. 20:5).*

36.5.3. אִישׁ, אָדָם *and* נֶפֶשׁ

The common nouns אִישׁ (#a-b), אָדָם (#c) and נֶפֶשׁ (#d) may be used to refer to an unspecified, representative person. נֶפֶשׁ may also be used as a collective (#e).

a   אִם־יוּכַל אִישׁ לִמְנוֹת...   If *one* could count... (Gen. 13:16).*

b   לְכוּ אִישׁ לְעִירוֹ   Go, *every man* to his city (1 Sam. 8:22).*

c   אָדָם כִּי־יַקְרִיב מִכֶּם קָרְבָּן   When *any man* of you brings an לַיהוָה...   offering to the LORD... (Lev. 1:2).

d   נֶפֶשׁ כִּי־תֶחֱטָא...   If *anyone* sins... (Lev. 4:2).*

e   וַיִּקַּח אַבְרָם אֶת־שָׂרַי אִשְׁתּוֹ   And Abram took Sarai his wife, וְאֶת־לוֹט בֶּן־אָחִיו   and Lot his brother's son, and all וְאֶת־כָּל־רְכוּשָׁם אֲשֶׁר רָכָשׁוּ   their possessions that they had וְאֶת־הַנֶּפֶשׁ אֲשֶׁר־עָשׂוּ בְחָרָן   gathered, and *the people* that they had acquired in Haran (Gen. 12:5).*

36.5.4. דָּבָר

The common noun דָּבָר may be used to refer to an indefinite item or notion.

הֲיִפָּלֵא מֵיהוָה דָּבָר   Is *anything* too hard for the LORD? (Gen. 18:14).*

36.5.5. *Unspecified third person verb*

An unspecified third person verb may be used to indicate an indefinite subject when the verbal form is singular active (#a), singular passive (#b) or plural active (#c).

a	וַיְהִ֗י אַחֲרֵי֙ הַדְּבָרִ֣ים הָאֵ֔לֶּה וַיֹּ֣אמֶר לְיוֹסֵ֔ף...	And then, after these events *some-body* told Joseph... (Gen. 48:1).*
b	עַל־כֵּן֙ יֵֽאָמַ֔ר בְּסֵ֖פֶר מִלְחֲמֹ֣ת יְהוָ֑ה	Therefore, it will be said in the book of the wars of the LORD (Num. 21:14).
c	כִּ֣י מִן־הַבְּאֵ֤ר הַהִוא֙ יַשְׁק֔וּ הָעֲדָרִ֑ים	For from that well *they* watered the flocks (Gen. 29:2).*

36.5.6. מְאוּמָה

מְאוּמָה is a negative polarity item. It only occurs within negative contexts.

וְאַל־תַּ֤עַשׂ לוֹ֙ מְא֔וּמָה And do not do *anything* to him (Gen. 22:12).*

§37. Numerals

§37.1. Introduction

Numerals are quantifiers (like *each*, *every*, *all* etc.; see §36.5) which specify the number or the amount of referents indicated by the nouns which with they collocate. Numerals differ from determiners (e.g., *a*, *the*, *this* and *that*), which indicate which part of a subgroup or group of entities is being referred to (Naudé 2011a: 409). Numeral quantifiers express numbers and are dealt with as a separate word type on that basis. Numbers in the Biblical Hebrew text are always fully written out in words; in other varieties of ancient Hebrew, the letters of the alphabet are used to symbolize numbers.

On the basis of form and their combination with other words, two kinds of numerals may be distinguished: cardinals and ordinals.

§37.2. Cardinals

37.2.1. *Forms*

The numerals 1 to 19 have different forms when qualifying masculine and feminine words.

37.2.1.1. *One to ten*

Status absolutus and *status constructus* forms are differentiated with the numerals 1 to 10.

	With a masculine noun		With a feminine noun	
	St. abs.	St. cs.	St. abs.	St. cs.
1	אֶחָד	אַחַד	אַחַת	אַחַת
2	שְׁנַיִם	שְׁנֵי	שְׁתַּיִם	שְׁתֵּי
3	שְׁלֹשָׁה	שְׁלֹשֶׁת	שָׁלֹושׁ	שְׁלֹשׁ
4	אַרְבָּעָה	אַרְבַּעַת	אַרְבַּע	אַרְבַּע
5	חֲמִשָּׁה	חֲמֵשֶׁת	חָמֵשׁ	חֲמֵשׁ
6	שִׁשָּׁה	שֵׁשֶׁת	שֵׁשׁ	שֵׁשׁ
7	שִׁבְעָה	שִׁבְעַת	שֶׁבַע	שְׁבַע
8	שְׁמֹנָה	שְׁמֹנַת	שְׁמֹנֶה	שְׁמֹנֶה
9	תִּשְׁעָה	תִּשְׁעַת	תֵּשַׁע	תְּשַׁע
10	עֲשָׂרָה	עֲשֶׂרֶת	עֶשֶׂר	עֶשֶׂר

37.2.1.2. *Eleven to nineteen*

(1) The numerals 11 to 19 are simply combinations of the unit (1–9) and a form for 10 (as in English *thirteen, seventeen,* etc.).

(2) The first component of the combination, the unit, takes a shortened form which usually looks like the *status constructus*. The phrases for 11 and 12 occur in two different forms.

	With a masculine noun	*With a feminine noun*
11	אַחַד עָשָׂר עַשְׁתֵּי עָשָׂר	אַחַת עֶשְׂרֵה עַשְׁתֵּי עֶשְׂרֵה
12	שְׁנֵים עָשָׂר שְׁנֵי עָשָׂר	שְׁתֵּים עֶשְׂרֵה שְׁתֵּי עֶשְׂרֵה
13	שְׁלֹשָׁה עָשָׂר	שְׁלֹשׁ עֶשְׂרֵה
14	אַרְבָּעָה עָשָׂר	אַרְבַּע עֶשְׂרֵה
15	חֲמִשָּׁה עָשָׂר	חֲמֵשׁ עֶשְׂרֵה
16	שִׁשָּׁה עָשָׂר	שֵׁשׁ עֶשְׂרֵה
17	שִׁבְעָה עָשָׂר	שְׁבַע עֶשְׂרֵה
18	שְׁמֹנָה עָשָׂר	שְׁמֹנֶה עֶשְׂרֵה
19	תִּשְׁעָה עָשָׂר	תְּשַׁע עֶשְׂרֵה

37.2.1.3. *Tens*

The tens look like (masculine) plural forms of singular numbers.

20	עֶשְׂרִים	60	שִׁשִּׁים
30	שְׁלֹשִׁים	70	שִׁבְעִים
40	אַרְבָּעִים	80	שְׁמֹנִים
50	חֲמִשִּׁים	90	תִּשְׁעִים

37.2.1.4. *Larger units (100, 1000 and 10,000)*

The numerals for larger units have distinct singular, dual and plural forms. In the case of the singular and plural forms for 100 and 1000 there is also a *status constructus* form in addition to the normal *status absolutus* form. The word for 10,000 is not used much and there is no distinction between a *status absolutus* and a *status constructus* form.

		St. abs.	*St. cs.*
100		מֵאָה	מְאַת
200	*dual*	מָאתַיִם	
	plural	מֵאוֹת	מְאוֹת
1000		אֶלֶף	אֶלֶף
2000	*dual*	אַלְפַּיִם	
	plural	אֲלָפִים	אַלְפֵי
10,000		רִבּוֹ or רִבּוֹא or רְבָבָה	
20,000	*dual*	רִבּוֹתַיִם	
	plural	רִבּוֹת or רִבּוֹאת	

37.2.1.5. *Compound numbers*

Compound numbers are expressed by combinations of the above-mentioned cardinals. When a numeral between 3 and 10 combines with מֵאָה or רְבָבָה, it takes the form it would take with a feminine noun, and when it combines with אֶלֶף, it takes the form it would take with a masculine noun. There is no rigid sequence for the different elements within the compound number. The following numbers will serve as examples:

31	שְׁלֹשִׁים וְאַחַת	2 Kgs 22:1
33	שָׁלוֹשׁ וּשְׁלֹשִׁים	Ezek. 41:6
150	מֵאָה וַחֲמִשִּׁים	1 Chron. 8:40
212	מָאתַיִם וּשְׁנֵים עָשָׂר	1 Chron. 9:22
250	חֲמִשִּׁים וּמָאתַיִם	2 Chron. 8:10
675	שֵׁשׁ מֵאוֹת חָמֵשׁ וְשִׁבְעִים	Num. 31:37
2700	אַלְפַּיִם וּשְׁבַע מֵאוֹת	1 Chron. 26:32
42,360	אַרְבַּע רִבּוֹא אֲלָפִים שְׁלֹשׁ־מֵאוֹת וְשִׁשִּׁים	Neh. 7:66
44,760	אַרְבָּעִים וְאַרְבָּעָה אֶלֶף וּשְׁבַע־מֵאוֹת וְשִׁשִּׁים	1 Chron. 5:18

37.2.2. *Syntax*[30]

The cardinals can combine with nouns in the ways listed below:

37.2.2.1. *One*

(1) The number one acts syntactically as an adjective.

The numeral follows the noun and agrees with it in gender, number and definiteness. This *attributive* construction occurs only with the cardinal אֶחָד.

מָנָה אַחַת   *one* part (1 Sam. 1:5)*

הַטּוּר הָאֶחָד   the *first* row (Exod. 39:10)

(2) The numeral in the *status constructus* can also stand before a noun in the *status absolutus*.

Only in the case of the numeral אֶחָד does the noun that follows a numeral in the *status constructus* take the article.

אַחַד הֶהָרִים   *one* of the mountains (Gen. 22:2)

(3) The numeral אֶחָד in the *status absolutus* can also follow a noun in the *status constructus*.

This combination is, however, rare.

מִשְׁפָּט אֶחָד   *one* judgment (Lev. 24:22)*

37.2.2.2. *Two*

(1) The number two acts as a noun and can be placed before or after the plural noun.

(2) The gender of the numeral two agrees with the gender of the noun with which it stands.

This construction has all the characteristics of an *appositional* relationship (see §29).

יָמִים שְׁנַיִם   *two* days (2 Sam. 1:1)

---

30. For a more exhaustive explanation of the syntax of numerals, see Richter (1979: 26).

(3) If the numeral two is placed before the noun, it can also occur in the *status constructus* form.

    a   שְׁנֵי בָנִים   *two* sons

The numeral two can also combine with a pronominal suffix.

    b   שְׁנֵיהֶם   the *two* of them (Est. 2:23)*

37.2.2.3. *Three to ten*

The numbers three to ten act as nouns and can be placed before or after the plural form of the noun.

(1) Reversed gender
The numerals for the numbers three to ten take the characteristic feminine ending (הָ◌) if the noun is masculine.

                                  שְׁלֹשָׁה בָנִים   *three* sons (Gen. 29:34)

If the noun is feminine, the numeral has no ending (as is normally the case with masculine nouns).

(2) Appositional relationship
- The numeral and a noun – both in the *status absolutus* – stand next to each other and have the form of an *appositional relationship* (see §29). Although the numeral *usually* precedes the noun (#*a*), it often *also follows* the noun (#*b*).

    a   שְׁלֹשָׁה בָנִים   *three* sons (Gen. 29:34)
    b   עָרִים אַרְבַּע   *four* cities (Josh. 21:18)*

(3) Construct relationship
- The cardinals 3–10 in the *status constructus* can also stand before a noun in the *status absolutus*.
- The rules for agreement in gender between the numeral and the noun (as set out above) still apply. The noun is usually in the plural.

    a   וּשְׁנֵי לְאֻמִּים   *two* nations (Gen. 25:23)
    b   שְׁלֹשֶׁת יָמִים   *three* days (Josh. 2:16)

37.2.2.4. *Eleven to nineteen*

With the numbers 11 to 19 the teens as well as the units (1–2) have the same gender as the noun, while the units (3–9) have the opposite gender.

עָרִים שֵׁשׁ־עֶשְׂרֵה   *sixteen* cities (Josh. 15:41)*

37.2.2.5. *Tens*

(1) The tens (20, 30, 40, etc.) are used with masculine and feminine nouns without changing the form of the numerals.

a	שְׁלֹשִׁים וּשְׁנַיִם מֶלֶךְ *thirty-two* kings (1 Kgs 20:1)
b	עָרִים אַרְבָּעִים וּשְׁמֹנֶה *forty-eight* cities (Josh. 21:41)*

(2) With double-digit numbers the units (1–9) or the tens (20, 30, 40 etc.) can be written first.

(3) The tens look like masculine plural forms of the singular numbers and are used with masculine and feminine nouns without distinction.

37.2.2.6. *Larger units (100 and 1000)*

(1) מֵאָה (100) acts as a feminine noun and אֶלֶף (1000) as a masculine noun. They do not change form according to the gender of the accompanying noun. *These numerals always precede the noun.*

a	מֵאָה פְעָמִים *a hundred* times (2 Sam. 24:3)*
b	וּמֵאָה צֹאן and a *hundred* sheep (1 Kgs 5:3)*
c	אֶלֶף פְּעָמִים *a thousand* times (Deut. 1:11)
d	אֶלֶף גֶּפֶן *a thousand* vines (Isa. 7:23)

(2) The cardinal 100 in the *status constructus* can also stand before a noun in the *status absolutus*.

The rules for congruency in gender between the numeral and the noun (as set out above) still apply.

בֶּן־מְאַת שָׁנָה   a *hundred* years old [lit. a son of *hundred* year] (Gen. 11:10)*

Note the following:

(a) With numerals having a semantic value greater than one, the noun is
usually in the plural. The collective use of nouns with numerals is,
however, common – especially with words such as שָׁנָה, נֶפֶשׁ, אִישׁ,
שֶׁקֶל, זָהָב, לֶחֶם, בָּקָר, עִיר, יוֹם, חֹדֶשׁ and אַמָּה. There are thus several
examples of nouns in the singular with numerals greater than one.
Compare also the following two cases:

a	שְׁלֹשׁ־עֶשְׂרֵה עָרִים	*thirteen* cities (Josh. 21:19)*
b	שְׁלֹשׁ־עֶשְׂרֵה עִיר	*thirteen* cities (Josh. 21:33)*

(b) In constructions including a numeral the noun is usually indefinite,
although there are exceptions.

a	שְׁלֹשׁ־מֵאוֹת הַשּׁוֹפָרוֹת	the *three hundred* trumpets (Judg. 7:22)
b	וַחֲמֵשֶׁת עָשָׂר בָּנָיו	and his *fifteen* sons (2 Sam. 19:18)

(3) With compound numbers the noun is often *repeated*.

a	שְׁתַּיִם וְשִׁשִּׁים שָׁנָה וּמְאַת שָׁנָה	*one hundred and sixty-two* years (Gen. 5:18)*
b	שְׁתַּיִם וּשְׁמוֹנִים שָׁנָה וּשְׁבַע מֵאוֹת שָׁנָה	*seven hundred and eight-two* years (Gen. 5:26)*

37.2.3. *Semantics*

Cardinals can fulfil various semantic functions.

(1) The most common use is indicating a specific number or quantity.

a	שִׁבְעַת בָּנָיו	*seven* of his sons (1 Sam. 16:10)
b	אַרְבָּעָה מְלָכִים אֶת־הַחֲמִשָּׁה	*four* kings against *five* (Gen. 14:9)

(2) The numeral אֶחָד is often used to mark an indefinite noun as a certain
specific someone/something (see §24.4.1).

אִישׁ אֶחָד מִן־הָרָמָתַיִם	a *certain* man of Ramathaim (1 Sam. 1:1)

(3) Cardinals are often used to express priority.

In the case of numerals greater than 10, priority can only be expressed by means of the cardinals as Biblical Hebrew does not have separate ordinals for these numbers. If cardinals are used to express priority, they precede the noun. The numeral אֶחָד is an exception to this rule as it can stand in an attributive relationship to the noun.

a   הַטּוּר הָאֶחָד   the *first* row (Exod. 39:10)

b   וַיְהִי בְּאַרְבָּעִים שָׁנָה   And then, in the fortieth year, on
        בְּעַשְׁתֵּי־עָשָׂר חֹדֶשׁ בְּאֶחָד   the *first* day of the eleventh month
                              לַחֹדֶשׁ   [lit. in the eleventh month on the
                                        first (day) of the month] (Deut.
                                        1:3).*

(4) Cardinals are often used to express multiples – whether with the ordinary form of the numeral, or through a form of the numeral that looks like a dual.

a   פַּעַם וּשְׁתָּיִם   once or *twice* (Neh. 13:20)

b   וְאֶת־הַכִּבְשָׂה יְשַׁלֵּם אַרְבַּעְתָּיִם   And the lamb he must restore
                                        fourfold (2 Sam. 12:6).*

(5) Cardinals are also used to express distribution by means of the following constructions (see §24.3.2.(4) and §29.3.(8)):

(a) *Repetition* of the numeral (and the noun)

                        שְׁנַיִם שְׁנַיִם   *two by two* (Gen. 7:9)*

(b) By joining two numerals *with the conjunction* וַ (§24.3.2.(4))

        וְאֶצְבְּעֹת יָדָיו וְאֶצְבְּעֹת רַגְלָיו   and *six* fingers on *each* hand, and
                          שֵׁשׁ וָשֵׁשׁ   *six* toes on *each* foot (2 Sam. 21:20)

(c) Or with the *preposition* לְ (§39.11.(6)(a))

              אַחַת לְשָׁלֹשׁ שָׁנִים   *once every three* years (1 Kgs
                                        10:22)

§37.3. Ordinals

37.3.1. *Forms*

Only the first ten numbers have separate forms for ordinals. Except for the ordinal "first," all the other ordinals end in characteristically masculine and feminine forms.

	Masculine	*Feminine*
first	רִאשׁוֹן	רִאשׁוֹנָה
second	שֵׁנִי	שֵׁנִית
third	שְׁלִישִׁי	שְׁלִישִׁית
fourth	רְבִיעִי	רְבִיעִית
fifth	חֲמִישִׁי	חֲמִישִׁית
sixth	שִׁשִּׁי	שִׁשִּׁית
seventh	שְׁבִיעִי	שְׁבִיעִית
eighth	שְׁמִינִי	שְׁמִינִית
ninth	תְּשִׁיעִי	תְּשִׁיעִית
tenth	עֲשִׂירִי	עֲשִׂירִית

37.3.2. *Syntax*

Ordinals act as attributive adjectives. They follow the noun and agree with it in gender and definiteness.

> בַּשָּׁנָה הַתְּשִׁיעִית בַּחֹדֶשׁ הָעֲשִׂירִי in the *ninth* year, in the *tenth* month (Ezek. 24:1)

37.3.3. *Semantics*
Ordinals always express sequence or priority.

Chapter 6

The Other Word Classes

§38. Introduction

Apart from nominals and verbs, traditional grammars of Biblical Hebrew also distinguish a third main word class, namely, particles. Particles represent a class of words with diverse features. Many *traditional grammars* identify the following particles:

- prepositions,
- conjunctions,
- adverbs and
- interjections.

Since the term "particle" is ambiguous,[1] this grammar prefers (where possible) the designation "other word classes" rather than "particles." The *other word classes* include the following:

- prepositions
- conjunctions
- adverbs (with the sub-classes: "ordinary adverbs," modal adverbs, focus particles, conjunctive adverbs and negatives)
- predicators of existence
- interrogatives
- discourse markers
- interjections and
- oaths[2]

---

1. Some regard "particle" as "a wide reaching term, including all indeclinable word classes such as adverbs, conjunctions, prepositions and other particles classes such as scaler particles, discourse markers, modal particles, interjections" while others assign them a narrower sense, viz. "all invariant words which are not adverbs, conjunctions or prepositions, i.e. scaler particles, discourse markers, modal particles and interjections" (Bussmann et al. 1996: 352).

2. Oaths do not represent a word class, but rather a pragmatic category in which many of the "other word classes" are used in formulaic types of expressions.

Most of the above-mentioned word classes have members that also function as members of one of the other classes. Although there are exceptions (e.g. בַּעֲבוּר, לְמַעַן), Biblical Hebrew prepositions are syntactically (viz. they govern a noun phrase) and semantically (viz. they have a basic spatial sense) a fairly homogenous class. The same could be said of interrogatives, predicators of existence and interjections. For this reason, prepositions (§39), interrogatives (§42), predicators of existence (§43) and interjections (§44) are treated in this grammar as distinct categories.

However, adverbs, conjunctions, and discourse markers are more heterogeneous and sometimes difficult to classify. To allow users an immediate overview of the various uses of each of the lexemes that are classified as belonging to one of these "problematic" word classes, these lexemes are listed alphabetically under the heading "conjunctions, adverbs and discourse markers" (§40). Since the semantic value of negation unites a number of the lexemes in §40, they are grouped together in §41 under the heading "negatives."

Therefore, for heuristic purposes, this grammar distinguishes seven clusters, with cross references where applicable:

- prepositions
- conjunctions, adverbs and discourse markers
- negatives
- interrogatives
- predicators of existence
- interjections
- oaths

§39. Prepositions

§39.1. Introduction

39.1.1. *Morphology: prepositions plus pronominal suffixes*

When Biblical Hebrew employs a pronoun in a prepositional phrase, e.g. to *you*, under *her*, the pronoun is affixed to the preposition as a pronominal suffix. This may be accomplished by the addition of the suffixes that are normally attached either to singular or to plural nouns. The following classes are distinguished on the basis of the suffixes and the morphological patterns of the prepositions + suffixes:

39.1.1.1. *Prepositions with the pronominal suffixes of singular nouns*

(1) The prepositions בְּ, לְ, כְּ, אֵת, עִם, אֵצֶל, נֶגֶד and בַּעַד decline with the suffixes attached to singular nouns.

Person	Singular		Plural	
1 c.	לִי	to me	לָנוּ	to us
2 m.	לְךָ	to you	לָכֶם	to you
2 f.	לָךְ	to you	לָכֶן	to you
3 m.	לוֹ	to him	לָהֶם	to them
3 f.	לָהּ	to her	לָהֶן	to them

(2) Before the suffixes the prepositions כְּ, אֵת and עִם become כְּמוֹ-, אֵת- and עִמָּ-, respectively.

(3) In certain cases the linking vowel between the preposition and the suffix is a *qāmeṣ*, e.g. לָכֶם as opposed to אֶתְכֶם.

(4) The bisyllabic prepositions such as אֵצֶל and נֶגֶד do not decline exactly like segholate nouns with /ֶ/ as stem vowel, e.g. נֶגְדִּי (see §27.3).

However, בַּעַד declines like a segholate noun with /ַ/ as stem vowel (i.e. an a-stem) and a guttural as middle consonant (see §27.3.3.(5), Table 46).

39.1.1.2. *Prepositions with the pronominal suffixes of plural nouns*

The prepositions אֶל, עַל, עַד, תַּחַת, אַחַר and סָבִיב decline with the suffixes attached to plural nouns.

Person	Singular		Plural	
1 c.	אֵלַי	to me	אֵלֵינוּ	to us
2 m.	אֵלֶיךָ	to you	אֲלֵיכֶם	to you
2 f.	אֵלַיִךְ	to you	אֲלֵיכֶן	to you
3 m.	אֵלָיו	to him	אֲלֵיהֶם	to you
3 f.	אֵלֶיהָ	to her	אֲלֵיהֶן	to you

(1) Before the suffixes, the above prepositions become עֶד־, עֲל־, אֶל־ and respectively.

(2) Before the suffixes, תַּחַת and אַחַר act like segholate words with a /◌ֲ/ as stem vowel and a guttural as middle consonant, e.g. אַחֲרֵי (see §27.3.3.(5), Table 46).

    In some cases the *šəwā'* under the guttural is not replaced by a *ḥaṭēp̄* vowel, e.g. תַּחְתַּי.

(3) סָבִיב acts like a noun with a variable vowel in the first syllable, e.g. סְבִיבַי (see §27.2.2.(1), Table 38a).

39.1.1.3. *The preposition* בֵּין

The preposition בֵּין has a variable declension pattern in that it utilizes the suffixes of both singular and plural nouns, e.g. בֵּינִי and בֵּינָיו.

39.1.1.4. *The preposition* מִן

The preposition מִן declines with the suffixes affixed to singular nouns. Why the preposition has such a relatively complicated morphology is not certain.[3]

Person	Singular			Plural		
1 c.	מִנִּי	מִמֶּֽנִּי	from me		מִמֶּֽנּוּ	from us
2 m.		מִמְּךָ	from you		מִכֶּם	from you
2 f.		מִמֵּךְ	from you		מִכֶּן	from you
3 m.	מֶֽנְהוּ	מִמֶּֽנּוּ	from him	מֵהֵֽמָּה מִנְּהֶם	מֵהֶם	from them
3 f.		מִמֶּֽנָּה	from her	מֵהֵֽנָּה	מֵהֶן	from them

39.1.2. *Morphology: prepositions prefixed to other words*

(1) The prepositions בְּ, לְ and כְּ are *joined directly* to the subsequent word.

    (a) If the word begins with יְ, the two audible *šəwā'*s combine to form בִּי, כִּי or לִי (see §8.1.1).

        יְהוּדָה   plus   בְּ = בִּיהוּדָה

---

3. See Bauer–Leander §81p′-y′.

(b) If the word begins with any consonant other than י and is followed by a *šəwāʾ*, the two audible *šəwāʾ*'s combine to form a single closed syllable (see §8.1.1).

שְׁמוּאֵל   plus   כְּ   =   כִּשְׁמוּאֵל

(c) If the noun begins with a guttural, which is followed by a *ḥaṭēp̄* vowel, the preposition takes the corresponding full vowel (see §8.1.1).

חֲלוֹם   plus   בְּ   =   בַּחֲלוֹם

(d) The prepositions לְ and בְּ are sometimes vocalized with a /ָ/. This happens especially with words in which the first syllable is accented:

תֵּת   plus   לְ   =   לָתֵת

זֶה   plus   בְּ   =   בָּזֶה

בֶּטַח   plus   לְ   =   לָבֶטַח

(2) If a *definite* article is prefixed to the noun, *the preposition and the article combine* (see §24.4.2.(4)).

לְ   plus   הַ   =   לַ (not לְהַ)

(3) *The preposition* מִן *may be attached directly to or written apart from the subsequent word. If it is attached directly to the subsequent word, the following rules apply:*

(a) The *nûn* assimilates with the first consonant of the subsequent word (see §4.2.4.2). This consonant then doubles accordingly:

מִן   plus   מֶלֶךְ   =   מִמֶּלֶךְ

(b) If מִן is attached to a word beginning with a guttural or *rêš*, the guttural cannot double. Compensatory lengthening then occurs. The /ִ/ of מִן changes to /ֵ/ (see §8.2.2):

מִן   plus   עִיר   =   מֵעִיר

(c) If מִן is attached to a word beginning with a י, then מִן and י combine to form מִי:

מִן   plus   יְהוּדָה   =   מִיהוּדָה

39.1.3. *Syntax*

Prepositional phrases may be used in several syntactic positions (see §32.2).

(1) Prepositional phrases may function as predicates of nominal clauses.

אֲרִי בֵּין הָרְחֹבוֹת A lion is *in* [lit. *between*] *the streets* [lit. *the plains*] (Prov. 26:13).*

(2) Prepositional phrases can function as complements (see §32.2.(2)).

    (a) As *direct objects* (prepositional objects).
    The prepositions לְ, אֶל־ and בְּ can mark the direct object.

וַיִּבְחַר בָּכֶם And he chose *you* (Deut. 7:7).*

    (b) As indirect objects
    The prepositions לְ, אֶל־, אֵת, עַל can mark the indirect object.

לְזַרְעֲךָ אֶתֵּן אֶת־הָאָרֶץ הַזֹּאת *To your descendants* I will give this land (Gen. 12:7).*

    (c) As complements of prepositional verbs

וְהוּא נִלְחַם בְּמֶלֶךְ מוֹאָב הָרִאשׁוֹן And he fought *against the former king of Moab* (Num. 21:26).*

(3) Prepositional phrases can function as adjuncts (see §32.2.(3)).

    (a) As optional adverbial modifier

וַיִּזְבַּח יַעֲקֹב זֶבַח בָּהָר And Jacob offered a sacrifice *on the mountain* (Gen. 31:54).*

    (b) As *agents of a passive verb*. This can be marked by בְּ, לְ, מִן.

שֹׁפֵךְ דַּם הָאָדָם בָּאָדָם דָּמוֹ יִשָּׁפֵךְ Whoever sheds the blood of human – *by a human* shall his blood be shed (Gen. 9:6).*

(4) Prepositional phrases can function as adjectival qualifications.

אִישׁ מִבֵּית לֶחֶם יְהוּדָה a man *of* [lit. *from*] Bethlehem, Judah (Ruth 1:1)*

39.1.4. *Semantics*

In Biblical Hebrew the semantic relationship indicated by the preposition אֶל can also be expressed by the so-called *hē' locale* (see §28.1).

> הַשְׁלִיכוּ אֹתוֹ אֶל־הַבּוֹר הַזֶּה   Throw him *into this pit* (Gen. 37:22).
>
> וַיַּשְׁלִכוּ אֹתוֹ הַבֹּרָה   And they threw him *into* the pit (Gen. 37:24).*

(1) The relationships expressed by Biblical Hebrew prepositions are limited.
    Prepositions express primarily the spatial relationships between trajectors and landmarks, e.g. a pitched tent in a landscape consisting of a mountain in the background may be profiled in different ways:

(a) The tent (trajector *x*) is *on* the ground (landmark *y*)

(b) The mountain (trajector *x*) is *behind* (or *at the back of*) the tent (landmark *y*)

(c) The tent (trajector *x*) is pitched *below* (or *in front of*) the mountain (landmark *y*).

Speakers determine the nature of the spatial relationship that they want to profile by indicating which entity is the trajector *x* and which one is the landmark *y*. Compare the difference between (a) and (c) above.
    The primary spatial relationship that a specific preposition profiles is called its *proto-scene*.
    The spatial relationships between entities that are expressed by prepositions are often mapped onto the temporal relationships between events. Metaphorical extensions and extensions to other relationships between events are also possible, e.g. cause and purpose.

(2) Three degrees of semantic specialization can be distinguished (Jenni 1992: 18):

(a) Very general, e.g.:

בְּ, לְ and כְּ.

(b) Less general with (especially spatial) oppositional pairs. e.g.:

עַל	on	תַּחַת	under
לִפְנֵי	before	אַחֲרֵי	after/behind
מִן	from	אֶל־	to

(c) More specialized

עַד   until

אֵ֫צֶל   next to

Compound prepositions consisting of more than one preposition are also usually more specialized, e.g.:

מִמַּ֫עַל לְ   at the top of

Note the following:
- Some semantic functions that are attributed to prepositions are largely due to the verbs that govern those prepositions. This feature of some prepositions has not been dealt with systematically in this grammar.
- The predominantly semantic description of the prepositions offered here is not complete, but it does cover about 80% of the cases in the Hebrew Bible. A dictionary should be used in conjunction with this grammar.[4]

§39.2. אַחַר and אַחֲרֵי

The root אחר occurs 899 times in the Hebrew Bible. The verbal usage is attested only 18 times (#a). As a noun (#b) or adjective (#c), the root is used 146 times. Its relational uses as a preposition are most frequent. The composite, אַחֲרֵי־כֵן, functions as an adverbial.

a   וַיֹּ֫אמֶר אֲלֵהֶם אַל־תְּאַחֲרוּ אֹתִי And he said to them, "*Do not delay* me" (Gen. 24:56).*

b   סֹב אֶל־אַחֲרָי Go around to *my back* (2 Kgs 9:18).*

c   וַעֲבַדְתֶּם אֱלֹהִים אֲחֵרִים And you serve *other* gods (Josh. 23:16).*

---

4. The works by Jenni (1992, 1994, 2000) are a very useful source of information on the less specialized prepositions בְּ, לְ and כְּ. The semantic model underlying our treatment benefitted much from the studies of Rodriguez (2011), Lyle (2012 and 2013), Mena (2012) and Lee (2016). See also Lamprecht (2015) on spatial cognition.

(1) Indicates spatial positioning: behind (very frequent)

The translation of the spatial equivalent of the preposition אַחַר and אַחֲרֵי is "*behind y*" or "*after y*." It usually stands in opposition to לִפְנֵי ("*before* x").

The trajector *x* may be in a static position "behind" the landmark *y* (#*a*), or both *x* and *y* may be moving (#*b*). The movement in battle scenes may have a high velocity (#*c*).

The notion of "following behind" is often used metaphorically to refer to the devotion of the trajector *x* "*after y*" (#*d*) or "to *y*" (#*e*).

a הִנֵּה־זֶה עוֹמֵד אַחַר כָּתְלֵנוּ Look, there he stands *behind* our wall (Song 2:9).

b וָאֹמַר אֶל־אֲדֹנִי אֻלַי לֹא־תֵלֵךְ הָאִשָּׁה אַחֲרָי And I said to my master, "Perhaps the woman will not follow me [lit. come *after* me]" (Gen. 24:39).

c וַיָּנָס אֲדֹנִי בֶזֶק וַיִּרְדְּפוּ אַחֲרָיו And Adoni-bezek fled, but they pursued *after* him (Judg. 1:6).*

d לֹא תֵלְכוּן אַחֲרֵי אֱלֹהִים אֲחֵרִים You shall not go *after* other gods (Deut. 6:14).*

e וְעַבְדִּי כָלֵב עֵקֶב הָיְתָה רוּחַ אַחֶרֶת עִמּוֹ וַיְמַלֵּא אַחֲרָי But my servant Caleb, because another spirit was with him, he remained true *to* me (Num. 14:24).*

(2) Indicates temporal positioning: after (very frequent)

a אַחַר הַדְּבָרִים הָאֵלֶּה הָיָה דְבַר־יְהוָה אֶל־אַבְרָם *After* these events the word of the LORD came to Abram (Gen. 15:1).*

b וַיהוָה אָמַר אֶל־אַבְרָם אַחֲרֵי הִפָּרֶד־לוֹט מֵעִמּוֹ... And the LORD said to Abram *after* Lot had parted from him... (Gen. 13:14).*

The adverbial phrase, אַחֲרֵי־כֵן, is typically fronted (#*c*). In only a few cases, אַחֲרֵי־כֵן does not occur sentence initially (#*d*).

c וַיֹּאמֶר יְהוָה אֶל־מֹשֶׁה עוֹד נֶגַע אֶחָד אָבִיא עַל־פַּרְעֹה וְעַל־מִצְרַיִם אַחֲרֵי־כֵן יְשַׁלַּח אֶתְכֶם מִזֶּה And the LORD said to Moses, "Still one plague I will bring upon Pharaoh and upon Egypt; *afterward* he will release you from here" (Exod. 11:1).*

d   וַיַּעֲשׂוּ כֹּל אֲשֶׁר־צִוָּה הַמֶּלֶךְ   And they did all that the king had
       וַיֵּעָתֵר אֱלֹהִים לָאָרֶץ   commanded, and God responded to
       אַחֲרֵי־כֵן׃   prayers [lit. was entreated] for the
       land *afterward* (2 Sam. 21:14).*

(3) Indicates a causal relationship (rare)

Motivated by (2) are instances where a clause introduced by אַחֲרֵי refers to
the grounds of a main clause.

       וַיֹּאמֶר פַּרְעֹה אֶל־יוֹסֵף אַחֲרֵי   Then Pharaoh said to Joseph, "*Since*
       הוֹדִיעַ אֱלֹהִים אוֹתְךָ   God has made all of this known to
       אֶת־כָּל־זֹאת אֵין־נָבוֹן וְחָכָם   you, there is no one as discerning
       כָּמוֹךָ׃   and wise as you" (Gen. 41:39).*

§39.3. אֶל

The preposition אֶל occurs 5,518 times. It is the shorter version of an older
form אֱלֵי. The latter occurs only in Job (5 times). When pronominal suffixes
are used with אֶל, they are added to אֵלַי. The prepositions עַל and אֶל are
sometimes interchanged, especially in the books of Ezekiel and Jeremiah.

(1) Indicates the goal of a movement or process (usually with reference to a
    specific person or place).[5]

    (a) The trajector *x* is a living being moving towards a physical landmark
        y.

    a   וַתָּשָׁב אֵלָיו אֶל־הַתֵּבָה   And it [lit. she] returned *to* him *to*
                                     the ark (Gen. 8:9).

    In some contexts, the process of movement may have a hostile conno-
    tation (like עַל).

    b   קוּמוּ עֲלוּ אֶל־גּוֹי שְׁלֵיו יוֹשֵׁב   Rise up, advance *against* a nation at
           לָבֶטַח   ease, that lives secure (Jer. 49:31).

    (b) The landmark *y* may be a container.

               וּבָאתָ אֶל־הַתֵּבָה   And you shall come *into* the ark
                                  (Gen. 6:18).

---

5. For a discussion of the difference between אֶל and לְ, see Jenni (1992: 21–24).

(c) The landmark *y* may be the goal of an act of observation or that of an emotional process.

a	לִהְיוֹת עֵינֶךָ פְתֻחוֹת אֶל־הַבַּיִת הַזֶּה	that your eyes may be open *toward* this house (1 Kgs 8:29).*
b	וְאֶל־אִישֵׁךְ תְּשׁוּקָתֵךְ	And your desire shall be *for* your husband (Gen. 3:16).*

In some contexts, the emotional process may have a hostile connotation (like עַל).

	לִסְפּוֹת עוֹד עַל חֲרוֹן אַף־יְהוָה אֶל־יִשְׂרָאֵל:	to increase still more the fierce anger of the LORD *against* Israel (Num. 32:14).*

(2) Closely related to (1) are instances where אֶל indicates the recipient of a transfer process.
In acts of transfer, a trajector *x* is transferred to a recipient (i.e. the landmark) *y*.

a	וַיִּתְּנוּ אֶל־יַעֲקֹב אֵת כָּל־אֱלֹהֵי הַנֵּכָר אֲשֶׁר בְּיָדָם	And they gave to Jacob all the foreign gods that they had with them (Gen. 35:4).*

In processes of saying, the content of an act of saying is conceptualized as being transferred to a recipient or addressee (the landmark *y*).

b	וְרִבְקָה אָמְרָה אֶל־יַעֲקֹב בְּנָהּ	Then Rebekah said *to* Jacob her son (Gen. 27:6).*

(3) Indicates spatial positioning (like עַל).
The path of a movement may be downplayed and only the final goal profiled.

a	וַיִּשְׁחָטוּהוּ אֶל־מַעְבְּרוֹת הַיַּרְדֵּן	And they slaughtered him *at* the fords of the Jordan (Judg. 12:6).*
b	וַיַּבְרֵךְ הַגְּמַלִּים מִחוּץ לָעִיר אֶל־בְּאֵר הַמָּיִם	And he made the camels kneel down outside the city *by* the well [lit. the well of water] (Gen. 24:11).*

(4) Indicates the *joining together* of entities (like עַל) (rare)

    (a) Indicates accompaniment: "together with."

וְלֹא־תֶחֶטְאוּ לַיהוָה לֶאֱכֹל אֶל־הַדָּם	And do not sin against the LORD by eating (it) *with* the blood (1 Sam. 14:34).*

    (b) Indicates addition to: "to, with."

הוֹסַפְתָּ חָכְמָה וָטוֹב אֶל־הַשְּׁמוּעָה אֲשֶׁר שָׁמָעְתִּי׃	Your wisdom and prosperity surpass the report which I have heard [lit. you have added wisdom and prosperity *to* the report which I have heard] (1 Kgs 10:7).*

(5) Gives the ground (motivational reason) upon which a certain process is based (like עַל).

כִּי־הִתְאַבֵּל שְׁמוּאֵל אֶל־שָׁאוּל	but Samuel grieved *over* Saul (1 Sam. 15:35).

§39.4. אֵצֶל

The preposition occurs 53 times.

The most typical semantic relationship in which אֵצֶל occurs is trajector x = landmark y and y refers to a location *next to, beside* or *near x. Y* is typically a person (#a-b). It is also often an artifact (#c) or building (#d). In a few instances, y is a geographical space (#e).

a	וַיַּעֲזֹב בִּגְדוֹ אֶצְלִי	And he left his garment *beside* me (Gen. 39:15).*
b	וַיֵּלֶךְ מֵאֶצְלוֹ	(When) he went from him [lit. from *next to* him] (1 Kgs 20:36).*
c	וְשָׂמוֹ אֵצֶל הַמִּזְבֵּחַ	And put them [lit. him] *beside* the altar (Lev. 6:3).*
d	כִּי הוּא קָרוֹב אֵצֶל בֵּיתִי	For it is close by, *next to* my house (1 Kgs 21:2).*
e	וַיִּזְבַּח אֲדֹנִיָּהוּ צֹאן וּבָקָר וּמְרִיא עִם אֶבֶן הַזֹּחֶלֶת אֲשֶׁר־אֵצֶל עֵין רֹגֵל	And Adoniah sacrificed sheep and goats, oxen and fatlings at the Zoheleth stone which is *near* En-rogel (1 Kgs 1:9).*

§39.5. אֵת

The preposition אֵת occurs 284 times[6] in the Pentateuch.[7] It is a near synonym of the preposition עִם which occurs 243 times in the same corpus (see §39.21).

(1) Indicates a *general shared proximity* in space between a trajector *x* and a landmark *y*.

    (a) *Shared presence*

        The most concrete function (proto-scene) of אֵת is to indicate that a trajector *x* is located in general spatial proximity to a landmark *y* (#*a*). Sometimes אֵת indicates that a trajector *x* is in the company of a landmark *y* (#*b*)

a	וַיִּזְכֹּר אֱלֹהִים אֶת־נֹחַ וְאֵת כָּל־הַחַיָּה וְאֶת־כָּל־הַבְּהֵמָה אֲשֶׁר אִתּוֹ בַּתֵּבָה	But God remembered Noah and all the wild animals and all the livestock that were *with* him in the ark (Gen. 8:1).*
b	וְנָתַנּוּ אֶת־בְּנֹתֵינוּ לָכֶם וְאֶת־בְּנֹתֵיכֶם נִקַּח־לָנוּ וְיָשַׁבְנוּ אִתְּכֶם	Then we will give our daughters to you, and we will take your daughters for ourselves, and we will settle *among* you (Gen. 34:16).*

    (b) *In front of*

        Related to (a) are instances where אֵת indicates that a trajector *x* is positioned in front of a landmark *y*. The landmark *y* is animate (#*a*) or inanimate (#*b*) and preceded by פְּנֵי. This combination with פְּנֵי is typically restricted to אֵת.

a	לֹא יֵרָאֶה אֶת־פְּנֵי יְהוָה רֵיקָם:	They must not appear *before* the LORD empty-handed (Deut. 16:16).*
b	וַיִּחַן אֶת־פְּנֵי הָעִיר:	and he camped *before* the city (Gen. 33:18).

---

  6. When they do not have a pronominal suffix the preposition אֵת and the object marker אֵת are homographs (see §33.4.(1)).

  7. This section is based on analysis of the uses of אֵת and עִם in the Pentateuch (Lyle 2012). While the prepositions are synonyms in the Penteuch, in the rest of the Hebrew Bible, עִם became the default preposition to refer to all of the senses identified here.

(c) *Possession*

אֵת indicates that a trajector *x* is in spatial proximity to a landmark *y* which is understood as indicating the landmark's possession of the trajector.

מַה אִתָּנוּ What do we have? [lit. What is *with* us?] (1 Sam. 9:7).

(2) Related to (1), are instances that represent a shift from profiling spatial proximity to *interaction* between living beings.

(a) *Shared activity*

The preposition אֵת indicates the shared participation of an activity between a trajector *x* and a landmark *y*. Typically the shared participation is an act of going (#*a*). However, other acts of shared activity include acts of communication (#*b*) or collaboration (#*c-d*).

a	וַיָּבֹא נֹחַ וּבָנָיו וְאִשְׁתּוֹ וּנְשֵׁי־בָנָיו אִתּוֹ אֶל־הַתֵּבָה	And Noah with his sons and his wife and his sons' wives went into the ark (Gen. 7:7).
b	וַיֵּצֵא חֲמוֹר אֲבִי־שְׁכֶם אֶל־יַעֲקֹב לְדַבֵּר אִתּוֹ	And Hamor the father of Shechem went out to Jacob to speak *with* him (Gen. 34:6).
c	וְהָקֵל מֵעָלֶיךָ וְנָשְׂאוּ אִתָּךְ:	So it will be easier for you, and they will bear the burden *with* you (Exod. 18:22).
d	לֹא אֶת־אֲבֹתֵינוּ כָּרַת יְהוָה אֶת־הַבְּרִית הַזֹּאת כִּי אִתָּנוּ	Not *with* our ancestors did the Lord make this covenant, but *with* us (Deut. 5:3).

(b) *Recipient*

Closely related to #*d* in (2)(a) are instances where אֵת profiles a landmark *y* who is the human recipient of the activity of a trajector *x*. In contrast to #*d* in (2)(a), the shared activity between *x* and *y* appears to be absent.

כְּכֹל אֲשֶׁר עָשָׂה אִתְּכֶם בְּמִצְרַיִם לְעֵינֵיכֶם: Just as he did *for* you in Egypt before your eyes (Deut. 1:30).*

(c) *Support*

Also related to (a) are instances where אֵת profiles an inferior landmark *y* in shared presence/activity with a superior trajector *x* in which support is rendered by the latter to former.

וַיֹּאמֶר אֵלַי יְהֹוָה אֲשֶׁר־הִתְהַלַּכְתִּי לְפָנָיו יִשְׁלַח מַלְאָכוֹ אִתָּךְ וְהִצְלִיחַ דַּרְכֶּךָ	But he said to me, "The LORD, before whom I walk, will send his angel *with* you and make your way successful" (Gen. 24:40).

(d) *Devotion*

Closely related to (c) are instances where אֵת profiles a superior landmark *y* in shared presence/activity with an inferior trajector *x* in which religious compliance is rendered by the latter to the former.

וַיִּתְהַלֵּךְ חֲנוֹךְ אֶת־הָאֱלֹהִים	And Enoch walked *with* God (Gen. 5:22).*

(3) Addition

In a few instances, no concrete spatial proximity could be postulated. אֵת indicates that a trajector *x* is coupled with a landmark *y* as far as an activity *z* is concerned. The activity is typically of a destructive nature.

הִנְנִי מַשְׁחִיתָם אֶת־הָאָרֶץ׃	Look, I am going to destroy them *with* the earth (Gen. 6:13).*

§39.6. בְּ

The preposition occurs 15,570 times. In 1,365 instances it governs a pronominal suffix.

The most typical semantic relationship in which בְּ occurs involves a trajector *x* = landmark *y* and *y* refers to a location in space. The proto-scene for the English preposition "in" involves a trajector that is enclosed by a landmark, and the functional aspect of "containment" (Tyler and Evans 2003: 26). Since בְּ is often unspecified as to whether the trajector is located inside or outside the landmark (Jenni 1992: 179), it may be argued that a similar containment proto-scene should not be postulated for בְּ.[8]

---

8. A counter-argument may be that "location in time" in Biblical Hebrew is predominantly mapped in terms of "location in space" within specific boundaries (landmarks), in other words, a containment proto-scene.

(1) Indicates *localization* (about 60%)

The translation of the most typical spatials equivalent of the preposition בְּ is more or less "trajector x is *in* or *at* landmark y."

(a) Indicates spatial localization – the so-called *beth locale*

(i) *In* or *on* a surface (very frequent)

a   וַיֵּשֶׁב אַבְשָׁלוֹם בִּירוּשָׁלַםִ   And Absalom lived *in* Jerusalem (2 Sam. 14:28).*

b   וַיִּזְבַּח יַעֲקֹב זֶבַח בָּהָר   And Jacob offered a sacrifice *on* the mountain (Gen. 31:54).*

Unlike English, Biblical Hebrew does not lexicalize the distinction between dynamic (#c) and static location (#a).

c   וַיַּעֲבֹר בְּאֶרֶץ־שָׁלִשָׁה וְלֹא מָצָאוּ   And they [lit. he (unusual singular)] passed *through* the land of Shalishah, but they did not find (them) (1 Sam. 9:4).

(ii) *On, in, along, beside* or *near* a path (often)

Closely related to (i) are instances where the landmark y is also a flat surface. However, it has the semantic feature of a path or route (#a-c). The preposition בְּ is unspecified as to whether the trajector x is inside the outer border of a surface (#a), or just outside of it (#b).

Metaphorical extensions of this type of relationship between the trajector x and landmark y are frequent (#c).

a   בְּדֶרֶךְ הַמֶּלֶךְ נֵלֵךְ   *Along* the road of the king we will go (Num. 21:22).*

b   וָאֶקְבְּרֶהָ שָּׁם בְּדֶרֶךְ אֶפְרָת   And I will bury her there *near/ beside* the road to Ephrath (Gen. 48:7).*

c   אִם־לֹא תִשְׁמְעוּ אֵלַי לָלֶכֶת בְּתוֹרָתִי   If you do not listen to me by going *in* my law (Jer. 26:4).*

(iii) *Within* a multi-dimensional space (very frequent)

The trajector x is contained in the landmark y. The landmark y is predominantly a construction.

וּשְׁמוּאֵל שֹׁכֵב בְּהֵיכַל יְהֹוָה   And Samuel was lying down *in* the temple of the LORD (1 Sam. 3:3).

(iv) Indicates localization *within* (*among*) a group (often)

אוֹדְךָ בָעַמִּים | אֲדֹנָי I will praise you, my Lord, *among* the peoples (Ps. 57:10).*

(b) Localizes through indicating contact with an *x*

In a significant number of instances a trajector x = בְּ, the landmark *y* does not involve the existence of *x* in, on, at, near or among the landmark *y*, but an action (חזק "take hold of," לחם Ni. "fight," נגע "touch," נכה Hi. "strike," תפש "seize," שלח "send [a hand against]") in which *y* is physically or figuratively touched. The latter is typical of בחר "choose," חפץ "delight in," משל "rule over," שמע "listen." The landmark *y* is typically not an open surface that can contain *x*, but a close "localized object" that presents the location that has come in contact with *x*.

(i) Material contact: *person or thing* (frequent)

The contact may be direct (#*a*) or indirect (#*b*).

a   <div dir="rtl">וַיִּפְגַּע־בּוֹ וַיָּמֹת:</div> And he struck *him* down, and he died (1 Kgs 2:25).*

b   <div dir="rtl">וְהִכְרַתִּי לְיָרָבְעָם מַשְׁתִּין בְּקִיר</div> And I will cut off from Jeroboam those pissing *against* a wall (1 Kgs 14:10).*

(ii) Figurative contact by means of mental processes (frequent)

Observation may be by means of the eyes (#*a*) or ears (#*b*). Mental processes, e.g. of observation (#*c*), choosing (#*d*) or rejection (#*d*) may also be involved.

a   <div dir="rtl">וַתֵּצֵא דִינָה בַּת־לֵאָה אֲשֶׁר יָלְדָה לְיַעֲקֹב לִרְאוֹת בִּבְנוֹת הָאָרֶץ:</div> And Dina, the daughter of Leah whom she bore to Jacob, went out to visit [lit. look *over*] the daughters of the land (Gen. 34:1).*

b   <div dir="rtl">אִם־אֶשְׁמַע עוֹד בְּקוֹל שָׁרִים וְשָׁרוֹת</div> Or can I still hear the voice of the singing men and women? (2 Sam. 19:36).*

c   <div dir="rtl">יָדַעְתָּ בְּצָרוֹת נַפְשִׁי</div> You took note *of* the distress of my inner being (Ps. 31:8).*

d   <div dir="rtl">וַיִּמְאַס בְּאֹהֶל יוֹסֵף וּבְשֵׁבֶט אֶפְרַיִם לֹא בָחָר:</div> Then he rejected the tent of Joseph, and he did not choose the tribe of Ephraim (Ps. 78:67).*

Although the construction שָׁמַע בְּקוֹל in #b and #e is the most frequent (99 times), שָׁמַע לְקוֹל (#f) is also attested (15 times). The former construction is typically associated with both a general ability to hear something (#b) as well as complete compliance, even to specific requests (#e). However, the latter (#f) is associated only with compliance to specific concrete requests (Jenni 1992: 250–51).

e	עֵקֶב אֲשֶׁר שָׁמַעְתָּ בְּקֹלִי׃	Because you obeyed my voice (Gen. 22:18).*
f	וַיִּשְׁמַע אַבְרָם לְקוֹל שָׂרָי׃	And Abram listened *to* [lit. the voice of] Sarai (Gen. 16:2).*

(iii) *Social* contact (frequent)
A feature of members of this category is that both trajector *x* and landmark *y* are persons, and the contact involved is in the form of a complex relationship. This relationship often has a negative effect on the landmark *y* (#a-c).

a	אִם־מָשׁוֹל תִּמְשֹׁל בָּנוּ	Or are you indeed to rule *over* us? (Gen. 37:8).*
b	וַיִּמְרֹד צִדְקִיָּהוּ בְּמֶלֶךְ בָּבֶל	And Zedekiah rebelled *against* the king of Babylon (Jer. 52:3).*
c	רְאוּ הֵבִיא לָנוּ אִישׁ עִבְרִי לְצַחֶק בָּנוּ	See, my husband brought a Hebrew man to make fun *of* us (Gen. 39:14).*

(iv) Contact with *part of a whole* (retaining a perspective of the whole) (occasionally)
In contrast to trajector *x* = מִן landmark *y* (the so-called partitive מִן), the focus of trajector *x* = בְּ landmark *y* is not *x* as an entity separated from *y*, but *x* as a part of the bigger entity *y*. Participation in a meal (#a) or reading part of a document (#b) are typical uses of this category.

a	לְכוּ לַחֲמוּ בְלַחֲמִי וּשְׁתוּ בְּיַיִן מָסָכְתִּי׃	Come, eat *of* my bread and drink *of* the wine I have mixed (Prov. 9:5).
b	וְהָיְתָה עִמּוֹ וְקָרָא בוֹ כָּל־יְמֵי חַיָּיו	And it must be with him and he must read *from* it all the days of his life (Deut. 17:19).*

(2) Indicates a *temporal frame* (very frequent)

In the relationship trajector $x = $ בְּ landmark y, y is a time frame in which an event or state of affairs needs to be positioned. The frame may be lexically (#a) or deictically (#b) specified. The preposition בְּ + infinitive construct often refers to events that provide the temporal frame of an event or events (#c) referred to in a subsequent sentence. (Compare in contrast, the preposition כְּ + infinitive construct in §39.10.(4).)

a	וַיְהִי בִשְׁנַת הַתְּשִׁיעִית לְמָלְכוֹ בַּחֹדֶשׁ הָעֲשִׂירִי בֶּעָשׂוֹר לַחֹדֶשׁ בָּא נְבֻכַדְנֶאצַּר מֶלֶךְ־בָּבֶל	And then, *in* the ninth year of his reign, *in* the tenth month, *on* the tenth (day) of the month Nebuchadnezzar, the king of Babylon, came (2 Kgs 25:1).*
b	וּדְבַר־יְהוָה הָיָה יָקָר בַּיָּמִים הָהֵם	And the word of the LORD was rare *in* those days (1 Sam. 3:1).*
c	בְּלֶכְתְּךָ הַיּוֹם מֵעִמָּדִי וּמָצָאתָ שְׁנֵי אֲנָשִׁים	*When* you depart from me today you will meet two men (1 Sam. 10:2).*

(3) Realizes an action by locating one of the following:[9]

(a) Instrument – the so-called *beth instrumenti* (very frequent)

The instrument is typically non-living entities, e.g. an implement (#a). The instrument may also be a living being (#b). The body part used is often governed by בְּ (#c), while the expression בְּיַד became a secondary preposition to refer to an agent (#d). Also a special case is the use of the preposition to indicate the means or norm with which something is measured (#e).

a	בַּשֵּׁבֶט יַכּוּ עַל־הַלְּחִי אֵת שֹׁפֵט יִשְׂרָאֵל:	*With* a rod they strike upon the cheek the ruler of Israel (Mic. 4:14).*
b	שֹׁפֵךְ דַּם הָאָדָם בָּאָדָם דָּמוֹ יִשָּׁפֵךְ	Whoever sheds the blood of a human, *by* a human shall his blood be shed (Gen. 9:6).*
c	בִּזְרֹעוֹ יְקַבֵּץ טְלָאִים	*With* his arms he will gather (the) lambs (Isa. 40:11).*

---

9. See further Jenni (1992: 71–170).

d כַּאֲשֶׁר דִּבֶּר יְהוָה בְּיַד־מֹשֶׁה: Just as the Lord had spoken
            through Moses (Exod. 9.35).*

e וְשָׁקַל אֶת־שְׂעַר רֹאשׁוֹ מָאתַיִם And he used to weigh the hair of
    שְׁקָלִים בְּאֶבֶן הַמֶּלֶךְ: his head, two hundred shekels *by*
            the king's weight (2 Sam. 14:26).*

It is hard to motivate the secondary preposition in #f (occurring 309
times) as a metaphoric extension of localization of a space. It most
probably became conventionalized via the instrumental use of בְּ. It
represents a metonymically extended fixed expression for "in *x*'s
opinion."

f עֲשִׂי־לָהּ הַטּוֹב בְּעֵינָיִךְ Do to her what is right *in* your eyes
            (Gen. 16:6).*

(b) Cause – the so-called *beth causa* (frequent)
  Closely related to (a) are instances where the "instrument" is not used
  by an agent to realize an action. Instead, the entity ("instrument")
  governed by בְּ is the ground or cause of the situation referred to in an
  intransitive clause. Typically the ground of joy (#*a*) or the ground of a
  sinful state of affairs (#*b*) are involved.

a וְשָׂמַחְתָּ בְכָל־הַטּוֹב אֲשֶׁר And you shall rejoice *in* (or:
    נָתַן־לְךָ יְהוָה אֱלֹהֶיךָ *because of*) all the good which the
           Lord your God has given to you
           (Deut. 26:11).*

b כִּי כַפֵּיכֶם נְגֹאֲלוּ בַדָּם For your hands are defiled *with*
            blood (Isa. 59:3).

(c) *Beth communicationis* (often)
  Also related to (a) is the *beth communicationis*. While words of saying
  typically have a valency of three, i.e. a speaker, addressee and the
  content of the address, acts of speaking may also be completed by
  means of constructions with בְּ that refer to the human "instrument"
  (#*a*). Also attested are instances where the instrument used to communicate with God, i.e. calling on his name, is governed by בְּ (#*b*).
  Probably related to the latter use, are the following: cases where בְּ
  governs the reference to a spiritual being (mainly God) from which an
  oracle is sought (#*c*) and where somebody is called by his name, i.e.
  mentioning his name (#*d*).

Often the (reference to the) person on whose behalf something is said (#e), or whose authority (#f) is invoked in an act of swearing, is governed by בְּ.

a   הֲלֹא גַּם־בָּנוּ דִבֶּר   Has he not spoken *through* us also? (Num. 12:2).

b   וּבְשֵׁם־יְהוָה אֶקְרָא   But I called *on* the name of the LORD (Ps. 116:4).*

c   וַיִּשְׁאַל דָּוִד בַּיהוָה   And David inquired *of* the LORD (1 Sam. 30:8).*

d   קָרָאתִי בְשִׁמְךָ לִי־אָתָּה   I have called you *by* your name, you are mine (Isa. 43:1).*

e   בֵּרַכְנוּ אֶתְכֶם בְּשֵׁם יְהוָה   We bless you *in* the name of the LORD (Ps. 129:8).*

f   נִשְׁבַּעְתָּ בַּיהוָה אֱלֹהֶיךָ לַאֲמָתֶךָ   You swore *by* the LORD your God to your (maid)servant (1 Kgs 1:17).*

(d) Price – the so-called *beth pretii* (often)

תְּנָה־לִּי אֶת־כַּרְמְךָ בְּכֶסֶף   Sell [lit. give] me your vineyard *for* money (1 Kgs 21:6).*

(e) Accompanying entity (comitative) – the so-called *beth comitantiae* (occasionally)
A distinctive feature of this category is that an act of movement is involved.

וַתָּבֹא יְרוּשָׁלְַמָה בְּחַיִל כָּבֵד מְאֹד   And she came to Jerusalem *with* a very great retinue (1 Kgs 10:2).*

(f) *Beth essentia* (occasionally)
A distinctive feature of this category is that in trajector x = בְּ landmark y, x is equated to y. This is in contrast to all other uses of x = בְּ y.

a   כִּי־אֱלֹהֵי אָבִי בְּעֶזְרִי   for the God of my father was my help (Exod. 18:4).*

b   נַעֲשֶׂה אָדָם בְּצַלְמֵנוּ כִּדְמוּתֵנוּ   Let us make human *as* our image, according to our likeness (Gen. 1:26).*

(4) Describe *the mode of an action* (frequent)

The distinctive feature of this category is that בְּ "locates" an event in terms of its mode. It may be a mode of quality (#*a*) or a mode of performance (#*b*).

a	וְשָׁפַט בְּצֶדֶק דַּלִּים	And he shall judge the poor *with* righteousness (Isa. 11:4).*
b	וְדָוִד וְכָל־בֵּית יִשְׂרָאֵל מַעֲלִים אֶת־אֲרוֹן יְהוָה בִּתְרוּעָה וּבְקוֹל שׁוֹפָר	And David and all Israel were bringing up the ark of the LORD *with* shouting and *with* the sound of a horn (2 Sam. 6:15).*

§39.7. בֵּין

The preposition בֵּין occurs 408 times. This includes 14 instances of the form בֵּנוֹת. Contra the suggestion by many scholars, the choice between either the masculine singular or feminine plural form cannot be related to any semantic considerations (Barr 1978: 12–18). The only difference between these forms is that בֵּנוֹת never occurs in the combinations referred to below. The combination בֵּין...וּבֵין is attested 128 times, and בֵּין...לְבֵין 30 times.

Semantically the preposition בֵּין has primarily a locative function, viz. a region intermediate to a trajector *x* and landmark *y* (i.e. two points in space) is referred to.

(1) Indicates spatial location

(a) A region "between" two points (often)

Typically בֵּין is repeated before each point in space (#*a*). Only in three instances from later books is the second בֵּין replaced by לְ (#*b*). In the case of paired body parts, בֵּין is not repeated (#*c*).

a	בֵּין בֵּית־אֵל וּבֵין הָעָי	*between* Bethel and Ai (Gen. 13:3)
b	בֵּין הָאוּלָם וְלַמִּזְבֵּחַ יִבְכּוּ הַכֹּהֲנִים	*Between* the vestibule and the altar the priests weep (Joel 2:17).
c	וַיַּךְ אֶת־יְהוֹרָם בֵּין זְרֹעָיו	And he shot Joram *between* his shoulders (2 Kgs 9:24).*

(b) A region "among" various points (seldom)

The points may be frames or surfaces (#*a*), or a collection of entities (#*b*).

a	אָמַר עָצֵל שַׁחַל בַּדָּרֶךְ אֲרִי בֵּין הָרְחֹבוֹת:	The lazy one says there is a lion in the road, a lion is *in* [lit. *between*] the streets [lit. *the plains*] (Prov. 26:13).*
b	וְהוּא עֹמֵד בֵּין הַהֲדַסִּים	And he was standing *among* the myrtle trees (Zech. 1:8).*

(2) Indicates a *temporal location* (very rare)

This use of בֵּין is limited to one expression, i.e. when בֵּין governs the dual form of עֶרֶב.

וְשָׁחֲטוּ אֹתוֹ כֹּל קְהַל עֲדַת־יִשְׂרָאֵל בֵּין הָעַרְבָּיִם:	Then the whole assembly of the congregation of Israel shall slaughter it *at* twilight (Exod. 12:6).*

(3) Indicates a *conceptual distinction* "between" entities (frequent)

The spatial distance "between" the entities is extended to that of a conceptual distinction between entities. Typically a reciprocal relationship between the entities is involved (#*a*). The construction בֵּין...וּבֵין (#*a*) is predominantly used. When בֵּין...לְבֵין is used, a distinction is typically made between unspecified classes (#*b*).

a	וַהֲקִמֹתִי אֶת־בְּרִיתִי בֵּינִי וּבֵינֶךָ וּבֵין זַרְעֲךָ	And I will establish my covenant *between* me and you and *between* your descendants (Gen. 17:7).*
b	וְשָׁפַטְתִּי בֵּין שֶׂה לָשֶׂה	And I will judge *between* one sheep and another [lit. *between* sheep and sheep] (Ezek. 34:22).*

§39.8. בַּעֲבוּר

See §40.19.

§39.9. בְּעַד

The preposition בְּעַד occurs 105 times. Semantically, the preposition has the following meanings:

(1) Indicates the *spatial location of a path* (often)

The preposition בְּעַד has primarily a locative function. It positions a trajector *x* as far as a landmark *y*, and *y* is an opening (e.g. window or door) in a wall. However, most instances in the Bible appear to represent a metaphorical extension from this locative sense.

(a) Trajector *x* moves (or is caused to move) בְּעַד landmark *y*.

A physical movement may be involved (#*a*) or the physical movement of an entity is extended to refer to the path of a perception (#*b*).

a	וַתּוֹרִדֵם בַּחֶבֶל בְּעַד הַחַלּוֹן	And she let them down by a rope *through* the window (Josh. 2:15).*
b	וּמִיכַל בַּת־שָׁאוּל נִשְׁקְפָה ׀ בְּעַד הַחַלּוֹן	And Michal, Saul's daughter, looked down *through* the window (2 Sam. 6:16).*

(b) A landmark *z* closes trajector *x* בְּעַד landmark *y* (or *z*) (often).

The landmark *y*, a path (typically a door) that provides access to trajector *x*, is closed (#*a*). In a few cases, the singular path of access is extended metaphorically to any access, whether in (#*b*) or out (#*c*).

a	וַיִּסְגֹּר דַּלְתוֹת הָעֲלִיָּה בַּעֲדוֹ	And he closed the doors of the upper-room *upon/behind* him (Judg. 3:23).*
b	הֲלֹא־אַתְּ שַׂכְתָּ בַעֲדוֹ וּבְעַד־בֵּיתוֹ וּבְעַד כָּל־אֲשֶׁר־לוֹ מִסָּבִיב	Have you yourself not put a fence *around* him and *around* his house and *around* all that he has – on every side? (Job 1:10).*
c	כִּי־סָגַר יְהוָה בְּעַד רַחְמָהּ	because the LORD had closed her womb (1 Sam. 1:6).*

(2) Indicates involvement of *x to the benefit of y*: for the sake of, for (frequent).

כִּי־נָבִיא הוּא וְיִתְפַּלֵּל בַּעַדְךָ	In fact, he is a prophet, and he will pray *for* you (Gen. 20:7).*

§39.10. כְּ

The preposition כְּ occurs 3,038 times, including 56 instances of the long form כְּמוֹ. The long form appears mainly in poetry and can be regarded as an archaic form of the language.

In 104 instances, כְּ governs a pronominal suffix and in most cases the pronouns are suffixed to the long form. The combination כַּאֲשֶׁר is attested 590 times. Like the prepositions בְּ and לְ, כְּ also combines with the definite article. However, ten instances are attested where this is not the case, hence the form כְּהַיּוֹם.[10]

In contrast to most other prepositions, כְּ has no spatial connotation. Generally speaking, the preposition כְּ has a fairly limited semantic potential, namely, it indicates agreement between a trajector *x* and a landmark *y*.

(1) Indicates *similarity* (very frequent)

Typically כְּ is used to indicate that a trajector *x* is (or will be made) similar to a landmark *y*.

וּבִעַרְתִּי אַחֲרֵי בֵית־יָרָבְעָם כַּאֲשֶׁר יְבַעֵר הַגָּלָל עַד־תֻּמּוֹ	And I will burn up the house of Jeroboam *as* one burns up dung until it is consumed (1 Kgs 14:10).*

(2) Indicates *comparability* (frequent)

X is comparable כְּ "with" *y*. The point of the comparison (#a), or lack of comparison (#b), has to be gleaned from the context.

a	עֵינָיו כְּיוֹנִים עַל־אֲפִיקֵי מָיִם	His eyes are *like* doves at streams of water (Song 5:12).*
b	וְאָנֹכִי לֹא אֶהְיֶה כְּאַחַת שִׁפְחֹתֶיךָ:	And I am not *like* one of your servant girls (Ruth 2:13).*

(3) Indicates *quantitative* agreement (occasionally)

Most typical of this category are instances where *an approximate* number is indicated by means of כְּ (#a). In a number of instances, the construction כְּאִישׁ אֶחָד appears to have developed into a fixed expression which could be interpreted as "as if one person" (#b). The preposition כְּ may also indicate agreement between portions (#c) or a quantitative agreement between an aspect of the propositional content of a clause *x* with that of a clause *y* (#d).

a	וְהֵמָּה כִּשְׁלֹשִׁים אִישׁ:	And they were *about* thirty persons (1 Sam. 9:22).*

---

10. For a detailed description of the syntagmatic distribution of כְּ, see Jenni (1994: 16–23).

b	וַיֵּצְאוּ כְּאִישׁ אֶחָד	And they came out *as* one man (1 Sam. 11:7).*
c	וַיְחַלֶּק־שָׁם יְהוֹשֻׁעַ אֶת־הָאָרֶץ לִבְנֵי יִשְׂרָאֵל כְּמַחְלְקֹתָם	And Joshua divided the land there for the Israelites *according* to their tribal divisions (Josh. 18:10).*
d	מַלֵּא אֶת־אַמְתְּחֹת הָאֲנָשִׁים אֹכֶל כַּאֲשֶׁר יוּכְלוּן שְׂאֵת	Fill the sacks of the men with as much food *as* they are able to carry [lit. with food *according* to they can carry] (Gen. 44:1).*

(4) Indicates *proximity in time* (often)

כְּ + temporal construction is used to indicate that an event referred to in the main clause, which typically follows the temporal clause with the כְּ + temporal construction, *immediately follows it in time*. The כְּ + temporal construction can typically be translated "as soon as," "just when," etc. Often "when" is also adequate.

This use of כְּ + temporal construction can be contrasted with בְּ + temporal construct that provides the temporal frame of the event referred to in the main clause (see §39.6.(2)).

The most typical constructions to be used are temporal clauses with כַּאֲשֶׁר + finitive verb (#a) or כְּ + infinitive construction (#b). Also attested are instances where כְּ is followed by a nominal construction that refers to a notion of time (#c). These constructions are typically used to indicate a point immediately proximate ("now immediately" or "first") to the time of speaking.

a	וַיְהִי כַּאֲשֶׁר קָרַב אֶל־הַמַּחֲנֶה וַיַּרְא אֶת־הָעֵגֶל	And then, *as soon as* he approached the camp, he saw the calf (Exod. 32:19).*
b	וַיְהִי כְּהַזְכִּירוֹ אֶת־אֲרוֹן הָאֱלֹהִים וַיִּפֹּל מֵעַל־הַכִּסֵּא	And then, *the moment that* he mentioned the ark of God, he (Eli) fell from his seat (1 Sam. 4:18).*
c	וַיֹּאמֶר יַעֲקֹב מִכְרָה כַיּוֹם אֶת־בְּכֹרָתְךָ לִי׃	And Jacob replied, "*First*, [lit. *as* the day] sell me your birthright" (Gen. 25:31).*

§39.11. לְ

The preposition לְ occurs 20,725 times. In 4,433 instances, it governs a pronominal suffix. לְ is often part of secondary prepositions and even conjunctions and question words, e.g. לִפְנֵי is attested 1,104 times, לְמַעַן (270 times), לָכֵן (200 times) and לָמָּה (180 times). Complex prepositions in which לְ follows מִן occur 144 times, e.g. מִלִּפְנֵי (72 times), מִלְּבַד (34 times) and מִלְמַעְלָה (24 times).

The preposition לְ does not have a specialized meaning. It indicates a very general relationship between two entities that can at best be described as "*x* as far as *y* is concerned."

In Biblical Hebrew, לְ is used often to characterize relationships that are marked by the dative form in Latin and Greek. In Late Biblical Hebrew, under the influence of Aramaic, אֶל was supplanted by לְ and עַל as the spatial locative "to."

(1) Indicates an indirect object relationship

    (a) With verbs of giving

        The most prototypical function of the preposition לְ is to indicate the indirect object of an action. Someone does something that *causes a relation of belonging* between a trajector *x* (the indirect object) and a landmark *y* (the object). What is done can broadly speaking be regarded as an act of giving (#*a-c*).

a	וַיִּתֶּן־לוֹ אֶת־כָּל־אֲשֶׁר־לוֹ	And he has given *to* him everything he owns (Gen. 24:36).*
b	וַיִּזְבְּחוּ־זֶבַח לַיהוָה	Then they offered a sacrifice *to* the Lord (Jonah 1:16).*
c	שִׂימָה־לָּנוּ מֶלֶךְ	Appoint *for* us a king (1 Sam. 8:5).*

Equally frequent are instances where no action is involved, but only a relationship of belonging between a trajector *x* and a landmark *y* is ascribed to the trajector *x* (#*d-e*).

d	וּלְרִבְקָה אָח	And Rebekah had a brother [lit. and *for* Rebekah (was) a brother] (Gen. 24:29).*
e	לַיהוָה אָנִי	I belong *to* the Lord (Isa. 44:5).*

(b) With verbs of saying

The valency of verbs of saying resembles that of verbs of giving. They have a subject (speaker/giver), an object (content of speech/what was given) and an indirect object (hearer/recipient). This applies when something is said (#*a*). Often the content of the communication is implied by the content of the verb so that it has a valency of two and not three (#*b*). The syntactic pattern also differs when a noun of saying is involved (#*c*), and when what is communicated does not concern a hearer, but a theme (#*d*).

a　　　　וַיֹּאמֶר לָהּ מַלְאַךְ יְהֹוָה הִנָּךְ הָרָה　And the messenger of the LORD said *to* her, "Look, you are pregnant" (Gen. 16:11).*

b　　　　הוֹדוּ לַיהוָה　Thank (*to*) the LORD (Isa. 12:4).*

c　　　　וַיְהִי דְבַר־שְׁמוּאֵל לְכָל־יִשְׂרָאֵל　And the word of Samuel came *to* all Israel (1 Sam. 4:1).

d　　　　אִמְרִי־לִי אָחִי הוּא　Say *concerning* me, "He is my brother" (Gen. 20:13).*

The hearer is, however, not always signaled by לְ, but may instead be signaled by אֶל. Jenni (1999) has established that when somebody of a higher social status speaks to someone of a lower status, only לְ is used (#*a*). When somebody of a lower status speaks to somebody of a higher status, אֶל is more often used (#*e*).

e　　　　וַיֹּאמֶר מֹשֶׁה אֶל־יְהֹוָה...　Then Moses said *to* the LORD... (Exod. 4:10).*

(2) Indicates an experienced relationship

Closely related to (1) are instances where the action performed does not result in a relationship of belonging. A state of affairs or event *y*, is *related to the experiencer x by means of a verb*. The construction עשׂה + לְ (#*a*) is the most typical one. However, the act of doing may be specified in various ways (#*b*). It may even include forms of social (#*c*) and mental contact (#*d*).

a　　　　וְאֶת־אֹתֹתָיו וְאֶת־מַעֲשָׂיו אֲשֶׁר עָשָׂה בְּתוֹךְ מִצְרָיִם לְפַרְעֹה　And his signs and deeds which he did in Egypt *to* Pharaoh (Deut. 11:3).*

b	וְהוֹשִׁ֫יעָה לָּ֫נוּ	And save *us* (Josh. 10:6).
c	וַתִּשַּׁק לָהֶן	Then she kissed *them* (Ruth 1:9).*
d	וְלֹא יִשְׁמְעוּ לְק֣וֹל אֲבִיהֶ֑ם	But they did not listen *to* the voice of their father (1 Sam. 2:25).*

Under the influence of Aramaic the preposition לְ is relatively often used in Late Biblical Hebrew before direct objects (#e).

e	וַיַּמְלִ֫יכוּ שֵׁנִית֙ לִשְׁלֹמֹ֤ה בֶן־דָּוִ֔יד	And they made *Solomon* the son of David king for a second time (1 Chron. 29:22).

Slightly less frequent are instances where a trajector *x*, a qualitative, quantitative or relational feature, state of affairs or event, is related to a landmark *y*, *an experiencing person or thing in a non-causative way*. For these purposes an adjective (#f), a noun phrase (#g), or an interjection (#h) is used.

f	וְהָֽאֲנָשִׁ֗ים טֹבִ֥ים לָ֖נוּ מְאֹ֑ד	And the men were very good *to* us (1 Sam. 25:15).
g	וַיֹּ֨אמֶר הָאִ֤ישׁ הַזָּקֵן֙ שָׁל֣וֹם לָ֔ךְ	And the old man said, "Peace *to* you" (Judg. 19:20).
h	אֽוֹי־לִ֣י כִֽי־נִדְמֵ֗יתִי	Woe *to* me, for I am lost (Isa. 6:5).

(3) לְ + infinitive (see also §20.1)

   (a) Embedded as complement in a nominal clause

      (i) Predicate of a nominal clause (rare)

         When לְ + infinitive is used as the predicate of a nominal clause, often deontic modality (predominantly in Late Biblical Hebrew texts) (#a), epistemic modality (#b) and in a few instances an imminent event (#c) are involved.

a	מַה־לַּעֲשׂוֹת֙ בָּאִ֔ישׁ אֲשֶׁ֥ר הַמֶּ֖לֶךְ חָפֵ֥ץ בִּיקָרֽוֹ	What *should be done* for the man whom the king wishes to honor? (Est. 6:6).*
b	שֹׁמֵ֣ר תְּבוּנָ֑ה לִמְצֹא־טֽוֹב	The one who preserves understanding *is likely to find* prosperity (Prov. 19:8).*
c	וַיְהִ֤י הַשֶּׁ֨מֶשׁ֙ לָב֔וֹא	and as the sun was *about to go down* (Gen. 15:12).*

(ii) Part of subject of a nominal clause (seldom)

וְאִם רַע בְּעֵינֵיכֶם לַעֲבֹד   And if it is wrong in your eyes *to*
אֶת־יהוה...   *serve the* LORD... (Josh. 24:15).*

(iii) Embedded as complement in a verbal clause (frequent)
לְ + infinitive is embedded as the complement of three types of verbs: verbs referring to one aspect of an action, e.g. a temporal phase (#a), a quantitative (#b-c) or qualitative dimension (#d); verbs referring to ability (#e) and verbs referring to (un)willingness (#f-g):

a   אֲדֹנָי יהוה אַתָּה הַחִלּוֹתָ   O LORD God, you yourself have
לְהַרְאוֹת אֶת־עַבְדְּךָ   begun *to show* your servant your
אֶת־גָּדְלְךָ   greatness (Deut. 3.24).*

b   וַיְמַהֵר פַּרְעֹה לִקְרֹא לְמֹשֶׁה   And Pharaoh hurriedly summoned
וּלְאַהֲרֹן   [lit. he hurried *to summon*] Moses
and Aaron (Exod. 10:16).*

c   וַיֹּסִפוּ בְּנֵי יִשְׂרָאֵל לַעֲשׂוֹת   And the Israelites did *again* [lit.
הָרַע בְּעֵינֵי יהוה   added *to do*] what was evil in the
eyes of the LORD (Judg. 3:12).

d   וּשְׁמַרְתֶּם לַעֲשֹׂתָם...   And you must observe (them)
carefully [lit. observe *to do them*]...
(Deut. 5:1).*

e   וְלֹא יָכְלוּ בְּנֵי יִשְׂרָאֵל   And the Israelites were not able *to*
לָקוּם לִפְנֵי אֹיְבֵיהֶם   *stand* before their enemies (Josh.
7:12).*

f   וְלֹא־אָבָה דָוִד לְהָסִיר   And David was not willing *to let*
אֵלָיו אֶת־אֲרוֹן יהוה   the ark of the LORD *turn* aside to
him (2 Sam. 6:10).*

g   וַיְמָאֵן לְהִתְנַחֵם   But he refused *to be consoled* (Gen.
37:35).

(b) As adjunct
In this section, the matrix clause with which the לְ + infinitive has a relationship is the landmark *y*. The לְ infinite clause is the trajector *x*. See also §20.1.
(i) Purpose (very frequent)
The landmark *y* refers typically to an intentional activity which involves movement from one location to the other (#a). Instances where other intentional actions are referred to are also often

attested, e.g., acts of communication (#b). Also relatively frequent
are instances where the purpose of the landmark y (referred to in
the matrix clause) is that of enablement (#c). A significant feature
of all the above-mentioned cases is that the trajector x follows in
time the landmark y.

a   וַיָּבֹא הַבַּיְתָה לַעֲשׂוֹת מְלַאכְתּוֹ   And he went into the house *to do*
                                         his work (Gen. 39:11).*

b   יִקְרָא אֶל־הַשָּׁמַיִם מֵעָל   He summons the heavens above,
     וְאֶל־הָאָרֶץ לָדִין עַמּוֹ   and the earth, *in order to judge* his
                                         people (Ps. 50:4).*

c   כִּי לָכֶם נָתַתִּי אֶת־הָאָרֶץ   for to you I give the land *so that*
     לָרֶשֶׁת אֹתָהּ   *you may possess* it [lit. her] (Num.
                                         33:53).*

(ii)   Explicative (frequent)

Typical of this category is that the finite verb of the landmark y
has no specific terminal point, i.e., it is atelic. The trajector x does
not follow in time on the landmark y.

     The trajector x explicates the landmark x in various ways, viz.
by narrowing it down – specification (#a), by giving one example
of it – exemplification (#b) or by explaining it – epexegesis (#c).

a   וַיָּשֶׁב אֱלֹהִים אֵת רָעַת   And God repaid Abimelech for the
     אֲבִימֶלֶךְ אֲשֶׁר עָשָׂה לְאָבִיו   evil he did to his father *by murder-*
     לַהֲרֹג אֶת־שִׁבְעִים אֶחָיו׃   *ing* his seventy brothers (Judg.
                                         9:56).*

b   וַיֶּאֱהַב שְׁלֹמֹה אֶת־יְהוָה   And Solomon loved the LORD *by*
     לָלֶכֶת בְּחֻקּוֹת דָּוִד אָבִיו   *walking* in the statutes of David his
                                         father (1 Kgs 3:3).*

c   זָכוֹר אֶת־יוֹם הַשַּׁבָּת לְקַדְּשׁוֹ   Remember the Sabbath day *by*
                                         keeping it holy (Exod. 20:8).*

(iii)   Consequence (seldom)

Significant features of members of this category are the following:
The landmark x refers to a situation that is atelic and gradable.
The trajector x follows the landmark y in time. Typically the
landmark y refers to an aspect of an entity's being, e.g. his/her
mental (#a) or physical state (#b).

a   וַתִּקְצַ֥ר נַפְשׁ֖וֹ לָמֽוּת׃   And he was *so* fed-up *he could die* [lit. his inner-being was impatient, *to die*] (Judg. 16:16).*

b   חָלָ֥ה חִזְקִיָּ֖הוּ לָמֽוּת   Hezekiah became *terminally* ill [lit. Hezekiah became ill, *to die*] (2 Kgs 20:1).*

(4) Indicates a *re-evaluation*

(a) Reclassification (very frequent)

A feature of this category is that trajector *x* and landmark *y* refer to the same entity, but in different capacities or roles.

a   וְהָיָה֩ הַדָּ֨ם לָכֶ֜ם לְאֹ֗ת עַ֤ל הַבָּתִּים֙   And the blood shall be for you a sign [lit. *as* a sign] on the houses (Exod. 12:13).*

b   וָאֶקַּ֥ח אֹתָ֛הּ לִ֖י לְאִשָּׁ֑ה   And I took her for me *as* my wife (Gen. 12:19).*

(b) Re-identification: whole/part (occasionally)

Sometimes not a qualitative re-classification, but rather a quantitative re-identification, can be distinguished. This re-identification could be generalizing (#*a*) or specifying (#*b*).

a   וַיְכַסּ֣וּ אֶת־הָרֶ֗כֶב וְאֶת־הַפָּ֣רָשִׁ֔ים לְכֹל֙ חֵ֣יל פַּרְעֹ֔ה   And they (the waters) covered the chariotry and the charioteers, the entire army of Pharaoh [lit. *to* the entire army of Pharaoh] (Exod. 14:28).*

b   וַיֹּ֤אמֶר יְהוֹשֻׁ֙עַ֙ אֶל־בֵּ֣ית יוֹסֵ֔ף לְאֶפְרַ֖יִם וְלִמְנַשֶּׁ֑ה   And Joshua said to the house of Joseph, *namely*, to Ephraim and Manasseh (Josh. 17:17).*

(c) Re-identification: principle of division (often)

Related to (a) are instances where a collection *x* is re-identified in terms of its parts.

        בְּנֵ֥י גֵרְשׁ֖וֹן לִבְנִ֣י וְשִׁמְעִ֑י לְמִשְׁפְּחֹתָֽם׃   The sons of Gershon: Libni and Shimei, *according to* their clan (Exod. 6:17).*

(d) Actualization: typically with verbs of movement (seldom)

Showing also some resemblance with (a) are instances of what is traditionally called "*dativus ethicus*."[11] Typically an addressee *x* is re-identified in terms of his/her current location (e.g. you, there where you are now) and directed to relocate, i.e. get *away* from where you are now (#*a*). The notion of "actualization" is also extended metaphorically (#*b*). In most instances, the personal responsibility of the addressees to comply with an appeal is profiled.

a   לֶךְ־לְךָ מֵאַרְצְךָ וּמִמּוֹלַדְתְּךָ וּמִבֵּית אָבִיךָ   Get *yourself* out, away from your land and from your relatives and from the house of your father (Gen. 12:1).*

b   הִשָּׁמֶר לְךָ פֶּן־תָּשִׁיב אֶת־בְּנִי שָׁמָּה   Take care that you do not take back my son there (Gen. 24:6).*

(5) Indicates a reference to a place and time

The preposition לְ often occurs in expressions that refer to the *place* or *time* of a state of affairs or an event.

(a) Adverbial expression of spatial orientation (often)

In these expressions the subject is the deictic center. The spatial orientation, typically with verbs of movement, is often where the subject lives (#*a*). Sometimes it is the direction he/she takes after meeting with somebody (#*b*). Also frequent is a vertical (#*c*) or horizontal (#*d*) orientation.

a   יֵלֵךְ וְיָשֹׁב לְבֵיתוֹ   Let him go and return *to* his house (Deut. 20:5).*

b   וְיַעֲקֹב הָלַךְ לְדַרְכּוֹ   So Jacob went *on* his way (Gen. 32:2).*

c   שְׂאוּ לַשָּׁמַיִם עֵינֵיכֶם   Lift up *to* heaven your eyes (Isa. 51:6).*

d   שֵׁב לִימִינִי   Sit *at* my right hand (Ps. 110:1).

---

11. Jenni (2000: 48–52) provides convincing arguments why the notion "*dativus ethicus*" should be abandoned. Naudé (2013a: 656) remarks: "an ethical dative is to be considered an anaphoric (specifically, reflexive) clitic, which can be translated as '-self'."

(b) Directional in Late Biblical Hebrew (seldom)

וְיַ֫עַל לִירוּשָׁלַ֫ם And let him go up *to* Jerusalem (Ezra 1:3).

(c) לְ + fossilized infinitives (occasionally)

The most frequent construction is לִקְרַאת (121 times). Typically it follows the reference to a movement of a person/people *x* to meet a person/people *y* (*#a*). Sometimes, with the arrangement of two entities at a specific location, a nuance of "over against," is expressed (*#b*).

a   וַיֵּצְאוּ֒ לִקְרַאת יֵהוּא So they went out *to meet* Jehu (2 Kgs 9:21).*

b   וַיִּתֵּן אִישׁ־בִּתְרוֹ לִקְרַאת רֵעֵהוּ And he laid each half *over against* the other (Gen. 15:10).*

(d) לְ + relative location = body part as preposition (very frequent)

A relative location refers to one section of a bigger space. Relative locatives across languages are typically formed by means of body parts. In Biblical Hebrew, the combination פָּנִים + לְ is very productive. This secondary preposition is predominantly used to express the notion *x before y* (*#a*). For more detail about this construction, see §39.13. Other body parts are also used (*#b-c*).

a   וַיִּפְּלוּ֒ לִפְנֵי יוֹנָתָן And they fell *before* Jonathan (1 Sam. 14:13).*

b   לְךָ֒ נְתַתִּ֫יהָ לְעֵינֵי בְנֵי־עַמִּי For you I hereby give it *in the presence of* my people [lit. *before* the eyes of my people] (Gen. 23:11).*

c   וַיְבָ֫רֶךְ יְהוָה אֹתְךָ֒ לְרַגְלִי And the LORD blessed you wherever I worked [lit. *at* my feet] (Gen. 30:30).*

(e) The combination: מִן *x* + לְ *y* (occasionally)

The item *x* can be preposition (*#a*) or locative noun (*#b*) (occasionally).

a   וַיַּ֫עַל | מֵעַל לְיוֹנָה And made it grow up *over* Jonah (Jon. 4:6).*

b   וַיַּנִּחֻ֫הוּ מִחוּץ לָעִיר: And they left him *outside* the city (Gen. 19:16).*

(f) Temporal frames of limited duration (occasionally)

לְ combines with constructions that refer to temporal frames of limited duration, e.g. a specific day (#a) or time of the day (#b).

a   וְהָיוּ נְכֹנִים לַיּוֹם הַשְּׁלִישִׁי   And be prepared *by* the third day (Exod. 19:11).*

b   בַּבֹּקֶר יֹאכַל עַד וְלָעֶרֶב   In the morning he devours (his) prey, and *by* the evening he divides (his) spoil (Gen. 49:27).*

           יְחַלֵּק שָׁלָל:

(g) Temporal references with unlimited duration (often)

     בֵּינִי וּבֵין בְּנֵי יִשְׂרָאֵל אוֹת   Between me and the Israelites it is a sign *forever* (Exod. 31:17).*

     הוּא לְעֹלָם

(6) Indicates a mode or a manner

(a) Quantitative relationships (often)

The quantitative modification of a proposition *x* by לְ + *y*, may have a distributional character (#a). Sometimes לְ + *y* refers to the criterion of distribution (#b).

a   וְיִקְחוּ לָהֶם אִישׁ שֶׂה   And they must take for themselves each person a lamb *per* family, a lamb *per* household (Exod. 12:3).*

     לְבֵית־אָבֹת שֶׂה לַבָּיִת

b   אֲשֶׁר יְהוָה אֱלֹהֶיךָ נֹתֵן לְךָ   which the LORD your God is giving to you *according to* your tribes (Deut. 16:18).*

     לִשְׁבָטֶיךָ

(b) Qualitative relationships (occasionally)

The qualitative modification of a proposition *x* by לְ + *y* may specify the quality of a circumstance. Also relatively frequent are instances where the quality resides in the extent of the quantity involved (#b).

a   וַיֵּשֶׁב יְהוּדָה וְיִשְׂרָאֵל לָבֶטַח   And Judah and Israel lived securely [lit. *as far as* confidence] (1 Kgs 5:5).*

b   וַיִּזְבַּח שׁוֹר וּמְרִיא־וְצֹאן לָרֹב   And he sacrificed oxen and fatted cattle and sheep *in* abundance [lit. *as far as* multitude] (1 Kgs 1:19).

(c) Normative relationships (seldom)

The norm *y* in terms of which a proposition *x* is modified, may be that of concrete (#*a*) or abstract actions (#*b*).

a   וַיַּחֲלֹשׁ יְהוֹשֻׁעַ אֶת־עֲמָלֵק   And Joshua defeated Amalek and
     וְאֶת־עַמּוֹ לְפִי־חָרֶב: his army *with* the sword [lit. *with* the mouth of the sword] (Exod. 17:13).*

b   וְיִסַּרְתִּיךָ לַמִּשְׁפָּט   And I will discipline you in a just measure [lit. *according to* justice] (Jer. 30:11).*

(d) Purpose relationships (occasionally)

וְאִם־אַתָּה לֹא־תַעֲבֹר אֵלַי   And that you will not pass beyond
אֶת־הַגַּל הַזֶּה וְאֶת־הַמַּצֵּבָה   this heap and this pillar *to* harm me
הַזֹּאת לְרָעָה: [lit. *for* evil] (Gen. 31:52).*

(e) Result relationships (rare)

עֲרֹב עַבְדְּךָ לְטוֹב   Be responsible for your servant so that it may go well with him [lit. *for* good] (Ps. 119:122).

(f) Causal relationships (seldom)

וַיֹּאמְרוּ אֵלָיו מֵאֶרֶץ רְחוֹקָה   And they said to him, "From a very
מְאֹד בָּאוּ עֲבָדֶיךָ לְשֵׁם יְהוָה   distant country your servants have
אֱלֹהֶיךָ   come, *because* of the name of the LORD your God" (Josh. 9:9).*

§39.12. לְמַעַן

See §40.36.

§39.13. לִפְנֵי

לִפְנֵי is a preposition that is formed through the combination of the preposition לְ and the construct form of the noun פָּנִים. It occurs 1,103 times. In nearly 40% of its occurrences לִפְנֵי governs a pronominal suffix. In 77 instances לִפְנֵי is governed by the preposition מִן.

Apart from the books of Obadiah and Zephaniah, לִפְנֵי occurs in all the books of the Hebrew Bible. However, it occurs significantly more frequently in non-poetic texts than in poetic texts.

(1) Indicates frontal location

  (a) Directly frontal location (occasional)

    The most concrete function of the preposition לִפְנֵי is to indicate that a trajector *x* is located (#*a*), makes a gesture (#*b*), or is presented (#*c*) to be directly "in front of" a landmark *y*.

a	וַיַּחֲנוּ לִפְנֵי מִגְדֹּל	And they camped *before* Migdol (Num. 33:7).
b	וַיִּשְׁתַּחוּ לוֹ עַל־אַפָּיו אַרְצָה לִפְנֵי הַמֶּלֶךְ	And he bowed down to him upon his face to the ground *before* the king (2 Sam. 14:33).*
c	וַיִּקַּח חֶמְאָה וְחָלָב וּבֶן־הַבָּקָר אֲשֶׁר עָשָׂה וַיִּתֵּן לִפְנֵיהֶם	Then he took curds and milk and the calf that he had prepared and put these *before* them (Gen. 18:8).*

The trajector *x* is also often moving "in front of" a moving landmark *y* (#*d*). Related to this use are cases where hostile forces fell (#*e*), are defeated or subdued (#*f*) "before" humans or God.

d	וַיֵּלְכוּ לִפְנֵי הָעָם:	And they went *ahead of* the people (Josh. 3:6).*
e	וּרְדַפְתֶּם אֶת־אֹיְבֵיכֶם וְנָפְלוּ לִפְנֵיכֶם לֶחָרֶב	And you will pursue your enemies and they will fall *before* you by the sword (Lev. 26:7).*
f	וְהוּא יַכְנִיעֵם לְפָנֶיךָ	And he himself will subdue them *before* you (Deut. 9:3).*

  (b) Closely related to (a), and the most typical use of לִפְנֵי is the location of observable proximity, i.e. *x* is in the presence of *y*.

    By far the most frequent are instances where *x* לִפְנֵי *y* indicates that *x* is "in the observable presence" of *y*. *Y* is typical God or the symbols that represent him (#*a*) or humans. The latter is often of a higher status, e.g. a king, priest or a prophet (#*b*).

a	וַיַּעַל הַנֵּרֹת לִפְנֵי יְהוָה כַּאֲשֶׁר צִוָּה יְהוָה אֶת־מֹשֶׁה:	And he lit the lamps *before* the LORD as the LORD had commanded Moses (Exod. 40:25).*

b   וּמֹשֶׁה וְאַהֲרֹן עָשׂוּ   And Moses and Aaron did all these
   אֶת־כָּל־הַמֹּפְתִים הָאֵלֶּה לִפְנֵי   wonders *before* Pharaoh (Exod.
            פַּרְעֹה   11:10).*

The following constructions appear to have specific connotations that
are motivated by this category, viz. "to stand לִפְנֵי *y*" typically is "to
stand in attendance of" or "to serve" *x* (#c); to stand לִפְנֵי *x* in a hostile
context is to "resist" or "endure before" *y* (#d); to הלד (typically Hitp.,
but sometimes Qal) לִפְנֵי God is to "live openly before" or "closely
to" God (#e); to be or serve לִפְנֵי a human of a higher status is to
serve "under the supervision of" *y* (#f); the expression that God gives
compassion to *x* לִפְנֵי *y* is to be understood as "God disposes *y* to show
x compassion" (#g); and in a frame of evaluation, לִפְנֵי *y*, is to be understood as "in *y*'s opinion" (#h).

c   וְיוֹסֵף בֶּן־שְׁלֹשִׁים שָׁנָה בְּעָמְדוֹ   And Joseph was thirty years old
   לִפְנֵי פַּרְעֹה מֶלֶךְ־מִצְרָיִם   when he entered the service of
            Pharaoh [lit. when he stood *before*
            Pharaoh] the king of Egypt (Gen.
            41:46).*

d   וַיִּמְכְּרֵם בְּיַד אוֹיְבֵיהֶם מִסָּבִיב   And he gave them over [lit. sold]
   וְלֹא־יָכְלוּ עוֹד לַעֲמֹד לִפְנֵי   into the hand of their enemies
            אוֹיְבֵיהֶם: around them and they were not able
            to resist [lit. to stand *before*] their
            enemies (Judg. 2:14).*

e   זְכָר־נָא אֵת אֲשֶׁר   Remember how I *have lived openly*
   הִתְהַלַּכְתִּי לְפָנֶיךָ בֶּאֱמֶת   [lit. walked around] *before* you in
            faithfulness (2 Kgs 20:3).*

f   וְהַנַּעַר שְׁמוּאֵל מְשָׁרֵת   And the boy Samuel was serving
            אֶת־יהוה לִפְנֵי עֵלִי   the LORD *under the supervision of*
            [lit. *before*] Eli (1 Sam. 3:1).*

g   וַיִּתֵּן הָאֱלֹהִים אֶת־דָּנִיֵּאל   And God disposed the chief officer
   לְחֶסֶד וּלְרַחֲמִים לִפְנֵי   to be kind and compassionate
            שַׂר הַסָּרִיסִים: toward Daniel [lit. God gave Daniel
            for kindness and mercy *before* the
            chief officer] (Dan. 1:9).*

h   וְנַעֲמָן שַׂר־צְבָא מֶלֶךְ־אֲרָם   And Naaman, the commander of
   הָיָה אִישׁ גָּדוֹל לִפְנֵי אֲדֹנָיו   the army of the king of Aram was
            a great man *in the opinion of* [lit.
            before] his master (2 Kgs 5:1).*

(2) Indicates an anterior temporal location (rare)

This use of לִפְנֵי represents a mapping from its spatial use in #a in (1). Related to this use of לִפְנֵי, is the use of לְפָנִים (as adverb) to refer to unspecified period of time, anterior to the point of speaking (#b).

a	וַיָּכֶן דָּוִיד לָרֹב לִפְנֵי מוֹתוֹ	So David made extensive preparations *before* his death (1 Chron. 22:5).*
b	וְשֵׁם חֶבְרוֹן לְפָנִים קִרְיַת אַרְבַּע	And the name of Hebron was *formerly* Kiriath-arba (Josh. 14:15).*

§39.14. מִן

The preposition occurs 7,555 times. In 307 instances it governs a pronominal suffix (for the morphology, see §39.1.1.4). In poetic texts, the form מִנִּי is sometimes used (30 times, of which 19 are in Job). The combination מִפְּנֵי is attested 184 times and מִלִּפְנֵי is attested 77 times. In 24 cases מִן is preceded by לְ.

(1) Indicates *detachment* (very frequent)[12]

The most typical spatial function of the preposition מִן is movement "*away from y*." It usually stands in opposition to אֶל "*to y*" or עַד "up to."

(a) Detachment: movement from a space, person or situation (nearly 50% of all occurrences)

The most typical instances are those where a trajector *x* moved from landmark *y*, which is a geographical space (#a). However, the notion movement must be understood in a very wide sense. It may involve any action where a trajector *y* moves or is caused to move from one point in space to another, e.g. take (#b).

When movement from a person or part of a person is involved, typically a second preposition is used to specify the location of the entity that moved (#c). When the landmark *y* is a person, movement is often implied by verbs of taking, seeking and hiding (#d).

---

12. The frequencies referred to in this section are based on a study of the 2,056 occurrences of מִן in the books of Genesis, Exodus, 2 Kings, Isaiah, Psalms and 2 Chronicles. Examples used as illustrations in the grammar, however, are not necessarily limited to this corpus.

Sometimes the notion of movement is extended figuratively to acts of redemption from an oppressing person (typically "from the hand," #e) or a threatening or negative situation (#f).

a   וַיַּעַל אַבְרָם מִמִּצְרַיִם   And Abraham went up *from* Egypt (Gen. 13:1).*

b   וַתִּקַּח־לוֹ אִמּוֹ אִשָּׁה מֵאֶרֶץ   And his mother took a wife for מִצְרָיִם   him *from* the land of Egypt (Gen. 21:21).*

c   וַתֵּלֶךְ מֵאִתּוֹ   So she went *from* [lit. *from* with] him (2 Kgs 4:5).*

d   וְאַל־תַּסְתֵּר פָּנֶיךָ מֵעַבְדֶּךָ   And do not hide your face *from* your servant (Ps. 69:18).*

e   אִישׁ מִצְרִי הִצִּילָנוּ מִיַּד   An Egyptian man saved us *from* הָרֹעִים   the hand of the shepherds (Exod. 2:19).*

f   כִּי הוּא יַצִּילְךָ מִפַּח יָקוּשׁ   For he himself will deliver you *from* the snare of the fowler (Ps. 91:3).*

(b) Detachment: location from which a person originates (occasionally)
Related to (a) are instances where the landmark *y* is the place from which a person (#a) originates.[13]

וַיִּמְלֹךְ תַּחְתָּיו יוֹבָב בֶּן־זֶרַח   Jobab son of Zerah *from* Bozrah מִבָּצְרָה: succeeded him as king (Gen. 36:33).*

(c) Detachment: location and/or source of sensority or mental activity (occasionally)
Related to (b) are instances where the landmark *y* is the place or person from which a sensory or mental activity *x* emanates (#a). Often the landmark *y* is a person who is conceptualized as the source of a positive or negative activity or attitude *x* (#b).

a   וַיִּקְרָא אֵלָיו מַלְאַךְ יְהוָה   But the angel of the LORD called out מִן־הַשָּׁמַיִם   to him *from* heaven (Gen. 22:11).*

b   מֵיהוָה יָצָא הַדָּבָר   It is *from* the LORD that this has gone out (Gen. 24:50).*

---

13. See Lemmer (2014: 93–94).

(d) Detachment: location and/or source of an attitude (seldom)
Related to (b) and (c) are uses that are associated with an attitude of
fear (#a). See also §39.15.(1)(b).

יְהֹוָה | אוֹרִי וְיִשְׁעִי מִמִּי אִירָא
יְהֹוָה מָעוֹז־חַיַּי מִמִּי אֶפְחָד:

The LORD is my light and my
salvation, *whom* shall I fear? The
LORD is the stronghold of my
life, *of whom* shall I be afraid?
(Ps. 27:1).*

(e) Detachment from a source as a bigger unit: partitive (often)
The most typical instances are those where a countable (#a) or
uncountable part *x* (#b) is taken in a broad sense of the word from
countable bigger units or an uncountable bigger mass *y* respectively.
See in contrast §39.6.(1)(b)(iv).

a   וַחֲמִשִּׁים אִישׁ מִבְּנֵי הַנְּבִיאִים הָלְכוּ...   And the fifty members *of* the prophetic guild went... (2 Kgs 2:7).*

b   וַיֵּשְׁתְּ מִן־הַיַּיִן וַיִּשְׁכָּר   And he drank *some of* the wine and became drunk (Gen. 9:21).*

(f) Detachment from a point in time (occasionally)
The category is closely related to (a) and represents a mapping of
detachment in space to that of time.

מִן־הַיּוֹם אֲשֶׁר הוֹצֵאתִי
אֶת־עַמִּי מֵאֶרֶץ מִצְרַיִם
לֹא־בָחַרְתִּי בְעִיר

From the day that I brought my
people out of Egypt, I have not
chosen a city (2 Chron. 6:5).*

(2) Indicates orientation in space or time
   (a) Orientation in space
The typical pattern is מִן trajector *x* (and *x* = spatial orientation) ... לְ
landmark *y* (and *y* = spatial location) (#a). The spatial location *y* is
sometimes not specified. This probably gave rise to the constructions
in which it appears as if מִן has lost is connotation of detachment. This
happens relatively often where the activity of "positioning" (#b) or
"standing" (#c) is involved. Though it happens only rarely, with verbs
of movement the dislocative sense of מִן is unambiguously neutralized
(#d).

a	וַיַּשְׁכֵּן מִקֶּדֶם לְגַן־עֵדֶן אֶת־הַכְּרֻבִים	And he placed *at* the east of the garden of Eden the cherubim (Gen. 3:24).*
b	וַיִּטַּע יְהוָה אֱלֹהִים גַּן־בְּעֵדֶן מִקֶּדֶם	And the LORD God planted a garden in Eden, *in* the east (Gen. 2:8).
c	וַיָּנֻעוּ וַיַּעַמְדוּ מֵרָחֹק:	And they trembled and stood *at* a distance (Exod. 20:18).*
d	וַיִּסַּע לוֹט מִקֶּדֶם	Lot then journeyed eastward (Gen. 13:11).*

(b) Orientation in time

Since it appears that מִן has also lost its primary sense of detachment in a number of instances where spatial indications are involved, it is assumed that also happens with temporal orientations. The construction with the widest distribution is מִקֵּץ + specification of a duration of time (#*a*). Furthermore, a number of other "fixed" expression has also to be postulated (#*b-c*).

a	וַיְהִי מִקֵּץ אַרְבָּעִים יוֹם וַיִּפְתַּח נֹחַ אֶת־חַלּוֹן הַתֵּבָה אֲשֶׁר עָשָׂה:	And then, *at the end of* forty days, Noah opened the window of the ark he had made (Gen. 8:6).*
b	וַיְהִי מִמָּחֳרָת וַתֹּאמֶר הַבְּכִירָה אֶל־הַצְּעִירָה...	And then, *the next day*, the firstborn daughter said to the younger one... (Gen. 19:34).*
c	וַיְהִי מִדֵּי עָבְרוֹ יָסֻר שָׁמָּה לֶאֱכָל־לָחֶם:	So, *whenever* he passed by, he would go [lit. turn off] there to eat (2 Kgs 4:8).*

(3) Indicates disassociation

(a) Comparison (occasionally)

The preposition מִן denotes that an entity *x* (object or event) is beyond that of another entity *y* in terms of quality or quantity. Instances where entities are compared as far as their quality (#*a*) or quantity (#*b*) is concerned are typical.

a	וְהַנָּחָשׁ הָיָה עָרוּם מִכֹּל חַיַּת הַשָּׂדֶה	Now the serpent was *the shrewdest of* all the wild creatures [lit. *shrewd from* all of the wild creatures] (Gen. 3:1).*
b	הִנֵּה עַם בְּנֵי יִשְׂרָאֵל רַב וְעָצוּם מִמֶּנּוּ:	Look, the Israelite people are *more* numerous and *more* powerful *than* we are (Exod. 1:9).*

(b) Privative (occasionally)

With verbs referring to the termination of an activity *y*, the preposition מִן denotes the activity from which the disassociation takes place (#*a*). Often somebody is caused to refrain or held back from an activity *y* (#*b*).

a	וַתַּעֲמֹד מִלֶּדֶת:	Then she stopped having children (Gen. 29:35).*
b	לָמָּה מֹשֶׁה וְאַהֲרֹן תַּפְרִיעוּ אֶת־הָעָם מִמַּעֲשָׂיו	Why, Moses and Aaron, do you distract the people *from* their tasks? (Exod. 5:4).*

(4) Indicates involvement

(a) Instrument (rare)

Related to instances where the preposition denotes the emanating source of an activity (§39.14.(1)(a)-(b)), are a few instances where the "source" is involved as the instrument of an accomplishment.

בֹּא־נָא אֶל־שִׁפְחָתִי אוּלַי אִבָּנֶה מִמֶּנָּה	Please go and sleep with my maid-servant [lit. go to my maidservant]. Perhaps, I will have children *through* her [lit. I will be built *from* her] (Gen. 16:2).*

(b) Ground (occasionally)

More frequent than (a) are instances where מִן denotes the grounds of an event or state of affairs. Typically a negative (#*a*) or threatening force (#*b*) is involved.

a	כִּי־עֲוֹנִי אַגִּיד אֶדְאַג מֵחַטָּאתִי:	After all, I confess my guilt and I am worried *because of* my sins (Ps. 38:19).*
b	מִן־גַּעֲרָתְךָ יְנוּסוּן מִן־קוֹל רַעַמְךָ יֵחָפֵזוּן:	*At* your rebuke they fled, *at* the sound of your thunder they hurried off (Ps. 104:7).*

§39.15. מִפְּנֵי

מִפְּנֵי is a preposition that is formed through the combination of the preposition מִן and the construct form of the noun פָּנִים. It represents a lexically specified use of מִן. It occurs 308 times and has a more restricted distribution than מִן.

The referents of the constituents governed by מִפְּנֵי are primarily (although not exclusively) living beings, and a frame of hostility and/or threat dominates the contexts in which it is used.

מִפְּנֵי is not an absolute synonym of מִלִּפְנֵי. In contexts where no frame of hostility is involved, the latter tends to be the preferred form for "*x* moves from the presence of *y*" (e.g. Gen. 41:46).

Apart from the books of Obadiah, Jonah, Daniel, Ezra, Song and Esther, מִפְּנֵי occurs in all the books of the Hebrew Bible. It is relatively often used in Joshua (23 times) and Jeremiah (45 times), while it is used only five times in Ezekiel.

(1) Indicates detachment

(a) Detachment: movement from a threatening person or situation (frequent)

The most concrete use of מִפְּנֵי involves instances where a trajector *x* moves away (e.g. flees or hides) from the presence of a landmark *y* (#*a*) Also frequent are instances where *z* causes *x* to move away from *y*. *Z* is typically God who drives out, dispossesses or exterminates the enemies of his people "before them" (#*b*).

a	וַיִּרְדְּפֵהוּ אֲבִימֶלֶךְ וַיָּנָס מִפָּנָיו	And Abimelech pursued him and he fled *before* him (Judg. 9:40).*
b	כִּי־אוֹרִישׁ גּוֹיִם מִפָּנֶיךָ	For I will drive out nations *before* you (Exod. 34:24).*

(b) Detachment as an attitude (fear, awe, respect or submission) (seldom). Considering (#*a*), it appears as if this category is a near synonym of מִן (see §39.14.(1)(d)). Typical of this use of מִפְּנֵי are instances where humans are afraid or terrified by *y* and *y* refers to other humans who pose an immediate threat to them (#*b*).

a	עַל־כֵּן מִפָּנָיו אֶבָּהֵל אֶתְבּוֹנֵן וְאֶפְחַד מִמֶּנּוּ׃	Therefore I am horrified *by his presence*, and when I consider, I dread him (Job 23:15).*
b	וַיַּרְא שָׁאוּל אֲשֶׁר־הוּא מַשְׂכִּיל מְאֹד וַיָּגָר מִפָּנָיו׃	When Saul saw that he (David) had great success, he was afraid *of* (or, felt threatened *by*) him (1 Sam. 18:15).*

(2) Indicates involvement

    (a) Ground (often)

        Closely related to both §39.14.4(b) and §39.15.(1)(b) are instances where a situation *x* is clearly caused by *y* (and not merely prompted by the presence of *y*). Instances where the negative (immoral) actions of humans are the cause of *x* are typical.

        וְאֵין מְכַבֶּה מִפְּנֵי רֹעַ מַעַלְלֵיכֶם   And there will be nobody to quench it, *because of* your wicked deeds (Jer. 4:4).*

§39.16. נֶגֶד

The preposition occurs 151 times. It is used in most books of the Bible, but is absent from Leviticus and most of the minor prophets. Its highest concentration is in the Psalms (36 times).

    The lexeme often (52 times) takes a pronominal suffix. It also frequently combines with the prepositions מִן (24 times) and לְ (32 times). In two instances it is governed by עַד.

(1) Indicates frontal opposition

    (a) Spatial (frequent)

        The most concrete function of the preposition נֶגֶד is to indicate that a trajector *x* is positioned (or acting) directly "opposite" a landmark *y*. *Y* is typically a person (#*a*) or a building or part of a building (#*b*).

    a   וַיָּבֹאוּ שְׁנֵי הָאֲנָשִׁים   Then two scoundrels came and sat
         בְּנֵי־בְלִיַּעַל וַיֵּשְׁבוּ נֶגְדּוֹ   *opposite* him (1 Kgs 21:13).*

    b   אַחֲרָיו הֶחֱזִיק צָדוֹק   After them, Zadok son of Immer
         בֶּן־אִמֵּר נֶגֶד בֵּיתוֹ   repaired *in front of* his house (Neh. 3:29).*

With verbs of movement, the construction with נֶגֶד gives the connotation of "straight ahead" (#*c*).

    c   וְעָלוּ הָעָם אִישׁ נֶגְדּוֹ   And the people shall go up, each *straight ahead* (Josh. 6:5).*

(b) Mental (seldom)

Closely related to (a) are instances where the trajector *x* is not concrete, but moral codes. In other words, *x* is cognitively salient to the landmark *y*.

כִּי כָל־מִשְׁפָּטָיו לְנֶגְדִּי   For all his judgments are *before* me (Ps. 18:23).*

(2) Indicates observable proximity

(a) Spatial (often)

Related to (1) are instances where the trajector *x* does not occupy a concrete position "directly in front of" the landmark *y*, but a position in the observable presence of *y* (#*a*). The position may even be specified as remote (#*b*).

a   הִנְנִי עֲנוּ בִי נֶגֶד יְהוָֹה וְנֶגֶד   Here am I, testify against me, *in*
        מְשִׁיחוֹ   *the presence of* the Lord and *in the presence of* his anointed one (1 Sam. 12:3).*

b   וַחֲמִשִּׁים אִישׁ מִבְּנֵי   And the fifty members of the
        הַנְּבִיאִים הָלְכוּ וַיַּעַמְדוּ   prophetic guild went and stood *oppo-*
        מִנֶּגֶד מֵרָחֹק   *site* them at a distance (2 Kgs 2:7).*

(b) Mental (rare)

Metaphorically mapped from (a) are instances where the trajector *x* is engaged in typically immoral behavior that takes place in "the presence or sight of" the landmark *y*.

וְלֹא־נִצְפַּן עֲוֺנָם מִנֶּגֶד עֵינָי   And their iniquity is not concealed from [lit. from *before*] my sight (Jer. 16:17).*

§39.17. נֹכַח

The preposition occurs 15 times in the Hebrew Bible, in Classical Biblical Hebrew as well as in Late Biblical Hebrew.

In its primary spatial sense, נֹכַח indicates a direct frontal opposition, i.e. "right opposite." The trajector may be a physical object *x* that is "right opposite" the landmark *y* (#*a*). When a physical or figurative object *x* is "right opposite" a landmark *y* which is a person or God, that object is "fully exposed" to the living landmark (#*b-c*).

a   וַיָּשֶׂם אֶת־הַמְּנֹרָה בְּאֹהֶל   And he put the lampstand in the tent
מוֹעֵד נֹכַח הַשֻּׁלְחָן   of meeting, *opposite* the table (Exod.
40:24).*

b   וּמֶלֶךְ יִשְׂרָאֵל הָיָה מַעֲמִיד   And the king of Israel was propped
בַּמֶּרְכָּבָה נֹכַח אֲרָם   up in his chariot *facing* [lit. *right
עַד־הָעֶרֶב   opposite*] the Arameans until even-
ing (2 Chron. 18:34).*

c   אַתָּה יָדַעְתָּ מוֹצָא שְׂפָתַי   You yourself know what came from
נֹכַח פָּנֶיךָ הָיָה׃   my lips; it is *open before* you [lit.
it was *right before* your face] (Jer.
17:16).*

§39.18. סָבִיב

The lexeme occurs 334 times in the Hebrew Bible. The lexeme is not very
evenly distributed; for example, it occurs 112 times in the book of Ezekiel[14]
and three times in Isaiah.[15]

    The lexeme has a restricted semantic potential. It typically refers to a
trajector *x* that encompasses a landmark *y*.

    Broadly speaking סָבִיב could be regarded as a relational. The lexeme is
typically used as an adverb (#*a-c*).

a   תָּקְעוּ עָלֶיהָ אֹהָלִים סָבִיב   They shall pitch (their) tents against
her, *all around* (Jer. 6:3).*

b   וַיִּזְרֹק מֹשֶׁה אֶת־הַדָּם   And Moses dashed the blood against
עַל־הַמִּזְבֵּחַ סָבִיב׃   the altar, *on all sides* (Lev. 8:24).*

c   וּמְדָדוֹ סָבִיב ׀ סָבִיב׃   And he measured it *all around*
(Ezek. 42.15).*

It may also be used as a preposition. When סָבִיב is used as preposition, it is
predominantly in the feminine plural construct form, that is סְבִיבֹ(ו)ת (#*d*).
Sometimes the combination לְ + סָבִיב is also used as a preposition (#*e*).

d   וַיַּעֲמֵד אֹתָם סְבִיבֹת הָאֹהֶל׃   And he stationed them *all around*
the tent (Num. 11.24).*

---

14. Of these 112 instances, 52 are in the format סָבִיב סָבִיב. The bulk of this repetitive
construction occurs in Ezek. 40–43.

15. For a more detailed analysis of סָבִיב, see van der Merwe (2011b).

e　　　　　　וְסָבִיב לַמִּשְׁכָּן יַחֲנוּ　And *all around* the tabernacle they must camp (Num. 1.50).*

סָבִיב may also follow the noun phrase that it modifies as a postposition (#f). Often the noun phrase is part of a *status constructus* construction (#g).

f　　　　וְאֻסַּף חֵיל כָּל־הַגּוֹיִם סָבִיב　And the wealth of all the nations *round about* shall be collected (Zech. 14:14).*

g　　　　כָּל־קַלְעֵי הֶחָצֵר סָבִיב שֵׁשׁ מָשְׁזָר:　All the curtains of the court *round about* were of fine twisted linen (Exod. 38:16).*

In a few rare cases, סָבִיב is used as a noun (#h-i).

h　　נֻדוּ לוֹ כָּל־סְבִיבָיו וְכֹל יֹדְעֵי שְׁמוֹ　Show some sympathy to him all *you who are around him* and all who know his name (Jer. 48:17).*

i　　וּבָאוּ מֵעָרֵי־יְהוּדָה וּמִסְּבִיבוֹת יְרוּשָׁלַם　And they shall come from the towns of Judah and from the *surroundings* of Jerusalem (Jer. 17:26).*

§39.19. עַד

The lexeme occurs 1,269 times. The form עֲדֵי is attested 12 times in poetic texts. In only 14 instances the lexeme takes a pronominal suffix. The set of suffixes that are normally added to plural nouns are used with עֲדֵי as base form.

(1) Indicates "up to" a point in *space* (often)

The preposition typically positions the activities of a trajector *x*, which may be living beings or the extent of non-living entities (e.g. land or border of a land) "up to" a landmark *y*, which is a terminal point in space. Typically, *x* moves (#a) or stretches (#b) as far as point *y*. Although point *y* is predominantly a geographical location, it may also be a more limited point in space (#c). Sometimes, when *y* is God and the verb of movement is שׁוּב, a type of fixed expression may be involved (#d).

a　　　　וַיַּעֲבֹר אַבְרָם בָּאָרֶץ עַד מְקוֹם שְׁכֶם　And Abram passed through the land (up) *to* the place of Shechem (Gen. 12:6).*

b   וַיְהִי גְּבוּל נַחֲלָתָם עַד־שָׂרִיד: And the boundary of their inheritance reached *as far as* Sarid (Josh. 19:10).*

c   הוֹשִׁיעֵנִי אֱלֹהִים כִּי בָאוּ מַיִם עַד־נָפֶשׁ:   Save me, God, for the water reached my neck [lit. came *up to* my neck] (Ps. 69:2).*

d   וְשַׁבְתָּ עַד־יְהוָה אֱלֹהֶיךָ וְשָׁמַעְתָּ בְקֹלוֹ   And return *to* the LORD your God and listen to his voice (Deut. 30:2).

(2) Indicates "up to" a point in *time* (very frequent)

The preposition profiles an event along a stretch of time that reaches "up to" a terminal point *y*. This landmark *y* is often a lexically specified unit of time (#*a*). Instances where the culmination of an event referred to by means of an infinitive (#*b*) or finite verb (#*c*) specifies the terminal point are equally frequent. In the majority of the latter cases, עַד is followed by אֲשֶׁר, כִּי, אִם, or בִּלְתִּי. In a few instances, the stretch of time provides the frame within which something happens (#*d*).

a   וְלֹא־תוֹתִירוּ מִמֶּנּוּ עַד־בֹּקֶר   And you shall not leave anything of it *until* the morning (Exod. 12:10).*

b   וְלֹא אָשׁוּב עַד־כַּלּוֹתָם: And I did not turn back *until* they perished (2 Sam. 22:38).

c   וַיִּגְדַּל הָאִישׁ וַיֵּלֶךְ הָלוֹךְ וְגָדֵל עַד כִּי־גָדַל מְאֹד   And the man became rich. He became richer and richer *until* he was extremely wealthy (Gen. 26:13).*

d   וַיְהִי עַד דִּבֶּר שָׁאוּל אֶל־הַכֹּהֵן וְהֶהָמוֹן אֲשֶׁר בְּמַחֲנֵה פְלִשְׁתִּים וַיֵּלֶךְ הָלוֹךְ וָרָב   But then, *while* Saul spoke to the priest the tumult which was in the camp of the Philistines kept on increasing (1 Sam. 14:19).*

(3) Indicates that an event or a state of affairs *extends to an extreme dimension* (occasionally)

Related to (1) and (2) are instances where the sense of reaching up to a terminal spatial or temporal point is extended to a figurative landmark *y*. This landmark may be an extreme dimension of an event or state of affairs (#*a-b*). It may also be represented by the *inclusion of specific entities* as far as a particular collection is concerned (#*c*).

a	וַיִּשְׂמַח שָׁם שָׁאוּל וְכָל־אַנְשֵׁי יִשְׂרָאֵל עַד־מְאֹד	And Saul and all the men of Israel rejoiced there greatly [lit. *until* very] (1 Sam. 11:15).*
b	לֹא נִשְׁאַר עַד־אֶחָד	Not *even* a single one was left (Judg. 4:16).*
c	וַיִּתְּנֵהוּ לְדָוִד וּמַדָּיו וְעַד־חַרְבּוֹ וְעַד־קַשְׁתּוֹ וְעַד־חֲגֹרוֹ:	And he gave it to David, and his robe, and *even* his sword, and *even* his bow and *even* his belt (1 Sam. 18:4).*

§39.20. עַל

The preposition עַל occurs about 5,765 times. It is the shorter version of an older form עֲלֵי. The latter occurs about 35 times, predominantly in poetry. When pronominal suffixes are used with עַל, they are added to עֲלֵי.[16] The prepositions עַל and אֶל are sometimes interchanged – especially in the books of Ezekiel and Jeremiah.

(1) Indicates a horizontal spatial relationship (frequent)

The most typical relationship profiled by עַל is one where a trajector x is higher than a landmark y within the same sphere of influence.

(a) x is "above" y

The trajector x may be in contact (#a) or not (#b) with the landmark y. The trajector x may (or be caused to) cover or influence y, in either a physical (#c-d) or a figurative sense (#e).

a	וּבְכָל־הָרֶמֶשׂ הָרֹמֵשׂ עַל־הָאָרֶץ:	And over every moving thing that moves *upon* the earth (Gen. 1:26).*
b	וְרוּחַ אֱלֹהִים מְרַחֶפֶת עַל־פְּנֵי הַמָּיִם	And the spirit of God was hovering *over* the surface of the waters (Gen. 1:2).*
c	אָנֹכִי מַמְטִיר עַל־הָאָרֶץ	I will send rain *upon* the earth (Gen. 7:4).*
d	וַתְּכַס עָלֵינוּ בְצַלְמָוֶת	And you covered us with deep darkness (Ps. 44:19).*
e	יְהִי־חַסְדְּךָ יְהוָה עָלֵינוּ	Let your loyal love, O LORD, be *upon* us (Ps. 33:22).*

---

16. This section is based on Mena (2012). The statistics are based on the 1,065 instances of עַל that occurs in Genesis, Psalms and 1 and 2 Chronicles.

(b) *x* is "(with)in" *y*

Related to (a) are instance where a trajector *x* is "on" the landmark *y*, but in a sense contained "within" the boundaries of the landmark *y* (#a-b). In some instances the combination עַל־יַד acquired the sense of "in the care of" (#c).

a   וְהִנָּם כְּתוּבִים עַל־סֵפֶר מַלְכֵי יִשְׂרָאֵל   And look, they were written *in* the book of the kings of Israel (1 Chron. 9:1).*

b   וָאֶתֵּן אֶת־הַכּוֹס עַל־כַּף פַּרְעֹה: Then I placed the cup *into* the hand of Pharaoh (Gen. 40:11).*

c   וַיִּתְּנוּהוּ עַל־יַד הַמֻּפְקָדִים   And they gave it *into* the hand of the overseers (2 Chron. 34:17).*

(c) *x* is "at" *y*

Also closely related to (a) are instances which could be regarded as "contingent locative." The trajector *x* is not horizontally above the trajector *y*, but in close proximity to it (#a-b). In a few rare cases, this sense extent to that of "accompaniment" (#c).

a   הִנֵּה אָנֹכִי נִצָּב עַל־עֵין הַמָּיִם   Look, I am standing *by* the spring of water (Gen. 24:43).*

b   אֲדֹנָי עַל־יְמִינְךָ   The Lord is *at* your right hand (Ps. 110:5).

c   וְלֹא שָׁתָם עַל־צֹאן לָבָן: And he did not put them *with* the flocks of Laban (Gen. 30:40).*

(2) Related to (1) are figurative extensions that imply "higher is more" (often).

(a) Superior ("over")

A trajector *x* that is in a higher position than a landmark *y* is regarded as superior to the landmark *y*.

כִּי אֵל גָּדוֹל יְהוָה וּמֶלֶךְ גָּדוֹל עַל־כָּל־אֱלֹהִים: For the LORD is a great God, and a great king *above* all gods (Ps. 95:3).*

(b) Control ("over")

A living being (trajector) *x* who is in a socially high position often exerts control over a landmark *y*.

אַתָּה תִּהְיֶה עַל־בֵּיתִי   You shall be *over* my house (Gen. 41:40).*

(c) "More than" (rare)
Height implies an increase in volume and quantity so that a trajector *x* acquires the sense of "more than" a landmark *y*.

> וַאֲנִי נָתַתִּי לְךָ שְׁכֶם אַחַד   And I now give to you one portion
> עַל־אַחֶיךָ   *more than* (to) your brothers (Gen.
>   48:22).*

(3) Indicates a direction to a goal (often)
   (a) Movement towards ("to") (similar to אֶל; see §39.3.(1)).
   The trajector *x* is directed towards the landmark *y*. Often a verb of movement in space is involved.

> וְאִם־לֹא הַגִּידוּ לִי וְאֶפְנֶה   And if not, tell me, so that I may
> עַל־יָמִין אוֹ עַל־שְׂמֹאל   turn *to* the right or *to* the left (Gen.
>   24:49).*

   (b) Hostility ("against")
   The movement of a trajector *x* to a landmark *y*, may be with hostile intentions (a#). In the process the preposition acquired a sense that profiles a hostile relationship between the trajector *x* and the landmark *y* (#*b*).

> *a*   וַיַּעֲמֹד שָׂטָן עַל־יִשְׂרָאֵל   And Satan rose up *against* Israel
>   (1 Chron. 21:1).
>
> *b*   וְהוּא עַל־לָכִישׁ   He was *against* Lachish (2 Chron.
>   32:9).*

   (c) Indirect goal ("for the sake of")
   A directed action may also have an indirect goal, i.e. of benefitting the landmark *y*.

> הִתְפַּלֵּל יְחִזְקִיָּהוּ עֲלֵיהֶם   Hezekiah had prayed *for* them
>   (2 Chron. 30:18).*

(4) Indicates a causal relationship (rare)
The landmark *y* is understood as the basis upon which the trajector *x* acts.

> *a*   פֶּן־יַהַרְגֻנִי אַנְשֵׁי הַמָּקוֹם   lest the men of the place kill me
>   עַל־רִבְקָה   *because* of Rebecca (Gen. 26:7).*
>
> *b*   פַּלְגֵי־מַיִם יָרְדוּ עֵינָי עַל   Streams of water flow down from
>   לֹא־שָׁמְרוּ תוֹרָתֶךָ:   my eyes, *because* they do not heed
>   your law (Ps. 119:136).*

(5) Indicates a norm (rare)

Related to (4) are instances where a trajector *x* is to meet a norm established by the landmark *y*.

וַיַּעֲמִידוּ אֶת־בֵּית הָאֱלֹהִים עַל־מַתְכֻּנְתּוֹ וַיְאַמְּצֻהוּ׃	And they restored the house of God *according to* its appropriate measurements and strengthened it (2 Chron. 24:13).*

(6) Indicates a focus of attention (seldom)

The vantage point is the trajector *x* and the landmark *y* is the focus of attention. This use is typical with activities of speech (#*a*) and the expression of emotions by a trajector *x* (#*b*).

a	וַתְּדַבֵּר עַל־בֵּית־עַבְדְּךָ לְמֵרָחוֹק	And you have spoken *about* the future of the house of your servant (1 Chron. 17:17).*
b	וַיִּתְאַבֵּל עַל־בְּנוֹ יָמִים רַבִּים׃	And he mourned *for* his son many days (Gen. 37:34).*

(7) Indicates an instrument (rare)

In a few rare cases, the trajector *x* refers to the means or manner with which the landmark *y* performs an activity.

וְעַל־חַרְבְּךָ תִחְיֶה וְאֶת־אָחִיךָ תַּעֲבֹד	But *by* your sword you shall live, and you shall serve your brother (Gen. 27:40).

§39.21. עִם

The preposition עִם occurs 243 times in the Pentateuch.[17] The form עִמָּדִי occurs 19 times in the Pentateuch. It is typically used where עִם needs a first person suffix. It is a near synonym of the preposition אֵת in the Pentateuch, which occurs 284 times in that corpus (see §39.5).

---

17. This section is based on the use of אֵת and עִם in the Pentateuch (Lyle 2012). While the prepositions are synonyms in this corpus, in the rest of the Hebrew Bible, עִם became the default preposition to express the senses identified here.

(1) Indicates a *general shared proximity* in space between a trajector *x* and a landmark *y*.

    (a) Shared presence

    The most concrete function of עִם is to indicate that a trajector *x* is located in general proximity to a landmark *y* (#*a*). Sometimes the trajector *x* is "among" a landmark *y* (#*b*).

a	וַתִּתֵּן גַּם־לְאִישָׁהּ עִמָּהּ וַיֹּאכַל	And she also gave some to her husband, (who was) *with* her, and he ate (Gen. 3:6).*
b	תְּנוּ לִי אֲחֻזַּת־קֶבֶר עִמָּכֶם	Give me burial property *among* you (Gen. 23:4).*

    (b) Possession

    עִם indicates that a trajector *x* is in spatial proximity to a landmark *y* which is understood as indicating the landmark's possession of the trajector.

וַתֹּאמֶר אֵלָיו גַּם־תֶּבֶן גַּם־מִסְפּוֹא רַב עִמָּנוּ	And she said to him, "We have both plenty of straw and fodder [lit. *with* us]" (Gen. 24:25).*

(2) Related to (1), are instances that represent a shift from profiling spatial proximity to *human interaction*.

    (a) Shared activity

    The preposition עִם indicates the sharing of an activity between a trajector *x* and a landmark *y*. Typically the activity is an act of going (#*a*). However, other acts of shared activity may be acts of communication (#*b*) and collaboration (#*c*). It may also be the shared activity of sexual intercourse (#*d*) or death (#*e*).

a	וַיַּעַל אַבְרָם מִמִּצְרַיִם הוּא וְאִשְׁתּוֹ וְכָל־אֲשֶׁר־לוֹ וְלוֹט עִמּוֹ הַנֶּגְבָּה׃	And Abram went up from Egypt, he and his wife, and all that he had, and Lot *with* him, into the Negeb (Gen. 13:1).*
b	עוֹדֶנּוּ מְדַבֵּר עִמָּם וְרָחֵל בָּאָה עִם־הַצֹּאן אֲשֶׁר לְאָבִיהָ	While he was still speaking *with* them, Rachel arrived with her father's sheep (Gen. 29:9).*

c   וַיֹּ֕אמֶר הִנֵּ֣ה דַם־הַבְּרִ֗ית   And he said, "Here is the blood
     אֲשֶׁ֨ר כָּרַ֤ת יְהוָה֙ עִמָּכֶ֔ם   of the covenant that the LORD has
                                        made *with* you" (Exod. 24:8).*

d   וְכִֽי־יְפַתֶּ֣ה אִ֗ישׁ בְּתוּלָ֛ה אֲשֶׁ֥ר   And when a man seduces a virgin
     לֹא־אֹרָ֖שָׂה וְשָׁכַ֣ב עִמָּ֑הּ   who is not engaged to be married,
     מָהֹ֛ר יִמְהָרֶ֥נָּה לֹּ֖ו לְאִשָּֽׁה׃   and lies *with* her, he must give the
                                        bride-price for her and make her his
                                        wife (Exod. 22:15).*

e   וְשָֽׁכַבְתִּי֙ עִם־אֲבֹתַ֔י וּנְשָׂאתַ֙נִי֙   And when I lie down *with* my
     מִמִּצְרַ֔יִם וּקְבַרְתַּ֖נִי בִּקְבֻרָתָ֑ם   ancestors (i.e. I die), carry me out
                                        of Egypt and bury me in their burial
                                        place (Gen. 47:30).*

(b) Recipient

Closely related to #*d* in (a) are instances where עִם profiles a landmark
y who is the human recipient (often beneficiary) of the activity of a
trajector *x* (#*a*). In contrast to #*d* in (a), the shared activity between
x and *y* appears to be absent. In a few instances the recipient is not a
benefactor (#*b*).

a   וַעֲשֵׂה־חֶ֖סֶד עִ֣ם אֲדֹנִ֑י   And show loyal love *to* my master
     אַבְרָהָֽם׃   Abraham (Gen. 24:12).

b   מַעֲשִׂים֙ אֲשֶׁ֣ר לֹא־יֵעָשׂ֔וּ   Things that ought not to be done,
     עָשִׂ֖יתָ עִמָּדִֽי׃   you have done *to* me (Gen. 20:9).*

(c) Support

Related to (b) are instances where עִם profiles an inferior landmark *y*
in shared presence/activity with a superior trajector *x* in which support
is rendered by the latter to the former.

אֱלֹהִ֣ים עִמְּךָ֔ בְּכֹ֥ל אֲשֶׁר־אַתָּ֖ה   God is *with* you in all that you do
עֹשֶֽׂה   (Gen. 21:22).

(d) Devotion

Closely related to (c) are instances where עִם profiles a superior
landmark *y* in a shared presence/activity with an inferior trajector *x*
in which religious compliance is rendered by the latter to the former.

וּמָה־יְהֹוָה דּוֹרֵשׁ מִמְּךָ כִּי And what does the LORD ask from אִם־עֲשׂוֹת מִשְׁפָּט וְאַהֲבַת חֶסֶד you but to do justice, and to love וְהַצְנֵעַ לֶכֶת עִם־אֱלֹהֶיךָ kindness [lit. loyal love], and to walk humbly *with* your God? (Mic. 6:8).*

(3) Addition

In a few instances, no concrete spatial proximity could be postulated. עִם indicates that a trajector *x* is coupled with a landmark *y* as far as an activity *z* is concerned.

חָלִלָה לְּךָ מֵעֲשֹׂת | כַּדָּבָר Far be it from you to do such a thing הַזֶּה לְהָמִית צַדִּיק עִם־רָשָׁע as this, to kill the righteous *with* the wicked (Gen. 18:25).*

§39.22. תַּחַת

The preposition תַּחַת occurs 511 times in the Hebrew Bible.[18] It derives from the substantive תַּחַת "underpart" that occurs 33 times.[19]

(1) Indicates vertical space below (frequent)

(a) Trajector *x* is תַּחַת landmark *y*, and *x* is vertically below *y*.
In a few instances, the landmark *y* is elided and implied by the position of the speaker (#c)

a   וַיְכֻסּוּ כָּל־הֶהָרִים הַגְּבֹהִים So that all the high mountains which אֲשֶׁר־תַּחַת כָּל־הַשָּׁמָיִם: were *under* the whole heaven were covered (Gen. 7:19).*

b   וַיִּקְחוּ־אֶבֶן וַיָּשִׂימוּ תַחְתָּיו Then they took a stone and put it וַיֵּשֶׁב עָלֶיהָ *under* him and he sat on it (Exod. 17:12).*

c   בִּרְכֹת תְּהוֹם רֹבֶצֶת תָּחַת blessings of the deep that lies *below* (Gen. 49:25).*

(b) The trajector *x* is sometimes not directly vertically below the landmark *y*, a vertically high-rising object, but close to its base (rare).

וַתִּקְרְבוּן וַתַּעַמְדוּן תַּחַת הָהָר And you came near and stood *at* the foot of the mountain [lit. *under* the mountain] (Deut. 4:11).*

---

18. This section is based on Rodriguez (2011).
19. יָבֹאוּ בְּתַחְתִּיּוֹת הָאָרֶץ "They will go to *the lower parts of* the earth" (Ps. 63:10).

(c) When the trajector *x* remains at (#*a*) or comes in contact (#*b*) with the space *y* occupied by *x*, that point in space is profiled as a "specific spot" (i.e. *x*'s place) (rare).

a	וַיֵּשְׁבוּ תַחְתָּם בַּמַּחֲנֶה עַד חֲיוֹתָם	And they remained *in their places* in the camp until they were healed (Josh. 5:8).*
b	וְנָפְלָה חוֹמַת הָעִיר תַּחְתֶּיהָ	And the wall of the city will collapse [lit. fall *under it*] (Josh. 6:5).*

(2) Indicates control (rare)

Related to (1)(a) are instances where the spatial notion of *x* is below *y* is mapped onto the domain of the human power relationships.

וְיִצְבְּרוּ-בָר תַּחַת יַד-פַּרְעֹה	And let them store up grain *under* the authority [lit. hand] of Pharaoh (Gen. 41:35).*

(3) Indicates substitution (frequent)

Related to (1)(c) are instances where the notion of "*x*'s place" is abstracted to an acquired substitution sense, i.e. *y* is "in the place of" *x*.

וַיִּמְלֹךְ יְהוֹרָם תַּחְתָּיו	And Jehoram became king *in his place* (2 Kgs 1:17).*

(4) Indicates exchange (rare)

Related to the substitution frame are instances where landmark *y* is "exchange for" trajector *x*.

וְנָתַתָּה נֶפֶשׁ תַּחַת נָפֶשׁ:	Then you shall give life *for* life (Exod. 21:23).

(5) Indicate causation (rare)

Related to (1)(a) are instances where trajector *x* is "under" landmark *y* and *y* "causes a downwards pressure on" *x*.

כִּי-תִרְאֶה חֲמוֹר שֹׂנַאֲךָ רֹבֵץ תַּחַת מַשָּׂאוֹ...	If you see the donkey of someone who hates you fallen down *under/ because of* his (its) load... (Exod. 23:5).

§40. Conjunctions, Adverbs and Discourse Markers

§40.1. Introduction

40.1.1. *Why one cluster?*

Prototypical conjunctions (§40.1.2) and ordinary adverbs (§40.1.3.1.(1)) are distinctive categories. However, conjunctions, on the one hand, are often used to do more than connecting words, phrases and clauses. For example, conjunctions may also be used as discourse markers to connect chunks of information. Such connections are subjective construals of the speakers of a language and may give a conjunction a modal sense – an element of meaning that is rather associated with adverbs.[20] Adverbs, on the other hand, have always been a problematic word class. Ordinary adverbs that modify an adjective or the predicate of a clause form a straightforward category. However, members of other categories that are often subsumed under the heading "adverbs," e.g. modal adverbs, conjunctive adverbs, focus particles and negatives are less homogenous – and often belong to more than one word class.

In particular, the category "discourse marker" is problematic (see §40.1.4). It typically draws its members from other categories, especially "conjunctions" or "adverbs." Due to the fact that the borders between adverbs and conjunctions are sometimes blurred, and members of both categories can be used as discourse markers, the lexemes that belong to these categories are listed alphabetically in §40.2–41 as one cluster.

40.1.2. *Conjunctions*

There are two classes of conjunctions, namely, coordinating and subordinating conjunctions (see §11.5).

(1) *Coordinating conjunctions* are conjunctions that link syntactically equal entities, whether they be clauses or parts of a word chain (see §31.1). In Biblical Hebrew, only וְ and אוֹ can be regarded as fully coordinating conjunctions. אִם and כִּי are only sometimes used as coordinating conjunctions.

(2) *Subordinating conjunctions* are conjunctions that introduce clauses which as a rule cannot be used to carry out a speech act. A distinction can be made between (1) complementary conjunctions (also referred to as complementizers), which introduce clauses that are clause constituents, for example, an object clause, and (2) supplementary conjunctions. In Biblical

---

20. See Degand et al. (2013).

Hebrew subordinate clauses often have the same syntactic structure as coordinating clauses. It is thus sometimes difficult to distinguish between coordinating conjunctions and subordinating conjunctions.

40.1.3. *Adverbs*

Traditionally, the term "adverb" has been accorded a very broad definition. The concept has included adverbs, modal adverbs, negatives, questions and discourse markers – which all are dealt with as distinct categories in this grammar. (Joüon–Muraoka §102 is a good example of the traditional approach.) In this grammar adverbs are also regarded as members of an inclusive word class that *can modify a word, a constituent or clause* (see §11.6). Sub-classes are distinguished primarily according to the nature of the modification.

(1) *Ordinary adverbs*: adverbs that only modify a clause or a constituent

(2) *Modal adverbs* and *conjunctive adverbs*: adverbs that modify a clause

(3) *Focus particles*: adverbs that can modify a word, a constituent and a clause

A semantic criterion has been adopted to distinguish a fourth class of adverbs, namely:

(4) *Negatives*: adverbs that negate a constituent or a clause

40.1.3.1. *Ordinary Adverbs*

(1) Ordinary adverbs usually modify an adjective or the predicate of a clause. Biblical Hebrew has only a few ordinary adverbs.
Morphological distinctions may be drawn between the following types:
  (a) So-called primitive adverbs
    • כֹּה (so), פֹּה (here), כֵּן (so), שָׁם (there), and אָז (then)
  (b) Derived adverbs *with* adverbial suffixes
    • with םָ◌, e.g. יוֹמָם (daily), רֵיקָם (vainly, in vain), חִנָּם (without reason) with םָ◌, e.g. פִּתְאֹם (suddenly)
  (c) Derived adverbs *without* adverbial suffixes
    • הַרְבֵּה (many), הֵיטֵב (good), הַרְחֵק (far), הַשְׁכֵּם (early) and מַהֵר (fast), which are primarily infinitive absolute forms used as adverbs
    • מְאֹד (many) and מְעַט (few), which were originally nouns, but now function mostly as adverbs
    • מַר (bitterly), which is primarily an adjective, but can also be used as an adverb

(d) Derived adverbs: preposition plus noun
- לָרֹב (many), לְשָׁלוֹם (peacefully), לָבֶטַח (safely)

(2) *Semantically* ordinary adverbs function as follows:

(a) Adverbs that modify verbs *describe the time, place or manner* of the action to which the verb refers.

(b) Adverbs that modify adjectives usually describe a *degree* of the attribute involved.

Most ordinary adverbs have a very specific lexical meaning. Those adverbs that also are used as conjunctive adverbs or discourse markers are most prominently treated in this grammar.

40.1.3.2. *Modal adverbs*

As opposed to ordinary adverbs, modal adverbs usually relate to an entire clause. In fact, an outstanding feature of modal adverbs is that they involve the subjective judgments of speakers in the content of clauses.

40.1.3.3. *Conjunctive adverbs*

Like modal adverbs, conjunctive adverbs usually relate to an entire clause. Distinctive features of conjunctive adverbs are that they occupy the sentence initial position (often preceded by the conjunction וְ), and link the content of the clause that they govern to that of another clause. They are also often used as discourse markers.

40.1.3.4. *Focus particles*

Focus particles can modify a word (as part of a coordinated phrase or of a constituent), a constituent or a clause. They are called focus particles because they place a particular focus on the entity or clause that follows them. A prominent feature of focus particles is that their meaning always indicates that the referent to which they refer *is an addition to* or *limitation of another referent.* Some scholars refer to focus particles as scalar particles.

40.1.3.5. *Negatives*

A feature of all the words belonging to this class is that they *negate* a constituent or sentence.

40.1.4. *Discourse markers*[21]

The category "discourse marker" is strictly speaking not a grammatical word class.[22] In other words, its members are not identified on the basis of their morphological features (i.e. their form) or syntactic features (i.e. how they combine with other clause constituents). Members of this category are distinguished on the basis of the function they fulfill in a text or discourse. A typical feature of discourse markers is that they have a discourse deictic function and often belong to other word classes too (e.g. conjunctions, adverbs and even verbs).

Onodera (2011: 615) defines a discourse marker as follows:

> A discourse marker signals the speaker's view/attitude/judgement with respect to the relationship between the chunks of discourse that precede and follow it, typically in the sentence (utterance)-initial positions.

In this grammar it is assumed that Biblical Hebrew speakers used discourse markers to comment on the content of a phrase, clause and/or clauses from a meta-level. In this way the content of a phrase, clause or clauses is anchored in the discourse in a particular way.

---

21. Weydt (2006: 205–206) lists a range of labels that are associated with what we call discourse markers: "pragmatic markers, interpersonal markers, argumentative markers, presentative particles, parentheticality markers, modal particles, adverbial connectives, connectives, modal discourse particles, elusive particles, particles of truth, contrastive and set-evoking particles, sentence-structure particles, down-toners." It is widely accepted that the definition of most of these terms is closely related to the theoretical frame of reference used and whether conversation or written texts are investigated. According to Fischer (2006: 8–12) discourse particles in conversation are primarily items constituting independent utterances. They function mainly to manage conversations and their host units can constitute the topic structure, extra-linguistic activities or participation frameworks of a conversation. However, in written and spoken texts, discourse particles are typically considered to be integrated into host utterances; they have a connecting function and their host units are aspects of utterances (Fischer 2006: 10–11). Our corpus is a written text (often based on oral traditions). Although our corpus often includes conversations, it is assumed that those conversations have been molded as "spoken texts."

22. Mosegaard-Hansen (2006: 27) remarks: "I do not conceive of discourse markers as constituting a part of speech, for it seems that very few linguistic items are exclusively devoted to this function."

§40.2. אֲבָל

אֲבָל is conjunctive adverb which is also used as a discourse marker.

אֲבָל occurs eleven times. Of these, five occur in the books Genesis, 2 Samuel, 1 and 2 Kings and six are attested in 2 Chronicles, Ezra and Daniel. Nine of the eleven instances are in reported speech. The lexeme does not combine with any other lexeme or proform.

אֲבָל occurs always in clause initial position. The clause often represents a speech turn (#*a*). However, it may also introduce a speech internal or narrative internal turn (#*b*).

אֲבָל introduces one speaker's response in which it is conceded what another one has said, but which provides an alternative perspective in a diplomatic way (#*a*). In Late Biblical Hebrew, the alternative perspective has a more contradictory nature (#*b*).

a	¹⁸וַיֹּאמֶר אַבְרָהָם אֶל־הָאֱלֹהִים לוּ יִשְׁמָעֵאל יִחְיֶה לְפָנֶיךָ: ¹⁹וַיֹּאמֶר אֱלֹהִים אֲבָל שָׂרָה אִשְׁתְּךָ יֹלֶדֶת לְךָ בֵּן	¹⁸ Then Abraham said to God, "If only Ishmael might live before you." ¹⁹God replied, "*Instead,* Sarah your wife is about to bear a son for you" (Gen. 17:18–19).*
b	¹⁶ וַיִּבֶן אֶת־מִזְבַּח יְהוָֹה וַיִּזְבַּח עָלָיו זִבְחֵי שְׁלָמִים וְתוֹדָה וַיֹּאמֶר לִיהוּדָה לַעֲבֹד אֶת־יְהוָה אֱלֹהֵי יִשְׂרָאֵל: ¹⁷ אֲבָל עוֹד הָעָם זֹבְחִים בַּבָּמוֹת רַק לַיהוָה אֱלֹהֵיהֶם:	¹⁶And he restored the altar of the LORD and offered sacrifices of well-being and thanksgiving on it. He told Judah to serve the LORD, the God of Israel. ¹⁷*Nevertheless* the people still sacrificed on the heights, though only to the LORD their God (2 Chron. 33:16–17).*

§40.3. או

או is primarily a coordinating conjunction. In some rarely occurring constructions, it acquires a modal sense (#*d-e*).

או occurs 321 times in the Hebrew Bible, predominantly in prescriptive (legal) texts in the Pentateuch. It is never affixed or prefixed to another lexeme.

או typically coordinates two or more phrases (#*a-b*) or clauses (#*c*). In a few instances, each coordinated phrase (#*d*) or clause (#*e*) is headed by או.

The conjunction lists *alternatives* (#a-c) When it heads each of the coordinated phrases, it is used correlatively in order to specify that *all the alternatives* preceded by אוֹ are of particular importance in the context in which they occur (#d-e).

a	כִּי־יִתֵּן֩ אִ֨ישׁ אֶל־רֵעֵ֜הוּ חֲמ֨וֹר אוֹ־שׁ֤וֹר אוֹ־שֶׂה֙...	If a person gives to his neighbor a donkey *or* an ox *or* a sheep... (Exod. 22:9).*
b	פֶּן־יִפְגָּעֵ֔נוּ בַּדֶּ֖בֶר א֥וֹ בֶחָֽרֶב	so that he does not strike us with pestilence *or* with the sword (Exod. 5:3).*
c	וְכִֽי־יִפְתַּ֨ח אִ֜ישׁ בּ֗וֹר א֠וֹ כִּֽי־יִכְרֶ֨ה אִ֤ישׁ בֹּר֙ וְלֹ֣א יְכַסֶּ֔נּוּ...	If a person opens a pit *or* if a person digs a pit and does not cover it... (Exod. 21:33).*
d	אֽוֹ־יֹמַ֨יִם אוֹ־חֹ֜דֶשׁ אוֹ־יָמִ֗ים בְּהַאֲרִ֨יךְ הֶעָנָ֤ן עַל־הַמִּשְׁכָּן֙ לִשְׁכֹּ֣ן עָלָ֔יו יַחֲנ֥וּ בְנֵֽי־יִשְׂרָאֵ֖ל וְלֹ֥א יִסָּֽעוּ	*Whether* it was for two days, *or* a month, *or* a longer time that the cloud prolonged to stay on the tabernacle by resting on it, the Israelites remained encamped, they did not set out (Num. 9:22).*
e	וַיֹּ֤אמֶר דָּוִד֙ חַי־יְהֹוָ֔ה כִּ֥י אִם־יְהֹוָ֖ה יִגְּפֶ֑נּוּ אֽוֹ־יוֹמ֤וֹ יָבוֹא֙ וָמֵ֔ת א֥וֹ בַמִּלְחָמָ֖ה יֵרֵ֥ד וְנִסְפָּֽה:	And David said, "As the LORD lives, the LORD will surely strike him, *either* his day will come and he will die, *or* he will go down in battle and perish" (1 Sam. 26:10).*

§40.4. אוּלַי

אוּלַי is primarily a modal adverb.

The lexeme אוּלַי (also written אֻלַי) occurs 43 times, predominantly in reported speech of narrative material. It is relatively evenly distributed in the Hebrew Bible. אוּלַי does not combine with any other lexeme or take any suffix.

אוּלַי typically heads a clause with *yiqtōl*/imperfect. Sometimes it heads a nominal clause, and in two instances a clause with *qātal*/perfect.

A speaker typically uses אוּלַי to express his or her attitude concerning an event or state of affairs, in particular the epistemic modality of *uncertainty* or *possibility*. אוּלַי is often used after a directive (#a-c). In the utterance with אוּלַי, the speaker typically expresses his or her hope concerning the outcome of an appeal (#a-c). However, sometimes only the speaker's doubt is expressed (#d).

a	קְחוּ צֳרִי לְמַכְאוֹבָהּ אוּלַי תֵּרָפֵא:	Get balm for her wound, *perhaps* she would be healed (Jer. 51:8).*
b	וַתֹּאמֶר שִׁפְחָתְךָ אֲדַבְּרָה־נָּא אֶל־הַמֶּלֶךְ אוּלַי יַעֲשֶׂה הַמֶּלֶךְ אֶת־דְּבַר אֲמָתוֹ:	And your servant thought [lit. said], "Let me speak with the king, *perhaps* the king will tend to the matter of his servant" (2 Sam. 14:15).*
c	יִתֵּן בֶּעָפָר פִּיהוּ אוּלַי יֵשׁ תִּקְוָה:	Let him put his mouth in the dust, *perhaps* there is hope (Lam. 3:29).*
d	כִּי אָמַר אִיּוֹב אוּלַי חָטְאוּ בָנַי	For Job said, "*Perhaps* my children have sinned" (Job 1:5).*

§40.5. אוּלָם

אוּלָם is conjunctive adverb that often features as a discourse marker.

אוּלָם occurs 19 times (17 times as וְאוּלָם). About one half of the occurrences are in Genesis to Kings. The other half are confined to the book of Job. Only one instance is attested in the prophetic books, viz. in the book of Micah. Seventeen of the instances are in reported speech.

אוּלָם occurs only in a clause initial position (#a-c). In reported speech it is always speech internal (#a-b).

After assertions *x*, אוּלָם typically introduces assertions *y*. Assertion *y* strongly contravenes *x* and speakers are strongly committed to what is asserted (#a-b). In narrative, the assertions *y* appear not to be strong (#c).

| a | וַיִּשָּׁבַע עוֹד דָּוִד וַיֹּאמֶר יָדֹעַ יָדַע אָבִיךָ כִּי־מָצָאתִי חֵן בְּעֵינֶיךָ וַיֹּאמֶר אַל־יֵדַע־זֹאת יְהוֹנָתָן פֶּן־יֵעָצֵב וְאוּלָם חַי־יְהוָה וְחֵי נַפְשְׁךָ כִּי כְפֶשַׂע בֵּינִי וּבֵין הַמָּוֶת: | And David also swore and said, "Your father knows well that you like me [lit. I have found favor in your eyes], and he thought, 'Do not let Jonathan know this, lest he will be grieved'. *However*, as the LORD lives and as you live, there is only a small step between me and death" (1 Sam. 20:3).* |
| b | אוּלָם אֲנִי אֶדְרֹשׁ אֶל־אֵל וְאֶל־אֱלֹהִים אָשִׂים דִּבְרָתִי: | *However*, as for me, I would seek God, and to God I would commit my case (Job 5:8).* |

c　　　　　וַיִּקְרָא אֶת־שֵׁם־הַמָּקוֹם And he called the name of that
הַהוּא בֵּית־אֵל וְאוּלָם לוּז place Beth-el, *but* the name of
שֵׁם־הָעִיר לָרִאשֹׁנָה: the city was formerly Luz (Gen.
28:19).*

§40.6. אָז/אֲזַי

אָז is primarily an adverb of time, but it is also used as a conjunctive adverb.

The lexeme אָז occurs 141 times (122 times as אָז and 18 times as מֵאָז and three times as אֲזַי in the Psalms). אָז is fairly evenly distributed throughout the entire corpus. Of the 18 occurrences of מֵאָז, eight are in the book of Isaiah.

Only the preposition מִן is prefixed to אָז. This happens 19 times, 18 times as מֵאָז and once as מִן־אָז.

The following categories of use can be distinguished

(1) Adverb of time

(a) אָז typically functions as an adverb to indicate a specific anaphoric duration in time (frequent).

Typically the stretch in time referred to is that of the duration of events in the immediately preceding context. In most cases the adverb occupies a clause-initial position (#a), but this is not always the case (#b). In a few cases, a point in time is referred to. This point in time is typically specified by an immediately following *qātal*/perfect clause (#c).

In cases where אָז is followed by a *yiqtōl*/imperfect form that refers to events in the past (#a), a new paragraph is often introduced.

a　　　　　אָז יַעֲלֶה חֲזָאֵל מֶלֶךְ אֲרָם At that time Hazael the king of
וַיִּלָּחֶם עַל־גַּת וַיִּלְכְּדָהּ Aram went up and fought against
Gath and captured it (2 Kgs 12:18).*

b　　　　　וְהַכְּנַעֲנִי אָז בָּאָרֶץ: And the Canaanites were *at that
time* in the land (Gen. 12:6).*

c　　　　　וַיְהִי מֵאָז הִפְקִיד אֹתוֹ And, from *the time* that he
בְּבֵיתוֹ וְעַל כָּל־אֲשֶׁר appointed him [lit. from *then*, i.e.
יֶשׁ־לוֹ וַיְבָרֶךְ יְהוָה he appointed him] in his house and
אֶת־בֵּית הַמִּצְרִי בִּגְלַל over all that he owned, the LORD
יוֹסֵף blessed the house of the Egyptian
for Joseph's sake (Gen. 39:5).*

(b) אָז (in the construction מֵאָז) functions as an adverb to refer to a duration of time in the distant past (seldom).

In a few instances of מֵאָז the preposition מִן appears to have lost its meaning, so that אָז and מֵאָז are near synonyms.

a	נָכוֹן כִּסְאֲךָ מֵאָז מֵעוֹלָם אָתָּה	Your throne is established *from long ago*, from eternity you are (Ps. 93:2).*
b	זֶה הַדָּבָר אֲשֶׁר דִּבֶּר יְהוָה אֶל־מוֹאָב מֵאָז:	This is what [lit. word] the LORD spoke about Moab, *long ago* (Isa. 16:13).*

(2) Conjunctive adverb

(a) אָז functions as a conjunctive adverb to refer to a point in time subsequent to other events referred to in the preceding context (often).

It typically occupies a clause-initial position (#*a-c*). In cases where אָז is followed by a *yiqtōl*/imperfect form that refers to events in the past (#*b*), a new paragraph is typically introduced.

a	אָז אָמַר אֲחַזְיָהוּ בֶן־אַחְאָב אֶל־יְהוֹשָׁפָט...	*Then* Ahaziah son of Ahab said to Jehoshaphat... (1 Kgs 22:50).
b	אָז יָשִׁיר־מֹשֶׁה וּבְנֵי יִשְׂרָאֵל אֶת־הַשִּׁירָה הַזֹּאת לַיהוָה	*Thereafter* Moses and the Israelites sang this new song to the LORD (Exod. 15:1).*
c	רַע רַע יֹאמַר הַקּוֹנֶה וְאֹזֵל לוֹ אָז יִתְהַלָּל:	"Bad, bad" says the buyer. He goes away [and] *then* he boasts (Prov. 20:14).*

(b) Closely related to (a) are instances where אָז functions as a conjunctive adverb to introduce the logical outcome of the accomplishment of an event (often).

The event may be reported in a statement (#*a*) or referred to in a directive (#*b*), a real or unreal condition (#*c*) or a wish (#*d*).

a	וַיַּעֲזָר־לוֹ אֲבִישַׁי בֶּן־צְרוּיָה וַיַּךְ אֶת־הַפְּלִשְׁתִּי וַיְמִיתֵהוּ אָז נִשְׁבְּעוּ אַנְשֵׁי־דָוִד לוֹ...	But Abishai son of Zeruiah helped him and attacked the Philistine and killed him. *So* David's men swore to him... (2 Sam. 21:17).*

b	אַל־תְּשַׁלְּחוּ אֹתוֹ רֵיקָם כִּי־הָשֵׁב תָּשִׁיבוּ לוֹ אָשָׁם אָז תֵּרָפְאוּ	Do not send it empty, but by all means return him a guilt offering, *then* you will be healed (1 Sam. 6:3).*
c	לוּלֵי תוֹרָתְךָ שַׁעֲשֻׁעָי אָז אָבַדְתִּי בְעָנְיִי:	If your law had not been my delight, *then* I would have perished in my misery (Ps. 119:92).*
d	אַחֲלֵי אֲדֹנִי לִפְנֵי הַנָּבִיא אֲשֶׁר בְּשֹׁמְרוֹן אָז יֶאֱסֹף אֹתוֹ מִצָּרַעְתּוֹ:	If only my lord were before the prophet who is in Samaria, *then* he would have cured him from his skin disease (2 Kgs 5:3).*

§40.7. אַיִן

See §41.2 and §43.2.

§40.8. אַךְ

אַךְ is primarily a focus particle, governing one constituent ("*only* x"). However, it is often used as a conjunctive adverb, governing a sentence or sentences ("however," "only"),[23] and in a number cases it is used as a modal adverb that governs a clause ("surely").[24]

This particle occurs 166 times throughout the Hebrew Bible. This is in contrast with its near synonym, רַק (§40.41), which occurs predominantly in narrative material. A significant feature of אַךְ is that it is rarely preceded by וְ.

אַךְ may govern a phrase, clause or sentences immediately following it. The entity may be a person, a thing, an attribute, an action or state of affairs, but it is often a piece of information.

The following categories of use can be distinguished:

(1) Indicates *limitation* (very frequent)

    (a) אַךְ + constituent

    In limiting/excluding *something or someone* with respect to something or someone in the preceding context (#*a*). Often when a predication is limited to a particular entity, a universe of other possible entities are implied (#*b*).

---

23. When אַךְ governs more than one sentence (e.g. Gen. 27:13), it can be argued that אַךְ functions as a discourse marker.

24. In this regard אַךְ differs from רַק. רַק is only rarely used as a modal word.

a   וְהַנַּעַר לֹא־יָדַע מְאוּמָה   But the lad knew nothing; *only*
     אַךְ יְהוֹנָתָן וְדָוִד יָדְעוּ   <u>Jonathan and David</u> knew the
     אֶת־הַדָּבָר: matter (1 Sam. 20:39).*

b   וַאֲדַבְּרָה אַךְ־הַפַּעַם   And let me speak again *only* <u>this
     once</u> (Gen. 18:32).*

(b) אַךְ + sentence(s)

Sets a limit with *respect to the implications of the content* of a directly preceding utterance.[25]

a   וַיַּעַן אָכִישׁ וַיֹּאמֶר אֶל־דָּוִד   And Achish answered David, "I
     יָדַעְתִּי כִּי טוֹב אַתָּה בְּעֵינַי   know that you are as blameless
     כְּמַלְאַךְ אֱלֹהִים   in my eyes as an angel of God;
     אַךְ שָׂרֵי פְלִשְׁתִּים אָמְרוּ   *however*, <u>the commanders of the
     לֹא־יַעֲלֶה עִמָּנוּ בַּמִּלְחָמָה: Philistines have said, 'He shall not
     go up with us into the battle'"</u>
     (1 Sam. 29:9).*

b   וַתֹּאמֶר לוֹ אִמּוֹ עָלַי קִלְלָתְךָ   And his mother said to him, "Let
     בְּנִי אַךְ שְׁמַע בְּקֹלִי   your curse be on me, my son; *only*
     וְלֵךְ קַח־לִי: <u>obey my voice, and go, get them
     for me</u>" (Gen. 27:13).*

(2) Modality: certainty (seldom)

Expresses conviction as to the correctness of an observation or evaluation (#a). In a few cases, the conviction of a poet is expressed without an explicit verb of saying (#b).

a   וַיְהִי כִּרְאוֹת שָׂרֵי הָרֶכֶב   And then, when the commanders of
     אֶת־יְהוֹשָׁפָט וְהֵמָּה אָמְרוּ   the chariots saw Jehoshaphat, they
     אַךְ מֶלֶךְ־יִשְׂרָאֵל הוּא   said, "*Surely* this [lit. he] <u>is the king
     of Israel</u>" (1 Kgs 22:32).*

b   אַךְ | קָרוֹב לִירֵאָיו יִשְׁעוֹ   *Surely* <u>his salvation is close for
     those who revere him</u> (Ps. 85:10).*

---

25. According to Levinsohn (2011: 105), אַךְ has only a limiting function, while רַק is limiting and countering something in the context.

(3) Affirmation (rare)

Confirms possible implications of a preceding assertion.

הִנֵּה טְפָחוֹת∣ נָתַתָּה יָמַי וְחֶלְדִּי	Look, you have made my days a
כְאַיִן נֶגְדֶּךָ אַךְ כָּל־הֶבֶל כָּל־אָדָם	few handbreadths, and my lifetime
נִצָּב	is as nothing before you. *Indeed everyone stands as a mere breath* (Ps. 39:6).*

§40.9. אָכֵן

אָכֵן is a modal adverb that is often used as a conjunctive adverb with a modal sense.

The lexeme occurs 18 times. It is relatively widely distributed, but confined to reported speech. It does not combine with any other lexeme

As a modal adverb a speaker may use אָכֵן to confirm a conviction that the content of a statement is true (#a-b). In some instances, the correctness of a new realization is affirmed (#c). However, the most typical use of אָכֵן is to affirm the truth of the content of a statement that overrules implications to the contrary that were invoked by a previous statement (#d).[26]

a	וַיֹּאמַר אָכֵן נוֹדַע הַדָּבָר:	And he thought [lit. said], "*Surely* the matter is known" (Exod. 2:14).*
b	לֹא־תָבֹאוּ בָהֶם וְהֵם לֹא־יָבֹאוּ בָכֶם אָכֵן יַטּוּ אֶת־לְבַבְכֶם אַחֲרֵי אֱלֹהֵיהֶם	You must not go to them, and they must not come to you. They will *certainly* incline your hearts to follow their gods (1 Kgs 11:2).*
c	וַיִּיקַץ יַעֲקֹב מִשְּׁנָתוֹ וַיֹּאמֶר אָכֵן יֵשׁ יְהוָה בַּמָּקוֹם הַזֶּה וְאָנֹכִי לֹא יָדָעְתִּי:	Then Jacob woke from his sleep and said, "*Surely*, the LORD is indeed in this place and I did not know it" (Gen. 28:16).*
d	⁶אֲנִי־אָמַרְתִּי אֱלֹהִים אַתֶּם וּבְנֵי עֶלְיוֹן כֻּלְּכֶם: ⁷אָכֵן כְּאָדָם תְּמוּתוּן וּכְאַחַד הַשָּׂרִים תִּפֹּלוּ:	⁶ I am the one who thought [lit. said], "You are gods, sons of Elyon, all of you." ⁷ *However*, like humans you will die, and fall like one of the high officials (Ps. 82:6–7).*

---

26. Garr (2007) provides a detailed discussion.

§40.10. אַל

See §41.3.

§40.11. אִם

אִם is primarily a subordinating conjunction. It may also function as coordinating conjunction and a modal word (in oaths).

The lexeme occurs 797 times, and is relatively evenly distributed in the Hebrew Bible

The following categories of use are distinguished:

(1) As conjunction

    (a) Introduces a real condition[27] as subordinating conjunction.

a	אִם־אֶמְצָא בִסְדֹם חֲמִשִּׁים צַדִּיקִם בְּתוֹךְ הָעִיר וְנָשָׂאתִי לְכָל־הַמָּקוֹם בַּעֲבוּרָם:	*If* I find at Sodom fifty righteous persons in the city, I will forgive the whole place for their sake (Gen. 18:26).*

When אִם is used as an apparent near synonym of כִּי, אִם specifies the details of a general condition that has been introduced by כִּי (see also §40.29.1/1).

b	²דַּבֵּר אֶל־בְּנֵי יִשְׂרָאֵל וְאָמַרְתָּ אֲלֵהֶם אָדָם כִּי־יַקְרִיב מִכֶּם קָרְבָּן לַיהוָה מִן־הַבְּהֵמָה מִן־הַבָּקָר וּמִן־הַצֹּאן תַּקְרִיבוּ אֶת־קָרְבַּנְכֶם: ³אִם־עֹלָה קָרְבָּנוֹ מִן־הַבָּקָר זָכָר תָּמִים יַקְרִיבֶנּוּ	²Speak to the Israelites and say to them, "When anyone among you brings an offering to the LORD, bring as your offering an animal from either the herd or the flock, ³ *if* the offering is a burnt offering from the herd, you are to offer a male without defect" (Lev. 1:2–3).

    (b) Introduces a concession as subordinating conjunction.

אִם־צָדַקְתִּי לֹא אֶעֱנֶה	*Though* I am in the right, I cannot answer (him) (Job 9:15).*

---

27. Bivin (2017) regards the prototypical function of אִם as that of "a hypothetical mental space builder." Following Dancygier and Sweetser (2005), he distinguishes between content conditionals, speech act conditionals and epistemic conditionals.

(c) Introduces an alternative as coordinating conjunction.

  (i) Typically in a question where only the second alternative is preceded by אִם.

הֲתָבוֹא לְךָ שֶׁבַע שָׁנִים ׀   Shall a seven-year famine come
רָעָב ׀ בְּאַרְצֶךָ אִם־שְׁלֹשָׁה   to you in your land? *Or* will you
חֳדָשִׁים נֻסְךָ לִפְנֵי־צָרֶיךָ   flee three months before your foes? (2 Sam. 24:13).*

  (ii) אִם precedes both alternatives.
      A speaker uses אִם correlatively to indicate that *both alternatives* preceded by אִם are of particular importance in the context in which they occur. (See also §40.3; §40.20.(3) and §40.23.3.1.(2).)

זִבְחֵי הַזֶּבַח אִם־שׁוֹר   those offering a sacrifice, *whether* it
אִם־שֶׂה   be an ox *or* a sheep (Deut. 18:3).*

(2) As modal adverb in oaths[28]

  (a) Marks a process that will not occur.
      This construction is used primarily in a *sworn oath*.

חַיֶּךָ וְחֵי נַפְשְׁךָ אִם־אֶעֱשֶׂה   As you live, and as your inner
אֶת־הַדָּבָר הַזֶּה: being lives, I will *not* do this thing! (2 Sam. 11:11).*

  (b) With לֹא marks a process that will occur (primarily in a sworn oath).
      This construction is used primarily in a *sworn oath* (#a). This is, however, not always the case (#b).

  a   וַיִּשָּׁבַע מֹשֶׁה בַּיּוֹם הַהוּא   And Moses swore on that day,
        לֵאמֹר אִם־לֹא הָאָרֶץ אֲשֶׁר   "*Surely* the land on which your foot
        דָּרְכָה רַגְלְךָ בָּהּ לְךָ תִהְיֶה   has trodden shall be an inheritance
        לְנַחֲלָה וּלְבָנֶיךָ עַד־עוֹלָם   for you and your children forever" (Josh. 14:9).

---

28. This use of אִם can be linked to oaths that have been shortened, see §41.8.(1)(c) and §45.1–2.

b   כִּי֩ לֹ֨א אֶל־עַ֜ם עִמְקֵ֣י שָׂפָ֗ה   [5] For you are not sent to a people of
וְכִבְדֵ֤י לָשׁוֹן֙ אַתָּ֣ה שָׁל֔וּחַ   obscure speech and a hard language,
אֶל־בֵּ֖ית יִשְׂרָאֵֽל: 6 לֹ֣א| but to the house of Israel – [6] not to
אֶל־עַמִּ֤ים רַבִּים֙ עִמְקֵ֣י   many peoples of foreign speech and
שָׂפָ֣ה וְכִבְדֵ֣י לָשׁ֔וֹן אֲשֶׁ֥ר   a hard language, whose words you
לֹֽא־תִשְׁמַ֖ע דִּבְרֵיהֶ֑ם אִם־לֹ֤א   cannot understand. *Surely*, if I sent
אֲלֵיהֶם֙ שְׁלַחְתִּ֔יךָ הֵ֖מָּה   you to such, they would listen to
יִשְׁמְע֥וּ אֵלֶֽיךָ:   you (Ezek. 3:5–6).*

§40.12. אָמְנָה

The modal adverb אָמְנָה occurs only twice and both instances are in reported
speech. It expresses a speaker's *confirmation of the truth* of a discourse active
proposition.

a   וְגַם־אָמְנָ֗ה אֲחֹתִ֤י בַת־אָבִי֙ הִ֔וא   And what is more, she is *indeed*
my sister, the daughter of my father
(Gen. 20:12).*

b   וַיַּ֧עַן עָכָ֛ן אֶת־יְהוֹשֻׁ֖עַ וַיֹּאמַ֑ר   Achan then answered Joshua, "*It*
אָמְנָ֗ה אָנֹכִ֤י חָטָ֙אתִי֙ לַֽיהוָ֔ה   *is true*, I am the one that sinned
אֱלֹהֵ֖י יִשְׂרָאֵ֑ל   against the LORD the God of Israel"
(Josh. 7:20).*

§40.13. אָמְנָם/אָמְנָ

אָמְנָם/אָמְנָ is primarily a modal adverb.

The lexeme אָמְנָ occurs nine times, of which six instances are in the book
of Job. The lexeme is restricted to reported speech. אָמְנָ sometimes occurs
clause initially (#*a*), but may also be preceded by אַף (#*b*), אִם (#*b*) or כִּי.
The variant אָמְנָם occurs five times, only in reported speech, and is always
governed by a yes–no question word (#*c*).

אָמְנָם expresses a speaker's confirmation of the truth of a discourse active
proposition or set of propositions (#*a*). Sometimes the truth of the discourse
active proposition is conceded (#*b*).[29] A speaker uses אָמְנָם to challenge the
truth of a discourse active proposition (#*c*).

---

29. Ruth 3:12a is difficult to interpret. Zewi (2007: 144) suggests that the verse can be
translated as "And now it is true that I am a near kinsman."

a   אָמְנָם יְהוָה הֶחֱרִיבוּ מַלְכֵי   *Truly*, O LORD, the kings of Assyria
     אַשּׁוּר אֶת־הַגּוֹיִם וְאֶת־אַרְצָם: have laid waste the nations and
                                        their lands (2 Kgs 19:17).

b   ⁴וְאַף־אָמְנָם שָׁגִיתִי אִתִּי תָּלִין   ⁴And, what's more, if *indeed* I had
     מְשׁוּגָתִי: ⁵אִם־אָמְנָם עָלַי   strayed, it is with me that my error
     תַּגְדִּילוּ וְתוֹכִיחוּ עָלַי חֶרְפָּתִי: remains. ⁵If *indeed* you magnify
     ⁶דְּעוּ־אֵפוֹ כִּי־אֱלוֹהַּ עִוְּתָנִי   yourself against me and make my
                                        humiliation an argument against
                                        me, ⁶know then that it is God who
                                        has wronged me (Job 19:4–6).*

c   הַאֻמְנָם לֹא אוּכַל כַּבְּדֶךָ:   Am I *really* not able to reward you?
                                        [lit. *Is it true* that I am not able to
                                        honor you?] (Num. 22:37).*

§40.14. אַף

אַף is primarily a conjunctive adverb that governs a sentence.[30] When it governs more than one sentence, it functions as discourse marker (seldom). It may also be used as a focus particle that governs an entity *x* (mostly a clause constituent). In a few instances, it governs a clause as a modal adverb.

אַף occurs 134 times in the Hebrew Bible, predominantly in poetic texts.[31] However, the combination כִּי אַף, which occurs 24 times, is evenly distributed in poetic and narrative texts.

אַף often marks the entity immediately following it (its syntactic domain) as a "noteworthy addition" ("also," "even," "moreover," "what's more" or "what's worse"). The entity may be concrete (a person or thing), but is typically a piece of information.

The following categories of use can be distinguished:

(1) Noteworthy addition (most frequent)

(a) אַף + sentence(s)

אַף signals that the information referred to in a sentence (#*a*) or sentences (#*b*) *y* needs to be considered. In addition to information referred to in an immediately preceding sentence (or sentences) *x*, *y* should be considered with respect to an explicit or implicit notion *z*. The information to be added represents predominantly the most

---

30. For a more detailed description, see Van der Merwe (2009a).
31. A high concentration is found Isa. 26–48, viz. 30 instances.

conclusive or compelling information of what is asserted in the context. In other words, it can often be translated as "moreover," "what's more" or "what's worse."

a	וְגָדַלְתִּי וְהוֹסַפְתִּי מִכֹּל שֶׁהָיָה לְפָנַי בִּירוּשָׁלָ͏ִם אַף חָכְמָתִי עָמְדָה לִּי:	So I became great and surpassed all who were before me in Jerusalem; *what's more*, <u>my wisdom remained with me</u> (Eccl. 2:9).*
b	⁴³הֲרִימוֹתָ יְמִין צָרָיו הִשְׂמַחְתָּ כָּל־אוֹיְבָיו: ⁴⁴אַף־תָּשִׁיב צוּר חַרְבּוֹ וְלֹא הֲקֵימֹתוֹ בַּמִּלְחָמָה:	⁴³You have raised the right hand of his foes, you have made all his enemies rejoice. ⁴⁴*What's worse*, <u>you turned back the edge of his sword and did not support him in the battle</u> (Ps. 89:43–44).*

(b) אַף כִּי + sentence (with an ellipsed predicate or main clause)

Although this relatively frequently occurring expression developed into a fixed expression with its own specialized meaning, it did retain two features of אַף, viz., it signals a connection between two pieces of information, and the second piece of information is the most compelling or conclusive of the two, hence the translation values "how much more" (#*a*) and "how much less" (#*b*). For this reason, the fixed expression can be semantically classified under the heading "noteworthy addition." However, the semantic function of the expression will be defined as follows: אַף כִּי points to "evidence *y*" that substantiates even more conclusively an assertion *z* than "evidence *x*." Evidence *x* was presented in an immediately preceding utterance as an already valid substantiation of (a predominantly implicit) assertion *z*.

a	וַיֹּאמְרוּ אַנְשֵׁי דָוִד אֵלָיו הִנֵּה אֲנַחְנוּ פֹה בִיהוּדָה יְרֵאִים וְאַף כִּי־נֵלֵךְ קְעִלָה אֶל־מַעַרְכוֹת פְּלִשְׁתִּים:	But David's men said to him, "Look, we are afraid here in Judah; *how much more* <u>then if we go to Keilah against the armies of the Philistines</u>?" (1 Sam. 23:3).
b	הִנֵּה הַשָּׁמַיִם וּשְׁמֵי הַשָּׁמַיִם לֹא יְכַלְכְּלוּךָ אַף כִּי־הַבַּיִת הַזֶּה אֲשֶׁר בָּנִיתִי:	Look, heaven and the highest heavens cannot contain you, *how much less* <u>this house that I have built</u>? (1 Kgs 8:27).*

(c) אַף + constituent (rare)

אֲבָרֵךְ אֶת־יְהוָה אֲשֶׁר יְעָצָנִי I bless the LORD who gives me
אַף־לֵילוֹת יִסְּרוּנִי כִלְיוֹתָי counsel, *even* <u>during the nights</u> my
kidneys instruct me (Ps. 16:7).*

(d) אַף + clause // אַף + clause (// אַף + clause)[32]

In this category, אַף is used as a correlative conjunction. This use of אַף represents a category that is synonymous with a frequent occurring category of גַּם (§40.20.(3)). This use of אַף as a correlative conjunction is regarded as a "noteworthy inclusion" since it signals that the information referred to in each sentence preceded by אַף carries equal weight as far as the substantiation of an explicit or implicit assertion is concerned.

מִי־הִגִּיד מֵרֹאשׁ וְנֵדָעָה Who declared it from the beginning,
וּמִלְּפָנִים וְנֹאמַר צַדִּיק אַף so that we might know, and before-
אֵין־מַגִּיד אַף אֵין מַשְׁמִיעַ אַף hand, so that we might say, "He is
אֵין־שֹׁמֵעַ אִמְרֵיכֶם: right"? <u>There was *neither* one who</u>
<u>declared it</u>, *nor* <u>one who proclaimed,</u>
nor <u>one who heard your words</u> (Isa.
41:26).*

(2) Affirmation

(a) אַף + sentence(s)

אַף signals in a number of instances that the information referred to in a sentence (or sentences) *y*, affirms the information referred to in an immediately preceding sentence (or sentences).

...מְפַלְּטִי מֵאֹיְבָי אַף מִן־קָמַי ...who delivered me from my
תְּרוֹמְמֵנִי מֵאִישׁ חָמָס תַּצִּילֵנִי: enemies; *indeed,* <u>you exalted me</u>
<u>above my adversaries; you delivered</u>
<u>me from the violent</u> (Ps. 18:49).

(b) Yes–no question word אַף + clause (rare)

אַף is used as a modal adverb in questions. In each instance the factuality of an event ("is indeed"?) (#*a*) or state of affairs (#*b*) is questioned.

---

32. This use is restricted to five verses in the book of second Isaiah – Isa. 40:10 (two times, 24 (three times); 41:26; 44:15 (two times); 46:11 (three times).

a   וַיִּגַּשׁ אַבְרָהָם וַיֹּאמַר   Then Abraham came closer and said,
       הַאַף תִּסְפֶּה צַדִּיק עִם־רָשָׁע: "Will you *indeed* sweep away the
                                                   righteous with the wicked?" (Gen.
                                                   18:23).*

b   הַאַף אֵין־זֹאת בְּנֵי יִשְׂרָאֵל   "Is it not *indeed* so, Israelites?"
                        נְאֻם־יְהוָה: declares the LORD (Amos 2:11).*

(3) Addition (seldom)

(a) אַף + constituent

Another less frequent, but not rare, use of אַף is one that corresponds with the most prototypical use of גַּם, i.e. "neutral" addition (§40.20.(1)(a)).

       וְהַנִּשְׁאָרִים בָּכֶם יִמַּקּוּ בַּעֲוֺנָם   And those who remain among you
       בְּאַרְצֹת אֹיְבֵיכֶם וְאַף בַּעֲוֺנֹת   will rot away in the lands of your
                  אֲבֹתָם אִתָּם יִמָּקּוּ:   enemies because of their iniquity,
                                                   and *also* <u>because of the iniquities of
                                                   their ancestors with them</u> they will
                                                   rot away (Lev. 26:39).*

(b) אַף + noun phrase in coordinated phrase

a   כְּלָבִיא שָׁכֵן וְטָרַף זְרוֹעַ   He lives like a lion and tears apart
                        אַף־קָדְקֹד: arm *as well as* <u>scalp</u> (Deut. 33:20).*

b   וְיוֹדוּ שָׁמַיִם פִּלְאֲךָ יְהוָה   Let the heavens praise your wonders,
            אַף־אֱמוּנָתְךָ בִּקְהַל   O LORD, *as well as* <u>your faithfulness</u>
                        קְדֹשִׁים: in the assembly of the holy ones
                                                   (Ps. 89:5).*

§40.15. אֶפֶס

The lexeme is mainly used as a noun and predicator of non-existence (a negative). In a few instances אֶפֶס is used as a conjunctive adverb.

The lexeme occurs 44 times in the corpus.[33] In more than 40% of its occurrences, אֶפֶס functions as a noun in the *status constructus* form אַפְסֵי־אָרֶץ (concentrated in the Psalms). In its other uses, אֶפֶס can sometimes combine with the conjunction וְ, take a preposition (mainly בְּ) and a pronominal suffix (only first person).

---

33. One-third of these occurrences are in Isa. 40–55.

The following patterns of use can be distinguished:

(1) Noun

אֶפֶס indicates extreme points in space. The expression אַפְסֵי־אָרֶץ "ends of the earth" implies the entire earth including its farthest "corners" (#*a*). In most of its uses, אַפְסֵי־אָרֶץ is a metonym for all the people of the earth, including those who live in its remotest corners (#*b*).

a	מִי הֵקִים כָּל־אַפְסֵי־אָרֶץ	Who established all the *ends* of the earth? (Prov. 30:4).*
b	יְהוָה יָדִין אַפְסֵי־אָרֶץ	The LORD will judge the *ends* of the earth (1 Sam. 2:10).

(2) Predicator of non-existence (for more detail, see §41.4)

In some instances, אֶפֶס is clearly a near synonym of אַיִן.

וְאֵין עוֹד אֱלֹהִים וְאֶפֶס כָּמוֹנִי:	And there is no other God, and *there is not* any like me (Isa. 46:9).*

(3) Conjunctive adverb

אֶפֶס indicates the restriction of invoked expectations. When used with this meaning, אֶפֶס כִּי (#*a*) or אֶפֶס (#*b*) governs a clause as a conjunctive adverb.

a	וְהִשְׁמַדְתִּי אֹתָהּ מֵעַל פְּנֵי הָאֲדָמָה אֶפֶס כִּי לֹא הַשְׁמֵיד אַשְׁמִיד אֶת־בֵּית יַעֲקֹב	And I will destroy them [lit. her] from the surface of the earth. *However*, I will not utterly destroy the house of Jacob (Amos 9:8).*
b	וְאֶפֶס אֶת־הַדָּבָר אֲשֶׁר־אֲדַבֵּר אֵלֶיךָ אֹתוֹ תְדַבֵּר	*However*, the word which I speak to you, that only you shall speak (Num. 22:35).*

§40.16. בַּל

See §41.5.

§40.17. בְּלִי

See §41.6.

§40.18. בִּלְתִּי

See §41.7.

§40.19. בַּעֲבוּר,

בַּעֲבוּר is a compound of the preposition בְּ and the noun עֲבוּר. How the noun's meaning, i.e. "harvest" could be related to that of the compound is not clear. בַּעֲבוּר is typically used as a preposition and sometimes as conjunction.

בַּעֲבוּר occurs 49 times. The combination לְבַעֲבוּר is attested three times (Exod. 20:20; 2 Sam. 14:20; 17:14).

The lexeme is not distributed evenly throughout the Hebrew Bible. It occurs only in Genesis (15 times), Exodus (7 times), 1 and 2 Samuel (14 times), Jeremiah (1 time), Amos (2 times), Micah (2 times), Psalms (3 times), Job (1 time) and 1 and 2 Chronicles (4 times). The absence of בַּעֲבוּר from the books in which לְמַעַן is frequent, i.e. Deuteronomy (23 times), 1 Kings (13 times), Isaiah (18 times), and Ezekiel (24 times), is significant.

בַּעֲבוּר typically governs a noun phrase or an infinitive clause. In a number of instances it governs a *yiqṭōl*/imperfect clause. In most cases a verb of motion is used in the matrix clause.

The following categories of use can be distinguished:[34]

(1) Purpose

Typically the agent of the verb of the event A referred to in a matrix clause performs an action with the intention to bring about an event B introduced by בַּעֲבוּר. The events involved may refer to what happened in the real world (#a-b). The purpose of the event in the matrix clause may also be of an epistemic nature, i.e. "so that *x* may know" (#c). Often the events involved may provide the purpose of the speech act referred to in the matrix clause (#d).

a	וַיֹּאמֶר יְהוָה אֶל־מֹשֶׁה הִנֵּה אָנֹכִי בָּא אֵלֶיךָ בְּעַב הֶעָנָן בַּעֲבוּר יִשְׁמַע הָעָם בְּדַבְּרִי עִמָּךְ	Then the LORD said to Moses, "Look, I am going to come to you in a dense cloud, *so that* the people may hear when I speak with you" (Exod. 19:9).*
b	וַיֹּאמֶר מֹשֶׁה אֶל־הָעָם אַל־תִּירָאוּ כִּי לְבַעֲבוּר נַסּוֹת אֶתְכֶם בָּא הָאֱלֹהִים	And Moses said to the people, "Do not be afraid; for God has come only *to* test you" (Exod. 20:20).*

---

34. This section benefitted from Yoo (2013).

c   כִּי | בַּפַּעַם הַזֹּאת אֲנִי שֹׁלֵחַ אֶת־   For this time I am sending all my
כָּל־מַגֵּפֹתַי אֶל־לִבְּךָ וּבַעֲבָדֶיךָ   plagues upon you yourself [lit. to
וּבְעַמֶּךָ בַּעֲבוּר תֵּדַע כִּי אֵין   your heart], and upon your officials,
כָּמֹנִי בְּכָל־הָאָרֶץ: and upon your people, *so that* you
may know that there is no one like
me in all the earth (Exod. 9:14).*

d   קוּם־נָא שְׁבָה וְאָכְלָה מִצֵּידִי   Please sit up and eat of my game,
בַּעֲבוּר תְּבָרֲכַנִּי נַפְשֶׁךָ:   *so that* you may bless me (Gen.
27:19).*

Often, a noun phrase is used to refer (metonymically) to the purpose of
the action referred to in the matrix clause. This construction is typically
translated as "for the sake of" (#e).

e   אִם־אֶמְצָא בִסְדֹם חֲמִשִּׁים   If I find at Sodom fifty righteous
צַדִּיקִם בְּתוֹךְ הָעִיר וְנָשָׂאתִי   persons in the city, I will forgive
לְכָל־הַמָּקוֹם בַּעֲבוּרָם: the whole place *for their sake*
(Gen. 18:26).*

(2) Reason[35]

A significant feature of this category is that the construction noun phrase
+ בַּעֲבוּר is always used. Furthermore, a speaker or narrator provides the
reason of the events referred to in the matrix clause. The reason is typically
due to a feature of a person (#a) or object (#b) or the result of what has
happened in the past (#c).

a   וּלְאַבְרָם הֵיטִיב בַּעֲבוּרָהּ   And with Abram he dealt well
because of her (Gen. 12:16).*

b   בֵּרַךְ יְהוָה אֶת־בֵּית   The LORD has blessed the household
עֹבֵד אֱדֹם וְאֶת־כָּל־אֲשֶׁר־לוֹ   of Obed-edom and all that belongs
בַּעֲבוּר אֲרוֹן הָאֱלֹהִים   to him, *because of* the ark of God
(2 Sam. 6:12).

c   אֲרוּרָה הָאֲדָמָה בַּעֲבוּרֶךָ   Cursed is the ground *because of*
you (Gen. 3:17).

---

35. The shift from *purpose* to *reason* is not hard to motivate. In the case of *purpose*, the
accomplishment of the event in the matrix clause is motivated by a goal in future, while
in the case of "reason," the event in the matrix clause is motivated by a current state of
affairs or something that already happened.

§40.20. גַּם

גַּם is primarily a focus particle.[36] It may also be used as conjunctive adverb, a correlative conjunction, a discourse marker, and in a few rare instances as a simple coordinating conjunction.

This particle occurs 769 times. It is evenly distributed throughout the Hebrew Bible. It is most typically used in the syntactic pattern גַּם + constituent. In these cases it can be translated as "also, too, even." גַּם is a near synonym of אַף (§40.14). The latter occurs more often in poetic material.

A significant feature of the syntax of גַּם is that it can modify a phrase, a constituent, a sentence or sentences. גַּם almost always directly precedes the constituent or sentences which it governs (its domain). A pronoun is often directly repeated after גַּם (usually as an independent personal pronoun) to indicate that the antecedent of the pronoun lies in the domain of גַּם.

a	פֶּן־יָמוּת גַּם־הוּא כְּאֶחָיו	otherwise *he too* might die, like his brothers! (Gen. 38:11).*
b	בָּרֲכֵנִי גַם־אָנִי אָבִי	Bless *me also*, my father! (Gen. 27:34).

גַּם typically marks the entity immediately following it (its syntactic domain) for addition ("also," "too," "moreover") or inclusion ("both…as well as") as far as a state of affairs or event *z* is concerned. The entity may be concrete (a person or thing) or abstract (a piece of information).

The following categories of use can distinguished:

(1) Addition (typical)

The most typical use of גַּם (over 50% of the cases) is the one that could be associated with the syntactic pattern גַּם + constituent, and which could be translated (predominantly) by "also" or (to a lesser extent) by "even."

(a) גַּם + constituent

גַּם typically signals that an entity *y*, governed by גַּם, must be added to an entity *x*, as far as a predication *z* is concerned. If the reference to *x* occurs in a previous expression, an audience would find it strange if the speakers or writers did not indicate that the entity *y* after גַּם has to be added to the entity in the preceding expression. In other words, the use of גַּם may contribute toward constituting a well-formed text or discourse (#*a-b*). If the entity that has to be added is something that is possible, but which represents an extreme case, גַּם is translated as *even* (#*c*).

---

36. For a more detailed description of גַּם, see van der Merwe (2009b).

a	וַיְהִי עֵר בְּכוֹר יְהוּדָה רַע בְּעֵינֵי יְהוָה וַיְמִתֵהוּ יְהוָה... ¹⁰וַיֵּרַע בְּעֵינֵי יְהוָה אֲשֶׁר עָשָׂה וַיָּמֶת גַּם־אֹתוֹ:	⁷But Er, Judah's firstborn, was wicked in the eyes of the LORD; and the LORD killed him… ¹⁰And what he (Onan) did was wicked in the eyes of the LORD, and he killed <u>him</u> *also* (Gen. 38:7, 10).*
b	וְאָמַרְתָּ גַּם עַבְדְּךָ אוּרִיָּה הַחִתִּי מֵת:	And you must say, "*Also* <u>your servant Uriah, the Hittite</u> is dead." (2 Sam. 11:24).*
c	וְעַתָּה אָנֹכִי נָתַתִּי אֶת־כָּל־הָאֲרָצוֹת הָאֵלֶּה בְּיַד נְבוּכַדְנֶאצַּר מֶלֶךְ־בָּבֶל עַבְדִּי וְגַם אֶת־חַיַּת הַשָּׂדֶה נָתַתִּי לוֹ לְעָבְדוֹ:	So now I have given all these lands into the hand of Nebuchadnezzar, king of Babylon, my servant. And, *even* <u>the wild animals of the field</u> I have given to him to serve him (Jer. 27:6).*

(b) גַּם + sentence(s)

גַּם signals that the information *y* that is referred to in a sentence (#*a*) or a cluster of sentences (#*b*)[37] needs to be considered in addition to information referred to in an immediately preceding sentence (or sentences) *x* are far as an explicit or implicit notion *z* is concerned.

In these cases גַּם could be translated by "also, furthermore, besides" or "moreover, what's more, what's worse." The utterance following גַּם may refer to *a conclusive or compelling piece of information.*[38] It is not always easy to judge whether a "noteworthy addition" or not is involved, e.g. #*a-b* could be interpreted as instances of "neutral" addition, while #*c-e* are "noteworthy additions."

a	וַיִּתֵּן יְהוָה אֶת־חֵן הָעָם בְּעֵינֵי מִצְרַיִם גַּם ׀ הָאִישׁ מֹשֶׁה גָּדוֹל מְאֹד בְּאֶרֶץ מִצְרַיִם בְּעֵינֵי עַבְדֵי־פַרְעֹה וּבְעֵינֵי הָעָם	And the LORD gave the people favor in the eyes the Egyptians. *Furthermore*, <u>the man, Moses, was very highly regarded in Egypt, by the officials of Pharaoh and the people [lit. Moses, was very great in the land of Egypt, in the eyes of the officials of Pharaoh and the eyes of the people]</u> (Exod. 11:3).*

---

37. This use of גַּם is rare and confined to poetic texts.

38. In contrast, when אַף is used, nearly always *a conclusive or compelling piece of information*, i.e. a "noteworthy addition" is involved.

b	וְגַם מָה־אַתֶּם לִי צֹר	And, *furthermore*, <u>what are you to</u>
	וְצִידוֹן וְכֹל גְּלִילוֹת פְּלָשֶׁת	<u>me, O Tyre and Sidon and all the</u>
	הַגְּמוּל אַתֶּם מְשַׁלְּמִים עָלָי	<u>regions of Philistia? Are you paying</u>
	וְאִם־גֹּמְלִים אַתֶּם	<u>me back for something? If you are</u>
	עָלַי קַל מְהֵרָה אָשִׁיב	<u>paying me back, I will turn your</u>
	גְּמֻלְכֶם בְּרֹאשְׁכֶם:	<u>deeds back upon your own heads</u> <u>swiftly and speedily</u> (Joel 4:4).*
c	¹¹אָמַרְתִּי רַק אֵין־יִרְאַת	¹¹I thought [lit. said], there is certainly
	אֱלֹהִים בַּמָּקוֹם הַזֶּה	no fear of God in this place, and they
	וַהֲרָגוּנִי עַל־דְּבַר אִשְׁתִּי:	will kill me because of my wife.
	¹²וְגַם־אָמְנָה אֲחֹתִי	¹²And, *what is more*, <u>she is indeed</u>
	בַת־אָבִי הִוא	<u>my sister, the daughter of my father</u> (Gen. 20:11–12).*
d	כִּי־נָכְרִי אַתָּה וְגַם־גֹּלֶה	For you are a foreigner, and, *what*
	אַתָּה לִמְקוֹמֶךָ:	*is worse*, <u>you are an exile from your</u> <u>home</u> (2 Sam. 15:19).*
e	וַיֹּאמֶר לֹא מְצָאתִיהָ וְגַם	And he said, "I have not found her;
	אַנְשֵׁי הַמָּקוֹם אָמְרוּ	and, *moreover*, <u>the men of the place</u>
	לֹא־הָיְתָה בָזֶה קְדֵשָׁה:	<u>said, 'There has been no prostitute</u> <u>here'"</u> (Gen. 38:22).*

(c) גַּם + member of a coordinated phrase
The specific inclusion of the entity or entities governed by וְגַם usually reflects *some special role* that the inclusion plays in the context (seldom).

וַיִּיטַב בְּעֵינֵי כָל־הָעָם וְגַם	And this was good in the eyes of all
בְּעֵינֵי עַבְדֵי שָׁאוּל:	the people and *also* <u>in the eyes of</u> <u>Saul's servants</u> (1 Sam. 18:5).*[39]

(2) Corresponding reaction (seldom)
Closely related to (1)(a) are instances where it cannot be said that "also *x*" does *y*, but what *x* does, is a corresponding reaction to what *z* did (#*a*). A negative reciprocal action in a judgment speech is often involved (#*b*).[40]

---

39. See in contrast 2 Sam. 17:4 where גַּם is not used.
40. See Lyavdansky (2004).

a   וְעַתָּה הִשָּׁבְעוּ־נָא לִי   So now, swear to me by the LORD
בַּיהוָה כִּי־עָשִׂיתִי עִמָּכֶם   that as I have dealt kindly with you,
חֶסֶד וַעֲשִׂיתֶם גַּם־אַתֶּם   you will *also* deal kindly with my
עִם־בֵּית אָבִי חֶסֶד   father's house (Josh. 2:12).*

b   זֶה גוֹרָלֵךְ מְנָת־מִדַּיִךְ ²⁵   ²⁵ This is your lot, the portion I have
מֵאִתִּי נְאֻם־יְהוָה אֲשֶׁר   measured out to you, declares the
שָׁכַחַתְּ אוֹתִי וַתִּבְטְחִי   LORD, because you have forgotten
בַּשָּׁקֶר: ²⁶וְגַם־אֲנִי חָשַׂפְתִּי   me and trusted in lies. ²⁶ I, *in turn*,
שׁוּלַיִךְ עַל־פָּנָיִךְ וְנִרְאָה   will lift up your skirts over your
קְלוֹנֵךְ:   face, and your shame will be seen
(Jer. 13:25–26).*

(3) Multiple inclusion (often)

Multiple inclusion is associated with the syntactic pattern x + גַּם / y + גַּם.
X may be objects (#*a*) or sentences (#*b*). Speakers may make it clear that
the inclusion of *each* entity preceded by גַּם *is of special importance* in
a particular context, i.e. "both," "as well as." Sometimes the entities are
two or more pieces of information that carry equal weight in substanti-
ating a statement (#*b*). See also §40.3, §40.11.(1)(b)(ii), §40.14.(1)(d) and
§40.23.3.1.(2).

a   מְשָׁל־בָּנוּ גַּם־אַתָּה   Rule over us, *both* you, *as well as*
גַּם־בִּנְךָ גַּם בֶּן־בְּנֶךָ   your son *and also* your grandson
(Judg. 8:22).*

b   וַיֹּאמֶר אֲבִימֶלֶךְ לֹא   And Abimelech said, "I do not
יָדַעְתִּי מִי עָשָׂה אֶת־הַדָּבָר   know who has done this thing.
הַזֶּה וְגַם־אַתָּה לֹא־הִגַּדְתָּ   *Neither* did you tell me, *nor* have
לִּי וְגַם אָנֹכִי לֹא שָׁמַעְתִּי   I heard of it until today" (Gen.
בִּלְתִּי הַיּוֹם: 21:26).*

(4) Affirmation (rare)

In a few instances גַּם has an affirmative connotation.

a   סַבּוּנִי גַם־סְבָבוּנִי   They surround me, *yes*, they
surrounded me (Ps. 118:11).*

b   וַיִּקָּבְצוּ יְהוּדָה לְבַקֵּשׁ   And Judah gathered to seek [help]
מֵיהוָה גַּם מִכָּל־עָרֵי יְהוּדָה   from the LORD, *indeed*, from all the
בָּאוּ לְבַקֵּשׁ אֶת־יְהוָה: towns of Judah they came to seek
the LORD (2 Chron. 20:4).*

(5) "Apparent" neutral enumeration (rare)

In a few instances גַּם appears to function as a near synonym of וְ (#a-b). As a semantically empty coordinating conjunction it can also connect clauses whose content is contrastive (#c).

a	רְעֵבִים גַּם־צְמֵאִים נַפְשָׁם בָּהֶם תִּתְעַטָּף	Hungry *and* thirsty, their soul fainted within them (Ps. 107:5).
b	צִיָּה גַם־חֹם יִגְזְלוּ מֵימֵי־שֶׁלֶג שָׁאוֹל חָטָאוּ׃	Drought *and* heat snatch away the snow waters; so does Sheol those who have sinned (Job 24:19).
c	רַבַּת צְרָרוּנִי מִנְּעוּרַי גַּם לֹא־יָכְלוּ לִי׃	Since my youth they have often attacked me, *but* they have never overcome me (Ps. 129:2).*

§40.21. הֵן

The scope of הֵן is very often more than just the clause or sentence following it. Therefore, it is not a typical modal adverb, but functions predominantly as a discourse marker.[41]

הֵן occurs 100 times in the Hebrew Bible (exclusively in reported speech). Not one instance of הֵן is attested in Joshua through 2 Kings, but it occurs 32 times in Job and 24 times in Isaiah 40–66. Two instances are attested in Jeremiah, one in Ezekiel and one in the minor prophets.

הֵן has a simple morphology. Except for two instances (Exod. 4:1 and 2 Chron. 7:13), הֵן does not combine with the conjunction וְ. It is never preceded by any other conjunction or clause adverbial. הֵן never takes a pronominal suffix and is never immediately followed by a participle (in stark contrast to הִנֵּה).

הֵן *always* immediately precedes the entity or entities it governs. The syntactic scope of הֵן is predominantly more than one sentence (#a). Although not frequent, a number of instances of the type הֵן + sentence הֵן + sentence are attested (#b).

---

41. At first glance הֵן appears to be a short form of הִנֵּה. However, although הֵן has, like הִנֵּה, primarily a deictic or demonstrative character and is in some contexts a near synonym of הִנֵּה, it differs in many ways from הִנֵּה. הֵן, for example, has more the character of a modal adverb than הִנֵּה since it expresses the attitude of a speaker as far as the epistemic modality of the content of an utterance is concerned. In the words of Garr (2004: 343), "הִנֵּה presents: הֵן affirms or confirms."

a   הֵן הֶרְאָנוּ יְהוָה אֱלֹהֵינוּ   *Look*, the LORD our God has shown
        אֶת־כְּבֹדוֹ וְאֶת־גָּדְלוֹ וְאֶת־קֹלוֹ   us his glory and his greatness, and
        שָׁמַעְנוּ מִתּוֹךְ הָאֵשׁ הַיּוֹם הַזֶּה   we heard his voice from the fire.
        רָאִינוּ כִּי־יְדַבֵּר אֱלֹהִים   Today we have seen that God may
        אֶת־הָאָדָם וָחָי: speak to a human and he/she may
            live (Deut. 5:24).*

b   [13]עִמּוֹ חָכְמָה וּגְבוּרָה לוֹ עֵצָה   [13] With him (God) are wisdom and
        וּתְבוּנָה: [14] הֵן יַהֲרוֹס וְלֹא   strength; he has counsel and under-
        יִבָּנֶה יִסְגֹּר עַל־אִישׁ וְלֹא   standing. [14] *Look*, if he tears down,
        יִפָּתֵחַ: [15] הֵן יַעְצֹר בַּמַּיִם   no one can rebuild; if he shuts
        וְיִבָשׁוּ וִישַׁלְּחֵם וְיַהַפְכוּ אָרֶץ: someone in, no one can open up.
            [15] *Look*, if he withholds the waters,
            they dry up; if he sends them out,
            they overwhelm the land (Job
            12:13–15).*

הֵן, like הִנֵּה, has a deictic (i.e. a pointing) function. Speakers or narrators use הֵן in reported speech to draw the attention of hearers to the propositional content of typically more than one clause, but also to that of a clause or a phrase. A speaker affirms with the use of הֵן the factuality or truth of the utterance.

The following patterns of use can be distinguished:

(1) Affirmation (typical)

   (a) Pointing to information which the speaker affirms as factual/true. What is affirmed modifies the content or implications of (mainly) preceding utterances (#a). What is affirmed by means of הֵן typically establishes the ground for assertions (#b) or directives (#c) that are the logical consequence or implication thereof. In a few rare instances, the grounds of questions are affirmed (#d).

a   [28]וְאֵרֶא וְאֵין אִישׁ וּמֵאֵלֶּה וְאֵין   [28]And I looked, but there was
        יוֹעֵץ וְאֶשְׁאָלֵם וְיָשִׁיבוּ דָבָר: nobody, and among them, there is
        [29]הֵן כֻּלָּם אָוֶן אֶפֶס מַעֲשֵׂיהֶם   no counselor so that I may ask them
        רוּחַ וָתֹהוּ נִסְכֵּיהֶם: פ   and they answer me. [29] *After all*, all
            of them are nothing, their works
            are nothing, their metal images are
            empty wind (Isa. 41:28–29).*

b   הֵן הֶרְאָנוּ יְהֹוָה אֱלֹהֵינוּ אֶת־כְּבֹדוֹ וְאֶת־גָּדְלוֹ וְאֶת־קֹלוֹ שָׁמַעְנוּ מִתּוֹךְ הָאֵשׁ הַיּוֹם הַזֶּה רָאִינוּ כִּי־יְדַבֵּר אֱלֹהִים אֶת־הָאָדָם וָחָי: *Look,* the LORD our God has shown us his glory and his greatness, and we heard his voice from the fire. Today we have seen that God may speak to a human and he/she may live (Deut. 5:24).*

c   הֵן־שָׁכַבְתִּי אֶמֶשׁ אֶת־אָבִי נַשְׁקֶנּוּ יַיִן גַּם־הַלַּיְלָה   *Look,* I have slept with my father last night, let us give him also tonight wine (Gen. 19:34).*

d   וְכִי תֹאמְרוּ מַה־נֹּאכַל בַּשָּׁנָה הַשְּׁבִיעִת הֵן לֹא נִזְרָע וְלֹא נֶאֱסֹף אֶת־תְּבוּאָתֵנוּ:   And if you would ask, "What shall we eat in the seventh year *since* we shall not sow or we shall not gather our crop?" (Lev. 25:20).*

(b) Confirming that a request has been granted (rare)

וַיֹּאמֶר לָבָן הֵן לוּ יְהִי כִדְבָרֶךָ:   And Laban said, "*Fine,* let it be as you have said" (Gen. 30:34).*

(2) Presentative (rare)

Pointing to (i.e. presenting) an entity in order to say something about it.

הֵן עַבְדִּי אֶתְמָךְ־בּוֹ בְּחִירִי רָצְתָה נַפְשִׁי   *Look*: my servant whom I support, my chosen one in whom I delight (Isa. 42:1).*

§40.22. הִנֵּה[42]

40.22.1. *Word class*

The word class to which הִנֵּה belongs has always been a problem for grammarians. Some have described it as an interjection while others think it is an adverb. Yet it does not really fit in either of these classes. As opposed to interjections and most ordinary adverbs, it can take a pronominal suffix and,

---

42. Due to the high frequency and complex nature of הִנֵּה, it is treated in more detail than most of the other lexemes listed in §40. The insights gained in this section benefitted much from a collaborate project between C. L. Miller-Naudé and C. H. J. van der Merwe. See Miller-Naudé and Van der Merwe (2011). After reading a draft of the latter publication, J. A. Naudé made some valuable observations.

as opposed to ordinary adverbs, it may have scope over a clause or multiple clauses. In fact, it always precedes the clause upon which it has a bearing. Semantically it also differs from the class *modal adverbs* as identified in this grammar. It does involve the speaker in the content of the clause, but it does not necessarily refer to his or her opinion on the degree of probability of the events or state of affairs.

Since most instances of the particle in the Hebrew Bible reflect the evaluation of the speaker(s) concerning the newsworthiness of an imminent action, event or the information conveyed in a clause or clauses, it is classified in this grammar as a deictic particle that predominantly functions as a "discourse marker." However, the particle is not necessarily always a typical discourse marker; for example, when the scope of הִנֵּה is limited to that of a nominal entity, it sometimes has the character of a presentative.

40.22.2. *Morphology and distribution*

The lexeme הִנֵּה occurs around 1,060 times in the Bible.

Person	Singular		Plural	
1 c.	הִנְנִי הִנֵּנִי הִנֶּ֫נִּי	Look, I	הִנְנוּ הִנֶּ֫נּוּ הִנֶּ֫נּוּ	Look, we
2 m.	הִנְּךָ וְהִנְּךָ הִנְּכָה הִנֶּ֫ךָּ	Look, you	הִנְּכֶם	Look, you
2 f.	הִנָּךְ	Look, you	(Not attested)	
3 m.	הִנּוֹ הִנֵּ֫הוּ	Look, he	הִנָּם	
3 f.	(Not attested)			

Personal pronouns may be suffixed to הִנֵּה (#*a*) and וְהִנֵּה (#*b*). Instead of the suffixed personal pronoun, independent personal pronouns may also be used (#*c*). Cases with the independent personal pronouns occur less frequently. Why independent personal pronouns are used is not clear. No difference in meaning or distribution has yet been determined.

In a few cases an independent personal pronoun precedes הִנְנִי (#*d*). In these cases the fronted pronoun serves to reactivate a discourse active participant in order to compare his/her activities with that of another, hence the translation "as for me."

a	הִנְנִי מַפְרְךָ	*Look, I* am going to make you fruitful (Gen. 48:4).*
b	¹³וְהִנְנִי מַשְׁחִיתָם אֶת־הָאָרֶץ׃ ¹⁴עֲשֵׂה לְךָ תֵּבַת עֲצֵי־גֹפֶר	¹³And, *look, I* am about to destroy them with the earth. ¹⁴Make for yourself an ark of cypress wood (Gen. 6:13–14).*
c	הִנֵּה אָנֹכִי מֵת... וְעַתָּה אֶעֱלֶה־נָּא	*Look, I* am about to die… Therefore let me go up (Gen. 50:5).*
d	וַאֲנִי הִנְנִי מֵקִים אֶת־בְּרִיתִי אִתְּכֶם	*As for me, look, I* am establishing my covenant with you (Gen. 9:9).*

40.22.3. Syntax

The scope of הִנֵּה (and sometimes וְהִנֵּה) in *reported speech* can be the content of a noun phrase (#*a*) or a clause (#*b*). The clause may be a nominal clause (#*b*), a verbal clause (#*c-d*) or clauses (#*e*).

a	וַיַּגִּידוּ לַמֶּלֶךְ לֵאמֹר הִנֵּה נָתָן הַנָּבִיא	And they told the king, "*Look!* <u>Nathan the prophet</u>" (1 Kgs 1:23).*
b	וַיֻּגַּד לְשָׁאוּל לֵאמֹר הִנֵּה דָוִד בְּנָוִת בָּרָמָה׃	And it was reported to Saul, "*Look*, <u>David is at Naioth in Ramah</u>" (1 Sam. 19:19).*
c	הִנְנִי מֵבִיא רָעָה עַל־הַמָּקוֹם הַזֶּה	*Look*, <u>I am about to bring disaster over this place</u> (Jer. 19:3).*
d	הִנֵּה אָנֹכִי שֹׁלֵחַ מַלְאָךְ לְפָנֶיךָ לִשְׁמָרְךָ בַּדָּרֶךְ	*Look*, <u>I am sending an angel before you to guard you on your way</u> (Exod. 23:20).*
e	הִנֵּה יָמִים בָּאִים וְגָדַעְתִּי אֶת־זְרֹעֲךָ וְאֶת־זְרֹעַ בֵּית אָבִיךָ	*Look*, <u>a time</u> [lit. <u>days</u>] <u>is coming when</u> [lit. <u>and</u>] <u>I will cut off your strength</u> [lit. <u>arm</u>] <u>and the strength</u> [lit. <u>arm</u>] *of the house of your father* (1 Sam. 2:31).*

When וְהִנֵּה is used in *narrative* its scope is sometimes the content of an object clause (#*f*), but in most cases its scope is that of a clause – either a nominal (#*g*) or a verbal clause (#*h*), and in some cases the content of more than one clause (#*i*).

f	וְהוּא יָצָא וַעֲבָדָיו בָּאוּ וַיִּרְאוּ וְהִנֵּה דַּלְתוֹת הָעֲלִיָּה נְעֻלוֹת	And after he had gone, his servants came and saw, *to their surprise,* the doors of the upper room were locked! (Judg. 3:24).*
g	רָאִיתִי אֶת־הָעָם הַזֶּה וְהִנֵּה עַם־קְשֵׁה־עֹרֶף הוּא:	I observed this people, *and indeed,* they are stiff-necked (Exod. 32:9).*
h	וַיַּרְא אֱלֹהִים אֶת־הָאָרֶץ וְהִנֵּה נִשְׁחָתָה	And God observed the earth, *and indeed,* it was corrupt (Gen. 6:12).*
i	וְרָאָהוּ הַכֹּהֵן בַּיּוֹם הַשְּׁבִיעִי וְהִנֵּה הַנֶּגַע עָמַד בְּעֵינָיו לֹא־פָשָׂה הַנֶּגַע בָּעוֹר וְהִסְגִּירוֹ הַכֹּהֵן שִׁבְעַת יָמִים שֵׁנִית:	And the priest must then examine it on the seventh day, and if *it turned out* the infection has stayed the same in his eyes and has not spread on the skin, then the priest shall confine the person for another seven days (Lev. 13:5).*

40.22.4. *Semantics and pragmatics*

40.22.4.1. *Points to a newsworthy event or situation*[43]

(1) הִנֵּה is used in direct speech to point an addressee to *something in the speech situation* that is newsworthy (about 35%).
The newsworthiness predominantly resides in the fact that an unexpected threat (#*a*), or sometimes negative information, is pointed out to the addressees. Less frequent, but still in a significant number of instances, a promise or positive information is pointed out to the addressees (#*b-c*). The newsworthiness of the events or state of affairs is sometimes evident from the reaction of the addressees (#*d*). When a speaker points out his/

---

43. We make a distinction between the notions "newsworthy" and "noteworthy." By "newsworthy," we mean (1) something the addressees did not know, (2) something they were unprepared for (e.g. something surprising or different from what they expected) or (3) it may be confirming something they already know. By "noteworthy," we mean something a speaker wants his/her addressee to take note of since it establishes a common ground of another speech act (e.g. a command, a request, an assertion, a question). Something "noteworthy" may be "newsworthy," but it need not be.

her performative action, often a positive gesture to the advantage of the addressee is involved (#e). A feature of this category is the immediacy of the events that are pointed out, typically by means of a participle (#a-c).

a	הִנְנִי מֵבִיא רָעָה עַל־הַמָּקוֹם הַזֶּה	*Look*, <u>I am about to bring disaster over this place</u> (Jer. 19:3).[44]
b	הִנֵּה שֶׁבַע שָׁנִים בָּאוֹת שָׂבָע גָּדוֹל בְּכָל־אֶרֶץ מִצְרָיִם:	*Look*, <u>seven years of great abundance are about to come in all the land of Egypt</u> (Gen. 41:29).*
c	הִנְנִי אֹסִפְךָ אֶל־אֲבֹתֶיךָ וְנֶאֱסַפְתָּ אֶל־קִבְרֹתֶיךָ בְּשָׁלוֹם	*Look*, <u>I will gather you to your ancestors</u> and you shall be gathered to your grave in peace (2 Chron. 34:28).*
d	וַיַּגֵּד לְיַעֲקֹב וַיֹּאמֶר הִנֵּה בִּנְךָ יוֹסֵף בָּא אֵלֶיךָ וַיִּתְחַזֵּק יִשְׂרָאֵל וַיֵּשֶׁב עַל־הַמִּטָּה:	And someone reported to Jacob and said, "*Look*, <u>your son Joseph has come to you</u>." Then Israel strengthened himself and sat up on his bed (Gen. 48:2).*
e	וַיֹּאמֶר אֱלֹהִים הִנֵּה נָתַתִּי לָכֶם אֶת־כָּל־עֵשֶׂב זֹרֵעַ זֶרַע	And God said: "*Look*, <u>I hereby give to you every seed-bearing plant</u>" (Gen. 1:29).*

Sometimes the location of somebody (#f-g) or something (#h) is pointed out. In a few cases, the presence or arrival of a person is pointed out (#i).

f	וַיֹּאמְרוּ אֵלָיו אַיֵּה שָׂרָה אִשְׁתֶּךָ וַיֹּאמֶר הִנֵּה בָאֹהֶל:	And they asked him, "Where is Sarah your wife?" and he answered: "*There*, <u>in the tent</u>!" (Gen. 18:9).
g	וַיֹּאמֶר־לוֹ הַמֶּלֶךְ אֵיפֹה הוּא וַיֹּאמֶר צִיבָא אֶל־הַמֶּלֶךְ הִנֵּה־הוּא בֵּית מָכִיר בֶּן־עַמִּיאֵל בְּלוֹ דְבָר:	And the king asked [lit. said to] him, "Where is he?" Ziba answered the king, "He is *there* <u>in the house of Makir, the son of Ammiel in Lo-Debar</u>!" (2 Sam. 9:4).*

---

44. Instances where הִנֵּה plus participle is headed by לָכֵן in the announcement of punishments or promises appear to represent a special category. The grounds of punishments or promises introduced by לָכֵן are typically spelled out in so much detail that it is hard to argue that the audience was unprepared for the announcement introduced by לָכֵן (see §40.35).

h	וָאֶקָחֵם וְהִנָּם טְמוּנִים בָּאָרֶץ בְּתוֹךְ הָאָהֳלִי	And I took them, and *there* <u>they are</u>, <u>hidden in the ground in the middle of my tent</u>! (Josh. 7:21).
i	וַיַּגִּידוּ לַמֶּלֶךְ לֵאמֹר הִנֵּה נָתָן הַנָּבִי	And they told the king, "*Look!* <u>Nathan the prophet</u>" (1 Kgs 1:23).

(2) וְהִנֵּה is used by a narrator (only sometimes a speaker) to *put the addressee in the perspective of the observing character* (about 25%)

    (a) The observing character (and sometimes speaker) is confronted with a new situation.

        Typically, one or another type of movement and/or change of scene is involved so that the observers are confronted with a new situation which is *surprising* to them (#*a-e*); linguists refer to the linguistic means for indicating surprise on the part of the speaker as *mirativity*. Often, when a situation is closely observed, the "new" perspective is a surprise to the observer (#*f*).

a	וַיָּשָׁב רְאוּבֵן אֶל־הַבּוֹר וְהִנֵּה אֵין־יוֹסֵף בַּבּוֹר	And Reuben returned to the pit *and to his surprise*, <u>Joseph was not in the pit</u> (Gen. 37:29).*
b	וְהוּא יָצָא וַעֲבָדָיו בָּאוּ וַיִּרְאוּ וְהִנֵּה דַּלְתוֹת הָעֲלִיָּה נְעֻלוֹת	And after he had gone, his servants came and saw *to their surprise*, <u>the doors of the upper room were locked</u>! (Judg. 3:24).*
c	וַיְהִי בְּהִקָּהֵל הָעֵדָה עַל־מֹשֶׁה וְעַל־אַהֲרֹן וַיִּפְנוּ אֶל־אֹהֶל מוֹעֵד וְהִנֵּה כִסָּהוּ הֶעָנָן וַיֵּרָא כְּבוֹד יְהוָה:	And then, when the assembly gathered against Moses and Aaron, they turned to the tent of meeting, *just then* <u>the cloud had covered it and the glory of the LORD appeared</u>! (Num. 17:7).*
d	וַיְהִי כִּי־בָאנוּ אֶל־הַמָּלוֹן וַנִּפְתְּחָה אֶת־אַמְתְּחֹתֵינוּ וְהִנֵּה כֶסֶף־אִישׁ בְּפִי אַמְתַּחְתּוֹ	And then, when we arrived at the lodging place and opened our sacks, *to our surprise*, <u>the money of each was in the mouth of his sack</u>! (Gen. 43.21).*
e	וַיָּסַר נֹחַ אֶת־מִכְסֵה הַתֵּבָה וַיַּרְא וְהִנֵּה חָרְבוּ פְּנֵי הָאֲדָמָה:	And Noah removed the covering of the ark, and saw, *to his surprise*, <u>the surface of the ground was dry</u>! (Gen. 8:13).*

f   וָאָקֻ֤ם בַּבֹּ֙קֶר֙ לְהֵינִ֣יק אֶת־בְּנִ֔י   And when I rose in the morning to
וְהִנֵּה־מֵ֑ת וָאֶתְבּוֹנֵ֤ן אֵלָיו֙   nurse my son, <u>he was dead</u>! However,
בַּבֹּ֔קֶר וְהִנֵּ֕ה לֹֽא־הָיָ֥ה בְנִ֖י   when I looked at him closely in
אֲשֶׁ֥ר יָלָֽדְתִּי׃   the morning, *to my surprise*, <u>it was</u>
<u>not my son to whom I gave birth</u>
(1 Kgs 3:21).*

(b) Related to (a), are instances where what observed is not surprising, but a confirmation of something that was expected.

Sometimes a situation is reconsidered and וְהִנֵּה is used to point out how the observers experienced the findings of their observations. In most cases it is not possible to argue that the findings were necessarily unexpected or surprising to the observers. It merely confirms what they expected.

וַיִּתְפָּקֵ֣ד הָעָ֔ם וְהִנֵּ֥ה אֵֽין־שָׁ֖ם אִ֑ישׁ   And the people were counted, and
מִיּוֹשְׁבֵ֖י יָבֵ֥שׁ גִּלְעָֽד׃   *indeed*, <u>there was no one from the</u>
<u>inhabitants of Jabesh-gilead</u> (Judg.
21:9).*

40.22.4.2. *Points to <u>noteworthy information</u>*

(1) הִנֵּה *points to and confirms* information which provides or prepares the grounds of something else that is being said (about 15%).

a   הִנֵּ֣ה שָׁמַ֔עְתִּי כִּ֥י יֶשׁ־שֶׁ֖בֶר   *Look*, <u>I have heard that there is</u>
בְּמִצְרָ֑יִם רְדוּ־שָׁ֙מָּה֙   <u>grain in Egypt</u>, go down there
וְשִׁבְרוּ־לָ֣נוּ מִשָּׁ֔ם   and buy grain for us there (Gen.
42:2).*

b   הִנֵּ֤ה שִׁפְחָתֵךְ֙ בְּיָדֵ֔ךְ   *Look*, <u>your slave-girl is in your</u>
עֲשִׂי־לָ֖הּ הַטּ֥וֹב בְּעֵינָֽיִךְ   <u>hands</u> [lit. hand], do to her what
is right in your eyes (Gen. 16:6).*

c   הִנֵּ֨ה חָפֵ֤ץ בְּךָ֙ הַמֶּ֔לֶךְ   *Look*, <u>the king is pleased with you</u>
וְכָל־עֲבָדָ֖יו אֲהֵב֑וּךָ וְעַתָּ֖ה   <u>and all his servants like you</u>. So
הִתְחַתֵּ֥ן בַּמֶּֽלֶךְ   then, become the king's son-in-law
(1 Sam. 18:22).*

d   הִנֵּה֩ שְׁנֵ֨י הַמְּלָכִ֜ים לֹ֤א עָֽמְדוּ֙   *Look,* two kings could not withstand
         לְפָנָ֔יו וְאֵ֖יךְ נַעֲמֹ֥ד אֲנָֽחְנוּ׃   him, how can we withstand [lit.
         stand]? (2 Kgs 10:4).*

e   הִנֵּ֣ה ׀ אַתָּ֣ה עָשִׂ֗יתָ אֶת־הַשָּׁמַ֙יִם֙   *Look,* you yourself made the heaven
         וְאֶת־הָאָ֔רֶץ בְּכֹֽחֲךָ֙ הַגָּד֔וֹל   and the earth with your great power
         וּבִזְרֹעֲךָ֖ הַנְּטוּיָ֑ה לֹֽא־יִפָּלֵ֥א   and your outstretched arm. Nothing
         מִמְּךָ֖ כָּל־דָּבָֽר׃   is impossible for you (Jer. 32:17).*

(2) הִנֵּה points to information *x* to *relate* it to information *y* which *x* then
modifies (about 10%).

הִנֵּה points to information which a speaker or author regards to *be
noteworthy as far as other discourse active information* is concerned. The
information presented modifies the content or implications of statements
in the *preceding* co-text.[45] This modification may be the confirmation (#*a*)
or the denial of an expectation (#*b*) thereof.

a   אֽוֹדְךָ֣ יְהוָ֔ה כִּ֥י אָנַ֖פְתָּ   [1] I praise you, Lᴏʀᴅ, for (though)
         בִּ֛י יָשֹׁ֥ב אַפְּךָ֖ וּֽתְנַחֲמֵֽנִי׃   you were angry with me your anger
         הִנֵּ֨ה אֵ֧ל יְשׁוּעָתִ֛י אֶבְטַ֖ח[2]   subsided and you comforted me.
         וְלֹ֣א אֶפְחָ֑ד   [2] *Yes,* God is my deliverer. I will trust
         and not be afraid (Isa. 12:1–2).*

b   וַיֹּ֨אמֶר שְׁמוּאֵ֤ל אֶל־יִשַׁי֙   Then Samuel asked Jesse, "Are
         הֲתַ֣מּוּ הַנְּעָרִ֔ים וַיֹּ֗אמֶר ע֚וֹד   those all the young men?" He
         שָׁאַ֣ר הַקָּטָ֔ן וְהִנֵּ֥ה רֹעֶ֖ה   replied, "The youngest still remains,
         בַּצֹּ֑אן   but he is keeping the sheep"
         (1 Sam. 16:11).*

40.22.4.3. *Used as a presentative*

(1) A speaker or speakers present(s) an entity (including themselves) to an
addressee (7%). What is presented typically prepares the ground for a
subsequent utterance (#*a-b*).

a   וְעַתָּ֕ה הִנֵּ֥ה אִשְׁתְּךָ֖ קַ֥ח וָלֵֽךְ׃   Now then, *here is* your wife, take
         (her) and go (Gen. 12:19).*

---

45. A significant difference between §40.22.4.2.(1) and §40.22.4.2.(2) is that all
instances of §40.22.4.2.(2) follow the utterance(s) of which the informational content is
modified.

b   הִנֵּה־רֹאשׁ אִישׁ־בֹּשֶׁת   *Here is* the head of Ish-boshet, the
     בֶּן־שָׁאוּל אֹיִבְךָ אֲשֶׁר בִּקֵּשׁ   son of Saul your enemy who sought
   אֶת־נַפְשֶׁךָ וַיִּתֵּן יְהוָה לַאדֹנִי   your life. So then the LORD has
   הַמֶּלֶךְ נְקָמוֹת הַיּוֹם הַזֶּה   avenged my lord the king this day
      מִשָּׁאוּל וּמִזַּרְעוֹ: ס   on Saul and on his descendants
                                     (2 Sam. 4:8).*

(2) A speaker or speakers present him-/herself or themselves to the addressee(s)
   as available to participate in an event or to fulfill a particular role.

a   הִנֶּנּוּ עֲבָדִים לַאדֹנִי   *Here* we *are*, my lord's slaves
                                          (Gen. 44:16).

b   וָאֶשְׁמַע אֶת־קוֹל אֲדֹנָי אֹמֵר   Then I heard the voice of the Lord
     אֶת־מִי אֶשְׁלַח וּמִי יֵלֶךְ־לָנוּ   saying: "Whom shall I send and
      וָאֹמַר הִנְנִי שְׁלָחֵנִי: who shall go for us." And I said:
                                     "*Here am* I, send me" (Isa. 6:8).

(3) A speaker presents him-/herself after being addressed or called by another
   speaker.
       These instances are similar to (2), but they appear to represent a conven-
   tionalized formula for responses, and indicate that the addressees are ready
   to be addressed. The responding speaker is often (#*a*), but not always (#*b*),
   already in the immediate proximity of the one calling.

a   וַיֹּאמֶר יִצְחָק אֶל־אַבְרָהָם אָבִיו   Then Isaac said to Abraham his
     וַיֹּאמֶר אָבִי וַיֹּאמֶר הִנֶּנִּי בְנִי   father, "My father" and he replied
                                     "*Yes* [lit. *here I am*], my son" (Gen.
                                     22:7).*

b   וַיֹּאמֶר אֵלָיו אַבְרָהָם וַיֹּאמֶר   He called to him, "Abraham," and
      הִנֵּנִי: he answered, "*Here I am*" (Gen.
                                     22:1).*

40.22.4.4. *Used as an expressive*

In seven instances, positive or negative feelings about a state of affairs are
presented. In these cases הִנֵּה functions as a discourse marker that a speaker
uses, not to relate propositional content of two utterances or sets of utterances,
but his/her feelings and the propositional content of his/her utterance.

a   הִנָּךְ יָפָה רַעְיָתִי   *Wow*, (how) beautiful you are, my love! (Song 1:15).*

b   וַאֲמַרְתֶּם הִנֵּה מַתְּלָאָה   And you say, "*Wow*, (how) tiresome (it is)!" (Mal. 1:13).*

40.22.4.5. *Used in fixed expressions and specific contexts*

(1) הִנְנִי אֶל and הִנְנִי עַל (21 times)

These constructions occur only in the books of Jeremiah, Ezekiel and Nahum. They are "challenging or threat formulas" with a mirative sense. They are regarded as fixed expressions on the following grounds[46]:

(a) The first item is always הִנְנִי. In other words, the suffixed personal pronoun is never substituted or modified by a nominal or independent pronominal element.

(b) The subject referent of the suffixed pronoun is always God.

(c) A participle is never used, despite the fact that an imminent threat is typically involved.

(d) הִנְנִי אֶל/עַל is typically followed by a vocative and then a description of the nature of the punitive action and/or reason for the threat.

a   דַּבֵּר וְאָמַרְתָּ כֹּה־אָמַר|
אֲדֹנָי יְהוִה הִנְנִי עָלֶיךָ
פַּרְעֹה מֶלֶךְ־מִצְרַיִם הַתַּנִּים
הַגָּדוֹל הָרֹבֵץ בְּתוֹךְ יְאֹרָיו
אֲשֶׁר אָמַר לִי יְאֹרִי וַאֲנִי
עֲשִׂיתִנִי: Speak, and say, Thus says the LORD God: *Look* I am going to deal with you [lit. *Look*, I am against you], Pharaoh king of Egypt, the great dragon sprawling in the midst of its channels, saying, "My Nile is my own; I made it for myself" (Ezek. 29:3).*

b   הִנְנִי אֵלַיִךְ יֹשֶׁבֶת הָעֵמֶק
צוּר הַמִּישֹׁר נְאֻם־יְהוָה
הָאֹמְרִים מִי־יֵחַת עָלֵינוּ   *Look*, I am against you, inhabitants [lit. inhabitant] of the valley, rock of the plain, declares the LORD [lit. oracle of the LORD], who say, "Who can swoop down on us?" (Jer. 21:13).*

---

46. See Humbert (1933).

(2) הִנָּם + Participle passive + prepositional phrase (21 times)

It appears that in its capacity to point out information, הִנֵּה became part of a conventionalized expression. The fact that historical information is recorded at a specific location is typically pointed out. The translation equivalent of this formula is uncertain.[47]

וְיֶ֙תֶר֙ דִּבְרֵ֣י יָרָבְעָ֔ם אֲשֶׁ֤ר נִלְחַם֙ — And the rest of the acts of Jeroboam, וַאֲשֶׁ֣ר מָלָ֔ךְ הִנָּ֣ם כְּתוּבִ֔ים עַל־סֵ֖פֶר — how he fought and how he reigned, דִּבְרֵ֥י הַיָּמִ֖ים לְמַלְכֵ֥י יִשְׂרָאֵֽל׃ — *look,* they are written in the scroll of the annals of the kings of Israel (1 Kgs 14:19).*

(3) הִנֵּה and וְהִנֵּה in dream reports (28 times)[48]

A feature of dream reports in Biblical Hebrew is that they may abound with the use of הִנֵּה and וְהִנֵּה. The syntax and semantics of these instances are in accordance with §40.22.4.1. The main difference is that וְהִנֵּה is used much more frequently than in ordinary language. The following types of uses occur:

(a) A speaker presents/announces his/her dream by means of הִנֵּה.

וַיֹּ֣אמֶר הִנֵּ֗ה חָלַ֤מְתִּי חֲלוֹם֙ עוֹד — And he said, "*Look,* I have had another dream" (Gen. 37:9).*

(b) A speaker narrates his/her dream and points to each separate state of affairs[49] or event that is observed by means of וְהִנֵּה.

וַֽיַּחֲלֹ֗ם וְהִנֵּ֤ה סֻלָּם֙ מֻצָּ֣ב אַ֔רְצָה — And he dreamed *and look,* a ladder וְרֹאשׁ֖וֹ מַגִּ֣יעַ הַשָּׁמָ֑יְמָה וְהִנֵּה֙ — was set on the ground and its top מַלְאֲכֵ֣י אֱלֹהִ֔ים עֹלִ֥ים וְיֹרְדִ֖ים בּֽוֹ׃ — reached to heaven, *and look,* angels of God were going up and down on it! (Gen. 28:12).*

---

47. In this construction, הִנֵּה is sometimes apparently used as alternative of הֲלֹא. See 1 Kgs 11:41 and also Deut. 3:11. See §42.2.1.(3)(c) for the views of Moshavi (2007a and 2007b) and Snyman and Naudé (2003: 258–64).

48. Only explicitly described dream reports are considered here. See also the vision reports, e.g. Jer. 24:1; 38:22; Ezek. 1:4.

49. See Gen. 40:9, 16.

(c) A narrator points to experience of the dreamer, i.e. his/her dream realization by means of וְהִנֵּה.

וַיִּיקַץ פַּרְעֹה וְהִנֵּה חֲלוֹם: And Pharaoh woke up, and *look* <u>a dream</u>
[i.e. and he realized *to his surprise*, it
was a dream!] (Gen. 41:7).*

§40.23. וְ

Only the so-called *wāw* copulative will be dealt with here.[50]

40.23.1. *Word class*

וְ is primarily a coordinating conjunction. It typically coordinates syntactically equal phrasal constituents and clauses. The translation values in English
of some clauses that are connected suggest a relationship of main clause +
dependent clause. In a number instances, וְ has no translation equivalent in
English. In some contexts וְ functions as a discourse marker, i.e. the speech-
initial וְ.[51] In poetry it may function as a signal of text level transition.[52]

40.23.2. *Morphology and distribution*

וְ is the most frequent word in the Hebrew Bible. It occurs 51,152 times (out of
a total of 475,862 words).[53]

As far as its morphology is concerned (see also §31.1.1), the following can
be observed:

(1) It is affixed to a word

אִישׁ וְסוּס   a man and a horse

(2) Before בּ, וּ, מ, פּ it becomes וּ.

סוּס וּפָרָשׁ   a horse and a rider

(3) Before a syllable with an audible *šəwāʾ* it also becomes וּ.

וּסְדֹם   and Sodom

---

50. Due to the high frequency of וְ, it is also treated in more detail than most of the other
lexemes listed in §40. This section benefitted much from insights gleaned from Steiner
(2000).

51. See Miller (1999).

52. See Bandstra (1995).

53. According to Vanoni (1991: 562).

(4) It combines with the syllable יְ to form וִי.

וִירִיחוֹ   in Jericho (יְרִיחוֹ)

(5) With concepts that *are closely related* (provided the first syllable of the second word is stressed), it becomes וָ.

יוֹם וָלַיְלָה   day and night

40.23.3. *Syntax of* וְ

40.23.3.1. *Phrase level*

(1) Every entity (#*a*), groups of entities (#*b*) or only the last entity in the list (#*c*) to be added, is preceded by וְ. In negated clauses or conditional clauses, a list of "apparent" alternatives may be involved (#*d*).

a	כִּי אָנֹכִי נָתַתִּי לָהּ הַדָּגָן וְהַתִּירוֹשׁ וְהַיִּצְהָר	that it was I who gave her the grain, the wine [lit. *and* the wine], *and* the oil (Hos. 2:10).
b	נֹתְנֵי לַחְמִי וּמֵימַי צַמְרִי וּפִשְׁתִּי שַׁמְנִי וְשִׁקּוּיָי׃	who give (me) my bread *and* my water, my wool *and* my flax, my oil *and* my drink (Hos. 2:7).*
c	כָּל־מְשׂוֹשָׂהּ חַגָּהּ חָדְשָׁהּ וְשַׁבַּתָּהּ	all her mirth, her feast(s), her new moon(s) *and* her sabbath(s) (Hos. 2:13)
d	לֹא־תַעֲשֶׂה כָל־מְלָאכָה אַתָּה וּבִנְךָ־וּבִתֶּךָ עַבְדְּךָ וַאֲמָתְךָ וּבְהֶמְתֶּךָ וְגֵרְךָ אֲשֶׁר בִּשְׁעָרֶיךָ׃	You shall not do any work, you, *or* your son, *or* your daughter, your manservant, *or* your maidservant, *or* your cattle, *or* the sojourner who is within your gates (Exod. 20:10).*

Sometimes (#*e*) the phrases to be coordinated by וְ are split (called split coordination).

e	וְעָבְדוּ אֹתוֹ כָּל־הַגּוֹיִם וְאֶת־בְּנוֹ וְאֶת־בֶּן־בְּנוֹ	And they shall serve him, all the nations, *and* his son *and* the son of his son (Jer. 27:7).*

Sometimes (#*f*) two words form a type of fixed compound. (If the word that is preceded by וְ is short then וָ is used instead of וְ.)

f	טוֹב וָרָע	good *and* evil (Gen. 2:17)

(2) Sometimes both the first and the second entity of a coordinated phrase are preceded by וְ.

It is then regarded as *a correlative conjunction* (see §31.1.3.(3)).

וּבְיִשְׂרָאֵל וּבָאָדָם

both in Israel *and* among all human-kind (Jer. 32:20).*

(3) An apparently superfluous use of וְ (rare)

וַתֵּשֶׁב תָּמָר וְשֹׁמֵמָה בֵּית אַבְשָׁלוֹם אָחִיהָ

So Tamar, [lit. *and*] a desolate woman, dwelt in the house of Absalom, her brother (2 Sam. 13:20).*

40.23.3.2. *Clause level*

(1) Connecting two (or more) clauses

The clause(s) that is/are connected may commence with a verbal constituent (#a), or a non-verbal constituent (#b) of a verbal clause, any constituent of a nominal clause (#c), or a sentence governing particle (#d). The two clauses connected may also be the protasis and apodosis of a conditional sentence (#e-f).

a	<div dir="rtl">וְאֶתְּנָה בְרִיתִי בֵּינִי וּבֵינֶךָ וְאַרְבֶּה אוֹתְךָ בִּמְאֹד מְאֹד:</div>	*And* I will make my covenant between me and you, *and* I will multiply you greatly (Gen. 17:2).*
b	<div dir="rtl">נִחַמְתִּי כִּי עֲשִׂיתִם:⁷ ⁸וְנֹחַ מָצָא חֵן בְּעֵינֵי יְהוָה:</div>	⁷I am sorry that I have made them. ⁸*But* Noah found favor in the eyes of the Lᴏʀᴅ (Gen. 6:7–8).*
c	<div dir="rtl">רִבְקָה יֹצֵאת...וְכַדָּהּ עַל־שִׁכְמָהּ:</div>	Rebekah was coming out…with her water jar [lit. *and* her water jar was] upon her shoulder (Gen. 24:15).*
d	<div dir="rtl">¹²וְאַתָּה אָמַרְתָּ יְדַעְתִּיךָ בְשֵׁם וְגַם־מָצָאתָ חֵן בְּעֵינָי ¹³וְעַתָּה אִם־נָא מָצָאתִי חֵן בְּעֵינֶיךָ הוֹדִעֵנִי נָא אֶת־דְּרָכֶךָ</div>	¹²And you yourself said, "I know you by name, *and* moreover, you have found favor in my eyes. ¹³So [lit. *and*] now, if I found favor in your eyes, please let me know your way" (Exod. 33:12–13).*

e   וַיֹּאמֶר לוֹ דָּוִד אִם עָבַרְתָּ אִתִּי וְהָיִתָ עָלַי לְמַשָּׂא׃   And David said to him, "If you go further with me, [lit. *and*] you will be a burden to me" (2 Sam. 15:33).*

f   וַנֹּאמֶר אֶל־אֲדֹנִי לֹא־יוּכַל הַנַּעַר לַעֲזֹב אֶת־אָבִיו וְעָזַב אֶת־אָבִיו וָמֵת׃   And we said to my lord, "The boy cannot leave his father, [lit. *and*] if he leaves his father, [lit. *and*] his father [lit. he] will die" (Gen. 44.22).*

(2) Dislocated constituent + clause

A dislocated constituent may be connected to its matrix clause by means of וְ. In this way a dislocated construction is indicated as separate from its matrix clause (see also §48.1.1.(2)).

וַיֹּאמֶר הַמֶּלֶךְ הַמְדַבֵּר אֵלַיִךְ וַהֲבֵאתוֹ אֵלָי   And the king said, "He who speaks to you, [lit. *and*] bring him to me" (2 Sam. 14:10).*

40.23.3.3. *Discourse level*

(1) Speech initial וְ

Speeches of different speakers (#a) or the same speaker (#b) may be joined by וְ (see Miller 1999).

a   [21]וַתֹּאמֶר יֻתַּן אֶת־אֲבִישַׁג הַשֻּׁנַמִּית לַאֲדֹנִיָּהוּ אָחִיךָ לְאִשָּׁה׃[22]וַיַּעַן הַמֶּלֶךְ שְׁלֹמֹה וַיֹּאמֶר לְאִמּוֹ וְלָמָה אַתְּ שֹׁאֶלֶת אֶת־אֲבִישַׁג הַשֻּׁנַמִּית לַאֲדֹנִיָּהוּ וְשַׁאֲלִי־לוֹ אֶת־הַמְּלוּכָה   [21] And she said, "Let Abishag the Shunammite be given to Adonijah, your brother, as wife." [22] The king, Solomon, answered his mother, "*And* why do you request Abishag the Shunammite for Adonijah? Then you may ask (as well) for him the kingdom!" (1 Kgs 2:21–22).*

b   [2] וַיֹּאמֶר הַמֶּלֶךְ אֶל־צִיבָא מָה־אֵלֶּה לָּךְ וַיֹּאמֶר צִיבָא הַחֲמוֹרִים לְבֵית־הַמֶּלֶךְ...[3] וַיֹּאמֶר הַמֶּלֶךְ וְאַיֵּה בֶּן־אֲדֹנֶיךָ   [2] And the king asked Ziba, "What are you doing with these things?" And Ziba replied, "The donkeys are for the household of the king…" [3] The king then asked, "*And* where is the son of your master?" (2 Sam. 16:2–3).*

(2) Text level connection in poetry

   A clause or clauses is joined by וֹ with a preceding textual unit.

הַבִּ֤יטָֽה עֲנֵ֨נִי יְהוָ֣ה אֱלֹהָ֑י	[4] Consider! Answer me, O LORD,
הָאִ֥ירָה עֵ֝ינַ֗י פֶּן־אִישַׁ֥ן הַמָּֽוֶת:	my God. Enlighten my eyes, lest I
[5]פֶּן־יֹאמַ֣ר אֹיְבִ֣י יְכָלְתִּ֑יו	sleep the sleep of death, [5] lest my
צָרַ֥י יָ֝גִ֗ילוּ כִּ֣י אֶמּֽוֹט:	enemy say, "I have prevailed," my
[6]וַאֲנִ֤י ׀ בְּחַסְדְּךָ֣ בָטַחְתִּי֮	foes rejoice since I am upended. [6] *But* for me, in your loyal love (alone) I trust (Ps. 13:4–6).*

40.23.4. *Semantics and pragmatics of* וֹ

Some scholars believe וֹ has a number of different semantic functions. However, there is a growing consensus that וֹ is semantically speaking relatively empty. Many of the "meanings" that are distinguished, scholars argue, are merely possible translation equivalents, or the lack thereof in modern languages. These "meanings" therefore merely reflect a possible translation value of a semantic relationship between the two entities that וֹ coordinates or connects.

40.23.4.1. *Phrase level*

(1) List two or more entities as additions.

כִּ֤י אָֽנֹכִי֙ נָתַ֣תִּי לָ֔הּ הַדָּגָ֖ן וְהַתִּיר֑וֹשׁ וְהַיִּצְהָ֗ר	that it was I who gave her the grain, [lit. *and* the] wine, *and* the oil (Hos. 2:10).

(2) List two or more entities as "apparent" alternatives.

לֹֽא־תַעֲשֶׂ֣ה כָל־מְלָאכָ֡ה אַתָּ֣ה ׀	You shall not do any work, you, *or*
וּבִנְךָֽ־וּבִתֶּ֡ךָ עַבְדְּךָ֣ וַאֲמָֽתְךָ֩	your son, *or* your daughter, your
וּבְהֶמְתֶּ֗ךָ וְגֵרְךָ֙ אֲשֶׁ֣ר בִּשְׁעָרֶֽיךָ:	manservant, *or* your maidservant, *or* your cattle, *or* the sojourner who is within your gates (Exod. 20:10).*

(3) Links two entities in a coordinated phrase that form a hendiadys (rare).

הַבְּרִ֖ית וְהַחֶ֑סֶד	the covenant of grace (Deut. 7:9).*

(4) When the same word is repeated with *wāw* the construction indicates diversity (see §24.3.2.(5) and §29.3.(9)).

אֶבֶן וָאָבֶן two *kinds of* weights [lit. stone *and* stone] (Deut. 25:13).

(5) A speaker uses the correlative conjunction to indicate that both the entities preceded by ו are of particular importance in the context in which they occur (see §40.14.(1)(d) and §40.20.(3)).

וּבְיִשְׂרָאֵל וּבָאָדָם *both* in Israel *and* among humanity (Jer. 32:20).*

40.23.4.2. *Clause level*

Clauses joined by ו can be in a variety of semantic relationships.

(1) The content of the clauses with ו refers to a list of events that happened (#*a*) or will happen (#*b*). It may also refer to things that need to be done (#*c*).

a	הוּא־הִכָּה אֶת־אֱדוֹם בְּגֵיא־הַמֶּלַח...וְתָפַשׂ אֶת־הַסֶּלַע בַּמִּלְחָמָה	He is the one that defeated Edom in the Valley of Salt...*and* captured Sela in battle (2 Kgs 14:7).*
b	וְאֶתְּנָה בְרִיתִי בֵּינִי וּבֵינֶךָ וְאַרְבֶּה אוֹתְךָ בִּמְאֹד מְאֹד:	*And* I will make my covenant between me and you, *and* I will multiply you greatly (Gen. 17:2).*
c	תְּיַסְּרֵךְ רָעָתֵךְ וּמְשֻׁבוֹתַיִךְ תּוֹכִחֻךְ וּדְעִי וּרְאִי כִּי־רַע וָמָר	Your wickedness will chastise you and your apostacies will punish you. *Then* consider *and* realize how evil and bitter (it is) (Jer. 2:19).*

(2) The content of the clause with ו is contrasted[54] with that of the other (frequent).

נִחַמְתִּי כִּי עֲשִׂיתִם:⁷ ⁷I am sorry that I have made them.
וְנֹחַ מָצָא חֵן בְּעֵינֵי יְהוָה:⁸ ⁸*But* Noah found favor in the eyes of the LORD (Gen. 6:7–8).*

---

54. The contrast is typically a "denial of expectation."

(3) The content of the clause with ו refers to events that will occur one after the other; in other words, it links sequential events (rare).

וְכָל־הָעָם יִשְׁמְעוּ וְיִרָאוּ   And all the people shall hear *and* fear (Deut. 17:13).

(4) The content of the clause with ו refers to the purpose of the content of the preceding clause (see also §21.5.3).

אָסֻרָה־נָּא וְאֶרְאֶה אֶת־הַמַּרְאֶה הַגָּדֹל הַזֶּה   I must go across *to see* [lit. *and* see] this great sight (Exod. 3:3).*

(5) The content of the clause with ו alludes to the result of the content of the preceding clause.

זֹאת עֲשׂוּ וִחְיוּ   *Do* this *so that* you may [lit. *and*] live (Gen. 42:18).*

(6) The content of the clause with ו refers to circumstances that prevailed at the same time as those described in the other clause (verbal + nominal clause = action followed by an event).

רִבְקָה יֹצֵאת...וְכַדָּהּ עַל־שִׁכְמָהּ:   Rebecca was coming out…with her water jar [lit. *and* her water jar was] upon her shoulder (Gen. 24:15).*

(7) The content of the clause with ו refers to a motivation for the other.

וְגֵר לֹא תִלְחָץ וְאַתֶּם יְדַעְתֶּם אֶת־נֶפֶשׁ הַגֵּר   You shall not oppress a stranger *for* [lit. *and*] you know the heart of a stranger (Exod. 23:9).*

(8) The content of the clause with ו introduces background information necessary for understanding the previous clause better.

גְּאַל־לָךְ אַתָּה אֶת־גְּאֻלָּתִי כִּי לֹא־אוּכַל לִגְאֹל: וְזֹאת לְפָנִים בְּיִשְׂרָאֵל עַל־הַגְּאוּלָּה   [6]Take my right of redemption yourself, for I cannot redeem it. [7]*Now* this was the custom in former times in Israel concerning redeeming (Ruth 4:6–7).

(9) The content of the clause with ׀ refers to a comparison with the other clause (rare).

הַדֶּלֶת תִּסּוֹב עַל־צִירָהּ
וְעָצֵל עַל־מִטָּתוֹ:

A door turns on its hinges *and so* does a sluggard on his bed (Prov. 26:14).*

(10) The content of the clause with ׀ describes more fully the content of the preceding one (the so-called epexegetical or explicative *wāw*).

כִּי־גוֹי אֹבַד עֵצוֹת הֵמָּה
וְאֵין בָּהֶם תְּבוּנָה:

For they are a nation void of counsel, [lit. *and*] there is no discernment in them (Deut. 32:28).*

40.23.4.3. *Discourse level*[55]

(1) Dispreferred response
The speech-initial ׀ "is used to connect a quotation by one speaker to an immediately preceding quotation by a different speaker" (Miller 1999: 172). The function of this type of speech-initial ׀ is to mark a dispreferred response.

21וַתֹּאמֶר יֻתַּן אֶת־אֲבִישַׁג
הַשֻּׁנַמִּית לַאֲדֹנִיָּהוּ אָחִיךָ לְאִשָּׁה:
22וַיַּעַן הַמֶּלֶךְ שְׁלֹמֹה וַיֹּאמֶר לְאִמּוֹ
וְלָמָה אַתְּ שֹׁאֶלֶת אֶת־אֲבִישַׁג
הַשֻּׁנַמִּית לַאֲדֹנִיָּהוּ וְשַׁאֲלִי־לוֹ
אֶת־הַמְּלוּכָה

[21]And she said, "Let Abishag the Shunammite be given to Adonijah, your brother, as wife." [22]The king, Solomon, answered his mother, "*And* why do you ask for Abishag the Shunammite for Adonijah? Then you may ask (as well) for him the kingdom!" (1 Kgs 2:21–22).*

(2) Connect to similar speech event
According to Miller (1999: 180), a speech-initial ׀ that connects two speeches of the same speaker within the same exchange that are not continuous, "signals to the hearer/reader to examine the preceding dialogue for a similar speech event by the same speaker."

---

55. Categories (1) to (3) are based on the insights from Miller (1999).

וַיֹּאמֶר הַמֶּלֶךְ אֶל־צִיבָא² ²And the king asked Ziba, "What are you doing with these things?" מָה־אֵלֶּה לָּךְ וַיֹּאמֶר צִיבָא הַחֲמוֹרִים לְבֵית־הַמֶּלֶךְ... And Ziba replied, "The donkeys are for the household of the king..." וַיֹּאמֶר הַמֶּלֶךְ וְאַיֵּה בֶּן־אֲדֹנֶיךָ³ ³The king then asked, "*And* where is the son of your master?" (2 Sam. 16:2–3).*

(3) Highlight a change of topic

A speech-initial ו may connect a string of quotations by the same speaker in a context of multiple quotative frames. "The discourse pragmatic function of *wāw* intersects with the use of word order to highlight a change of topic relating to one of the speech participants" (Miller 1999: 184).

וַיֹּאמֶר אֵלָיו אֲנִי־אֵל שַׁדַּי הִתְהַלֵּךְ¹ ¹And he said to him, "I am El לְפָנַי וֶהְיֵה תָמִים: Shaddai. Walk before me and be וַיִּפֹּל אַבְרָם עַל־פָּנָיו וַיְדַבֵּר אִתּוֹ³ blameless." ³And Abraham fell on אֱלֹהִים לֵאמֹר: אֲנִי הִנֵּה בְרִיתִי⁴ his face. God then spoke to him, אִתָּךְ וְהָיִיתָ לְאַב הֲמוֹן גּוֹיִם: ⁴ "As for me, look, my covenant וַיֹּאמֶר אֱלֹהִים אֶל־אַבְרָהָם⁹ is with you and you shall be the וְאַתָּה אֶת־בְּרִיתִי תִשְׁמֹר... ancestor of a multitude of nations." ⁹ And God said to Abraham, "*And,* as for you, you shall keep my covenant,..." (Gen. 17:1, 3–4, 9).*

(4) Text level disjunction

A *wāw* + pronoun signals a text level *disjunction* in a poetic text.[56]

הַבִּיטָה עֲנֵנִי יְהוָה אֱלֹהָי⁴ ⁴Consider! Answer me, O LORD, הָאִירָה עֵינַי פֶּן־אִישַׁן הַמָּוֶת: my God. Enlighten my eyes, lest פֶּן־יֹאמַר אֹיְבִי יְכָלְתִּיו⁵ I sleep the sleep of death, ⁵lest my צָרַי יָגִילוּ כִּי אֶמּוֹט: enemy say, "I have prevailed." My וַאֲנִי | בְּחַסְדְּךָ בָטַחְתִּי⁶ foes rejoice since I am upended. ⁶*But* for me, in your loyal love (alone) I trust (Ps. 13:4–6).*

---

56. See Bandstra (1995).

§40.24. וְהָיָה

וְהָיָה is primarily a verb. However, when it immediately precedes a temporal expression, it plays a role in the temporal organization of a narration. In those instances וְהָיָה may be regarded as a discourse marker.

וְהָיָה occurs 397 times in the Hebrew Bible, mainly in reported speech.[57] As the nuclear verb of a clause, its number, person and gender tend to agree with that of the subject of the clause.

When וְהָיָה functions as discourse marker, it typically does not decline and is an optional element that occurs at the left-hand border of a clause.[58]

The following categories of use can be distinguished:

(1) Ordinary verb

Reference is typically to events that are projected in the future. (For uses of the *wəqātal* form, see §21.3.)

a	וְהָיָה צֶדֶק אֵזוֹר מָתְנָיו וְהָאֱמוּנָה אֵזוֹר חֲלָצָיו:	And righteousness *will be* the belt of his waist, and faithfulness the belt of his loins (Isa. 11:5).*
b	וְהָיָה לְאוֹת בְּרִית בֵּינִי וּבֵינֵיכֶם:	And it *will be* a sign of the covenant between me and you (Gen. 17:11).*

(2) Discourse marker

In a sequence of main line events that are projected in the future, וְהָיָה[59] creates a generic space "and then."[60] This space may be used to update the reference time of a subsequent main line event (#*a-f*). The temporal expression with וְהָיָה is often a constituent which is separated from the main sentence (#*a-c*). However, this is also often not the case (#*d-f*). The generic space "and then" may also be used to specify a topic (#*g*) or conditions (#*h-i*) of a subsequent main line event.

---

57. The highest concentration of וְהָיָה is found in Isaiah (66 times) and Deuteronomy (41 times) and the lowest in Psalms (once), Job (3 times), 2 Kings (3 times) and 1 and 2 Chronicles (3 times). Not one instance is attested in Habakuk, Malachi, Proverbs, Ecclesiastes, Song of Songs or Lamentations.

58. In terms of the two divisions made by Even-Shoshan (1981: 288–89), in 50% of the occurrences of וְהָיָה in the Hebrew Bible it is used as a discourse marker.

59. Sometimes וְהָיָה occurs where וַיְהִי is expected. For a discussion of these "problematic" uses of וְהָיָה, see Stipp (1991).

60. It is often difficult to "interpretively resemble" this use of וְהָיָה in an idiomatic English translation.

The function of וְהָיָה is to indicate that an event whose reference time, topic or conditions had to be modified, must be construed as part of a main line of events projected in the future.

a   וְהָיָה כִּרְאוֹתוֹ כִּי־אֵין הַנַּעַר וָמֵת   *And then*, <u>the moment that he sees the boy is not there</u>, he will die (Gen. 44:31).*

b   וְהָיָה בַּתְּבוּאֹת וּנְתַתֶּם חֲמִישִׁית לְפַרְעֹה   *And then*, <u>in the harvest</u>, you shall give one-fifth to Pharaoh (Gen. 47:24).*

c   לִינִי הַלַּיְלָה וְהָיָה בַבֹּקֶר אִם־יִגְאָלֵךְ טוֹב יִגְאָל   Stay for the night, *and then* <u>in the morning</u>, if he will act as next-of-kin, good, let him do it (Ruth 3:13).*

d   וְהָיָה אַחֲרֵי נָתְשִׁי אוֹתָם אָשׁוּב וְרִחַמְתִּים   *And then*, <u>after I have plucked them up</u>, I again will have compassion on them (Jer. 12:15).*

e   וְהָיָה בַּאֲכָלְכֶם מִלֶּחֶם הָאָרֶץ תָּרִימוּ תְרוּמָה לַיהוָה׃   *And then*, <u>whenever you eat from the food of the land</u>, you shall raise up (i.e. present) a contribution to the LORD (Num. 15:19).*

f   וְהָיָה בַּיּוֹם הַהוּא שֹׁרֶשׁ יִשַׁי אֲשֶׁר עֹמֵד לְנֵס עַמִּים אֵלָיו גּוֹיִם יִדְרֹשׁוּ   *And then*, <u>in that day</u> the root of Jesse shall stand as an ensign to the peoples; him shall the nations seek (Isa. 11:10).*

g   וְהָיָה הַמָּקוֹם אֲשֶׁר־יִבְחַר יְהוָה אֱלֹהֵיכֶם בּוֹ לְשַׁכֵּן שְׁמוֹ שָׁם שָׁמָּה תָבִיאוּ אֵת כָּל־אֲשֶׁר אָנֹכִי מְצַוֶּה אֶתְכֶם   *And then*, <u>the place which the LORD your God has chosen to let dwell his name there</u>, there you should bring everything that I am commanding you (Deut. 12:11).*

h   וְהָיָה כַּאֲשֶׁר שָׁקַדְתִּי עֲלֵיהֶם לִנְתוֹשׁ וְלִנְתוֹץ וְלַהֲרֹס וּלְהַאֲבִיד וּלְהָרֵעַ כֵּן אֶשְׁקֹד עֲלֵיהֶם לִבְנוֹת וְלִנְטוֹעַ   *And then*, <u>just as I have watched over them to pluck out, to break down, to destroy and to bring evil</u>, so I watch over them to build and to plant (Jer. 31:28).*

i   וְהָיָה אִם־לֹא יַאֲמִינוּ לָךְ וְלֹא יִשְׁמְעוּ לְקֹל הָאֹת הָרִאשׁוֹן וְהֶאֱמִינוּ לְקֹל הָאֹת הָאַחֲרוֹן׃   *And so*, <u>if they do not believe you and do not heed the first sign</u>, they may believe the latter sign (Exod. 4:8).*

§40.25. וַיְהִי

וַיְהִי is primarily a verb. However, when it immediately precedes a temporal expression, it plays a role in the temporal organization of a narration. In those instances וַיְהִי may, as a counterpart of וְהָיָה, be regarded as a discourse marker.

וַיְהִי occurs 864 times[61] in the Hebrew Bible, mainly in narrative.[62] According to Harmelink (2004: 147), in 458 (i.e. 53%) of the cases it functions as a verb. In those cases it displays the normal morphology of a Qal *yiqtōl*/imperfect verb form of היה. As the nuclear verb of a clause, its number, person and gender tend to agree with that of the subject of the clause.

When וַיְהִי functions as discourse marker, it typically does not decline and is an optional element that occurs at the beginning of a clause.

The following categories of use can be distinguished:

(1) Ordinary verb

When וַיְהִי functions as a verb, in other words, the *wayyiqtol* form of היה, it has a semantic potential that is similar to that of other lexemes in the *wayyiqtōl* (see §21.2).

a	וַיְהִי־נֹחַ בֶּן־חֲמֵשׁ מֵאוֹת שָׁנָה	And Noah *was* five hundred years old (Gen. 5:32).*
b	וַיְהִי דְבַר־יְהֹוָה אֶל־יֵהוּא בֶּן־חֲנָנִי	And the word of the LORD *came* [lit. *was*] to Jehu the son of Hanani (1 Kgs 16:1).*[63]

(2) Discourse marker

וַיְהִי typically signals, on the one hand, that an event or scene *follows* on a preceding event or scene and, on the other hand, that *the reference time* of the event or scene *is being updated (and by implication specified)*. The detail of the update is provided by the temporal expression following וַיְהִי.[64]

---

61. Included here are 86 instances of וַתְּהִי.

62. The highest concentration of וַיְהִי is found in Genesis (130 times) and the lowest in Leviticus (once) and the Psalms (6 times). Not one instance is attested in Amos, Joel, Micah, Nahum, Zephaniah, Malachi, Proverbs, Ecclesiastes, Song of Songs or Lamentations. For more detail, see Harmelink (2004: 137–46).

63. This is a typical formulaic expression to announce a message that came to a prophet, e.g. 1 Sam. 15:10; 2 Chron. 11:2. Except for the book of Isaiah, where it occurs only once (Isa. 38:4), the formula occurs in most of prophetic books, e.g., 21 times in Jeremiah and 39 times in Ezekiel (see also Harmelink 2004: 158–76). The use of וַיְהִי in prophetic contexts is typical, but not necessarily obligatory, see Jer. 1:1–2 and 14:1.

64. A feature of the וַיְהִי + temporal expression construction is that it is typically followed by a *wayyiqtol* clause. However, the subsequent clause may also be a *we-x-qātal/*

וַיְהִי + temporal expression has the semantic potential to anchor an event or scene of which the reference time needs to be updated or specified to the main stream of events in a scene, episode or narrative. Two classes can be distinguished.

(a) וַיְהִי + temporal expression that describes the reference time of a scene

The scene may be the onset of a new episode (#*a*), a development in an episode (#*b*) or a scene which concludes an episode (#*c*).

a	וַיְהִי הַיּוֹם וַיָּבֹא שָׁמָּה וַיָּסַר אֶל־הָעֲלִיָּה וַיִּשְׁכַּב־שָׁמָּה:	*And then*, <u>one day</u>, he came there, and turned aside to the upper room and lay down there (2 Kgs 4:11).*
b	וַיְהִי בַבֹּקֶר וַיִּכְתֹּב דָּוִד סֵפֶר אֶל־יוֹאָב	*And then*, <u>in the morning</u>, David wrote a letter to Joab (2 Sam. 11:14).*
c	וַיְהִי אַחֲרֵי מוֹת אַבְרָהָם וַיְבָרֶךְ אֱלֹהִים אֶת־יִצְחָק בְּנוֹ וַיֵּשֶׁב יִצְחָק עִם־בְּאֵר לַחַי רֹאִי:	*And then*, <u>after Abraham's death</u> God blessed Isaac, his son, and Isaac settled near Beer-lahai-roi (Gen. 25:11).*

(b) וַיְהִי + temporal expression that updates the reference time of a scene

In most cases the updated reference time provides the temporal frame of a subsequent event (#*a-b*). In cases where *the immediate temporal proximity of two events on the time line* is involved (usually expressed by means of the preposition כְּ + infinitive construct, see §39.10.(4)), וַיְהִי allows speakers to describe the immediate temporal proximity of two events, without breaking the main stream of events in the scene (#*c*). These constructions are often used at the climax of a scene in order to signal what triggered a climactic event.

a	וַיְהִי כִּי עָלִינוּ אֶל־עַבְדְּךָ אָבִי וַנַּגֶּד־לוֹ אֵת דִּבְרֵי אֲדֹנִי:	*And then*, <u>when we went up to your servant my father</u>, we told him the words of my lord (Gen. 44:24).

---

perfect clause (e.g. Gen. 22:1), or a clause introduced by a *qātal*/perfect form (e.g. Gen. 40:1). For a list instances where וַיְהִי + temporal expression is followed by a *qātal*/perfect and not a *wayyiqtol* form, see Harmelink (2004: 339–449). Many of the temporal expressions refer to very specific points in time, e.g. Gen. 8:13; Exod. 40:17; 2 Kgs 25:25.

b	וַיְהִי מִמׇּחֳרָת וַתֹּאמֶר הַבְּכִירָה אֶל־הַצְּעִירָה...	*And then*, <u>the next morning</u>, the firstborn daughter said to the younger... (Gen. 19:34).*
c	וַיְהִי כְּהַזְכִּירוֹ ׀ אֶת־אֲרוֹן הָאֱלֹהִים וַיִּפֹּל מֵעַל־הַכִּסֵּא	*And then*, <u>the moment that he mentioned the ark of God</u>, he (Eli) fell from his seat (1 Sam. 4:18).*

§40.26. טֶרֶם

See §41.8.

§40.27. יֵשׁ

See §43.3.

§40.28. כֹּה

כֹּה is primarily a cataphoric adverb.

כֹּה occurs 577 times in the Hebrew Bible. It is fairly evenly distributed, but has a higher concentration of occurrences in the prophetic books (in particular Jeremiah and Ezekiel). While כֹּה is relatively often preceded by כִּי (66 times) and לָכֵן (67 times), it is less often preceded by וְ (22 times). In only three instances, כֹּה is governed by the preposition עַד.

Near synonyms of כֹּה are כֵּן and כָּכָה. In contrast to the cataphoric character of כֹּה, כֵּן tends to point "backwards" (i.e. it is anaphoric).

The following classes of use can be distinguished:

(1) כֹּה is predominantly a *cataphoric* adverb

כֹּה points to the content of direct speech which immediately follows: *thus* (#a). In a relatively frequently occurring fixed expression, כֹּה refers cataphorically to the content of an oath (#b) (see also §45.2.3).

a	כֹּה אָמַר אֲדֹנָי יְהוִה לֹא תָקוּם וְלֹא תִהְיֶה:	*Thus* says the LORD God, "It shall not stand, and it shall not come to pass" (Isa. 7.7).
b	כֹּה־יַעֲשֶׂה אֱלֹהִים וְכֹה יוֹסִף כִּי־מוֹת תָּמוּת יוֹנָתָן:	Thus and more may God do [lit. *thus* may God do and *thus* may he add], you shall certainly die, Jonathan (1 Sam. 14:44).*

(2) כֹּה sometimes functions as an anaphoric adverb (seldom)
In most cases reference is made to *the mode of a verb of doing* (#a). Only rarely is a verb of saying involved. In one instance a fixed expression is involved (#b).

a	כֹּה עָשׂוּ אֲבֹתֵיכֶם	*Thus* your ancestors did (Num. 32:8).*
b	וַיֹּאמֶר זֶה בְּכֹה וְזֶה אֹמֵר בְּכֹה׃	And the one said *this* and the other says *that* (1 Kgs 22:20).*

(3) כֹּה as adverb of spatial deixis (rare)
כֹּה points to a proximate location *here*, or to a less proximate location *there* (#a). In one instance a fixed expression is involved (#b).

a	וַיֹּאמֶר אֶל־בָּלָק הִתְיַצֵּב כֹּה עַל־עֹלָתֶךָ וְאָנֹכִי אִקָּרֶה כֹּה	And he said to Balak, "Stand *here* by your burnt offering, and I will meet (the LORD) over *there*" (Num. 23:15).*
b	וַיִּפֶן כֹּה וָכֹה	And he looked *this* way and *that* way [lit. he turned *here* and *here*] (Exod. 2:12).*

(4) כֹּה as adverb of temporal deixis
כֹּה points only twice to a proximate point in time ("now"), in each case governed by the preposition עַד (#a and #b).

a	וְהִנֵּה לֹא־שָׁמַעְתָּ עַד־כֹּה׃	And, look, until *now* you did not listen (to me) (Exod. 7:16).
b	וַיְהִי עַד־כֹּה וְעַד־כֹּה וְהַשָּׁמַיִם הִתְקַדְּרוּ עָבִים וְרוּחַ	And then, *in no time* [lit. until *now* and until *now*], the sky grew dark with clouds and wind (1 Kgs 18:45).*

§40.29. כִּי

כִּי is primarily a conjunction. It is used both as a subordinating and coordinating conjunction. It is also used as a modal adverb and discourse marker.

The lexeme occurs about 4,500 times in the Bible.

The following patterns of used can be distinguished.[65]

---

65. Follingstad (2001: 320) is of the opinion that "The core function of כִּי is the same throughout all its contexts. It shifts viewpoint to the propositional contents being structured, 'mentioning' it metarepresentationally as the object of discourse – marking it as a

40.29.1. כִּי + *Main Clause*

(1) Introduces the protasis of a condition

It introduces as subordinating conjunction the protasis of a condition and may then be translated *when* or *if* (#a). In legal texts כִּי often does not stand at the beginning of the clause (#b).

כִּי and אִם are sometimes apparently used as synonyms. However, כִּי normally introduces the *general conditions* whereas אִם introduces *the details* of these general conditions (see also §40.11.(1)(a)). It is rare that the protasis introduced by כִּי follows the apodosis (#c); אִם is more frequently found in that position.

a	וְכִי־יִגַּח שׁוֹר אֶת־אִישׁ אוֹ אֶת־אִשָּׁה וָמֵת סָקוֹל יִסָּקֵל הַשּׁוֹר	And *if* an ox gores a man or a woman to death, the ox must be stoned (Exod. 21:28).*
b	אִשָּׁה כִּי תַזְרִיעַ וְיָלְדָה זָכָר וְטָמְאָה שִׁבְעַת יָמִים	*If* a woman conceives, and bears a male child, then she will be unclean seven days (Lev. 12:2).*
c	וּבִקַּשְׁתֶּם מִשָּׁם אֶת־יְהוָה אֱלֹהֶיךָ וּמָצָאתָ כִּי תִדְרְשֶׁנּוּ בְּכָל־לְבָבְךָ וּבְכָל־נַפְשֶׁךָ:	But from there you will seek the LORD your God and you will find him, *if* you search after him with all your heart and with all your soul (Deut. 4:29).*

In a few instances, the protasis introduced by כִּי has a concessive sense (#d).

d	כִּי יָצֻמוּ אֵינֶנִּי שֹׁמֵעַ אֶל־רִנָּתָם	*Though* they fast, I do not listen to their cry (Jer. 14:12).*

(2) Introduces a temporal clause ("when")

Functions as a subordinating conjunction to introduce a temporal clause that refers to a process occurring simultaneously with the main clause. In such cases כִּי may be translated "when." The distinction between a temporal clause and a conditional clause is sometimes vague. A temporal clause usually refers to a process that has a good chance of being realized.

---

propositional content (thought or utterance) entertained *about* some state of affairs, rather than a description of them." We do not find this highly schematic category very helpful. An exhaustive systematic study of the categories that we are proposing, however, needs still to be done.

כִּי יְבִיאֲךָ֣ יְהוָ֣ה אֱלֹהֶ֔יךָ¹   ¹*When* the LORD your God brings
אֶל־הָאָ֑רֶץ... ²וְהִכִּיתָ֞ם הַחֲרֵ֤ם   you into the land... ²and you defeat
תַּחֲרִים֙ אֹתָ֔ם   them, then you must utterly destroy
them (Deut. 7:1–2).

(3) Introduces a cause

Introduces as subordinating conjunction the cause[66] of a condition or process. The reason that the clause referring to the cause comes first in the sentence is that the speaker/narrator wishes to remove any doubt about the grounds of a situation.

כִּי עָשִׂ֣יתָ זֹּאת֒ אָר֤וּר אַתָּה֙   *Because* you have done this, cursed
are you (Gen. 3:14).

40.29.2. *Main clause* + כִּי

(1) Complementizer

Introduces an object clause after the following verbs: שבע, ראה, שמע, ידע, עוד and אמן, זכר, נגד. It may then be translated "that."

דַּ֕ע כִּי־מ֖וֹת תָּמֽוּת   Know *that* you will surely die
(Gen. 20:7).*

(2) Introduces a clause (sentence or sentences) that provides causal grounds

(a) Provides the reason for a state of affairs

The causal relation is due to laws of nature. כִּי may be translated "for" or "because."

וְלֶ֤חֶם אֵין֙ בְּכָל־הָאָ֔רֶץ   And there was no food in all the
כִּי־כָבֵ֥ד הָרָעָ֖ב מְאֹ֑ד   land, *for* the famine was very severe
(Gen. 47:13).

(b) Provides the grounds for a preceding expression or expressions by marking with כִּי the motivation given by speakers to explain something they have said or asked.

---

66. In some contexts it is not clear whether a temporal or causal relation is involved, e.g. Judg. 2:18 and Ps. 32:3. Sometimes כִּי is preceded by יַ֫עַן (1 Kgs 13:21), תַּ֫חַת (Deut. 4:37) or עֵ֫קֶב (Amos 4:12) to specify that a causal relation is indeed involved.

Speakers base the ground for a directive action (request, command, summons, exhortation, etc.) on what they or someone else is doing, has done or will do (#a), or what the speakers know (#b). Speakers may also construe the grounds of an assertion as due to a condition (#c). Sometimes, an inference made from what they have observed, is provided as grounds and evidence by means of כִּי (#d). כִּי may also introduce a clause that follows a question that asks about the background to (i.e. the grounds of) events referred to by the clause introduced by כִּי (#e).

Instances where speakers provide the grounds of speech acts by means of כִּי sometimes involve clusters of utterances. When כִּי is used in this way, translations sometimes leave כִּי untranslated because it does not entirely make sense on a grammatical level. In (#f) the psalmist gives the reason in v. 6 for what is said in vv. 1–5. In this way the psalmist provides the grounds for the assertions made in vv. 1–5.

In the above-mentioned instances, the English translation value depends on how a speaker assesses the information status of what is presented to addressees. If what is presented refers to new information, "for" or "because" is a typical translation value (#a). In cases where it is clear that speakers consider that the grounds on which they base a speech act are difficult to contest, thus suggesting the force of their conviction, one can translate כִּי "in fact," "the fact of the matter" or "yes" (#b). If speakers believe that their motivation contains information that is generally known, כִּי may be translated "after all" (#c). In secondary communication situations such as the one in which modern interpreters of the Hebrew Bible find themselves, however, it is often difficult to identify such pragmatic information.

a   וַיֹּאמֶר יְהוָה אֶל־מֹשֶׁה   But the LORD said to Moses, "Do not
    אַל־תִּירָא אֹתוֹ כִּי בְיָדְךָ   fear him; *for* into your hand I have
    נָתַתִּי אֹתוֹ   given him" (Num. 21:34).*

b   וְעַתָּה הָשֵׁב אֵשֶׁת־הָאִישׁ   Now then restore the man's wife; *in
    כִּי־נָבִיא הוּא וְיִתְפַּלֵּל   fact*, he is a prophet, and he will pray
    בַּעַדְךָ   for you (Gen. 20:7).*

c   וָאֹמַר אֲהָהּ אֲדֹנָי יְהוִֹה   Then I said, "Oh, LORD God! Look, I
    הִנֵּה לֹא־יָדַעְתִּי דַּבֵּר   do not know how to speak, *after all*,
    כִּי־נַעַר אָנֹכִי   I am only a boy" (Jer. 1:6).*

d   וַיֹּאמֶר֙ נָתָ֣ן אֲדֹנִ֣י הַמֶּ֔לֶךְ   [24]And Nathan said, "My lord the
      אַתָּ֣ה אָמַ֔רְתָּ אֲדֹנִיָּ֖הוּ יִמְלֹ֣ךְ   king, have you said, 'Adonijah
      אַחֲרָ֑י וְה֖וּא יֵשֵׁ֥ב עַל־כִּסְאִֽי: shall reign after me, and he shall sit
      [25]כִּ֣י יָרַ֣ד הַיּ֗וֹם וַ֠יִּזְבַּח שׁ֥וֹר   upon my throne'? [25]*For* he has gone
      וּֽמְרִיא־וְצֹאן֮ לָרֹב֒ וַיִּקְרָא֙   down today, and has sacrificed oxen,
      לְכָל־בְּנֵ֤י הַמֶּ֙לֶךְ֙ וּלְשָׂרֵ֣י   fatlings, and sheep in abundance,
      הַצָּבָ֔א וּלְאֶבְיָתָ֖ר הַכֹּהֵ֑ן   and has invited all the king's sons,
                                          the commanders of the army,
                                          and Abiathar the priest" (1 Kgs
                                          1:24–25).*

e   מֶה־עָשִׂ֣יתָ לָּ֔נוּ   What have you done to us? And how
      וּמֶֽה־חָטָ֤אתִי לָךְ֙ כִּֽי־הֵבֵ֧אתָ   have I sinned against you, *that* you
      עָלַ֛י וְעַל־מַמְלַכְתִּ֖י   have brought a great sin upon me
      חֲטָאָ֣ה גְדֹלָ֑ה   and my kingdom? (Gen. 20:9).*

f   כִּֽי־יוֹדֵ֣עַ יְהוָ֭ה דֶּ֣רֶךְ צַדִּיקִ֑ים   *For* the LORD takes care of [lit.
      וְדֶ֖רֶךְ רְשָׁעִ֣ים תֹּאבֵֽד: knows] the way of the righteous, but
                                          the way of the wicked will perish
                                          (Ps. 1:6).*

(3) Expresses a counter-statement after a negative statement

This use of כִּי (#*a*) is typically translated as "but." כִּי אִם is sometimes used instead of כִּי. With כִּי אִם the speaker makes it very clear that not only is an alternative involved, but that it is the only possible alternative (#*b*).

a   שָׂרַ֣י אִשְׁתְּךָ֔ לֹא־תִקְרָ֥א   As for Sarai your wife, you shall not
      אֶת־שְׁמָ֖הּ שָׂרָ֑י כִּ֥י שָׂרָ֖ה   call her name Sarai, *but* Sarah shall
      שְׁמָֽהּ:   be her name (Gen. 17:15).

b   לֹ֤א יֵאָמֵר֙ ע֣וֹד שִׁמְךָ֔   Your name shall no more be called
      כִּ֖י אִם־יִשְׂרָאֵ֑ל   Jacob, *but* Israel (Gen. 32:29).*

(4) Functions as a modal adverb[67]

כִּי expresses confirmation (primarily in a context of swearing an oath). In these instances it may be translated *indeed*, *truly*, *surely*.

      חֵ֣י פַרְעֹ֔ה כִּ֥י מְרַגְּלִ֖ים אַתֶּֽם   By the life of Pharaoh, you are
                                          certainly spies (Gen. 42:16).*

---

67. This use of כִּי probably goes back to its use in oaths, in which it is postulated that the "I swear" has been elided, as in Gen. 42:16: "*By the life of Pharaoh*, [I swear] *that* you are spies." Without "I swear" the utterance is used to expressed the speakers' conviction about what they regard as true about a situation, "You are *certainly* spies." See §45.2.1.

§40.30. כֵּן

כֵּן is primarily an anaphoric adverb. In a few instances כֵּן is used as an adjective.

כֵּן occurs about 340 times and is fairly evenly distributed throughout the Hebrew Bible. (Instances where כֵּן occurs in the combinations לָכֵן, אַחֲרֵי־כֵן and עַל־כֵּן are not included in these statistics.) כֵּן can be immediately preceded by וּ. In about 40% of its occurrences כֵּן is used in combination with the preposition כְּ. Near synonyms of כֵּן are כָּכָה and כֹּה. In contrast to the anaphoric character of כֵּן, the latter tends to point "forward" (cataphorically).

כֵּן occurs in a number of syntactic configurations.[68] A distinction is made between instances where the lexeme is unambiguously an anaphoric deictic adverb and those few cases where it does not have this deictic connotation.

The following classes of use can be distinguished:

(1) As anaphoric adverb (more than 90% of instances)

כֵּן occurs predominantly in verbal clauses, and in particular verbal clauses with the lexeme עשׂה (#a). כֵּן signals that the behavior of entities is (was/will be/must be) executed in the same mode, or in accordance with, that of a discourse active action, event or state of affairs (#a). In some cases, it is an event that accords with a discourse active one (#b). Often the point of correspondence is overtly marked by means of the preposition כְּ, and the mode involved is the focus of the subsequent assertion (#c).

a	וַיַּעֲשׂוּ־כֵן בְּנֵי יִשְׂרָאֵל	And the sons of Israel did *so* (Gen. 45:21).*
b	וַיְהִי־כֵן	And it happened *accordingly* (2 Kgs 15:12).*
c	כַּאֲשֶׁר צִוָּה יְהוָה אֹתָם כֵּן עָשׂוּ	*According* to what the LORD commanded them, *so* they did (Exod. 7:6).*

(2) As adjective (rare)

כֵּן indicates that the quality of entities accords to a positive norm.

כֻּלָּנוּ בְּנֵי אִישׁ־אֶחָד נָחְנוּ כֵּנִים	All of us are the sons of one man, we are *honest* (Gen. 42:11).*

---

68. Mulder (1981: 207) distinguishes 26 different patterns.

§40.31. לֹא

See §41.9.

§40.32. לְבַד

לְבַד is a combination of the preposition לְ and the noun בַּד. The latter lexeme occurs only twice in the Hebrew Bible and refers to a "portion" (see Exod. 30:34). לְבַד is typically used as a "quantifying" adverb.

לְבַד occurs 156 times and is relative evenly distributed in the Hebrew Bible. The lexeme often takes a pronominal suffix.

The following patterns of use can be distinguished.

(1) לְבַד indicates the singularity of entity *x*, i.e. *x* "alone."

A feature of the construction is that the modified noun phrase is referred back to "superfluously" by means of a pronominal suffix which agrees with it in gender and number. לְבַד with the pronominal suffix typically immediately follows the noun that its modifies (#a-b), but this is not always the case (#c).

a	וְנִגַּשׁ מֹשֶׁה לְבַדּוֹ אֶל־יְהֹוָה	But Moses *alone* is to approach the LORD (Exod. 24:2).*
b	וְאָחִיו מֵת וַיִּוָּתֵר הוּא לְבַדּוֹ לְאִמּוֹ	And his brother is dead; he *alone* is left to his mother (Gen. 44:20).*
c	וַיֹּאמֶר אֵלִיָּהוּ אֶל־הָעָם אֲנִי נוֹתַרְתִּי נָבִיא לַיהוָה לְבַדִּי	Then Elijah said to the people, "I am left as a prophet of the LORD, *I alone*" (1 Kgs 18:22).*

(2) Related to (1), are instances where לְבַד indicates separation from a collection *x*.

In these constructions, the preposition מִן typically governs the collection (#a). לְבַד itself may also be governed by the preposition מִן (#b-d).

a	וַיִּסְעוּ בְנֵי־יִשְׂרָאֵל מֵרַעְמְסֵס סֻכֹּתָה כְּשֵׁשׁ־מֵאוֹת אֶלֶף רַגְלִי הַגְּבָרִים לְבַד מִטָּף:	And the Israelites journeyed from Rameses to Succoth, about six hundred thousand men on foot, *besides* children (Exod. 12:37).*
b	⁶⁴כָּל־הַקָּהָל כְּאֶחָד אַרְבַּע רִבּוֹא אֲלָפַיִם שְׁלֹשׁ־מֵאוֹת שִׁשִּׁים: ⁶⁵מִלְּבַד עַבְדֵיהֶם וְאַמְהֹתֵיהֶם אֵלֶּה	⁶⁴ The whole assembly together was forty-two thousand three hundred sixty, ⁶⁵ *besides* their male and female servants (Ezra 2:64–65).

c אַתָּה הָרְאֵתָ לָדַעַת כִּי יְהוָה
הוּא הָאֱלֹהִים אֵין עוֹד מִלְבַדּוֹ:
You were shown (these things) so that you would acknowledge that the LORD, he is God; there is no other *besides him* (Deut. 4:35).*

d וַיַּקְרֵב אֶת־הַמִּנְחָה וַיְמַלֵּא כַפּוֹ
מִמֶּנָּה וַיַּקְטֵר עַל־הַמִּזְבֵּחַ מִלְבַד
עֹלַת הַבֹּקֶר:
And he presented the grain offering, and, taking a handful of it, he turned it into smoke on the altar, *in addition* to the burnt offering of the morning (Lev. 9:17).*

§40.33. לוּ

לוּ is primarily a subordinating conjunction that introduces the protasis of a hypothetical condition. It developed into an expression of a wish (always לוּ + *qātal*/perfect)

לוּ occurs 23 times and is fairly evenly distributed throughout the Hebrew Bible. The lexeme is also attested a few times with the spelling לוּא. The lexeme occurs predominantly in reported speech.

In more than 60% of its uses, לוּ governs a *qātal*/perfect form. It often governs a nominal clause, but rarely a *yiqtōl*/imperfect form.

The following patterns of use can be distinguished:

(1) Introducing a hypothetical condition
    לוּ relatively frequently introduces the protasis of a hypothetical condition (#a-c). When used with *qātal*/perfect, the hypothetical condition is unreal (#a), but with *yiqtōl*/imperfect it could still be realized (#b).

a לוּ חָכְמוּ יַשְׂכִּילוּ זֹאת
If they had been wise, they would understand this (Deut. 32:29).

b וַיִּרְאוּ אֲחֵי־יוֹסֵף כִּי־מֵת
אֲבִיהֶם וַיֹּאמְרוּ לוּ יִשְׂטְמֵנוּ
יוֹסֵף וְהָשֵׁב יָשִׁיב לָנוּ אֵת
כָּל־הָרָעָה אֲשֶׁר גָּמַלְנוּ אֹתוֹ:
When the brothers of Joseph realized that their father was dead, they said, "*If* Joseph would (still) bear a grudge against us, he will certainly repay us all the harm which we did to him" (Gen. 50:15).*

c לוּ־יֵשׁ נַפְשְׁכֶם תַּחַת נַפְשִׁי
אַחְבִּירָה עֲלֵיכֶם בְּמִלִּים
If you were in my place, I could pile up words against you (Job 16:4).*

(2) Expressing a wish

In a number of instances, mainly when לֹו is followed by a *qātal*/perfect form, a wish that a speaker typically does not expect to be fulfilled, is expressed.

לוּ־מַ֫תְנוּ בְּאֶ֫רֶץ מִצְרַ֫יִם אֹו   If only we *had died* in the land of
בַּמִּדְבָּ֥ר הַזֶּ֖ה לוּ־מָ֫תְנוּ׃   Egypt or if only *we had died* in this

wilderness (Num. 14:2).*

§40.34. לוּלֵי

See §41.10.

§40.35. לָכֵן

לָכֵן is a conjunctive adverb that is predominantly used as a discourse marker.

לָכֵן is a combination of the preposition לְ and the anaphoric deictic כֵּ (see §40.30). The 200 instances of לָכֵן in the Hebrew Bible are not very evenly distributed, viz. it occurs predominantly in the prophetic books (166 times). Furthermore, among the prophetic books it occurs 63 times in Ezekiel, 55 times in Jeremiah and 27 times in Isaiah. It occurs only once in later texts, viz. 1 Chron. 18:18 (parallel to 1 Kgs 22:19). In the parallel to 1 Kgs 22:20, viz. 2 Chron. 34:18, לָכֵן is omitted. לָכֵן occurs, with one exception (1 Sam. 27:6) exclusively in reported speech.

לָכֵן must be understood from the perspective its components provide, viz. "as far as" + "these *x*." In other words, it has the deictic value of "under these circumstances" (Jenni 2000: 283).[69]

The following patterns of use can be distinguished:

(1) לָכֵן pointing to the grounds of prophetic announcements

Announcements introduced by לָכֵן are made only after a speaker has explicitly established a firm common ground between himself and his addressee. A range of linguistically marked constructions are used, e.g. rhetorical questions (#*a*) and infinitive constructions (#*b*). A stated ground is also often explicitly marked by means of יַ֫עַן (#*c*). The firmly established grounds are sometimes profiled in more detail in the utterance(s) following לָכֵן (#*d*).

---

69. For a detailed analysis of לָכֵן, see Van der Merwe (2014).

The announcements themselves may be prompted by directives to listen, to declare and/or authenticators (#e). The announcements themselves are often pointed out by means of הִנֵּה and refer vividly to what will or is about to happen – or not (#e).

The confrontational sense of לָכֵן is sometimes exploited by a staggering of the discourse marker to make highly emotional appeals (#e).

a	¹³וַיֹּאמֶר שִׁמְעוּ־נָא בֵּית דָּוִד הַמְעַט מִכֶּם הַלְאוֹת אֲנָשִׁים כִּי תַלְאוּ גַּם אֶת־אֱלֹהָי: ¹⁴לָכֵן יִתֵּן אֲדֹנָי הוּא לָכֶם אוֹת הִנֵּה הָעַלְמָה הָרָה וְיֹלֶדֶת בֵּן וְקָרָאת שְׁמוֹ עִמָּנוּ אֵל:	¹³ Then he said: "Hear then, O house of David! <u>Is it too little for you to weary mortals, that you weary my God also?</u> ¹⁴ *Therefore* the Lord himself will give you a sign. Look, the young woman is with child and shall bear a son, and you shall name him Immanuel (Isa. 7:13–14).*
b	הֹבִשׁוּ כִּי תוֹעֵבָה עָשׂוּ גַּם־בּוֹשׁ לֹא־יֵבֹשׁוּ וְהִכָּלֵם לֹא יָדָעוּ לָכֵן יִפְּלוּ בַנֹּפְלִים בְּעֵת פְּקֻדָּתָם יִכָּשְׁלוּ אָמַר יְהוָה: ס	"<u>They acted shamefully, yes they committed abomination; what is worse, they were not at all ashamed, they did not know how to blush.</u> *Therefore* they shall fall among those who fall; at the time when I punish them, they shall be overthrown," says the LORD (Jer. 8:12).*
c	וַיֹּאמֶר יְהוָה אֶל־מֹשֶׁה וְאֶל־אַהֲרֹן יַעַן לֹא־הֶאֱמַנְתֶּם בִּי לְהַקְדִּישֵׁנִי לְעֵינֵי בְּנֵי יִשְׂרָאֵל לָכֵן לֹא תָבִיאוּ אֶת־הַקָּהָל הַזֶּה אֶל־הָאָרֶץ אֲשֶׁר־נָתַתִּי לָהֶם:	But the LORD said to Moses and Aaron, "<u>Because you did not trust in me, to acknowledge my holiness before [lit. to treat me as holy before the eyes of] of the Israelites, *therefore* you will not bring this assembly into</u> the land that I have given them" (Num. 20:12).*
d	¹⁰שָׂנְאוּ בַשַּׁעַר מוֹכִיחַ וְדֹבֵר תָּמִים יְתָעֵבוּ: ¹¹לָכֵן יַעַן בּוֹשַׁסְכֶם עַל־דָּל וּמַשְׂאַת־בַּר תִּקְחוּ מִמֶּנּוּ בָּתֵּי גָזִית בְּנִיתֶם וְלֹא־תֵשְׁבוּ בָם	¹⁰They hate the one who reproves in the gate, and they detest the one who speaks the truth. ¹¹*Therefore* <u>because you trample on the poor and take from them levies of grain, you have built houses of hewn stone, but you shall not live in them</u> (Amos 5:10–11).*

e

לָכֵן כֹּה־אָמַר יְהוָה²¹
עַל־אַנְשֵׁי עֲנָתוֹת הַמְבַקְשִׁים
אֶת־נַפְשְׁךָ לֵאמֹר לֹא תִנָּבֵא
בְּשֵׁם יְהוָה וְלֹא תָמוּת בְּיָדֵנוּ:
לָכֵן כֹּה אָמַר יְהוָה צְבָאוֹת²²
הִנְנִי פֹקֵד עֲלֵיהֶם הַבַּחוּרִים
יָמֻתוּ בַחֶרֶב בְּנֵיהֶם וּבְנוֹתֵיהֶם
יָמֻתוּ בָּרָעָב:

²¹*Therefore* thus says the LORD concerning the people of Anathoth, who seek your life, and say, "You shall not prophesy in the name of the LORD, or you will die by our hand" – ²² *therefore* thus says the LORD of hosts: I am going to punish them; the young men shall die by the sword; their sons and their daughters shall die by famine (Jer. 11:21–22).

The strong argumentative conclusive sense of לָכֵן neutralizes the adversative relationship that could be postulated between the grounds and consequences of the otherwise typical announcement that we find in (#f).

f

וּפָקַדְתִּי עָלֶיהָ אֶת־יְמֵי¹⁵
הַבְּעָלִים אֲשֶׁר תַּקְטִיר
לָהֶם וַתַּעַד נִזְמָהּ וְחֶלְיָתָהּ
וַתֵּלֶךְ אַחֲרֵי מְאַהֲבֶיהָ וְאֹתִי
שָׁכְחָה נְאֻם־יְהוָה: פ
לָכֵן הִנֵּה אָנֹכִי מְפַתֶּיהָ¹⁶
וְהֹלַכְתִּיהָ הַמִּדְבָּר וְדִבַּרְתִּי
עַל־לִבָּהּ:

¹⁵"And I will punish her for the festival days of the Baals, when she burned incense to them and decked herself with her ring and jewelry, and went after her lovers, and forgot me," declares the LORD. ¹⁶"*Therefore*, look I am now going to allure her, and bring her into the wilderness, and speak tenderly to her" (Hos. 2:14–15).*

(2) לָכֵן in argumentative dialogues

לָכֵן occurs only in a few instances in dialogues, predominantly in non-prophetic contexts. Typically, a speaker *x* makes a strongly asserted statement (#a-b). Speaker *y* then acknowledges the validity of the assertion by means of לָכֵן, "that being so, granted, all right" and present an answer to counter (#a) or confirm (#b) what has been asserted.

a

וַתֹּאמֶר לָהּ הַמְעַט קַחְתֵּךְ
אֶת־אִישִׁי וְלָקַחַת גַּם
אֶת־דּוּדָאֵי בְּנִי וַתֹּאמֶר
רָחֵל לָכֵן יִשְׁכַּב עִמָּךְ
הַלַּיְלָה תַּחַת דּוּדָאֵי
בְנֵךְ:

But she said to her, "Wasn't it enough that you took away my husband? Will you take also my son's mandrakes?" Then Rachel responded, "*Very well*, he can sleep with you tonight in return for your son's mandrakes" (Gen. 30:15).*

b

וַיֹּאמֶר אָכִישׁ אֶל־דָּוִד יָדֹעַ [1]
תֵּדַע כִּי אִתִּי תֵּצֵא בַמַּחֲנֶה
אַתָּה וַאֲנָשֶׁיךָ: [2]וַיֹּאמֶר דָּוִד
אֶל־אָכִישׁ לָכֵן אַתָּה תֵדַע
אֵת אֲשֶׁר־יַעֲשֶׂה עַבְדֶּךָ
וַיֹּאמֶר אָכִישׁ אֶל־דָּוִד
לָכֵן שֹׁמֵר לְרֹאשִׁי
אֲשִׂימְךָ כָּל־הַיָּמִים:

[1]And Achish said to David, "You know very well that you and your men are to go out with me in the army." [2] David said to Achish, "*Very well*, then you will see [lit. know] for yourself what your servant can do." Achish said to David, "*Very well*, I will make you my bodyguard for life" (1 Sam. 28:1–2).*

(3) לָכֵן in "fact reporting" contexts

In a few instances, typically introducing a clause headed by *qātal*/perfect, both in the first person (*#a*) and the third person (*#b*), לָכֵן is used to explain the grounds of factual situations. In this use of לָכֵן, it is a near synonym of עַל־כֵּן (§40.38).

a

וּמִצְרַיִם הֶבֶל וָרִיק יַעְזֹרוּ
לָכֵן קָרָאתִי לָזֹאת רַהַב
הֵם שָׁבֶת:

And Egypt's help is worthless and empty, *therefore* I have called her, "Rahab who sits still" (Isa. 30:7).*

b

וַיִּתֶּן־לוֹ אָכִישׁ בַּיּוֹם הַהוּא
אֶת־צִקְלָג לָכֵן הָיְתָה צִקְלַג
לְמַלְכֵי יְהוּדָה עַד הַיּוֹם
הַזֶּה:

So Achish gave him Ziklag that day; *therefore* Ziklag has belonged to the kings of Judah to this day (1 Sam. 27:6).*

§40.36. לְמַעַן [70]

לְמַעַן is a subordinating conjunction that is also used secondarily as a preposition.

The noun מַעַן is not attested in the Hebrew Bible, but appears to be related to the verbal root ענה, "to be concerned about." For the noun the meaning "concerning" is postulated (Jenni 2000: 289). In the combination מַעַן + לְ "as far as" + "concerning" results in a pleonastic emphasis of the notion "for the sake of" according to Jenni (2000: 289).

The lexeme לְמַעַן occurs 270 times. It is evenly distributed throughout the Bible, but is most prevalent in the books of Deuteronomy, 1 Kings, Isaiah, Ezekiel and the Psalms.

---

70. This section benefitted much from Yoo (2013).

In more than 50% of its occurrences, לְמַעַן introduces a clause with *yiqtōl/* imperfect.[71] In the rest of the instances of לְמַעַן, it heads either an infinitive clause[72] or a noun phrase. The clause or noun phrase with לְמַעַן typically follows the matrix clause. However, it may be fronted to mark the content of the לְמַעַן construction as the focus of an utterance.

When לְמַעַן is followed by an infinitive or *yiqtōl/*imperfect, the matrix clauses typically contain atelic verbs – and not concrete telic verbs that refer to a change of place and that serve as preparation for an intentional action. In the latter instances, the preferred construction is לְ plus infinitive (Jenni 2000: 291). See §39.11.(3)(b)(i).

The following categories of use can be distinguished:

(1) Purpose (very frequent)

(a) Positive purpose

Typically the agent of the verb of the events *x* referred to in a matrix clause performs an action with the intention to bring about an event *y* introduced by לְמַעַן. The events involved may refer to what will happen (#*a*), happened (#*b*) or should happen (#*c*). The purpose of the event in the matrix clause may also be of an epistemic nature, e.g. "so that *x* may know" (#*d-e*). Often a speaker (#*f-g*), and, in a few instances, a narrator (#*h*), provides the purpose of speech act(s) referred to in the matrix clause(s). A significant feature of the latter category is that the matrix often comprises more than one sentence (#*g-h*).

a	וּמָל יְהוָה אֱלֹהֶיךָ אֶת־לְבָבְךָ וְאֶת־לְבַב זַרְעֶךָ לְאַהֲבָה אֶת־יהוה אֱלֹהֶיךָ בְּכָל־לְבָבְךָ וּבְכָל־נַפְשְׁךָ לְמַעַן חַיֶּיךָ:	And the Lord your God will circumcise your heart and the heart of your descendants, so that you will love the Lord your God with all your heart and with all your soul, *in order that* you may live [lit. *for the sake of* your life] (Deut. 30:6).*
b	כִּי־הִקְשָׁה יְהוָה אֱלֹהֶיךָ אֶת־רוּחוֹ וְאִמֵּץ אֶת־לְבָבוֹ לְמַעַן תִּתּוֹ בְיָדְךָ כַּיּוֹם הַזֶּה	For the Lord your God had hardened his spirit and made his heart defiant *in order to* hand him over to you, as it is this day (Deut. 2:30).*

---

71. Typically the subject of the לְמַעַן + *yiqtōl/*imperfect clause is not the same as that of the matrix clause. Furthermore, this construction occurs predominantly in discourse (see Yoo 2013: 164).

72. This construction occurs predominantly in narration (see Yoo 2013: 164.)

c וּבָחַרְתָּ֙ בַּֽחַיִּ֔ים לְמַ֥עַן תִּֽחְיֶ֖ה אַתָּ֥ה וְזַרְעֶֽךָ׃

So choose life *so that* you may live, you and your descendants (Deut. 30:19).*

d וְהִפְלֵיתִ֣י בַיּ֣וֹם הַה֗וּא אֶת־אֶ֤רֶץ גֹּ֙שֶׁן֙ אֲשֶׁ֣ר עַמִּ֣י עֹמֵ֣ד עָלֶ֔יהָ לְבִלְתִּ֥י הֱיֽוֹת־שָׁ֖ם עָרֹ֑ב לְמַ֣עַן תֵּדַ֔ע כִּ֛י אֲנִ֥י יְהוָ֖ה בְּקֶ֥רֶב הָאָֽרֶץ׃

But I will set apart on that day the land of Goshen, where my people live, so that no swarms of flies will be there, *that* you may know that I, the LORD, am in the midst of this land (Exod. 8:18).*

e בְּאַחֲרִ֣ית הַיָּמִ֣ים תִּֽהְיֶ֔ה וַהֲבִאוֹתִ֖יךָ עַל־אַרְצִ֑י לְמַ֜עַן דַּ֤עַת הַגּוֹיִם֙ אֹתִ֔י

In the latter days it will happen: I will bring you against my land, *so that* the nations may know me (Ezek. 38:16).*

f וַיֹּ֗אמֶר הַגִּ֤שָׁה לִּי֙ וְאֹ֣כְלָ֔ה מִצֵּ֥יד בְּנִ֖י לְמַ֥עַן תְּבָרֶכְךָ֖ נַפְשִׁ֑י

Then he said, "Serve [lit. bring] me and let me eat some of the game of my son, *so that* I [lit. my soul] may bless you" (Gen. 27:25).*

g תָּֽבוֹא־נָ֞א תָּמָ֣ר אֲחוֹתִ֗י וּתְבָרֵ֣נִי לֶ֔חֶם וְעָשְׂתָ֤ה לְעֵינַי֙ אֶת־הַבִּרְיָ֔ה לְמַ֗עַן אֲשֶׁ֤ר אֶרְאֶה֙ וְאָכַלְתִּ֖י מִיָּדָֽהּ

Please let Tamar my sister come and give me food to eat. Let her prepare the food in my sight, *so that* I may see it and eat it from her hand (2 Sam. 13:5).*

h וַיֹּ֣אמֶר אֲלֵהֶ֣ם ׀ רְאוּבֵ֗ן אַל־תִּשְׁפְּכוּ־דָם֙ הַשְׁלִ֣יכוּ אֹת֗וֹ אֶל־הַבּ֤וֹר הַזֶּה֙ אֲשֶׁ֣ר בַּמִּדְבָּ֔ר וְיָ֖ד אַל־תִּשְׁלְחוּ־ב֑וֹ לְמַ֗עַן הַצִּ֤יל אֹתוֹ֙ מִיָּדָ֔ם לַהֲשִׁיב֖וֹ אֶל־אָבִֽיו׃

And Reuben said to them, "Shed no blood; throw him into this pit in the wilderness, but lay no hand on him" – *that* he might rescue him out of their hand to restore him to his father (Gen. 37:22).*

Often, a noun phrase is used to refer (metonymically) to the purpose of the action referred to in the matrix clause that benefits the referent of the noun phrase. This construction typically can be translated as "for the sake of" (#i).

i וְגַנּוֹתִ֛י עַל־הָעִ֥יר הַזֹּ֖את לְמַ֣עֲנִ֔י וּלְמַ֖עַן דָּוִ֥ד עַבְדִּֽי׃

And I will shield this city *for my sake* and *for the sake of* David my servant (2 Kgs 20:6).*

(b) Negative purpose (seldom)

In negative purpose constructions, the matrix clause(s) refers to precautionary situations (#*a*) or actions (or #*b*) in order to prevent undesirable events from happening.

a	יְהִי־לִבִּי תָמִים בְּחֻקֶּיךָ לְמַעַן לֹא אֵבוֹשׁ:	Let my heart be blameless in your statutes, *so that* I may *not* be put to shame (Ps. 119:80).*
b	¹⁷כִּי־הַחֲרֵם תַּחֲרִימֵם... כַּאֲשֶׁר צִוְּךָ יְהוָה אֱלֹהֶיךָ: ¹⁸לְמַעַן אֲשֶׁר לֹא־יְלַמְּדוּ אֶתְכֶם לַעֲשׂוֹת כְּכֹל תּוֹעֲבֹתָם אֲשֶׁר עָשׂוּ לֵאלֹהֵיהֶם וַחֲטָאתֶם לַיהוָה אֱלֹהֵיכֶם: ס	¹⁷But you must completely annihilate them...just as the LORD your God has commanded, ¹⁸*so that* they may *not* teach you to do all the abhorrent things that they do for their gods, and you thus sin against the LORD your God (Deut. 20:17–18).*

(2) Result (seldom)

A distinctive feature of this category is that in the matrix, which typically comprises more than one clause, no intentional action is involved. And, in the clauses introduced by לְמַעַן, reference is to an achieved result. In about two-thirds of the instances, לְמַעַן governs an infinitive (#*a*), and in the other third, a *yiqtōl*/imperfect (#*b*). In only one case, a noun phrase is governed by לְמַעַן (#*c*).

a	תַּחַת ׀ אֲשֶׁר עֲזָבוּנִי וַיְקַטְּרוּ לֵאלֹהִים אֲחֵרִים לְמַעַן הַכְעִיסֵנִי בְּכֹל מַעֲשֵׂה יְדֵיהֶם	Because they have abandoned me and burned incense to other gods, *so that* they have provoked me to anger with all the work of their hands (2 Kgs 22:17).*
b	לְךָ לְבַדְּךָ ׀ חָטָאתִי וְהָרַע בְּעֵינֶיךָ עָשִׂיתִי לְמַעַן תִּצְדַּק בְּדָבְרֶךָ תִּזְכֶּה בְשָׁפְטֶךָ	Against you, you alone, have I sinned, and done what is evil in your eyes, *so that* you are justified in your sentence and blameless when you pass judgment (Ps. 51:6).*
c	הַאֹתִי הֵם מַכְעִסִים נְאֻם־יְהוָה הֲלוֹא אֹתָם לְמַעַן בֹּשֶׁת פְּנֵיהֶם: ס	"Is it I whom they provoke?" declares the LORD. "Is it not themselves, *to* their own disgrace [lit. the shame of their faces]?" (Jer. 7:19).*

(3) Reason (sometimes)

A significant feature of this category, is that the construction noun phrase + לְמַעַן is predominantly used. Furthermore, a speaker or narrator provides (metonymically) the reason for the events referred to in the matrix clause. The matrix may refer to events that happened in the real world (#*a*) or to a directive speech act (#*b*).

a	וַיִּתְעַבֵּר יְהוָה בִּי לְמַעַנְכֶם וְלֹא שָׁמַע אֵלָי	But the LORD was angry with me *because of* you and would not listen to me (Deut. 3:26).*
b	שׁוּבָה יְהוָה חַלְּצָה נַפְשִׁי הוֹשִׁיעֵנִי לְמַעַן חַסְדֶּךָ:	Turn, O LORD, and deliver me; save me *because of* your unfailing love (Ps. 6:5).*

§40.37. עוֹד

עוֹד is primarily an ordinary adverb. However, it may take a pronominal suffix. It may also be governed by a preposition. In a few instances עוֹד is used as an conjunctive adverb. In the latter cases, עוֹד is a near synonym of גַּם.

The lexeme עוֹד occurs about 490 times. It is relatively evenly distributed throughout the Hebrew Bible

Pronominal suffixes are attached to עוֹד in 39 instances. These suffixes are as a rule the subject of a clause. The following patterns are attested:

Person	Singular		Plural	
1 c.	עוֹדֶנִּי/עוֹדִי	still, I	עוֹדֵינוּ	still, us
2 m.	עוֹדְךָ	still, you		
2 f.	עוֹדֵךְ	still, you		
3 m.	עוֹדֶנּוּ	still, he	עוֹדָם	still, them
3 f.	עוֹדָהּ/עוֹדֶנָּה	still, she		

In the majority of instances, עוֹד follows the finite verbal form that it modifies (#*a-b*). It is also used often in, or at the head of, a temporal clause (#*c-e*) or phrase (#*f*) – often governed by the preposition בְּ (#*c-d* and #*f*).

a	וַיֹּאמֶר עוֹד אֱלֹהִים אֶל־מֹשֶׁה...	And God *also* said to Moses... (Exod. 3:15).*
b	וַיֵּרָא אֱלֹהִים אֶל־יַעֲקֹב עוֹד	And God *again* appeared to Jacob (Gen. 35:9).*

c	וַיֹּאמֶר בְּעוֹד הַיֶּלֶד חַי צַמְתִּי וָאֶבְכֶּה	And he answered, "While the child was *still* alive, I fasted and cried" (2 Sam. 12:22).*
d	וַיְשַׁלְּחֵם מֵעַל יִצְחָק בְּנוֹ בְּעוֹדֶנּוּ חַי	And he sent them away from his son Isaac while he was *still* alive (Gen. 25:6).*
e	עוֹדֶנּוּ מְדַבֵּר עִמָּם וְרָחֵל ׀ בָּאָה...	While he was *still* speaking with them, Rachel arrived... (Gen. 29:9).*
f	בְּעוֹד ׀ שְׁלֹשֶׁת יָמִים יִשָּׂא פַרְעֹה אֶת־רֹאשֶׁךָ	*Within* three days Pharaoh will lift up your head (Gen. 40:13).*

The following classes of use can be distinguished:

(1) Repetition of an event (very frequent)

עוֹד is used to indicate that an event was repeated, i.e. happened *again*, (#a) or was not repeated (#b). Often עוֹד appears to be semantically redundant (#c). The most frequent use of עוֹד in the Hebrew Bible is in utterances about future situations (e.g. in announcements, promises, appeals) to indicate what will or should *not happen again* or *any longer* (#d). Strictly speaking a state will prevail during which an action will not be repeated – hence the translation value "any longer."

a	וַתַּהַר עוֹד וַתֵּלֶד בַּת	And she conceived *again* and gave birth to a daughter (Hos. 1:6).*
b	וְלֹא־קָם נָבִיא עוֹד בְּיִשְׂרָאֵל כְּמֹשֶׁה	And not *again* there has risen a prophet in Israel like Moses (Deut. 34:10).*
c	וַיֹּסֶף עוֹד לְדַבֵּר אֵלָיו...	And he *again* spoke to him [lit. he continued to speak *again* to him...] (Gen. 18:29).*
d	לֹא־יֹאמְרוּ עוֹד אֲרוֹן בְּרִית־יְהֹוָה	They will *no longer* say, "The ark of the covenant of the LORD" (Jer. 3:16).*

(2) Endurance of a state of affairs (seldom)

Semantically closely related to (1) are instances where עוֹד is used to assert (#a-b) or question (#c) the continuation or endurance of an identifiable or discourse active state of affairs. In a number of instances, the endurance of an event referred to in a temporal frame is involved (#d).

a	עוֹדֶנּוּ חָי	He is *still* alive (Gen. 43:28).
b	עוֹד הָעָם מְזַבְּחִים וּמְקַטְּרִים בַּבָּמוֹת:	The people were *still* sacrificing and offering incense on the high places (1 Kgs 22:44).*
c	הַעוֹדֶנּוּ חָי	Is he still alive? (Gen. 43:27).*
d	עוֹדֶנּוּ מְדַבֵּר עִמָּם וְרָחֵל ׀ בָּאָה...	While he was *still* speaking with them, Rachel arrived... (Gen. 29:9).*

(3) Extension of the number of a collection (seldom)

Related to (2) are instances where עוֹד signals that an entity is the extension of a discourse active collection (#*a*). In a few cases, עוֹד is used to question the completeness of a discourse active collection (#*b*). The constructions אֵין עוֹד and אֶפֶס אֵין confirm the non-existence of any extension to a collection of "one."

a	וַיֹּאמֶר שְׁמוּאֵל אֶל־יִשַׁי הֲתַמּוּ הַנְּעָרִים וַיֹּאמֶר עוֹד שָׁאַר הַקָּטָן...	Then Samuel asked Jesse, "Are those all the young men?" He replied, "The youngest *still* remains..." (1 Sam. 16:11).*
b	וַיֹּאמְרוּ הָאֲנָשִׁים אֶל־לוֹט עֹד מִי־לְךָ פֹה	And the two men asked Lot, "Have you *still* anyone else here?" (Gen. 19:12).*
c	כִּי יְהוָה הוּא הָאֱלֹהִים אֵין עוֹד:	that the LORD, he is God, there is no *other* (1 Kgs 8:60).
d	וַתֹּאמְרִי בְלִבֵּךְ אֲנִי וְאַפְסִי עוֹד:	And you said in your heart, "I am, and besides me, there is no *other*" (Isa. 47:10).*

(4) Extension of the quantity of a state (very rare)

Related to (2) and (3) are instances where עוֹד signals the extension of the degree of a discourse active state.

	וַיּוֹסִפוּ עוֹד שְׂנֹא אֹתוֹ:	And they hated him *even more* (Gen. 37:5).*

(5) Duration to be quantified (rare)

Also related to (2) and (3) are instances where the duration of a state is quantified. Often עוֹד is governed by the preposition בְּ (#*a*). In a few cases, the preposition is absent, and the temporal adjunct is syndetically connected with its matrix clause (#b). A fixed expression, עוֹד מְעַט, is also attested (#c).

a	בְּעוֹד ׀ שְׁלֹשֶׁת יָמִים יִשָּׂא פַּרְעֹה אֶת־רֹאשֶׁךָ	*Within* three days Pharaoh will lift up your head (Gen. 40:13).*
b	וַיֹּאמַר עוֹד אַרְבָּעִים יוֹם וְנִינְוֵה נֶהְפָּכֶת:	And he said, "*Another* forty days, and Nineveh will be destroyed" (Jon. 3:4).*
c	וְעוֹד מְעַט וְאֵין רָשָׁע	And *another* little while [lit. *yet* a little while], and the wicked will be no more (Ps. 37:10).*

(6) An unspecified long duration (very rare)

a	אָשִׁירָה לַיהוָה בְּחַיָּי אֲזַמְּרָה לֵאלֹהַי בְּעוֹדִי:	I will sing to the LORD as I live, I will sing praise to God *as long as I exist* [lit. *at my duration*] (Ps. 104:33).*
b	הֲלוֹא אָנֹכִי אֲתֹנְךָ אֲשֶׁר־רָכַבְתָּ עָלַי מֵעוֹדְךָ עַד־הַיּוֹם הַזֶּה	Am I not your jenny [lit. she-ass] that you have ridden *all your life* to this day? (Num. 22:30).*

(7) Addition (very rare)

עוֹד indicates that the information referred to in a sentence *y* must be added to that of a sentence *x* in the immediately preceding context as far as an argument *z* is concerned. עוֹד functions as a near synonym of גַּם (as a conjunctive adverb). See §40.20.(1)(b).

עוֹד זֹאת עָשׂוּ לִי	*Moreover*, this they have done to me (Ezek. 23:38).*

§40.38. עַל־כֵּן

עַל־כֵּן is a conjunctive adverb that is often used as a discourse marker.

עַל־כֵּן is a combination of the preposition עַל and the anaphoric deictic כֵּן (see §40.30). The phrase עַל־כֵּן occurs 155 times. It is relatively evenly distributed throughout the Hebrew Bible, used in both narrative and discourse. Unlike לָכֵן, it does not occur predominantly in prophetic announcements.

עַל־כֵּן must be understood from the perspective its components provide, viz. "over" or "because of" + "these *x*." In other words, it has the deictic value of "because of these."

The lexeme typically governs either *qātal*/perfect or *yiqtōl*/imperfect clauses. However, these clauses are very often connected to a cluster of preceding utterances. In these utterances reference is made to the grounds of the factual outcome (or result) that עַל־כֵּן introduces.

The following patterns of use can be distinguished:

(1) עַל־כֵּן points to the grounds of a factual statement

After stating the grounds in one (#*a*) or (typically) more utterances (#*b*), the factual outcome thereof is introduced by עַל־כֵּן. In this way an explanation of the name of a place (#*a*) or a custom (#*b*) are provided. It may also be used to explain the grounds of why something happened (#*c*) or will happen (#*d*).[73]

a	וְיַעֲקֹב נָסַע סֻכֹּתָה וַיִּבֶן לוֹ בָּיִת וּלְמִקְנֵהוּ עָשָׂה סֻכֹּת עַל־כֵּן קָרָא שֵׁם־הַמָּקוֹם סֻכּוֹת: ס	But Jacob journeyed to Succoth, and built himself a house, and made booths for his livestock; *therefore* the place is called Succoth (Gen. 33:17).*
b	⁴וַיַּשְׁכִּמוּ בַבֹּקֶר מִמָּחֳרָת וְהִנֵּה דָגוֹן נֹפֵל לְפָנָיו אַרְצָה לִפְנֵי אֲרוֹן יְהוָה וְרֹאשׁ דָּגוֹן וּשְׁתֵּי כַּפּוֹת יָדָיו כְּרֻתוֹת אֶל־הַמִּפְתָּן רַק דָּגוֹן נִשְׁאַר עָלָיו: ⁵עַל־כֵּן לֹא־יִדְרְכוּ כֹהֲנֵי דָגוֹן וְכָל־הַבָּאִים בֵּית־דָּגוֹן עַל־מִפְתַּן דָּגוֹן בְּאַשְׁדּוֹד עַד הַיּוֹם הַזֶּה: ס	⁴But when they rose early on the next morning, to their surprise [lit. and look] Dagon had fallen on his face to the ground before the ark of the LORD, and the head of Dagon and both his hands were lying cut off upon the threshold; only the trunk of Dagon was left to him. ⁵*That is why* the priests of Dagon and all who enter the house of Dagon do not step on the threshold of Dagon in Ashdod to this day (1 Sam. 5:4–5).*
c	כַּאֲשֶׁר לֹא־שָׁמַעְתָּ בְּקוֹל יְהוָה וְלֹא־עָשִׂיתָ חֲרוֹן־אַפּוֹ בַּעֲמָלֵק עַל־כֵּן הַדָּבָר הַזֶּה עָשָׂה־לְךָ יְהוָה הַיּוֹם הַזֶּה:	Because you did not listen to the voice of the LORD, and did not carry out his fierce wrath against Amalek, *therefore* the LORD has done this thing to you today (1 Sam. 28:18).*

---

73. Instances where עַל־כֵּן introduces events that are projected in the future are relatively few.

d	לֹא־כֵן הָרְשָׁעִים כִּי[4]	[4] No so are the wicked, but they
	אִם־כַּמֹּץ אֲשֶׁר־תִּדְּפֶנּוּ רוּחַ׃	are like chaff that the wind drives
	עַל־כֵּן ׀ לֹא־יָקֻמוּ רְשָׁעִים[5]	away. [5]*Therefore* the wicked will
	בַּמִּשְׁפָּט	not stand in the judgment (Ps.
		1:4–5).*

(2) A specialized use of (1) in the construction כִּי־עַל־כֵּן

This construction is used by speakers to convince their addressees that the grounds that they construe for a factual situation is correct and that they should maintain the same point of view (Jenni 2005c: 129).

וַיַּכֵּר יְהוּדָה וַיֹּאמֶר צָדְקָה מִמֶּנִּי	Then Judah acknowledged them
כִּי־עַל־כֵּן לֹא־נְתַתִּיהָ לְשֵׁלָה בְנִי	and said, "She is more in the right
וְלֹא־יָסַף עוֹד לְדַעְתָּהּ	than I, *after all*, I did not give her
	to Shelah, my son." And he did not
	lie with her again (Gen. 38.26).*

§40.39. וְעַתָּה and עַתָּה

עַתָּה is primarily an adverb that refers to a point in time concurrent with the speech time of an utterance, i.e. "now." In the Hebrew Bible, וְעַתָּה = עַתָּה + וְ is predominantly a conjunctive adverb functioning as a discourse marker ("so now," "so then," "therefore").

עַתָּה occurs 433 times in the Hebrew Bible, more in the narrative sections than in poetic ones, but nearly always in reported speech. The prepositions מִן and עַד may govern עַתָּה – in the format מֵעַתָּה (13 times) and עַד־עַתָּה (8 times), respectively.

The following patterns of use can be distinguished:[74]

(1) עַתָּה and וְעַתָּה as discourse markers (very frequent)

After a short (#a-b) or long exposition (#c-d) of a situation *x*, וְעַתָּה (or sometimes עַתָּה) is used to point to the implications of *x* for the here and now of a speaker or addressee. It is not uncommon for the exposition to be marked by means of הֵן or הִנֵּה (#a-b).

---

74. Instances like 1 Sam. 25:7 are hard to categorize. See also Garr (forthcoming).

Typically the grounds of an action to be taken are introduced (#*a-d*). Sometimes it is the grounds of a question (#*e*) or an assertion (#*f*).

a	⁴²וַתֹּאמֶר אֵלָיו הִנֵּה עֵשָׂו אָחִיךָ מִתְנַחֵם לְךָ לְהָרְגֶךָ: ⁴³וְעַתָּה בְנִי שְׁמַע בְּקֹלִי	⁴²And she said to him, "Look, Esau your brother is plotting to get revenge [against you] by killing you. ⁴³*So now*, my son, listen to my voice" (Gen. 27:42–43).*
b	וַיֹּאמְרוּ אֵלָיו הִנֵּה אַתָּה זָקַנְתָּ וּבָנֶיךָ לֹא הָלְכוּ בִּדְרָכֶיךָ עַתָּה שִׂימָה־לָּנוּ מֶלֶךְ לְשָׁפְטֵנוּ כְּכָל־הַגּוֹיִם:	And they said to him, "Look you are old and your sons do not follow your ways, *so* appoint *now* for us a king to govern us like all the nations" (1 Sam. 8:5).*
c	⁶וַיֹּאמֶר אֵלָיו הָאֱלֹהִים בַּחֲלֹם גַּם אָנֹכִי יָדַעְתִּי כִּי בְתָם־לְבָבְךָ עָשִׂיתָ זֹּאת וָאֶחְשֹׂךְ גַּם־אָנֹכִי אוֹתְךָ מֵחֲטוֹ־לִי...⁷וְעַתָּה הָשֵׁב אֵשֶׁת־הָאִישׁ	⁶Then God said to him in the dream, "I too know that you have done this in the integrity of your heart, and it was also I who kept you from sinning against me... ⁷*Therefore* restore the man's wife" (Gen. 20:6–7).*
d	וְעַתָּה יִשְׂרָאֵל שְׁמַע אֶל־הַחֻקִּים וְאֶל־הַמִּשְׁפָּטִים	*Therefore*, O Israel, listen to the statutes and the ordinances (Deut. 4:1).[75]*
e	וְאַבְשָׁלוֹם אֲשֶׁר מָשַׁחְנוּ עָלֵינוּ מֵת בַּמִּלְחָמָה וְעַתָּה לָמָה אַתֶּם מַחֲרִשִׁים לְהָשִׁיב אֶת־הַמֶּלֶךְ:	But Absalom, whom we anointed over us died in the battle. *So now* why are you slack to bring back the king? (2 Sam. 19:11).*
f	וַיֹּאמְרוּ כָל־הַנְּשִׂיאִים אֶל־כָּל־הָעֵדָה אֲנַחְנוּ נִשְׁבַּעְנוּ לָהֶם בַּיהוָה אֱלֹהֵי יִשְׂרָאֵל וְעַתָּה לֹא נוּכַל לִנְגֹּעַ בָּהֶם	But all the leaders said to the whole community, "We have sworn to them by the LORD, the God of Israel, *therefore* we cannot touch them" (Josh. 9:19).*

In those instances where two instances of וְעַתָּה are used in tandem, the first וְעַתָּה predominantly points to a current development that emanates from a preceding exposition. This current development provides the ground of the subsequent directive introduced by the second וְעַתָּה (#*g*).

---

75. The exposition comprises the content conveyed in Deut. 1–3.

g	וַיֹּאמֶר יְהוָה רָאֹה רָאִ֫יתִי	[7]Then the LORD said, "I have
	אֶת־עֳנִי עַמִּי אֲשֶׁר בְּמִצְרָ֑יִם	carefully observed the misery of
	וְאֶת־צַעֲקָתָם שָׁמַ֫עְתִּי	my people who are in Egypt; I
	מִפְּנֵי נֹגְשָׂיו כִּי יָדַ֫עְתִּי	have heard their cry on account of
	אֶת־מַכְאֹבָיו׃ ....[9]וְעַתָּה	their taskmasters. Yes, I know their
	הִנֵּה צַעֲקַת בְּנֵי־יִשְׂרָאֵל	sufferings."... [9]*And now*, look, the
	בָּ֫אָה אֵלָ֑י וְגַם־רָאִ֫יתִי	cry of the Israelites has come to me;
	אֶת־הַלַּ֫חַץ אֲשֶׁר מִצְרַ֫יִם	I have also seen how the Egyptians
	לֹחֲצִים אֹתָם׃ [10]וְעַתָּה לְכָה	oppress them. [10]*So* come, I will
	וְאֶשְׁלָחֲךָ אֶל־פַּרְעֹה וְהוֹצֵא	send you to Pharaoh and he will
	אֶת־עַמִּי בְנֵי־יִשְׂרָאֵל	bring my people, the Israelites, out
	מִמִּצְרָ֫יִם׃	of Egypt" (Exod. 3:7, 9–10).*

(2) עַתָּה and וְעַתָּה as an adverb (often)

Mainly עַתָּה, but also וְעַתָּה, refer to a point in time simultaneous with the speech time of an utterance (#*a-c*).

a	וּמָלַךְ יְהוָה עֲלֵיהֶם בְּהַר	And the LORD will reign over
	צִיּוֹן מֵעַתָּה וְעַד־עוֹלָם׃	them on Mont Zion from *now* until
		eternity (Mic. 4:7).
b	וְעַתָּה הֵנִ֫יחַ יְהוָה אֱלֹהֵיכֶם	And *now* the LORD your God has
	לַאֲחֵיכֶם	given rest to your kinsmen (Josh.
		22:4).*
c	בְּשִׁבְעִים נֶ֫פֶשׁ יָרְדוּ	With seventy persons your
	אֲבֹתֶ֫יךָ מִצְרָ֑יְמָה וְעַתָּה	ancestors went down to Egypt, but
	שָׂמְךָ יְהוָה אֱלֹהֶ֫יךָ	*now* the LORD your God has made
	כְּכוֹכְבֵי הַשָּׁמַ֫יִם לָרֹב׃	you as numerous as the stars of
		heaven (Deut. 10:22).*

(3) וְעַתָּה introducing the main body of a letter

וַיָּבֵא הַסֵּ֫פֶר אֶל־מֶ֫לֶךְ יִשְׂרָאֵל	And he brought the letter to the
לֵאמֹר וְעַתָּה כְּבוֹא הַסֵּ֫פֶר הַזֶּה	king of Israel, saying, "*And now*,
אֵלֶ֫יךָ הִנֵּה שָׁלַ֫חְתִּי אֵלֶ֫יךָ אֶת־נַעֲמָן	when this letter reaches you, look
עַבְדִּי וַאֲסַפְתּוֹ מִצָּרַעְתּוֹ׃	I have sent to you Naaman, my
	servant, that you may cure him of
	his leprosy" (2 Kgs 5:6).*

§40.40. פֶּן

See §41.11.

§40.41. רַק

רַק is primarily a focus particle, governing a constituent ("*only* x"). However, it is often used as a conjunctive adverb, governing a sentence ("however," "only"), and in a few cases it is used as modal adverb ("surely").

This particle occurs 108 times, predominantly in narrative material. This is in contrast with its near synonym, אַךְ (§40.8), which often occurs in poetic material. A significant feature of רַק is that it is never preceded by וְ.

רַק marks the entity immediately following it (its syntactic domain) primarily for "limitation." The entity may be a person, a thing, an attribute, an action or state of affairs, but it is often a piece of information. According to Levinsohn (2011: 105), רַק is limiting and countering something in the context, while אַךְ has only a limiting function.

The following patterns of use can distinguished:

(1) Indicates limitation with a countering effect

(a) רַק + constituent (frequent)

Excludes *something or someone* with respect to something or someone in the preceding context.

וַיִּקְרָא פַרְעֹה אֶל־מֹשֶׁה וַיֹּאמֶר לְכוּ עִבְדוּ אֶת־יְהֹוָה רַק צֹאנְכֶם וּבְקַרְכֶם יֻצָּג גַּם־טַפְּכֶם יֵלֵךְ עִמָּכֶם:	Then Pharaoh summoned Moses and said, "Go, serve the LORD. *Only* <u>your flocks and herds</u> shall remain behind; even your children can go with you" (Exod. 10:24).*

(b) רַק + sentence(s) (frequent)

Sets a limit and counters the implications of the content of a directly preceding utterance.

a	וְאִם־לֹא תֹאבֶה הָאִשָּׁה לָלֶכֶת אַחֲרֶיךָ וְנִקִּיתָ מִשְּׁבֻעָתִי זֹאת רַק אֶת־בְּנִי לֹא תָשֵׁב שָׁמָּה:	But if the woman is not willing to follow you, then you will be free from this oath of mine; *only* <u>do not take my son back there</u> (Gen. 24:8).*

b	וַיֹּ֣אמֶר פַּרְעֹ֗ה אָנֹכִ֞י אֲשַׁלַּ֤ח	So Pharaoh said, "I will allow you
	אֶתְכֶם֙ וּזְבַחְתֶּ֤ם לַֽיהוָה֙	to go to sacrifice to the Lord your
	אֱלֹֽהֵיכֶם֙ בַּמִּדְבָּ֔ר רַ֛ק	God in the wilderness, *however*,
	הַרְחֵ֥ק לֹא־תַרְחִ֖יקוּ לָלֶ֑כֶת	<u>you shall by no means go far</u>"
		(Exod. 8:24).*

(2) Expresses conviction as to the correctness of an observation or evaluation (rare).

וַיֹּ֙אמֶר֙ אַבְרָהָ֔ם כִּ֣י אָמַ֗רְתִּי	And Abraham responded, "Because
רַ֚ק אֵין־יִרְאַ֣ת אֱלֹהִ֔ים בַּמָּק֖וֹם	I thought, *surely* <u>there is not fear of</u>
הַזֶּ֑ה	<u>God in this place</u>" (Gen. 20:11).*

§41. Negatives

§41.1. Introduction

Biblical Hebrew has a series of negatives (or, negators), which form a special class of adverbs. Each one is used to negate a specific grammatical form. In certain contexts, the negatives may also function as conjunctions, rather than adverbs. Two types of negation have been identified in Biblical Hebrew: (1) sentential negation and (2) constituent negation.[76] Word order in verbal clauses, especially the placement of the negative, may affect the meaning and scope of the negative.[77]

Sentential negation implies that the negative form has scope over (i.e. it negates) the whole subsequent phrase or sentence that follows. Constituent negation implies that the negative form is subcategorized for a specific lexical category (i.e. it applies to a specific category of words), hence it takes a specific category as its complement and thus has scope over this category only. Both kinds of scope can be observed in Hos. 1:6, each introduced by לֹא, the most common negative in Biblical Hebrew (occurring 5,188 times, including orthographic varieties).[78]

---

76. See especially Snyman (2004), based on Minimalist Syntax. For a different model, which posits three different types (item negation, constituent negation, and clausal negation), see Waltke and O'Connor §39.3.1d. See also Miller (2005a), Naudé and Rendsburg (2013) and Miller-Naudé and Naudé (forthcoming).

77. Snyman and Naudé (2003: 258–64); see also Moshavi (2007a and 2007b).

78. Cited in Waltke and O'Connor §39.3.1d.

קְרָא שְׁמָהּ לֹא רֻחָמָה כִּי לֹא Call her name *Lo*-Ruḥama/
אוֹסִיף עוֹד אֲרַחֵם אֶת־בֵּית Not-Pitied, for I will *not* continue
יִשְׂרָאֵל any more to have pity on the house
of Israel (Hos. 1:6).

The first לֹא serves as a constituent negative (as part of the proper name Lo-Ruḥama, "Not-Pitied"); while the second לֹא functions as sentential negative (negating the clause introduced by כִּי "for, because"; note the placement of לֹא before the verb).

§41.2. אֵין

אֵין occurs 747 times.

Technically speaking, אֵין is the construct form of אַיִן. When a sentence with אֵין has a pronominal subject, it always appears as a pronominal suffix (103 times).

Person	*Singular*		*Plural*	
1 c.	אֵינֶנִּי	not I	אֵינֶנּוּ	not us
2 m.	אֵינְךָ	not you	אֵינְכֶם	not you
2 f.	אֵינֵךְ	not you	(not attested)	not you
3 m.	אֵינֶנּוּ	not he	אֵינָם	not they
3 f.	אֵינֶנָּה	not she	(not attested)	not they

אֵין functions typically as a sentence negative, and sometimes as a constituent negative or substantive indicating non-existence.

The following patterns of use can be distinguished:

(1) Sentential negative

אֵין is typically used as a sentential negative to negate nominal clauses, and therefore functions as a (negative) predicator of existence. It denies the existence of the referent of an undetermined subject in a nominal clause (#*a*).[79]

---

79. אֵין also serves as the opposite of the positive predicator of existence, יֵשׁ ("there is/ are"), which occurs 140 times; see §43.3.

אַיִן as sentential negative negates responses to sentences predicated with the predicator of existence (#*b*). In this case, the negative response to the yes–no question predicated with יֵשׁ is אַיִן. The choice of the negative depends upon the previous utterance with which it is paired. אַיִן is also used as a sentential negative to negate the participle (#*c*).

a	וְהַבּוֹר רֵק אֵין בּוֹ מָיִם	And the pit was empty (with implied copula); *there was no* water in it (Gen. 37:24).*
b	וְהָיָה אִם־אִישׁ יָבוֹא וּשְׁאֵלֵךְ וְאָמַר הֲיֵשׁ־פֹּה אִישׁ וְאָמַרְתְּ אָיִן:	And then, if anyone comes and asks you, "*Is anyone here?*" you must say, "*No one*" (Judg. 4:20).*
c	אֵינֶנִּי שֹׁמֵעַ	I am *not* listening (Isa. 1:15).*

(2) Constituent negative

אַיִן is used as a constituent negative when it precedes a noun (#*a*) or an implicit noun (#*b*) or when it occurs as אָיִן following a noun (#*c*) (see Miller-Naudé and Naudé 2015b: 177–78).

a	וּלְשָׁלוֹם אֵין־קֵץ	And to peace (there will be) *no* end (i.e. there will be endless peace) (Isa. 9:6).*
b	וַיֹּאמֶר אֵלֶיהָ קוּמִי וְנֵלֵכָה וְאֵין עֹנֶה	And he said to her, "Get up and let's go!" But *no* (one) was answering (Judg. 19:28).*
c	יָמִים אֵין מִסְפָּר	days *without* number (Jer. 2:32)

(3) A substantive indicating non-existence

The absolute form אָיִן (attested 42 times) occurs with different word order (the noun appears before the negative particle, suggesting that אָיִן serves as a substantive indicating non-existence).

וְאָדָם אַיִן לַעֲבֹד אֶת־הָאֲדָמָה:	And there was *no* human to till the ground (Gen. 2:5).*

§41.3. אַל

אַל occurs 730 times. It typically functions as a sentential negative and rarely as a constituent negative.

(1) Sentential negative

It is used as a sentential negative in negative commands or prohibitions (§19.5.2.1), especially one-time prohibitions, with the first person cohortative (#*a*) (§15.4) where a desire is negated, with the second person jussive as the negation of a command (#*b*) (the imperative is never negated; see §15.3), and with the third person jussive (#*c*) (see §15.5).[80]

a	כִּי אָמְרָה אַל־אֶרְאֶה בְּמוֹת הַיֶּלֶד	For she said, "Let me *not* look upon the death of the child" (Gen. 21:16).
b	אַל־תִּירְאִי	Do *not* fear [lit. may you not fear] (Gen. 21:17).*
c	אַל־יֵרַע בְּעֵינֶיךָ	Let it *not* be bad in your eyes (Gen. 21:12).*

אַל may be used as a sentential negative when the prohibition is elided (#*d*). The choice of the negative depends upon the previous utterance with which it is paired. אַל negates responses to volitive sentences (contrast the use of אַיִן as a negative response to a sentence with the existential יֵשׁ in Judg. 4:20 above).

Sometimes, when the directive is elided, it looks as if a constituent is negated (#*e-f*).

d	⁹וַיֹּאמֶר עֵשָׂו יֶשׁ־לִי רָב אָחִי יְהִי לְךָ אֲשֶׁר־לָךְ: ¹⁰וַיֹּאמֶר יַעֲקֹב אַל־נָא אִם־נָא מָצָאתִי חֵן בְּעֵינֶיךָ וְלָקַחְתָּ מִנְחָתִי מִיָּדִי	⁹But Esau said, "I have plenty, my brother; keep what you have for yourself." ¹⁰Jacob said, "No, please; if I find favor in your eyes, then accept my present from my hand" (Gen. 33:9–10).*
e	אַל־טַל וְאַל־מָטָר	(Let there be) *no* dew and *no* rain (2 Sam. 1:21).
f	קְחוּ־מוּסָרִי וְאַל־כָּסֶף	Receive my instruction, and (do) *not* (receive) silver (Prov. 8:10).*

---

80. The domains of לֹא and אַל appear to overlap sometimes. See Qimron (1983: 475; 1986: 80).

(2) Constituent negative[81]

יְהֹוָה אַל־בְּאַפְּךָ תוֹכִיחֵנִי

O Lᴏʀᴅ, rebuke me *not in your anger* (Ps. 6:2).*

§41.4. אֶפֶס

In some instances, אֶפֶס is a near synonym of אֵין. In (#a) the two negatives occur in parallel poetic lines with essentially the same meaning. It may also take a pronominal suffix (#b) or a preposition (#c). In one instance אֶפֶס is governed by a yes–no question word (#d).

a	<div dir="rtl">וְאֵין עוֹד אֱלֹהִים וְאֶפֶס כָּמוֹנִי:</div>	And there is no other God, and *there is not* any like me (Isa. 46:9).*
b	<div dir="rtl">אֲנִי וְאַפְסִי עוֹד</div>	I am, and *there is no one* besides me (Isa. 47:8).
c	<div dir="rtl">וַיִּכְלוּ בְּאֶפֶס תִּקְוָה:</div>	And they came to an end *without* hope [lit. at *there is not* hope] (Job 7:6).*
d	<div dir="rtl">וַיֹּאמֶר הַמֶּלֶךְ הַאֶפֶס עוֹד אִישׁ לְבֵית שָׁאוּל</div>	Then the king asked, "*Is there not* another person of the house of Saul left?" (2 Sam. 9:3).*

For the other uses of אֶפֶס, see §40.15.

§41.5. בַּל

בַּל (76 times) is used as a sentential negative in poetry as an analogue to לֹא in narrative. It is used especially before a *yiqtōl*/imperfect verb, in particular the Niṗ‘al form of מ-ו-ט "shake" (for reasons which are not readily transparent) (#a)[82] or before a nominal clause (#b).

---

81. Joüon-Muraoka §160oa claims that אַל may negate nouns, especially when an "added volitional nuance" is suggested. Rendsburg (2003: 24) suggests that this may be an Israelian Hebrew feature.

82. This particle may occur more frequently in Israelian (northern) Hebrew compositions (Rendsburg 2003: 20), especially given the fact that the neighboring Phoenician dialect uses בל regularly (in fact, לא is not attested in Phoenician).

a   אָמַר בְּלִבּוֹ בַּל־אֶמּוֹט   He thinks in his heart: I shall *not* be
                                             moved (Ps. 10:6).*

b   וְלִבּוֹ בַּל־עִמָּךְ:   But his heart is *not* with you (i.e.
                                             he does not mean it) (Prov. 23.7).*

§41.6. בְּלִי

בְּלִי occurs 25 times, especially in poetic texts.

(1) Sentential negative

a   עַל־בְּלִי הִגִּיד לוֹ כִּי בֹרֵחַ   in that he did *not* tell him that he
         הוּא: was fleeing (Gen. 31:20).*

b   בְּלִי נִשְׁמָע קוֹלָם: their voice is *not* heard (Ps. 19:4).

(2) Constituent negative

As a constituent negative בְּלִי negates the referent of a noun and can be
translated as "without."

אֲשֶׁר יִרְצַח אֶת־רֵעֵהוּ בִּבְלִי־דַעַת   who kills his neighbor *without*
                                             knowledge (i.e. unintentionally)
                                             (Deut. 4:42).*

§41.7. בִּלְתִּי

בִּלְתִּי occurs 112 times, 78 times with the preposition לְ.

(1) Sentential negative

In *infinitive clauses* בִּלְתִּי occurs with the preposition לְ to negate the
infinitive construct (#a).[83]

a   הֲמִן־הָעֵץ אֲשֶׁר צִוִּיתִיךָ לְבִלְתִּי   Have you eaten of the tree of
         אֲכָל־מִמֶּנּוּ אָכָלְתָּ:   which I commanded you *not to*
                                             eat? (Gen. 3:11).*

Usually with the preposition עַד the form בִּלְתִּי negates adverbial clauses
(#b). בִּלְתִּי may also serve as a sentential negative to negate the predicate
of a nominal clause (#c).

---

83. In a few instances בִּלְתִּי negates a finite verb, e.g. Exod. 20:20 and 2 Sam. 14:14.

b	וַיַּכּוּ אֹתוֹ ...עַד־בִּלְתִּי הִשְׁאִיר־לוֹ שָׂרִיד	So they slew him...until there was *not* left to him a survivor (Num. 21:35).*
c	כִּי אָמַר מִקְרֶה הוּא בִּלְתִּי טָהוֹר הוּא	For he thought, "Something has befallen him; he is *not* clean" (1 Sam. 20:26).

(2) Constituent negative

In some cases the events or states of affairs referred to by the expression following בִּלְתִּי are exceptions to a generalization in the preceding expression and בִּלְתִּי indicates exclusion: "only," "unless." In (#*a*) the scope of the focus is a clause, and in (#*b*) a constituent (the temporal adjunct).

a	לֹא־תִרְאוּ פָנַי בִּלְתִּי אֲחִיכֶם אִתְּכֶם:	You will not see my face, *unless* your brother is with you (Gen. 43:3).*
b	וַיֹּאמֶר אֲבִימֶלֶךְ לֹא יָדַעְתִּי מִי עָשָׂה אֶת־הַדָּבָר הַזֶּה וְגַם־אַתָּה לֹא־הִגַּדְתָּ לִּי וְגַם אָנֹכִי לֹא שָׁמַעְתִּי בִּלְתִּי הַיּוֹם:	And Abimelech said, "I do not know who has done this thing. Neither did you tell me, nor have I heard of it *until* today" (Gen. 21:26).

§41.8. טֶרֶם

The lexeme טֶרֶם occurs 56 times. It is relatively evenly distributed through the corpus, but absent in a number of books associated with Late Biblical Hebrew, e.g. Esther, Ecclesiastes, Ezra, Nehemiah, 1 and 2 Chronicles and Zechariah.

טֶרֶם very often combines with the preposition בְּ. The combination בְּטֶרֶם is attested 39 times. In 12 cases טֶרֶם occurs with no other morpheme attached to it. One instance each of וְטֶרֶם, הֲטֶרֶם and מִטֶּרֶם is attested. טֶרֶם is predominately followed by a *yiqtōl*/imperfect form and only rarely by *qātal*/perfect.

טֶרֶם may serve as a sentential negative to connote "not yet." Or put differently, טֶרֶם refers to *a point in time prior* to that of the referent of the construction in its scope, irrespective of the time frame involved.

a   וְגֵר אֱלֹהִים֙ טֶ֣רֶם יִכְבֶּ֔ה וּשְׁמוּאֵ֖ל שֹׁכֵ֑ב בְּהֵיכַ֥ל יְהוָ֖ה   And the lamp of God was *not yet* extinguished, and Samuel was lying down in the temple of the LORD (1 Sam. 3:3).*

b   בְּטֶ֨רֶם יָבֹ֤א הַמַּלְאָךְ֙ אֵלָ֔יו וְה֥וּא ׀ אָמַ֖ר אֶל־הַזְּקֵנִ֑ים...   *Before* the messenger came to him, he said to the elders... (2 Kgs 6:32).

§41.9. לֹא

לֹא is the most common negative (5,188 times) in the Hebrew Bible. It is typically used as a sentential negative (4,403 times), but also as a constituent negative (778 times).

(1) Sentence negative

    (a) Negation of a statement

       As a sentential negative, לֹא is typically used to negate independent verbal clauses which act as statements, either with a *qātal*/perfect (#a) or *yiqtōl*/imperfect (#b) form of the verb.

       In replying to a statement (or directive) by a previous speaker, the negative may negate the elided statement. The choice of the negative depends upon the previous utterance with which it is paired (#c). The negative particle itself may also be elided, especially in texts characterized by poetic parallelism (#d). Sentential negation is typically involved (Miller 2005b).

a   וְלֹא־מָצְאָה֩ הַיּוֹנָ֨ה מָנ֜וֹחַ לְכַף־רַגְלָ֗הּ   And the dove did *not* find a resting-place for its feet (Gen. 8:9).*

b   לֹ֥א יִֽירָשְׁךָ֖ זֶ֑ה   This one will *not* inherit you (Gen. 15:4).*

c   ¹¹כֻּלָּ֛נוּ בְּנֵ֥י אִישׁ־אֶחָ֖ד נָ֑חְנוּ כֵּנִ֣ים אֲנַ֔חְנוּ לֹא־הָי֥וּ עֲבָדֶ֖יךָ מְרַגְּלִֽים: ¹²וַיֹּ֖אמֶר אֲלֵהֶ֑ם לֹ֕א כִּֽי־עֶרְוַ֥ת הָאָ֛רֶץ בָּאתֶ֖ם לִרְאֽוֹת: ¹¹ We are all sons of one man; we are honest men; your servants have never been spies." ¹² But he said to them, "*No*, it is the nakedness of the land that you have come to see!" (Gen. 42:11–12).*

d   כִּ֣י לֹ֣א שְׁא֣וֹל תּוֹדֶ֑ךָּ מָ֖וֶת יְהַלְלֶ֑ךָ   For Sheol *cannot* acclaim you, Death (*cannot*) praise you (Isa. 38:18).*

(b) Negation of a directive

לֹא is used as sentential negative to negate a command which is expressed with a *yiqṭōl*/imperfect verbal form. The command then acquires a generally valid character, i.e. a prohibition (see §15.3 and §19.5.2.1).

וּמֵעֵץ הַדַּעַת טוֹב וָרָע לֹא תֹאכַל מִמֶּנּוּ	And from the tree of the knowledge of good and evil, you shall *not* eat from it (Gen. 2:17).

(c) Negation in oaths

An oath depends on the suppression of an imprecation upon a person so that when אִם introduces oath content, a negative statement is expressed: "(May God curse me) if I do this" = "I will not do this." Contrastively, when אִם־לֹא, lit. "if not," introduces oath content, a positive statement is expressed: "(May God curse me) if I do not do this" = "I will do this" (Gesenius–Kautzsch–Cowley §149b; Conklin 2011: 9). See also §40.11.(2) and §45.2.

The phrases introduced by אִם (#a) and אִם־לֹא (#b) function thus as protases of incomplete conditional clauses – the former for negative oaths and the latter for positive oaths – as illustrated by (#a) and (#b), respectively.

a	²²וַיֹּאמֶר אַבְרָם אֶל־מֶלֶךְ סְדֹם הֲרִימֹתִי יָדִי אֶל־יְהוָה אֵל עֶלְיוֹן קֹנֵה שָׁמַיִם וָאָרֶץ: ²³אִם־מִחוּט וְעַד שְׂרוֹךְ־נַעַל וְאִם־אֶקַּח מִכָּל־אֲשֶׁר־לָךְ	²²And Abram said to the king of Sodom, "I raise my hand to the LORD, El Elyon, creator of heaven and earth ²³(and swear that) if from a thread to a sandal thong, if I take anything of yours (may I be cursed) (i.e. I will not take anything of yours, from thread to sandal thong)" (Gen. 14:22–23).*
b	יְהוָה יִהְיֶה שֹׁמֵעַ בֵּינוֹתֵינוּ אִם־לֹא כִדְבָרְךָ כֵּן נַעֲשֶׂה	The LORD will be a witness [lit. one who hears] between us, if we do not act in accordance with your proposal, (may we be cursed) (i.e. we will act) (Judg. 11:10).*

(d) Negation and כָּל

The construction לֹא...כָּל followed by an undetermined noun phrase expresses an absolute negation.[84] In addition, the particle כָּל acts as a negative polarity item in negative statements. In other words, instead of meaning "each," when כָּל is negated it means "no" (#a).[85]

When כֹּל precedes a determined noun phrase it has the sense of a collective universal quantifier and indicates "the totality of the (specific) group or whole." (See the section on the quantifier, §36.5.1.) In the singular it bears the nuance of individualization. In a negative sentence it means "none" or "nothing" in the plural (#b) and "any" in the singular (#c).

a	וְלֹא־יִכָּרֵת כָּל־בָּשָׂר עוֹד מִמֵּי הַמַּבּוּל	And *no* flesh will be cut off again by the waters of the flood (Gen. 9:11).*
b	כִּי כָל־דְּבָרָיו לֹא־יַעֲנֶה	that he will answer *none* of his words (Job 33:13).*
c	לֹא תֹאכְלוּ מִכֹּל עֵץ הַגָּן	You shall not eat of *any* tree of the garden (Gen. 3:1).*[86]

(e) Negation of a marked relative clause

לֹא may be employed to negate a relative clause.

מִכֹּל הַבְּהֵמָה הַטְּהוֹרָה תִּקַּח־לְךָ שִׁבְעָה שִׁבְעָה אִישׁ וְאִשְׁתּוֹ וּמִן־הַבְּהֵמָה אֲשֶׁר לֹא טְהֹרָה הִוא שְׁנַיִם אִישׁ וְאִשְׁתּוֹ׃	Of every clean animal you shall take for you by sevens [lit. seven by seven], a male and his female; and of the animals *that are not clean* two, a male and his female (Gen. 7:2).*

(f) Negation of a zero relative clause

לֹא may be employed to negate a zero relative clause (see §36.3.1.1.(3)). The relative clause may have both an overt subject and predicate (#a) or only an overt predicate (#b) (see Miller-Naudé and Naudé 2015b: 89–192).

---

84. Naudé (2011a: 413; forthcoming).

85. In this construction כֹּל functions as a distributive quantifier (i.e. it means "each" rather than "all") and its semantic nuance is non-specific and implicitly inclusive.

86. See also 1 Chron. 4:27.

a   אַתְּ אֶרֶץ לֹא מְטֹהָרָה הִיא   You are a land (*which*) *it is not clean* (Ezek. 22:24).*

b   זָכַרְתִּי לָךְ חֶסֶד נְעוּרַיִךְ   I remember you with respect to the
     אַהֲבַת כְּלוּלֹתָיִךְ לֶכְתֵּךְ   loyalty of your youth, your love as
     אַחֲרַי בַּמִּדְבָּר בְּאֶרֶץ   a bride by following after me in the
     לֹא זְרוּעָה: desert, in a land (*which it*) *is not sown* (Jer. 2:2).*

(2) Constituent negative

לֹא may be employed as a constituent negative to negate non-verbal lexical categories, including noun phrases (#a), proper names (#b), adjectives (#c) and prepositional phrases (#d). (See Miller-Naudé and Naudé 2016b.)[87] An instance of ellipsis of the predicate (#e) stresses the constituent negation.

a   לֹא אִישׁ דְּבָרִים אָנֹכִי   I am *no* <u>man</u> of words (Exod. 4:10).*

b   לֹא־אֵל   *no*-<u>god</u> (Deut. 32:21).*

c   לֹא חָכָם   *non*-<u>wise</u> (Deut. 32:6).*

d   כִּי| לֹא עַל־צִדְקֹתֵינוּ אֲנַחְנוּ   For *not* <u>on the ground of our</u>
     מַפִּילִים תַּחֲנוּנֵינוּ לְפָנֶיךָ   <u>righteousness</u> do we present our
     supplication before you (Dan. 9:18).*

e   כִּי חֶסֶד חָפַצְתִּי וְלֹא־זָבַח   For faithful love I desire, and *not*
     וְדַעַת אֱלֹהִים מֵעֹלוֹת   <u>sacrifice</u> (I desire); and knowledge
     of God (I desire) more than burnt-offerings (Hos. 6:6).*

§41.10. לוּלֵי

לוּלֵי occurs 14 times. It occurs only in Genesis to 2 Kings, the Psalms and Isaiah. The lexeme is attested three times with the spelling לוּלֵא. The lexeme occurs predominantly in reported speech.

לוּלֵי typically introduces a hypothetical condition, i.e. *if* something had *not* happened, then... (#a). This often takes places in a context where strong assertions are made, e.g. in oaths (#b). In a few cases, the protasis follows the apodosis (#c). In one case the apodosis is lacking (#d).

---

87. לֹא may also negate adverbs, numerals, and pronouns. See Snyman and Naudé (2003: 253) and Waltke and O'Connor §39.3.3.

a
לוּלֵא חֲרַשְׁתֶּם בְּעֶגְלָתִי
לֹא מְצָאתֶם חִידָתִי׃
If you had *not* ploughed with my heifer, you would not have solved my riddle (Judg. 14:18).*

b
וַיֹּאמֶר יוֹאָב חַי הָאֱלֹהִים
כִּי לוּלֵא דִּבַּרְתָּ כִּי
אָז מֵהַבֹּקֶר נַעֲלָה הָעָם
אִישׁ מֵאַחֲרֵי אָחִיו׃
And Joab said, "As God lives, *if* you had *not* spoken, then only in [lit. from] the morning the army would have stopped pursuing their kinsmen [lit. the army would have pulled back each from after his brother]" (2 Sam. 2:27).*

c
²⁶אָמַרְתִּי אַפְאֵיהֶם
אַשְׁבִּיתָה מֵאֱנוֹשׁ זִכְרָם׃
²⁷לוּלֵי כַּעַס אוֹיֵב אָגוּר
[26]I thought, "I want to cut them to pieces, I want to blot out their memory from humankind. [27]*If not* it was for the provocation of the enemy that I feared" (Deut. 32:27).*

d
לוּלֵא הֶאֱמַנְתִּי לִרְאוֹת
בְּטוּב־יְהוָה בְּאֶרֶץ חַיִּים׃
If I had *not* believed to experience to goodness of the LORD in the land of the living (I would have been lost) (Ps. 27:13).*

§41.11. פֶּן[88]

פֶּן is a subordinating conjunction.

The lexeme פֶּן occurs 133 times in the Hebrew Bible. It occurs predominantly in discourse in Genesis to 2 Kings. However, a number of cases are attested in the Psalms, Proverbs, Isaiah and Jeremiah. In Job, two cases occur and one instance is found in Hosea, Amos, Malachi and 1 Chronicles, respectively.

פֶּן is nearly always followed by a *yiqtōl*/imperfect form of the verb. The clause (#a) or clauses (#b) governed by פֶּן usually follow their matrix clause(s). In a few cases, a כִּי clause is used between the matrix and the פֶּן clause (#c). The matrix clause of a פֶּן clause is sometimes elided (#d).

In the majority of cases, the person of the subject of the verb of the matrix clause is second person. In more than 60% of the instances, the subject(s) of the matrix and פֶּן clauses differ (#b).

---

88. This section is based on Yoo (2013).

a   וּמִפְּרִי הָעֵץ אֲשֶׁר בְּתוֹךְ־הַגָּן
אָמַר אֱלֹהִים לֹא תֹאכְלוּ
מִמֶּנּוּ וְלֹא תִגְּעוּ בּוֹ פֶּן־תְּמֻתוּן:
    But from the fruit of the tree *which* (it) is in the midst of the garden, God said, "You shall not eat from it, nor shall you touch it, *lest* you die" (Gen. 3:3).*

b   וְאָנֹכִי לֹא אוּכַל לְהִמָּלֵט
הָהָרָה פֶּן־תִּדְבָּקַנִי הָרָעָה
    But I cannot flee to the mountains, *lest* the disaster overtake me (Gen. 19:19).*

c   וְכִלְכַּלְתִּי אֹתְךָ שָׁם כִּי־עוֹד
חָמֵשׁ שָׁנִים רָעָב פֶּן־תִּוָּרֵשׁ אַתָּה
וּבֵיתְךָ וְכָל־אֲשֶׁר־לָךְ:
    And I will provide for you there, because there are still five years of famine – *lest* you and your household and all that you have become destitute (Gen. 45:11).*

d   וַיִּקְרָא אֲבִימֶלֶךְ לְיִצְחָק וַיֹּאמֶר
אַךְ הִנֵּה אִשְׁתְּךָ הִוא וְאֵיךְ
אָמַרְתָּ אֲחֹתִי הִוא וַיֹּאמֶר אֵלָיו
יִצְחָק כִּי אָמַרְתִּי פֶּן־אָמוּת
עָלֶיהָ:
    And Abimelech called Isaac and said, "Surely, look, she *is* your wife. And how then could you say, 'She *is* my sister'?" And Isaac said to him, "Because I thought, '(I have to do so) *lest* I would die on account of her'" (Gen. 26:9).*

פֶּן indicates the negative purpose of a matrix clause, i.e. the prevention of a possible event. It nearly always can be translated as "lest" or "so that not."[89]

In most cases, a directive speech act is suggested in the matrix clause in order to prevent an undesirable event from happening (#*e*). The prevention may also be based on epistemic reasoning (#*f*) or events in the world (#*g*).

e   וַיֹּאמְרוּ הָבָה | נִבְנֶה־לָּנוּ
עִיר וּמִגְדָּל וְרֹאשׁוֹ בַשָּׁמַיִם
וְנַעֲשֶׂה־לָּנוּ שֵׁם פֶּן־נָפוּץ
עַל־פְּנֵי כָל־הָאָרֶץ
    And they said, "Come, let us build for ourselves a city and a tower whose top reaches to the heavens. And let us make a name for ourselves, *lest* we be scattered over the face of the whole earth" (Gen. 11:4).*

---

89. In Prov. 5:6 and Jer. 51:46, פֶּן is used as a simple negation word.

f　וַיַּעַן יַעֲקֹב וַיֹּאמֶר לְלָבָן כִּי יָרֵאתִי
כִּי אָמַרְתִּי פֶּן־תִּגְזֹל אֶת־בְּנוֹתֶיךָ
מֵעִמִּי

Then Jacob answered and said to Laban, "Because I was afraid, for I thought, '*Lest* you take your daughters from me by force'" (Gen. 31:31).*

g　וַיֹּאמֶר יְהוָה אֶל־גִּדְעוֹן רַב
הָעָם אֲשֶׁר אִתָּךְ מִתִּתִּי אֶת־מִדְיָן
בְּיָדָם פֶּן־יִתְפָּאֵר עָלַי יִשְׂרָאֵל
לֵאמֹר יָדִי הוֹשִׁיעָה לִּי:

And the Lord said to Gideon, "The troops that are with you are too many for me to give Midian into their hands; *lest* Israel will boast, saying, 'My hand has delivered me'" (Judg. 7:2).*

§42. Interrogatives

§42.1. Introduction

The writing system of the Hebrew Bible does not orthographically indicate questions; in other words, unlike English and Modern Hebrew, Biblical Hebrew has no question mark. In Biblical Hebrew questions requiring a content answer (who? what? when? where? why?) and yes–no questions requiring a positive or negative reply are introduced with an interrogative (see §11.9). Although content questions are usually introduced with an interrogative pronoun and could have been dealt with in §36, they are discussed here for the sake of covering questions as a whole.

Each type of question may be used as a rhetorical question in Biblical Hebrew. In addition to expressing a question, rhetorical questions serve additional rhetorical and communicative functions within the discourse.

§42.2. Yes–no questions

Yes–no questions ask the addressee to indicate whether the implied assertion is true or false.[90] Among the languages of the world, there are three main types of yes–no question–answer systems (see Miller 2005b). One type, like English, is a "yes–no answering system" in which a positive particle stands for or accompanies a positive answer and a negative particle stands for or accompanies a negative answer.

---

90. Waltke and O'Connor §40.3 refer to yes–no question as "polar questions" in that they question the polarity of the statement as positive or negative.

A second type is an "agreement–disagreement system," in which the positive particle is used for an answer that agrees with the polarity of the question; a negative particle disagrees with the polarity of the question. For example, in Japanese, to the question "Are you not going?," a reply with the positive particle means, "Yes (I *agree* with the proposition that I am not going)." A reply with the negative particle means, "No (I *disagree* with the proposition that I am not going)." Contrast English, where "Yes" would mean "Yes, I am going" whereas "No" would mean "No, I am not going."

A third type, like Welsh, is an "echo system." A positive answer repeats the verb of the question with or without additional material; a negative answer uses the negative particle and often repeats the verb of the question. Of these three types, Biblical Hebrew is an echo system in which no special word for "yes" is used. The repetition of some or all of the question in the answer is simply the normal way to express a positive reply and should not be seen as forceful or emphatic. (Modern Hebrew, in contrast to Biblical Hebrew, has a yes–no answering system in which כֵּן has become grammaticalized as a positive particle of response.)

In exegesis of a question–answer sequence (e.g. 1 Sam. 23:2; Jon. 4:9), the repetition of the question in the answer does not, in contrast to English pragmatics, mean that the person replying is angry or obstinate – this is the normal means for providing an affirmative, cooperative answer in Biblical Hebrew (Miller 1997, 2005b).

42.2.1. הֲ or הֲלֹא

Yes–no questions may be positively framed and introduced with the interrogative particle הֲ. They may also be negatively framed and introduced with the interrogative particle הֲ followed by the negative particle לֹא. For yes–no questions that are not marked with the interrogative particle, see §42.2.2 below.

(1) Morphology

    (a) Before words that begin with a guttural, the interrogative particle is vocalized with a /ֶ/.

        הַאֵלֵךְ וְקָרָאתִי לָךְ אִשָּׁה מֵינֶקֶת   Shall I go and call for you a nurse?
                                    (Exod. 2:7).*

(b) Before words that begin with a guttural and in which the first vowel is a /ְ◌/ or /◌ֲ/, the interrogative particle is vocalized with a /◌ֶ/.

כִּי־אֶל־אֵל הֶאָמַר... For has anyone said to God...? (Job 34:31).

(2) Syntax

The interrogative particle הֲ is typically attached to the first word of the sentence (#*a*).

a   הֲשָׁלוֹם לַנַּעַר לְאַבְשָׁלוֹם Is it well with the young man, with Absalom? (2 Sam. 18:32).*

When the interrogative particle is followed by the negative, the interrogative particle occurs at the beginning of the sentence. The negative marker may immediately follow the interrogative particle (#*b*) or it may occur immediately before the portion of the sentence that is negated (#*c*).

b   וַיֹּאמֶר יִפְתָּח לְזִקְנֵי גִלְעָד But Jephthah said to the elders הֲלֹא אַתֶּם שְׂנֵאתֶם אוֹתִי of Gilead, "Are you not the one וַתְּגָרְשׁוּנִי מִבֵּית אָבִי who hated me and drove me out form my father's house?" (Judg. 11:7).*

c   הֲשֹׁפֵט כָּל־הָאָרֶץ לֹא Will the judge of all the earth not יַעֲשֶׂה מִשְׁפָּט: do justice? (Gen. 18:25).*

(3) Semantic and pragmatic functions

(a) Introduce a yes–no question

וַיִּשְׁאַל דָּוִד בַּיהוָה לֵאמֹר הַאֵלֵךְ And David inquired of the LORD, וְהִכֵּיתִי בַּפְּלִשְׁתִּים הָאֵלֶּה "Shall I go and attack these Philistines?" (1 Sam. 23:2).*

(b) Introduce direct or indirect alternative questions

Alternate questions are usually introduced with הֲ ... (וְ) אִם. See also §40.11.(1)(c)(i).

a   הֲמָלֹךְ תִּמְלֹךְ עָלֵינוּ Are you indeed to reign over us? אִם־מָשׁוֹל תִּמְשֹׁל בָּנוּ Or are you indeed to rule over us? (Gen. 37:8).*

b	לָדַעַת הֲהִצְלִיחַ יְהוָה דַּרְכּוֹ אִם־לֹא	to learn whether the LORD had prospered his journey or not (Gen. 24:21).*

(c) Introduce a rhetorical question

Rhetorical questions are questions which do not seek information, but instead are used for rhetorical and persuasive effect. Often rhetorical questions are used to make an assertion which cannot easily be contested by the person addressed; the assertion reverses the polarity of the rhetorical question (#*a–c*).

a	וַיֹּאמֶר יְהוָה הַהֵיטֵב חָרָה לָךְ:	And the LORD said, "Is it right for you to be angry?" (i.e. it is not right for you to be angry) (Jon. 4:4).
b	הֲלֹא הוּא אָמַר־לִי אֲחֹתִי הוּא	Did he not himself say to me (i.e. he himself certainly said to me), "She is my sister?" (Gen. 20:5).
c	וַיַּעַן הַמַּלְאָךְ הַדֹּבֵר בִּי וַיֹּאמֶר אֵלַי הֲלוֹא יָדַעְתָּ מָה־הֵמָּה אֵלֶּה	Then the angel who talked with me answered and said to me, "Do you not know what these are?" (i.e. you certainly know who these are) (Zech. 4:5).*

Although rhetorical questions function semantically and pragmatically to accomplish speech acts in addition to questions, the semantics of a question remain.[91] The fact that rhetorical questions are still questions and that negation functions normally within them can be seen in (#*d*) with two yes–no questions introduced by the particle הֲ.[92] The second question has constituent negation at the beginning (הֲלֹא) as well as sentence negation before the verb (see §42.2.1.(2)).

---

91. Contrast the viewpoint of Moshavi (2007a and 2007b) that some rhetorical questions introduced with הֲלֹא are neither questions nor negative.

92. See Snyman and Naudé (2003) and Naudé and Rendsburg (2013).

d   וַאֲמַרְתֶּם לֹא יִתָּכֵן דֶּרֶךְ   And you say, "The way of the
אֲדֹנָי שִׁמְעוּ־נָא בֵּית יִשְׂרָאֵל   Lord does not measure up." Listen,
הֲדַרְכִּי לֹא יִתָּכֵן הֲלֹא   O house of Israel: "Is it my way
דַּרְכֵיכֶם לֹא יִתָּכֵנוּ׃   (which) does not measure up? Isn't
               it your ways (which) do not measure
               up?" (Ezek. 18:25).*

In a few cases, positive rhetorical questions do not reverse the polarity of the question (#e). Because they do not reverse polarity, these questions have been described not as rhetorical questions but as "conducive questions" in which the speaker wants to lead the hearer to a correct conclusion (Moshavi 2011).

e   וַיֹּאמֶר מֶלֶךְ־יִשְׂרָאֵל   And the king of Israel said to his
אֶל־עֲבָדָיו הַיְדַעְתֶּם   servants, "Do you know that Ramoth
כִּי־לָנוּ רָמֹת גִּלְעָד   Gilead belongs to us? And yet we
וַאֲנַחְנוּ מַחְשִׁים מִקַּחַת   hesitate to take it from the hand of the
אֹתָהּ מִיַּד מֶלֶךְ אֲרָם׃   king of Aram" (1 Kgs 22:3).*

42.2.2. *Unmarked yes–no questions*

Some yes–no questions are not introduced with the interrogative הֲ marker. If one considers #a and #b, it appears that there is not a significant semantic or pragmatic difference in unmarked yes–no questions.

a   וַיֹּאמֶר הַמֶּלֶךְ שָׁלוֹם לַנַּעַר   And the king said, "Is it well with
לְאַבְשָׁלוֹם   the young man, with Absalom?"
               (2 Sam. 18:29).

b   וַיֹּאמֶר הַמֶּלֶךְ אֶל־הַכּוּשִׁי   And the king said to the Cushite,
הֲשָׁלוֹם לַנַּעַר לְאַבְשָׁלוֹם   "Is it well with the young man, with
               Absalom?" (2 Sam. 18:32).*

Unmarked yes–no questions were probably intonationally indicated, but the intonational patterns of ancient Hebrew cannot be reconstructed with certainty at this stage.

42.2.3. *Answers to yes–no questions*

In English, yes–no question can be answered positively or negatively in a minimal way with "yes" or "no." (Similarly, Modern Hebrew uses כֵּן and לֹא.) In Biblical Hebrew, however, the response "echoes" the question and there is no comparable word to express "yes."

(1) A direct positive reply to a yes–no question is expressed as the positive
restatement of at least the predicate of the question.[93]

a

וַתֹּ֤אמֶר אֲחֹתוֹ֙
אֶל־בַּת־פַּרְעֹה֙ הַאֵלֵ֗ךְ
וְקָרָ֤אתִי לָךְ֙ אִשָּׁ֣ה מֵינֶ֔קֶת
מִן הָעִבְרִיֹּ֑ת וְתֵינִ֥ק לָ֖ךְ
אֶת־הַיָּ֑לֶד׃ וַתֹּֽאמֶר־לָ֥הּ
בַּת־פַּרְעֹ֖ה לֵֽכִי

[7] And his sister said to Pharaoh's
daughter, *"Shall I go and call for
you a nurse from the Hebrew women
so that she may nurse the child for
you?"* [8] Pharaoh's daughter said to
her, *"Go!"* (Exod. 2:7–8).*

b

וַיִּשְׁאַ֨ל דָּוִ֤ד בַּֽיהוָה֙ לֵאמֹ֔ר
הַאֵלֵ֗ךְ וְהִכֵּ֖יתִי בַּפְּלִשְׁתִּ֣ים
הָאֵ֑לֶּה ס וַיֹּ֨אמֶר יְהוָ֤ה
אֶל־דָּוִד֙ לֵ֣ךְ וְהִכִּ֣יתָ
בַפְּלִשְׁתִּ֔ים וְהוֹשַׁעְתָּ֖
אֶת־קְעִילָֽה׃

And David inquired of the LORD,
*"Shall I go and attack these Philis-
tines?"* The LORD said to David, *"Go
and attack the Philistines* and rescue
Keilah" (1 Sam. 23:2).*

(2) A direct negative reply is minimally expressed with the negative particle
and may echo more of the question as well.

Note that which negative particle is used depends upon the kind of
question posed; a verbless (nominal) clause will have the existential
negative אַ֫יִן (#c) rather than the indicative negative לֹא (#a-b).

a

וְהָיָ֡ה כִּ֣י יֹאמְרוּ֩ פְּלִיטֵ֨י
אֶפְרַ֜יִם אֶעֱבֹ֗רָה וַיֹּ֨אמְרוּ
ל֜וֹ אַנְשֵֽׁי־גִלְעָ֤ד הַֽאֶפְרָתִי֙
אַ֔תָּה וַיֹּ֖אמֶר ׀ לֹֽא׃
וַיֹּ֤אמְרוּ לוֹ֙ אֱמָר־נָ֣א
שִׁבֹּ֔לֶת וַיֹּ֣אמֶר סִבֹּ֔לֶת
וְלֹ֥א יָכִ֖ין לְדַבֵּ֣ר כֵּ֑ן

[5] And when any of the fugitives of
Ephraim said, *"Let me go over,"*
the men of Gilead said to him,
"Are you an Ephraimite?" When
he said, *"No,"* [6] they said to him,
"Then say Shibboleth," and he
said, "Sibboleth," for he could not
pronounce it right (Judg. 12:5–6).*

b

וַיֹּ֤אמֶר מֶֽלֶךְ־יִשְׂרָאֵל֙
אֶל־אֱלִישָׁ֔ע כִּרְאֹת֖וֹ אוֹתָ֑ם
הַאַכֶּ֥ה אַכֶּ֖ה אָבִֽי׃
וַיֹּ֙אמֶר֙ לֹ֣א תַכֶּ֔ה הַאֲשֶׁ֣ר
שָׁבִ֗יתָ בְּחַרְבְּךָ֙ וּֽבְקַשְׁתְּךָ֔
אַתָּ֖ה מַכֶּֽה

[21] And the king of Israel said to
Elisha when he saw them, *"Shall I
strike (them), shall I strike (them),
my father?"* [22] He said to him, *"Do
not strike (them)!* Would you strike
down those whom you have taken
captive with your sword and with
your bow?" (2 Kgs 6:21–22).*

---

93. See Greenstein (1989) and Miller (2005b).

c	וַיֹּאמֶר אֵלֶיהָ עֲמֹד פֶּתַח הָאֹהֶל וְהָיָה אִם־אִישׁ יָבוֹא וּשְׁאֵלֵךְ וְאָמַר הֲיֵשׁ־פֹּה אִישׁ וְאָמַרְתְּ אָיִן:	And he said to her, "Stand at the opening of the tent, and then, if anyone comes and asks you, '*Is anyone here?*' you must say, '*No one*'" (i.e. *No*) (Judg. 4:20).*

(3) A pragmatic response to a yes–no question may not echo the question at all, but may instead give a reason or explanation for the positive (#*a*) or negative response (#*b-c*).

Pragmatic responses are especially common when they are dispreferred; in other words the answer to the yes–no question is a negative one which the addressee does not want to hear.

a	וַיִּשְׁאֲלוּ־עוֹד בַּיהוָה הֲבָא עוֹד הֲלֹם אִישׁ וַיֹּאמֶר יְהוָה הִנֵּה־הוּא נֶחְבָּא אֶל־הַכֵּלִים:	And they inquired of the LORD again, "Has anyone else come here?" The LORD said, "Look, he is hiding among the baggage" (1 Sam. 10:22).*
b	וַיֹּאמֶר שְׁמוּאֵל אֶל־יִשַׁי הֲתַמּוּ הַנְּעָרִים וַיֹּאמֶר עוֹד שָׁאַר הַקָּטָן וְהִנֵּה רֹעֶה בַּצֹּאן	Then Samuel asked Jesse, "Are those all the young men?" He replied, "The youngest still remains, but he is keeping the sheep" (1 Sam. 16:11).*
c	וַיֹּאמֶר הַמֶּלֶךְ אֶל־הַכּוּשִׁי הֲשָׁלוֹם לַנַּעַר לְאַבְשָׁלוֹם וַיֹּאמֶר הַכּוּשִׁי יִהְיוּ כַנַּעַר אֹיְבֵי אֲדֹנִי הַמֶּלֶךְ וְכֹל אֲשֶׁר־קָמוּ עָלֶיךָ לְרָעָה:	And the king said to the Cushite, "Is it well with the young man, with Absalom?" The Cushite answered, "May the enemies of my lord the king and all who rise up against you for evil be like that young man" (2 Sam. 18:32).*

§42.3. Content (or WH-) Questions

Content questions are introduced with an interrogative word which question the person (who?), item (what?), place (where?), time (when?), reason (why?) or manner (how?) of an assertion. Because the interrogatives *who, what, where, when,* and *why* all begin with "wh" in English, these questions are sometimes described as "WH-questions."

Content questions are introduced by the following interrogatives in Biblical Hebrew. The predicate of the sentence immediately follows the interrogative word – in a verbal question the verb follows the interrogative; in a nominal clause the nominal predicate follows the question.

Content questions may also serve as rhetorical questions. By highlighting the expressive nature of the question, rhetorical questions often serve a persuasive function and may mitigate or soften criticism or directives (see Moshavi 2014).

42.3.1. אֵי

(1) Inquires as to the place where someone or something is: *where?*

> אֵי הֶבֶל אָחִיךָ *Where* is Abel your brother? (Gen. 4:9).*

(2) Inquires (with or without preposition) as to the place from which or along which movement has occurred: *from where? along which?*

> אֵי־מִזֶּה בָאתָ *Where* have you come *from?* (Gen. 16:8).

> אֵי־זֶה הַדֶּרֶךְ הָלַךְ *Which* way did he go? (1 Kgs 13:12).

42.3.2. אַיֵּה

Inquires about the place *in which* someone or something is: *where?*
אַיֵּה is never used to inquire about the place in which *an event* took place.

> אַיֵּה שָׂרָה אִשְׁתֶּךָ *Where* is Sarah your wife? (Gen. 18:9).*

42.3.3. אֵיכָה and אֵיךְ

Strictly speaking these words are not interrogative pronouns but interrogative adverbs.

(1) Inquires about the manner in which something occurred: *how?*
This apparently basic function is, however, seldom used to pose an ordinary question.

> *a*   אֵיכָה יַעַבְדוּ הַגּוֹיִם הָאֵלֶּה *How* did these nations serve their
> אֶת־אֱלֹהֵיהֶם   gods? (Deut. 12:30).*

Sometimes אֵיךְ and אֵיכָה are used in indirect questions (#*b*).

> *b*   הַגֶּד־נָא לָנוּ אֵיךְ כָּתַבְתָּ Tell us, *how* did you write all these
> אֶת־כָּל־הַדְּבָרִים הָאֵלֶּה   words? (Jer. 36:17).*

(2) Functions primarily in rhetorical questions (almost half the occurrences in the Hebrew Bible).

In these cases the rhetorical question is used to *make it clear to listeners that some happening or state of affairs is out of the question.* אֵיךְ and אֵיכָה are then usually followed by a *yiqtōl*/imperfect form (#a-b). Sometimes the rhetorical question can be used to *reproach* the person addressed (#c).

a	אֵיכָה אֶשָּׂא לְבַדִּי טָרְחֲכֶם...	How *can I bear* all by myself your troubles...? (Deut. 1:12).*
b	הֵן אֲנִי עֲרַל שְׂפָתַיִם וְאֵיךְ יִשְׁמַע אֵלַי פַּרְעֹה:	Look, I am of uncircumcised lips; *how* then will Pharaoh listen to me? (Exod. 6:30).*
c	וְאֵיךְ אָמַרְתָּ אֲחֹתִי הִוא	And *how* then could you say, "She is my sister?" (Gen. 26:9).*

(3) Functions as exclamations to introduce the nature of a particular state of affairs or events.

Speakers often use such constructions to express *their disappointment* (#a-b), *satisfaction* or *amazement* (#c) about a situation.

a	אֵיךְ נָפְלוּ גִבּוֹרִים:	*How* are the mighty fallen! (2 Sam. 1:19).*
b	אֵיכָה הָיְתָה לְזוֹנָה	*How* she (the faithful city) has become a harlot! (Isa. 1:21).*
c	אֵיךְ חַתָּה הֵילִילוּ אֵיךְ הִפְנָה־עֹרֶף מוֹאָב בּוֹשׁ	*How* it is broken! (How) they wail! *How* Moab has turned his back in shame! (Jer. 48:39).

42.3.4. אֵיפֹה

Inquires about the place *in which* someone or something is to be found (#a) or in which events occur: *where* (#b).

a	אֵיפֹה שְׁמוּאֵל וְדָוִד	*Where* are Samuel and David? (1 Sam. 19:22).
b	אֵיפֹה לִקַּטְתְּ הַיּוֹם	*Where* did you glean today? (Ruth 2:19).

42.3.5. אָן and אָנָה[94]

(1) Inquires about the place to which someone is going: *where to?*

a	וְאָנָה תֵלֵכִי	And *where* are you going? (Gen. 16:8).
b	אָן הֲלַכְתֶּם	*Where* did you go? (1 Sam. 10:14).

(2) In exceptional cases אָנָה is used to inquire about the place in which an event occurred: *where?*

וְאָנָה עָשִׂית	And *where* have you worked? (Ruth 2:19).

(3) עַד־אָנָה is used to inquire about the duration of events: *until when? how long still?*

עַד־אָנָה מֵאַנְתֶּם	*How* long do you refuse? (Exod. 16:28).*

42.3.6. מַה

Morphologically מַה changes to מָה if it precedes א, ה or ר. מַה changes to מֶה if it precedes ח or ע. (Some dictionaries regard מָה as the basic form.) If מַ precedes any other consonant, no lengthening of the vowel occurs and the following consonant doubles, e.g. מַה־זֹּאת. It resembles the patterns of the definite article, see §24.4.2.

(1) Inquires about the nature of a thing or event

a	מֶה עָשִׂיתָ	*What* have you done? (Gen. 4:10).

The question sometimes acquires emotional weight by the addition of זֶה or זֹאת (#b). Speakers may, for example, express a degree of irritation. (See also §36.2.2.(6).)

b	וַיֹּאמֶר יְהוָה אֱלֹהִים לָאִשָּׁה מַה־זֹּאת עָשִׂית	Then the LORD God said to the woman. "*What* is this that you have done?" (Gen. 3:13).

---

94. אָן occurs only twice in the Hebrew Bible.

The event or state of affairs that is inquired about is sometimes to *the benefit or disadvantage* of someone. In such cases מַה is followed by the preposition לְ (#c).

c   מַה־לָּךְ הָגָר   *What* troubles you, Hagar? (Gen. 21:17).

(2) Inquires sometimes about the reason for a state of affairs or an event

a   מָה אֲנַחְנוּ יֹשְׁבִים פֹּה   *Why* do we sit here? (2 Kgs 7:3).*

The question sometimes acquires emotional weight by the addition of זֶה or זֹאת. Speakers may, for example, express a degree of irritation (#b).

b   מַה־זֶּה רוּחֲךָ סָרָה   *Why* is your spirit so vexed? (1 Kgs 21:5).*

(3) Functions as an introduction to a rhetorical question in which a speaker usually expresses a value judgment about something or someone. This value judgment is usually negative.

a   כִּי מֶה עַבְדְּךָ הַכֶּלֶב כִּי יַעֲשֶׂה   For *what* is your servant, who is but
       הַדָּבָר הַגָּדוֹל הַזֶּה   a dog, that he should do this great thing? (2 Kgs 8:13).*

Sometimes the rhetorical question indicates a *strong denial* (#b).

b   מַה־לָּנוּ חֵלֶק בְּדָוִד   *What* portion have we in David? (1 Kgs 12:16).*

(4) Functions as an introduction to an exclamation in which a speaker usually expresses a value judgment about something.

            מָה־אַדִּיר שִׁמְךָ בְּכָל־הָאָרֶץ   *How* majestic is your name in all the earth! (Ps. 8:2).

(5) Functions also as an indefinite pronoun (see §36.5).

       מַה־תֹּאמַר נַפְשְׁךָ וְאֶעֱשֶׂה־לָּךְ:   *Whatever* you want [lit. *whatever your soul says*] I will do for you (1 Sam. 20:4).*

42.3.7. Preposition + מָה

(1) לָמָה

Inquires as to the *reason* for a state of affairs or an action: *why?*

לָמָּה חָרָה לָךְ   *Why* are you angry? (Gen. 4:6).

(2) בַּמָּה

Inquires about the *manner* in which something is to be done: *how?*

בַּמָּה אֵדָע   *How* am I to know? (Gen. 15:8).

(3) עַד־מָה

Inquires about the *duration* of a state of affairs or events: *how long?*

עַד־מָה יְהוָה תֶּאֱנַף לָנֶצַח   *How long,* O LORD? Will you be angry forever? (Ps. 79:5).

(4) עַל־מָה

Inquires about the *reason* or *motivation* for a state of affairs or action: *why?*

עַל־מָה הִכִּיתָ אֶת־אֲתֹנְךָ   *Why* have you struck your jenny [lit. female donkey] (Num. 22:32).*

42.3.8. מִי

(1) Inquires about the identity of a person (#*a*).

a   מִי־הָאִישׁ הַלָּזֶה   *Who* is this man? (Gen. 24:65).*

The question sometimes acquires some emotional weight by the addition of זֶה (#*b*) or זֹאת. One could also speak here of the speaker's *attitude* that emerges in relation to the content of the question.

b   בֶּן־מִי־זֶה הַנַּעַר   *Whose* son is this youth? (1 Sam. 17:55).*

The question may sometimes be posed *indirectly* (#*c*).

c   שְׁאַל אַתָּה בֶּן־מִי־זֶה הָעָלֶם: Inquire *whose* son the stripling is (1 Sam. 17:56).

(2) Inquires about the identity of a group of people (#*a*) or the name of a person (#*b*).

a כִּי מִי־גוֹי גָּדוֹל אֲשֶׁר־לוֹ אֱלֹהִים For *what* great nation is there that has gods? (Deut. 4:7).*

b מִי שְׁמֶךָ *What* is your name? (Judg. 13:17).

(3) Introduces a rhetorical question in which a speaker usually expresses a value judgment about himself or someone else.

וַיֹּאמֶר מִי דָוִד וּמִי בֶן־יִשָׁי And he said, "*Who* is David? *Who* is the son of Jesse?" (1 Sam. 25:10).*

(4) Expresses a *wish* (rare)

a וַיֹּאמֶר אַבְשָׁלוֹם מִי־יְשִׂמֵנִי שֹׁפֵט בָּאָרֶץ And Absalom said, "*Oh* that I were [lit. who would make me a] judge in the land!" (2 Sam. 15:4).*

Sometimes a fixed expression מִי יִתֵּן is used (#*b*). This construction, which functions as an interjection, expresses *a positive wish* (see §44.9). In the fixed expression מִי יוֹדֵעַ, the outcome of the wish is doubtful (#*c*).

b בַּבֹּקֶר תֹּאמַר מִי־יִתֵּן עֶרֶב In the morning you will say, "*Would that it were* evening!" (Deut. 28:67).*

c אָמַרְתִּי מִי יוֹדֵעַ יְחַנַּנִי יְהוָה I said, "*Who knows? Maybe* the LORD will be gracious to me" (2 Sam. 12:22).*

(5) Functions as an indefinite pronoun

a מִי־יָרֵא וְחָרֵד יָשֹׁב *Whoever* is fearful and trembling, let him return (Judg. 7:3).*

Sometimes מִי is followed by אֲשֶׁר (#*b*) or even הָאִישׁ אֲשֶׁר (#*c*). In a few instances מִי is used after אֶת as the object of a clause (#*d*).

b מִי אֲשֶׁר חָטָא־לִי אֶמְחֶנּוּ מִסִּפְרִי: *Whoever* has sinned against me, I will blot him out of my book (Exod. 32:33).*

c	מִי־הָאִישׁ אֲשֶׁר בָּנָה בַיִת־חָדָשׁ...	*Whoever* that has built a new house… (Deut. 20:5).*
d	בַּחֲרוּ לָכֶם הַיּוֹם אֶת־מִי תַעֲבֹדוּן	Choose today *whom* you will serve (Josh. 24:15).*

§43. Predicators of Existence

§43.1 Introduction

Predicators of existence relate to an entire clause. Furthermore, predicators of existence have only two members, and their use is restricted to nominal clauses (i.e. verbless clauses and participle clauses).

§43.2. אֵין

See §41.2.

§43.3. יֵשׁ

יֵשׁ occurs 138 times in the Hebrew Bible, both in poetic and prose material. It is absent from the books of Leviticus, Joshua, Ezekiel and most of the smaller prophets. Its highest concentration is in the book of Ecclesiastes (16 times).

יֵשׁ may take a pronominal suffix, but this does not happen frequently. It sometimes combines with the yes–no question word הַ and the conjunction וְ.

The following categories can be distinguished:

(1) Expresses existence of an undetermined entity

In nearly 85% of the occurrences, יֵשׁ is used to refer to the existence of an undetermined entity or entities. The entity may be concrete (#a and #c), abstract (#b) or a quality (#d).

a	אוּלַי יֵשׁ חֲמִשִּׁים צַדִּיקִם בְּתוֹךְ הָעִיר	Perhaps *there are* fifty righteous within the city (Gen. 18:24).*
b	יֵשׁ רָעָה אֲשֶׁר רָאִיתִי תַּחַת הַשָּׁמֶשׁ	*There is* an evil that I saw under the sun (Eccl. 6:1).*
c	וַנֹּאמֶר אֶל־אֲדֹנִי יֶשׁ־לָנוּ אָב זָקֵן	And we said to my lord, "We have an aged father" [lit. *There is* for us a father, an old man] (Gen. 44:20).*

d   וַיֹּאמֶר עֵשָׂו יֶשׁ־לִי רָב   But Esau said, "I have plenty"
                                               [lit. *There is* for me plenty] (Gen.
                                               33:9).*

(2) Affirms the presence or involvement of an identifiable entity in a situation.[95]
     The involvement may entail the presence of an identifiable entity at a
     location (#*a*). It may also entail that the entity is involved in an action
     (#*b*).

a   אָכֵן יֵשׁ יְהוָה בַּמָּקוֹם הַזֶּה   Surely, the Lord *is indeed* in this
                                                place (Gen. 28:16).*

b   וַיֹּאמֶר גִּדְעוֹן אֶל־הָאֱלֹהִים   Then Gideon said to God, "If *indeed*
             אִם־יֶשְׁךָ מוֹשִׁיעַ בְּיָדִי   you are going to deliver Israel by
           אֶת־יִשְׂרָאֵל כַּאֲשֶׁר דִּבַּרְתָּ:   my hand as you have said" (Judg.
                                                 6:36).*

§44. Interjections

§44.1. Introduction

Interjections do not form part of a constituent or a clause (see §11.10). They
also do not modify a constituent or clause.

§44.2. אֲהָהּ

Expresses *sorrow and regret*

        אֲהָהּ בִּתִּי הַכְרֵעַ הִכְרַעְתִּנִי   *Oh*, my daughter! You have brought
                                                me very low (Judg. 11:35).*

§44.3. אוֹי

אוֹי is usually followed by לְ plus pronominal suffix and expresses the
experience of a threat

        אוֹי לָנוּ כִּי לֹא הָיְתָה כָּזֹאת   *Woe* to us! For nothing like this has
                 אֶתְמוֹל שִׁלְשֹׁם: happened before (1 Sam. 4:7).

---

95. See also Muraoka (1985: 77–82).

§44.4. אַחֲלַי and אַחֲלֵי

Expresses a positive wish

אַחֲלֵי אֲדֹנִי לִפְנֵי הַנָּבִיא   *If only* my lord were before the
אֲשֶׁר בְּשֹׁמְרוֹן אָז יֶאֱסֹף אֹתוֹ   prophet who is in Samaria, then
מִצָּרַעְתּוֹ   he would have cured him from his
skin disease (2 Kgs 5:3).*

§44.5. אָנָּא/אָנָּה

Expresses an urgent request: *I/we beg you*

אָנָּא שָׂא נָא פֶּשַׁע אַחֶיךָ   *I beg you*, please forgive the trans-
gression of your brothers (Gen.
50:17).*

§44.6. בִּי

בִּי is always followed by אֲדֹנָי or אֲדֹנִי and expresses a request to be excused:
pardon/excuse me/us

בִּי אֲדֹנָי מָה אֹמַר   *Excuse me*, Lord, but what can I
say (Josh. 7:8).*

§44.7. הוֹי

Expresses the experience of a threat. Twelve of the 50 instances in which this
interjection is used in the Hebrew Bible occur in the book of Isaiah.

הוֹי אֹמֵר לְאָב מַה־תּוֹלִיד   *Woe* to him who says to a father:
What are you begetting? (Isa.
45:10).*

§44.8. חָלִילָה

(1) Expresses a speaker's refusal to accept a state of affairs or course of events.

וַיֹּאמֶר לוֹ חָלִילָה לֹא תָמוּת   And he said to him, "*Far from it*!
You shall not die" (1 Sam. 20:2).*

(2) A speaker uses the expression to distance himself from a situation or action.

This expression is more commonly the predicate of a nominal clause, i.e. syntactically speaking it is not an interjection.

וַיֹּאמֶר חָלִילָה לִּי מֵעֲשׂוֹת זֹאת But he said, "*Far be it* from me that I should do so!" (Gen. 44:17).*

§44.9. מִי יִתֵּן

Expresses a positive wish (see §42.3.1.(4)).

וּמִי יִתֵּן אֶת־הָעָם הַזֶּה בְּיָדִי And *if only* that this people were under my command [lit. hand]! (Judg. 9:29).

§44.10. ־נָא

Expresses a polite request: *please* (see §19.5.2.2).

נַעְבְּרָה־נָּא בְאַרְצֶךָ *Please* let us pass through your land (Num. 20:17).*

§45. Oaths

§45.1. Introduction

A distinction must be made between vows and oaths. The former typically do not involve special formulaic language.[96] According to Conklin (2011: 12), there are "some 170 passages that contain oath formulas" in the Hebrew Bible. Oaths may be mentioned, e.g. "somebody swore that..." or used, e.g. "I hereby swear."[97] Typically oaths contain an authenticating element, e.g. "as surely as the LORD lives," "I swear," and the content of the oath, e.g. "If I do this, may I be cursed."

What is attested across languages is that elements like "I swear" and "may I be cursed" are often elided.

---

96. See Naudé (2013d).
97. Most of this section is based on Conklin (2011).

§45.2. Authenticating Elements

According to Conklin (2011: 13), five different types of authenticating elements are attested.

45.2.1. *(By) the life (חֵי/חַי) of x*

Occurring 76 times, this is by far the most frequent authenticator in the Hebrew Bible. It is concentrated in the book of Samuel, Kings, Jeremiah and Ezekiel (Conklin 2011: 26). It is typically used to make an oath (#*a-e*). Sometimes the oath is only "mentioned" (#*g*).

Most frequent are instances where חַי־יְהֹוָה is used as authenticator (#*a*). In eight cases, חַי־יְהֹוָה is part of a double authenticator (#*c*). חֵי is used when *x* is not the Israelite god (#*d-e*). The construction חַי־אָנִי (#*b* and #*f*) occurs 23 times, predominantly in the book of Ezekiel (16 times).

The formula literally reads "(by) the life of *x*," but is typically translated as "as surely as *x* lives." Such a translation implies that the living existence of *x* is affirmed as the basis of the truthfulness of the oath.

Two types of content that follow the authenticating formula can be distinguished. Firstly, "By the life of *x*, (I swear) that, ..." (#*a-d*). Sometimes a speaker uses this type of oath to express his/her conviction that his/her assessment of a state of affairs is correct (#*d*). Secondly, "By the life of *x*, if *y* (or not *y*) ... (may I be cursed)" (#*e*).

a	כִּי חַי־יְהֹוָה הַמּוֹשִׁיעַ אֶת־יִשְׂרָאֵל כִּי אִם־יֶשְׁנוֹ בְּיוֹנָתָן בְּנִי כִּי מוֹת יָמוּת	For *by the life of the* LORD *who saves Israel*, (I swear) that, if it is indeed Jonathan, my son, then he will certainly die (1 Sam. 14:39).*
b	חַי־אָנִי נְאֻם־יְהוָה כִּי אִם־יִהְיֶה כָּנְיָהוּ בֶן־יְהוֹיָקִים מֶלֶךְ יְהוּדָה חוֹתָם עַל־יַד יְמִינִי כִּי מִשָּׁם אֶתְּקֶנְךָּ:	"*By my life*," declares the LORD, "(I swear) that even if King Coniah son of Jehoiakim of Judah were the signet ring on my right hand, then even from there I would tear you off" (Jer. 22:24).*
c	חַי־יְהֹוָה וְחֵי אֲדֹנִי הַמֶּלֶךְ כִּי אִם־בִּמְקוֹם אֲשֶׁר יִהְיֶה־שָּׁם׀ אֲדֹנִי הַמֶּלֶךְ אִם־לְמָוֶת אִם־לְחַיִּים כִּי־שָׁם יִהְיֶה עַבְדֶּךָ:	*By the life of the* LORD, *and the life of my lord the king*, (I swear) that wherever my lord the king may be, whether for death or for life, then there also your servant will be (2 Sam. 15:21).*

d   חֵי פַרְעֹה כִּי מְרַגְּלִים אַתֶּם   By the life of Pharaoh, (I swear) that you are spies (Gen. 42:16).*[98]

e   וַיֹּאמֶר אַבְנֵר חֵי־נַפְשְׁךָ הַמֶּלֶךְ   Abner said, "By the life of your inner being, O king, if I know (may I be cursed)" (1 Sam. 17:55).*
אִם־יָדָעְתִּי׃

f   לָכֵן חַי־אָנִי נְאֻם אֲדֹנָי יְהוִה   "Therefore, by my life," declares the LORD God, "if not, because you have defiled my sanctuary with all your detestable things and with all your abominations, I also cut you down and my eye not spare, and I also have no pity (may I be cursed)" (Ezek. 5:11).*
אִם־לֹא יַעַן אֶת־מִקְדָּשִׁי
טִמֵּאת בְּכָל־שִׁקּוּצַיִךְ
וּבְכָל־תּוֹעֲבֹתָיִךְ וְגַם־אָנִי
אֶגְרַע וְלֹא־תָחוֹס עֵינִי
וְגַם־אֲנִי לֹא אֶחְמוֹל׃

g   אִם חַי־יְהֹוָה יֹאמֵרוּ לָכֵן לַשֶּׁקֶר   If they say, "By the life of the LORD," then they swear falsely (Jer. 5:2).*
יִשָּׁבֵעוּ׃

45.2.2. *Swearing* (שבע)

The Niṗ῾al of שבע plus the entity that is sworn by, governed by בְּ, is prototypically used to make an oath (#a) or to solicit an oath from another person (#b). In a number of cases the same verbal root is used to "mention" the making of an oath (#c).

a   כִּי בַיהוָה נִשְׁבַּעְתִּי כִּי־אֵינְךָ יוֹצֵא   For by the LORD *I hereby swear* that if you do not go out, not a man will be left with you to stay the night [lit. if a man stays with you the night (may I be cursed)] (2 Sam. 19:8).*
אִם־יָלִין אִישׁ אִתְּךָ הַלַּיְלָה

b   וְעַתָּה הִשָּׁבְעָה לִּי בֵאלֹהִים   So now *swear* to me here by God, if you deal falsely with me or with my offspring or my posterity (may you be cursed) (Gen. 21:23).*
הֵנָּה אִם־תִּשְׁקֹר לִי וּלְנִינִי
וּלְנֶכְדִּי

---

98. If one argues that this construction has also become a conventionalized way of expressing "certainty" (epistemic modality), this expression can be translated as "By the life Pharaoh, you are certainly spies" (see §40.29.2.(4)).

c   וַיִּשָּׁבַע שָׁאוּל חַי־יְהוָה   And Saul *swore*, "(By) the life of the
אִם־יוּמָת: Lord, (I swear that), if he is killed
    (may I be cursed)" (1 Sam. 19:6).*

45.2.3. *"Thus will x do to y and thus will he add"*

This formula occurs 12 times. It is regarded as the apodosis of a conditional
clause in which the protasis is elided: "(If this oath is false), thus will God do
to me." What exactly will be done to the one who utters the oath is not stated,
but gestures may have accompanied each of the deictics ("thus").[99]

a   וַיֹּאמֶר כֹּה־יַעֲשׂוּן לִי אֱלֹהִים   And he said, *"Thus will the gods do*
וְכֹה יוֹסִפוּ אִם־יִשְׂפֹּק עֲפַר   *to me and thus they will add*; if the
שֹׁמְרוֹן לִשְׁעָלִים לְכָל־הָעָם   dust of Samaria is enough for all the
אֲשֶׁר בְּרַגְלָי: people who are under me to have
    handfuls, (may I be cursed)" (1 Kgs
    20:10).*

b   יִשָּׁבַע דָּוִד לֵאמֹר כֹּה   David swore, *"Thus will God to me*
יַעֲשֶׂה־לִּי אֱלֹהִים וְכֹה יֹסִיף   *and thus will he add*: (I swear) that,
כִּי אִם־לִפְנֵי בוֹא־הַשֶּׁמֶשׁ   if I eat bread or anything else before
אֶטְעַם־לֶחֶם אוֹ   the sun comes up, (may I be cursed)"
כָל־מְאוּמָה: (2 Sam. 3:35).*

c   כֹּה־יַעֲשׂוּן אֱלֹהִים וְכֹה   *Thus the gods will do to me and thus*
יוֹסִפוּן כִּי־כָעֵת מָחָר   *they will add*, (I swear) that tomorrow
אָשִׂים אֶת־נַפְשְׁךָ כְּנֶפֶשׁ   I will make your life like the lives of
אַחַד מֵהֶם: one like them (1 Kgs 19:2).*

45.2.4. *Raising of the hand*

The raising of the hand could refer to the act of swearing (#a) or be used to
swear (#b).

a   וְהֵבֵאתִי אֶתְכֶם אֶל־הָאָרֶץ   And I will bring you to the land which
אֲשֶׁר נָשָׂאתִי אֶת־יָדִי לָתֵת   *I lifted my hand* (in an oath) to give it
אֹתָהּ לְאַבְרָהָם לְיִצְחָק   to Abraham, Isaac and Jacob (Exod.
וּלְיַעֲקֹב   6:8).*

---

99. See Conklin (2011: 22–24).

b וַיֹּאמֶר אַבְרָם אֶל־מֶלֶךְ [22]

22 And Abram said to the king of Sodom, "*I raise my hand* to the LORD, El Elyon, creator of heaven and earth, 23(and swear that) I will not take anything of yours, from thread to sandal thong [lit. if from thread to sandal thong, if I take anything of yours (may I be cursed)]" (Gen. 14:22–23).*

סְדֹם הֲרִימֹתִי יָדִי אֶל־יְהוָה
אֵל עֶלְיוֹן קֹנֵה שָׁמַיִם וָאָרֶץ:
אִם־מִחוּט וְעַד [23]
שְׂרוֹךְ־נַעַל וְאִם־אֶקַּח
מִכָּל־אֲשֶׁר־לָךְ

45.2.5. *Invocation of witnesses*

יְהוָה יִהְיֶה שֹׁמֵעַ בֵּינוֹתֵינוּ
אִם־לֹא כִדְבָרְךָ כֵּן נַעֲשֶׂה:

The LORD will be a witness [lit. one who hears] between us, if we do not act in accordance with your proposal, (may we be cursed) (Judg. 11:10).*

§45.3. Contents of Oaths

The contents of oaths are typically introduced by אִם (46 times), אִם־לֹא (12 times), or כִּי (43 times).[100] Less frequently, a complementizer introduces the content – twice with אֲשֶׁר (#a) and twice with מַה (#b). In the remaining ten cases, no formal marker is used (#c).

a וְאַשְׁבִּיעֲךָ בַּיהוָה אֱלֹהֵי

And I will make you swear by the LORD, the God of the heaven and the earth, *that you will not take a wife for my son from the daughters of the Canaanites* (Gen. 24:3).*

הַשָּׁמַיִם וֵאלֹהֵי הָאָרֶץ אֲשֶׁר
לֹא־תִקַּח אִשָּׁה לִבְנִי מִבְּנוֹת
הַכְּנַעֲנִי

b הִשְׁבַּעְתִּי אֶתְכֶם בְּנוֹת

I adjure you, O daughters of Jerusalem, *do not stir up or awaken love until it is ready*! (Song 8:4).

יְרוּשָׁלַםִ מַה־תָּעִירוּ|
וּמַה־תְּעֹרְרוּ אֶת־הָאַהֲבָה
עַד שֶׁתֶּחְפָּץ:

c עַל־כֵּן נָשָׂאתִי יָדִי עֲלֵיהֶם

"Therefore I have sworn concerning them [lit. I have lifted my hand concerning them]," declares the LORD God, "*that they shall bear their punishment*" (Ezek. 44:12).*

נְאֻם אֲדֹנָי יְהוִה וְנָשְׂאוּ
עֲוֹנָם

---

100. See §40.11.(2) and §40.29.2.(4), respectively.

Chapter 7

WORD ORDER

§46. Syntax of Word Order

§46.1. Syntax of Word Order in Verbal Clauses

46.1.1. *Introduction*

Statistically speaking most finite verbal clauses in the Hebrew Bible commence with a verb.[1] The reasons for this are the following:

- In the *qātal*/perfect and *yiqtōl*/imperfect forms of Biblical Hebrew verbs, person (first, second or third person) is not marked by means of an independent personal pronoun, as it is in most European languages. In other words, Biblical Hebrew has no direct equivalent for "*I* wrote the book." The morpheme that marks person is part of the verbal conjugation, e.g. כָּתַבְתִּי אֶת־הַסֵּפֶר. (See also §15.)
- The *wəqātal* and *wayyiqtōl* constructions that are frequently used in Biblical Hebrew also indicate person as part of their verbal conjugation. In addition, these forms do not allow a constituent (e.g. subject, object, or prepositional phrase) to precede the verb.

It is therefore understandable that Biblical Hebrew is regarded as a verb-initial language. In verb-initial languages, the verb normally takes the initial position in a clause and is followed by the subject and object (in cases where the valency of the verb establishes the need for an object). This order of constituents is regarded as the unmarked word order in Biblical Hebrew. If the verb is, however, preceded by the subject or any other constituent, the word order of that clause is regarded as "marked."[2]

---

1. In narrative material, about 75% of clauses start with a verb. For a discussion of studies illustrating the statistical dominance of clauses that commence with a finite verb in Biblical Hebrew, see Moshavi (2010: 11–13). In a comparison of about 1200 verbal clauses from a selection of narrative portions with a similar number in a selection of poetic texts, Lunn (2006: 8) found that 85% of the verbal clauses in narrative texts and 66% of those in poetic texts begins with a finite verb.

2. In the field of linguistic typology, scholars have distinguished for many years between Verb-Subject-Object (=VSO), Subject-Verb-Object (=SVO) and Subject-Object-Verb (=SOV) languages (Song 2011: 257–59). Due to the fact that in many languages, pronominal subjects of finite verbs may form (morphologically speaking) part of the verb, as is indeed the case in Biblical Hebrew, in the recent years the value of these distinctions

In many traditional grammars of Biblical Hebrew only the semantic function of "emphasis" is attributed to this marked constructions. In this grammar it is assumed that a more nuanced view of the semantic-pragmatic functions of Biblical Hebrew word order is possible.[3]

46.1.2. *Marked and unmarked word order*

In determining whether the word order of a verbal clause is marked or unmarked, the following considerations must be kept in mind:

(1) With marked and unmarked word order, reference is made to the linear sequence of clause constituents that are marked or unmarked.

In other words, only the linear sequence of the complements (i.e. verb, subject, object, indirect object, etc.) and adjuncts (i.e. adjuncts of time, place and manner) of a clause are involved. Lexical items like conjunctions, some adverbs, negatives and discourse marker typically do not come into play when establishing the word order of a clause. In terms of their word order, the clauses in #*a-g* could therefore be regarded as verb initial (i.e. unmarked). Furthermore, the infinitive absolute of an infinitive absolute construction is part of the verb of a clause, and should not be regarded as a fronted clause constituent (#*h*).

a	בָּאנוּ אֶל־אָחִיךָ אֶל־עֵשָׂו	We came to your brother Esau (Gen. 32:7).

---

has been called into question. Distinguishing only between VO (i.e. SVO and VSO) and OV (i.e. SOV) languages is therefore preferred by many linguistic typologists (see Velupillai 2012: 295–300, and Song 2011: 259–62). For an analysis of the marked word order of Biblical Hebrew in the book of Joel, see Van der Merwe and Wendland (2010).

Most Biblical Hebrew scholars regard the language as a VSO language (see the discussion in Holmstedt 2011: 1–4). Holmstedt (2011, 2013b) strongly argues against this "canonical" view. We do not regard a final word on this debate as crucial for the purposes of this grammar. Firstly, the fact that pronominal subjects of finite verbs cannot be utilized in establishing its status as SVO or VSO languages, limits the value of this type of typology for the interpretation of Biblical Hebrew word order patterns. Secondly, since speakers of a language tend to regard patterns that they encounter most often as the unmarked instances of those constructions, we settle for distinguishing only between instances of unmarked word order and instances of marked word order. For the theoretical model that undergirds the semantic-pragmatic functions of unmarked and marked word order in this grammar, see §47.1.

3. Although the word order in Biblical Hebrew poetry can often be explained in terms of the same rules that apply to non-poetical texts, some word order sequences in poetical texts can be explained in terms of regular patterns that are characteristic of Biblical Hebrew poetic texts (see Lunn 2006).

b	הִנֵּה שָׁמַעְתִּי כִּי יֶשׁ־שֶׁבֶר בְּמִצְרָיִם רְדוּ־שָׁמָּה וְשִׁבְרוּ־לָנוּ מִשָּׁם	*Look,* I have heard that there is grain in Egypt, go down there and buy grain for us there (Gen. 42:2).*
c	וְעַתָּה הִנֵּה יָדַעְתִּי כִּי מָלֹךְ תִּמְלוֹךְ	*So now, look,* I know that you will certainly be king (1 Sam. 24:21).*
d	וּבֵרַכְתִּי אֹתָהּ וְגַם נָתַתִּי מִמֶּנָּה לְךָ בֵּן	And I will bless her, and *what is more,* I will give you a son by her (Gen. 17:16).*
e	אוּלַי יַחְסְרוּן חֲמִשִּׁים הַצַּדִּיקִם חֲמִשָּׁה	*Perhaps* five of the fifty righteous are lacking (Gen. 18:28).*
f	לֹא יָדַעְתִּי מִי עָשָׂה אֶת־הַדָּבָר הַזֶּה	I do *not* know who has done this thing (Gen. 21:26).*
g	וְטֶרֶם יִגָּלֶה אֵלָיו דְּבַר־יְהוָה:	And the word of the Lord had *not yet* been revealed to him (1 Sam. 3:7).
h	כִּי־בָרֵךְ אֲבָרֶכְךָ	*For* I will bless you richly (Gen. 22:17).*

(2) A distinction must be made between fronting[4] and left dislocation.[5]

A clause with a fronted constituent and a clause with a left dislocated constituent are both marked constructions. However, they differ structurally. They also tend to have different semantic-pragmatic functions.

With fronting, a non-verbal clause constituent, e.g. the subject (#*a*) or object (#*b*), occupies the position in front of the verb. More than one clause constituent may also be fronted (#*c*).

a	בֵּיתְךָ וּבֵית אָבִיךָ יִתְהַלְּכוּ לְפָנַי עַד־עוֹלָם	*Your household and the household of your father* will walk before me forever (1 Sam. 2:30).*
b	אֹתִי שָׁלַח יְהוָה לִמְשָׁחֲךָ לְמֶלֶךְ	*Me (and no-one else)* has the Lord sent to anoint you as king (1 Sam. 15:1).*

---

4. Moshavi (2010) prefers the notion "preposing" to that of "fronting." For a discussion of the notion "fronting," see Van der Merwe (2013b). In generative circles, "fronting" is referred to as "topicalization," see Naudé (1994a, 1994b).

5. In linguistic terminology, "left" refers to the beginning of a sentence and "right" to the end of a sentence.

c   וְהַנִּשְׁאָרִים הֶרָה נָּסוּ׃   *And the rest* [lit. *those who remained over*] fled *to the mountain* (Gen. 14:10).*

With left dislocation, a clause constituent occurs in a position outside the left-hand border of a clause. That clause constituent is typically resumed in the subsequent matrix clause (see also §48.1). The resumed constituent may (#d) or may not (#e) be fronted in the matrix clause.

d   אֵת כָּל־הַדָּבָר אֲשֶׁר אָנֹכִי   *Everything I am commanding you* מְצַוֶּה אֶתְכֶם אֹתוֹ תִשְׁמְרוּ   *today*, <u>that</u> you must take care to do לַעֲשׂוֹת   (Deut. 13:1).*

e   וְלָאֲתֹנוֹת הָאֹבְדוֹת לְךָ   *As for the donkeys that were lost to* הַיּוֹם שְׁלֹשֶׁת הַיָּמִים   *you three days ago*, give no further אַל־תָּשֶׂם אֶת־לִבְּךָ לָהֶם כִּי   thought <u>to them</u>, for they have been נִמְצָאוּ   found (1 Sam. 9:20).*

(3) Postverbal word order

A distinction must be made between marked constructions as signaled by means of fronting and left dislocation and marked constructions in the post verbal field (i.e. linear sequence of constituents following the verb) (see §47.2.2).

(4) Marked and unmarked constructions

Marked constructions are positively marked in any context for specific functions. Unmarked constructions do not specify whether a feature is present or not. As an illustration, compare the semantics of the word "dog," which is unmarked for gender, with the word "bitch," which is marked for gender. A "dog" may be either male or female. However, if a "dog" is contrasted with a "bitch," "dog" will be understood as referring to a male. The marked word "bitch," however, can only refer to a female animal.

46.1.3. *Postverbal word order*[6]

46.1.3.1. *Typical order of constituents*

(1) Shorter constituents with a deictic function stand as close to the verb as possible.

The shorter constituents, which may be expressed by means of a preposition + pronominal suffix or אֵת + pronominal suffix, typically stand as close to the verb as possible (#a). However, if the subject constituent

---

6. This section benefitted from Gross (1996).

consists of a *status constructus* phrase and the pronominal suffix refers to the referent of the *status absolutus*, the preposition + pronominal suffix cannot precede the subject (#*b*). Constituents that are expressed by means of deictic adverbs also stand as close to the verb as possible (#*c*). The adverb עוֹד often stands as close to the verb as possible (#*d*).

a	וַיֹּאמֶר אֵלָיו הָאֱלֹהִים...	And God said *to him*... (Gen. 20:6).*
b	וַתֵּלֶד אֵשֶׁת־גִּלְעָד לוֹ בָּנִים	And *Gilead's* wife also bore *him* sons (Judg. 11:2).*
c	וַיַּכֵּם שָׁם דָּוִד	And David defeated them *there* (2 Sam. 5:20).
d	כִּי לוֹא־יַעֲשֶׂה עוֹד עַבְדְּךָ עֹלָה וָזֶבַח לֵאלֹהִים אֲחֵרִים	For your servant will not offer *again* burnt offering or sacrifice to other gods (2 Kgs 5:17).*

(2) Long constituents tend to occur at the end of a clause.

The long constituents may be a relative complementizer + clause (#*a*) or a coordinated phrase (#*b*). However, if the coordinated phrase is the subject (and in a few cases the object) of the clause, it tends not to stand at the end of the clause (#*c*).

a	כִּי־לָקַח מֶלֶךְ בָּבֶל מִנַּחַל מִצְרַיִם עַד־נְהַר־פְּרָת כֹּל אֲשֶׁר הָיְתָה לְמֶלֶךְ מִצְרָיִם:	For the king of Babylon had taken from the Brook of Egypt to the river Euphrates all *that belonged to the king of Egypt* (2 Kgs 24:7).*
b	וְנָתַן לַכֹּהֵן הַזְּרֹעַ וְהַלְּחָיַיִם וְהַקֵּבָה:	And they must give to the priest *the shoulder and the two cheeks and the stomach* (Deut. 18:3).*
c	וַתָּשַׁר דְּבוֹרָה וּבָרָק בֶּן־אֲבִינֹעַם בַּיּוֹם הַהוּא...	Then sang *Deborah and Barak the son of Abinoam* on that day... (Judg. 5:1).*

46.1.3.2. *Unmarked and marked word order*

(1) The unmarked order when all the constituents are lexicalized is:[7]
Subject + object + indirect object + prepositional object + other complement/ adjunct + complement/adjunct (place) + adjunct (time).

---

7. This is a theoretical template that is reconstructed from the postverbal patterns in clauses with a variety of verbal lexemes.

(2) Marked order

Mark order is involved when a constituent stands further away from the verb than usual, e.g. a lexicalized subject is moved to the end of a clause (#*a*). When a constituent that normally occurs at the end of a clause, e.g. a temporal adjunct, is moved closer to the verb, it is also an instance of marked order (#*b*).

a   כִּי נִמְנַע מִבֵּית אֱלֹהֵיכֶם   For withheld from the house of
                  מִנְחָה וָנָסֶךְ:   your God is *grain offering and drink offering* (Joel 1:13).*

b   וָאוֹלֵךְ אֶתְכֶם אַרְבָּעִים   And I have led you *forty years* in
                 שָׁנָה בַּמִּדְבָּר   the wilderness (Deut. 29:4).

§46.2. Syntax of Word Order in Nominal Clauses

46.2.1. *Introduction*

When considering the constituent order of nominal clauses, it must be taken into account whether a verbless clause or participle clause is involved.[8] In the case of verbless clauses, a clear distinction must be made between the subject and predicate.[9] As in the case of verbal clauses, a dislocated constituent may be used on the left-hand border of nominal clauses.

46.2.2. *Syntax of word order of participle clauses*

A participle clause is a clause in which the main verb is a participle.

46.2.2.1. *Unmarked word order*

A typical unmarked participle clause displays the constituent order: subject + participle. This sequence occurs in approximately 80% of the cases of participle clauses.[10] (See also §20.3.2.1.)

---

8. See also §20.3.2.1.

9. The empirical status of these two constituents, as well as the criteria to determine them, are not uncontroversial. See Zewi and Van der Merwe (2001). In this grammar the more formal criteria suggested by Talstra and Dyk (1999: 152) are used as the point of departure. Definiteness is regarded as representing a continuum, and when the two poles of a verbless clause are both noun phrases, the relatively more definite phrase is regarded as the subject. See also Buth (1999: 100–101).

10. These statistics are based on Joosten (1989: 140).

a　　　　　　וַיֹּ֣אמֶר אֵלָ֗יו אֲדֹנִ֤י יֹדֵ֨עַ֙ But he said to him, "*My lord*
כִּֽי־הַיְלָדִ֣ים רַכִּ֔ים *knows* that the children are frail"
(Gen. 33:13).*

b　　　　　　וְכָל־עֲבָדָיו֙ עֹבְרִ֣ים עַל־יָד֔וֹ And *all his servants* pass by before
him (2 Sam. 15:18).*

46.2.2.2. *Marked word order*

The marked order is participle + subject (#*a-b*). A non-subject complement or
adjunct may also be fronted. In such a case, the fronted constituent precedes
the subject (#*c*).

a　　　　　　וַתֹּ֖אמֶר חֹלֶ֥ה הֽוּא And she said, "He *is ill*" (1 Sam.
19:14).*

b　　　　　　דַּבֵּ֣ר יְהוָ֔ה כִּ֥י שֹׁמֵ֖עַ עַבְדֶּ֑ךָ Speak, Lord, for your servant *is
listening* (1 Sam. 3:9).

c　　　　　　מָֽה־אַתָּ֥ה רֹאֶ֖ה יִרְמְיָ֑הוּ "What are you seeing, Jeremiah?"
וָאֹמַ֕ר מַקֵּ֥ל שָׁקֵ֖ד אֲנִ֥י and I answered, "I am seeing *an
רֹאֶֽה: almond stick*" (Jer. 1:11).*

46.2.3. *Syntax of word order in verbless clauses*

46.2.3.1. *Unmarked word order*

The most typical unmarked order is subject + predicate.[11] The predicate may
be a noun phrase (#*a-b*), adjective phrase (#*c*) or prepositional phrase (#*d*).

a　　　　　　שֵׁ֥ם הַגְּדֹלָה֙ לֵאָ֔ה The name of the elder (daughter)
was Leah (Gen. 29:16).*

b　　　　　　אַתֶּ֣ם עֵדַ֔י You are *my witnesses* (Isa. 43:10).

c　　　　　　גַּ֣ם ׀ הָאִ֣ישׁ מֹשֶׁ֗ה גָּד֤וֹל Furthermore, the man Moses *was
great* (Exod. 11:3).*

d　　　　　　וּשְׁנֵ֥י נְעָרָ֖יו עִמּֽוֹ: And his two servants *were with him*
(Num. 22:22).

---

11. In accordance with Buth (1999), the distinction between descriptive and identi-
ficational verbless clauses is regarded as having only a heuristic value. They do not have
different types of unmarked word order.

46.2.3.2. *Marked word order*

The marked order is predicate + subject (#*a*). The adjunct of a verbless clause may also be fronted (#*b*). A dislocated constituent often precedes the verbless clause with the marked order (#*c*).

a	מְרַגְּלִים אַתֶּם	You are nothing *but spies* [lit. *Spies* are you] (Gen. 42:9).*
b	זֶה | אַרְבָּעִים שָׁנָה יְהוָה אֱלֹהֶיךָ עִמָּךְ	*These forty years* the LORD your God has been with you (Deut. 2:7).
c	אֶרֶץ מִצְרַיִם לְפָנֶיךָ הִוא	The land of Egypt, it *is in front of you* (Gen. 47:6).

§47. Semantic-Pragmatic Functions of Word Order

§47.1. Introduction

The *semantic-pragmatic* function of word order refers to the contribution that the order of constituents makes to the interpretation of a clause. Often, there is no one-to-one correlation between the order of constituents and the function that is expressed by means of it. Its function can only be determined if the communicative context in which the clause was uttered is taken into consideration. For this reason we refer to the semantic-pragmatic function of word order rather than merely to its semantic function. In order to determine which particular semantic-pragmatic function is involved, the following general remarks need to be taken into consideration:

(1) Participants in a communicative situation, i.e. the interlocutors, each have a cognitive world of their own. This world, among other things, consists of mental representations of persons, things and places (entities), as well as states of affairs and events (propositions). These mental representations make up their knowledge of the world.

(2) When two parties communicate they are normally unconscious of their entire knowledge of the world. At a particular point in a conversation, only a part of their conceptual world is (or can be) activated. This is because the short-term memory of humans has a limited capacity. In the case of a narrative, the composite parts of the conceptual world (e.g. characters, things, places, states of affairs and events, etc.) may be introduced or activated throughout its course. However, only those entities and propositions that are in the short-term memory of the interlocutors are active

at a particular point in a discourse; they are referred to as being discourse active.[12]

(3) When one analyzes the utterances of a narrative, it is usually evident that most of the utterances are about somebody or something which is already *discourse active*. The entity or entities about which an utterance says something is referred to as the *topic* of that utterance.[13] A discourse active topic is normally referred to by means of a pronominal reference that is the subject of the sentence involved, e.g.:

וַיֵּצֵא הָרֹוּחַ וַיַּעֲמֹד לִפְנֵי יְהוָה   And a (particular) spirit [lit. the spirit] came forward and (*he*) stood before the LORD (1 Kgs 22:21).

(4) What is said about the discourse active topic of an utterance presents the most salient information conveyed by a particular utterance. This section of the utterance is referred to as the focus of the utterance. In the case of 1 Kgs 22:21, it is the section in italics: "…and (he) *stood before the LORD*." In this utterance the predicate is the focus of the utterance. Across languages, utterances with predicate focus are those that are the most unmarked as far as the sequence of clause constituents is concerned; for example, in English, it is the sequence subject-verb-object (SVO) and in Biblical Hebrew and Arabic it is verb-subject-object (VSO). (See also §46.1.1–2.)

(5) The focus of an utterance is considered to be that section of an utterance that carries the most salient information in that utterance, relative to all the information provided by that utterance in a given context.[14] The focus of an utterance is also defined as that event (e.g. He *stood before the LORD*),

---

12. Identifiable discourse active entities do not necessarily imply that interlocutors know much about them, viz., that much can be presupposed about them.

13. This concept can be more technically formulated: "Topic is seen as a cognitive-pragmatic concept, the concept or referent in the user's mind *about* which something is asserted in a particular communication situation" (Floor 2004: 73).

14. This concept can be more technically formulated: the focus of an utterance is "the semantic component of a pragmatically structured proposition whereby the assertion differs from the proposition" (Lambrecht 1994: 213). Heimerdinger (1999: 64) also observes: "As focus is a relational pragmatic category, the property of being new in discourse, i.e. not previously mentioned is not defining focus… The 'newness' required for focus is not the newness of the constituent, but the newness of the role of the constituent in the abstract presupposed proposition." One could go one step further and reformulate Heimerdinger as follows: the "newness" required for focus is not the newness of the constituent, but the newness or *saliency* (in the sense of being *confirmed or modified*) of the role of the constituent in the abstract presupposed proposition.

that aspect of an event (e.g. *At exactly four o'clock*, we completed the race), that entity (e.g. *Peter* did it) or that attribute of an entity (e.g. The *old* dog did it, not the young one) that represents a particular choice in a context where more than one alternative is possible, whether this choice be explicit or implicit.

The choice made by a speaker may affect the knowledge of the addressee in primarily three ways: firstly, the focus may *complete* a proposition of which the identity of one or more of the entities involved in the proposition is not shared by the interlocutors;[15] secondly, the focus may *confirm* the identity of an entity or aspect of a proposition that is already shared by the interlocutors;[16] or thirdly, the focus may *modify* a proposition shared by the interlocutors by replacing,[17] restricting,[18] expanding[19] or negating[20] an aspect of it.

(6) From the above-mentioned definition of focus it is obvious that not only the predicate may be the focus of an utterance. When an event or state of affairs is discourse active, the referent (or attribute of the referent) of one of a sentence's complements (i.e. subject, object, indirect object) or adjuncts (i.e. adverbial of time, place or manner) may also be the focus of that utterance. The most obvious instances of this type of focus are manifested in answers to questions. For example, the question "What were you singing?" may be answered in English as follows: (1) "OB-LA-DI-OB-LA-DA"; (2) "We were singing OB-LA-DI-OB-LA-DA"; (3) "What we were singing was, OB-LA-DI-OB-LA-DA" or (4) "It was OB-LA-DI-OB-LA-DA that we were singing." It is significant that in each case a special or marked construction is involved. In Biblical Hebrew, fronting is one of the constructions used to signal that an entity or attribute of an entity is the focus of an utterance.

(7) An utterance typically does not have more than one primary topic, but often may have more than one focus. For example, in the utterance "*At this very moment tomorrow, I will send a Benjaminite to you*" both the adjunct of time, "At this very moment tomorrow," and predicate, "will

---

15. In Judg. 1.1–2 the speaker knew somebody must go up in war, but did not know who in particular; hence the question: "WHO must go up?" In the answer "JUDAH must go up" the item marked for focus specifies the identity of the unknown entity.

16. "Did SHE tell you?" "Yes, SHE HERSELF did."

17. "We did not spend the night IN THEIR HOUSES. We slept IN OUR TENTS."

18. "He destroyed ALL PLACES OF BAAL WORSHIP IN JUDAH, *only* THE ASHERAH POLES he did not demolish."

19. "He killed ONAN. He killed *also* HIS BROTHER."

20. "Joseph RECOGNIZED HIS BROTHERS, but they DID *not* RECOGNIZE HIM."

send a Benjaminite to you," can be the foci of the utterance.[21] Also, while the utterance only has one primary topic (i.e. "I"), a secondary topic may be identified as part of the predicate focus (i.e. "you").

(8) When the topic of an utterance is discourse active, it is normally referred to by means of a pronoun or another unmarked construction (see (3) above). However, when the topic of an utterance is not discourse active and needs to be newly introduced, or reactivated, a special construction may be involved again. In English, the phrase "as far as TOPIC is concerned…" may be used. Left dislocation may also be used, e.g. "The TOPIC which…, I love *it*" (see §48).

(9) One or two already discourse active topics are often "apparently unnecessarily" reactivated as topics. However, the reactivation is required in order to compare or contrast two different topics, e.g. "HE (topic a) STAYED in the hills, but SHE (topic b) LEFT for town."

(10) The question may arise: Can only the predicate of a discourse active topic (predicate focus), the constituent of a discourse active or discourse inferable proposition (constituent focus) be the focus of an utterance? Is it not also possible for an entire sentence to be the focus of an utterance (sentence focus)? Lambrecht (1994: 307–23) indeed makes such a distinction. However, this only happens in so-called presentative ("There was once a young girl") and event-reporting sentences ("A group of men arrived in our city last night"). It is significant, according to Lambrecht (1994: 307), that across languages constructions with sentence focus tend to display the same surface-level features as those with constituent focus.

§47.2. Semantic-Pragmatic Functions of Word Order in Verbal Clauses

47.2.1. *Functions of fronting*

(1) Topic (re-)activation
The fronted constituent signals the activation or reactivation of an identifiable entity or entities. The entity is (re-)activated to signal a topic or topic shift in a context where it is part of a set of entities that are involved in the same discourse context.

(a) (Re-)activated characters (or entities) are *compared* (#*a*) or *contrasted* (#*b-c*). In some instances, both entities to be compared or contrasted are fronted (#*a*).

---

21. In such cases, the event involved is not necessarily discourse active as in the cases referred to in (6).

a   אַבְרָם יָשַׁב בְּאֶרֶץ־כְּנָעַן וְלוֹט יָשַׁב בְּעָרֵי הַכִּכָּר   *Abram* lived in Canaan, and *Lot* lived in the cities of the plain (Gen. 13:12).*

b   ²¹וַיַּעַל הָאִישׁ אֶלְקָנָה... ²²וְחַנָּה לֹא עָלָתָה...   ²¹And the man, Elkanah, went up… ²²But *Hannah* did not go up (1 Sam. 1:21–22).*

c   וָאָבִיא אֶת־אֲגַג מֶלֶךְ עֲמָלֵק וְאֶת־עֲמָלֵק הֶחֱרַמְתִּי: And I have brought Agag the king of Amalek, but *the Amalekites* I have utterly destroyed (1 Sam. 15:20).*

Less typical examples of this category are instances in which actions or events that should or did take place at a particular point in time are described. This point in time follows a duration of time during which actions or events of a different (#d) or opposite (#e) nature should be done or were done.

d   שִׁבְעַת יָמִים יִהְיֶה עִם־אִמּוֹ בַּיּוֹם הַשְּׁמִינִי תִּתְּנוֹ־לִי: Seven days it shall be with his mother, *on the eight day* you shall give it to me (Exod. 22:29).*

e   שֵׁשֶׁת יָמִים תַּעֲשֶׂה מַעֲשֶׂיךָ וּבַיּוֹם הַשְּׁבִיעִי תִּשְׁבֹּת   Six days you must do your work, but *on the seventh day* you shall rest (Exod. 23:12).*

(b) Activating an identifiable entity in order to comment on different entities that are *involved in the same situation* (#a). The shifted topic may also be a different person or audience addressed (#b-c).

a   וַתִּקַּח תָּמָר אֵפֶר עַל־רֹאשָׁהּ וּכְתֹנֶת הַפַּסִּים אֲשֶׁר עָלֶיהָ קָרָעָה   And Tamar put ashes on her head, and *the long robe that she was wearing*, she tore (2 Sam.13:19).*

b   וּלְשָׂרָה אָמַר הִנֵּה נָתַתִּי...   And *to Sarah* he said, "Look, I hereby give…" (Gen. 20:16).*

c   ²²אַל־תִּירְאוּ בַּהֲמוֹת שָׂדַי כִּי דָשְׁאוּ נְאוֹת מִדְבָּר כִּי־עֵץ נָשָׂא פִרְיוֹ תְּאֵנָה וָגֶפֶן נָתְנוּ חֵילָם: ²³וּבְנֵי צִיּוֹן גִּילוּ וְשִׂמְחוּ בַּיהוָה אֱלֹהֵיכֶם   ²² Do not be afraid, wild animals, for the pastures of the wilderness are green, yes, the tree bears its fruit, the fig tree and vine give their full yield. ²³And *children of Zion*, be glad and rejoice in the LORD, your God (Joel 2:22–23).*

Often the different topics that are involved have the character of a *list*.

d   אָנֹכִי נֹתֵן אֶת־כֻּלָּם חֲלָלִים   I will give over all of them, slain,
לִפְנֵי יִשְׂרָאֵל אֶת־סוּסֵיהֶם   to Israel; *their horses* you shall
תְּעַקֵּר וְאֶת־מַרְכְּבֹתֵיהֶם   hamstring, and *their chariots* you
תִּשְׂרֹף בָּאֵשׁ:   shall burn with fire (Josh. 11:6).*

Genealogical lists represent an atypical type of list, for it is not different topics that are involved in the same situation that are listed, but a chronological chain of descendants.

e   וַיִּוָּלֵד לַחֲנוֹךְ אֶת־עִירָד   And to Enoch was born Irad;
וְעִירָד יָלַד אֶת־מְחוּיָאֵל   and *Irad* fathered Mehujael, and
וּמְחִיָּיאֵל יָלַד אֶת־מְתוּשָׁאֵל   *Mehujael* fathered Methushael,
וּמְתוּשָׁאֵל יָלַד אֶת־לָמֶךְ:   and *Methushael* fathered Lamech
   (Gen. 4:18).*

(c) Reactivating entities to be the topics of utterances that are the *summary* of a paragraph, episode or narrative

a   וַיִּשְׂמַח כָּל־עַם־הָאָרֶץ   So all the people of the land
וְהָעִיר שָׁקָטָה   rejoiced; and *the city* was quiet
וְאֶת־עֲתַלְיָהוּ הֵמִיתוּ   and *Athaliah* they had killed by the
בַחֶרֶב   sword (2 Kgs 11:20).*

b   מֹשֶׁה עֶבֶד־יְהוָה וּבְנֵי   *Moses, the servant of the* LORD,
יִשְׂרָאֵל הִכּוּם   *and the Israelites* defeated them
   (Josh. 12:6).

(2) Constituent focus

Fronting signals that an entity, an aspect of an entity or an event is *the focus of an utterance*.

(a) Providing (#*a*) or describing (#*b*) the *identity* of an entity (e.g. a character, a point in time or place, or the manner) involved in a discourse active event or state of affairs.

Since the answer to a content question (e.g. who? what? where? or how?) provides the identity of somebody or something, the reference to it is usually fronted. In these cases the rest of the proposition is obviously discourse active, e.g. "Somebody must go up for us against the Canaanites."

a   מִי יַעֲלֶה־לָּנוּ אֶל־הַכְּנַעֲנִי ¹   ¹Who shall go up first for us against
        בַּתְּחִלָּה לְהִלָּחֶם בּוֹ:   the Canaanites, to fight against them?
        ²וַיֹּאמֶר יְהוָה יְהוּדָה יַעֲלֶה   ²The LORD answered, *Judah* shall go
                                   up (Judg. 1:1–2).*

b   לֹא־אֲדֹנִי שְׁמָעֵנִי הַשָּׂדֶה   No, my lord, hear me; *the field* I
        נָתַתִּי לָךְ וְהַמְּעָרָה אֲשֶׁר־בּוֹ   hereby give you, *and the cave* that is
        לְךָ נְתַתִּיהָ לְעֵינֵי בְנֵי־עַמִּי   in it, *to you* I give it; *in the presence*
        נְתַתִּיהָ לָךְ קְבֹר מֵתֶךָ:   *of my people* I give it to you; bury
                                     your dead (Gen. 23:11).*

(b) *Modifying* the identity, features or extent of (the referent of) a
constituent of an explicit or implicit discourse active proposition

The modification may have the character of confirming the identity
in the sense of restricting it to a particular entity (#*a-d*), purpose
(#*e*), quality (#*f*) or quantity (#*g-h*). The modification sometimes has
the character of specifying (#i), replacing (#j) or expanding (#k) the
identity of the referent(s).

a   אֹתִי שָׁלַח יְהוָה לִמְשָׁחֲךָ   *Me* (*and no one else*) has the LORD
        לְמֶלֶךְ   sent to anoint you as king (1 Sam.
                                     15:1).*

b   וְלֹא תֹאמַר אֲנִי הֶעֱשַׁרְתִּי   so that you cannot say, "*I* (or *it
        אֶת־אַבְרָם: is I who*) made Abram rich" (Gen.
                                     14:23).*

c   וַיֹּאמְרוּ אֱלֹהֵי הָעִבְרִים   And they said, "*The God of the
        נִקְרָא עָלֵינוּ   Hebrews himself* revealed himself to
                                     us" (Exod. 5:3).*

d   וַיֵּרָא יְהוָה אֶל־אַבְרָם   And the LORD appeared to Abram
        וַיֹּאמֶר לְזַרְעֲךָ אֶתֵּן   and said, "*To your descendants* I will
        אֶת־הָאָרֶץ הַזֹּאת   give this land" (Gen. 12:7).*

e   וַיֹּאמְרוּ אֶל־פַּרְעֹה לָגוּר   And they said to Pharaoh, "*Only to
        בָּאָרֶץ בָּאנוּ   sojourn in the land* we have come"
                                     (Gen. 47:4).*

f   בְּתָם־לְבָבִי וּבְנִקְיֹן כַּפַּי   *In the integrity of my heart and the
        עָשִׂיתִי זֹאת: innocence of my hands* I have done
                                     this (Gen. 20:5).*

g   כָּל־הָעָם הַיֹּצֵא מִמִּצְרַיִם   *All the males coming out of Egypt,
        הַזְּכָרִים כֹּל אַנְשֵׁי   all the soldiers* died in the wilderness
        הַמִּלְחָמָה מֵתוּ בַמִּדְבָּר   (Josh. 5:4).*

h	שֵׁ֣שֶׁת יָמִים֮ תַּעֲבֹד֒ וְעָשִׂ֣יתָ כָּל־מְלַאכְתֶּ֔ךָ	*For six days* you shall labor and do all your work (Exod. 20:9).*
i	²⁷בְּנֵ֣י יַעֲקֹ֗ב בָּ֚אוּ עַל־הַ֣חֲלָלִ֔ים וַיָּבֹ֖זּוּ הָעִ֑יר אֲשֶׁ֥ר טִמְּא֖וּ אֲחוֹתָֽם׃ ²⁸אֶת־צֹאנָ֧ם וְאֶת־בְּקָרָ֛ם וְאֶת־חֲמֹרֵיהֶ֖ם וְאֵ֧ת אֲשֶׁר־בָּעִ֛יר וְאֶת־אֲשֶׁ֥ר בַּשָּׂדֶ֖ה לָקָֽחוּ׃	²⁷The [other] sons of Jacob came upon the slain and they looted the city which defiled their sister. ²⁸*Their sheep, their cattle, their donkeys and whatever was in the city and in the field* they took (Gen. 34:27–28).*
j	זָרְע֤וּ חִטִּים֙ וְקֹצִ֣ים קָצָ֔רוּ	They have sown wheat, but what they reaped were *thorns* (Jer. 12.13).*
k	וְכָל־אַנְשֵׁ֣י בֵית֗וֹ יְלִ֣יד בָּ֚יִת וּמִקְנַת־כֶּ֖סֶף מֵאֵ֣ת בֶּן־נֵכָ֑ר נִמֹּ֖לוּ אִתּֽוֹ׃	And *all the men of his house, those born in the house and those bought with money from a foreigner*, were circumcised with him (Gen. 17.27).*

The nuance of the modification, e.g. expanding (#*l-m*) or replacing (#*n*), may also be specified by an overt particle.[22]

l	וְעַתָּ֗ה אָנֹכִי֙ נָתַ֜תִּי אֶת־כָּל־הָאֲרָצ֣וֹת הָאֵ֗לֶּה בְּיַ֛ד נְבוּכַדְנֶאצַּ֥ר מֶֽלֶךְ־בָּבֶ֖ל עַבְדִּ֑י וְגַ֤ם אֶת־חַיַּ֤ת הַשָּׂדֶה֙ נָתַ֣תִּי ל֖וֹ לְעָבְדֽוֹ׃	So now I have given all these lands into the hand of Nebuchadnezzar, king of Babylon, my servant. *And even the wild animals of the field* I have given to him to serve him (Jer. 27.6).*
m	אֲבָרֵ֗ךְ אֶת־יְהוָ֥ה אֲשֶׁ֣ר יְעָצָ֑נִי אַף־לֵ֝יל֗וֹת יִסְּר֥וּנִי כִלְיוֹתָֽי׃	I bless the LORD who gives me counsel, *even during the nights* my kidneys instruct me (Ps. 16.7).*
n	וַיֹּ֜אמֶר הִנֶּ֣ה נָּֽא־אֲדֹנַ֗י ס֣וּרוּ נָ֠א אֶל־בֵּ֨ית עַבְדְּכֶ֤ם וְלִ֔ינוּ...וַיֹּאמְר֣וּ לֹּ֔א כִּ֥י בָרְח֖וֹב נָלִֽין׃	And he said, "Consider, please, my lord, please turn aside to the house of your servant and spend the night..." And they replied, "No, rather *in the town square* we will spend the night" (Gen. 19:2).*

---

22. According to Moshavi (2010: 135), "Focusing by preposing, as we have seen, relates to an activated but not necessarily presupposed proposition. The focusing adverb [viz. the 'focus particle'], in contrast, may relate to a proposition that is presupposed but not activated."

When the entity to be replaced is governed by a negation word, the negation word + entity is fronted. The "replacing" entity typically (#o), but not necessarily always (#p), follows in a clause with an ellipsed predicate.

o	וְעַתָּה לֹא־אַתֶּם שְׁלַחְתֶּם אֹתִי הֵנָּה כִּי הָאֱלֹהִים	So now, *it is not you* that sent me here, *but God* (Gen. 45:8).*
p	אַלְמָנָה וּגְרוּשָׁה וַחֲלָלָה זֹנָה אֶת־אֵלֶּה לֹא יִקָּח כִּי אִם־בְּתוּלָה מֵעַמָּיו יִקַּח אִשָּׁה:	A widow, a divorced woman or one defiled, that is a prostitute: *these* he must not marry [lit. take], but *a virgin from his people* he must take as wife (Lev. 21:14).*

(c) Motivated by (b) are cases where a forward (#a) or backwards pointing (#b) deictic reference is fronted to confirm the exact nature of its reference.

a	בְּזֹאת תִּבָּחֵנוּ חֵי פַרְעֹה אִם־תֵּצְאוּ מִזֶּה כִּי אִם־בְּבוֹא אֲחִיכֶם הַקָּטֹן הֵנָּה:	*This is how* you will be tested: As Pharaoh lives, you will not go out from here unless your younger brother comes here (Gen. 42:15).
b	שְׁמֹנָה אֵלֶּה יָלְדָה מִלְכָּה לְנָחוֹר אֲחִי אַבְרָהָם:	*These eight* Milkah bore to Nahor, the brother of Abraham (Gen. 22:23).*

(d) Most probably also motivated by (b) are cases where an oath is taken (#a-b).

a	[23] וְעַתָּה הִשָּׁבְעָה לִּי בֵאלֹהִים הֵנָּה אִם־תִּשְׁקֹר לִי... [24]וַיֹּאמֶר אַבְרָהָם אָנֹכִי אִשָּׁבֵעַ:	[23]So now, swear to me here by God that you will not break faith with me.... [24]And Abraham said, "*I swear*" (Gen. 21:23–24).*
b	וַיֹּאמֶר בִּי נִשְׁבַּעְתִּי נְאֻם־יְהוָה	And he said, "*By myself* I swear," declares the LORD (Gen. 22:16).*

(3) Sentence focus

In Biblical Hebrew, the subject of a sentence with sentence focus is typically fronted. In other words, on the surface level it may look like the constructions with constituent focus or topic (re-)activation.

A construction with sentence focus reports on something that happened at a particular point in time or place.[23] In other words, a construction with sentence focus is not in the first place about "what a discourse active referent did," but "what happened."[24] The subject of the sentence is often indeterminate and/or lexically explicated. The predicate is typically a verb of movement or another intransitive verb.[25] Verbs of saying may also be involved.

A report about an event or state of affairs may be used as follows:

(a) Opens a report in direct speech.

וַיֹּאמְרוּ אֵלָיו אִישׁ ׀ עָלָה	And they replied [lit. said to him],
לִקְרָאתֵנוּ וַיֹּאמֶר אֵלֵינוּ	"*A man came up to meet us* and he
לְכוּ שׁוּבוּ אֶל־הַמֶּלֶךְ	said to us, 'Go back to the king who
אֲשֶׁר־שָׁלַח אֶתְכֶם	sent you'" (2 Kgs 1:6).*

(b) Opens the first scene of an new episode.

a

וּבֶן־הֲדַד מֶלֶךְ־אֲרָם קָבַץ	And *Ben-hadad the king of Syria*
אֶת־כָּל־חֵילוֹ וּשְׁלֹשִׁים	gathered all his army together.
וּשְׁנַיִם מֶלֶךְ אִתּוֹ וְסוּס	Thirty-two kings were with him,
וָרָכֶב וַיַּעַל וַיָּצַר עַל־שֹׁמְרוֹן	and horses and chariots. And he
וַיִּלָּחֶם בָּהּ:	went up and closed in on Samaria
	and fought against it (1 Kgs 20:1).*

---

23. The latter point in time and/or place may be regarded as the topic (referred to as the "stage topic") about which something is said (Erteschik-Shir 2007: 16).

24. Lambrecht (2000: 623) states, "In a SF [Sentence Focus] sentence, the subject referent is not conceptualized as actively involved in some situation but as appearing on the 'scene' of the discourse."

25. According to Lambrecht (1994: 144), sentence focus can be used to express both a presentation and an event-reporting function. The difference, he says, "between the presentational and event-reporting type is that in presentational sentences proper the newly introduced element is an entity (a discourse referent) while in event-reporting sentence it is an event, which necessarily involves an entity." An example of the presentational type is Job 1:1, אִישׁ הָיָה בְאֶרֶץ־עוּץ, "There was a man in the land of Uz." This way of introducing "brand new" entities is extremely rare in Biblical Hebrew. See also Heimerdinger (1999: 141–55) and Moshavi (2010: 46). More typical are instances where a brand-new entity follows a verb of movement in the *wayyiqtol*, e.g. Exod. 2:2, וַיֵּלֶךְ אִישׁ מִבֵּית לֵוִי וַיִּקַּח אֶת־בַּת־לֵוִי, "And a man from the house of Levi went and married a Levite woman." See also Exod. 1:8; 1 Sam. 2:27; 11:1; 17:4–5.

b

וְאִישׁ אֶחָד מִבְּנֵי הַנְּבִיאִים
אָמַר אֶל־רֵעֵהוּ בִּדְבַר יְהוָה
הַכֵּינִי נָא וַיְמָאֵן הָאִישׁ
לְהַכֹּתוֹ:

And *a certain man, a member of the prophets*, said to his companion through the word of the LORD, "Hit me." However, the man refused to hit him (1 Kgs 20:35).*

(c) Opens the presentation of background information or a flashback. The background information may be provided at the beginning of an episode (#*a*) or scene (#*b*). It may also provide the background of a preceding (#*c*) or subsequent event (#*d*).

a

¹וְשָׂרַי אֵשֶׁת אַבְרָם לֹא
יָלְדָה לוֹ וְלָהּ שִׁפְחָה מִצְרִית
וּשְׁמָהּ הָגָר: ²וַתֹּאמֶר
שָׂרַי אֶל־אַבְרָם...

¹*And Sarah, Abram's wife, bore him no children. However, she had an Egyptian slave-girl and her name was Hagar.* ²So Sarah said to Abram… (Gen. 16:1–2).*

b

וַיָּמָת אֱלִישָׁע וַיִּקְבְּרֻהוּ
וּגְדוּדֵי מוֹאָב יָבֹאוּ בָאָרֶץ
בָּא שָׁנָה:

Then Elisha died, and they buried him. *Now bands of Moabites used to invade the land in the spring of the year* (2 Kgs 13:20).*

c

⁴וַתִּקַּח הָאִשָּׁה אֶת־שְׁנֵי
הָאֲנָשִׁים וַתִּצְפְּנוֹ וַתֹּאמֶר |
כֵּן בָּאוּ אֵלַי הָאֲנָשִׁים וְלֹא
יָדַעְתִּי מֵאַיִן הֵמָּה:
⁵וַיְהִי הַשַּׁעַר לִסְגּוֹר בַּחֹשֶׁךְ
וְהָאֲנָשִׁים יָצָאוּ לֹא יָדַעְתִּי
אָנָה הָלְכוּ הָאֲנָשִׁים רִדְפוּ
מַהֵר אַחֲרֵיהֶם כִּי תַשִּׂיגוּם:
⁶וְהִיא הֶעֱלָתַם הַגָּגָה
וַתִּטְמְנֵם בְּפִשְׁתֵּי הָעֵץ
הָעֲרֻכוֹת לָהּ עַל־הַגָּג:

⁴ But the woman took the two men and hid them. Then she said, "Yes [lit. thus], the men came to me, but I did not know where they came from. ⁵ And when it was time to close the gate at dark, the men went out. Where the men went I do not know. Pursue them quickly, for you can overtake them." ⁶ *She had, however, brought them up to the roof and hidden them with the stalks of flax that she had laid out on the roof* (Josh. 2:4–6).*

d

³וַיֹּאמֶר לוֹ הִנְּךָ מֵת
עַל־הָאִשָּׁה...⁴וַאֲבִימֶלֶךְ
לֹא קָרַב אֵלֶיהָ וַיֹּאמַר
אֲדֹנָי...

³And he said to him, "You are about to die because of the woman…" ⁴Now *Abimelech had not gone near her*; so he said, "Lord…" (Gen. 20:3–4).*

(d) Comments on a temporal frame.

a	עוֹדֶ֖נּוּ מְדַבֵּ֣ר עִמָּ֑ם וְרָחֵ֣ל׀ בָּ֗אָה עִם־הַצֹּאן֙ אֲשֶׁ֣ר לְאָבִ֔יהָ	While he was still speaking with them, *Rachel arrived with her father's sheep* (Gen. 29:9).*
b	וַיְהִ֗י מֶ֣לֶךְ יִשְׂרָאֵל֙ עֹבֵ֣ר עַל־הַחֹמָ֔ה וְאִשָּׁ֖ה צָעֲקָ֣ה אֵלָ֣יו לֵאמֹ֑ר הוֹשִׁ֖יעָה אֲדֹנִ֥י הַמֶּֽלֶךְ׃	And then, while the king of Israel was passing by on the wall, *a woman cried to him saying, "Help, my lord the king"* (2 Kgs 6:26).*

(4) Grounds utterance (often with a deictic expression), either temporally (#*a*) or spatially (#*b*).

a	בָּעֵ֣ת הַהִ֔יא חָלָ֖ה אֲבִיָּ֥ה בֶן־יָרָבְעָֽם׃	*At that time* Abijah, Jeroboam's son, fell sick (1 Kgs 14:1).*
b	מִן־הָאָ֥רֶץ הַהִ֖וא יָצָ֣א אַשּׁ֑וּר וַיִּ֙בֶן֙ אֶת־נִ֣ינְוֵ֔ה	*From that land* he went to Assyria and built Nineveh (Gen. 10:11).*

(5) The fronted subject signals a special type of temporal construction where immediately simultaneous or nearly simultaneous actions are involved.

a	הֵ֗מָּה בָּ֚אוּ בְּאֶ֣רֶץ צ֔וּף וְשָׁא֥וּל אָמַ֛ר לְנַעֲר֥וֹ אֲשֶׁר־עִמּ֖וֹ לְכָ֥ה וְנָשׁ֑וּבָה	*When they came to the land of Zuph*, Saul said to his servant who was with him, "Come, let us go back" (1 Sam. 9:5).*
b	הִ֣וא מוּצֵ֗את וְהִ֨יא שָׁלְחָ֤ה אֶל־חָמִ֙יהָ֙ לֵאמֹ֔ר...	As she was being brought out, *she sent (a message) to her father-in-law...* (Gen. 38:25).*

(6) A formal pattern in poetry
In poetic texts fronting can fulfil the same functions as in non-poetic texts. Yet one must take into account the fact that poets can sometimes use the order of elements to create formal patterns, for example, a chiastic pattern AB / B′A′ (verb + X / X + verb).

לֹא־יָב֥וֹא עוֹד֙ שִׁמְשֵׁ֔ךְ וִירֵחֵ֖ךְ לֹ֣א יֵאָסֵ֑ף	Your sun shall no more go down, nor *your moon* withdraw itself (Isa. 60:20).*

47.2.2. *Functions of marked word order in verbal clauses*

To mark an entity as a focus of the utterance in which it occurs.

(1) Confirming *the quality* of an event

הִנֵּה יָמִים בָּאִים נְאֻם־יְהוָה וְכָרַתִּי אֶת־בֵּית יִשְׂרָאֵל וְאֶת־בֵּית יְהוּדָה בְּרִית חֲדָשָׁה:	Look, the days are coming, declares the Lord, when I will make with the house of Israel and with the house of Judah *a new covenant* (Jer. 31:31).*

(2) Confirming *the identity* of an entity

כִּי נִמְנַע מִבֵּית אֱלֹהֵיכֶם מִנְחָה וָנָסֶךְ:	For withheld from the house of your God is *grain offering and drink offering* (Joel 1:13).*

§47.3. Semantic-Pragmatic Functions of Word Order in Nominal Clauses

47.3.1. *Functions of marked word order in participle clauses*[26]

(1) Predicate focus

a	וַתֹּאמֶר חֹלָה הוּא	And she said, "He *is ill*" (1 Sam. 19:14).*
b	דַּבֵּר יְהוָֹה כִּי שֹׁמֵעַ עַבְדֶּךָ	Speak, Lord, for your servant *is listening* (1 Sam. 3:9).

(2) Constituent focus

מָה־אַתָּה רֹאֶה יִרְמְיָהוּ וָאֹמַר מַקֵּל שָׁקֵד אֲנִי רֹאֶה:	"What are you seeing Jeremiah?" And I answered, "I am seeing *an almond stick*" (Jer. 1:11).*

47.3.2. *Functions of marked word order in verbless clauses*

(1) Predicate focus
Marks an entity as the focus of the utterance in which it occurs. It establishes or confirms the nature (#*a*), identity (#*b*), state or features (#*c-d*), or the location (#*e*) of the discourse active subject of a verbless clause.

---

26. See also §20.3.2.1.

a	מְרַגְּלִים אַתֶּם	You are nothing *but spies* [lit. *Spies are you*] (Gen. 42:9).*
b	וַיֹּאמֶר אַבְרָהָם אֶל־שָׂרָה אִשְׁתּוֹ אֲחֹתִי הִוא	And Abraham said concerning Sarah his wife, "She is *my sister*" (Gen. 20:2).*
c	וַיֵּדְעוּ כִּי עֵירֻמִּם הֵם	And they realized that they *were naked* (Gen. 3:7).*
d	תְּנוּ־נָא כִּכְּרוֹת לֶחֶם לָעָם אֲשֶׁר בְּרַגְלִי כִּי־עֲיֵפִים הֵם	Please give some loaves of bread to the people who follow me [lit. who are in my feet], for they *are exhausted* (Judg. 8:5).*
e	כִּי כָל־הָעֵדָה כֻּלָּם קְדֹשִׁים וּבְתוֹכָם יְהוָה	For all of the congregation, all of them, are holy and *in their midst* is the LORD (Num. 16:3).

(2) Constituent focus

The duration of a state of affairs, referred to by a fronted temporal adjunct, may be the focus of an utterance in a context where the state of affairs is already discourse active.

זֶה ׀ אַרְבָּעִים שָׁנָה יְהוָה אֱלֹהֶיךָ עִמָּךְ	*These forty years* the LORD your God has been with you (Deut. 2:7).

§48. Left Dislocation

Left dislocation (also referred to *status pendens*) should not be mistaken for the fronting (or, topicalization) of a clause constituent. In the case of the former, a constituent stands outside the border of a clause. The dislocated constituent is referred to in the clause by another element (called the resumptive), e.g. "*That big house*, I am still going to buy *it* for us."

A dislocated construction may be preceded by discourse markers (וַיְהִי, וְהָיָה, לָכֵן, הִנֵּה, הֵן, וְעַתָּה), conjunctions (וְ, כִּי), focus particles (רַק, גַּם, אַף, אַךְ) or yes–no question words (הֲלֹא and הֲ).

§48.1. Syntax of Dislocation

48.1.1. *In verbal clauses*[27]

Although the most typical dislocated construction may be the one associated with the English example referred to above, a variety of constructions with dislocated constituents can be distinguished in Biblical Hebrew.

(1) The dislocated constituent is resumed in the matrix clause.

The *first major type* are those cases where a constituent is dislocated and then resumed in the matrix clause. This constituent may be a subject (#*a*). In most cases, however, it is an object (#*b*). The resumed constituent is often fronted in the matrix clause. This is not always the case (#*c*). Sometimes, another constituent is fronted in the matrix clause (#*d*).

a	כִּי־עַבְדְּךָ יוֹאָב הוּא צִוָּנִי	For *your servant Joab*, <u>it was he who</u> commanded me (2 Sam. 14:19).*
b	אֵת כָּל־הַדָּבָר אֲשֶׁר אָנֹכִי מְצַוֶּה אֶתְכֶם אֹתוֹ תִשְׁמְרוּ לַעֲשׂוֹת	*Everything I am commanding you today*, <u>that</u> *you must take care to do* (Deut. 13:1).*
c	הַמִּטָּה אֲשֶׁר־עָלִיתָ שָּׁם לֹא־תֵרֵד מִמֶּנָּה	*The bed to which you have gone*, you will not come down from <u>it</u> (2 Kgs 1:4).*
d	כִּי אֶת־כָּל־הָאָרֶץ אֲשֶׁר־אַתָּה רֹאֶה לְךָ אֶתְּנֶנָּה וּלְזַרְעֲךָ עַד־עוֹלָם:	*For all the land that you are seeing*, to you I will give <u>it</u>, and to your descendants forever (Gen. 13:15).*

(2) Dislocated constituent is separated by a *wāw* from the matrix clause and resumed within it.

The *second major category* involves cases where the dislocated constituent is separated by a *wāw* from its matrix clause. The dislocated constituents are also resumed (#*a*).

a	וַיֹּאמֶר הַמֶּלֶךְ הַמְדַבֵּר אֵלַיִךְ וַהֲבֵאתוֹ אֵלַי	And the king said, "*He who speaks to you*, bring <u>him</u> to me" (2 Sam. 14:10).*

---

27. This section benefitted much from the insights of Westbury (2014).

(3) A constituent is separated by a *wāw* from the matrix clause and is not resumed within it.

The *third* category involves cases where the initial constituent is separated by a *wāw* from the matrix clause and not resumed within it (#*a-d*).

a	הַנְּבִיאִים אֲשֶׁר הָיוּ לְפָנַי וּלְפָנֶיךָ מִן־הָעוֹלָם וַיִּנָּבְאוּ אֶל־אֲרָצוֹת רַבּוֹת	*The prophets who were before me and you from ancient times*, they prophesied against many countries (Jer. 28:8).*
b	וּדְבַר מַה־יַּרְאֵנִי וְהִגַּדְתִּי לָךְ	And the *word that he shows me*, I will tell you (Num. 23:3).*
c	כְּשָׁמְעֲכֶם אֶת־קוֹל הַשֹּׁפָר וַאֲמַרְתֶּם מָלַךְ אַבְשָׁלוֹם בְּחֶבְרוֹן:	*The moment that you hear the sound of the horn*, you must say, "Absalom has become king in Hebron" (2 Sam. 15:10).*
d	בַּיּוֹם הַשְּׁלִישִׁי וַיִּשָּׂא אַבְרָהָם אֶת־עֵינָיו	*On the third day*, Abraham lifted up his eyes (Gen. 22:4).*

The analysis of this construction is problematic because it shares a characteristic of fronting (i.e. lack of resumption within its matrix clause) and a characteristic of left dislocation (i.e. separation of the initial constituent from its matrix clause by a *wāw*). As a result there are two analyses of this construction.

One viewpoint regards resumption as the most critical syntactic feature, because resumption demonstrates that the initial constituent occurs *outside* of the boundary of the clause.[28] Therefore, they view this construction as being a kind of fronting (or, topicalization) in that there is no resumption of the initial constituent within the matrix clause and the initial constituent is structurally part of the clause. In order to distinguish this construction from ordinary fronting in which no *wāw* intervenes between the initial constituent and its matrix clause, the construction has been called "heavy topicalization" by Holmstedt (2014).

The other viewpoint regards the fact that the initial constituent is separated from the sentence by a *wāw* as the most critical syntactic feature for identifying left dislocation and not necessarily resumption. This construction is then seen as a kind of left dislocation.[29]

---

28. Baltin (1982), Bayer (2004), Lohnstein and Trissler (2004) and others form the basis of Naudé (1990) and Holmstedt (2014).

29. Westbury (2014) is based on Lambrecht (2001). See also López (2016: 427–30).

Temporal adjuncts often occur in this construction and clearly constitute a class of their own (#c-d). See also §40.24.(2) and 40.25.(2) for the use of this type of construction after וַיְהִי or וְהָיָה.

(4) Other minor categories (rare)

Two minor *categories*, each of which are concentrated in specific genres, may also be distinguished: (1) instances where the dislocated constituent is separated from the rest of the clause by means of a question word (#a) (see Miller-Naudé and Naudé 2015a). These occur mainly in poetic texts. (2) Instances in legal texts where the dislocated items are separated from their matrix clauses by means of כִּי (#b). These matrix clauses are, as a rule, a conditional sentence with a protasis and an apodosis.

a	תַּאֲנָתָהּ מִי יְשִׁיבֶנָּה	Her lust, who can restrain *it*? (Jer. 2.24).*
b	אִישׁ כִּי־יָמוּת וּבֵן אֵין לוֹ וְהַעֲבַרְתֶּם אֶת־נַחֲלָתוֹ לְבִתּוֹ׃	If a man dies and he has no son [lit. *a man*, that he dies and a son does not exist to *him*], you must transfer his inheritance to his daughter (Num. 27:8).*

48.1.2. *In participle clauses*

The syntax of dislocation in participle clauses and verbal clauses is very similar. In most instances the subject is dislocated. The dislocated constituent is then resumed by means of an independent personal pronoun (#a-b) or pronominal suffix (#c-d). In a number of instances fixed expressions are involved (#d-e).

a	וְחַנָּה הִיא מְדַבֶּרֶת עַל־לִבָּהּ	And *Hannah*, she was praying by herself [lit. she was speaking on her heart] (1 Sam. 1:13).*
b	יְהוָה אֱלֹהֶיךָ הוּא עֹבֵר לְפָנֶיךָ הוּא־יַשְׁמִיד אֶת־הַגּוֹיִם הָאֵלֶּה מִלְפָנֶיךָ	The LORD your God, he will cross over before you, he shall destroy these nations before you (Deut. 31:3).*
c	וַאֲנִי הִנְנִי מֵבִיא אֶת־הַמַּבּוּל מַיִם עַל־הָאָרֶץ	And, *as for me*, look I am going to bring a flood of waters on the earth (Gen. 6:17).*

d	וְיֶ֜תֶר דִּבְרֵ֤י יָֽרָבְעָם֙ אֲשֶׁ֣ר נִלְחַ֔ם וַאֲשֶׁ֣ר מָלָ֔ךְ הִנָּ֣ם כְּתוּבִ֗ים עַל־סֵ֛פֶר דִּבְרֵ֥י הַיָּמִ֖ים לְמַלְכֵ֥י יִשְׂרָאֵֽל׃	And *the rest of the acts of Jeroboam, how he fought and how he reigned*, look, <u>they</u> are written in the scroll of the annals of the kings of Israel (1 Kgs 14:19).*
e	וְיֶ֨תֶר דִּבְרֵ֤י שְׁלֹמֹה֙ וְכָל־אֲשֶׁ֣ר עָשָׂ֔ה וְחָכְמָת֑וֹ הֲלֽוֹא־הֵ֣ם כְּתֻבִ֔ים עַל־סֵ֖פֶר דִּבְרֵ֥י שְׁלֹמֹֽה׃	And *the rest of the acts of Solomon, all that he did as well and his wisdom*, are <u>they</u> not written on the scroll of the acts of Solomon? (1 Kgs 11:41).*

48.1.3. *In verbless clauses*

Like verbal and participle clauses, verbless clauses may also have a dislocated constituent.

However, the status of configurations like (#*a*) and (#*b*) as being verbless clauses with a dislocated constituent has been debated.[30] Naudé (1994b, 2002a, 2002b, 2013b) argues that the pronoun in (#*a*) is a pronominal clitic which is prosodically dependent upon the preceding subject, because it does not have stress and it is joined to the subject with a conjunctive accent. The function of the so-called tripartite nominal clause is to disambiguate subject and predicate in verbless (nominal) clauses as a "last resort" strategy. By contrast, in (#*b*) the third person pronoun is separated prosodically from the preceding noun. The construction involves dislocation of the noun and the pronoun is the resumed subject. See also §36.1.1.2.(4).

a	אַתָּה־ה֣וּא מַלְכִּ֣י אֱלֹהִ֑ים	You are my king, O God (Ps. 44:5).*
b	יְהוָה֙ ה֣וּא הָאֱלֹהִ֔ים	*The LORD*, <u>he</u> is God (Deut. 4:35).*

Two constituent orders involving dislocated constituents can be distinguished, viz. dislocated item // predicate + independent personal pronoun (#*c-d*) and dislocated item // independent personal pronoun + predicate (#*e*). Some other configurations are also attested, e.g. (#*f*).

c	שַׁל־נְעָלֶ֙יךָ֙ מֵעַ֣ל רַגְלֶ֔יךָ כִּ֣י הַמָּק֗וֹם אֲשֶׁ֤ר אַתָּה֙ עֹמֵ֣ד עָלָ֔יו קֹ֥דֶשׁ הֽוּא	Remove the sandals from your feet, for *the place where you are standing upon it, it* is holy (Josh. 5:15).*

---

d   וְעַתָּ֡ה שְׁנֵֽי־בָנֶ֡יךָ הַנּוֹלָדִ֣ים   So now, *your two sons who were*
     לְךָ֩ בְּאֶ֨רֶץ מִצְרַ֜יִם עַד־בֹּאִ֧י   *born for you in Egypt before I came*
     אֵלֶ֛יךָ מִצְרַ֖יְמָה לִי־הֵ֑ם   *to you in Egypt*, <u>they</u> shall be mine
                                          (Gen. 48:5).*

e   וְהָיָ֗ה הָאִ֛ישׁ אֲשֶׁר־יִבְחַ֥ר   And then, *the man whom the LORD*
     יְהוָ֖ה ה֣וּא הַקָּד֑וֹשׁ   *chooses*, <u>he</u> shall be the holy one
                                          (Num. 16:7).*

f   וַאֲנִ֖י הִנְנִ֣י בְיֶדְכֶ֑ם   But, *as for me*, look, <u>I</u> am in your
     עֲשׂוּ־לִ֛י כַּטּ֥וֹב וְכַיָּשָׁ֖ר   hands. Do to me as is good and
     בְּעֵינֵיכֶֽם׃   right in your eyes (Jer. 26:14).*

§48.2. Semantic-Pragmatic Functions of Left Dislocation

48.2.1. *In verbal clauses*[31]

The prototypical function of most of the two major types of dislocated constructions in prose texts is "the (re)activation of referents that are assumed to entertain low degrees of accessibility in the minds of addressees" (Westbury 2014: 340). In this way dislocated constituents are typically "topic announcing" constructions.[32]

Most typical are instances where the activated referent is the primary topic of the subsequent clause (#*a-b*).[33] It may also be the secondary topic (#*c*).

a   וְהָאִ֞ישׁ אֲשֶׁר־יַעֲשֶׂ֣ה בְזָד֗וֹן   And *anyone who presumes to*
     לְבִלְתִּ֨י שְׁמֹ֤עַ אֶל־הַכֹּהֵן֙   *disobey the priest appointed to*
     הָעֹמֵ֞ד לְשָׁ֤רֶת שָׁם֙ אֶת־יְהוָ֣ה   *minister there to the LORD your*
     אֱלֹהֶ֔יךָ א֖וֹ אֶל־הַשֹּׁפֵ֑ט וּמֵת֙   *God, or the judge*, <u>that person</u> shall
     הָאִ֣ישׁ הַה֔וּא   die (Deut. 17:12).*

b   וַאֲנִ֗י הִנְנִי֩ מֵבִ֨יא אֶת־הַמַּבּ֥וּל   And *as for me*, look <u>I</u> am going to
     מַ֨יִם֙ עַל־הָאָ֔רֶץ   bring a flood of waters on the earth
                                          (Gen. 6:17).*

---

31. Since the left dislocated constituent appears to function similarly in finite verbal clauses and participle clauses, the two syntactic classes are examined together in this section.

32. The necessity for using dislocation constructions in these instances is most probably motivated by the "principle of the separation of reference and role." See Lambrecht (1994: 184–88). According to Lambrecht (1994: 185), this principle "can be captured in the form of a simple maxim: 'Do not introduce a referent and talk about it in the same clause.'"

33. The primary topic may sometimes be the topic of an entire discourse unit, e.g. Num. 4:29.

c　　　וְלָאֲתֹנוֹת הָאֹבְדוֹת לְךָ And, *as for the donkeys that were lost*
　　　הַיּוֹם שְׁלֹשֶׁת הַיָּמִים *to you three days ago*, give no further
　　　אַל־תָּשֶׂם אֶת־לִבְּךָ לָהֶם thought to them, for they have been
　　　כִּי נִמְצָאוּ found (1 Sam. 9:20).*

In some instances, a discourse active referent is "reactivated" in order to profile
how it compares (#*d*) or contrast (#*e*) with another discourse active referent.

d　　　²⁶וַיִּקֹּד הָאִישׁ וַיִּשְׁתַּחוּ ²⁶And the man bowed his head and
　　　לַיהוָה: ²⁷וַיֹּאמֶר בָּרוּךְ worshipped the LORD ²⁷and said,
　　　יְהוָה אֱלֹהֵי אֲדֹנִי אַבְרָהָם "Blessed be the LORD, the God of
　　　אֲשֶׁר לֹא־עָזַב חַסְדּוֹ my master Abraham, who has not
　　　וַאֲמִתּוֹ מֵעִם אֲדֹנִי אָנֹכִי forsaken his loyal love and his faith-
　　　בַּדֶּרֶךְ נָחַנִי יְהוָה בֵּית fulness toward my master. *As for me,*
　　　אֲחֵי אֲדֹנִי: the LORD has led me on the way to the
　　　 house of my master's kinsmen" (Gen.
　　　 24:26–27).*

e　　　כִּי | הַגּוֹיִם הָאֵלֶּה אֲשֶׁר Although these nations that you are
　　　אַתָּה יוֹרֵשׁ אוֹתָם about to dispossess do give heed to
　　　אֶל־מְעֹנְנִים וְאֶל־קֹסְמִים soothsayers and diviners, *as for you,*
　　　יִשְׁמָעוּ וְאַתָּה לֹא כֵן the LORD your God has not allowed
　　　נָתַן לְךָ יְהוָה אֱלֹהֶיךָ: you to do so (Deut. 18:14).*

A discourse active topic may be reactivated with a specific profile in order
to act as the focus of the matrix clause (#*f-g*).

f　　　וַיֹּאמֶר הָאָדָם הָאִשָּׁה And the man said, *"The woman whom*
　　　אֲשֶׁר נָתַתָּה עִמָּדִי הִוא *you gave to be with me*, she gave to
　　　נָתְנָה־לִּי מִן־הָעֵץ וָאֹכֵל: me from the tree, and I ate" (Gen.
　　　 3:12).*

g　　　וַיֹּאמֶר הַמֶּלֶךְ הֲיַד יוֹאָב And the king asked, "Is the hand of
　　　אִתָּךְ בְּכָל־זֹאת וַתַּעַן Joab with you in all this?" The woman
　　　הָאִשָּׁה וַתֹּאמֶר חֵי־נַפְשְׁךָ answered and said, "As surely as you
　　　אֲדֹנִי הַמֶּלֶךְ אִם־אִשׁ | live, my lord the king, one cannot turn
　　　לְהֵמִין וּלְהַשְׂמִיל מִכֹּל right or left from anything that my lord
　　　אֲשֶׁר־דִּבֶּר אֲדֹנִי הַמֶּלֶךְ the king has said. For *your servant*
　　　כִּי־עַבְדְּךָ יוֹאָב הוּא צִוָּנִי *Joab*, it was he who commanded
　　　וְהוּא שָׂם בְּפִי שִׁפְחָתְךָ me; and it was he who put all these
　　　אֵת כָּל־הַדְּבָרִים הָאֵלֶּה: words into the mouth of your servant"
　　　 (2 Sam. 14:19).*

48.2.2. *In verbless clauses*

(1) Topic identification

(a) An identifiable entity is established as the topic of a subsequent classifying or qualifying predication.

The predication is typically the focus of the matrix clause (#*a-e*). The dislocated constituent is typically used to *present the identifiable entity, often in terms of specific features, as the topic of an utterance.* Specifying the topic requires a separate matrix clause so that a predication about the topic can be made.

a	שַׁל־נְעָלֶ֙יךָ֙ מֵעַ֣ל רַגְלֶ֔יךָ כִּ֣י הַמָּק֗וֹם אֲשֶׁ֤ר אַתָּה֙ עֹמֵ֣ד עָלָ֔יו קֹ֥דֶשׁ ה֖וּא	Remove the sandals from your feet, for *the place where you are standing upon it,* it is holy (Josh. 5:15).*
b	הָאֲנָשִׁ֨ים הָאֵ֜לֶּה שְׁלֵמִ֧ים הֵ֣ם אִתָּ֗נוּ	*These men,* they were friendly with us (Gen. 34:21).*
c	אַ֣ךְ־כָּל־חֵ֡רֶם אֲשֶׁ֣ר יַחֲרִם֩ אִ֨ישׁ לַֽיהוָ֜ה מִכָּל־אֲשֶׁר־ל֗וֹ מֵאָדָ֤ם וּבְהֵמָה֙ וּמִשְּׂדֵ֣ה אֲחֻזָּת֔וֹ לֹ֥א יִמָּכֵ֖ר וְלֹ֣א יִגָּאֵ֑ל כָּל־חֵ֗רֶם קֹֽדֶשׁ־קָֽדָשִׁ֥ים ה֖וּא לַיהוָֽה׃	However, nothing that a person owns that has been devoted to destruction for the Lord, be it human or animal, or inherited landholding, may be sold or redeemed; *every devoted thing* most holy is it to the Lord (Lev. 27:28).*
d	וְכֹל֙ שֶׁ֣רֶץ הָע֔וֹף טָמֵ֥א ה֖וּא לָכֶ֑ם לֹ֥א יֵאָכֵֽלוּ׃	And *every flying insect,* it is unclean for you. They may not be eaten (Deut. 14:19).*
e	וְכֹ֣ל ׀ הוֹלֵ֣ךְ עַל־כַּפָּ֗יו בְּכָל־הַֽחַיָּ֛ה הַהֹלֶ֥כֶת עַל־אַרְבַּ֖ע טְמֵאִ֥ים הֵ֛ם לָכֶ֑ם	*And (also) all those going on paws among the animals that walk on fours,* they are unclean for you (Lev. 11:27).*

(b) An entity is established as the topic of a subsequent utterance. In the subsequent utterance the topic *x* is identified as the sole entity to whom the predication (#*a-d*) or identity (#*e*) could be attributed.

a	וְהָיָ֗ה הָאִ֛ישׁ אֲשֶׁר־יִבְחַ֥ר יְהוָ֖ה ה֣וּא הַקָּד֑וֹשׁ	And then, *the man whom the Lord chooses,* he shall be the holy one (Num. 16:7).*

b	רַק חֲזַק לְבִלְתִּי אֲכֹל הַדָּם כִּי הַדָּם הוּא הַנָּפֶשׁ	However, be resolute not to eat the blood, for *the blood* <u>that</u> [lit. <u>it</u>] is the life (Deut. 12:23).*
c	אַתָּה הָרְאֵתָ לָדַעַת כִּי יְהוָה הוּא הָאֱלֹהִים אֵין עוֹד מִלְבַדּוֹ:	You, yourself have been shown (these things) so that you would realize that *the LORD*, <u>he</u> is God, there is no one besides him (Deut. 4:35).*

(2) Shift in topic

וַאֲנִי הִנְנִי בְיֶדְכֶם עֲשׂוּ־לִי כַּטּוֹב וְכַיָּשָׁר בְּעֵינֵיכֶם:	But, *as for me*, look, <u>I</u> am in your hands. Do to me as is good and right in your eyes (Jer. 26:14).*

GLOSSARY

The glossary contains the metalanguage that is used in this grammar which is mainly linguistic in character. Terms that are themselves explained elsewhere in the glossary are indicated by capital letters in the definitions.

A   An abbreviation for *adjective*. See AP (ADJECTIVE PHRASE).

ABLATIVE   In languages that express grammatical relations explicitly by DECLENSIONS (inflection) this term indicates the form of the word (normally a NOUN or pronoun). For example, in Latin the ablative indicates the word form of the CASE that expresses the medium or instrument with which an action is carried out or which indicates a place or source. In Biblical Hebrew the ablative is not indicated explicitly as in Latin, and similar functions are expressed by way of other constructions, especially with prepositions.

ACCUSATIVE   In languages that express grammatical relations explicitly by DECLENSIONS (inflection) this term indicates the form of the word (normally a NOUN or pronoun). For example, in Latin the accusative indicates the word form of the CASE that expresses the (DIRECT) OBJECT of the VERB. In Biblical Hebrew the accusative is not indicated explicitly as in Latin, and similar functions are expressed by other grammatical means.

AD SENSUM   See *CONSTRUCTIO AD SENSUM*.

ADJECTIVE PHRASE (AP)   AP refers to an adjective phrase, a PHRASE with an A (adjective) as head. The phrase *incredibly clever* in the clause *The student is incredibly clever* is the AP with the A *clever* as head.

ADJUNCT   The term *adjunct* refers to an optional or secondary element in a construction. On the syntactic level, adjuncts refer to optional, omissible, non-verbal elements in the PREDICATE or verb phrase (VP). An adjunct can be removed from the predicate without influencing the structural identity of the rest of the construction, for example, *yesterday* in *Yesterday John kicked the ball*. Adjuncts are adverbs and prepositional phrases (and sometimes also noun phrases) that are added to or combined with VERBS, although the verb itself does not require its presence. Adjuncts are in contrast to COMPLEMENTS, which are obligatory elements in the verb phrase, for example, the DIRECT OBJECT.

ADVERBIAL ACCUSATIVE   In languages with explicit CASE endings the adverbial ACCUSATIVE indicates an adverbial modifier consisting of a NOUN in the accusative. In Biblical Hebrew this function is fulfilled by nominal ADJUNCTS which exhibit the normal form of the noun and which can fulfil different SEMANTIC functions, e.g. the indication of time, location, manner and regard.

AFFECTED   The term *affected* refers to the entity (person or thing) that, although it does not cause the action or event indicated by the VERB, is somehow directly involved. In active CLAUSES the affected item and the grammatical OBJECT normally refer to the same person or thing. The affected entity existed before the action, and it is only influenced by the action, e.g. *the table* in *He broke the table.* See EFFECTED.

AFFIX   An affix is a MORPHEME that cannot act independently, but has to be combined with another morpheme to form one word. There are three kinds of affixes, i.e. PREFIXES, INFIXES and SUFFIXES.

AGENT   The term *agent* refers to the acting person or thing that causes the action expressed by the VERB or PREDICATE. In active CLAUSES the agent and the grammatical SUBJECT normally refer to the same entity. Contrast PATIENT.

AGREEMENT   Agreement, concord or congruency indicates the similarity of the formal elements in two or more words with reference to number, gender and person (and sometimes definiteness), for example, the agreement of the adjective with the NOUN, the agreement of the demonstrative pronoun with the noun, or the agreement of the VERB with the grammatical SUBJECT.

AKTIONSART   *Aktionsart* [lit. kind of action], which can usually be deduced from the VERB, indicates the manner in which the structure of a situation or event is understood in relation to durativity (= durative progress, e.g. *The sun shines*), iterativity (= interrupted, consecutive, repeated moments of progress, e.g., *The watch ticks continuously*), causativity (e.g. *The alarm clock wakes us up in the morning*), and other similar factors.

ALLOPHONE   Allophones are conditioned phonetic variants of a PHONEME (phonemes are linguistically distinctive speech sounds within a specific language, i.e. speech sounds that are used to contrast meaning). In English the two [p] sounds in *paper*, are allophones of the phoneme /-p/. The first one is aspirated and the second one is not, but aspirated and non-aspirated [p] are conditioned variants in English. In Biblical Hebrew the PLOSIVE and FRICATIVE pronunciations of the *beḡaḏkep̄aṯ* letters (§4.2.2) are phonetic variants or allophones.

ANAPHORA   An *anaphor* (plural *anaphora*) is a grammatical element without any independent reference. For its reference it depends on a previous element (the ANTECEDENT) in the same structural unit (normally a CLAUSE). *Anaphors* include REFLEXIVE pronouns (e.g. *myself*) and RECIPROCAL pronouns (e.g. *each other*). In contrast to anaphora, other pronouns refer independently (i.e. without an antecedent in the same structural unit, e.g. *he* in *He is ill*). See also ANTECEDENT.

ANAPHORIC   See ANAPHORA.

ANTECEDENT   An antecedent is an element in a CLAUSE to which another word that follows it, e.g. an anaphoric pronoun, refers. For example, in the sentence *Mary washes herself*, *Mary* is the antecedent for the anaphoric pronoun *herself*. See also ANAPHORA.

AP   See ADJECTIVE PHRASE.

APODOSIS   The *apodosis* is the second (*then*) part of a conditional construction (*if–then*). The *apodosis* is the consecutive main clause that follows the conditional subordinate clause or *PROTASIS* (the *if*-part) of this construction.

APPOSITION   Apposition is the juxtaposition of (placing next to or opposite to) an element (usually a NOUN or noun PHRASE) as a descriptive and/or explanatory modifier to another element (usually a noun or noun phrase) (the head). Nouns in apposition have the same reference and SYNTACTIC function as the head. Usually they also agree in number and gender with the head. In the CLAUSE *He called Sarah, his wife* the PHRASE *his wife* is in apposition to *Sarah*.

ASPECT   Aspect is used, like the notions tense and MOOD, in the grammatical description of verbs. It typically refers to grammatical forms of verbs which mark them as incomplete, durative, on-going (IMPERFECTIVE) or as complete (PERFECTIVE).

ASSIMILATION   Assimilation indicates a process where one segment (a discrete sound unit) adopts the characteristics of an adjacent segment and by which the two sounds become more similar. A consonant may take up the characteristics of a vowel, and a vowel may take up the characteristics of a consonant. A consonant may influence another consonant, and a vowel may influence another vowel. The equalization may be total or partial. Assimilation usually happens at the border of two MORPHEMES or words. In the word *cupboard* the [p]-sound takes over the characteristics of the adjacent [b]-sound. Usually the change occurs in both the spelling and pronunciation. For example, in the following examples the final consonant of a PREFIX adopted the characteristics of the initial consonant of the root word: *in+legal > illegal*; *in+mortal > immortal*. Progressive assimilation occurs when a sound adapts itself to a preceding one. Regressive assimilation occurs when a sound adapts itself to a following one.

ASYNDETIC   Asyndetic constructions involve a connection of words, PHRASES or CLAUSES without the normal coordinating or subordinating conjunction, for example, *In the days of Uzziah, Jotham, Ahaz...* instead of *In the days of Uzziah and Jotham and Ahaz...* Contrast SYNDETIC.

ATELIC   The term *atelic* refers to an event or activity which has no clear temporal boundary, e.g. English "he looks around." It is typically used in the grammatical description of the ASPECT of verbs. Contrast TELIC.

ATTRIBUTIVE   The term *attributive* refers to the manner in which adjectives qualify. In English the placing of an adjective or other adjectival modifier before the qualified NOUN indicates an attributive adjective, e.g. *red* in *He sits on the red chair*. In Biblical Hebrew an attributive adjective agrees with its noun in number, gender and definiteness, and it follows the noun, e.g. הַסּוּס הַגָּדוֹל. The term PREDICATIVE is used in contrast to attributive.

BACKGROUND   Background is a PRAGMATIC term that is used to refer to information that does not carry a narrative forward. Background information, however, typically provides information that is important to fully understand what is narrated. Contrast FOREGROUND.

BETH CAUSA   If the Biblical Hebrew preposition בְּ indicates the *cause* or *reason* for an action, it is called the *beth causa*.

BETH COMITANTIAE   If the Biblical Hebrew preposition בְּ indicates the person or entities that *accompany* the acting person, or that are *joined* or *associated* with him/her, it is called the *beth comitantiae*. See COMITATIVE.

BETH COMMUNICATIONIS   If the Biblical Hebrew preposition בְּ indicates the *instrument* (mainly human) of an act of speaking, it is called the *beth communicationis*.

BETH ESSENTIA   If the Biblical Hebrew preposition בְּ is used to equate a TRAJECTOR *x* with a LANDMARK *y*, it is called the *beth essentia.*

BETH INSTRUMENTI   If the Biblical Hebrew preposition בְּ indicates the *instrument* or *means* with which an action is realized, it is called the *beth instrumenti.*

BETH LOCALE   If the Biblical Hebrew preposition בְּ indicates the *place* where an action is realized, it is called the *beth locale.*

BETH PRETII   If the Biblical Hebrew preposition בְּ indicates the *price* for which an action is realized, it is called the *beth pretii.*

CASE   Case indicates a grammatical category that is used to identify the SYNTACTIC relations between words in a CLAUSE. In languages that express grammatical relations explicitly by DECLENSIONS (inflection), cases indicate the different functions of a word (normally a NOUN or pronoun). In languages like Biblical Hebrew with abstract case (not expressed explicitly as in Latin) other grammatical means are used to mark the SYNTACTIC relations between words.

CASUS PENDENS   See DISLOCATION CONSTRUCTION.

CATAPHOR   A cataphor is a grammatical element that is dependent for its reference on another element occurring later in a structural unit, usually a CLAUSE. In *Here is the news* the word *here* is a cataphor for that which follows in the UTTERANCE.

CATAPHORIC   See CATAPHOR.

CAUSATIVE   A causative indicates a grammatical construction or form (usually a VERB) that expresses cause or causality. Examples of causative verbs are *declare holy/consecrate, kindle, bring back* (= *cause to go back*).

CLAUSE   A clause is considered by some to be a grammatically organized unit, smaller than a sentence, but larger than a PHRASE, e.g. *who lived in Canaan* in *Jacob, who lived in Canaan, loved Joseph.* In this grammar a clause is regarded as a meaningful series of words that has a subject and a predicate. See also SENTENCE.

CLITIC A clitic is an unstressed word that normally occurs only in combination with another word, for example *m* in *I'm.*

COHESION   Cohesion refers to those qualities of a text that bind CLAUSES and sentences together, e.g. the cross-references of pronouns and NOUNS when people and things are referred to.

COMITATIVE   Comitative indicates the combining of a person or thing with another person or thing by accompanying it or by associating with it, or by causing an action in its presence.

COMPLEMENT   In grammatical theory this term refers to an obligatory element in a construction. On the SYNTACTIC level complements refer to obligatory, non-omissible, non-verbal parts of the PREDICATE or verb phrase (VP). If a complement is removed from the predicate, the structural identity of the rest of the construction is affected, for example, *bread* and *sons* cannot be omitted in the sentence *John gives his sons bread*. Complements are NOUNS or prepositional phrases that are added to or combined with verbs because the VERB requires its presence. They differ from ADJUNCTS that are optional, secondary PHRASES in the verb phrase. The noun (or other element) that is obligatory after a preposition is the complement of that preposition.

COMPLEMENT CLAUSE   A complement CLAUSE is subordinate, but non-omissible, e.g. a subject clause and an object clause.

COMPLEMENTIZER   A complementizer is a word or MORPHEME that marks an embedded clause as functioning as a COMPLEMENT to the matrix clause, that is, as a COMPLEMENT CLAUSE. In English, complementizers are typically a subordinating conjunction (e.g. *that*) or infinitival *to*.

COMPLEX SENTENCE   A complex sentence indicates the type of sentence where a clause stands in a coordinate relation to the so-called main clause (*John is ugly, but Mary is beautiful*), or in a subordinate relation (*When John saw Mary, he was infatuated*).

CONCORD   See AGREEMENT.

CONGRUENCY   See AGREEMENT.

CONJUGATION   A conjugation is the collection of the different forms of a VERB. In Biblical Hebrew verbs do not show different forms for MOODS like the INDICATIVE, SUBJUNCTIVE and OPTATIVE. Tense and MOOD both are expressed by the *QĀTAL*/PERFECT and *YIQTŌL*/ IMPERFECT FORMS. FINITE verbs have a STEM FORMATION, conjugation (tense/MOOD), person, gender and number. Non-finite verbs like the participle do not have person; the infinitive has neither person nor gender and number. The following finite conjugations are found: *QĀTAL*/

PERFECT, *YIQTŌL*/IMPERFECT, SHORT *YIQTŌL*, cohortative, imperative; and the following non-finite (without person) conjugations: infinitive construct, infinitive absolute, participle.

CONJUNCTIVE ADVERB   Conjunctive adverb is a sub-category of the WORD CLASS of adverbs. It occupies the sentence initial position (often preceded by the conjunction ׳), and links the content of the clause that it governs to that of another clause. It is also often used as a DISCOURSE MARKER.

CONSONANTAL SUFFIX   A consonantal SUFFIX indicates a pronominal suffix starting with a consonant. Contrast VOCALIC SUFFIX.

CONSTITUENT   In contrast to PHRASES which refer to the SYNTACTIC composition of a word group, e.g. noun phrase, adjective phrase, verb phrase, adverbial phrase and prepositional phrase, constituents are the word groups that form the functional units of the CLAUSE, e.g. SUBJECT, OBJECT, INDIRECT OBJECT, etc.

CONSTITUENT FOCUS   When a constituent of a sentence, e.g. the SUBJECT, OBJECT, INDIRECT OBJECT, ADJUNCT represents the most salient information in an utterance, relative to all the information provided by that utterance in a given context, that CONSTITUENT is the FOCUS of the UTTERANCE.

CONSTITUENT ORDER   The linear order of the CONSTITUENTS (e.g. the SUBJECT, VERB, OBJECT and INDIRECT OBJECT) of a sentence is called its CONSTITUENT ORDER. Languages are sometimes compared in terms of their most typical constituent order, e.g. does the OBJECT typically precede the VERB (an OV language) or does it typically follow the verb in a sentence (a VO language). The term word order is widely used as a synonym of CONSTITUENT ORDER.

CONSTRUCT PHRASE   A construct phrase is a PHRASE consisting of one or more NOUNS in the *STATUS CONSTRUCTUS*, followed by a noun (or its equivalent) which is called the *STATUS ABSOLUTUS* (or "GENITIVE"). A number of SEMANTIC relations can exist between the two elements of a construct phrase.

CONSTRUCTIO AD SENSUM   *Constructio ad sensum* refers to the forming of a grammatical construction in accordance with the meaning rather than the SYNTAX of the grammatical form. Usually the grammatical form of the SUBJECT determines the person, gender and number of the PREDICATE. However, a plural predicate is often used with nouns that have a collective meaning, but a singular form (thus the predicate only agrees in meaning with the subject), e.g. יָדְעוּ הָעָם (*The people know*).

COPULA   A *copula* is that element in a NOMINAL CLAUSE which connects the SUBJECT and the PREDICATE. Together the *copula* and predicate form the PREDICATE of such a clause, e.g. הָיָה and בְּאֶרֶץ־עוּץ in אִישׁ הָיָה בְאֶרֶץ־עוּץ. In Biblical Hebrew the *copula* is often omitted, e.g. אִיּוֹב שְׁמוֹ.

CONTINGENT USE   The contingent use of a construction refers to the fact that its function is underdetermined and depends on the meaning of another construction (usually in the preceding context). In Biblical Hebrew, the contingent use of the *WƏQĀTAL* means its interpretation depends on whether it follows an imperative or *YIQTŌL*.

CORRELATIVE CONJUNCTIONS   Words that can be used to link items and precede each member of the coordinated construction (i.e. each word, each phrase or each sentence) are regarded as correlative conjunctions. In other words, they link items in the format conj+*x* conj+*y* (conj+*z*) and not only *x* conj *y*. In Biblical Hebrew, אוֹ, אִם, אַף, גַּם and וְ can be used as correlative conjunctions.

DATIVE   In languages that express grammatical relations explicitly by DECLENSIONS (inflection) this term indicates the form of the word (normally a NOUN or pronoun) that expresses the INDIRECT OBJECT or the receiver of something or an action. In Biblical Hebrew the dative is not indicated explicitly; instead, the functions of the dative are expressed by other grammatical means, for example, by prepositions.

DECLENSION   A declension is the collection of the different forms of a NOUN. In Biblical Hebrew nouns do not show CASE endings, but they do have masculine and feminine forms in the singular, dual and plural; and they may exhibit the *STATUS ABSOLUTUS* and *STATUS CONSTRUCTUS*. Singular, plural and dual nouns all can be combined with pronominal SUFFIXES. Thus a word with masculine and feminine forms (like סוּס and סוּסָה) can theoretically have 72 different forms. In the declension the noun can undergo different vowel and consonantal changes, on the basis of which five main declension types are distinguished.

DEICTIC   See DEIXIS.

DEIXIS   *Deixis* refers to a system of words that depends on the concrete situation in which language is used for its meaning or interpretation (i.e. the speaker, addressee, time and location). For example, the referents of personal PRONOUNS (e.g. *I, we, you, he/she/they*) depend upon the speaker(s) and addressee(s), the referents of *this/that, here/there* and *now/then* depend upon the time and/or location of the speaker. Thus, the meaning *deictics* (grammatical elements involving *deixis*) is relative to the situation in which they occur.

DETACHMENT   Detachment is a semantic category that refers to the relationship between a TRAJECTOR *x* that moves (or is caused to move) away from a LANDMARK *y*. In Biblical Hebrew, this is the most typical function of the preposition מִן.

DIACHRONY   Diachrony is concerned with the way in which something, especially language, has developed, changed and evolved through time. Often contrasted with SYNCHRONY.

DIRECT OBJECT   A direct object refers to one of the two grammatical relations that functions as an objective element in the CLAUSE structure. The other is the INDIRECT OBJECT. In English the difference between the direct object and the indirect object on the SYNTACTIC level is that the direct object cannot be marked by a preposition, for example, *I gave the book to John* and *I gave John the book*. SEMANTICALLY the direct object refers to the entity that is affected or effected by the action. For example, in the clause *John kicks the ball* the entity affected by the action is *the ball*.

DIRECTIVE   A directive is a SPEECH ACT with which a person intends to cause people to do something, e.g. a command, hint or suggestion.

DISCOURSE ACTIVE Discourse active is a PRAGMATIC category that describes the information status of items in a communication event. Items that are available in the short-term memory of participants in a communication event, so that reference can be made to them, are discourse active.

DISCOURSE LINGUISTICS   See TEXT LINGUISTICS.

DISCOURSE MARKER   The term refers to a category of linguistic expressions that signals the speaker's view/attitude/judgment with respect to the relationship between the chunks of discourse that precede and follow it, typically in the sentence (utterance)-initial position.

DISLOCATION CONSTRUCTION   A dislocation construction consists of a grammatical element, isolated to the left (beginning) or the right (end) of the CLAUSE (the dislocated CONSTITUENT), and a main clause containing an element (the RESUMPTIVE) that refers to the dislocated constituent, e.g. _This food – I will eat it all_.

DISTRIBUTION   Distribution refers to all the linguistic contexts or areas in which a grammatical element can occur.

DUAL   The term _dual_ is used for an inflection that indicates that a noun or pronoun refers to exactly _two_ people or things (as distinct from singular and plural).

EFFECTED   The term _effected_ refers to the entity (person or thing) that, although it does not cause the action or event indicated by the VERB, is somehow directly involved. In active CLAUSES the effected element and the grammatical OBJECT normally refer to the same person or thing. The effected entity did not exist before the action, but is created by the action, e.g. _the table_ in _He made the table_. See AFFECTED.

ENERGIC _NÛN_   The energic _nûn_ in Biblical Hebrew refers to the INFIXED _nûn_ before (objective) pronominal SUFFIXES in certain verbal forms. The syllable in which the _nûn_ occurs carries the accent. It has no SEMANTIC value. See SUFFIX.

EPEXEGETICAL   Epexegetical refers to the function of explaining the directly preceding material.

EPICENE NOUNS   Epicene noun (NOUNS of common gender) is the phenomenon involving words which MORPHOLOGICALLY have either a masculine or feminine form, but SEMANTICALLY refer to a mixed gender group. In Biblical Hebrew the word כֶּלֶב (dog) has a masculine form although it can refer to a bitch or a male dog. The word יוֹנָה (dove) has a feminine form even when it refers to a male dove.

EPISTEMIC MODALITY   Epistemic MODALITY is a type of modality that indicates the degree of certainty or the quality of evidence that a speaker has for what he/she says.

ERGATIVE SYSTEM   An ergative system refers to languages where the DIRECT OBJECT of a TRANSITIVE verb and the SUBJECT of an INTRANSITIVE verb show the same CASE, whereas the subjects of transitive VERBS are treated differently. In such a system the role of the subject in an intransitive CLAUSE like *The window broke* will be the same as the role of the direct object in the transitive clause *John broke the window*. The AGENT of the action is referred to as the ergative subject.

EXTENDED SENTENCE   An extended sentence is a sentence of which one CONSTITUENT is extended, for example, by a relative clause.

FACTITIVE   A factitive indicates a grammatical construction or form (normally a VERB) that refers to an action or event in which a cause produces a consequence or result, for example, *makes* in *He makes wine*.

FIENTIVE   A VERB that describes movement or a change of state, is called a fientive (or dynamic) verb. In these cases the SUBJECT performs an action. Contrast STATIVE.

FINITE   Finite refers to the grammatical classification of VERBS and CLAUSES. A finite verb is limited by person, and it can occur independently in a main clause. It allows contrasts in tense, ASPECT and MOOD. Non-finite verbs, however, occur only in subordinate clauses. Contrasts in time, ASPECT and MOOD are lacking. All conjugated forms of the Biblical Hebrew verb are finite except infinitives and participles. Clauses with finite verbs are finite clauses.

FOCUS   The focused entity in a CLAUSE represents the most salient information in terms of the total amount of information in that clause. Usually the focused element is specifically selected in a context where there is more than one alternative available. In Biblical Hebrew focus can be marked by CONSTITUENT ORDER, or by a focus particle.

FOREGROUND   Foreground is a PRAGMATIC term that is used to refer to events that carry a narrative foreword. It is sometimes used as a synonym for the "main line" or "backbone" of a story. In Biblical Hebrew narrative, FOREGROUND is often associated with the *WAYYIQTŌL* construction. In other text types, foregrounded material may be associated with other constructions. Contrast BACKGROUND.

FRICATIVE   This term refers to the manner of articulation of consonants that are formed by narrowing the speech canal at a certain place, thereby obstructing the outgoing breath in such a way that a clearly audible friction develops. In Biblical Hebrew the ב, ג, ד, כ, פ and ת are fricatives when they are pronounced with friction (the so-called *beḡaḏkep̄aṯ* letters).

FRONTING   If the PREVERBAL FIELD (i.e. the part of the CLAUSE that precedes the VERB) is occupied by a CONSTITUENT, this phenomenon is referred to as fronting of that constituent. Contrast DISLOCATION.

GENITIVE   In languages that express grammatical relations explicitly by DECLENSIONS (inflection) this term indicates the form of the word (normally a NOUN or pronoun) that often marks the possessor. In Biblical Hebrew the genitive is not indicated explicitly and the genitive function is expressed by way of other grammatical means like the CONSTRUCT PHRASE.

GLIDE   This term refers to the manner of articulation of certain consonants that are formed when the air stream is obstructed only slightly. Glides have more in common with vowels than with consonants. Therefore, they are sometimes also called transitional sounds. In Biblical Hebrew the consonants ה, י and ו are sometimes pronounced as glides.

GNOMIC *QĀTAL*/PERFECT   When the *QĀTAL*/PERFECT FORM expresses actions, events and/or facts that are timeless or usually true, it is called the gnomic *QĀTAL*/PERFECT. It is usually used for general experiential descriptions or verdicts where the idea of time has been moved totally to the background. In Biblical Hebrew the VERB *keeps* in the sentence *The swallow keeps its migration pattern* will be in the *QĀTAL*/PERFECT form.

GRAMMATICALIZATION   Grammaticalization is a process by which a lexical item or a construction changes in form and/or meaning into one that serves a grammatical function.

HAPAX LEGOMENON   The term *hapax legomenon* [lit. read once] refers to a word or combination of words (an expression) that is known only from a single citation in a given piece of literature.

HENDIADYS   *Hendiadys* [lit. one through two] refers to the presentation of a single idea by a coordinate combination of words, *inter alia* two NOUNS, two VERBS or two adjectives, e.g. *nice and warm* for *nicely warm*.

IMMINENT CONNOTATION   Imminent connotation has the quality: to be on the point of happening, about to happen.

IMPERFECT FORM   See *YIQTŌL* FORM

IMPERFECTIVE   *Imperfective* refers to one of the SEMANTIC functions of a VERB form (e.g. the *YIQTŌL*/IMPERFECT), viz., that an action or event is viewed as incomplete. Contrast PERFECTIVE.

INDICATIVE   The indicative is a MOOD of the VERB that expresses a fact in the form of a statement or question. However, it is not expressed in Biblical Hebrew by a separate CONJUGATION, but the *QĀTAL*/ PERFECT FORM (and sometimes also the *YIQTŌL*/IMPERFECT FORM) is often used for this.

INDIRECT OBJECT   An indirect object refers to one of the two grammatical relations that function as objective element in the CLAUSE structure. The other is the DIRECT OBJECT. In English the difference between the indirect object and the direct object on the SYNTACTIC level is that the indirect object can be marked by a preposition or not, for example, *I gave the book to John* and *I gave John the book*. SEMANTICALLY the indirect object refers to the entity that receives the indirect effect of an action (e.g. (*to*) *John* above).

INFINITIVE ABSOLUTE CONSTRUCTION   An infinitive absolute that is followed (and sometimes preceded) by a finite verb with the same root is called an infinitive absolute construction. This construction is referred to also as the "tautological infinite" or the "paronomastic infinitive."

INFIX   An infix is an AFFIX that is inserted into the ROOT of a word itself, in contrast to other affixes which are inserted before the root (PREFIX) or after the root (SUFFIX).

INFORMATION STRUCTURE   Information structure is a SEMANTIC-PRAGMATIC concept that refers to the way in which information is packaged within a sentence, as either what is "given" (or assumed to be given) in the addressee's mind or what is "new" and not assumed in the prior discourse. In many languages (like Biblical Hebrew), the CONSTITUENT ORDER of a sentence reflects its information structure. See also TOPIC and FOCUS.

INGRESSIVE   The ingressive refers to the function of a verbal form that emphasizes the beginning or transitional phase of the event indicated by the VERB.

INTERROGATIVE   An interrogative is a grammatical element that introduces a question. Questions with yes–no answers are marked with the interrogative הֲ/הֲלֹא. Questions with factual answers are marked by interrogative pronouns and adverbs (the so-called WH-interrogatives or content questions). There is no punctuation such as a question mark in Biblical Hebrew for indicating that a sentence is a question. Interrogatives can also introduce indirect questions. See also WH-QUESTIONS.

INTRANSITIVE   This term indicates VERBS that do not require a DIRECT OBJECT, e.g. *John walks*. Contrast TRANSITIVE.

JUSSIVE   Jussive refers to an indirect command to the third or second person.

JUSSIVE FORM   See SHORT *YIQTŌL*.

LANDMARK   The terms LANDMARK and TRAJECTOR are used to describe an asymmetric relationship between two entities, in which one, the TRAJECTOR, is described relative to another one, the LANDMARK. The LANDMARK is the relatively stationary entity with respect to which the position of the less stationary TRAJECTOR is profiled. See TRAJECTOR.

LEXEME   Lexeme refers to the smallest, distinguishable meaningful unit in the SEMANTIC system of language. The words *wrote* and *written* are manifestations of the lexeme *write*.

LEXICAL ENTRY   Lexical entry refers to any entry of a word in a lexicon or a dictionary article. Such an entry contains the distinguishable information (e.g. PHONOLOGICAL, MORPHOLOGICAL, SYNTACTIC and SEMANTIC information) of the word.

LEXICAL CLASS   Lexical class refers to a set or category of the words or vocabulary of a language having some property or attribute in common and differentiated from others by kind, type or quality. For example, in Biblical Hebrew, the segholate nouns constitute a lexical class based upon their phonological and morphological features, whereas kinship terms constitute a lexical class based upon their semantic features. Contrast PARTS OF SPEECH and WORD CLASSES.

LONG *YIQTŌL*   See SHORT *YIQTŌL* and *YIQTŌL*.

MAIN FIELD   The main field of a Biblical Hebrew CLAUSE is that part of the clause that is introduced by the VERB. The part of the clause that precedes the verb is the PREVERBAL FIELD.

MAIN VERB   The *main verb* of a CLAUSE or SENTENCE is a FINITE verb.

MARKED   An entity is marked when it is distinguished by a particular feature. In English, the term *drake* is semantically marked for gender (i.e. it indicates masculine), whereas the term *duck* is unmarked for gender (i.e. it may be used to refer to a male or female animal). Contrast UNMARKED.

MATRIX CLAUSE   A *matrix clause* is a clause of which one or more constituents are extended, for example, by a relative clause, or in which one or more clauses are embedded, for example, as a COMPLEMENT CLAUSE or an infinitival complement. In this grammar, the notion MATRIX CLAUSE is also used to refer to the clause in which a dislocated constituent is resumed or the clause with which a dislocated constituent could be associated.

MEANING POTENIAL   See SEMANTIC POTENTIAL

METAPHORIC EXTENSION   The term *metaphoric extension* refers to a process during which an original metaphorical use of an expression becomes encoded as part of the meaning of the expression on the basis of some *similarity* between their referents. For example, the English word "mouse" meaning "a small rodent" has been metaphorically extended to refer to the "pointing device of a computer" on the basis of the visual similarity between a computer mouse and its cord to a rodent with its tail.

METONYMIC EXTENSION   The term *metonymic extension* refers to a process during which an original metonymical use of an expression becomes encoded as part of the meaning of the expression on the basis of a strong association between their referents. For example, English "wheels" may refer to circular rubber objects or, by metonymic extension, to a "car."

METATHESIS   Metathesis indicates a process where the sequence of two segments (discrete sound units) is switched. A consonant may be interchanged with a vowel, a vowel with a consonant, a consonant with another consonant, or a vowel with another vowel. It usually occurs at the border of two MORPHEMES or words, e.g. pr<u>e</u>vent is pronounced as p<u>er</u>vent. In Biblical Hebrew the change usually occurs in the pronunciation, as well as in the spelling, e.g. תִּתְשַׁכְּרִין* is written and pronounced as תִּשְׁתַּכְּרִין.

MIRATIVITY   The term *mirativity* refers to the grammatical means for indicating surprise or unexpectedness on the part of the speaker(s).

MODAL ADVERB   Modal adverbs are a sub-category of the WORD CLASS of adverb and modify entire sentences. They involve the subjective judgments of speakers concerning the possibility, necessity and obligation of what is said. See also MODALITY and EPISTEMIC MODALITY.

MODAL PARTICLE   See MODAL ADVERB

MODALITY   Modality as a SEMANTIC category refers to the speaker's subjective judgment concerning the factuality of the events, for example, the possibility, potentiality, (un)desirability of events. In English, modal auxiliary VERBS like *can/could, will/would, should, may, must*, etc. are used to express the subjective judgment of a speaker concerning the factuality of the events, e.g. *John would have sung now*. In Biblical Hebrew the *YIQTŌL*/IMPERFECT FORM is used especially to express modalities: usually the relevant events are non-factual. See EPISTEMIC MODALITY.

MOOD   The term *mood* refers to certain CONJUGATIONS of the VERB in languages that express mood explicitly, e.g. the INDICATIVE, SUBJUNCTIVE and OPTATIVE in Greek.

MORPHEME   The term *morpheme* refers to the smallest unit of a language with independent meaning and/or grammatical function; a meaningful morphological unit of a language that cannot be further divided (e.g., the English word *incoming* consists of three morphemes: *in, come, ing*).

MORPHOLOGY   Morphology as a component of grammar is the study of the forms of words in a language. The distinction of WORD CLASSES is part of the morphology.

N   See NOUN.

NARRATIVE   The term *narrative* refers to a spoken or written account of connected events – a story, involving events, characters, and what the characters say and do. It can also refer to the narrated part or parts of a literary work as distinct from dialogue.

NOMINAL CLAUSE   Nominal CLAUSES refer to clauses in Biblical Hebrew that do not contain a FINITE form of the VERB and where the *COPULA is* has to be inserted in English, e.g. *Jacob (is) old*. Nominal clauses are also referred to as *verbless clauses*.

NOMINATIVE   In languages that express grammatical relationships explicitly by DECLENSIONS (inflection), the NOMINATIVE indicates the
form of the word (normally a NOUN or pronoun) that usually expresses
the SUBJECT of the VERB. In Biblical Hebrew the nominative is not
indicated explicitly, and similar functions are expressed by way of other
grammatical ways (or it is simply unmarked).

NOUN   The noun (abbreviated N) is a term in the grammatical classification
of words that traditionally refers to a class of words indicating persons or
things. The noun includes the following main classes: SUBSTANTIVES,
pronouns and numerals.

NOUN PHRASE (NP)   NP refers to a noun phrase, a PHRASE with N
(a noun) as head. The phrase *the student* in the clause *The student is
incredibly clever* is the NP with the N *student* as head.

NP   See NOUN PHRASE.

OBJECT   See DIRECT OBJECT and INDIRECT OBJECT.

OPTATIVE   The optative is a MOOD of the VERB that expresses non-factual
or UNREAL events and states. Biblical Hebrew does not distinguish
between the optative and SUBJUNCTIVE. See INDICATIVE.

P   An abbreviation of *preposition*. See PREPOSITIONAL PHRASE (PP).

PARADIGMATIC DISTRIBUTION   The term *paradigmatic distribution*
refers to the relationship between a set of linguistic items that are
MORPHOLOGICALLY, SYNTACTICALLY, or SEMANTICALLY
similar, and which can be substituted for one another as mutually
exclusive choices in particular linguistic roles; it also refers to the vertical
relationship between any linguistic item in a phrase or sentence and
other items that are similar and which can be substituted for it. Contrast
SYNTAGMATIC.

PART OF SPEECH   Part of speech is a synonym for WORD CLASS.

PARTICLE   Particle is an umbrella term that is sometimes used for a number
of parts of speech that are neither nouns nor verbs, viz. the article,
prepositions, conjunctions, adverbs, PREDICATORS OF EXISTENCE,
INTERROGATIVES, DISCOURSE MARKERS and interjections.

PARTITIVE   Partitive is a SEMANTIC term that indicates part-whole
relations.

PAST PERFECT   *Past perfect* or pluperfect refers to one of the SEMANTIC functions of a VERB form (e.g. *QĀTAL*/PERFECT), viz., distant past tense, i.e. an event or state that had been completed before another in the past. See PERFECT.

PATIENT   The SEMANTIC function of the AFFECTED or EFFECTED is called the patient. Contrast AGENT.

PENDENS   See DISLOCATION CONSTRUCTION.

PERFECT   *Perfect* refers to one of the SEMANTIC functions of a VERB form (e.g. *QĀTAL*/PERFECT FORM), viz., that an anterior event has current relevance. This may be the case in a present, past or future time frame. See PAST PERFECT.

PERFECT FORM   See *QĀTAL* FORM.

PERFECTIVE   *Perfective* refers to one of the SEMANTIC functions of a VERB form (e.g. the *QĀTAL*/PERFECT), viz., that an action or event is viewed as complete. Contrast IMPERFECTIVE.

PERFORMATIVE   *Performative* is a term that indicates that a certain action is carried out or accomplished by a linguistic UTTERANCE, e.g. *He declares you holy.* In Biblical Hebrew, the *QĀTAL*/PERFECT FORM is used especially for performative utterances. See SPEECH ACT.

PERSON SUFFIX   "Person suffix" (e.g. the verbal affixes) must be distinguished from "pronominal suffix" (e.g. the objective affixes on verbs or the possessive suffixes on nouns).

PHONEME   Any of the perceptually distinct units of sound in a specific language that distinguish one word from another. For example, English has the phonemes *p*, *b*, *d*, and *t* which can be demonstrated to be phonemes from the fact that they distinguish the words *pad, pat, bad, bat, dad, dab, tap, tab* and *tad*. Contrast ALLOPHONE.

PHONETICS   Phonetics is the study that describes the sounds of a language with respect to their acoustic and articulatory characteristics.

PHONOLOGY   Phonology is the study that explains the underlying sound structure of a language, for example, how the different forms of a word within the language are related (like מֶלֶךְ and מַלְכָּה) and how sound indicates distinctive meanings (like the difference between בָּאָה and בָּאָה) with the accent either on the first syllable (*QĀTAL*/PERFECT) or the last syllable (PARTICIPLE).

PHRASE   The smallest units with which a CLAUSE is built are words. Words are distinguished in different classes, e.g. VERB (V), NOUN (N), adjective (A) and preposition (P). Words can be grouped into larger units known as phrases. Phrases can again be distinguished in different classes, named according to the class of the head word in the phrase, e.g. NOUN PHRASE (NP), VERB PHRASE (VP), PREPOSITIONAL PHRASE (PP) and ADJECTIVE PHRASE (AP).

PLEONASTIC   A pleonastic expression is something that is said unnecessarily, i.e. a redundancy of words. A *tautology* (to say something twice) is an example of a *pleonastic expression.*

PLOSIVE   This term refers to the manner of articulation of consonants that are formed by completely blocking the breath stream somewhere in the speech canal for an important moment, followed by the sudden release of the suppressed breath so that a light explosion is heard. In Biblical Hebrew the sounds ב, ג, ד, כ, פ and ת are plosives or stops when they are pronounced with an occlusive sound (the so-called *beḡaḏkep̄aṯ* letters).

PLURALIS MAJESTATIS   If the plural form does not express a normal numerical plural, but indicates that something or someone is mighty, big, terrible or worthy of respect, it is called the *pluralis majestatis* or royal plural.

POLARITY   Polarity refers to the semantic feature of a linguistic item as either positive or negative. In Biblical Hebrew, rhetorical questions can be usually understood as assertions that reverse the polarity of the rhetorical question. A few words have inherent negative polarity.

PP   See PREPOSITIONAL PHRASE and PHRASE.

PRAGMATICS   *Pragmatics* involves the relationship between natural language expressions and their use in specific situations.

PRECATIVE   The precative refers to a rare SEMANTIC use of the *QĀTAL/ PERFECT FORM* to make a request. In Biblical Hebrew, it is usually found in prayers.

PREDICATE   The predicate is that CONSTITUENT of a CLAUSE – normally a verb phrase (VP) – that combines with the SUBJECT to form a (complete) clause. The predicate of NOMINAL CLAUSES in Biblical Hebrew is not formed by a verb phrase, but by a noun phrase (e.g. *Abraham (is) a prophet*), prepositional phrase (e.g. *Sarah (is) in the tent*) or adjective phrase (e.g. *Sarah (is) beautiful*).

PREDICATE FOCUS   Predicate focus is a type of FOCUS where the PREDICATE of a sentence represents the most salient information in terms of the total amount of information in that sentence.

PREDICATIVE   The term *predicative* refers to the manner in which adjectives qualify. In English the position of an adjective or other attribute after the qualified NOUN or pronoun (and connected with it by the copulative VERB *is*) indicates the predicative, e.g. *red* in *The chair is red*. In Biblical Hebrew a predicative noun agrees with the SUBJECT in number and gender, and it is always indefinite. Usually it follows the subject (and *COPULA*), but it can precede it. Contrast ATTRIBUTIVE.

PREDICATORS OF EXISTENCE   Predicators of existence are grammatical function words which are used to assert the existence or non-existence of person(s) or thing(s).

PREFIX   A prefix is an AFFIX attached to the beginning of a ROOT, for example, the MORPHEMES of the *YIQTŌL*/IMPERFECT FORMS that appear before the STEM CONSONANTS, in contrast to affixes which are inserted in the root itself (INFIX) or after the root (SUFFIX).

PREFIX CONJUGATION   See *YIQTŌL*/IMPERFECT FORM.

PREPOSING   Some scholars use *preposing* as a synonym for FRONTING.

PREPOSITIONAL PHRASE (PP)   A prepositional phrase is a phrase consisting of a preposition and its nominal or pronominal object (or COMPLEMENT).

PRESENTATIVES   *Presentatives* are a small set of grammatical function words that a speaker may use to present an entity to his/her audience.

PRETERITE   Preterite is a simple past tense form that is not marked for ASPECT, e.g. *saw, loved.*

PREVERBAL FIELD   The preverbal field is that part of a Biblical Hebrew CLAUSE that precedes the VERB. The part of the clause that is introduced by the verb, is called the MAIN FIELD.

PROCLITIC   Proclitic refers to the phenomenon that, in pronunciation, a syllable is combined so closely with the following word that it loses its own accent. In Biblical Hebrew proclisis is indicated by the *maqqēp* (raised hyphen between letters). Two words that are combined in this way form one accent unit, the accent being on the last part (normally on the last syllable of that part). *Proclisis* occurs especially after monosyllabic words, e.g. בֶּן instead of בֶּן in בֶּן־יִשְׂרָאֵל. Words that have undergone *proclisis* are called CLITICS.

PROPHETIC   *QĀTAL*/PERFECT The prophetic *QĀTAL*/PERFECT is a use of the *QĀTAL*/PERFECT FORM to present future events as if they have already happened. Here the use of the *QĀTAL*/PERFECT form to express completeness and factuality is so prominent that it is even used for a future event.

PROTASIS   The *protasis* is the first (*if-*) part of a condition – a subordinate, conditional clause. See APODOSIS.

PROTO-SCENE   The primary spatial relationship that a specific preposition profiles is called its proto-scene.

PROTOTYPE   Prototype is a term used in semantics to refer to the most typical member of a category. A sparrow or robin is, for example, a prototypical member of the category "bird," while an ostrich or penguin are non-prototypical members of the category "bird."

QĀTAL/PERFECT FORM   The *QĀTAL*/PERFECT form is one of the CONJUGATIONS in Biblical Hebrew that indicates the VERB's tense (past) and/or ASPECT (completeness) and/or MOOD (factuality). It is also called the suffix conjugation because the Qal *QĀTAL*/PERFECT conjugation only takes SUFFIXES. With reference to the third-person masculine singular of the pattern verb קָטַל, it is called the *QĀTAL*/PERFECT form. The *QĀTAL*/PERFECT is a FINITE form having person, number and gender. It is found in all STEM FORMATIONS (*binyanim*) and is used especially for the main verb in a CLAUSE.

QUANTIFIER   A quantifier is a determiner or pronoun indicative of quantity, e.g. *all*, *both*. It indicates the SCOPE of a term to which it is attached.

REAL CONDITION   A subordinate, conditional CLAUSE is real if it indicates a fact in the past, present or future, e.g. *If it rains, the streets are wet*. Contrast UNREAL.

RECIPROCAL   A construction is reciprocal if an action or relation applies mutually. The members of a plural SUBJECT carry out the action on one another, e.g. *they wash each other*. In Biblical Hebrew the Nip̄ʿal STEM FORMATION is sometimes used reciprocally.

REFERENT   A referent is that entity in the real or conceptual (conversa-
tional) world which is associated with a NOUN PHRASE in a specific
sentence or UTTERANCE.

REFLEXIVE   A construction is called reflexive when two noun PHRASES
in the construction have the same REFERENT, for example, *Liza washes
herself* in which *Liza* and *herself* refers to the same person.

REPORTED SPEECH   The term *reported speech* refers to a speaker's
words as reported by a reporting speaker. The reported words may be
represented indirectly in subordinate clauses governing by a reporting
verb with the required changes of person and tense (e.g. *he said that he
would go*, reporting *I will go*); also called indirect speech. The reported
words may be represented directly without subordination to a reporting
verb with the DEIXIS of the original speech maintained in the report (e.g.
he said, "I will go"); also called direct speech.

RESUMPTIVE   The resumptive is the element in a CLAUSE that repeats
the concord features (number and gender) of a previous element (the
ANTECEDENT of a relative clause or a dislocated element of a
DISLOCATION CONSTRUCTION), e.g. *The man, I saw him*.

ROOT   See STEM.

ROYAL PLURAL   See PLURALIS MAJESTATIS.

SCOPE   The term *scope* refers to the range of the effectiveness of an operator
such as a QUANTIFIER or a conjunction.

SECONDARY ACCENT   In Biblical Hebrew certain words receive a
secondary accent. Words consisting of three syllables with the primary
accent on the last syllable very often get secondary accentuation on the
third to last syllable.

SELECT   Select refers to the restriction that a VERB's lexical meaning has
on the CONSTITUENTS which can or must be used with it, for example,
the verb *to die* selects only a SUBJECT (*He died*). In contrast to this
the verb *to give* selects a subject, DIRECT OBJECT and INDIRECT
OBJECT (*[He]* gives *[the man]* *[bread]*). See VALENCY.

SEMANTIC POTENTIAL   The semantic potential of an expression, also
called its meaning potential, refers to all the information that are
connected to a linguistic expression. It is a result of its use(s) by an individual or linguistic community in specific contexts. Any of these senses
have the potential to be activated again in similar contexts.

SEMANTIC-PRAGMATIC FUNCTION   The term is used to refer to the functional value of (mainly syntactic) constructions where there is no one-to-one correlation between the construction and the function that is expressed by means of it. Its function can only be determined if the communicative context in which the clause was uttered is taken into consideration. In this grammar the term is used to refer to the contribution (i.e. the functional value) that the order of constituents makes to the interpretation of the INFORMATION STRUCTURE of a sentence (see CONSTITUENT ORDER, FOCUS and TOPIC). See also SEMANTIC POTENTIAL.

SEMANTICS   Semantics is the study of meaning in a language. Semantics describes not only the meaning of words, but also the meaning of relationships expressed in CLAUSES and SENTENCES, as well as the meaning of CLAUSES and SENTENCES.

SENTENCE   A sentence is regarded as the largest structural unit in terms of which the grammar of language is organized. See also CLAUSE.

SENTENCE FOCUS   Sentence focus is a SEMANTIC-PRAGMATIC term that refers to the INFORMATION STRUCTURE of sentences in which everything that is said represents new information. This happens typically in "event reports" in contexts where none of the participants is necessarily DISCOURSE ACTIVE, e.g. *A group of strangers arrived in our city last night.*

SHORT *YIQTŌL*   The short *yiqtōl* has traditionally been described as the jussive form. The epithet "short," qualifying the *yiqtōl*, differentiates it from a morphologically similar construction, known as *"YIQTŌL"* or *"LONG YIQTŌL."* It is not always possible to distinguish morphologically between long and short *yiqtōl* forms. This can be done only with the Hipꜥîl and some weak verbs, e.g. the III-*hēʾ*. Short *yiqtōl* forms typically have a DIRECTIVE function. See JUSSIVE.

SIBILANT   The term *sibilant* refers to the manner of articulation of consonants that are formed when the speech canal is narrowed and, as a result, the air stream passes through with an audible hiss. In Biblical Hebrew the sounds ז, ס, צ, שׁ and שׂ are sibilants.

SOCIOLINGUISTICS   Sociolinguistics is the study of language in relation to social factors, including differences of region, class, occupation, gender and age, and the use of more than one language (bilingualism) or variety of language (diglossia).

SPEECH ACT   A speech act is an act performed by a speaker's UTTERANCE: making an assertion, asking a question, giving a command, expressing encouragement or wish, etc. See PERFORMATIVE.

SPEECH TURN   The term *speech turn* refers to the speeches alternately spoken by speakers in a dialogue; the speech turn of one speaker is followed by the speech turn of another speaker.

SPLIT COORDINATION   See SPLIT PHRASE.

SPLIT PHRASE   (split SUBJECT, OBJECT, etc.) In Biblical Hebrew a split PHRASE indicates the grammatical pattern where other CLAUSE elements are inserted between the first and other parts of a constituent. For example, *moved away* is inserted between the parts of the split subject in the clause *A man* moved away, *he and his wife and his sons*.

STATIVE   Stative indicates a form or construction expressing a state or quality rather than an event. In the case of VERBS in Biblical Hebrew there is a MORPHOLOGICAL distinction between the conjugation of statives and events/actions. Stative verbs are usually used INTRANSITIVELY, and events/actions are usually TRANSITIVE. Contrast FIENTIVE.

STATUS ABSOLUTUS   The *status absolutus* is the normal form of the NOUN – singular, plural or dual; masculine or feminine. It is also called the נִפְרָד. A noun in the *status absolutus* can fulfil any SYNTACTIC function. The last element of a CONSTRUCT PHRASE or chain is also in the *status absolutus*. Compare STATUS CONSTRUCTUS and see CONSTRUCT PHRASE.

STATUS CONSTRUCTUS   The form of the first element of a CONSTRUCT PHRASE is shortened where possible. This form is the *status constructus* or נִסְמָךְ. The *status constructus* is sometimes also used as a binding form before other elements like prepositions. A word in the *status constructus* often loses its own accent (see PROCLITIC). Compare STATUS ABSOLUTUS and see CONSTRUCT PHRASE.

STEM   The stem or root of a word is a theoretical abstraction containing only the basic consonants of a word, without any of its PREFIXES, INFIXES, SUFFIXES and STEM VOWELS. The root of the VERB in Biblical Hebrew usually consists of three consonants.

STEM CONSONANT   A stem consonant is one of the three consonants forming the abstracted STEM or root of a VERB.

STEM FORMATION   Stem formation is a conjugational type of the VERB. Biblical Hebrew distinguishes seven basic stem formations: Qal, Niṗʿal, Piʿēl, Puʿal, Hiṯpaʿēl, Hiṗʿîl and Hoṗʿal. Sometimes stem formations are used to express VOICE, for example, the Niṗʿal can be the passive or REFLEXIVE of the Qal. However, the stem formations are not in absolutely fixed SEMANTIC relations to one other.

STEM SYLLABLE   The stem syllable is that syllable of a VERB that starts with the first STEM CONSONANT.

STEM VOWEL   A stem vowel is one of the characteristic vowels of a certain CONJUGATION; for example, the vowels ◌ and ◌ are the stem vowels of the Qal *QĀTAL*/PERFECT (כָּתַב, כָּתְבָה, כָּתַבְתָּ, כָּתַבְתִּי, etc.). With reference to NOUNS the stem vowel is one of the basic vowels of the word, for example, the stem vowel of מֶלֶךְ is /◌/ (מַלְךְ).

SUBJECT   The subject refers to the grammatical relation that functions as subjective element in the CLAUSE structure. On the SYNTACTIC level the subject is that part of the clause that agrees with the PREDICATE in number and gender (and person – if the verb is FINITE). SEMANTICALLY the subject refers to the one who carries out the action or who experiences the state, for example, in the clauses *John kicks the ball* and *John sleeps* the word *John* is the entity that carries out the action or experiences the state.

SUBJUNCTIVE   The subjunctive is a MOOD of the VERB expressing non-factualities like a wish, expectation or possibility. However, these are not expressed in Biblical Hebrew by a separate CONJUGATION. The *YIQTŌL*/IMPERFECT FORM is used to express modal functions like *can/could*, *want(ed) to*, and *may* or *have to*. See OPTATIVE.

SUBSTANTIVE   Substantive is a synonym for NOUN.

SUFFIX   A suffix is an AFFIX attached to the end of a STEM/ROOT, for example, the endings of the *QĀTAL*/PERFECT and the nominal endings for the singular, plural and dual; masculine and feminine; *STATUS ABSOLUTUS* and *STATUS CONSTRUCTUS*. Suffixes are in contrast to affixes which are inserted in the root itself (INFIX) or before the root (PREFIX). The possessive pronouns that are suffixed to NOUNS are called pronominal suffixes. A pronominal DIRECT OBJECT can also be expressed by a pronominal suffix to the VERB.

SUFFIX CONJUGATION   See *QĀTAL*/PERFECT FORM.

SUPPLEMENT CLAUSE   A supplement CLAUSE is a subordinate clause that acts as an ADJUNCT. It can be omitted without changing the meaning of the main clause. It is also called an adverbial, subordinate clause, e.g. conditional clause, circumstantial clause, temporal clause. A speaker cannot perform a SPEEECH ACT with a supplementary clause. See also COMPLEMENT CLAUSE.

SYNCHRONY   In terms of language study the term *synchrony* refers to the systematic interrelations of the components of a single language at a particular time. Contrast DIACHRONY.

SYNDETIC   When a CLAUSE, PHRASE or word is connected by a conjunction to another, it is connected syndetically to the first. Contrast ASYNDETIC.

SYNTACTIC DOMAIN   *Syntactic domain* refers to the collection of objects (word, PHRASE or CLAUSE) that are modified or related by a word (e.g. focus particle or quantifier). This is called the SCOPE of the word. For example, in Biblical Hebrew FOCUS particles have a syntactic domain, which is sometimes indicated by an independent personal pronoun.

SYNTAGM   Syntagm is a synonym for CONSTITUENT.

SYNTAGMATIC DISTRIBUTION   The term *syntagmatic distribution* denotes the relationship between two or more linguistic units used sequentially to make well-formed structures. It is also referred to as the horizontal relationship of sequences of elements. Contrast PARADIGMATIC.

SYNTAX   Syntax is the study of the structure of CLAUSES and sentences in a language, i.e. the formal connections and relations between the elements of clauses and sentences.

TELIC   *Telic* refers to an event or activity which has a clear terminal point, e.g. English *He kicks the ball over the post*. Telic is typically used in the grammatical description of the ASPECT of verbs. Contrast ATELIC.

TEXT LINGUISTICS   Text linguistics (also referred to as discourse analysis and/or text grammar) refers to the scientific study of the conventions in a specific language with regard to the way in which semantic relations between people and matters are brought about in a text so that it can be understood as a coherent text. It also refers to the way in which sentences in the language are organized (and depend on one another linguistically) to form texts.

TOPIC   The topic is the matter about which the sentence tells something. Usually but not necessarily, it coincides with the SUBJECT.

TOPICALIZATION   Topicalization is a synonym for FRONTING.

TRAJECTOR   The notions LANDMARK and TRAJECTOR are terms that are used to describe the image scheme of a asymmetric relationship between two entities, in which one, the TRAJECTOR, is described relative to another one, the LANDMARK. The LANDMARK is the relatively stationary entity with respect to which the position of the less stationary TRAJECTOR is profiled.

TRANSITIVE   This term indicates VERBS that take a DIRECT OBJECT, e.g. *write* a book. Contrast INTRANSITIVE.

TRIPARTITE NOMINAL CLAUSE   A tripartite nominal clause is a NOMINAL (or verbless) CLAUSE consisting of a third constituent (a pronoun) in addition to the other two constituents, namely the subject and predicate.

UNMARKED   An entity which is not positively marked for a particular feature is typified as unmarked. In English, the term *duck* is semantically unmarked for gender (i.e. it may refer to a male or female entity), whereas the term *drake* is marked for gender (it is masculine). Contrast MARKED.

UNREAL   Unreal refers to an event or situation that is not real, or which does not really exist, or which is hypothetical or impracticable. Contrast REAL CONDITION.

UTTERANCE   An utterance is anything that is said in language, including anything from a single sound to a word, exclamation or a whole sentence.

VALENCY   The valency of a VERB refers to the number and nature of the obligatory CONSTITUENTS required SYNTACTICALLY or SEMANTICALLY by the verb, for example, *give* has a valency of three: it SELECTS a SUBJECT, DIRECT OBJECT and INDIRECT OBJECT (semantically: AGENT, PATIENT, receiver).

VERB   Verb is a term in the grammatical classification of words that traditionally refers to a class of words which expresses actions, positions, processes and states. The following subclasses are found: INTRANSITIVE, TRANSITIVE, prepositional and copulative verbs. The STEM of a Biblical Hebrew verb normally has three consonants, and this is the dictionary form. FINITE verbs in Biblical Hebrew have the following characteristics: STEM FORMATION, CONJUGATION (tense/MOOD), person, gender, number. Non-finite verbs do not have person: the participle does have gender and number, and, strictly speaking, it is a verbal adjective. The infinitive does not have person, gender or number, and, strictly speaking, it is a verbal NOUN.

VERB CHAIN   Verb chain refers to a sequence of finite VERBS that are each directly preceded by a *WĀW* COPULATIVE. Contrast VERB SEQUENCE.

VERB PHRASE (VP)   The verb phrase refers to a phrase with V (a Verb) as head and including COMPLEMENTS (i.e. OBJECTS) and ADJUNCTS of the verb. The phrase *gave me his paper yesterday* in the clause *The student gave me his paper yesterday* is the VP with the V *gave* as head, *his paper* as COMPLEMENT (i.e. OBJECT) and *yesterday* as ADJUNCT of the verb.

VERB SEQUENCE   Verb sequence refers to a specific combination of VERBS (in the *QĀTAL*/PERFECT or SHORT *YIQTŌL* FORM) that are directly preceded by a *WĀW* CONSECUTIVE. Contrast VERB CHAIN.

VERBLESS CLAUSE   See NOMINAL CLAUSE.

VOCALIC SUFFIX   A SUFFIX (e.g. a verbal ending or pronominal SUFFIX) that begins with a vowel, is a vocalic suffix, e.g. ־ִי in סוּסִי. Contrast CONSONANTAL SUFFIX.

VOCATIVE   Vocative is the name of a CASE that occurs in certain languages like Greek and Latin. It is used to mark the addressee MORPHOLOGICALLY. In Biblical Hebrew the addressed person is either marked by the article ־ַה or not at all.

VOICE   Voice is the group of conjugated forms of a VERB that determines if the AGENT or the PATIENT will be the SUBJECT of the verb. Active, passive and REFLEXIVE forms are distinguished. In Biblical Hebrew STEM FORMATIONS are often used to express voice.

VOLITIONAL USE   Volitional use refers to linguistic expressions the main functions of which are to express the faculty or power of one's will, for example wish, desire, petition, and command.

VP   See VERB PHRASE.

WĀW CONSECUTIVE   The *wāw* consecutive is a special use of the
conjunction ו (and) before *QĀTAL*/PERFECT and SHORT *YIQTŌL*/
IMPERFECT FORMS. Before SHORT *YIQTŌL*/IMPERFECT forms the
wāw consecutive has the form ו with doubling of the following consonant
or compensational lengthening of the a-vowel of the ו. Before *QĀTAL*/
PERFECT forms the *wāw* consecutive has the normal form of the
conjunction ו. The *wāw* consecutive is also called by some scholars the
wāw conversive because it appears to change the tense of an *YIQTŌL*/
IMPERFECT form to past tense, and the tense of a *QĀTAL*/PERFECT to
future. However, the term *wāw* consecutive is used more widely, mainly
to express progression like temporal and logical sequence, as well as to
introduce new stories and to determine the flow of a story. Normally the
consecutive SHORT *YIQTŌL*/IMPERFECT (i.e. *WAYYIQTŌL*) follows
a *QĀTAL*/PERFECT or another *WAYYIQTŌL*, and the consecutive
QĀTAL/PERFECT (i.e. *WƏQĀTAL*) follows a *YIQTŌL*/IMPERFECT
or another *WƏQĀTAL*), but there are other possibilities as well.

WĀW COPULATIVE   The *wāw* copulative is the normal conjunction ו
(and) that can be prefixed to any word to connect words, PHRASES
or CLAUSES coordinately. Due to the form or meaning of the word to
which it is prefixed, the form can differ: ו, ו, ו, ו, ו, ו, וֹ, ו, ו. With the
QĀTAL/PERFECT FORM or *YIQTŌL*/IMPERFECT FORM the *wāw*
copulative has no SEMANTIC value of its own, except that of "and."
However, different underlying semantic relations between clauses can be
expressed by the *wāw* copulative on the surface.

WĀW COPULATIVE + *YIQTŌL*/IMPERFECT.   If the normal conjunction ו
is followed by the *YIQTŌL*/IMPERFECT FORM, the ו is used simply to
combine the CLAUSES coordinately. On its own this construction has
no further specific SEMANTIC value. However, following a command it
often expresses an underlying relation of purpose.

WAYYIQTŌL   *Wayyiqtōl* is a synonym for *WĀW* CONSECUTIVE + SHORT
YIQTŌL/IMPERFECT FORM.

WƏQĀTAL   *Wəqātal* is a synonym for *WĀW* CONSECUTIVE + *QĀTAL*/
PERFECT FORM.

WH-QUESTION   A WH-question is an interrogative sentence with a
factual answer. A WH-question is also called a content question. See
INTERROGATIVE. Contrast YES–NO QUESTION.

WORD CLASS   A word class (or PART OF SPEECH) is one of the categories in which words are divided, mainly on the basis of formal features and distributional patterns. The following main word classes are distinguished in Biblical Hebrew: NOUN, VERB, adjective, adverb, preposition, conjunction, interrogative, predicator of existence. Contrast LEXICAL CLASS.

WORD ORDER   See CONSTITUENT ORDER

YES–NO QUESTION   A yes–no question is one which asks the addressee whether the statement is true or false. See also WH-QUESTION and POLARITY.

YIQTŌL/IMPERFECT FORM   The *YIQTŌL* form is one of the CONJUGA-TIONS in Biblical Hebrew that indicates the VERB's tense (presence/future) and/or aspect (incompleteness) and/or MOOD (non-factuality). It is also called the prefix conjugation because the Qal *YIQTŌL*/IMPERFECT conjugation takes PREFIXES in all its forms (SUFFIXES also appear in five of the ten forms). With reference to the *YIQTŌL*/IMPERFECT third-person masculine singular of the pattern verb קטל it is called the *YIQTŌL* form. The *YIQTŌL*/IMPERFECT is a FINITE form having person, number and gender. It is found in all STEM FORMATIONS (*binyanim*) and is used especially for the main verb in a CLAUSE. See also SHORT *YIQTŌL* and LONG *YIQTŌL*.

Bibliography

Andersen, F. I. 1974. *The Sentence in Biblical Hebrew*. Janua Linguarum Series Practica 231. The Hague/Paris: Mouton.

Andersen, T. D. 2000. "The Evolution of the Hebrew Verbal System." *Zeitschrift für Althebräistik* 13, no. 1: 1–66.

Andrason, A. 2010. "The Panchronic Yiqtol: Functionally Consistent and Cognitively Plausible." *Journal of Hebrew Scriptures* 10: 1–63.

———. 2011a. "The Biblical Hebrew Verbal System in Light of Grammaticalization – the Second Generation." *Hebrew Studies* 53: 351–83.

———. 2011b. "The BH Weqatal: A Homogenous Form with No Haphazard Functions. Part 1." *Journal of Northwest Semitic Languages* 37, no. 2: 1–25.

———. 2011c. "Biblical Hebrew Wayyiqtol – a Dynamic Definition." *Journal of Hebrew Scriptures* 11: 1–50.

———. 2011d. "Making It Sound – the Performative Qatal and Its Explanation." *Journal of Hebrew Scriptures* 12: 1–58.

———. 2012a. "The BH Weqatal: A Homogenous Form with No Haphazard Functions. Part 2." *Journal of Northwest Semitic Languages* 38, no. 1: 1–30.

———. 2012b. "Thermodynamic Model of the Biblical Hebrew Verbal System." Pages 146–63 in *Grammaticalisation in Semitic*. Edited by D. Eades. Journal of Semitic Studies Supplement Series 29. Oxford: Oxford University Press.

———. 2012c. "The Dynamic Short Yiqtol." *Journal for Semitics* 21, no. 2: 308–39.

———. 2013. "The Gnomic Qatal." *Orientalia Suecana* 61: 5–53.

Andrason, A., and C. H. J. van der Merwe. 2015. "The Semantic Potential of Verbal Conjugations as a Set of Polysemous Senses: The Qatal in Genesis." *Hebrew Studies* 56: 71–88.

Baasten, M. F. J. 2003. "A Note on the History of Semitic." Pages 57–72 in *Hamlet on a Hill: Semitic and Greek Studies Presented to Professor T. Muraoka on the Occasion of His Sixty-Fifth Birthday*. Edited by M. F. J. Baasten and W. Th. van Peursen. Orientalia Lovaniensia Analecta 118. Leuven: Uitgeverij Peeters.

Baker, M. C. 2003. *Lexical Categories: Verbs, Nouns, and Adjectives*. Cambridge Studies in Linguistics 102. Cambridge: Cambridge University Press.

Baltin, M. R. 1982. "A Landing Site Theory of Movement Rules." *Linguistic Inquiry* 13: 1–38.

Bandstra, B. L. 1995. "Marking Turns in Poetic Text: 'Waw' in the Psalms." Pages 45–52 in *Narrative and Comment: Contributions to Wolfgang Schneider*. Edited by E. Talstra. Amsterdam: Societas Hebraica Amstelodamensis.

Barr, J. 1978. "Some Notes on Ben 'Between' in Classical Hebrew." *Journal of Semitic Studies* 23, no. 1: 1–22.

Bauer, H., and P. Leander. [1922] 1991. *Historische Grammatik der hebräischen Sprache des Alten Testaments*. Hildesheim: Georg Ohlms.

Bayer, J. 2004. "Decomposing the Left Periphery: Dialectical and Cross-Linguistic Evidence." Pages 59–95 in *The Syntax and Semantics of the Left Periphery*. Edited by H. Lohnstein and S. Trissler. Interface Explorations 9. New York: Mouton de Gruyter.

Bekins, P. 2013. "Non-Prototypical Uses of the Definite Article in Biblical Hebrew." *Journal of Semitic Studies* 58, no. 2: 225–40.

———. 2014. *Transitivity and Object Marking in Biblical Hebrew: An Investigation of the Object Preposition ʾet.* Harvard Semitic Studies 64. Winona Lake, IN: Eisenbrauns.

Benton, R. C., Jr. 2008. "The Niphal and Hitpael of ברך in the Patriarchal Narratives." *Kleine Untersuchungen zur Sprache des Alten Testaments und seiner Umwelt* 8–9: 1–17.

Bergen, R. D. 1994. *Biblical Hebrew and Discourse Linguistics.* Dallas, TX: SIL.

Bergsträsser, G. 1929. *Hebräische Grammatik. Wilhelm Gesenius' hebräische Grammatik.* Leipzig: Vogel.

———. [1923] 1983. *Introduction to the Semitic Languages.* Translated by P. T. Daniels. Winona Lake, IN: Eisenbrauns.

Bivin, W. E. 2017. "The Particle אם and Conditionality in Biblical Hebrew Revisited: A Cognitive Linguistic Account." PhD diss., Stellenbosch University, Stellenbosch.

Bodine, W. R. 1992. *Linguistics and Biblical Hebrew.* Winona Lake, IN: Eisenbrauns.

Borer, H. 2013. "Generative Grammar and Hebrew." Pages 23–42 in Vol. 2 of *Encyclopedia of Hebrew Language and Linguistics.* Edited by G. Khan. Leiden: Brill.

Brockelmann, C. 1956. *Hebräische Syntax.* Neukirchen: Neukirchener Verlag.

———. [1926] 1961. *Grundriss der vergleichenden Grammatik der semitischen Sprachen.* Hildersheim: Georg Olms.

Bussmann, H., K. Kazzazi and G. Trauth. 1996. *Routledge Dictionary of Language and Linguistics.* London: Routledge.

Buth, R. J. 1995. "Functional Grammar, Hebrew and Aramaic: An Integrated, Exegetically Significant, Textlinguistic Approach to Syntax." Pages 77–102 in *Discourse Analysis of Biblical Literature: What It Is and What It Offers.* Edited by W. R. Bodine. Semeia Studies. Atlanta: Scholars Press.

———. 1999. "Word Order in the Verbless Clause: A Generative-Functional Approach." Pages 79–108 in *The Verbless Clause in Biblical Hebrew: Linguistic Approaches.* Edited by C. L. Miller. Linguistic Studies in Ancient West Semitic 1. Winona Lake, IN: Eisenbrauns.

Bybee, J. L. 2010. *Language, Usage and Cognition.* Cambridge: Cambridge University Press.

———. 2011. "Usage-Based Theory and Grammaticalization." Pages 69–78 in *The Oxford Handbook of Grammaticalization.* Edited by H. Narrog and B. Heine. Oxford: Oxford University Press.

Bybee, J. L., R. Perkins and W. Pagliuca. 1994. *The Evolution of Grammar.* Chicago: The University of Chicago Press.

Callaham, S. N. 2010. *Modality and the Biblical Hebrew Infinitive Absolute.* Abhandlungen für die Kunde des Morgenlandes 71. Wiesbaden: Harrassowitz.

Coetzee, A. W. 1999. *Tiberian Hebrew Phonology: Focussing on Consonant Clusters.* Assen: Van Gorcum.

Conklin, B. W. 2011. *Oath Formulas in Biblical Hebrew.* Linguistic Studies in Ancient West Semitic 5. Winona Lake, IN: Eisenbrauns.

Cook, J. A. 2002. "The Biblical Hebrew Verbal System: A Grammaticalization Approach." PhD diss., University of Wisconsin-Madison, Madison.

———. 2012. *Time and the Biblical Hebrew Verb: The Expression of Tense, Aspect, and Modality in Biblical Hebrew.* Linguistic Studies in Ancient West Semitic 7. Winona Lake, IN: Eisenbrauns.

Crystal, D. 2008. *A Dictionary of Linguistics and Phonetics.* 6th ed. Malden, MA: Blackwell.

Dancygier, B., and E. Sweetser. 2005. *Mental Spaces in Grammar: Conditional Constructions.* Cambridge Studies in Linguistics. Cambridge: Cambridge University Press.

De Haan, F. 2011. "Typology of Tense, Aspect, and Modality Systems." Pages 445–64 in *The Oxford Handbook of Linguistic Typology*. Edited by J. J. Song. Oxford: Oxford University Press.

DeCaen, V. 1995. "On the Placement and Interpretation of the Verb in Standard Biblical Hebrew Prose." PhD diss., University of Toronto, Toronto.

Degand, L., B. Cornillie and P. Pietrandrea. 2013. "Modal Particles and Discourse Markers: Two Sides of the Same Coin?" Pages 1–18 in *Discourse Markers and Modal Particles: Categorization and Description*. Edited by L. Degand, B. Cornillie and P. Pietrandrea. Pragmatics & Beyond New Series. Amsterdam: John Benjamins.

Elliger, K., and W. Rudolph. 1997. *Biblia Hebraica Stuttgartensia*. 5th ed. Stuttgart: German Bible Society.

Ellis, N. C., and D. Larsen-Freeman. 2009. *Language as a Complex Adaptive System*. Oxford: Blackwell.

Erteschik-Shir, N. 2007. *Information Structure: The Syntax–Discourse Interface*. Oxford Surveys in Syntax and Morphology 3. Oxford: Oxford University Press.

Even-Shoshan, A. 1981. *A New Concordance of the Bible*. Jerusalem: Kiryat Sepher.

Faber, A. 1997. "Genetic Subgrouping of the Semitic Languages." Pages 3–15 in *The Semitic Languages*. Routledge Language Family Descriptions. Edited by R. Hetzron. London: Routledge.

Fassberg, S. E. 1999. "The Lengthened Imperative קָטְלָה in Biblical Hebrew." *Hebrew Studies* 55: 7–14.

Finch, G. 2005. *Key Concepts in Language and Linguistics*. 2nd ed. Palgrave Key Concepts. New York: Palgrave Macmillan.

Fischer, K. 2006. *Approaches to Discourse Particles*. Studies in Pragmatics 1. Amsterdam: Elsevier.

Floor, S. J. 2004. "From Information Structure, Topic and Focus, to Theme in Biblical Hebrew Narrative." PhD diss., University of Stellenbosch, Stellenbosch.

Follingstad, C. M. 2001. *Deictic Viewpoint in Biblical Hebrew Text: A Syntagmatic and Paradigmatic Analysis of the Particle* כִּי *(kî)*. Special Issue of *Journal of Text and Translation*. Dallas, TX: SIL.

Garr, W. R. 1985. *A Dialect Geography of Syria-Palestine, 1000 to 586 B.C.E.* Philadelphia: University of Pennsylvania.

———. 2004. "הֵן." *Revue biblique* 105: 321–44.

———. 2007. "אָכֵן." *Journal of Northwest Semitic Languages* 33, no. 2: 65–78.

———. 2009. "The Infinitive Absolute as Substitute for the Finite Verb." SBL Annual Meeting, Boston.

———. forthcoming. "וְעַתָּה 'Now'." In *May You Favor the Work of His Hands: Essays in Memory of M. O'Connor*. Edited by P. T. Daniels, E. L. Greenstein, J. Huehnergard, M. S. Leson and P. C. Schmitz. Winona Lake, IN: Eisenbrauns.

Geeraerts, D., and H. Cuyckens, eds. 2007. *The Oxford Handbook of Cognitive Linguistics*. New York: Oxford University Press.

Gemser, B. 1968. *Hebreeuse Spraakkuns: Vormleer, Sinsleer en Oefeninge*. Pretoria: Van Schaik.

Gesenius, W., E. Kautzsch and A. E. Cowley. 1910. *Gesenius' Hebrew Grammar: As Edited and Enlarged by the Late E. Kautzsch: Second English Edition Revised in According with the Twenty-Eighth German Edition (1909) by A. E. Cowley*. Oxford: Clarendon.

Greenberg, J. H. 1952. "The Afro-Asiatic (Hamito-Semitic) Present." *Journal of the American Oriental Society* 72: 1–9.

Greenstein, E. L. 1989. "The Syntax of Saying 'Yes' in Biblical Hebrew." *Journal of the Ancient Near Eastern Society* 19: 51–59.

Gross, W. 1996. *Die Satzteilfolge im Verbalsatz alttestamentlicher Prosa: Untersucht an den Büchern Dtn, Ri und 2Kön.* Forschungen zum Alten Testament 17. Tübingen: Mohr [Siebeck].

Harmelink, B. L. 2004. "Exploring the Syntactic, Semantic, and Pragmatic Uses of וַיְהִי in Biblical Hebrew." PhD diss., Westminster Theological Seminary, Philadelphia.

Haspelmath, M. 2012. "Escaping Ethnocentrism in the Study of Word-Class Universals." *Theoretical Linguistics* 38: 91–102.

Heimerdinger, J. M. 1999. *Topic, Focus and Foreground in Ancient Hebrew Narratives.* Library of Hebrew Bible/Old Testament Studies 295. Sheffield: Sheffield Academic.

Heine, B., U. Claudi and F. Hünnemeyer. 1991. *Grammaticalization: A Conceptual Framework.* Chicago: University of Chicago Press.

Hengeveld, K., and E. H. van Lier. 2010. "An Implicational Map of Parts-of-Speech." Pages 129–56 in *Semantic Maps: Methods and Applications.* Edited by A. Malchukov, M. Cysouw and M. Haspelmath Special issue of *Linguistic Inquiry* 7, no. 1.

Hetzron, R., ed. 1997. *The Semitic Languages.* Routledge Language Family Descriptions. London: Routledge.

Holmstedt, R. D. 2002. "The Relative Clause in Biblical Hebrew: A Linguistic Analysis." PhD diss., University of Wisconsin-Madison, Madison.

———. 2011. "The Typological Classification of the Hebrew of Genesis: Subject-Verb or Verb-Subject?." *Journal of Hebrew Scriptures* 11: 2–39.

———. 2013a. "Relative Clause: Biblical Hebrew." Pages 350–37 in Vol. 3 of *Encyclopedia of Hebrew Language and Linguistics.* Edited by G. Khan. Leiden: Brill.

———. 2013b. "Investigating the Possible Verb-Subject to Subject-Verb Shift in Ancient Hebrew: Methodological First Steps." *Kleine Untersuchungen zur Sprache des Alten Testaments und seiner Umwelt* 15: 3–31.

———. 2014. "Critical at the Margins: Edge Constituents in Biblical Hebrew." *Kleine Untersuchungen zur Sprache des Alten Testaments und seiner Umwelt* 17: 109–56.

———. 2016. *The Relative Clause in Biblical Hebrew.* Linguistic Studies in Ancient West Semitic 10. Winona Lake, IN: Eisenbrauns.

Holmstedt, R. D., and A. R. Jones. 2014. "The Pronoun in Tripartite Verbless Clauses in Biblical Hebrew: Resumption for Left-Dislocation or Pronominal Copula?" *Journal of Semitic Studies* 59, no. 1: 53–89.

Humbert, P. 1933. "Die Herausforderungsformel 'hinnenî êlékâ'." *Zeitschrift für die alttestamentliche Wissenschaft* 51: 101–108.

Jenni, E. 1992. *Die Hebraischen Präpositionen. Band 1: Das Präposition Beth.* Stuttgart: Kohlhammer.

———. 1994. *Die Hebräischen Präpositionen. Band 2: Das Präposition Kaph.* Stuttgart: Kohlhammer.

———. 1999. "Einleitung formeller und familiärer Rede im alten Testament durch ʾmr ʾl und ʾmr l-." Pages 17–33 in *Vielseitigkeit des Alten Testaments: Festschrift für Georg Sauer zum 70. Geburstag.* Edited by J. A. Loader and H. V. Kieweler. Frankfurt am Main: Lang.

———. 2000. *Die Hebräischen Präpositionen. Band 3: Die Präposition Lamed.* Stuttgart: Kohlhammer.

———. 2005a. "Untersuchungen zum hebräischen Kohortativ." Pages 166–226 in *Studien zur Sprachwelt des Alten Testaments II.* Edited by J. Luchinger, H.-P. Mathys and M. Saur. Stuttgart: Kohlhammer.

————. 2005b. "Verwendung Des Imperativs im biblish-Hebräischen." Pages 227–94 in *Studien zur Sprachwelt des Alten Testaments II*. Edited by J. Luchsinger, H.-P. Mathys and M. Saur. Stuttgart: Kohlhammer.

————. 2005c. "Eine hebräische Abtönungspartikel *ʿal-ken*." Pages 118–33 in *Studien zur Sprachwelt des Alten Testaments II*. Edited by J. Luchsinger, H.-P. Mathys and M. Saur. Stuttgart: Kohlhammer.

Joosten, J. 1989. "The Predicative Participle in Biblical Hebrew." *Zeitschrift für Althebraistik* 2, no. 2: 128–59.

————. 2012. *The Verbal System of Biblical Hebrew: A New Synthesis Elaborated on the Basis of Classical Prose*. Jerusalem Biblical Studies 10. Jerusalem: Simor.

Joüon, P., and T. Muraoka. 1991. *A Grammar of Biblical Hebrew*. Rome: Pontificio Istituto Biblio.

————. 2006. *A Grammar of Biblical Hebrew*. Revised English Edition, Second Print of Second Edition. Rome: Pontificio Istituto Biblico.

————. 2009. *A Grammar of Biblical Hebrew*. Revised English Edition, Third Reprint of Second Edition with Corrections. Rome: Pontificio Istituto Biblico.

Kaltner, J., and S. L. McKenzie, eds. 2002. *Beyond Babel: A Handbook for Biblical Hebrew and Related Languages*. Resources for Biblical Study 42. Atlanta: Society of Biblical Literature.

Kelley, P. H., D. S. Mynatt and T. G. Crawford. 1998. *The Masorah of Biblia Hebraica Stuttgartensia*. Grand Rapids, MI: Eerdmans.

Khan, G. 2013a. *A Short Introduction to the Tiberian Masoretic Bible and Its Reading Tradition*. Piscataway: Gorgias.

————, ed. 2013b. *Encyclopedia of Hebrew Language and Linguistics*. 4 vols. Leiden: Brill.

Kim, Y.-K. 2009. *The Function of the Tautological Infinitive in Classical Biblical Hebrew*. Harvard Semitic Studies 60. Winona Lake, IN: Eisenbrauns.

Kittel, R. 1937. *Biblia Hebraica Kittel*. Stuttgart: Bible Society of Württemberg.

Köhler, L., and W. Baumgartner. 1988. *The Hebrew and Aramaic Lexicon of the Old Testament; Subsequently Revised by Walter Baumgartner and Johann Jakob Stamm*. Grand Rapids, MI: Eerdmans.

König, F. E. [1881–1897] 1979. *Historisch-kritisches Lehrgebaude der hebräischen Sprache*. Vol. I–III. Hildesheim: Georg Olms.

Kutscher, E. Y. 1982. *A History of the Hebrew Language*. Jerusalem: Magnes.

Lambdin, T. O. 1971. *Introduction to Biblical Hebrew*. New York: Scribner.

Lambrecht, K. 1994. *Information Structure and Sentence From: Topic, Focus and the Mental Representation of Discourse Referents*. Cambridge Studies in Linguistics. Cambridge: Cambridge University Press.

————. 2000. "When Subjects Behave Like Objects: An Analysis of the Merging of S and O in Sentence-Focus Constructions Across Languages." *Studies in Language* 24, no. 3: 611–82.

————. 2001. "Dislocation." Pages 1050–78 in *Language Typology and Language Universals: An International Handbook*. Edited by M. Haspelmath, E. König, W. Oesterreicher, and W. Raible. Berlin: de Gruyter.

Lamprecht, A. 2015. "Spatial Cognition and the Death Metaphor in the Hebrew Bible." PhD diss., University of the Free State, Bloemfontein.

Lee, Y.-S. 2016. "Description of the BH Lexeme אַל: A Cognitive Approach." MA thesis, Stellenbosch University, Stellenbosch.

Lemmer, L. 2014. "The Polysemic Nature of the Preposition מִן (min) in Biblical Hebrew: A Study in the Book of Judges." MA thesis, North-West University, Potchefstroom.

Levinsohn, S. H. 2011. "רַק and אַךְ: Limiting and Countering." *Hebrew Studies* 52, no. 1: 83–105.

Lipiński, E. 2001. *Semitic Languages: Outline of a Comparative Grammar.* 2nd ed. Orientalia Lovaniensa Analecta 80. Leuven: Peeters.

———. 2014. *Semitic Languages in Historical Perspective.* Orientalia Lovaniensa Analecta 230. Leuven: Peeters.

Lohnstein, H., and S. Trissler. 2004. "Theoretical Developments of the Left Periphery." Pages 1–21 in *The Syntax and Semantics of the Left Periphery.* Edited by H. Lohnstein and S. Trissler. Interface Explorations 9. Berlin: Mouton de Gruyter.

Longacre, R. E. 2003. *Joseph: A Story of Divine Providence: A Text Theoretical and Textlinguistic Analysis of Genesis 37 and 39–48.* 2nd ed. Winona Lake, IN: Eisenbrauns.

López, L. 2016, "Dislocations." Pages 423–43 in *The Oxford Handbook of Information Structure.* Edited by C. Féry and S. Ishihara. Oxford Handbooks of Linguistics. Oxford: Oxford University Press.

Lunn, N. P. 2006. *Word-Order Variation in Biblical Poetry.* Paternoster Biblical Monographs. Milton Keynes: Paternoster.

Lyavdansky, A. 2004. "Gam in the Prophetic Discourse." *Babel und Bibel* 1: 231–50.

Lyle, K. A. 2012. "A Cognitive Semantic Assessment of עִם and אֶת's Semantic Potential." MA thesis, Stellenbosch University, Stellenbosch.

———. 2013. "A New Methodology for Ascertaining the Semantic Potential of Biblical Hebrew Prepositions." *Hebrew Studies* 54, no. 1: 49–67.

Malone, J. L. 1993. *Tiberian Hebrew Phonology.* Winona Lake, IN: Eisenbrauns.

McFall, L. 1982. *The Enigma of the Hebrew Verbal System: Solutions from Ewald to the Present.* Historic Texts and Interpreters in Biblical Scholarship 2. Sheffield: Press.

Mena, A. K. 2012. "The Semantic Potential of עַל in Genesis, Psalms, and Chronicles." MA thesis, Stellenbosch University, Stellenbosch.

Miller, C. L. 1996. *The Representation of Speech in Biblical Hebrew Narrative: A Linguistic Analysis.* Harvard Semitic Monographs 55. Atlanta: Scholars Press.

———. 1997. "In Conversation with *In Conversation with Jonah.*" *Journal of Hebrew Scriptures* 1. Online: http://www.arts.ualberta.ca/JHS/Articles/article2.htm.

———. 1999. "The Pragmatics of *Waw* as a Discourse Marker in Biblical Hebrew Dialogue." *Zeitschrift für Althebraistik* 12, no. 2: 165–91.

———. 2005a. "Ellipsis Involving Negation in Biblical Poetry." Pages 37–52 in *Seeking Out the Wisdom of the Ancients: Essays Offered to Honor Michael V. Fox on the Occasion of His Sixty-Fifth Birthday.* Edited by R. L. Troxel, K. G. Friebel and D. R. Magary. Winona Lake, IN: Eisenbrauns.

———. 2005b. "Linguistics." Pages 657–69 in *Dictionary of the Old Testament: Historical Books.* Edited by B. T. Arnold and H. G. M. Williamson. Downers Grove, IL: InterVarsity.

———. 2010a. "Definiteness and the Vocative in Biblical Hebrew." *Journal of Northwest Semitic Languages* 36, no. 1: 43–65.

———. 2010b. "Vocative Syntax in Biblical Hebrew Prose and Poetry: A Preliminary Analysis." *Journal of Semitic Studies* 55, no. 2: 347–64.

Miller-Naudé, C. L. 2014. "Mismatches of Definiteness between Appositional Noun Phrases Used as Vocatives in Biblical Hebrew." *Journal of Northwest Semitic Languages* 40, no. 2: 97–111.

Miller-Naudé, C. L., and J. A. Naudé. 2015a. "Negation and Edge Constructions." SBL Annual Meeting, Atlanta.

———. 2015b. "The Participle and Negation." *Kleine Untersuchungen zur Sprache des Alten Testaments und seiner Umwelt* 19: 165–99.

————. 2016a. "Is the Adjective Distinct from the Noun as a Grammatical Category in Biblical Hebrew?." *In die Skriflig / In Luce Verbi* 50, no. 4, a2005. http://dx.doi.org/10.4102/ids.v50i4.2005.

————. 2016b "The Intersection of Orality and Style in Biblical Hebrew: Metapragmatic Representations of Dialogue in Genesis 34." Pages 57–77 in *Doubling and Duplicating in the Book of Genesis: Literary and Stylistic Approaches to the Text.* Edited by E. R. Hayes and K. Vermuelen. Winona Lake, IN: Eisenbrauns.

————. 2017. "Word Classes, Linguistic Theory, Typology and Universals." Pages 331–76 in *From Ancient Manuscripts to Modern Dictionaries: Select Studies in Aramaic, Hebrew, and Greek.* Edited by T. Li and K. Dyer. Perspectives on Linguistics and Ancient Languages. Piscataway: Gorgias.

————. forthcoming. "The Scope of Negation Inside and Outside of the Biblical Hebrew Prepositional Phrase." In *Advances in Biblical Hebrew Linguistics: Data, Methods, and Analyses.* Edited by A. Moshavi and T. Notarius. Winona Lake, IN: Eisenbrauns.

Miller-Naudé, C. L., and C. H. J. van der Merwe. 2011. "הִנֵּה and Mirativity in Biblical Hebrew." *Hebrew Studies* 52, no. 1: 53–81.

Miller-Naudé, C. L., and Z. Zevit, eds. 2012. *Diachrony in Biblical Hebrew.* Linguistic Studies in Ancient West Semitic 8. Winona Lake, IN: Eisenbrauns.

Mosegaard-Hansen, M. B. 2006. "A Dynamic Polysemy Approach to the Lexical Semantics of Discourse Markers (with an Exemplary Analysis of French *Toujours*)." Pages 21–42 in *Approaches to Discourse Particles.* Edited by K. Fischer. Studies in Pragmatics 1. Amsterdam: Elsevier.

Moshavi, A. 2007a. "הֲלֹא as Discourse Marker of Justification in Biblical Hebrew." *Hebrew Studies* 48: 171–86.

————. 2007b. "Syntactic Evidence for a Clausal Adverb הֲלֹא in Biblical Hebrew." *Journal of Northwest Semitic Languages* 33, no. 2: 51–63.

————. 2010. *Word Order in the Biblical Hebrew Finite Clause: A Syntactic and Pragmatic Analysis of Preposing.* Linguistic Studies in Ancient West Semitic 4. Winona Lake, IN: Eisenbrauns.

————. 2011. "Can a Positive Rhetorical Question Have a Positive Answer in the Bible?" *Journal of Semitic Studies* 56, no. 2: 253–73.

————. 2014. "What Can I Say? Implications and Communication Functions of Rhetorical 'WH' Questions in Classical Biblical Hebrew Prose." *Vetus Testamentum* 64: 93–108.

Mulder, M. J. 1981. "Die Partikel כֵּן im Alten Testament." *Oudtestamentische Studiën* 21: 201–27.

Muraoka, T. 1985. *Emphatic Words and Structures in Biblical Hebrew.* Leiden: Brill.

Naudé, J. A. 1990. "A Syntactic Analysis of Dislocation in Biblical Hebrew." *Journal of Northwest Semitic Languages* 16: 115–30.

————. 1991. "On the Syntax of *dy*-Phrases in the Aramaic of 11QtgJob." *Journal of Northwest Semitic Languages* 17: 45–67.

————. 1993. "On Subject Pronoun and Subject Noun Asymmetry: A Preliminary Survey of Northwest Semitic." *South African Journal of Linguistics* 11, no. 1: 17–28.

————. 1994a. "The Asymmetry of Subject Pronouns and Subject Nouns in Qumran Hebrew and Cognates." *Journal of Northwest Semitic Languages* 20, no. 1: 139–63.

————. 1994b. "The Verbless Clauses with Pleonastic Pronoun in Biblical Aramaic." *Journal for Semitics* 6, no. 1: 74–93.

————. 1996a. "Resumptive Pronouns in Biblical Aramaic Relatives." Pages 125–47 in *South African Journal of Linguistics Supplement 29.* Edited by J. Maartens.

———. 1996b. "Independent Personal Pronouns in Qumran Hebrew Syntax." PhD diss., University of the Free State, Bloemfontein.

———. 1997. "The Syntactical Status of the Ethical Dative in Biblical Hebrew." *Journal for Semitics* 9: 129–65.

———. 1999. "Syntactic Aspects of Co-Ordinate Subjects with Independent Personal Pronouns." *Journal of Northwest Semitic Languages* 25, no. 2: 75–99.

———. 2001. "The Distribution of Independent Personal Pronouns in Qumran Hebrew." *Journal of Northwest Semitic Languages* 27: 91–112.

———. 2002a. "The Third Person Pronoun in Tripartite Verbless Clauses of Qumran Hebrew." Pages 161–82 in *Pronouns – Grammar and Representation*. Edited by H. J. Simon and W. Heike. Linguistics Today 52. Amsterdam: John Benjamins.

———. 2002b. "Verbless Clauses Containing Personal Pronouns in Qumran Hebrew." *Journal for Semitics* 11, no. 1: 126–68.

———. 2003a. "The Consonantal Root in Semitic Languages." *Journal of Northwest Semitic Languages* 29, no. 2: 15–32.

———. 2003b. "The Transitions of Biblical Hebrew in the Perspective of Language Change and Diffusion." Pages 189–215 in *Biblical Hebrew: Chronology and Typology*. Edited by I. Young. Journal for the Study of the Old Testament Supplement Series 369. Sheffield: Sheffield Academic.

———. 2006. "Review of Chomsky, N. 2002, On Nature and Language. Cambridge: Cambridge University Press." *South African Linguistics and Applied Language Studies* 24, no. 1: 125–27.

———. 2011a. "The Interpretation and Translation of the Biblical Hebrew Quantifier *kol.*" *Journal for Semitics* 22, no. 2: 408–21.

———. 2011b. "Syntactic Patterns of Quantifier Float in Biblical Hebrew." *Hebrew Studies* 52, no. 1: 121–36.

———. 2012a. "The Complexity of Language Change: The Case of Ancient Hebrew." *Southern African Linguistics and Applied Language Studies* 30, no. 3: 395–411.

———. 2012b. "Diachrony in Biblical Hebrew and a Theory of Language and Diffusion." Pages 61–81 in *Diachrony in Biblical Hebrew*. Edited by C. L. Miller-Naudé and Z. Zevit. Linguistic Studies in Ancient West Semitic 8. Winona Lake, IN: Eisenbrauns.

———. 2013a. "Dative." Pages 655–58 in Vol. 1 of *Encyclopedia of Hebrew Language and Linguistics*. Edited by G. Khan. Leiden: Brill.

———. 2013b. "Pronominalization." Pages 272–77 in Vol. 3 of *Encyclopedia of Hebrew Language and Linguistics*. Edited by G. Khan. Leiden: Brill.

———. 2013c. "Government and Binding." Pages 72–79 in Vol. 2 of *Encyclopedia of Hebrew Language and Linguistics*. Edited by G. Khan. Leiden: Brill.

———. 2013d. "Vow Formulae: Biblical Hebrew." Pages 976–79 in Vol. 3 in *Encyclopedia of Hebrew Language and Linguistics*. Edited by G. Khan. Leiden: Brill.

———. forthcoming. "Syntactic Features of *kol* as a Polarity Item in Negative Statements." In *May You Favor the Work of His Hands: Essays in Memory of M. O'Connor*. Edited by P. T. Daniels, E. L. Greenstein, J. Huehnergard, M. S. Leson and P. C. Schmitz. Winona Lake, IN: Eisenbrauns.

Naudé, J. A., and C. L. Miller-Naudé. 2011. "A New Biblical Hebrew Teaching Grammar for African Bible Translators: A Typological Approach." *Old Testament Essays* 24, no. 3: 690–707.

————. 2015. "Syntactic Features of כל in Qumran Hebrew." Pages 88–111 in *Hebrew of the Late Second Temple Period: Proceedings of a Sixth International Symposium on the Hebrew of the Dead Sea Scrolls and Ben Sira*. Edited by E. Tigchelaar and P. Hecke. Studies on the Texts of the Desert of Judah 114. Leiden: Brill.

Naudé, J. A., and G. A. Rendsburg. 2013. "Negation: Pre-Modern Hebrew." Pages 801–11 in Vol. 2 of *Encyclopedia of Hebrew Language and Linguistics*. Edited by G. Khan. Leiden: Brill.

Oakes, P. J. 2011. "The Social Pragmatics of the Two Forms of Directive Speech in Biblical Hebrew." *Journal of Northwest Semitic Languages* 37, no. 2: 49–68.

Onodera, N. O. 2011. "The Grammaticalization of Discourse Particles." Pages 614–24 in *The Oxford Handbook of Grammaticalization*. Edited by H. Narrog and B. Heine. Oxford: Oxford University Press.

Polak, F. H. 1998. "The Oral and the Written: Biblical Syntax, Stylistics and the Development of Prose Narrative." *Journal of the Ancient Near Eastern Society* 26: 59–105.

————. 2003. "Style Is More Than the Person: Sociolinguistics, Literary Culture, and the Distinction between Written and Oral Narrative." Pages 38–103 in *Biblical Hebrew: Studies in Chronology and Typology*. Edited by I. Young. Library of Hebrew Bible/Old Testament Studies 369. London: Continuum.

Qimron, E. 1983. "מלית השלישה אל במקורותינו הקדומים." In *Hebrew Language Studies Presented to Professor Zeev Ben-Ḥayyim*. Edited by M. Ben-Asher et al. Jerusalem: Magnes.

————. 1986. *The Hebrew of the Dead Sea Scrolls*. Harvard Semitic Studies 29. Atlanta: Scholars Press.

Rabin, C. 1974. *A Short History of the Hebrew Language*. Jerusalem: Haomanim.

Radford, A. 2004. *Minimalist Syntax: Exploring the Structure of English*. Cambridge Textbooks in Linguistics. Cambridge University Press.

Rendsburg, G. A. 2003. "A Comprehensive Guide to Israelian Hebrew." *Orient* 38: 5–35.

Rezetko, R., and I. Young. 2014. *Historical Linguistics and Biblical Hebrew: Steps Toward an Integrated Approach*. Ancient Near East Monographs 9. Atlanta: Society of Biblical Literature.

Richter, W. 1978. *Grundlagen einer althebräischen Grammatik. A. Grundfragen einer sprachwissenschaftlichen Grammatik. B. Beschreibungsebenen. I. Das Wort (Morphologie)*. Arbeiten zu Text und Sprache im Alten Testament 8. St. Ottilien: EOS.

————. 1979. *Grundlagen einer althebräischen Grammatik. B. II. Die Wortfügung (Morphosyntax)*. Arbeiten zu Text und Sprache im Alten Testament 10. St. Ottilien: EOS.

————. 1980. *Grundlagen einer althebräischen Grammatik. B. III. Der Satz*. Arbeiten zu Text und Sprache im Alten Testament 13. St. Ottilien: EOS.

Rodriguez, D. 2011. "תַּחַת: A Cognitive Linguistic Analysis of the Biblical Hebrew Lexeme." MA thesis, Stellenbosch University, Stellenbosch.

Rollston, C. A. 2010. *Writing and Literacy in the World of Ancient Israel: Epigraphic Evidence from the Iron Age*. SBL Archaeology and Biblical Studies 11. Atlanta: Society of Biblical Literature.

Rosenbaum, M. 1997. *Word-Order Variation in Isaiah 40–55: A Functional Perspective*. Studia Semitica Neerlandica 35. Assen: Van Gorcum.

Rubin, A. D. 2005. *Studies in Semitic Grammaticalization*. Harvard Semitic Studies 57. Winona Lake, IN: Eisenbrauns.

————. 2010. *A Brief Introduction to the Semitic Languages*. Gorgias Handbooks 19. Piscataway: Gorgias.

Sáenz-Badillos, A. 1993. *A History of the Hebrew Language*. Cambridge: Cambridge University Press.

Sanders, S. L. 2009. *The Invention of Hebrew*. Traditions. Urbana and Chicago, IL: University of Illinois Press.

Schäfer, R., and F. Voss. 2008. *Textual Research on the Bible: An Introduction to the Scholarly Editions of the German Bible Society*. Stuttgart: Deutsche Bibelgesellchaft

Schenker, A. et al. 2004–. *Biblia Hebraica Quinta*. Stuttgart: German Bible Society.

Schniedewind, W. M. 2004. *How the Bible Became a Book: The Textualization of Ancient Israel*. Cambridge: Cambridge University Press.

———. 2013. *A Social History of Hebrew: Its Origins Through the Rabbinic Period*. New Haven: Yale University Press.

Siebesma, P. A. 1991. *The Function of the Niph⁽al in Biblical Hebrew: In Relationship to Other Passive-Reflexive Verbal Stems and to the Pu⁽al and Hoph⁽al in Particular*. Studia Semitica Neerlandica 29. Assen: Van Gorcum.

Snyman, F. P. J. 2004. *The Scope of the Negative Loᵓ in Biblical Hebrew*. Bloemfontein: UV-Sasol-Biblioteek.

Snyman, F. P. J., and J. A. Naudé. 2003. "Sentence and Constituent-Negation in Biblical Hebrew." *Journal for Semitics* 12, no. 2: 237–67.

Song, J. J. 2011. "Word Order Typology." Pages 253–79 in *The Oxford Handbook of Linguistic Typology*. Edited by J. J. Song. Oxford: Oxford University Press.

Steiner, R. C. 2000. "Does the Biblical Hebrew Conjunction-ו Have Many Meanings, One Meaning, or No Meaning at All?" *Journal of Biblical Literature* 119, no. 2: 249–67.

Stipp, H.-J. 1991. "wᵉhayā für nichtiterative Vergangenheit? Zu syntaktischen Modernisierungen im masoretischen Jeremiabuch." Pages 521–47 in *Texte, Methode und Grammatik: Wolfgang Richter zum 65. Geburtstag*. Edited by W. Gross, H. Irsigler and T. Seidl. St. Ottilien: EOS.

Talstra, E., and J. W. Dyk. 1999. "Paradigmatic and Syntagmatic Features in Identifying Subject and Predicate in Nominal Clauses." Pages 133–85 in *The Verbless Clause in Biblical Hebrew*. Linguistic Studies in Ancient West Semitic 1. Edited by C. L. Miller. Winona Lake, IN: Eisenbrauns.

Taylor, J. R. 2003. *Linguistic Categorization*. 3rd ed. Oxford Textbooks in Linguistics. New York: Oxford University Press.

Tov, E. 2001. *Textual Criticism of the Hebrew Bible*. 2nd ed. Minneapolis: Fortress.

———. 2004. *Scribal Practices and Approaches Reflected in the Texts Found in the Judean Desert*. Studies on the Texts of the Desert of Judah 54. Atlanta: Society of Biblical Literature.

Tyler, A., and V. Evans. 2003. *The Semantics of English Prepositions: Spatial Scenes, Embodied Meaning and Cognition*. Cambridge: Cambridge University Press.

Van der Merwe, C. H. J. 1989. "Recent Trends in the Linguistic Description of Old Hebrew." *Journal of Northwest Semitic Languages* 15: 217–41.

———. 1994. "Discourse Linguistics and a Biblical Hebrew Grammar." Pages 13–49 in *Biblical Hebrew and Discourse Linguistics*. Edited by R. D. Bergen. Dallas, TX: Summer Institute of Linguistics.

———. 2003. "Some Recent Trends in Biblical Hebrew Linguistics: A Few Pointers Towards a More Comprehensive Model of Language Use." *Hebrew Studies* 44: 7–24.

———. 2009a. "The Biblical Hebrew Particle אַף." *Vetus Testamentum* 59: 266–83.

———. 2009b. "Another Look at the Biblical Hebrew Focus Particle גַּם." *Journal of Semitic Studies* 54, no. 2: 313–32.

———. 2011a. "The Difference Between הֵן, הִנֵּה and רְאֵה." Pages 237–56 in *"Ich werde meinen Bund mit euch niemals brechen!" (Ri 2,1). Festschrift für Walter Gross zum 70. Geburtstag*. Edited by E. Gass and H.-J. Stipp. Herder's Biblical Studies 62. Freiburg: Herder.

————. 2011b. "The Lexeme סָבִיב." Pages 399–415 in *Tradition and Innovation in Biblical Interpretation: Studies Presented to Professor Eep Talstra on the Occasion of His Sixty-Fifth Birthday*. Edited by J. Dyk and W. van Peursen. Studia Semitica Neerlandica 57. Leiden: Brill.

————. 2013a. "The Infinitive Absolute Reconsidered: A Review Article." *Journal of Northwest Semitic Languages* 39, no. 1: 61–84.

————. 2013b. "Fronting: Biblical Hebrew." Pages 931–35 in Vol. 1 of *Encyclopedia of Hebrew Language and Linguistics* 1. Edited by G. Khan. Leiden: Brill.

————. 2014. "The Challenge of Better Understanding Discourse Particles: The Case of לָכֵן." *Journal of Northwest Semitic Languages* 40, no. 2: 127–57.

Van der Merwe, C. H. J., and A. Andrason. 2014. "Finite Infinite? Finite uses of the Biblical Hebrew Infinitive Absolute and Their Rationale." *Journal of Semitic Studies* 59, no. 2: 255–96.

Van der Merwe, C. H. J., J. A. Naudé and J. H. Kroeze. 1999. *A Biblical Hebrew Reference Grammar*. Biblical Languages: Hebrew 3. Sheffield: Sheffield Academic.

Van der Merwe, C. H. J., and E. Wendland. 2010. "Marked Word Order in the Book of Joel." *Journal of Northwest Semitic Languages* 36, no. 2: 255–80.

Vanoni, G. 1991. "Zur Bedeutung der althebräischen Konjunktion W." Pages 561–76 in *Text, Methode und Grammatik: Wolfgang Richter zum 65. Geburtstag*. Edited by W. Gross, H. Irsigler and T. Seidl. St. Ottilien: EOS.

Velupillai, V. 2012. *An Introduction to Linguistic Typology*. Amsterdam: John Benjamins.

Waltke, B. K., and M. P. O'Connor. 1990. *An Introduction to Biblical Hebrew Syntax*. Winona Lake, IN: Eisenbrauns.

Weil, G. E., ed. 1971. *Massorah Gedolah: Iuxta Codicem Leningradensem B 19a*. Vol. 1. Rome: Pontificium Istitutum Biblicum.

Westbury, J. 2014. "Left Dislocation in Biblical Hebrew: A Cognitive Linguistic Account." PhD diss., Stellenbosch University, Stellenbosch.

Weydt, H. 2006. "What Are Particles Good For?" Pages 205–19 in *Approaches to Discourse Particles*. Edited by K. Fischer. Studies in Pragmatics 1. Amsterdam: Elsevier.

Winther-Nielsen, N. 1995. *A Functional Discourse Grammar of Joshua: A Computer-Assisted Rhetorical Structure Analysis*. Coniectanea Biblia Old Testament 40. Stockholm: Almqvist & Wiksell International.

Yoo, C.-K. 2013. "A Cognitive Linguistic Description of Purpose and Result Connectives in Biblical Hebrew." PhD diss., Stellenbosch University, Stellenbosch.

Young, I., R. Rezetko and M. Ehrensvärd. 2008. *Linguistic Dating of Biblical Texts*. Vol. 2, *A Survey of Scholarship: A New Synthesis and a Comprehensive Bibliography*. London: Equinox.

Zewi, T. 2000. "Is There a Tripartite Nominal Sentence in Biblical Hebrew?." *Journal of Northwest Semitic Languages* 26, no. 2: 51–63.

————. 2007. *Parenthesis in Biblical Hebrew*. Studies in Semitic Languages and Linguistics. Leiden: Brill.

Zewi, T., and C. H. J. Van der Merwe. 2001. "Biblical Hebrew Nominal Clause: Definitions of Subject and Predicate." *Journal of Northwest Semitic Languages* 27, no. 1: 81–99.

INDEX OF BIBLICAL REFERENCES

6:6	195	20:15	171	10:3	83		
6:8	488	20:18	363	11:4–5	219		
6:17	353	20:20	399, 461	11:27	517		
6:30	477	21:8	261	11:43	85		
7:6	437	21:22	79	11:44	85		
7:13	156	21:23	378	12:2	433		
7:16	432	21:28	180, 274,	13:5	410		
7:27	185		433	13:9	288		
8:4	198	21:33	384	13:51	274		
8:18	445	22:9	384	16:23	76		
8:24	456	22:11	178	20:3	92		
9:14	400	22:15	376	21:14	505		
9:27	157	22:29	501	24:22	316		
9:34	289	23:5	378	25:20	407		
9:35	341	23:9	424	26:7	358		
10:16	174, 351	23:12	501	26:39	397		
10:24	455	23:20	409	27:28	517		
11:1	330	23:22	278				
11:3	402, 496	24:2	438	*Numbers*			
11:10	359	24:8	376	1:50	369		
12:3	356	31:17	356	3:1	302		
12:6	344	32:1	302	4:29	515		
12:10	370	32:6	184	9:22	384		
12:13	353	32:9	410	10:34–36	43		
12:16	78	32:19	347	11:24	368		
12:37	438	32:33	311, 481	12:2	342		
13:7	283	33:12–13	420	13:17	195, 198		
14:28	353	33:14	209	14:2	158, 440		
15:1	387	34:3	171	14:22	303		
15:3	221	34:9	171	14:24	330		
15:4	272	34:23	211	15:19	428		
16:21	211	34:24	365	16:3	510		
16:28	478	34:32	279	16:7	515, 517		
17:12	285, 377	38:16	369	17:7	412		
17:13	357	39:10	316, 320	20:12	441		
18:1	187	40:13	82	20:15	190		
18:4	342	40:17	430	20:17	485		
18:22	335	40:24	368	21:9	282		
19:5	195	40:25	358	21:14	312		
19:9	165, 399			21:22	337		
19:11	356	*Leviticus*		21:26	276		
20:8	352	1:2–3	391	21:34	435		
20:9	195, 281,	1:2	311	21:35	462		
	504	4:2	311	22:22	496		
20:10	266, 419,	6:3	333	22:30	450		
	422	7:15–18	180	22:32	480		
20:12	165, 167	8:24	368	22:35	398		
20:13	164	9:17	439	22:37	394		

21:13	366	16:17	263	30:7	443
22:3	473	18:23	299	30:16	268
22:19	440	18:26–28	3	36:11–13	3
22:20	432, 440	18:33	180	38:4	429
22:21	498	19:16	197	38:18	463
22:25	304	19:17	394	40–66	405
22:32	389	20:1	175, 353	40–55	397
22:44	449	20:3	359	40:10	396
22:50	387	20:6	445	40:11	340
		22:1	315	41:26	396
2 Kings		22:10	176	41:28–29	406
1:2	167	22:17	446	42:1	407
1:4	511	24:7	494	42:7	267
1:6	506	25:1	340	42:18	286
1:17	378	25:15	212, 264	42:24	308
2:7	362, 367	25:25	430	43:1	342
2:16	163			43:10	496
2:17	83	*Isaiah*		44:5	348
3:10	302	1:15	280, 458	44:9	298
3:12	289	1:21	477	44:15	396
3:16	212	1:24	79	44:21	278
3:26	288	3:18	303	45:10	484
4:5	361	5:13	160	46:9	398, 460
4:8	363	6:3	302	46:11	396
4:11	430	6:5	350	47:8	460
5:1	359	6:8	415	47:10	449
5:3	388, 484	7:7	431	51:6	354
5:6	196, 454	7:11	181	53:11	269
5:17	494	7:13–14	441	59:3	341
6:5	283	7:23	318	60:20	508
6:21–22	474	8:17	309	65:2	81
6:26	508	9:1	224		
6:32	463	9:6	458	*Jeremiah*	
7:1	263	9:8	209, 288	1:1–2	429
7:3	479	9:16	211	1:6	435
7:12	171	11:1	196	1:11	496, 509
7:13	172	11:4	343	2:2	466
8	4	11:5	427	2:19	423
8:13	479	11:9	159, 224	2:21	299
9:18	329	11:10	428	2:24	513
9:21	355	12:1–2	414	2:32	458
9:24	343	12:1	166	3:16	448
10:4	414	12:4	349	4:4	366
11:20	502	16:13	387	5:2	487
12:18	162, 386	17:2	185	5:22	97
13:14	161	20:2	181	6:3	368
13:20	507	26–28	394	6:13	272
14:7	423	28:8	214, 310	7:13	183
15:12	437	29:11	301	7:19	446

Index of Authors

Index of Subjects

Page numbers with <u>underlining</u> refer to sections in the grammar where the subject referred to is the topic of a paragraph or subparagraph. Page numbers in **bold** refer to subjects that are entries in the glossary.

INDEX OF HEBREW WORDS

Page numbers with <u>underlining</u> refer to sections in the grammar where the Hebrew word in question is the topic of a paragraph or subparagraph.